PENGUIN  CLASSICS

# GUIDE TO GREECE VOLUME 2

### ADVISORY EDITOR: BETTY RADICE

PAUSANIAS was a doctor from Greek Asia Minor who devoted ten or twenty years to travelling in mainland Greece during and after the reign of Hadrian, in the brief golden age of the Roman Empire (second century AD). It was during this time that he wrote a detailed account of every Greek city and sanctuary with historical introductions and a record of local customs and beliefs.

PETER LEVI, a classical scholar, archaeologist and poet, was born in 1931. He has also translated *The Psalms* for the Penguin Classics, as well as a collection of Yevtushenko (with R. Milner-Gulland) for the Penguin Modern Poets. He has edited *The Penguin Book of English Christian Verse* and, for the Penguin Classics, Johnson's *A Journey to the Western Islands of Scotland* and Boswell's *The Journal of a Tour to the Hebrides*. *The Light Garden of the Angel King*, an account of his travels in Afghanistan, is published in the Penguin Travel Library and he is also the author of *The Penguin History of Greek Literature*. Peter Levi was Professor of Poetry at the University of Oxford from 1984 to 1989.

# PAUSANIAS
# GUIDE TO GREECE

## VOLUME 2
## *Southern Greece*

TRANSLATED WITH AN INTRODUCTION
BY PETER LEVI

*Illustrated with drawings from Greek coins*
*by John Newberry*
*Maps and plans by Jeffery Lacey*

PENGUIN BOOKS

PENGUIN BOOKS

Published by the Penguin Group
Penguin Books Ltd, 27 Wrights Lane, London W8 5TZ, England
Penguin Books USA Inc., 375 Hudson Street, New York, New York 10014, USA
Penguin Books Australia Ltd, Ringwood, Victoria, Australia
Penguin Books Canada Ltd, 10 Alcorn Avenue, Toronto, Ontario, Canada M4V 3B2
Penguin Books (NZ) Ltd, 182–190 Wairau Road, Auckland 10, New Zealand

Penguin Books Ltd, Registered Offices: Harmondsworth, Middlesex, England

This translation first published 1971
Reprinted with revisions 1979
7 9 10 8 6

Translation and Introduction copyright © Peter Levi, 1971
Coin drawings copyright © John Newberry, 1971
All rights reserved

Printed in England by Clays Ltd, St Ives plc
Set in Monotype Bembo

FOR

NANCY SANDARS

Quomodo obscuratum est aurum, mutatus est
color optimus, dispersi sunt lapides sanctuarii in
capite omnium platearum?
*Lamentations of Jeremiah* 4, 1

The work of which this is a translation
was conceived in an age of dictatorship
and false enlightenment, but is impregnated with that sense of a persistent religion, of the inevitable victories of
reason, and of the godlike resurrections
of liberty and democracy in Greece
which make Greek stones noble.

# CONTENTS

# LIST OF FIGURES

# ACKNOWLEDGEMENTS

Any commentary on Pausanias, even the thinnest, must rest on a huge structure of other people's knowledge; no one could possibly be his own expert in everything Pausanias talked about. It is inevitable that in some field or other, perhaps in many, one will have missed important recent or old contributions to the understanding of what Pausanias wrote. If I have made mistakes of this kind (as I am bound to have done) I would be most grateful to hear of them, and in the cause of public utility to correct them either in a future edition of this book or at least in a much fuller commentary on which I am now working.

I would like to thank friends and colleagues for tolerance and for assistance. I owe more than I can express to the kindness and encouragement of Professor E. R. Dodds and Professor Eduard Fraenkel. Without their blessing I should not have undertaken this or any other work on a classical author. This book owes its existence also to the friendly interest of Professor Martin Robertson and Mr John Boardman, and most of all to the delightful and inspiring conversation and sympathetic friendship of Miss Nancy Sandars.

It is hard to know how to thank one's friends whom one feels one ought always to be thanking, but over this book I do owe particular thanks to Mr John Newberry for his drawings, to Mr Philip Sherrard and to Canon Francis Bartlett, to Mr Cyril Connolly, Mr and Mrs Watson, Mr George Pavlopoulos, Mr Takis Loumiotis and to Sir Maurice Bowra. Within the charmed circle of Campion Hall, links are too close for thanks to be permitted. Finally I should like to express my sincere thanks to the members of the British School of Archaeology in Athens in 1965-7 for many constant pleasures and for constant and most practical help and advice, particularly to Mr Geoffrey Waywell, Miss Jeffery and Lord William Taylour.

*Campion Hall, Oxford*
*September 1969*

PAUSANIAS

# GUIDE TO GREECE

*Volume 2*

Corfu

Euboia

ATTICA

PHOKIS

Delphi

BOIOTIA

Patrai

Megara

Kephallenia

ACHAIA

Corinth

Athens

ELIS

Elis

ARKADIA

Salamis

Zakynthos

Argos

Olympia

Aigina

Megalopolis

Epidauros

Messene

Sparta

MESSENIA

LAKONIA

CORINTHIA

Kythera

# GREECE &
# ASIA MINOR

English miles

0                    100

# INTRODUCTION

Virtually everything we know about the author of this book depends on the internal evidence of the book itself. Pausanias seems to have lived for a time in an inland Greek city near Mount Sipylos in Asia Minor, presumably Magnesia, and was perhaps born there. He had already passed the middle of his life when he began to write, and worked on his *Guide to Greece* for at least fourteen years between the late fifties and the late seventies of the second century A.D., in what seems to us to be the lucid and inspiring afterglow of the Antonine age. He wrote for Roman philhellenes in the Greek language, sometimes elaborately and sometimes carelessly – there are passages in his work which read like hasty dictation – at a miraculously chosen moment. Nero had stolen some treasures, Akarnania and Achaia were poverty-stricken and depopulated to build Augustus's great Roman cities: Thebes of course had been broken to pieces by the Macedonians and ancient Corinth by Rome: but every other important monument of Greek antiquity was still standing in his time. Here and there a temple had been moved bodily, ivy had covered an inscription, a roof had fallen in, but his was the only lifetime in which the final embellishments of Hadrian and of Herod of Athens could be seen, yet the seventeen centuries of neglect had not begun. Pausanias was not the first to write this kind of book; Strabo, writing under Augustus, and the fragments of Dikaiarchos are enough to prove it was a recognized *genre*. But the value of Pausanias to archaeologists and to all classical scholars is unique and astonishing.

Of course he used textbooks and compilations which existed in his day but which have since perished. The marked variations in his prose style often reflect a change of sources. But we know that he actually visited the sites he talks about, since he tells us so in so many words. His criteria for what to believe and what not to believe involved observation and personal reasoning, but they were also conventional: they are clearly stated by his contemporary Artemidoros (*Oneirocrit.* 4, 47) with some of the same examples. In Athens he belonged to a circle of almost professional antiquaries; he worked in great libraries; he consulted the sacred officials and city guides whom Plutarch describes at Delphi and who existed in every city. Pausanias seems to have been a doctor; he was interested in questions of anatomy and personally devoted to the healing god Asklepios. When he was old he became addicted to bird-watching, and complained about steep hills and bad roads. He had the kind of interest in natural science one might expect in an early member of the Royal Society. As a young man he seems to have been an expert on Homeric questions, but the bitterness and malice of scholars in this field drove him to abandon literary criticism.

It is sometimes said that the educated sensibility of his period was essentially literary. When one comes to think of it this is an astonishing view: the architecture, the gardening, the philosophy and the less amiable pursuits of the Antonine age would hardly endorse it. Pausanias was certainly a man of letters, and very widely read: we owe to his *Guide to Greece* a large proportion of those fragments of Greek non-Homeric epic poetry which have survived at all. For certain subjects he is still important as a historian. He was devoted to the idea of Greek liberty and to Greek history as the history of liberty which was in the end lost. But his most devoted, obsessive interest was religion.

Pausanias was capable of entertaining a sophisticated and philosophical solution of religious difficulties, but his deepest engagement was in the local cults and legends and traditions of provincial Greece. There is no doubt that he was a true believer in the most sacred of these traditions: he accepted the warning of a dream and understood the punishment of a god. He was perhaps like his greatest editor, Sir James Frazer (whose entire lifework had its roots in Pausanias), in that all his scholarship and topography and encyclopedic curiosity were a burden undertaken in the attempt to satisfy a deeper anxiety which had once been apprehended in religious terms. The collapse of ancient religion or some deeper collapse was the unspoken object of his studies. If this anxiety had not ridden him as it did, or had he been a less patient and learned traveller, modern archaeology would be immeasurably poorer. Of course he had his limitations. To Pausanias a ruined building was hardly worth mentioning; it is an open question what he would have made of the recoveries we value so highly. As a geographer and natural historian he was almost ludicrously eager to add something to the records, yet for him Greece was even smaller than modern Greece: its gate was Thermopylai. His interest was in principle bounded by the limits of the Roman province of Achaia, though he had travelled in Italy, in Macedonia and in Palestine, and no doubt elsewhere.

Archaeologists and historians have made constant use of his work. I used to consider it probable that Cyriaco of Ancona in the fifteenth century brought the first knowledge of Pausanias to the West; it was widely copied in the late fifteenth and sixteenth centuries, but all the known manuscripts seem to be related to one rather faulty original, probably itself a fifteenth-century copy deriving ultimately like so many other treasures from the learned library of Archbishop Arethas of Caesarea in the late ninth or the early tenth century. The faults in the manuscript tradition are very likely even earlier than Arethas. Naturally Pausanias's descriptions, sketchy and selective as they sometimes are, have been much used for the location and identification of ancient sites; those scholars who have believed him to be mistaken on specific points have often (though not always) turned out to be wrong. The first use of Pausanias to identify ancient sites may be traced to Gemistos Plethon whom Cyriaco visited at Mistra, but that is a perplexed question.

There is a worse danger in the tendency to take him absolutely literally as an inch by inch commentator; it is often impossible to follow him step by step in his journeys. His habit, which is in fact a convention of the literary form in which he writes, is to arrange his material in alternative routes from the same focal point, sometimes without naming this point and with no warning when he retraces his steps. Neglect of this principle of method has led to some confusing modern controversies. There are certain refinements of information available to us which were not available to him. The exact study of epigraphy and, for example, the comparison of different kinds of builders' clamps used at Delphi have taught us more about the complicated history of the Delphic monuments than Pausanias could have discovered. We have a better theoretic grasp and a wider sense of background information even for the study of Greek religion; our art criticism is more acute and scholarly; our libraries of Greek literature may lack books but what survives is better organized. Nonetheless, when the average classical scholar is confronted by a badly mapped landscape and a heap of brute physical objects his advantages desert him; one could do a lot worse than take Pausanias for a guide.

Pausanias's *Guide to Greece* is in ten books. Since this translation of the entire work will fill two volumes, for the convenience of readers I have thought it best to change the order of books of the original, so that while Volume One contains the five provinces of central Greece this second volume contains southern Greece; Pausanias refers to northern Greece only in a few passing remarks. I have made a very few abridgements, all of the same kind: in certain lists of mythical or invented names, where the list has been bald and tediously long and the names so far as I can discover quite without significance, I have cut out all but the first and last, and substituted a formula like 'great-great-grandson' or 'in the seventh generation'. I have occasionally left out patronymics where they were otiose. There are no other abridgements. For the spelling of names I have kept as close as possible to the Greek, and except in cases like *Oedipus* and *Mycenae* I have avoided Latinized forms. One reason among many for this is that it may lessen confusion for travellers in Greece. I have sometimes altered the order of phrases in a sentence, and once or twice even that of sentence, for the sake of clarity.

In writing the footnotes I was preoccupied with brevity. Pausanias is an author who raises one's interest in every direction, but it seemed best to limit one's comments to an explanation of what he actually wrote, with some allusion to the results of archaeology. This raises many more problems than a limited commentary can discuss: virtually every major question in Greek archaeology would have to be treated somewhere in a full-scale commentary on the *Guide to Greece*. But space was limited; there was no room for argument and little for conjecture. I have generally given references only to classical texts, or to modern sources where something was explained beyond the scope of a footnote; these references are of course not exhaustive. But if any book other than a standard textbook has been particulary useful to me personally I have usually managed to refer to it somewhere by name. Readers who are puzzled by the names and the order of events to which Pausanias refers in the years following the death of Alexander the Great may find it useful to refer to a short appendix at the end of Volume One in which I have indicated very briefly the main happenings of those years.

In 1978 I made a few corrections and additions, many of them suggested by letters I have received, but some of them due to further reading or new discoveries. It has not been possible to acknowledge all the help I have had or to discuss everything that needs discussion.

# BOOK III
## LAKONIA

[1] Westward from the Hermai[1] you are already in 1
Lakonia.The Lakonians themselves say that Lelex who was a
child of the earth was the first king in this country, and that
the Leleges whom he governed were named after him.[2] Lelex
had a son called Myles and a younger son Polykaon. I shall
explain later where Polykaon went to and why he went away,
but, anyway, when Myles died his son Eurotas inherited
the sovereignty. It was Eurotas who channelled away the
marsh-water from the plains by cutting through to the

1. Pausanias crosses the mountains into Lakonia from the Argolid. At the
end of his Corinthian book (Bk II, 38 (7)) he had reached these Hermai on
Mount Parnon where the Roman boundaries of Arkadia, Lakonia and the
Argolid met, above the modern HAGIOS PETROS. The Hermai were three
mounds of stones and earth; their local name STOUS FONEMENOUS, the
Murdered Men, is medieval and derives from a romantic legend about an
imprisoned princess and her suitors from which many local landmarks in this
area took new names (e.g. Kastro tis Oraias and the hill named Sarantapsycho).
They were first noticed by the French survey expedition of 1829, and finally
excavated by a learned local antiquary, K. Romaios, in the summer of 1905.
His excavation (B.S.A., II. pp. 137–9) did not reveal the origin of the mounds,
only that they were at least as old as the sixth century B.C. He returned
several times to the same site, and finally discovered traces of a small shrine,
probably of Artemis, beside the mounds (cf. Romaios in Athena XX,
1908, Praktika, 1950, p. 235, Peloponnesiaka, 1955 and 1958–9). The inscribed stone Romaios found in 1905 is probably a dedication as W. Kolbe
supposed (I.G., V, 926), and not a gravestone. There is no trace of any
burial.

2. The name Leleges is obscure and widespread in Greece and Asia Minor.
Herodotos says that the Karians were Leleges, and Homer makes them Trojan
allies, and Pausanias knew (Bk I, 39 (6)) that several peoples in mainland
Greece shared this ancient name. It is also used in a fragment of Hesiod quoted
by Strabo (7, 7, 2; 322). The confusion of the early migrations it represents
is impenetrable. It should be understood that at least from Mycenaean times
the inhabitants of the Peloponnese were a mixture of races (Syriopoulos,
Proistoria tis Peloponnisou, 1964, pp. 555 f.).

sea,[3] and when the land was drained he called the river which was left running there the Eurotas. [2] As he had no male children he left the crown to Lakedaimon, whose mother was Taygete after whom the mountain was named and whose father is supposed to have been Zeus; Lakedaimon had married Sparta, the daughter of Eurotas. Once he was in power, he first of all renamed the country and the people after himself, and then founded a city and named it after his wife: the city is called Sparta to this day. [3] Lakedaimon's son Amyklas, who also wanted to leave something to be remembered by, founded a city in Lakonian territory. The youngest and most beautiful of his sons was Hyakinthos, who was fated to die before his father, and the tomb of Hyakinthos is in Amyklai under Apollo's statue. When Amyklas died power passed into the hands of his eldest son Argalos, and later when Argalos died it came to Kynortas. [4] Kynortas's son was Oibalos, who married Perseus's daughter Gorgophone from Argos, and had a son called Tyndareos. Hippokoon quarrelled with Tyndareos over the crown, thinking he should have it because he was older. Ikarios and the revolutionary party were on his side so he was much more powerful than Tyndareos and frightened him away. The Lakonians say he went to Pellana, but the Messenians have a legend about him in which Tyndareos goes into exile to Messenia with Aphareus the son of Perieres, who was Tyndareos's brother on his mother's side. They say Tyndareos lived at Thalamai in Messenia[4] and his sons were born there. [5] Some time later Herakles brought Tyndareos home, and he renewed his reign. The sons of Tyndareos became kings, and so did Menelaos son of Atreus who married Tyndareos's daughter, and

3. Presumably at the Eurotas gorge just north of SKALA, not far from the sea. An ancient commentary on Euripides (*Orestes*, 626) says this was a way of releasing the water after Deukalion's flood.

4. Thalamai is at KOUTIPHARI, south-east of PLATSA in the MANI. By Pausanias's time it belonged to Lakonia, but Messenia claimed it (cf. Bk III, 26 (1–3)). Augustus recognized these southern Lakonian towns as semi-independent of Lakonia; they were called the free Lakonians.

Orestes who married Menelaos's daughter Hermione. When the children of Herakles came home in the reign of Tisamenos son of Orestes, the countries of Messene and Argos were handed over to Kresphontes and Temenos respectively, but in Lakonia, because Aristodemos had twin sons, two royal families were founded. They say this was the Pythian priestess's solution. [6] The story is that Aristodemos himself had died at Delphi before the Dorians came home to the Peloponnese.[5] Some people dress his legend up by saying he was shot by Apollo for not approaching the oracle because he happened to meet Herakles on the way and found out from him there was going to be a return of the Dorians to the Peloponnese. But the truth is that Aristodemos was murdered by the sons of Pylades and Elektra, who were the cousins of Tisamenos son of Orestes.[6] [7] His sons were named Prokles and Eurysthenes, and though they were twin brothers they differed violently. In fact they were far advanced in mutual loathing, but they did cooperate to found a colony with Autesion's son Theras, who was acting as regent for them. He was a brother of their mother Argeia. Theras sent the colony to an island that was then called Kalliste,[7] where he hoped the descendants of Membliaros would be willing to resign the crown, [8] and so they did; they accepted the argument that Theras's family went right back to Kadmos, while their

5. Apollodoros (2, 8, 2) believed he was hit by a thunderbolt when the Dorians were embarking at Naupaktos. The source of Pausanias's more elaborate story has not been traced. Herodotos (6, 52) says that the Lakonians, 'with whom no poet agrees', claimed that Aristodemos had actually led the invasion of Lakonia.

6. Cf. Bk II, 16 (7). They were called Medon and Strophios.

7. This is SANTORINI, the southernmost of the Cyclades. The island is volcanic; it blew up with an enormous explosion in the period of the great Cretan palaces. There have been able and extensive excavations of classical Thera by German archaeologists, including Hiller von Gärtringen; the only good and properly illustrated modern guide is by Lois Knidlberger, in German (Munich, 1965). The evidence of cults, of tribal names and of dialect confirms the close connexion of the Therans with the Peloponnese, and they took the Lakonian side in the Peloponnesian War. For prehistoric Thera cf. preliminary reports of excavations by Marinatos (Athens, 1968 and 1969).

ancestor Membliaros was a man of the people, whom Kadmos had left in that island to take command of the islanders. Theras renamed the island after himself, and once a year to this day the Therans offer sacrifices to him as their founder. Prokles and Eurysthenes agreed in being well disposed to Theras, but they disagreed about every other subject. [9] But even supposing they were a harmonious couple, I should not have included all their descendants in a single list, as their generations did not always coincide: cousin with cousin for example, or cousins' children with cousins' children, and so on through their remoter descendants. So I shall go through both families separately without mixing them.

2   [1] They say that Aristodemos's elder son Eurysthenes had a boy called Agis; Eurysthenes' descendants are called the Agiadai after him. In Agis's time Patreus son of Preugenes founded a city in Achaia which is still called Patrai to this day after Patreus, and the Lakonians played a part in the settlement. They also assisted Gras the son of Echelas who was the son of Orestes' son Penthilos, when Gras set off with his fleet to make a colony. Gras was going to occupy the territory between the Ionians and the Mysians,[8] which is still called Aiolian; even earlier than this his ancestor Penthilos had taken the island lying opposite the mainland at the same point, that is Lesbos. [2] While Agis's son Echestratos was reigning at Sparta the Lakonians expelled all the Kynoureans of military age,[9] on the grounds that the Argives were their blood-relatives, yet brigands based on Kynourean territory were creating havoc in the Argolid, and the Kynoureans themselves were making open raids there. The Kynoureans are supposed to be Argives by blood; they say that their founder was Kynouros son of Perseus.

[3] Not many years after this Echestratos's son Labotas took

8. In Asia Minor.

9. Between Lakonia and the Argolid (cf. Herodotos, 8, 7, 3); he thought they were aboriginal inhabitants. The Lakonians were surrounded by subdued and semi-independent peoples more loosely organized than the central Lakonian state. This is perhaps the central fact of Spartan history.

over the throne of Sparta. Herodotos in the story of Kroisos says that during Labotas's boyhood Lykourgos the Law-giver was regent; but Herodotos calls him Leobotes instead of Labotas.[10] It was at this time the Lakonians first decided to go to war with Argos; Lakonia claimed that the Argives were making annexations in the Kynourean territory, that Lakonia was the occupying power, that the people of the province were Lakonian subjects, and that Argos was removing them from Lakonian allegiance. It is said that in this war neither side gained any very notable immediate success, [4] and neither of the kings who succeeded in that family, Labotas's son Doryssos and Doryssos's son Agesilaos, was destined to live long. But it was in the reign of Agesilaos that Lykourgos fixed the laws of Lakonia. Some people claim he composed laws for Lakonia following the advice of the Pythian priestess, but there are others who say he simply introduced the legal institutions of Crete.[11] The Cretans say these laws were fixed for them by Minos, and that Minos's deliberations in this matter were divinely inspired.[12] I believe that Homer in the following verses was hinting at Minos's laws:

> ... Knossos the great city where Minos
> who spoke with the great Zeus was nine years king.

[5] I shall speak about Lykourgos later. Agesilaos's son was Archelaos. In his reign the Lakonians fought, captured and

10. Herodotos, 1, 65. Pausanias's attempt to establish a firm date may be admired, but should be accepted with suspicion.

11. There is a fuller discussion of all this in Plutarch's *Life of Lykourgos*, which is partly based on a lost work of Aristotle, who apparently gives the Delphic version. The Spartans in the fifth century accepted the Cretan version (Herodotos, 1, 65). The prestige of the archaic aristocratic legal codes, by which parts of Crete continued to be governed right into the Hellenistic period, was very high, as one can see from Plato. Their social significance is discussed by R. F. Willetts in his recent edition of the Gortyn law-code.

12. Cf. Strabo, 10, 4, 8 (476); according to the *Marmor Parium* Minos founded Knossos and Kydonia, the modern CHANIA. The reference to Homer is to the *Odyssey* (19, 178). Ephoros had already noticed it, and Strabo uses it. Cf. also *Iliad*, 13, 450 and *Hymn to Apollo*, 393.

enslaved the provincial city of Aigys, on the suspicion that it
favoured Arkadia.[13] Charilaos who was king in the other
family helped Archelaos at the taking of Aigys; I shall record
what Charilaos did as a Lakonian commander on his own
when I come to deal with the Eurypontidai, as they were
called. [6] Archelaos's son was Teleklos, under whom the
Lakonians fought and captured the provincial cities of
Amyklai and Pharis and Geronthrai, which were still Achaian.[14] The people of Pharis and Geronthrai were terrified
when the Dorians marched on them and agreed to withdraw
from the Peloponnese under a truce; Amyklai did not fall at
the first assault, but after a resistance under arms and some by
no means inglorious battles. The Dorians on their side show
a trophy they raised over Amyklai, the most highly valued
trophy that they possessed in that age. Not long after this
Teleklos was killed by Messenians in the temple of Artemis.
This was a temple built at the place called Limnai on the
borders of Lakonia and Messenia. [7] When he died his son
Alkamenes assumed sovereignty; this was when the Lakonians sent Euthys's son the distinguished Spartan Charmidas to
Crete, to put an end to the civil wars there, and to persuade
the Cretans to abandon those of their cities which were too
far from the sea or weak in other ways, and bring them together into the maritime cities instead.[15] They also destroyed

13. Cf. Bk VIII, 27 (4), and 34 (5). Aigys was on the north-west edges of
Taygetos, south of LEONTARI, among the springs of the XERILOPOTAMOS
(Karneion), a tributary of the Alpheios. The Delphic oracle advised the
Spartans to dedicate half of its land to Apollo; cf. Parke, *Delphic Oracle*, n.
539.

14. Pharis and Amyklai are only five miles south of Sparta, but Geronthrai
is at YERAKI on Mount Parnon to the south-east. They are all mentioned
again; cf. Bk III, 18 (7); 20 (3); 22 (6). Distinctions between Dorians and
Achaians are a backward projection of later political and social grouping; they
are not to be taken seriously as history; for Homer's usage of 'Dorian',
'Achaian' and 'Hellene', cf. Allen, *Homer*, pp. 110–129.

15. We are now in the late eighth century. Nothing is known about
Charmidas's interesting expedition, but there is an illuminating discussion
of it in G. L. Huxley's *Early Sparta* (1962), pp. 27–8.

Helos, an Achaian town on the sea-coast, and fought and beat the Argives who came to relieve it.[16]

[1] When Alkamenes had died and his son Polydoros had 3 succeeded to the crown, Lakonia sent out an expedition of colonists to Italy: the settlement at Kroton and another at Lokroi at Cape Zephyrios;[17] it was also in the reign of Polydoros that the Messenian War reached its climax. The Lakonians and the Messenians give different accounts of the causes of this war. [2] As my story unfolds I shall explain the two versions and how the war ended; for the present I shall simply record that in their first war against the Messenians the Lakonians were mostly led by Theopompos son of Nikander, the king from the other family. When the Messenian War had been fought to its finish and Lakonia was already in armed occupation of Messenia, Polydoros, who was highly thought of in Sparta and particularly popular with the Lakonian people, since he never offended by arrogant language or by any kind of violence, and was just and even compassionate in his judgements – [3] Polydoros, whose name was by this time glorious all over Greece, was murdered; and it was a man of not undistinguished family in Lakonia, although rashly daring as this enterprise proved, who murdered him: Polemarchos. After his death Polydoros received many memorable honours from the Lakonians,[18] but there also exist at Sparta the grave and memorial of Polemarchos, either because his past life had been honourable or because his relatives secretly buried him.

[4] In the reign of Polydoros's son Eurykrates the Messen-

16. Cf. Bk III, 20 (6–7). Helos was a Homeric coastal city; cf. Note 219 perhaps.

17. Other literary authorities say that Kroton was an Achaian, not a Spartan settlement, except perhaps for Ovid (*Metamorphoses*, 15, 15). There was a district in Sparta where the people were called Krotanoi (Bk III, 14 (2)). The settlement seems to have been at the end of the eighth century. Some Spartans may well also have joined the Lokrian settlement, which was perhaps-not much later, but it was of course chiefly a settlement of the mainland Greek Lokrians, who lived on the borders of Phokis.

18. Cf. Bk III, 11 (10), and 12 (3).

ians stayed quiet as Lakonian subjects, nor was there any new trouble from the people of Argos, but under Eurykrates' son Anaxander destiny was already at work to drive the Messenians right out of the Peloponnese, and they rebelled against Lakonia. Their resistance lasted some time, but when they were beaten they left the Peloponnese under the terms of their surrender; the remnant who were left on Lakonian territory became serfs, with the single exception of the people of the coastal towns. [5] This history is not the right point for me to discuss the military events of the war that followed the Messenian rebellion. Anaxander's son was called Eurykrates the second, and the son of this second Eurykrates was called Leo. In their reigns Lakonia fought a largely unsuccessful war against Tegea,[19] but under Leo's son Anaxandrides the Lakonians got the upper hand over the Tegeans. This is how it happened. [6] A Lakonian called Lichas arrived in Tegea at a time when there was a truce. When he arrived they were looking for the bones of Orestes; that is, the Spartans were looking for these bones because of an oracle.[20] Lichas realized that they must be buried in a bronze-worker's forge. He realized this through connecting the things he saw in the forge with the prophecy from Delphi, the smith's bellows with the winds because they blew a violent stream of air, the hammer with striking and the anvil with striking back, and probably steel with human suffering, because they already used steel in battle, though in the age of heroes the god would have said it was bronze that was the suffering of mankind. [7] In later times an oracle like the one given to the Lakonians about Orestes' bones was given to Athens telling them to bring

19. For Tegea in Arkadia, cf. Bk VIII, 45–9.
20. Herodotos (1, 67) tells the story more clearly. The oracle said:

> There is a place in the Arkadian plain, Tegea is its name,
> with two winds breathing by hard necessity,
> blow on blow is struck there, grief is piled on grief,
> and in that place the life-giving earth
> holds the bones of the son of Agamemnon.
> Take them and you shall be master of Tegea.

back Theseus from Skyros, or else they would never capture it. It was Kimon the son of Miltiades who discovered Theseus's bones; he too used his intelligence in the matter, and he took Skyros soon afterwards.[21] [8] As for the weapons in the heroic age being all made of bronze, I could argue that from Homer, from the lines about Peisander's axe and Meriones' arrow; the opinion I have given can be proved anyway from the spear of Achilles, which is dedicated in the sanctuary of Athene at Phaselis, and Memnon's sword in the temple of Asklepios at Nikomedia: the blade and the butt of the spear and the whole of the sword are made of bronze.[22] [9] I know that this is the case.

Leo's son Anaxandrides was the only Lakonian to have two wives at once and live in two houses. The wife he lived with first was excellent in most ways but she happened not to conceive a child. The board of governors ordered him to send her away, but he was certainly not prepared to do that, and yielded only so far as to take another wife as well. The second wife bore a son called Kleomenes, and after Kleomenes was born the first wife who had not been pregnant before bore a child called Dorieus, then Leonidas and then Kleombrotos as well. [10] When Anaxandrides died, the Lakonians felt that Dorieus was better disposed and a better soldier than Kleomenes, but against their inclination they rejected him

21. Kimon saw an eagle tearing up the tumulus with its claws and beak. Cf. Plutarch, *Theseus*, 36.

22. It is true that bronze, which is a copper-tin alloy, was discovered far earlier, and for a long time more easily produced than iron or mild steel. Steel is carbonized iron; steel technology was very slow to progress except by infinite pains until the isolation of carbon in the late eighteenth century. Bronze had important advantages over the kind of iron available to the Greeks until a comparatively late period. It is hard to see why they changed from bronze to iron unless because iron became easier to obtain. The references to Homer are to *Iliad*, 13, 611 f. and 650. Homer does in fact mention iron weapons, and iron objects have been recovered from prehistoric Greek burials, but the overwhelming mass of offensive weapons down to the late Mycenaean period was in bronze. The anomalies of iron and bronze in the Homeric poems are interpreted and fully discussed in H. L. Lorimer's *Homer and the Monuments*, pp. 111–21. Phaselis and Nikomedia were both in Asia Minor.

and the sovereignty went legally and by seniority to Kleomenes.

4    [1] Dorieus could not bear to stay in Lakonia and obey Kleomenes, and went off to found a colonial settlement. Once Kleomenes was king he collected an army of Lakonians and their allies and immediately invaded the Argolid. The Argives came out against him under arms but Kleomenes won the battle, and since there was a wood near by, sacred to Argos the son of Niobe,[23] about five thousand of the Argives when they broke took refuge in the sacred wood. Kleomenes, who was a kind of madman, ordered fire to be brought against that wood and against everyone besieged in it. The flames consumed the whole area of the wood, and the men in sanctuary were burnt to death as the wood burnt. [2] He also took an army against Athens;[24] at first he brought freedom to the Athenians from the sons of Peisistratos and a good reputation all over Greece to himself and to Lakonia, but later he came to help an Athenian called Isagoras to establish a dictatorship in Athens. When this hope was disappointed, because the Athenians fought hard for their freedom, they claim that among other parts of the countryside Kleomenes destroyed the ground called Orgas, which is sacred to the Eleusinian goddesses.[25] He also went to Aigina and arrested the powerful figures there who had been responsible for the surrender to Persia, by persuading the people to give earth and water to King Darius. [3] While Kleomenes was spending time in Aigina, Demaratos the king from the other family was slandering Kleomenes to the people of Lakonia. When Kleomenes came home he set about getting Demaratos deposed. He bribed the Delphic prophetess to give the

23. Cf. Bk II, 22 (5).

24. Cf. Herodotos, 5, 64, 70 f.

25. Between Athenian (that is, Eleusinian) territory and Megara; cf. Bk I, 36 (3). The Megarians trespassing on it in the fifth century provoked a punitive decree from Perikles, which was one of the causes of the Peloponnesian War. A very solemn fourth-century Athenian decree about its administration has survived. (Cf. *B.C.H.*, 13, 1889, p. 433.) For the crimes of Kleomenes and their divine punishment, cf. Herodotos, 6, 75.

Lakonians whatever oracles about Demaratos he might dictate, and he got Leotychides, who belonged to the royal family on the same side as Demaratos, to put in a counter-claim to the throne. [4] Leotychides seized upon something Ariston had stupidly let slip about Demaratos when the child was born, denying that it was a son of his. At this point the Lakonians had recourse as they usually did to the oracle at Delphi; they took it their difficulty about Demaratos, but the priestess gave only the responses Kleomenes wanted. [5] So Demaratos was unjustly deprived of his crown because of the hostility of Kleomenes, who afterwards died raving mad. He took hold of a sword and wounded himself, chopping and disfiguring his whole body. The Argives say he died like this in revenge for the fugitives in the sanctuary of Argos, the Athenians say it was because he destroyed Orgas, and the Delphians say it was because of the bribes he gave to the priestess to tell lies about Demaratos. [6] It may be true that the vengeance of the divine heroes and of the gods together fell on Kleomenes, because at Elaious Protesilaos, who was a hero no better known than Argos, took revenge for a personal injury on a Persian called Artayktes,[26] nor were the Megarians ever able to placate the vengeance of the Eleusinian gods after once cultivating the sacred ground. As for corrupting the oracle, we know of absolutely no one but Kleomenes who ever dared to do it.

[7] As Kleomenes had no sons, the sovereignty passed to Leonidas the son of Anaxandrides, who was the full brother of Dorieus. That was when Xerxes brought his people against Greece, and Leonidas with three hundred Lakonians met him at Thermopylai. There have been many wars fought by Greeks and by the barbarians among themselves, and a fair number of them have become famous through the courageous behaviour of one man, like Achilles in the Trojan War and

26. Cf. Herodotos, 9, 116 f. Pausanias refers to Eleous and Protesilaos at Bk I, 34 (2). Artayktes sacked the sanctuary of the divine hero, which was very rich; he was later captured and terribly tortured to death. Elaious was the southernmost town in the Thracian Chersonese.

Miltiades in the battle of Marathon; but in my opinion the grandeur of the action of Leonidas has towered over the exploits of all earlier and later ages. [8] Xerxes above all the kings of the Medes and Persians who came after him used the greatest intellectual power; his achievements were glittering; yet Leonidas with the few men he brought to Thermopylai would have stopped him in his path, so that he would not even have seen Greece, and could never have burnt the city of Athens, if the Greeks had not been cut off and surrounded, when that Trachinian brought round Hydarnes' army over the path that cuts across Oite, Leonidas was overwhelmed, and the barbarians passed through into Greece.[27]

[9] Pausanias the son of Kleombrotos never became king; but as regent for Pleistarchos, the young son Leonidas had left, he took the Lakonians to Plataia and afterwards with a fleet to the Hellespont. I particularly praise Pausanias's behaviour over the Koan woman, the daughter of a not undistinguished father in Kos, Hegetorides the son of Antagoras; she was the unwilling concubine of a Persian called Pharandates the son of Teaspis. [10] When Mardonios fell in battle at Plataia and the barbarian army perished, Pausanias sent the woman home to Kos with her Persian jewellery and all her belongings. And Pausanias was unwilling to dishonour Mardonios's dead body, the suggestion of Lampon of Aigina.[28]

5    [1] Leonidas's son Pleistarchos died soon after inheriting the throne, and Pleistoanax became king; he was the son of the Pausanias who commanded at Plataia, and his own son was also called Pausanias. It was this Pausanias who went to Attica as the supposed enemy of Thrasyboulos and of Athens, but really to establish solidly the dictatorship of the government Lysander had appointed. He fought and beat the Athen-

27. The topography of Thermopylai is much more problematic than it sounds; the best modern discussion is scattered here and there in Y. Béquignon's *La Vallée du Spercheios* (1937).

28. Cf. Herodotos, 9, 76 and 78f.

ians who held Piraeus, but as soon as the battle was over he preferred to take his army home rather than bring the most abominable disgrace on Sparta by any increase in the dictatorial power of those ungodly men. [2] But because he had retreated from Athens after an ineffective battle, his enemies brought him to trial. The court to try a king of Lakonia consisted of the Elders, of whom there were twenty-eight, and the Governors, and the king from the other family sitting with them. Fourteen of the Elders, and Agis who was the king from the other family, found Pausanias guilty, but the rest of the court acquitted him.[29]

[3] Not long after this Lakonia collected an army against Thebes – I shall explain why in my account of Agesilaos – and Lysander entered Phokis, enlisted the entire Phokian people, and without a minute's delay invaded Boiotia and attacked the walls of Haliartos which was refusing to defect from Thebes. But some Thebans and Athenians had already smuggled themselves into the city; they made a sally and gave battle outside the fortress, and it was then that among other Lakonians Lysander fell.[30] [4] Pausanias was collecting forces from Tegea and all over Arkadia, and he was too late for the fight; when he entered Boiotia he heard of the defeat of Lysander's group, and of the death of Lysander, but, still, he took his army against Thebes and intended to give battle. The Thebans marched out against him at once, and a message came that Thrasyboulos with the Athenians was not far off, waiting for the Lakonians to open battle, in order to attack from behind when the battle had started. [5] Pausanias was frightened of being caught between two enemy forces, so he made a truce with Thebes, and buried the dead who had fallen below the walls of Haliartos. The Lakonians did not like the idea of this, but I praise him for it, and this is why: Pausanias knew very well that Lakonian defeats have always involved being trapped and cut off by their enemies, and what

29. We are now in the period after the Peloponnesian War; cf. Xenophon, Hellenika, 2, 4, 29f.

30. In 395. Cf. Bk IX, 32 (5).

happened at Thermopylai and on the island of Sphakteria gave him grounds to fear he might be responsible for a third catastrophe. [6] But the Spartans at the time blamed him for his slow arrival in Boiotia; he refused to appear in court, and the Tegeans accepted him as a fugitive in the sanctuary of Alean Athene. This sanctuary was respected by the whole Peloponnese from ancient times and gave particular security to its fugitives. The Lakonians showed this with Pausanias and even earlier with Leotychides, and the Argives with Chrysis, none of whom was even asked for while they stayed there in sanctuary.[31] [7] When Pausanias fled, his sons Agesipolis and Kleombrotos were still extremely young, so Aristodemos, who was a very close relative, was regent for them. The Lakonian success at Corinth happened under Aristodemos's command.[32]

[8] When Agesipolis grew up and took over authority, his first war was inside the Peloponnese with the Argives.[33] As he brought his army from Tegea into the Argolid, the Argives sent him a herald to renew a sacred ancestral truce that had existed between the Dorians from ancient times. Agesipolis refused to swear, advanced his army, and destroyed the countryside. Then the god quaked in the earth, but even so Agesipolis was not going to take away his forces, even though of all peoples in Greece the Lakonians like the Athenians were most terrified of divine warnings in nature. [9] He had already encamped under the walls of Argos, and still the god quaked underground, and soldiers in his army were struck down by thunderbolts, and some went crazy from the thunder and lightning. So, still unwillingly, he marched his army out of the Argolid; then he mounted an expedition against Olynthos. He was winning the war and had already taken most of the other Chalkidian cities, and was hoping to

31. For Chrysis, the priestess who burnt down the Heraion at Argos, cf. Bk II, 17 (7); for Leotychides cf. Herodotos, 6, 72, and Pausanias, Bk III, 7 (10). For the temple of Alean Athene at Tegea cf. Bk VIII, 45 (4f.).

32. In 394. Cf. Bk I, 29 (11).

33. Cf. Xenophon, *Hellenika*, 4, 7, 2. The invasion was in 387.

take Olynthos itself, when sudden sickness and death took it from his grasp.[34]

[1] Agesipolis died childless, and the crown went to 6 Kleombrotos. It was under his command they fought the Boiotians at Leuktra. Kleombrotos behaved well, and died very early in the battle. In great disasters the god first takes away the commander, as he took away Hippokrates son of Ariphron from the Athenians when he commanded them at Delion, and Leosthenes in Thessaly.[35] [2] Kleombrotos's elder son Agesipolis did nothing great and memorable; the younger son Kleomenes inherited the crown when his brother died. His sons were Akrotatos and Kleonymos, but Akrotatos payed the debt of our nature even before his father Kleomenes, and later, when Kleomenes died, there was a quarrel over the crown between his son Kleonymos and Akrotatos's son Areus. The Elders gave a judgement that the royal throne belonged by ancestry to Areus and not Kleonymos. [3] Kleonymos really blazed with fury to be driven out of his kingship, and the Governors tried to charm him with honours and made him general of the army, so that he could never turn into an enemy of Sparta. But in the end he was bold enough to take many most hostile actions against his country, and he brought in Pyrros son of Aiakides against Lakonia.[36]

[4] While Akrotatos's son Areus was reigning at Sparta, Antigonos son of Demetrios attacked Athens by land and sea. An Egyptian expeditionary force under Patroklos came to defend the Athenians, and the whole Lakonian people marched out to fight, with King Areus commissioned to command them. [5] Antigonos surrounded Athens and prevented the

34. OLYNTHOS was the rich and at this period very important city commanding the great gulf south-east of Thessalonike. It was a formidable barricade between Macedonia and Greece.

35. Leuktra (cf. Bk IX, 13) was in 371, Delion in 424; Leosthenes' defeat in Thessaly in command of an allied Greek army against Antipater at Lamia! was in 323 (cf. Bk I, 29 (13)).

36. For the career of the royal adventurer Pyrros, cf. Bk I, 11 (1f.); for this war cf. Bk I, 13 (4–6).

Athenian allies from entering the city, so Patroklos sent messengers to get Areus and the Lakonians to open a battle, promising he would himself attack the Macedonians from behind as soon as the battle started, but saying that it was not sensible for Egyptian sailors to make a first attack against Macedonians on dry land. Out of good will to Athens and out of their longing to do something future generations would remember, the Lakonians were ready to put themselves in danger, [6] but Areus withdrew his army, because his provisions were exhausted. He preferred to bottle up their careless courage for home consumption, and not pour it away so generously on other people's occasions. But Athens held out a very long time, and Antigonos made peace, with the condition that he installed a garrison in the MUSEUM.[37] As time went by, Antigonos withdrew the garrison of his own free will, and Areus had a son called Akrotatos and Akrotatos a son called Areus, who died of a sickness when he was just eight years old. [7] In the blood descent of Eurysthenes in the male line there was no one left but Leonidas son of Kleonymos, an extremely old man, and the Lakonians gave him the crown. As it happened, Lysander, the descendant of Aristokritos's son Lysander, had an implacable feud with Leonidas, and Lysander won over Kleombrotos, who was married to Leonidas's daughter. Once he had hold of Kleombrotos, he brought a number of accusations against Leonidas, including the charge that when he was a boy he took an oath to his father Kleonymos to destroy Sparta. [8] So Leonidas lost his kingdom, and Kleombrotos became king in his place. If Leonidas had given rein to his anger and gone off like Demaratos to the king of Macedon or of Egypt, then even if the

37. This war, which is called the Chremonidean War after the Athenian politician Chremonides, is difficult to date exactly and in several ways obscure. The fort of Korone on the headland south of PORTORAPHTI in Attica, the fort on Patroklos's island off Sounion, and a number of other Attic fortifications can be connected with it. The Museum is the hill now called PHILOPAPPOU which screens Athens from the sea and commanded the Long Walls. The fortress walls on the summit, which connect with the city circuit wall, can still be traced. Museum *mouseion* means place of the muses.

Spartans had changed their minds it would have done him no good; what in fact happened was that he was exiled by the people and went to Arkadia, and a few years afterwards the Lakonians brought him home and made him king all over again.

[9] I have already discussed in the story of Aratos of Sikyon the boldness of character and at the same time the courage of Leonidas's son Kleomenes, and how it was through him that the Spartans lost their kings. I also dealt with the way in which Kleomenes died in Egypt.[38]

[1] Kleomenes the son of Leonidas was the last of the family 7 of Eurysthenes, who were called the Agiadai, to reign in Sparta. What I have heard about the other family is as follows. Aristodemos's son Prokles called his son Soos. They say Soos's son Eurypon became so famous that this family, which until his time was called the Prokleidai, was afterwards called the Eurypontidai after Eurypon. [2] His son was called Prytanis. It was in his reign that Lakonian hostility against Argos began, and even earlier than that the Lakonians fought the Kynoureans. In the generations that followed, in the reigns of Prytanis's son Eunomos and Eunomos's son Polydektes, Sparta lived in peace. [3] But Polydektes' son Charillos devastated the Argive territory – it was he who invaded the Argolid – and not many years afterwards there was the Spartan expedition against Tegea with Charillos in command, when Lakonia hoped to uproot all the Tegeans and annex the Tegean plain from Arkadia. They attacked because of a treacherous oracle.[39]

[4] When Charillos died his son Nikander succeeded. In his reign the Messenians caught King Teleklos of the other family in the Limnaian sanctuary. Nikander also invaded the Argolid and did a lot of damage in the countryside. In this action the people of Asine worked with the Lakonians, and not long afterwards they paid the penalty to Argos in the terrible devastation of their own country and became fugi-

38. Cf. Bk II, 9 (1–3).
39. Cf. Bk VIII, 1 (6). This was apparently in the early eighth century.

25

tives.[40] [5] Nikander's son Theopompos who reigned after him will crop up again in this book in my essay on Messenia. While Theopompos still sat on the throne of Sparta there was fought the war between Lakonia and Argos over the land called the Thyreatis,[41] but Theopompos himself took no part in the action chiefly because of his grief and because of his age, because Archidamos had died in his lifetime. [6] Archidamos did not die childless; he left a son Zeuxidamos, whose son Anaxidamos succeeded in his turn. In his reign the Messenians lost the war against Sparta for a second time, and fled from the Peloponnese. Anaxidamos had a son Archidamos, who had a son Agesikles; both of them lived their whole lives in peace with no experience of war. [7] Agesikles' son Ariston married a woman who is said to have been the most unattractive virgin in Lakonia, but Helen made her the most beautiful woman.[42] After Ariston married her she bore a son Demaratos in only seven months; as he was sitting in council with the governors, in came a house-slave to say his son was born. Ariston forgot what the *Iliad* says about the birth of Eurystheus, or perhaps he had never known, and denied that the child was his because of the seven months. [8] He was sorry later for what he said then, but when Demaratos was king and glorious in Sparta among other things for helping Kleomenes to liberate Athens from the dictatorship of the

40. For Teleklos cf. Bk IV, 4 (2–3). The excavations show independently of literary sources that the great fortress of Asine was abandoned some time a little before 700 B.C. and not resettled before the Hellenistic period. Cf. G. L. Huxley, *Early Sparta*, p. 21 and note 79.

41. Cf. Bk·II, 38 (5).

42. Helen was worshipped as a goddess at Sparta like the Dioskouroi, who were her brothers. She had some of the characteristics of a tree-nymph, and she was associated with the dances of young girls. She is already an important and powerful divinity in the poetry of the archaic age; the origins of her cult are shadowy, but it seems that any Homeric elements in it are rather late. The pre-existence of Helen and perhaps Agamemnon as divinities must have been among the germs of the Homeric legends, which for many reasons and in many ways grew away from these conceptions; but the points where living legend and cult in the Greece of Pausanias came closest to Homeric poetry are usually cases of the influence of that poetry.

Peisistratidai, Ariston's thoughtlessness and Kleomenes' enmity made him a commoner. He went to King Darius of the Persians and they say his descendants lived on in Asia long afterwards.

[9] Leotychides who became king in his place worked with the Athenians and their general Xanthippos son of Ariphron in the action at Mykale, and afterwards fought a campaign against the Aleuadai in Thessaly.[43] He could have turned the whole of Thessaly upside down as he won every battle, but he took bribes from the Aleuadai. [10] He was brought to justice in Lakonia but went into voluntary exile in Tegea. There he stayed as a fugitive in the sanctuary of Alean Athene,[44] and as his son Zeuxidamos had died of sickness in his lifetime and before his exile, Zeuxidamos's son Archidamos succeeded. This was the Archidamos who did such terrible damage to the Athenians by invading Attica every year and methodically devastating it at every invasion, and who besieged and took the fortified city of Plataia, which was friendly to Athens. [11] But he did nothing at all to bring about the Peloponnesian War against Athens; on the contrary he did everything in his power to maintain the oaths of peace. The responsibility for the outbreak of war belongs principally to Sthenelaidas, who was always an important figure in Lakonia and at that moment was a Governor. Until then Greece had walked with its feet well planted on the ground, but that war shook it from its foundations like an earthquake, and afterwards Philip the son of Amyntas found it already rotted and unhealthy and ruined it altogether.

[1] When Archidamos died leaving two sons, his elder son 8 Agis succeeded and not his younger son Agesilaos. Archidamos also had a daughter called Kyniska who longed to do well in the Olympic games, and was the first woman to own race-horses and the first woman to win an Olympic victory.

43. The battle of Mykale was a naval action against Persia in the channel between Samos and Asia Minor in 479. The Aleuadai had collaborated with the Persians in Greece.
44. 5 (7) above, and Note 32.

Women after Kyniska's time and particularly Lakonian women have won Olympic victories, but no woman is more famous as an Olympic winner than Kyniska.[45] [2] The Spartans seem to me the least interested of all mankind in poetry and the praise that it can offer, because apart from the verse inscription someone or other wrote for Kyniska, and before that the inscription Simonides wrote for Pausanias inscribed on the tripod at Delphi, no composition is recorded by any poet for the Lakonian kings.[46]

[3] In the reign of Archidamos's son Agis the Lakonians had a number of quarrels with Elis; they were particularly furious because Elis banned Lakonia from the Olympic games and the Olympic sanctuary. So they sent a herald with an ultimatum to Elis to grant independence to the Lepreans and to all the other provincial peoples subject to Elis. Elis replied that when they saw freedom in the cities of the Spartan provinces there would be no delay about releasing their own; so the Lakonians under King Agis invaded Eleia.[47] [4] At that moment the god quaked in the earth and the army retreated after reaching Olympia and the Alpheios. The next year Agis raided and ruined in the countryside and took away most of the cattle, and an Elean called Xenias who was a private friend of Agis and a public friend of Lakonia led a rich men's revolution against the people; but before Agis and his army came to defend him the people's president in Elis, Thrasydaios, fought and beat Xenias and his friends and threw them out of the city. [5] When Agis withdrew his army, he left a

45. Cf. Bk VI, 1 (6). Her name means Puppy. A small Doric capital with her name on it, which apparently once held up a dedication to Helen, was found in Sparta in 1909 (I.G., V (i) 235).

46. Pausanias is wrong about poetry down to Pindar; until the emergence of democracy and the development of tragic poetry, Sparta has a more glittering record of poets than Athens. What his accusation amounts to is that Spartan kings have no verse epitaphs, which is both true and interesting. Kyniska's epigram was preserved as an example of a metrical anomaly in the thirteenth book of the *Palatine Anthology* (no. 16); cf. Bk VI, 1 (6). The epigram on Pausanias was recorded by Thukydides (1, 132). Cf. Bk X, 13 (9).

47. This was in 401 B.C. Cf. Bk V, 4 (8).

Spartan called Lysistratos with part of his forces and the Elean fugitives to make what havoc they could in the Leprean countryside. In the third year of the war Agis and his army were getting ready to invade Elea once again, but Thrasydaios and the Eleans, who were in the last stages of ruin, agreed to give up their authority in the provinces and to demolish the fortifications of their city,[48] and to let the Lakonians sacrifice to the god at Olympia and compete in the Olympic games. [6] Agis also continually invaded Attica and fortified a strongpoint against Athens at Dekeleia.[49] When the Athenian fleet was broken up at Aigospotamoi, Agis and Lysander broke a sacred oath which all Lakonia had sworn to Athens; but it was their own idea, independent of the Spartan people, to suggest to their allies the obliteration of Athens. [7] These were Agis's greatest military distinctions; but he repeated over his son Leotychides the rash behaviour of Ariston over Demaratos, and by some malicious providence it came to the attention of the Governors that he thought Leotychides was not his own. Agis like Ariston was overtaken by remorse, and as they were carrying him home sick from Arkadia he made the crowd of people at Heraia[50] his witnesses that he believed

48. But Elis had no fortifications at this time, as we learn from Xenophon (*Hellenika*, 3, 2, 27). It is hard to prove such a negative by excavation, but at least no such fortifications have been found. L. Dindorf had astutely pointed out that Pausanias's error could have arisen from a minute copyist's mistake in a manuscript of Xenophon, but it is likely on other grounds that Pausanias was not drawing directly on Xenophon but on some writer who followed him. Copyists' mistakes of this kind are by no means confined to the confused traditions of the Middle Ages; some of the worst tangles in the text of ancient authors already occur in the papyri; Dindorf is surely right.

49. The remains of this fort, now called PALAIOKASTRO, stand on the hill commanding a pass over Mount Parnes, about fifteen miles north-north-west of Athens; it is inaccessible, because it is inside the royal estate of TATOI; there are some ruins of an Athenian counter-fort built higher up on the hill overlooking the pass. This route (close to that of a modern minor road) carried an important ancient road between Athens and Euboia which can still be followed, though not without a map and compass, from the fields behind VARYBOMBI to the Boiotian plain.

50. He was on his way home from Delphi after consecrating the spoils of his war against Elis. For Heraia in Arkadia, cf. Bk VIII, 26 (1). Xenophon

Leotychides was most certainly his own son, and he demanded and implored in tears they should tell Lakonia what he said. [8] When Agis died Agesilaos reminded the Lakonians what he had once said about Leotychides, and wanted to drive Leotychides from the throne, but the Arkadians from Heraia came to bear witness for Leotychides about Agis's dying words. [9] Agesilaos and Leotychides argued even worse than before over the Delphic oracle given at that time. It went like this:

> *Boasting Sparta, be careful not to sprout*
> *a crippled kingship, you are sure-footed;*
> *unexpected troubles will overtake you,*
> *the lamentations of the storm of war*
> *destroyer of mankind.*

[10] Leotychides said this meant Agesilaos, who was lamed in one of his feet, but Agesilaos referred it to Leotychides being no true son of Agis. The Lakonians did not take the difficulty to Delphi even though it was them the oracle concerned; I think Lysander was responsible for this, as he used every means to bring the crown to Agesilaos.

9 [1] Agesilaos reigned as king, and the Lakonians decided to take a fleet and cross into Asia to remove Darius's son Artaxerxes.[51] They were told by their government that it was not Artaxerxes who gave them money for ships in the war against Athens, but Cyrus. Agesilaos was appointed to take the army over to Asia and to command the land forces. He sent round to the whole Peloponnese except Argos, and also to the mainland of Greece, to demand regiments. [2] The Corinthians were particularly eager to take part in the expedition against Asia, but suddenly their temple of Olympian Zeus was burnt to the ground;[52] they took this for an

---

(*Hellenika*, 3, 3, 1f.) says Agis, who was an old man, fell sick at Heraia and was carried home to Sparta to die. He says nothing about the Heraian witnesses.

51. He crossed into Asia in 396.

52. Cf. Bk II, 5 (5). The ruins of this temple were so effectively reduced that they have not been found. There is a possibility of identifying it with the meagre relics of an enormous but unidentified late fifth-century temple half

evil omen and unwillingly stayed at home. The Athenian excuse was that their city was recovering from the Peloponnesian War and the plague, to the prosperity it once had; but really they had news that Konon had gone up to see the king, and this was their chief reason for keeping quiet. [3] Aristomelidas was sent on an embassy to Thebes; he was Agesilaos's mother's father, and on familiar terms with the Thebans; at the fall of the fortress of Plataia he was one of the judges who condemned the prisoners to death.[53] The Thebans refused to help; they gave the same reply as the Athenians; but when the home and the allied armies had collected and the ships were ready, Agesilaos went to Aulis to sacrifice to Artemis, because that was where Agamemnon placated the goddess before he led the expedition against Troy.[54] [4] Agesilaos thought himself king of a richer city than Agamemnon and like him the lord of all Greece, and he believed that to overpower Artaxerxes and possess the riches of Persia would be a more glorious achievement than the destruction of the kingdom of Priam. But as he was making his sacrifice and the thigh meat of the victims was already in flames, he was attacked by armed Thebans; they scattered it from the altar and drove him from the sanctuary. [5] Agesilaos was grieved by the unfinished sacrifice, but all the same he crossed over to Asia and attacked Sardis. The greatest part of lower Asia at that time was Lydia, and SARDIS was its wealthiest and grandest city; it was the residence appointed for the satrap of the sea-coast, just as SOUSA was for the king. [6] Tisaphernes the satrap of Ionia gave battle in the Hermos plain;[55] Agesilaos overcame the Persian cavalry and the biggest force of infantry that had mustered since the army of Xerxes, and Darius's

a kilometre north-west of the temple of Apollo, discussed by W. B. Dinsmoor in *Hesperia*, Supp. VIII, 1949, p. 104f.

53. Cf. Bk IX, 1 (1f.).          54. Cf. Bk IX, 19 (6–8).

55. The Hermos is the modern GEDIZ, north of Smyrna (IZMIR). The rich ruins of Sardis are at SART on the ancient Paktolos, a tributary of the Hermos, a little west of SALIHLI, south of the main road from Izmir. For the ruins of Sousa, cf. Pauly-Wissowa, *Supplement VIII*, 1251–1274. It lies away beyond Iraq, inside the Persian border, south of Luristan and north of the Persian gulf.

army before him, against the Scythians and against Athens. The Lakonians were delighted by Agesilaos's eager activity and made him commander of the fleet as well. Agesilaos commissioned Peisander to be captain of the warships – he happened to be married to Peisander's sister – and he himself attended vigorously to the war on dry land. [7] But the evil eye of some divinity prevented him from fulfilling his plans. When Artaxerxes heard of the battles Agesilaos had won and his continual and overwhelming advances, in spite of good service in the past he condemned Tisaphernes to death, and sent Tithraustes, who was a cunning planner with a grudge against the Lakonians, to the coast. [8] Tithraustes came to Sardis, and at once thought of a way to force the Lakonians to recall their army from Asia. He sent a Rhodian called Timokrates to Greece with money and with orders to raise a war against Lakonia. In Argos, Kylon and Sodamas are supposed to have accepted this money, and in Thebes Androkleides, Ismenias and Amphithemis; Kephalos of Athens had a share, so did Epikrates, and the Argive party of Corinth, Polyanthes and Timolaos.[56] [9] But the open occasion for war came from the Lokrians of Amphissa. There was some disputed territory the Lokrians claimed from Phokis, and the Thebans around Ismenia egged them on to cut the ripe wheat from it and drive off the livestock. The Phokians invaded Lokris in full force and devastated the countryside.[57] [10] The Lokrians brought in Thebans to fight on their side and looted Phokis. So the Phokians went to Lakonia to complain about Thebes and said what the Thebans had done to them. The Lakonians decided to go to war with Thebes; one of their quarrels was the outrage at Aulis at Agesilaos's sacrifice. [11]

56. The source of this detailed information is certainly not Xenophon (*Hellenika*, 3, 5, 1) or Plutarch; it may possibly be Ephoros of Kyme, a fourth-century historian and pupil of Isokrates, who wrote a history of Greece from the Trojan War to his own times. Cf. W. Immerwahr, *Die Lakonika des Pausanias* (1899), p. 45, and pp. 26f.

57. Here again Pausanias disagrees with Xenophon. For the Ismenian sanctuary of Thebes, cf. Bk IX, 10. It was an oracle of Apollo (cf. Bk IV, 32 (5)), and the Lokrians were evidently encouraged by an oracular reply.

Athens knew in advance how Lakonia felt, and sent a request
to Sparta that no military force should be used against
Thebes, but that all the Spartan complaints should be decided
by trial; the Lakonians were furious and dismissed the ambassadors. I have already described what happened then, how
the Lakonians marched and how Lysander died, in the story
of Pausanias.[58] [12] The whole Corinthian War as it was
called grew and grew from the Lakonian march on Boiotia.
All this forced Agesilaos to bring his army back from Asia.
He crossed by ship from Abydos to Sestos,[59] passed through
Thrace and came to Thessaly, where to please Thebes the
Thessalians tried to obstruct his passage. Also they had an old
friendship with the city of Athens. [13] But Agesilaos drove
off their cavalry and passed through Thessaly. He crossed
Boiotia with a victory over the Thebans and their allies at
Koroneia; when the Boiotians were routed some of them
took refuge in the sanctuary of Itonian Athene, and although
Agesilaos was wounded in that battle, even so he committed
no sacrilege against the fugitives.[60]

[1] Not long afterwards the exiled Lakonian party from    10
Corinth held the Isthmian games; the people in the city were
frightened into keeping quiet by Agesilaos, but the city of
Corinth and the Argives held an Isthmian festival of their own
after he withdrew to Sparta.[61] He came back to Corinth in
force, but it was time for the Hyakinthia, so he let the Amyklaians go home to perform the traditional service for Apollo
and Hyakinthos. This division was attacked on the way and
wiped out by Athenians under Iphikrates.[62] [2] Agesilaos also

58. Cf. Bk III, 5 (3f.).
59. That is he crossed the narrow Hellespont from Asia to Europe.
60. Cf. Bk IX, 6 (4), and 34 (1).        61. In the spring of 390.

62. The Hyakinthia was a three-day festival probably celebrated in early
summer, but the arguments about its exact date are tortuous and vexing. A
description of the celebration at a rather late period from the *Lakonika* of the
lost author Polykrates has been preserved by Athenaios (4, 17; 139 c-f).
Hyakinthos is a pre-Greek name, but Apollo had taken over this festival almost
completely, cf. Bk III, 19 (3–5). There is an interesting English summary of
special studies of Hyakinthos by M. J. Mellink (Utrecht, 1943).

went over to help the Aitolians who were losing a war with Akarnania; he forced the Akarnanians to give up the war when they were close to taking KALYDON and all the Aitolian towns.[63] Later on he even sailed against Egypt to help a rebellion against the king of the Egyptians; his achievements in Egypt were numerous and memorable. And since he was an old man by this time, he died on that journey. His body was brought home, and the Lakonians buried him with greater honours than the other kings.

[3] In the reign of Agesilaos's son Archidamos the Phokians occupied the Delphic sanctuary. So the Thebans went to war with Phokis; the Phokians on their own account employed mercenaries, and the Lakonians and the Athenians fought for them as well, the Athenians because they were bound to Phokis by the memory of old services, the Lakonians on the same excuse of friendship, but really because they were anti-Theban. Theopompos says that Archidamos had touched money and that his wife Deinicha took a bribe from the influential circle in Phokis, and that this made Archidamos rather keener on the alliance.[64] [4] Taking holy money and defending the looters of the most famous of all prophetic sanctuaries are things I cannot put down to his credit, but I can praise him for this: the Phokians had dared to agree on the slaughter of every boy in Delphi of fighting age, the enslavement of the women and the children, and the utter destruction of the city, but Archidamos begged them off. [5] Later he crossed over to Italy to help Tarentum in a war against its barbarous neighbours. He was killed there by the savages, and Apollo had his revenge: the body never found a grave.[65] His elder son Agis died fighting Antipater and the

63. The ruins of Kalydon lie just north of EVINOCHORION, seven miles east of MISSOLONGHI, commanding the north shore of the gulf of Patrai. Cf. Bk VII, 21.

64. This happened in 357. For Theopompos of Chios, a mid-fourth-century historian, cf. Jacoby, *Fragments of the Greek Historians*, II B, n. 115 pp. 526f. This is Jacoby's Fr. 312 (p. 602).

65. The various ancient references to this divine punishment are discussed in Jacoby's note on Theopompos, Fr. 232–4 (II B. 2, p. 388).

Macedonians, but his younger son Eudamidas reigned in peace in Lakonia. My treatment of Sikyon has already given the story of Eudamidas's son Agis, and Agis's son Euryda-midas.[66]

[6] On the way from the Hermai the whole area is full of oak-trees; the place is called SKOTITAS, not because of the continuous darkness under the trees, but because Skotitas was a ritual title of Zeus, and a sanctuary of Zeus Skotitas lies more or less a mile and a quarter to the left of the road if you turn off.[67] If you come back to the main road and go on a little way and then turn off again to the left, there is a statue of Herakles and a trophy. Herakles is supposed to have put up the trophy after killing Hippokoon and his sons.[68] [7] The third turning off from the straight road goes to the right, to Karyai and the sanctuary of Artemis: the place belongs to Artemis and the nymphs and is called KARYAI; there is a statue of Artemis Karyatis standing in the open air, where the Lakonian girls come to dance a traditional local dance every year.[69] Turn back and follow the main road and you come to

66. Cf. Bk II, 8 (5), and 9 (1). It hardly needs saying that these lists of kings are of problematic historical value.

67. For the Hermai, cf. Bk III, Note 1. A succession of travellers and scholars since the French survey of 1829 have noticed a likely looking wood of oak-trees in this area. The site of the SANCTUARY is possibly a chapel of HAGIOS THEODOROS near BARBITZA on the slopes of PARNON, south-south-west of HAGIOS PETROS, but this traditional identification is really simply a guess. Lieutenant Gen. Jockmus's alternative site, which Frazer records, is almost certainly wrong, since it appears to be in the wrong direction from the Murdered Men (cf. Bk III, Note 1). Skotitas means the dark one; as a title of Zeus it must mean Zeus of the Underworld (there is a Plouton Skotios). The cult of Zeus as a dark god was by no means unknown in Greece.

68. Cf. Bk III, 15 (4), and 19 (7).

69. The modern KARYAI is a village once called ARACHOVA and recently renamed, south-west of HAGIOS PETROS. K. A. Romaios (in the periodical Peloponnesiaka, 1958–9, pp. 376f.) was confident that the ancient Karyai was somewhere just north of this village (and Artemis's sanctuary at a local chapel of the Panagia); but without a thorough archaeological survey of the entire region, such questions cannot be solved. The site called Analepsis west of Bourboura, which is not far away, and which Romaios (following Frazer and Loring) in 1902 believed was Karyai (cf. I.G., V, (i), p. 172 and Praktika, 1950,

the ruins of Sellasia. As I said before, it was captured by the Achaians when they won a battle against Lakonia under King Kleomenes, Leonidas's son.[70]

[8] At THORNAX, where you arrive if you go on, is a statue of Pythaian Apollo made in the same way as the one at Amyklai; I shall describe it at Amyklai. The Amyklaian

*1. Apollo at Amyklai*

Apollo holds a higher position in Lakonia: so that for example they used the gold Kroisos of Lydia sent to Pythaian Apollo to decorate the statue at Amyklai.[71]

---

pp. 234–41), appears to be just as likely or unlikely a candidate. Romaios came to think *Analepsis* was Iasos (cf. Bk VII, 13 (7)). There is a mythological explanation of the cult of Artemis Karyatis in Servius's commentary on Vergil (*Eclogues*, 8, 30). Karyai means the walnut-trees. The cult of Artemis Karyatis seems to be the origin of the architectural term Caryatid. There is perhaps the suggestion even in the Caryatids of the Erechtheion of a very solemn dance or procession.

70. Cf. Bk II, 9 (2f.). The ruins of SELLASIA can be identified with certainty, south-west of HAGIOS PETROS and of KARYAI, west of the main north–south road linking TRIPOLIS to Sparta, which it commands. The modern SELLASIA was once called VOURLIA; the fortress is two or three miles east of this village, on top of a hill called HAGIOS KONSTANTINOS.

71. For Apollo at Amyklai, cf. Bk III, 19 (2). He was a pillar-like armed man with a spear and bow. The Spartans sent to Sardis to buy gold for Apollo at

[1] Beyond Thornax you come to the city originally called 11
SPARTA which in the course of time came also to be called
Lakedaimon, the old territorial name. Before I speak about
the Spartans I must make the same clarification that I made in
my essay on Attica: I am not going through everything in
order, but selecting and discussing the really memorable
things. It has been the intention of this book from the beginning to discriminate what truly merited discussion from the
mass of worthless stories which every people will tell you
about themselves. Since my plan has been a good one there
is no change I can make in it.

[2] The Lakonians of Sparta have a MARKET-PLACE worth
seeing, and the council-house of the Elders and the government chambers of the Governors and the protectors of laws
and of the Bidiaioi are in the market-place.[72] The Elders are

Thornax, but Kroisos offered it as a present to the god (Herodotos 1, 69). The
Thornax shrine was evidently on level ground somewhere west of the river
Eurotas and south of Sellasia, (Xenophon, *Hellenika*, 6, 5, 27; cf. also Polybios,
16, 16). It must therefore have been very close to Sparta. The existence of some
such settlement has been confirmed by the evidence of pottery (Waterhouse and
Hope Simpson, *B.S.A.*, 55, 1960, p. 82). The shrine has not yet been found.
The title 'Pythaian' is a variant of 'Pythian'; cf. Note 78.

72. The site of Sparta lies almost in the shadow of the great Byzantine
fortress of MISTRA; it was called PALAIOKASTRO, the old castle, and was
never entirely abandoned. Its site became known to the west through Gemistos
Plethon of MISTRA, which was also called SPARTOVOUNO. Cyriaco of Ancona
visited it in September 1437. The area of ancient Sparta was then still littered
with fragments of antiquity, including inscriptions, though a great part of it
seems to have been deliberately destroyed by the Abbé Fourmont in the
eighteenth century, who ravaged Sparta with from forty to sixty workmen
for thirty days, in order to increase by rarity the value of the notes he took.
Much of what was left was taken by the villagers of another village for building
materials. The first building to be positively identified was the theatre, which
was discovered by the Russian military expedition of 1770 under Count Orlov,
while they were digging themselves in against the Turks. In the 1840s Ernst
Curtius discovered the ruins of the Eurotas bridge by which I suppose Pausanias entered the city. There is an interesting archaeological guide to Sparta in
modern Greek by C. A. Christou. The *agora*, the chief public square of
Pausanias's Sparta, seems to have been the level ground south-east of the
akropolis and the theatre. We know from Thukydides (1, 10) that classical

the principal political committee of Lakonia, and the rest are government officers. There are five Governors and five Bidiaioi; the Governors control the most important arrangements and years are named after them, just as one of the nine at Athens is eponymous officer; the Bidiaioi hold the games at the Planes and the other traditional games for lads past adolescence. [3] The most striking monument in the market-place is called the PERSIAN COLONNADE, built from the spoils of the Persian Wars.[73] It was altered in the course of time until it reached the size and the decorative splendour you now see. One of the Persians carved in marble on the pillars is Mardonios. There is also a sculpture of Artemisia, daughter of Lygdamis and queen of Halikarnassos. She is supposed to have volunteered to fight for Xerxes against Greece, and done great deeds in the sea-fight at Salamis.[74] [4] The TEMPLES on the market-place are consecrated to Caesar, the first Roman to set his heart on supreme sovereignty and the first founder of the established empire, and to Caesar's son Augustus, who established the empire more solidly and outdid his father in dignity and in power. His name was Augustus; in Greek it means 'august'. [5] By Augustus's altar they show you a bronze portrait of Agias. They say this Agias by his prophetic advice to Lysander took the whole Athenian fleet at Aigospotamoi except for ten warships that fled to Cyprus.[75] All the rest were caught by the Lakonians, ships and men. Agias was the son of Agelochos, whose father Tisamenos belonged to the Elean clan of the Iamidai.[76] [6] There was a prophecy that Tisamenos was going to carry off five very famous

Sparta was not physically impressive; Roman Sparta was certainly more elaborate, but very little of the agora is to be seen. Cf. B.S.A., 12, 1905–6, pp. 432–5 and the general map in B.S.A., 13.

73. The statues of the enemy held up the roof. Cf. Vitruvius, 1, 1, 6.

74. This history is told more fully by Herodotos (7, 99, and 8, 87f.); Pausanias combines as well as abbreviates the two passages and adds a seed of uncertainty. Herodotos, whom he trusts, is very likely not his direct source here.

75. The decisive battle of the Peloponnesian War.

76. They had prophetic powers; cf. Bk IV, 16 (1), etc. This story comes from Herodotos (1, 33–6).

contests, so he trained for the Olympic pentathlon but he was beaten, though he came first in two events. He beat Hieronymos of Andros in the running and the jumping, but he was beaten in the wrestling and lost his victory, so then he understood the oracle: the god was going to give him prophecy and victory in five battles. [7] The Lakonians had heard what the Pythian priestess had predicted for Tisamenos, and they persuaded him to move from Elis to prophesy for the Spartan people. Tisamenos won his five battles, first against the Persians at Plataia, second at Tegea in a battle the Lakonians fought against Tegeans and Argives, then at Dipaia, which is an Arkadian town in the region of Mainalos, against all Arkadia except for Mantineia; [8] the fourth time he fought against the rebel serfs from the isthmus[77] at Ithome – it was not all the serfs who rebelled, but the Messenians who split off from the old serfs, as I shall explain presently. Lakonia was persuaded by Tisamenos and the Delphic oracle to let the rebels get away under a truce. Finally Tisamenos prophesied for the Lakonians when they met the Athenians and the Argives at Tanagra.

[9] This was what I discovered about Tisamenos. The Spartans have statues in their market-place of Pythaian Apollo and Artemis and Leto.[78] This whole area is called the dancing-floor, because on the feast of the naked boys, which is the most solemn of all Lakonian festivals, this is where the boys of fighting age dance to Apollo. Not far from here is a sanctuary of Earth and of Market Zeus,[79] and one of Market

77. This peculiar phrase comes from Herodotos (9, 35). Perhaps Herodotos thought Messenia was an isthmus. There was a legendary Messenian King Isthmios (Bk IV, 3 (10)).

78. 'Pythaian' is a variant of 'Pythian' Apollo. 'Python' is usually the name for Apollo's original enemy, the monster that he killed; its etymology has to do with corruption (cf. Bk X, 6 (5)). Apollo is a god of institutional and ritual purity and its benefits; Apollo and Artemis were Leto's children. For the unconvincing figure of 'Pythaieus son of Apollo', cf. Bk II, 35 (2).

79. The *agora* is not simply a market: the word means the meeting-place and in Homer the assembly of the whole people. It is impossible to convey all the nuances of such a word by blunt translation; in fact it is often difficult to determine them.

Athene and the Poseidon called Safe Poseidon, and one of Apollo and Hera. There is a large statue of the People of Sparta. [10] The Lakonians have a sanctuary of the Fates as well, with the grave of Agamemnon's son Orestes beside it; when his bones were brought from Tegea through the oracle this is where they buried him.[80] Beside his grave is a portrait of Polydoros son of Alkamenes, a king so honoured that the officers of state seal every sealed document with his portrait.[81] [11] There is a Market Hermes holding the boy Dionysos, and the ancient sanctuary of the Governors as it was called, with the monuments of Epimenides the Cretan and Aphareus son of Perieres. I think that the Lakonian story about Epimenides is a more likely one than the Argos story.[82] The Lakonian Hearth goddess and Zeus of Strangers and Athene of Strangers are in the same place as the Fates.

12    [1] As you leave the market-place by LEAVING STREET you come to what they call the CATTLEPRICE; but I must deal first with the name of the street. They say Ikarios held a race for Penelope's lovers, and obviously Odysseus won, but the others were left behind in Leaving Street. [2] I imagine Ikarios got the idea of a race from Danaos, who did the same

80. Cf. Bk III, 3 (6).

81. Polydoros is an early king (cf. Bk III, 3 (1)). His house was also preserved (Bk III, 12 (3)). Since he is supposed to have been murdered, these traces of cult may have been originally a placation of his dangerous ghost; at any rate one should note his association with the magic bones of Orestes, and with the sanctuary of the Fates, who are closely related to the Furies. The seal, if it was not a modern 'portrait', may possibly have been a Minoan seal-stone; these seals survived in use, or were rediscovered, and one was found for example in the context of an archaic Lakonian sanctuary at Tocra in Libya.

82. This Hermes appears on the Roman coinage of Sparta. Epimenides the Cretan was a legendary holy man and prophet whom the Lakonians were supposed to have murdered after a war with Knossos; they claimed to possess his relics in this monument, but he had another grave at Argos; the Argives claimed to have taken home his dead body and buried it at a temple of Athene (cf. Bk II, 21 (3)). Aphareus was a legendary king of Messenia, where he was associated with the cult of the Great goddesses (cf. Bk III, 1 (4), and Bk IV, 2 (7)). No legends have survived about his death or his burial at Sparta, but his two sons were killed by the Dioskouroi.

thing for his daughters.[83] No one would marry them because they were criminals, so he announced he would give them away without a bride-price to anyone who thought they were beautiful; some men did turn up though not many, so he held a race for them, and the first home had first choice and the second home had second choice and so on down to the last. The girls left over had to wait for more lovers to arrive and another race. [3] On this road as I said before lies the Cattleprice, which was once King Polydoros's house; when he died they bought it with cattle from his widow. There was no silver or gold money in those days, and they still used to pay in the old-fashioned way with cattle and slaves and un-minted silver and gold. [4] The sailors on the ships that go to India say the Indians will give produce in exchange for a Greek cargo, but coins are meaningless to them, even though they have an enormous amount of gold and bronze.

Beyond the government chambers of the Bidiaioi there is a SANCTUARY OF ATHENE.[84] Odysseus is supposed to have installed the statue and called it Athene of the Road when he beat Penelope's lovers in the race. He installed three separate sanctuaries of Athene of the Road separately placed. [5] Farther along Leaving Street there are the shrines of the divine heroes Iops, who is thought to have lived in the time of Lelex or Myles, and Amphiaraos son of Oikles. They think this last was built for Amphiaraos by the sons of Tyndareos because he was their cousin.[85] There is another shrine to the divine

83. There was a religious cult of Penelope in eastern Arkadia, where she was supposed to have died (cf. Bk VIII, 12 (3)). There was a legend that she was the mother of the Arkadian god Pan (Herodotos, 2, 145). The story of Danaos and his daughters, who were all married off before lunch, is told in perhaps the most sparkling of all Pindar's odes, the ninth Pythian (193f.). Their crime was murdering the fifty sons of Aigyptos, who were their first husbands, on their wedding night.

84. For the Bidiaioi cf. Bk III, 11 (2), above.

85. No one knows anything at all about Iops; but there are local divine heroes of whom the same can be said everywhere in Greece. The prophet Amphiaraos was a cousin of the sons of Tyndareos, that is of Kastor and Poly-

hero Lelex himself, and not far off a sacred enclosure of
Poseidon with the title Poseidon of Tainaron, with a statue
of Athene quite close to it which they say was dedicated by
Taras and the colonial expedition that went to settle in
Italy.[86] [6] The story about the place called HELLENION is that
when Xerxes crossed into Europe and they were getting ready
to fight for Greece, this was where they planned their method
of defence. The other story is that the men who fought the
Trojan War for Menelaos made their plan here to sail to Troy
and punish Paris for the rape of Helen.

[7] Close to the Hellenion they point out Talthybios's
tomb. But the Achaians of Aigion show you what they, just
like the Lakonians, call Talthybios's tomb in their own
market-place. Talthybios's revenge for the murder of the
heralds who were sent to Greece to demand earth and water
for King Darius fell in Lakonia on the whole people, but in
Athens it struck privately at the family of one man, Miltiades
son of Kimon, because he was responsible for the heralds who
came to Attica being killed by the Athenians.[87]

---

deukes, the Dioskouroi, because Amphiaraos's mother Hypermnestra was their
mother Leda's sister.

86. For Lelex cf. Bk III, 1 (1), above. Tainaron is Cape MATAPAN, the southernmost point of the MANI, which is the central prong of southern Greece (cf. Bk
III, 25 (4–8), and Bk IV, 24 (5)). Poseidon of Tainaron was the god of a rich
and elaborate guild at Sparta which recorded its membership in three inscriptions now in the Sparta museum (n. 205–7, = 1G. V (i) 210–12). They were
found in June 1857 when a house was being built for Loukas Rallis 'in the
lowest part of the city towards the Eurotas'. Mr Rallis in the old Greek tradition built them into his walls above his front door '*come un piccolo museo di
statue ed inscrizioni*' (cf. Conze and Michaelis in *Annuali dell' Instituto di Corres-
pondenza Archaeologica* for 1861, pp. 41f.). Presumably all this rich material
marked the sanctuary of Poseidon and the direction of Pausanias's road, but the
place where it was found cannot now be pinpointed.

87. Talthybios is Agamemnon's herald in the *Iliad*. He was an important
divine hero, and legendary founder of the clan of Talthybiadai, the hereditary
heralds of Sparta (cf. Herodotos 7, 134). Pausanias records several instances of
religious cult attaching to the sacred statues of heralds. Since it was the function
of heralds to ask a truce for the burial of the dead, and since Hermes is a herald
as well as an underworld messenger, there may be a connexion with the cult of
Hermes.

[8] The Lakonians have an ALTAR OF APOLLO of the Peak, and a sanctuary of Earth called GASEPTON, above which is Apollo Maleates.[88] At the end of Leaving Street and very close to the ramparts there is a SANCTUARY OF DIKTYNNA, and the royal GRAVES OF THE EURYPONTIDAI are here. By the Hellenion is a sanctuary of Arsinoe, Leukippos's daughter, whose sisters were the wives of Kastor and Polydeukes. Near the Forts as they call them there is a TEMPLE OF ARTEMIS, and a little farther on you come to the monument of the prophets from Elis called the Iamidai.[89] [9] There is also a sanctuary of Maro and of Alpheios, who, it seems, fought best after Leonidas himself in the battle of Thermopylai. The SANCTUARY OF ZEUS of the Trophy was built by the Dorians after winning a war against the Amyklaians and against all those other Achaians who in those days held Lakonia.[90] The honours given to the SANCTUARY OF THE GREAT MOTHER are really extraordinary. Beyond it lie the shrines of the divine heroes, Theseus's son Hippolytos and Aulo the Arkadian who was a son of Tlesimenes. They say Tlesimenes was a brother of Parthenopaios son of Melanion, and Aulo's father.[91]

[10] There is another road out of the market-square; what they call the CANOPY stands on it; political assemblies take

88. Apollo Maleates had a sanctuary on the hill above the Asklepieion at Epidauros; he is also associated with Asklepios's cave at Trikka in Thessaly; cf. Bk II, 27 (7).

89. For Artemis's nymph Diktynna, patron of the great temple on Aigina, cf. Bk II, 30 (3). The topography of all these Spartan sanctuaries lacks a fixed point. For the Iamidai, cf. Book VI, 2 (5).

90. Pausanias presents a version of early Spartan history in which expansion towards the south came comparatively late, presumably because it was blocked by Amyklai only a few miles away. By Achaians he means non-Dorians, that is the inhabitants of southern Greece before the 'Dorian invasion', which he identifies with the 'return of the children of Herakles'. Historically this theory is of course worthless, but it is only by understanding how most of his views of early history arose from general principles that one can distinguish grains of specific fact and tradition like this one.

91. Aulo is quite unknown except for this passage. His name is a place-name, and there was an Aulonian Asklepios in Messenia (Bk IV, 36 (7); cf. Xenophon, *Hellenika*, 3, 2, 25).

place there to this day.[92] They say the Canopy was built by Theodoros of Samos; he was the first man to forge iron and make statues from it.[93] Here the Lakonians hung up the guitar played by Timotheos of Miletos, when they condemned him for adding four new strings to the old seven-stringed guitar.[94] [11] Beside the Canopy is a rotunda with statues of Olympian Zeus and Olympian Aphrodite. They say it was erected by Epimenides; they disagree with the Argives about Epimenides, and deny that they ever fought a war against Knossos.[95]

13     [1] Near by is the grave of Kynortas the son of Amyklas; KASTOR's TOMB is there, and he has a sanctuary as well as a tomb. They reckon it was not until forty years after their fight with Idas and Lynkeus that the sons of Tyndareos were accepted for gods. They show you the grave of Idas and Lynkeus near the Canopy.[96] According to probability Idas and Lynkeus were buried in Messenia, and not buried here; [2] but the calamities of history and the period of the Messenian exile from the Peloponnese have obliterated a great part of Messenian antiquity, even if you go down there; and since

92. The word is hard to translate; it means a building with a roof like a sun-hat or a parasol. The *Etymologicon Magnum* says this building was a music-hall, an *Odeion*.

93. Elsewhere he says this master worked in bronze (Bk VIII, 14 (8)). He also remarks (Bk X, 38 (6)) that he has never seen any of Theodoros's works, at least his bronze works. Theodoros lived in the mid sixth century.

94. This was a famous piece of Spartan austerity. Timotheos was born about 450 B.C. and seems to have lived to be ninety. Fragments of a rhetorical and grotesquely pretentious poem by him have survived on a papyrus of the fourth century B.C. He regarded himself as a revolutionary musician, which no doubt he was.

95. Cf. Note 82 above.

96. For Kynortas, cf. Bk III, 1 (3). Kastor and Polydeukes are the Dioskouroi, the legendary twin sons of Tyndareos, who came to be thought of as sons of Zeus. In the *Iliad* they are simple human beings and in fact dead and buried in Sparta (3, 237f.). but in the *Odyssey* they take it in turns to be dead or alive (11, 300f.). The fight was when the Dioskouroi carried off two girls, Leukippos's daughters; Leukippos's nephews Idas and Lynkeus were killed, but so was Kastor. The legend is that Kastor was human and Polydeukes was a god, but after Kastor's death they used Polydeukes' immortality on alternate days.

the Messenians have no real information, anyone who wants can contradict them.[97]

Opposite Olympian Aphrodite stands the TEMPLE OF THE MAID of Salvation, supposed to have been built by Thracian Orpheus, though some say Abaris came from the fabulous North to build it. [3] Karneios, whose title is Household Karneios, was worshipped at Sparta even before the return of the children of Herakles; his sanctuary was in the house of Krios son of Theokles, who was a prophet. One day some Dorian spies met Krios's daughter fetching water, and by talking to her they got to see Krios, who told them about the taking of Sparta. [4] All the Dorians have a tradition of the worship of Karnean Apollo, because of Karnos who was by blood an Akarnanian, and a prophet of Apollo. When Hippotes the son of Phylas killed Karnos, the vengeance of Apollo fell on the Dorian camp; Hippotes went into exile for the murder, and since that time the Dorians have had the tradition of placating the Akarnanian prophet. But the Lakonian Household Karneios is different; he is the god who was worshipped in the house of Krios the prophet when the Achaians still owned Sparta.[98] [5] Praxilla has written that Karneios was the son of Europa and Zeus, brought up by Apollo and Leto; and there is another story about him, saying that to make the wooden horse the Greeks cut down wild cherry-trees growing in Apollo's wood on the Trojan mount Ida; when they heard the god was angry with them they placated him with sacrifices and named him Karneian Apollo after the word *kraneia* (a wild cherry-tree), changing the position of the letter R in what is apparently an ancient way.[99]

97. All this is more fully treated in the next book.

98. The family of a hereditary priestess of Karneios in the Roman imperial period has been elaborated and charted on the evidence of inscriptions (*I.G.*, V, p. 131). The word *karnos* means a ram; so does the word *krios*, and rams were slaughtered at the Karneian festival.

99. Praxilla of Sikyon was a fifth-century poetess. The story about the wild cherry may not be as old as it looks; the etymology could easily be Alexandrian. (But cf. also Vergil, *Aeneid*, 3, 22f. and Plutarch, *Romulus*, 20.)

[6] Not far from Karneios is what they call the statue of the Starting god. This is where they say the race for Penelope's lovers began. There is a kind of square with colonnades which in the old days used to be the place for small trading. Beside it is an altar of Zeus of Counsel and Athene of Counsel and even the Dioskouroi of Counsel. [7] Opposite all this stands KOLONA with the temple of Dionysos of Kolona, with the sacred enclosure of a divine hero who is supposed to have shown Dionysos the way to Sparta. The daughters of Dionysos and of Leukippos sacrifice to this hero before sacrificing to the god. The other eleven who are also called daughters of Dionysos have a race in which they run; they took the tradition from Delphi.[100] [8] Not far from Dionysos's temple is a SANCTUARY OF ZEUS of good winds, on the right of which is a shrine of the divine hero Pleuro, ancestor of the sons of Tyndareos on their mother's side, because Asios says in his poetry that Leda's father Thestios was the son of Pluero's son Agenor.[101] Not far from his shrine a TEMPLE OF ARGIVE HERA stands on the top of a slope. It is supposed to have been founded by Lakedaimon's daughter Eurydike, who was Akrisios's wife. The sanctuary of Hera of the Raised Hands was built because of an oracle when the Eurotas was flooding badly.

[9] The ancient wooden idol is called Aphrodite Hera; the custom is for mothers to sacrifice to this goddess when a daughter marries.[102] On this same hillside along the road to

100. These 'daughters' are religious guilds. There is perhaps a remote analogy with the festival being celebrated in Alkman's *Partheneion*. If the Dionysos of Kolona of Pausanias and of his predecessor Polemo (cf. Athenaios 13, 574 c-d) is the same as Strabo's Dionysos in the Marshes (8, 5, 1; 363), then Kolona is presumably the hill between Artemis Orthia and the akropolis.

101. The manuscripts of Pausanias say this poet was called *Areios;* if they are right he seems to be a writer of genealogical hexameters of whom absolutely nothing is known. On the other hand we know that Pausanias quotes Asios elsewhere, and we know that Asios did write a genealogical poem (Bk IV, 2 (1)).

102. Plotinos (3, 5, 8) points out that the planet Venus (Aphrodite) is also Hera's star. The problem of a compound goddess Aphrodite Hera is best discussed by Hitzig and Blümner in their commentary on Pausanias, I (2), p. 782.

the right there is a portrait of Hetoimokles; he and his father Hipposthenes won the wrestling at Olympia eleven times between them; Hipposthenes won one more time than his son.[103]

[1] As you go from the market-place towards the setting sun, 14 you come to the empty monument of Brasidas the son of Tellis.[104] Not far away lies the THEATRE, which is marble and worth seeing. Opposite the theatre stands the MONUMENT OF PAUSANIAS who commanded at Plataia, and the MONUMENT OF LEONIDAS; Pausanias brought his bones home from Thermopylai forty years after the battle.[105] Every year they make speeches about them, and hold games in which only Spartans can enter. There is a stone tablet here with the names of all the men who fought out that battle, and their father's names.

[2] There is a place at Sparta called THEOMELIDA; the royal tombs of the Agiadai are in this part of the city, the Krotanian club is near the tombs, and the Krotanians belong to the Pitanatai; there is a sanctuary of Asklepios near the club called the sanctuary of Asklepios at the Agiadai.[106] Farther on you come to the MONUMENT OF TAINAROS, after whom the cape jutting out into the sea is supposed to have been named, and there are SANCTUARIES of Horse-breeding Poseidon and Artemis of the Goats. On the way back to the club you come to a sanctuary of Issorian Artemis; she also has the title of the Lake-goddess; she is not really Artemis, but Cretan Brito-

103. Cf. Bk V, 8 (9).

104. The fifth-century Brasidas, the greatest Spartan commander in the war with Athens. He was buried at Amphipolis. The Hellenistic THEATRE has been disengaged but its marble has not survived.

105. The traditional 'tomb of Leonidas' identified by early travellers is some distance from the theatre and the akropolis, just on the edge of the modern town. It is a small, massively built Hellenistic temple. These two tombs must have been close to the theatre; they have not been found.

106. The Pitanatai are the villagers of Pitane. The villages of which the city of Sparta, like old London, consisted were never completely integrated; these districts can be more or less accurately identified through a combined use of Pausanias and of the evidence of inscriptions (cf. Christou, *Archaia Sparte*, pp. 47–52). Two stamped tiles belonging to the Pitanatai have been recovered from a wall on KOKKINOKI; the area is now called MAGOULA.

martis, whom I discussed in my description of Aigina.[107] [3]
Very close to the monuments of the Agiadai you will see a
tablet engraved with the races won by a Lakonian called
Chionis, some of them at Olympia. He won seven times at
Olympia, four times over one length and three times over two;
the race with the shield at the end of the games did not yet
exist. They say Chionis took part in the expedition with Battos
of Thera and helped him found Kyrene and subdue the neighbouring Libyans.[108]

[4] This is the origin they give for the foundation of the
SANCTUARY OF THETIS. In the war against the Messenian
rebellion King Anaxander had invaded Messenia and taken
some women prisoners; one of these was Kleo, who was a
priestess of Thetis. Anaxander's wife asked him for Kleo, and
discovered that she had the wooden idol of Thetis, so she and
Kleo made a temple for the goddess. Leandris did this because
of what she saw in a dream.[109] [5] The wooden idol of Thetis
is kept hidden. The Lakonians claim they were taught to
worship Underground Demeter by Orpheus, but in my
opinion it was through the sanctuary at Hermione that the
tradition of Demeter as Underground goddess spread to
Lakonia.[110] There is also a Spartan SANCTUARY OF SARÁPIS,
which is extremely new, and of Zeus under the title of
Olympian.

[6] There is a place they call the RACE-COURSE, where the

107. Cf. Bk II, 30 (3). This sanctuary was a strongpoint and stood on a hill
(Plutarch, *Agesilaos*, 32). Issorion was the name of the hill, though 'Issorian
Artemis' was also worshipped at Teuthrone (cf. Bk III, 25 (4)), and there was a
festival called the Issoria. The hill may be KLARAKI, north-west of the akropolis.

108. Pausanias says he first won in 668 (cf. Bk IV, 23 (4), and Bk VI, 13 (2)).
This just fits the traditional foundation date of Kyrene at about 630 B.C.
Herodotos tells the story (4, 150 f.).

109. Thetis is an unusual goddess, but the Spartans were particularly
enthusiastic about sea-goddesses, and at least in southern Sparta people are still
interested in mermaids. There is a fascinating account of this phenomenon in
Patrick Leigh Fermor's classic work on southern Greece (*Mani*, p. 50, and pp.
169–70).

110. Cf Bk II, 35 (4f.).

young Lakonians practise running to this day.[111] If you proceed to the Race-course from the tomb of the Agiadai, the monument of Eumedes will be on your left. This Eumedes was another of the sons of Hippokoon. There is a statue of Herakles where sacrifices are offered by the Ball-players, adolescent boys just on the point of complete manhood. There are also gymnasia built on the Race-course, one of them dedicated by Eurykles the Spartan.[112] Outside the Race-course by Herakles' statue stands a house which in our own times is in private hands, but in antiquity it belonged to Menelaos. As you go on from the Race-course you come to a SANCTU-ARY of Dioskouroi and Graces, and one of Eileithuia and Karneian Apollo and Artemis the Guide. [7] The SANCTUARY OF AGNITES stands on the right of the Race-course. Agnites is a title of Asklepios, because the god had a wooden idol made of *agnus castus*; this is a kind of *vitex*, in the same way as buckthorn. Not far from Asklepios stands a trophy; the story is that Polydeukes put it up after beating Lynkeus, which seems to me another demonstration of how likely it is that the sons of Aphareus were not buried at Sparta.[113] By the beginning of the Race-course there are the Dioskouroi as Starting gods, and a little farther on you come to the shrine of the divine hero Alkon; they say he was a son of Hippokoon. By Alkon's shrine is a SANCTUARY OF POSEIDON under the title of House-god.[114]

[8] The place called THE PLANES is named after the plane-trees growing tall and dense all round it. This place, which is the traditional ground for the fight between adolescent boys,

111. This has not been found, and no one knows where it was. N. D. Papahadzis in his commentary on Pausanias (1963) argues persuasively that it lay to the west of the ancient city.

112. Perhaps the rich Augustan Spartan Eurykles (cf. Bk II, 3 (5)) who has a curious niche in history as having been a bad influence in the court of Herod the Great.

113. I suppose he means that if the fight was here Lynkeus would have been buried here? Cf. Note 96 above.

114. The hereditary priestess Damosthenia (cf. Note 98 above) was also a priestess of Poseidon the House-god.

is encircled by a moat as if it were an island in the sea; the entrances are bridges. On one of the bridges is a statue of Herakles, on the other a portrait of Lykourgos: among his other constitutional laws Lykourgos legislated for this fight between adolescent boys. They have these other rituals to go through as well: [9] before the fight they sacrifice in the PHOIBAION, which is outside the city, not far from Therapne;[115] each side sacrifices a puppy there to Enyalios, with the idea that the most aggressive tame animal will be the right victim for the most aggressive god. I know of no other Greeks who believe in sacrificing puppies except at Kolophon,[116] where they sacrifice a black bitch to Hekate. The sacrifice at Kolophon takes place at night, and so does the boys' sacrifice in Lakonia. [10] After the sacrifice the boys put down hand-reared fighting boars. The side whose boar wins is generally the one that wins at the Planes. That is all done at the Phoibaion; on the next day a little before mid-day they enter the ground I described over the bridges: the entrance each side comes in by was decided by picking straws during the night. They fight hand to hand and with running kicks, they bite and they gouge, man to man; one side flings itself at the other in general charges and they push one another into the water.[117]

15     [1] Kyniska the daughter of King Archidamos of Sparta has a divine hero's shrine by the Planes. She was the first woman to raise horses and the first woman to win with a team at Olympia.[118] There are some shrines of divine heroes behind

115. Therapne was south-east of Sparta, on or behind the high cliffs of the Eurotas; cf. Bk III, 19 (7). The Phoibaion has not been discovered, perhaps because there is an *embarras de richesses* of antiquities in this area, and scholars have been confused by inadequate literary sources.

116. Kolophon is in Asia Minor south of Izmir, north-west of Ephesos, and north-east of Samos. Cf. Bk VIII, 3 (1-4).

117. This is the object of the exercise. Cicero's jaundiced account of the violence of this game, which he once saw, is apparently heavily coloured by a context of philosophic argument. The principle is more or less that of the Eton wall game, only with more action.

118. Cf. Bk III, Note 45.

the COLONNADE which runs beside the Planes: one of Alkimos, one of Enaraiphoros, one of Dorkeus not far off, with one of Sebros.[119] [2] The spring near by is called the Dorkeian spring after Dorkeus's shrine, and the whole area is called the Sebrion after Sebros. On the right of the Sebrion is ALKMAN'S MONUMENT; the pleasure of the songs he composed is not at all spoilt by their being written in Lakonian, the least musical of languages.

[3] HELEN'S SANCTUARY is near Alkman's grave; HERAKLES' SANCTUARY is very close to the ramparts. It has an armed statue of Herakles; the story is that Herakles' statue is like this because of his battle with Hippokoon and his sons. Herakles is supposed to have been an enemy of Hippokoon and his family because of when he came to Sparta for purification after killing Iphitos, and they refused to let him be purified.[120] [4] There was another cause that contributed to the outbreak of this war: Herakles' nephew Oionos who was a boy at the time came to Sparta with his uncle. He was the son of Alkmene's brother Likymnios. Oionos was wandering about investigating the city and arrived at Hippokoon's house. Hippokoon's guard-dog attacked him, so he flung a stone and knocked the bitch over; Hippokoon's sons came rushing out of the house and beat him to death with their wooden staves. [5] This made Herakles absolutely infuriated with Hippokoon and his sons, and he came and fought them there and then with the anger still in him. On that occasion he was wounded and had to get away quietly, but later on he fought a war against Sparta and took vengeance for the murder of Oionos from Hippokoon and Hippokoon's sons. Oionos's monument stands beside the Herakleion.

119. Alkimos and his uncouth-sounding brethren are more of the sons of Hippokoon. The spelling of some of their names is uncertain and probably ought not to be regularized. The fragmentary papyrus of Alkman's Partheneion opens with a list of Hippokoon's sons; there is an attempt at a complete list in Apollodoros (3, 10, 5).

120. According to Homer, Herakles had treacherously murdered Iphitos in order to steal some mares and some mules (Odyssey, 21, 22f.).

[6] Going dead east from the Race-course you come to a path on your right leading to the SANCTUARY OF ATHENE of Vengeance Deserved, because when Herakles came back from giving Hippokoon and his sons what they had been asking for he founded a sanctuary of Athene with the title of Vengeance Deserved, vengeance being the old word for punishment. If you leave the Race-course by the road, you come to a different SANCTUARY OF ATHENE, which they say was founded by Theras son of Autesion, grandson of Tisamenos and great-grandson of Thersander, when he sent off his expedition of colonists to the island which still carries his name, though in ancient times it was called Kalliste.[121] [9] Near this is a shrine of Hipposthenes, the Hipposthenes who won so many wrestling matches. They worship Hipposthenes in honour of Poseidon; the cult was established by an oracle.[122] Just opposite this temple is an antique statue of Enyalios in chains. The Lakonians have the same idea about this statue as the Athenians have about Wingless Victory: in Lakonia they think the god of war will never desert them if they keep him in chains; in Athens they believe Victory will stay with them for ever because she has no wings.[123]

[8] That is the kind of cult-statue these cities have erected and that was the kind of belief in which they did so. At Sparta there is also the Painted MEETING-HOUSE with shrines beside it of the divine hero Kadmos son of Agenor and two of his descendants, Oiolykos the son of Theras and Aigeus the son of Oiolykos. The story is that these shrines were built by Maisis, Laias and Europas, the sons of Aigeus's son Hyraios. They built the one for Amphilochos too, because Amphilo-

121. Cf. Bk III, Note 7.

122. Cf. Bk III, 13 (9). It has been suggested that this Hipposthenes was simply a projection of Poseidon of Horses. His connexion with the god is certain at least after his death; but he must surely have been a human being.

123. There was an Aktaion in chains at Orchomenos (Bk IX, 38 (5)) and a chained Aphrodite at Sparta. Frazer in his commentary on Pausanias gives a long and persuasive list of ancient and modern analogies, but it is not clear that the chains were not simply dedications, like perhaps those on Oinomaos's pillar at Olympia.

chos's sister Demonasse was the mother of their ancestor Tisamenos.[124]

[9] The Lakonians are the only people in Greece who have the custom of calling Hera the Goat-eater and sacrificing goats to her. They say Herakles founded the sanctuary and was the first to sacrifice goats, because when he fought Hippokoon and his sons Hera made no trouble for him in the way he felt she opposed him on other occasions. They maintain that he sacrificed goats because he had no other victims.

[10] Not far from the theatre there is a SANCTUARY OF FAMILY POSEIDON, and there are shrines of the divine heroes Kleodaios son of Hyllos and Oibalos.[125] The grandest SANCTUARY OF ASKLEPIOS is at the Cattleprice, and to the left of it lies the shrine of the divine hero Teleklos, whom I shall be mentioning again in my treatment of Messenia.[126] Not far from here you will come to a hill, not very high, on which there is an ancient TEMPLE and an armed cult-statue of Aphrodite. This temple is unique so far as I know in having an upper storey consecrated to the Beautiful goddess. [11] The Beautiful goddess is a title of Aphrodite;[127] she is enthroned and veiled,

124. This genealogy is systematic (cf. also Bk V, 17 (7), and Bk IX, 5 (15)). The facts were already entangled with myth and religion in the time of Pindar (*Pythian Odes*, 5, 69–85). It has been plausibly suggested (Immerwahr, *Lakonika*, pp. 79–80) that Pausanias's doctrine had already been systematized by Ephoros in the fourth century. The personal name Damonassa was still in use on Thera until the Hellenistic period (on three inscriptions). Amphilochos and Demonasse (or Damonassa) were the son and daughter of the prophet Amphiaraos. Amphilochos inherited his father's powers; Pausanias mentions (Bk I, 34 (2)) that he had an altar at Athens and an oracle in Asia, and that his children shared their grandfather's great altar at Oropos.

125. These are both members of the earliest generations of the Dorian invaders.

126. Cf. Bk IV, 4 (2). He was a Spartan king.

127. That is, *Morpho*; the form of the word indicates a noun and not an adjective. An archaic temple of Aphrodite recently discovered in the Mani by Mr Delivorias (cf. Bk III, Note 255) was inscribed *Iostephano*, the goddess of the violet wreath, a title which occurs as an epithet in the Homeric hymns; it seems to have the same relation to Aphrodite as *Morpho* at Sparta.

with fetters on her feet. They say it was Tyndareos who put fetters on her, meaning that the relationship of women to their husbands was as absolute as fetters. As for the story that Tyndareos was taking vengeance on the goddess because he thought it was Aphrodite who disgraced his daughters, I shall not even discuss it.[128] It would have been utterly idiotic to make a doll of cedar-wood and call it Aphrodite, and then imagine he was striking a blow at the goddess.

16 [1] Near here there is a SANCTUARY OF HILAEIRA AND PHOIBE; the poet of the Kypria says they were Apollo's daughters. Their priestesses are virgin girls, who are called by the same name as the goddesses, Leukippides.[129] One of the statues was ornamented by a Leukippis who had served as a priestess. She gave it a face of contemporary artistry instead of its ancient one, but a dream forbade her to do the same for the other statue. There is an egg here hanging from the roof tied with ribbons; they say this is the legendary egg which was laid by Leda.[130]

[2] Every year the women weave a tunic for the Apollo at Amyklai, and they call the room where they weave it the TUNIC-HOUSE. There is a house near it which they say was first built by Tyndareos's sons, and later came into the possession of a Spartan called Phormion. The Dioskouroi came to visit him disguised as foreigners; they told him they had come from Kyrene and asked him to take them in and let them have the room they had loved most when they were among mankind. [3] He told them they could live wherever they liked in the rest of his house, but not in that room, because his daughter was a young virgin girl and she was living in it. The next morning the young girl and all her attendants vanished; and

128. Klytaimnestra murdered her husband Agamemnon, and Helen caused the Trojan war.

129. Leukippos's two daughters who were stolen by the Dioskouroi. The Kypria was an epic poem from which Herodotos, Pausanias and Athenaios have quoted a few fragments, and of which Proklos preserves the skeleton of the plot (Kinkel, Epic. Gr. Frag., pp. 15–31).

130. It was double-yoked and contained the heavenly twins, the Dioskouroi. To mate with Leda Zeus had taken the form of a swan.

statues of the Dioskouroi were found in the room, and also a
table with sylphium on it.[131]

[4] That is how they say it happened. On the way to the
gates from the Tunic-house is a shrine to the divine heroes
Chilon who had a reputation for wisdom and Athenodoros
who was a member of the Sicilian expedition with Dorieus
son of Anaxandridas.[132] This expedition sailed in the belief
that the Erykinian territories belonged to Herakles' descend-

*2. Silphium*

ants and not to the barbarians who lived there. The story is
that Herakles wrestled with Eryx on terms that if Herakles

131. The sons of Tyndareos are the Dioskouroi; Kyrene was a Lakonian
colony, and silphium was the foundation of its wealth. Although silphium is
clearly represented on the coinage of Kyrene, it has never been identified in
modern times. We know that it was precious and medically powerful, and
that it had magic properties.

132. Chilon was an influential mid-sixth-century Governor of Sparta and
one of the proverbial Seven Wise Men of the ancient world. He seems to have
been responsible for bringing home Orestes' bones. 'Athenodoros' was invented by Madvig to cover a confused and corrupt phrase in the manuscripts.
Although Dorieus's expedition (cf. Bk III, 3 (10), and 4 (1)) is described by
Herodotos (5, 42–8), 'Athenodoros' is not mentioned. This expedition ended
very badly, and it is hard to see how he alone came to be buried at home.
Perhaps there was really a shrine of all the Spartan dead whose bones were
brought back.

won he should have Eryx's land, and if he was beaten Eryx should take Geryon's cows, which Herakles was driving away at the time; [5] the cows had swum over to Sicily and Herakles had come across to find them at the crooked olive-tree. The gods did not favour Dorieus as they favoured Herakles: Herakles killed Eryx, but Dorieus and most of his army were massacred by the people of Egesta.

[6] The Lakonians have also made a god's SANCTUARY FOR LYKOURGOS the Law-giver.[133] Behind the temple lies the grave of his son Eukosmos, and beside the altar the graves of Lathria and Anaxandra, the twin sisters who were married to Aristodemos's twin sons. They were Thersander's daughters; Thersander's father was Agamedidas king of Kleonai, who was the fourth in line of descent from Herakles' son Ktesippos.[134] Opposite this temple are the memorials of Theopompos son of Nikander, and of Euribiadas who commanded the Lakonian battle fleet against the Persians at Artemision and at Salamis, and near by is what they call the hero's shrine of Astrabakos.[135]

[7] The place called the LAKE SANCTUARY is sacred to

133. This sanctuary already existed in the time of Herodotos (1, 66). The most fundamental Spartan laws were attributed to him; he is a shadowy, perhaps a legendary figure, and we know from many inscriptions he was not a divine hero but a god, like Herakles, although, a generation before Pausanias, Plutarch had written his biography. What might possibly be Lykourgos's altar was found by British archaeologists in the bed of the Eurotas in 1906 (B.S.A., 12, pp. 301–2). We depend for the laws on a lost work of Aristotle quoted by Plutarch; they have been much discussed (lucidly and I think most recently by W. G. Forrest in his History of Sparta, 1968); their language is so strange as to be suspicious (cf. Jeffery in Historia, 1961, and Hammond in Journal of Hellenic Studies, 1950, p. 43, n. 8: horas ex horas is a phrase for prayers and holy blessings and belongs to the liturgical language of annual festivals).

134. For Aristodemos and his twin sons cf. Bk III, 1 (5f.). Kleonai was a city on high ground between Corinth and Argos, not far from HAGIOS BASILIOS.

135. King Theopompos is associated with the first Messenian War (cf. Bk IV, 4 (4)), which was probably in the late eighth century; this makes him more or less a contemporary of Homer. We know from Section 9 below that Astrabakos was a dead ancestor once driven mad by Artemis; his shrine was at the gate of King Ariston's house, and the dead hero is supposed to have slept with Ariston's wife and generated Demaratos (Herodotos, 6, 69).

Standing Artemis.[136] They claim this as the idol that Orestes and Iphigeneia stole from the Taurians. The Lakonian story is that it was brought to Lakonia when Orestes was king here, and this seems to me more probable than the Athenian version, because why should Iphigeneia leave the statue behind at Brauron? And how is it that when the Athenians were getting ready to abandon their country they failed to load this statue on to a ship?[137] [8] To this day the Taurian goddess has so great a name that Cappadocians and the people on the shores of the Euxine claim to possess the same statue, the Lydians claim it at the sanctuary of Artemis Anaiitis, and the Athenians if you please are supposed casually to have watched it disappear as Persian loot: the statue from Brauron was taken to Sousa; later it was given as a gift by Seleukos; and the Syrians of Laodikea have it today.[138] [9] There is another piece of evidence that the Standing goddess of the Lakonians is the old barbarian idol: Astrabakos and Alopekos, the sons

136. East of the akropolis and left of the Eurotas bridge as you enter Sparta from Tripolis. This SANCTUARY was excavated by British archaeologists in the 1900s; a small amphitheatre had been noticed there ever since the eighteenth century; its significance emerged in 1906 through the appearance of some archaic lead figurines below the ruins where the Eurotas was eating away its banks. This theatre was in fact built in the third century A.D. to face the east end of a temple which had survived on the same foundations since about 600 B.C. The earliest deposits (corroded bronze and geometric pottery) were in the central and lowest area of a natural hollow; altar succeeded altar in the same position. The characteristic flat lead figurines from this sanctuary were recovered in huge numbers and are in many museums, but the principal finds are in the Sparta museum. For a fourth-century sacred building just north of the sanctuary, c.f. *Arch. Reports*, 1968–9, p. 17.

137. Cf. Bk I, 33 (1). The Athenians claimed to have lost it in the Persian wars (cf. Bk VIII, 46 (3)).

138. Strabo said it was at Komana in Cappadocia (12, 2, 3); the claimants on the Euxine are unknown. There seem to have been several cult-places of Artemis Anaiitis in Lydia, and others in Phrygia (*B.C.H.*, 4, 1880, p. 120). She was worshipped at Balkh in Bactria and by Parthians and Sakai as well as Greeks. She was the local water goddess of central Asia (Anahita. the Undefiled) with a thousand arms and a thousand canals, identical with the river Oxus (Amu Darya). cf. Tarn, *Greeks in Bactria and India* (1966), p. 102. For Sousa, cf. Bk III, Note 55. The Laodikean Artemis is represented on coins. Seleukos was one of Alexander's generals who became king of Syria.

of Irbos and the descendants of Agis through Amphikles and Amphisthenes, suddenly went mad when they found this statue, and when the Spartans of Limnai, Kynosouria, Mesoa and Pitane sacrificed to Artemis she cursed them through this statue with quarrels and then with murders; many of them died at her altar and disease devoured the rest.[139] [10] This is the reason why they bloody the altar with human blood. They used to slaughter a human sacrifice chosen by drawing lots; Lykourgos substituted the whipping of fully grown boys, and the altar still gets its fill of human blood.[140] The priestess with the idol stands beside them; the idol is small and light, [11] except that if ever the scourgers pull their strokes because of a boy's beauty or his rank, then the woman finds the idol heavy and hard to carry; she blames the scourgers and says they are hurting her: such a taste for human blood has survived in that statue from the time of the Taurian sacrifices. She is called not only the Standing one, but also Withy-tied, because she was found in a thick tangle of withies, with the withy-tree winding round the statue and keeping it standing.

17     [1] Not far from the Standing one is a SANCTUARY OF EILEITHUIA; they say they built it and recognized Eileithuia as a goddess by order of the Delphic oracle.[141]

The Lakonian AKROPOLIS is not so high as to be a landmark, like Theban Kadmeia and Argive Larisa, nor is it the only hill in the city, but the hill that rises highest into the air is called the akropolis. [2] There is a sanctuary built here of Athene of the City, who is also called BRONZEHOUSE

139. The people of the four districts or villages of which Sparta was composed.

140. What Pausanias says here about human sacrifice is nonsense based on Euripides. This primitive ritual beating had in the classical period the character of a kind of very rough initiation; in the Roman period the ancient disciplines of Sparta were not only revived but exaggerated to a horrifying degree. The disgusting third-century-A.D. addition of an amphitheatre for tourists to watch boys being savagely beaten can reasonably be related to the other entertainments of that age.

141. Eileithuia is the birth goddess. Perhaps cf. *Arch. Reports*, 1968–9, p. 17.

ATHENE.[142] According to the story it was Tyndareos who started the building of this sanctuary, and when he died his sons wanted to finish the building from the spoils of Aphidna, but like their father they died too soon, and it was the Lakonians many years afterwards who erected the temple and the bronze statue, which was made by a local man, Gitiadas.[143] Gitiadas also composed Dorian songs, including a hymn to the goddess. [3] The bronze is worked with numerous labours of Herakles, and numerous good deeds he did of his own free will, and the deeds of the sons of Tyndareos, including the carrying-off of Leukippos's daughters; there is also Hephaistos freeing his mother from the fetters: a story I have explained before in my records of Athens.[144] There is Perseus setting out for Libya to meet Medusa, with the nymphs giving him his cap and the sandals to travel through the air. And the story of Athene's birth is represented, with Amphitrite and Poseidon, in my opinion the most rewarding and the greatest figures of all. [4] There is also another sanctuary here to Athene of Work. If you go into the colonnade to the south you come to a shrine of Zeus the Marshal, in front of which is Tyndareos's memorial. The western colonnade has two eagles

142. It was found by British archaeologists early in 1907 at the west end of the akropolis, and excavated. The title Athene of the City occurs in a midfifth-century inscription, half of which was found here (*I.G.*, V, 1, 213), and the title Bronzehouse Athene is at least as early as Thukydides (1, 134f.). The excavators recovered a few splendid archaic bronzes; below the early or mid sixth-century sanctuary there was a rich level of geometric pottery which may perhaps indicate the earliest date of the cult. (In the whole of Sparta only the most insignificant traces of Mycenaean antiquities have been found, and it is unlikely that Sparta itself existed as a significant settlement in Mycenaean times.)

143. This statue perhaps appears on bronze Spartan coins of the third century A.D. Gitiadas would seem to have worked in the middle of the sixth century (cf. Note 158 below). For the spoils of Aphidna, cf. Bk I, 17 (5).

144. Bronze plates and nails (from the walls?) were found in the excavation, but all the bronze that survived was terribly corroded and was undecorated. For the myth (which figures in the first book of the *Iliad* and the first book of *Paradise Lost*), cf. Bk I, 20 (3). For the sons of Tyndareos, cf. Bk III, Note 96. The decoration of an archaic temple did not necessarily have anything to do with its cult.

carrying two Victories: they were dedicated by Lysander in memory of both his victories, the one at Ephesos when he beat the Athenian warships under Alkibiades' captain Antiochos, and the later one at Aigospotamoi when he destroyed the Athenian fleet.[145]

[5] On the left of Bronzehouse Athene they have erected a sanctuary of the Muses, because the Lakonians used to march out to battle not to the tune of trumpets, but with the music of flutes and the striking of harp-strings and guitars.[146] Behind Bronzehouse Athene is a TEMPLE OF APHRODITE of War; the cult-statues are as ancient as any in Greece.[147] [6] On the right of Bronzehouse Athene is a statue of Zeus the Highest, the oldest of all bronze statues, not cast in bronze in one piece, but each part made of beaten bronze and then fitted together and all held in place with bolts. They say this statue was made by Klearchos of Region, who is supposed to have been a pupil of Dipoinos and Skyllis, or some people say of Daidalos himself.[148] By the Tabernacle as they call it is

145. Presumably we are still on the akropolis, though true south would put us in the theatre. Lysander's victories ended the Peloponnesian War; they were in the last years of the fifth century.

146. No one but Pausanias mentions lyres and guitars ('lyre' and 'kithara'). A few lines of certain Spartan battle-songs have survived (cf. Page, P.M.G., n. 856–7), and there is a boy flute-player in a black tunic between two ranks of advancing soldiers among the magnificent decorations of the Chigi vase (cf. Arias-Hirmer, Greek Vase-painting, n. 16). The painting is Corinthian, but the custom survived longer in Sparta (cf. Thukydides, 5, 70, etc.).

147. Aphrodite of War is perhaps a Fury (cf. Wide, Lakonische Kulte, pp. 141–2). One would rationally expect any Spartan goddess of young people to to be identified with their warlike pursuits, but the origins of cults are not so easily categorized.

148. Klearchos is known only through Pausanias (cf. also Bk VI, 4 (4)). It seems obvious that he really existed, but his apprenticeship is a fabrication, since Daidalos is a creature of legend; for Dipoinos and Skyllis, in whom Pausanias was interested, cf. Bk II, 15 (1). The technique of this Zeus certainly sounds primitive and nothing like it has been found, though there are occasional sixth-century figures cut from thin sheet-bronze, which is then doubled to give two profiles (cf. W. Lamb, Greek and Roman Bronzes, pp. 99–100). Fragmentary inscriptions to Zeus the Highest have been found in more than one part of the akropolis.

the portrait of a woman the Lakonians call Euryleon's daughter, who won an Olympic race with a chariot and pair.

[7] Beside the altar of Bronzehouse Athene stand two portraits of Pausanias who commanded at Plataia. I shall not tell his story because people know it already; what earlier writers have written is quite accurate enough.[149] For myself, I shall simply add what I heard from a Byzantine: the only reason Pausanias's purposes were discovered, and that he alone could not obtain forgiveness by ritual application from Bronzehouse Athene, was a murderous stain that nothing could wash out. [8] When he was in the Hellespont with the Lakonian and all the Greek ships, he lusted for a virgin girl from Byzantion; as soon as night fell Kleonike, as she was called, was brought to him by his orders, but meanwhile Pausanias had been asleep and the noise woke him: as she came to him she accidentally upset the burning lamp. Pausanias, who was conscious of having betrayed Greece, and was troubled and panic-stricken at all times, leapt up and struck at the girl with his short sword. [9] Pausanias went through every kind of purification, he supplicated to Zeus of Escape and he even went to visit the necromantic priests at Phigalia in Arkadia,[150] but he could never get rid of the stain of this guilt. So he paid the penalty of justice to Kleonike and to the goddess. In fulfilment of a command from Delphi, the Lakonians erected these bronze portraits and honour the daemonic power of the Generous god, who they say turned away the curse of Zeus of Suppliants which fell on them because of Pausanias.

[1] Near the figures of Pausanias is a statue of Aphrodite 18

149. Thukydides, 1, 128–34. King Pausanias of Sparta was stoned to death with roof-tiles in this sanctuary in about 470 B.C.

150. Plutarch says it was at Herakleia (*Kimon*, 6). The standard commentaries on Pausanias give lists of necromantic shrines all over the Greek world, but nothing is known about one at Phigalia. It seems likely that it centred on the formidably deep and dark hole into which the river Neda disappears; as late as 1963 it was still the custom to throw things into this hole from the high cliffs of the Neda gorge on a certain day in the year. It is an impressive and snake-haunted spot.

the Turner-away-of-old-age, which was erected through an oracle, and statues of Sleep and Death, whom they believe to be brothers as the *Iliad* says.[151] [2] On the way to the ALPEION is a SHRINE OF ATHENE of Eyes;[152] the story is that Lykourgos dedicated it, because one of his eyes had been put out by Alkander, who disliked the laws he made. He escaped to this place, where the Lakonians protected him from losing the other eye, and so he built a shrine of Athene of Eyes. [3] Farther on you come to a SANCTUARY OF AMMON; the Lakonians seem to have used the Libyan oracle more than anyone else in Greece from the beginning. Also they say, when Lysander was besieging Aphytis in Pallene,[153] Ammon appeared to him in the night to warn him it would be better for himself and better for Lakonia to give up their war with Aphytis; so Lysander broke up the siege and made the Lakonians offer more worship to this god; Ammon is not more honoured by the Lybian Ammonians than he is at Aphytis.

[4] The legend of Knagian Artemis is this. They say Knageus was a local man who fought against Aphidna with the Dioskouroi; he was taken prisoner in the fighting and sold as a slave into Crete, to a place where the Cretans had a sanctuary of Artemis. In the course of time he ran away with the virgin priestess, and she brought the statue with her. This is supposed to be why they call her Knagian Artemis; [5] but in my view this Knageus must have gone to Crete in some

151. Plutarch quotes a line or two of a prayer to this Aphrodite (Page, *P.M.G.*, n. 872). Sleep and Death are the twin brothers who carry away Zeus's dead son Sarpedon in the sixteenth book of the *Iliad* (672). Sleep is identified with the Generous god at the Sikyonian Asklepieion (Bk II, 10 (2)).

152. Alpeion seems to have been the land north-west of the akropolis but south of the small river MOUSGA. Some tiles have been found there stamped for the colonnade in Alpeion.

153. The oracle of Zeus Ammon at the Siwa oasis in the Libyan desert has never been excavated. Zeus Ammon was a projection of the god of Egyptian Thebes, Amon Ra, who was originally the Libyan god Ammun. The oracle is treated in Parke's *Oracles of Zeus* (1967), p.p 194f., and by Oric Bates in *The Eastern Libyans*. Lysander seems to have had an inherited family friendship with the king of the Ammonites. APHYTIS was near Potidaia on the east side of the Pallene peninsula in Macedonia.

other way quite contrary to the Lakonian story, since I do not believe there was ever a battle at Aphidna while Theseus was held in Thesprotia and Athens was unfriendly and in fact rather inclined towards Menestheus. And even if there had been a fight, how is one to suppose that prisoners were taken from the winning side, particularly in the case of so over-whelming a victory that Aphidna actually fell?[154]

[6] That is enough discussion of this matter. On the way down to AMYKLAI from Sparta you come to the river Tiasa;[155] they believe she was Eurotas's daughter, and beside the river is a SANCTUARY OF THE GRACES Phaenna and Kleta just as Alkman says. They think it was Lakedaimon who built the Graces' sanctuary here and gave them their names.[156] [7] These are the interesting things at Amyklai. There is a stone tablet naming a champion of the pentathlon called Ainetos, who died (so they say) with his head still wreathed after winning at Olympia.[157] There is a portrait of him, and there are bronze tripods. The more antique tripods are said to be a tenth part of the spoils of the war against Messenia. [8] Under the first tripod stands a statue of Aphrodite, under the second is Artemis; these tripods and their decoration are by Gitiadas, but the third is by Kallon of Aigina, and below it stands a

154. For all the arguments, cf. Bk I, 17 (4f.). Artemis's title 'Knagian' seems to refer to white or perhaps more exactly to yellow billy-goats (cf. Nilsson, *Griechische Feste*, p. 231).

155. The site of AMYKLAI was something over three miles south of Sparta just west of the Eurotas, north-east of SLAVOCHORI, and north of MACHMOUT BEY which has now been christened AMYKLAI. The site lies to the left of the GYTHION road after the third substantial stream. (There is no saying which of these was the Tiasa.) The first authentic Amyklaian inscription appears to have been dug up by Lord Aberdeen in about 1803 (cf. Walpole's *Memoirs Relating to Turkey*, pp. 446f.) The editors of *I.G.*, V (i), have missed this, and possibly it never reached England.

156. Most unhappily we know nothing about Alkman's poem on this subject; but we do know from a piece of Polemo's *Lakonika* preserved by Athenaios (4, 138f-139b) that there was a sanctuary of Artemis not far away where on one day in the year people built brushwood shelters and ate a rather simple country feast.

157. Ainetos is unknown and undatable.

statue of the Maid, Demeter's daughter.[158] Aristandros of Paros made the woman with the harp, Sparta apparently, and Polykleitos of Argos made the Aphrodite of the Amyklaian, as they call her. These tripods are bigger than the others; they come from the victory at Aigospotamoi.[159] [9] Bathykles the Magnesian who made the Amyklaian's throne, dedicated the Graces on completing it, with a statue of Artemis of Good Thoughts. The question of who taught Bathykles and under what Lakonian king he worked is one I am leaving aside, but I saw this throne and I shall describe it.[160] [10] In front of it and behind it rise two Graces and two Seasons, on the left stand Echidna and Typhos, on the right there are Tritons.[161] It would weary my readers if I went through all its workmanship in detail, but to summarize, since anyway most of it is

158. Kallon's signature has been found on the Athenian akropolis and can be dated to about 500 B.C. (Raubitschek, *Dedications*, no. 85). Gitiadas can be tentatively dated by the earliest Bronzehouse Athene pottery to about 550 B.C. (cf. *B.S.A.*, 13, 1906–7, p. 139). The first Messenian War was in the eighth century, the second in the seventh and, the third in the fifth. So it looks as if Pausanias was misinformed about these tripods being spoils from the Messenian War.

159. Aristandros is probably the father of the famous Parian sculptor Skopas, whose son we know from inscriptions was also called Aristandros. If Pausanias's Aristandros is really Skopas's son whom we know and not his father of whom we know nothing, he lived too late to commemorate Aigospotamoi, since Skopas was still working after 351 and Aigospotamoi was in 405. Polykleitos worked in the second half of the fifth century. He was the most successful and influential of Pheidias's pupils. His signature has been found more than once at Olympia, but not one of his statues survives. They were mostly in bronze.

160. Bathykles sounds like an early or mid sixth-century master; he may have been sent with Kroisos's gift of gold – cf. Bk III, 10 (8). For the abundance and weird variety and probably for the style of the Amyklaian throne, the nearest surviving parallel is probably the Francois vase (*c.* 570 B.C.) or the work of Sophilos. There is a further analogy in a wooden throne of about 700 B.C. plated with an elaborate series of ivory reliefs and lined with gold, found in a royal grave at Salamis in Cyprus (*Illustrated London News*, December 1967). The Salamis throne is of a human size but the Amyklaian throne was really a gigantic throne-shaped statue-base. A similar throne-base is represented on the Hellenistic coinage of Ainos. The Amyklaion was excavated by German archaeologists in the 1920s (cf. *At. Mitteilungen*, 1927, p. 65).

161. Snake-footed giants and fish-footed sea-gods.

already familiar, Poseidon and Zeus are carrying Taygete daughter of Atlas and her sister Alkyone. Atlas is also engraved on it, and Herakles' single fight with Kyknos, and the battle of the Centaurs in Pholos's cave. [11] I do not understand why Bathykles carved the Minotaur bound and taken alive by Theseus; there is a Phaiakian dance on the throne and Demodokos is singing,[162] and there is Perseus's triumph over Medusa. There is the carrying-off of Leukippos's daughters, not to mention Herakles' fight with the giant Thourios and Tyndareos's with the giant Eurytos.[163] Hermes is carrying the child Dionysos to heaven, and Athene is bringing Herakles to live with the gods for ever after. [12] Peleus is handing over Achilles to be brought up by Chiron, as Achilles is supposed to have been one of his pupils; Kephalos is being carried off by the Dawn because of his beauty; the gods are bringing presents to Harmonia's wedding. There are figures of Achilles' single fight with Memnon,[164] and Herakles punishing Diomedes the Thracian and Nessos on the river Euenos. Hermes is taking the goddesses to be judged by Paris; Adrastos and Tydeus stop Amphiaraos and Lykourgos son of Pronax from fighting.[165] [13] Hera is looking at Io daughter of In-

162. Demodokos and the Phaiakians and their king Alkinoos are an important element in Homer's *Odyssey*, but this scene has no more necessarily to do with Homer than the eighth-century inscribed cup from Ischia which says 'I am Nestor's enormous tankard'.

163. Otherwise unknown. There have been attempts to correct some of Pausanias's identifications, but such attempts are often the merest and most flatulent conjecture. Some at least of the figures had their names written beside them. Cf. Note 171 below.

164. Memnon is a largely post-Homeric hero; the earliest surviving literary sources for his battle with Achilles, during which Zeus, or in another version Eos and Thetis, weighed the souls of the two heroes in a balance, appear to be Pindar and Aischylos. Zeus in the *Iliad* weighs Greeks and Trojans (8, 70) and Hektor and Achilles (22, 210) but Aischylos's lost *Psychostasia* was probably based on the post-Homeric epic *Aithiopis*. The weighing of Achilles and Memnon (never Hektor so far as I know) is quite a common theme for vase-painting.

165. I suppose in Arkadia before the battle of the Seven against Thebes. This incident is otherwise unknown, although there has been an attempt to relate it to the fifth book of Statius's *Thebais*.

achos, who has already turned into a heifer; Athene is escaping from Hephaistos who is coming after her.[166] Then there is a series of the great deeds of Herakles, Herakles and the hydra and how he brought home Hades' dog. Anaxias and Mnasinous are each on horseback, but Menelaos's son Megapenthes and Nikostratos are riding the same horse.[167] Bellerophon is destroying the Lykian monster, and Herakles is driving off Geryon's cows. [14] At the upper limits of the throne there are the sons of Tyndareos on horseback, one on either side. There are sphinxes under the horses and wild beasts with their heads raised, a lioness under Polydeukes and on the other side a leopard. On the very top of the throne is a dance of the Magnesians who worked on this throne with Bathykles. [15] Underneath the throne in behind the Tritons there is the hunt for the Kalydonian boar; Herakles is killing the sons of Aktor, and Kalais and Zetes are driving off the harpies from Phineus; Peirithous and Theseus have carried off Helen, and Herakles has the lion by the throat; Apollo and Artemis are shooting Tityos. [16] There are carvings of Herakles' fight with the centaur Oreios and Theseus's fight with the Minotaur; Herakles' wrestling match with Acheloos, and the legend of Hera bound by Hephaistos; the games Akastos gave for his father, and the story of Menelaos and Proteus the Egyptian from the *Odyssey*.[168] Finally Admetos is harnessing his chariot with a boar and a lion, and the Trojans are bringing pitchers to offer them to Hektor.

19   [1] The part of the throne where the god would sit is not a single continuous thing, but it has several seats with a space beside each of the seats; [2] the middle part is extremely broad, and that is where the statue stands. I know no one who has measured this, but at a guess you could say it was forty-five

166. In an attempted rape; he spilled his seed and Erichthonios or Erechtheus was born from the rocks where it fell.

167. The sons of the Dioskouroi and the sons of Menelaos, who was worshipped near by; cf. Note 178 below.

168. Akastos's father was Pelias, whom Medeia had persuaded Akastos's innocent and foolish sisters to murder. The story of Proteus occurs in the fourth book of the *Odyssey*, 384 f.

feet. It is not the work of Bathykles, but antique and made without artistry; apart from the faces and the tips of its feet and hands it looks just like a bronze pillar. It has a helmet on its head and a lance and a bow in its hands.[169] [3] The base of the statue is shaped like an altar, and Hyakinthos is said to be buried in it; at the Hyakinthia, before Apollo's sacrifice, they pass through a bronze door to dedicate the offerings of a divine hero to Hyakinthos in this altar; the door is on the left of the altar.[170] There is a figure of Biris worked on one side of the altar,[171] with Amphitrite and Poseidon on the other; Zeus and Hermes are talking together, with Dionysos and Semele standing near them and Io beside Semele. [4] Also on this altar are Demeter and the Maid and Pluto, the Fates and the Seasons and Aphrodite and Athene and Artemis; they are bringing Hyakinthos and Polyboia into heaven; they say she was his sister who died virgin. In this carving Hyakinthos has already grown hair on his face; but Nikias the son of Niko-demos has painted him as fantastically beautiful, which is a reference to the fact that Apollo was in love with him.[172]

169. It seems to be represented on the Lakonian coinage of Commodus.

170. For Hyakinthos, who in classical mythology was Apollo's murdered boy, but whose cult here is so early as to be pre-Greek; cf. Note 62 above. The Amyklaion itself and several other sites in this area have yielded abundant evidence of prehistoric occupation. The early pottery from the Amyklaion itself is mostly late or very late Mycenaean, with the significant exception of some fragments of palace style jars (B.S.A., 55, 1960, pp. 74–6, and pl. 17c, 1). The site was reoccupied comparatively soon after the end of the Mycenaean period (cf. Desborough, Last Myceneans and their Successors, p. 234).

171. Biris is evidently Iris; Pausanias is having understandable difficulties with the archaic Lakonian alphabet. Iris was a divine messenger and guide of souls.

172. Pausanias is noting the difference between a late-fourth-century Athenian painter and an archaic Lakonian. Nikias is the Nikias whose 320-B.C. theatre monument is built into the Beulé gate below the Athenian akropolis. Almost all of the manuscripts of Pausanias spell Nikias's father's name wrongly; Pausanias may possibly have got it wrong. Augustus looted Nikias's Hyakin-thos from Alexandria, and when he died Tiberius put it in Augustus's temple, where presumably Pausanias in his turn fell in love with it. Pliny says Nikias was more realistic than harmonious, not a flamboyant colourist and an accurate painter of women; he was interested in light and shade, and his figures stood out from the pictures (Natural History, 35, 131).

[5] Herakles is also carved on this altar being led into heaven by Athene and all the gods. Then there are Thestios's daughters, and the Muses and Seasons. The story of the West wind and of how Hyakinthos was killed by accident by Apollo and the legend about the flower may not really be true, but let it stand.

[6] Amyklai was uprooted by the Dorians; but the village which has survived there since that time has an interesting SANCTUARY OF ALEXANDRA with a statue; according to the Amyklaians Alexandra is Priam's daughter Kassandra. They also have a figure of Klytaimnestra there, and what they believe to be Agamemnon's tomb.[173] The people here worship the Amyklaian and Dionysos, whom they call Psilax, and quite rightly it seems to me, because *psila* is the Dorian word for wings, and humans are as much raised up by wine and their thoughts are as much lightened as any bird is by its wings.

173. In the Roman period and probably earlier, Amyklai was one of the constituent regions of Sparta. Amyklai was first taken for the Spartans by a certain Timomachos, apparently in the eighth century; Aristotle believed he was a Theban; at least as late as the fourth century his bronze breast-plate was carried in procession at the Hyakinthia (Artistotle, *Fr.* 532); presumably it had perished by Pausanias's time. There was an exploratory excavation of the Amyklaian village in 1961 (*Praktika*, 1961, p. 177). The site of the sanctuary of Alexandra has been more or less known since an inscription turned up in a garden near HAGIA PARASKEVI in 1878, but the sanctuary has never actually been found. The 'tomb of Agamemnon' was a cult-place like the Agamemnoneion at Mycenae, and pieces of pottery dedicated to Alexandra and to Agamemnon have been found there (*Archaiologikon Deltion* 16, pp. 102–3, and pl. 81b). One would like to know the date and relevance of the statue of Klytaimnestra. The cult of Agamemnon is apparently that of a divine hero, a kind of underground king. The first archaeological evidence of his name in connexion with the hero-cult at Mycenae (*B.S.A.*, 48, 30–68) is from the fourth century; the earliest evidence at Amyklai seems to be later still; but Stesichoros in the seventh or sixth century says Agamemnon died at Sparta, and Pindar in the early fifth says it was at Amyklai. There is a powerful archaic stone relief of Agamemnon and Klytaimnestra in the Sparta museum from MAGOULA inside the city of Sparta, which might be earlier than Stesichoros. It is sometimes said that these cults arose from the stimulus of Homer's *Iliad*, or even that they represent a continuous folk-memory of real Mycenaean monarchs; it seems to me likelier that this kind of cult has no reference or a minimal reference to history, but that it existed before Homer and fed the stock of traditional stories on which he drew.

That is all there was to remember at Amyklai; [7] the other road out of the city goes to THERAPNE; on the roadside is a cult-statue of Alean Athene, and before you cross the Eurotas they show you a SANCTUARY OF ZEUS of Wealth, slightly above the river-bank.[174] When you cross you come to a shrine of Pelvic Asklepios built by Herakles; he gave Asklepios the title Pelvic because he was cured of the wound in the pelvis he got in his first battle with Hippokoon and his sons.[175] But the most ancient of all the buildings on this road is the SANCTUARY OF ARES; it stands to the left of the road. The Dioskouroi are said to have brought the statue from the Kolchians: [8] they call it Theritas, after Thero, who they say was Ares' nurse, but they may have picked up the title Theritas from the Kolchians, as Ares' nurse Thero is unheard of in Greece.[176] In my view Ares took the title Theritas not from his nurse, but because a fighting man who comes to battle must have put away gentleness, as Homer says of Achilles:

> *his looks were lion-wild.*[177]

[9] The place called THERAPNE was named after Lelex's daughter; MENELAOS'S SHRINE is there, and the story is that Menelaos and Helen are buried there.[178] The Rhodians dis-

---

174. THERAPNE is across the Eurotas south-east of Sparta. Cf. Note 178 below. In the fourth century there was a considerable sanctuary of Alean Athene (Xenophon, *Hellenika*, 6, 5, 27). What may possibly have been its late remains were observed by a local schoolmaster, Mr K. Nestorides, but they had apparently disappeared in the late 1890s; Mr Nestorides (*Topographia Spartis*, p. 93) was already complaining in 1892 that the site, close beside the modern bridge, was being looted by builders. Trial trenches in 1908 produced only a hoard of Hellenistic coins (*B.S.A.*, 14, p. 149).

175. The place where Herakles was wounded has nothing to do with religion; it is a kind of wound that occurs several times in the *Iliad*. The nineteenth-century revolutionary hero Kolokotronis got his name (which means Stonebottom) from a similar incident.

176. The sanctuary has not been found, and the etymology of the title is still uncertain.

177. *Iliad*, 24, 41. *Ther* means a wild beast, or a satyr or a centaur.

178. The MENELAION was not difficult to discover, since there was ample evidence for its whereabouts in Livy (34, 28) and Polybios (5, 18, 21), and in

agree with the Lakonians over this: they say that when Menelaos died and while Orestes was still wandering, Helen was
exiled by Nikostratos and Megapenthes, and came to Rhodes
as a friend of Tlepolemos's wife Polyxo, [10] who was an
Argive by birth and blood, but being married to Tlepolemos
shared his exile to Rhodes, and now Polyxo was queen of the
island; she was a widow with an orphan son.[179] Now that
Polyxo had Helen in her power, the story goes that she
wanted to take vengeance on Helen for Tlepolemos's death;
while Helen was washing Polyxo sent slavewomen dressed
like the Furies who took her and hanged her on a tree, and
this is why the Rhodians have a sanctuary of Helen of the
Tree.[180] [11] Let me record also the legend about Helen that
I know they tell in Kroton and in Himera. There is an island
in the Euxine opposite the Danube estuary which is sacred
to Achilles; the island is called WHITE ISLAND, its shores are
two and a half miles round, the island is completely covered
with thick forest and full of wild and tame animals; there is
a temple of Achilles on it, and a statue.[181] [12] It is said that

---

several other classical writers. Ludwig Ross dug a little hole there in 1834 and
uncovered a little of it; an even smaller excavation which took place in 1841
in the presence of King Otto and Queen Amalia produced a number of small
lead figures, and the whole very impressive monument was uncovered in the
summer of 1900 by P. Kastriotis. The site was re-excavated by the British in
1909 and 1910, and yielded a wide variety of small finds from the eighth
century downwards, and an extensive late Mycenaean settlement which had
perished by fire.

179. Tlepolemos is a Homeric hero, son of Herakles and king of Argos. He
went overseas after killing his uncle Lykimnios, and was finally killed by
Sarpedon in the Trojan war. Nikostratos and Megapenthes were the sons of
Menelaos.

180. We know from Theokritos's eighteenth idyll, the wedding song of
Menelaos and Helen, that Helen was a tree-goddess, just as Agamemnon was a
daemonic underground power. The symbolism of hanged Helen is obscure;
its origin is surely in a magical belief (cf. perhaps Bk VIII, 23 (6)). Both
Thukydides (7, 57) and Pindar (*Olympian Odes*, 7, 9) record the connexion
between Argos and Rhodes.

181. Pausanias is mistaken about this island; it was off the estuary of the
Dnieper and not of the Danube (cf. Strabo, 2, 125 etc.). Certain cults of

the first man who ever sailed here was Leonymos of Kroton. There was a war between Kroton and the Italian Lokrians, and being related to the Lokrians of Opous, the Lokrians always call to Ajax son of Oileus to fight on their side.[182] Leonymos was general for Kroton; he attacked the enemy at a point where he heard that Ajax was standing in the battle line. He was wounded in the breast, and sickening from this wound he went to Delphi; the Pythian priestess sent him off to White Island and said Ajax would appear to him there and cure his wound. [13] When in the course of time he was cured and came back from the island, he said he had seen Achilles, with Ajax Oileus's son and Ajax Telamon's son, that Patroklos and Antilochos were with them, and that Helen was living with Achilles,[183] and commanded him to sail to Himera and tell Stesichoros the loss of his eyes was because of her curse: that was how Stesichoros wrote his Recantation.[184]

---

Achilles were observed by the rich coastal city of Olbia in the Crimea (Herodotos, 4, 55, Dio Chrysostomos, Or, 36). Pausanias's mistake appears to arise from a misleading phrase in the Augustan Greek story-teller Konon, who in the course of exactly the same story says 'if you sail past the Danube you come to Leuke off the Taurian coast'. But if Konon is Pausanias's direct source for this story, it is odd that for Pausanias's Leonymos Konon has Autoleon. (Photios, Bibl. p. 133, ed. Bekker.) For traces of antiquity on the island of Leuke, I know of no witness except B.C.H., 1885, p. 376, n. 1.

182. Until the fourth century the Italian and Greek Lokrians shared the duty of sending girls to the site of Troy to placate Athene for Ajax's sacrifice. The implication of this fact is far-reaching (cf. G. L. Huxley in Studies presented to V. Ehrenburg, 1966). Konon says they always left an empty place for Ajax in their line of battle, and that the ghost of Ajax fought there.

183. The White Island (Leuke) first appears in Pindar (Nemean Odes, 4, 49) and in Euripides Iphigeneia in Tauris, (434f., and cf. Herodotos, 4, 55). Philostratos tells a wild and beautiful story about its ghostly phenomena. Passing sailors could hear Achilles and Helen at night, singing the story of their lives in the verses of Homer. Achilles lived there for ever with Helen or Medea or Iphigeneia, or with Antilochos and Patroklos.

184. Stesichoros of Himera was a great and influential Doric choral poet of the late seventh and early sixth centuries. We have the merest fragments of his poetry, but every advance in their study has increased his stature. His poem about Helen seems to have been a rather full narrative including a rich treat-

20 [1] The spring at Therapne called MESSEIS is something I myself have seen. Other Lakonians have maintained the modern Polydeukeia rather than the spring at Therapne is the ancient Messeis; the POLYDEUKEIA is on the right of the road to Therapne, both the spring itself and Polydeukes' sanctuary.[185]

[2] Not far from Therapne is what they call the PHOIBAION, with a shrine of the Dioskouroi inside it; this is where the fully-grown boys sacrifice to the war-god.[186] Not far away is a SANCTUARY OF POSEIDON called the Earth-holder.[187] If you

---

ment of her wedding to Menelaos. The first words of the *Recantation* (Page, *P.M.G.*, 192–3) are quoted by Plato (*Phaidros*, 243A):

> *I say that this story was not true:*
> *you did not travel in the benched ships,*
> *you did not come to the fortress of Troy.*

Plato tells us that what went to Troy and caused the war was a ghost or *doppelgänger* of Helen, not the divine heroine herself, who seems in the end to have been stellified. It is hard to disentangle what really happened to Stesichoros. We only know that Lokrians worshipped Ajax and sent girls to the site of Troy, and that Stesichoros offended Helen or Aphrodite (Isokrates, *Helen*, 64), that he then lost his eyesight, and that his recovery was connected with the cults on the island of Leuke. Evidently around the year 600 there were confusions and conflicts over the relation of these cult-heroes with the Homeric poems. Stesichoros appears to have attacked both Homer and Hesiod. Punishment by loss of eyesight is a prerogative of nymphs and of Aphrodite, but nymphs are like Muses and it might easily happen to a poet.

185. Messeis is mentioned in the *Iliad* (6, 457). Hektor warns Andromache that the fall of Troy will mean slavery, fetching water from a spring like Messeis or working in Argos. The spring and the sanctuary have never been found; for a conjecture, cf. *B.S.A.*, 24, pp. 144–5.

186. Livy (34, 38) perhaps implies that the Phoibaion was across the Eurotas on the same bank as Sparta, but this is not necessarily so: what he says is that one Roman division attacked Sparta from the Phoibaion, and one each from two other directions, 'all of which places are open and unwalled'. We know from Herodotos that the Menelaion was 'above the Phoibaion', but all these directions are insufficiently clear and the Phoibaion has not been identified. It is at least certain that Pausanias does recross the Eurotas before the next sentence.

187. Poseidon the Earth-holder had a race-course near Sparta, on open ground on the west bank of the Eurotas. (Xenophon, *Hellenika*, 5, 27–30; cf. also *I.G.*, X (i), 213.)

go on beyond it towards Taygetos you come to a place called Grinding-ground; they say that Myles the son of Lelex who first invented the mill-stone ground with it in this grinding-ground. They have a shrine here to Taygetes' son, the divine hero Lakedaimon.[188] [3] From here if you cross the river Phellia and go by Amyklai straight towards the sea, you come to where the Lakonian city of PHARIS used to be, but if you turn off to the right from the river Phellia your road will take you to Mount Taygetos.[189] In the plain is the sacred enclosure of Messapean Zeus; they say it got this title from a man who was the god's priest.[190] From here as you come away from Taygetos you come to a place where the city of BRYSEAI once stood.[191] A TEMPLE OF DIONYSOS still survives there with a statue in the open air; only women are allowed to see the statue inside the temple; and all the ceremonies of sacrifice are performed in secret by women. [4] The peak of Taygetos above Bryseai is Taleton. They call it a sanctuary of the Sun, and there among other victims they sacrifice horses to the Sun; and I know the Persians sacrifice by the same tradition. Not far from Taleton is Euoras, which breeds wild animals, particularly wild goats. The whole of Taygetos provides excellent hunting; there are these goats and also boars, and an excellent supply of deer and of bear. [5] Between Taleton and Euoras is what they call THERAI, where they say

188. It has been suggested that Alesiai (grinding-ground) is the unidentified classical site a kilometre south of HAGIOS IANNIS, just south-east of TSAREMIO (B.S.A., 55, p.82).

189. Since Pharis was evidently a deserted town, and since it plays no part in the written history of Lakonia but occurs in the Iliad (2, 582), it has been plausibly identified with the very important Mycenaean settlements at VAPHIO and PALIOPYRGI, about five miles south of Sparta. There is no way of deciding which river the Phellia was.

190. Unidentified. Could it be the temple near KATSAROU, discovered and mapped by the French Survey? This question cannot be solved except in relation to the problem of Bryseai; cf. Note 191 below.

191. Bryseai is presumably north of the Eleusinion (cf. Note 192 below) which we know was near the KALYBIA TIS SOCHAS. It is not impossible but it seems to me unlikely that Bryseai is the site south of HAGIOS IANNIS (cf. Note 188 above). It must therefore be somewhere west of SKLAVOCHORI.

Leto ... from the crest of Taygetos ... is a SANCTUARY OF
DEMETER of Eleusis.[192] The Lakonians say that Asklepios hid
Herakles here while his wound was healing; there is a statue of
Orpheus as well, which is supposed to have been made by
Pelasgians; [6] and I know of another ceremony performed
there. There was a city called HELOS on the shore of the sea
mentioned by Homer in his list of Lakonians,

*men from Amyklai and Helos the sea city.*[193]

Helos was built by Perseus's youngest son Helios, but afterwards the Dorians besieged it and occupied it, and that people
was the first slave people of the Lakonian republic, and the
first to be called Helots, which is what they were.[194] The name
took hold, so that the slaves acquired later who were actually
Dorians from Messenia were also called Helots, just as the
whole Hellenic people were named after what was once
Hellas in Thessaly.[195] [7] On certain days they bring a cult-
statue of the Maid to the Eleusinion from Helos. Two
miles away from the Eleusinion stands the LAPITHAION,
which is named after a man called Lapithos who lived here.
The Lapithaion is on Taygetos, and not far away is the
DEREION where there is a statue of Artemis Dereatis standing
in the open air, with a spring they call Anonos beside it. About
two and half miles beyond the Dereion is HARPLEIA, which
extends right down to the plain.[196]

192. The text is mutilated beyond the possibility of restoration. The ELEU-
SINION has been identified and excavated above KALYBIA TIS SOCHAS
(*B.S.A.*, 16, pp. 12–14, and *B.S.A.*, 45, p. 261, with J. M. Cook's map). The
sanctuary is in an area of abundant natural springs. The identification is guaranteed by inscriptions.

193. *Iliad*, 2, 584. It lay to the east of the Eurotas estuary; Bk III, Note 219.

194. The word *Helotes* seems originally to have meant captives; considering
its usage in Lakonia, I have generally translated it as 'serfs'.

195. The words Hellas and Hellenes always have this limited meaning in the
Homeric poems. For the uncertain whereabouts of Homeric Hellas, cf. Wace
and Stubbings, *Companion to Homer*, pp. 296–7. For 'Hellenes' and 'Panhellenes'
in Homer, cf. T. W. Allen, *Homer* (1924), pp. 111 and 119.

196. Probably the Lapithaion is to be connected with the sparse but significant classical finds at ANOGEIA. But the Dereion and the Anonos spring have

[8] On the road from Sparta towards Arkadia there is a statue of Athene of the Cheeks in the open air, and beyond it a SANCTUARY OF ACHILLES, which by tradition is never opened; but there is a sacred law that fully-grown boys who are going to fight at the Plane-trees should sacrifice to Achilles before fighting. The Spartans say Prax built them this sanctuary; he was the grandson of Pergamos the son of Neoptolemos.[197] [9] Farther on is the HORSE'S GRAVE, where Tyndareos sacrificed a horse and made Helen's lovers swear an oath standing on the cut pieces of its meat: it was an oath to defend Helen and whoever should be picked to marry her against every injury; when the oath was sworn he buried the horse in this place. There are seven pillars not far from the grave which I believe are in the ancient pattern;[198] people say

---

not been found. Harpleia is very likely at XEROKAMPI, near the south-west corner of the central Spartan plain. There is a fine Hellenistic bridge here. The identification of Harpleia was first made in a clear and useful discussion of all these problems by H. von Prott in 1903 (*Ath. Mitt.* 29, 1904, pp. 13–14). But it will be seen by any reader of the articles or visitor to the sites that only the *deus ex machina* of an inscription can finally solve such questions. In this area we know of more antiquities than we have names to fit, nor are the most promising sites in the right places (cf. for example Waterhouse and Hope Simpson on HAGIOS BASILIOS, *B.S.A.*, 55, p. 80).

197. The road north from Sparta goes straight up the Eurotas. Athene *Pareia* could possibly mean 'Paris's Athene', but 'beautiful-cheeked' is a traditional Greek epithet. Achilles had a quite widespread religious cult in Lakonia (Wide, *Lak. Kalte.*, pp. 232f.). Euripides mentions a story that Achilles was one of Helen's lovers (*Helen*, 98f.). Neoptolemos was Achilles' son.

198. A great deal of nonsense is talked about the orientation of northern European monuments, including Stonehenge, by ancient astronomy, but astronomic calendars of big stones do exist in the North Balkans, and it is not impossible this might be one. If it consisted simply of rocks Pausanias would probably say so. But he would also tell us if there had been an inscription.

Kranios (in the line below) is Apollo Karneios. At his festival of the Karneia the priest was a running man wearing wreaths who prayed for the welfare of the whole people. Artemis is Apollo's sister, and she may well have the same connexion with mice that Apollo has (cf. Bk VIII, 18 (8)). But the word I translate as Mouse Artemis could be a geographical title, Mysian Artemis. The title is not otherwise known. Perhaps one of these holy places is to be associated with the cuttings in the rock above the east bank of the river below the KOPANOS bridge; cf. W. Loring in *Journal of Hellenic Studies*, 15, pl. 1.

they are statues of the planets. Along the road is a sacred EN-CLOSURE OF KRANIOS of the Wreath and a SANCTUARY OF MOUSE ARTEMIS. [10] The statue of Shame about four miles from the city was dedicated by Ikarios, and this is the story they tell about its erection.[199] When Ikarios gave Penelope to Odysseus to marry, he tried to settle Odysseus in Lakonia, but he failed, so then he begged his daughter to stay with him; she set out for Ithake but he followed her in a chariot and beseeched her. [11] Odysseus put up with this for a time, but in the end he told Penelope either to follow him of her own free will, or to choose her father and go home to Lakonia. The story is that she gave no reply, but simply hid her face with her veil, and Ikarios realized she wanted to go with Odysseus; so he let her go, and dedicated a statue of Shame. They say Penelope had come this far along the road when she hid her face.

21    [1] Two and a half miles farther on the Eurotas runs very close to the road, and at this point is LADAS'S MEMORIAL; he was the fastest runner of his time, and in fact he won the wreath for the long race at Olympia, and I suppose he sickened immediately after winning and was brought home, and because he died here his grave is above the highway.[200] According to the Elean Olympic victory records, the other man of the same name who also won at Olympia, but who won in the stadium race not in the long race, was an Achaian from Aigion. [2] On the way to PELLANA you come to what they call the BARRICADE, beyond which is the ancient site of the city of Pellana.[201] They say Tyndareos settled here when Hip-

199. It may well have stood in a niche near the entrance to the PHOURNOS cavern. It is very possible that Modesty or Shame (*Aidos*) would be worshipped with a nymph or nymphs, and a Penelope with her face hidden seems to me for reasons too complicated to argue here likelier than not to be associated with a cave cult.

200. Ladas's grave has not been found. It might have been somewhere on the hillside above the narrow point of the Eurotas valley where Loring found so many antiquities.

201. The BARRICADE is probably the fortification wall now locally called HELLENIKON (like many classical relics all over Greece). It is a solid piece of work at an angle with the river. Pellana was one of a series of three important and historic fortresses that guarded the approach to Sparta from the north:

pokoon and his sons drove him out of Sparta. The interesting things I saw here were ASKLEPIOS'S SANCTUARY and the spring called Pellanis. They say a young girl who was drawing water fell into this spring and disappeared, and her head-scarf came up in another spring called Lankia. [3] Twelve and a half miles from Pellana lies BELEMINA, the wettest place in the whole Lakonian territory, with the water of Eurotas running through it and plenty of natural springs.[202]

[4] On the way down to the sea at Gythion the Lakonians have a village called KROKEAI with a stone-quarry.[203] This is not a single continuous mass of rock, but they dig out stones shaped like river-pebbles, and very hard to work, but once

---

Pellana, Belemina (cf. Note 202 below), and Karystos (or possibly Aigys). Of these Karystos is still unidentified. The important but unexcavated classical site that was once called KALYBIA TOU GEORGITSOU, west of the river, north-east of GEORGITSI and south-east of LONGANIKO, was identified by Loring as Karystos, but its received identification is now Pellana, and the village has been renamed *Pellane*. W. M. Leake's and also Loring's site for Pellana was on the east bank near the VIVARI spring due west of Sellasia (*Journal of Hellenic Studies*, 15, pp. 44-5, pls. 1 and 3; Leake, *Travels in the Morea*, vol. 3, pp. 13-19). The springs and the distances seem to fit quite well.

202. BELEMINA itself lay south of the village of PETRINA, which is on a direct line between LONGANIKOS and MEGALOPOLIS, between the Taygetos range and Mount Chelmos. What is so well watered is not the town but the territory. It is the northern limit of Lakonia.

203. We are now heading south again from Sparta. Pausanias is crossing the mountains from the central Lakonian plain to reach the sea at the nearest point. LEBETSOBA, about a mile and a half beyond the great eastward bend of the modern Sparta-Gythion road, has been renamed 'Krokeai'; the ruins are south-east of this village near ALAÏMBEY. The quarry lies farther south at PSEPHI, and there are workings on both sides of the track from Alaïmbey to STEPHANIA. These quarries are the only source of the magnificent dark green porphyry called *lapis lacedaemonius*, or by a popular confusion *verde antico*. Hard as it is, it was already used in Crete and at Mycenae in the Bronze Age, and was massively exploited in the Roman imperial period. It was highly valued in the Renaissance, and in use as late as the eighteenth century: at that time it seems not to have been quarried, but classical blocks (not all from Lakonia) were reused. The cobble stones around the obelisk in St Peter's Square at Rome are made of alternate *verde antico* and *antica rosso*, and there is a *verde antico* table in the Ashmolean museum at Oxford.

worked those stones are used for decorating divine sanctuaries, and particularly for the beauty of swimming-baths[204] and water-sources. The gods they have here are a stone statue of Zeus of Krokeai erected in front of the village, and the Dioskouroi in bronze at the quarries.[205] [5] If you turn right after Krokeai, away from the direct road to Gythion, you come to a town called AIGIAI, though they say Homer in his epic called the same town Augeiai. Here there is a lake called Poseidon's lake, with a shrine and statue of the god beside the water.[206] The people are frightened to take fish from here, because they say any fisherman who disturbs these fish turns into a frogfish.[207]

[6] GYTHION is four miles away from Aigiai; it stands on the sea and you are already in the territory of the Free Lakonians, who were subjects of the Lakonians of Sparta released from slavery by the emperor Augustus.[208] Except for the

204. Pausanias says Eurykles used it for baths at Corinth (Bk II, 3 (5)) (cf. also Lucian, *Hippias*, 5).

205. A relief carving of the Dioskouroi with a Latin inscription by the *domus Augusti dispensator* has been found built into the stonework of the LEBETSOBA village spring (*C.I.G.*, V (i) p. 210). Ludwig Ross found it in the 1830s and wanted to buy it, but the village sensibly told him it was their guardian spirit. It was not properly published until 1904 (*B.S.A.*, 10, pp. 187–8), and so far as I know has never been photographed. An Augustan *dispensator* was an important official (cf. *C.I.L.*, 6, 8819–45), and it may well have been this *dispensator* who managed the quarries after the fall of Eurykles, since it was probably Eurykles who invested new capital in Lakonian quarries in the Augustan period and brought them back to life (Strabo, 8, 5, 7).

206. Now called PALAIOCHORA TIS LIMNIS, about five miles north-west of GYTHION, close to the BARDOUNIA river. Poseidon's lake had degenerated by the 1900s into a marsh, which was already beginning to be drained and reclaimed. Homer mentions his Augeiai in the list of cities in the *Iliad* (2, 583). There is no prehistoric site at Aigiai.

207. *Lophius piscatorius;* there is a fascinating discussion of this fish with a fearsome illustration by D'Arcy Thompson in his glossary of Greek Fishes (p. 28).

208. The ancient town stood rather north of the village of MARATHONISI, which is now modern GYTHION, on the coast south-west of the Eurotas estuary. An akropolis, a theatre, and a ragbag of miscellaneous antiquities survive, mostly from the Roman period. These Lakonian sea-ports were declared free by Titus Flamininus, and they were already confederated;

isthmus of Corinth, the whole Peloponnese is surrounded by sea, and the Lakonian coast has the best sea-shells in the world for purple dye, excepting only the Phoenician sea.[209] [7] There are eighteen Free Lakonian cities: the first as you come down from Aigiai to the sea-shore is Gythion, then Teuthrone and Las and Pyrrichos, and on Tainaron Kainepolis, Oitylos, Leuktra and Thalamai, and also Alagonia and Gerenia. On the other side of Gythion on the coast are Asopos, Akriai, Boiai, Zarax, Epidauros Harbour, Brasiai, Geronthrai, and Marios. From twenty-four Free Lakonian cities, these have survived.[210] I should make it clear that any other city I mention belongs to Sparta, and is not independent like the cities I have listed. [8] The people of Gythion say it was not a human being who founded their city, but when Herakles and Apollo fought over the tripod, after their quarrel was over they founded this city together. They have statues of Apollo and Herakles in the market-place with Dionysos near them.[211] Elsewhere they have Karneian Apollo and a SANCTU-ARY OF AMMON and a bronze statue of Asklepios, with no roof on his temple, and a WATER-SPRING that belongs to the god and a SANCTUARY sacred to Demeter and a statue of Poseidon

Augustus confirmed and guaranteed their independence of Sparta; my impression (based on the casual observation of local antiquities) is that they prospered under the early empire.

209. The Lakonian shellfish is *murex brandaris*, a spikier and more etiolated relative of the fat Phoenician *murex trunculus*. They are both called *sconciglio real* and both kinds are eaten (*m. brandaris* is better); D'Arcy Thompson believed there was no real difference in the quality of their purple, so that the difference must have been a matter of technique.

210. That is, eighteen had survived. Of the other six, we can name Kotyrta, Hippola (Bk III, 25 (9)), and Pherai (Bk IV, 30 (2)) and with even less certainty Kyphas, Leukas, Helos and Pephnos. (For references, see Kolbe's note under the year 21 in the skeletal history at the beginning of *C.I.G.*, V (i), p. xvi.)

211. It is hard to think Gythion was connected with Delphi by a lost and ancient link. The peculiar story of Herakles' fight with Apollo for the tripod – one backed by Athene and the other by Artemis – was a popular subject in sixth- and fifth-century art, but it is probably quite irrelevant in the myth of the foundation of Gythion, which sounds like a simple attempt to explain the joint cult of Herakles and of Apollo. It is not attested before the Roman period.

Earth-keeper.[212] [9] What the Gythion people call the Old Man, who they say lives in the sea, is Nereus, I discovered. They took his name originally from Homer in the *Iliad* in Thetis's speech:

> Go down under the sea's broad lap, visit
> the old man of the sea, your father's house.

There are gates here called Kastor's gates, and there is a shrine and statue of Athene in the AKROPOLIS.[213]

22    [1] Just about half a mile from Gythion is a rough stone, where they say Orestes sat and the madness left him, so this stone is called FALLEN ZEUS, which is Dorian Greek.[214] The island of KRANAE lies offshore of Gythion; Homer says that when Paris carried away Helen, it was on this island he first slept with her.[215] On the mainland opposite the island is a SANCTUARY OF APHRODITE of Sex [*Migonitis*], and this whole area is called the Migonion. [2] Paris is supposed to have built this sanctuary, and when Menelaos took Troy and came safely home eight years after it fell, he erected statues of Thetis and the goddess Praxidika close to Migonitis.[216] There

212. For Ammon, cf. Bk III, 18 (3). We have an inscription of about the year 100 B.C. recording the restoration of the ruined sanctuary of Apollo in the market-place at Gythion and the establishment of a hereditary priesthood (*C.I.G.*, V (i), 1144). A large part of ancient Gythion has been swallowed by the sea; there are spectacular underwater ruins. The market-place has been conjecturally identified on dry land south-west of the theatre.

213. *Iliad*, 18, 140f. In the *Iliad* the old man of the sea is Nereus, in the *Odyssey* (4, 384f.) the old man of the sea is Proteus, and in archaic and classical art he is apparently Triton, who fought with Herakles.

214. One of the oldest Latin formulas for an oath is to swear *per Iovem lapidem*. The cult of Zeus is often associated with a shaped block of stone (see for example the frontispiece to Cook's *Zeus*), but a natural rock is another matter; this case is rare but not unique. It must have been a meteorite (cf. A. B. Cook, *Zeus*, vol. 1, p. 520 note 2).

215. *Iliad*, 3, 443f. The island of MARATHONISI opposite the modern GYTHION. There is a chapel on the island standing on the foundations of a temple.

216. Praxidika is a strange and obscure underworld nymph (cf. Bk IX, 33 (3)), perhaps like Eurydike or Eurynome and the male demon Eurynomos. Thetis is a kind of deep-water nymph, the eldest of the Nereids.

is a holy mountain of Dionysos called Larysion above the Migonion; when spring begins they hold a festival for Dionysos, and among the stories about this festival and its ceremonies they say they find a bunch of ripe grapes on the mountain.[217]

[3] To the left of Gythion about four miles away and still on the mainland you come to the walls of THREE ISLANDS, which I think used to be a fort and not a city. I think it took its name from the three little offshore islets opposite this point.[218] About ten miles beyond Three Islands you would come to the remains of Helos, [4] and about four miles farther on lies the coastal city of AKRIAI, with an interesting stone statue and shrine of the Mother of gods.[219] The people of Akriai claim it as the oldest sanctuary of this goddess in the Peloponnese, though the Magnesians to the north of mount Sipylos have the most ancient of all statues of the Mother of gods, on the rock of Koddinos; the Magnesians say it was made by Tantalos's son Broteas.[220] [5] Akriai once produced a man called Nikokles who was a winner at Olympia; over

217. The hill now called KOUMARO, I suppose.

218. North-east along the coast before the mouths of the Eurotas; it was a fort to guard the estuary. Most of the WALLS have survived.

219. Helos (which means Marsh-meadows) lay in the marshy ground around the mouth of the Eurotas. In the Augustan period it was still a village; the *Iliad* (2, 584) lists it as a seaport. It may have been a site identified by the French Survey near KALYBIA, east of the Eurotas. It has so far as I know nothing to do with the estuary village now called Helos. Pausanias's distances at this point seem exaggerated; he may have used a ship's chart of distances by sea, or he may well have had to go round inland to avoid marshes; whatever the answer is, this coastline has certainly altered since his time. Akriai was the modern coastal village of KOKINIO. Its position was fixed by Philippe Le Bas, who visited the site in 1843 and found its one surviving inscription (*Revue archéologique*, 2, 1845, pp. 219–20).

220. Mount Sipylos and the ruins of Magnesia are north-east of IZMIR. The figure on the rock of Koddinos seems to be the *Tas Suret*, a Hittite monument carved in the face of the mountainside above *Akpinar*, about four miles east of MANISA. It really is the Hittite mother-goddess whom the Greeks called Kybele; there is an excellent discussion of it by G. E. Bean in his *Aegean Turkey* (1966), pp. 53f. and pl. 3. Pausanias appears to have been brought up at Magnesia, and very often mentions the antiquities and curiosities of the area.

two games he won five foot-races; his memorial was built
between the training-ground and the harbour wall.[221]

[6] GERONTHRAI lies fifteen miles inland from Akriai; it was
built before Herakles' children came to the Peloponnese, but
then the Dorians of Lakonia depopulated it, rooted out the
Achaians, and sent settlers of their own, though in my time
these people belonged to the Free Lakonians.[222] On the road
from Akriai to Geronthrai lies what they call the Old Village,
where the Geronthrians have a sacred wood and a TEMPLE OF
ARES. [7] Every year they hold a festival for him, when
women are not allowed into the sacred wood. Their springs
of drinking water are around the market-place; in the akropolis
they have a TEMPLE OF APOLLO and the head of a statue made
in ivory; the rest of the statue was destroyed by fire with the
earlier temple.

[8] MARIOS is another Free Lakonian town fifteen miles
from Geronthrai.[223] There is an ancient sanctuary there of all
the gods in common, with a sacred wood around it where
there are water-springs, and there are more springs in the
sanctuary of Artemis. If there was ever a place generously
supplied with water, that place is Marios. There is a village
above the town called GLYPIA, inland like the town itself;[224]

221. Incredibly, the base of this is the one inscription from Akriai that has
survived (C.I.G., V (i), 1108; cf. Note 219 above).

222. The site of Geronthrai is now GERAKI or YERAKI, in mountainous
country dead north from the estuary of the Eurotas, where the road branches
for LEONIDION or for Sparta. It was thoroughly explored and partly excavated
by British archaeologists in 1905, but none of Pausanias's antiquities were
identified (B.S.A., 11 pp. 91f.). The akropolis walls are said to be prehistoric,
perhaps even pre-Mycenaean, in which case they have survived on a scale
unique in Greece.

223. The modern MARI, east-north-east of GERAKI as a crow would fly,
behind the massive ridges of Mount Parnon. The akropolis is KASTELLI, a hill
in the very fertile valley below the village (B.S.A., 15, p. 166, survey by Wace
and Hasluck, with some conjectural identifications). It is a very ancient site.

224. Probably a rather unexplored site at the modern village of KOSMAS.
KOSMAS, MARI and GERAKI are the three points of an equilateral triangle
which contains Mount MAZARAKI. Kosmas and Mari represent alternative
routes from the area of Leonidion through wild mountains to the lower
Eurotas valley (B.S.A., 15, p. 165). In 1963 Mr Christou of the Greek archaeo-

there is also a two-and-a-half-mile road from Geronthrai to another village called SELINOUS.[225]

[9] All this lies inland from Akriai. Seven or eight miles from Akriai along the coast is the city of ASOPOS, where there is a temple of the Roman kings and about one and a half miles above the city a SANCTUARY OF ASKLEPIOS;[226] they call the god the People's Friend. The bones they worship at the training-ground are enormous but human. There is a SANCTUARY OF ATHENE in the akropolis under the title of Cypress Athene; and just at the foot of the citadel rock lie the ruins of what they called the city of the Cypress Achaians.[227] [10] In the same territory there is also a SANCTUARY OF ASKLEPIOS six miles or so from Asopos; the place where this Asklepieion is is called Hyperteleaton.[228] There is a cape projecting out to sea thirty miles from Asopos called the DONKEY'S JAW. There is a SANCTUARY OF ATHENE on it with no statue and no roof, supposed to have been built by Agamemnon, and Kinados's

---

logical service dug trial trenches and uncovered part of a fortified area north of the chapel of the Prophet Elias above the main Sparta–Leonidion road. Glyppia seems to be the Glympeis of Polybios (4, 36, 5, and 5, 20, 6). For a contrary view of the topography of this area, argued in detail and with some perversity, cf. Romaios, *Mikres Meletes*, 1955, p. 152.

225. Probably at NEROTRIVI near the ruined monastery of DAPHNI, about an hour's walk from Geraki (cf. *B.S.A.*, 24, p. 145, and fig. 1).

226. Asopos was on the promontory of XYLI south of the modern inland village of Asopos, probably on the site at PLYTRA at the head of the bay. The sanctuary of Asklepios must have been at the foot of the steep rock with the ruins of a monastery on it, a little way inland (*B.S.A.*, 14. pp. 163–4).

227. Strabo says there was a city of KYPARISSIA here (8, 5, 2) which had a harbour. Evidently Kyparissia (the akropolis) and Asopos (the main site) are the same city. The akropolis was the small hill of GOULAS. There is a helmeted Athene on the coins of Asopos.

228. An important SANCTUARY of Apollo Hyperteleates, which I think means Overdoing or Supereffective Apollo, has been identified from abundant inscriptions south of PHOINIKI, which is a few miles north-east of the ancient and east of the modern Asopos. It was the central sanctuary of the Free Lakonian Federation. No evidence of a cult of Asklepios there has turned up, but it would by no means be impossible, nor has the site ever been efficiently enough excavated.

memorial: he was Menelaos's steersman.[229] [11] Beyond the
cape is a bay called the gulf of Boiai, with the city of BOIAI on
the edge of the gulf.[230] It was built by Boios, one of the
children of Herakles, who is supposed to have gathered the
people from three cities: Etis, Aphrodisias and Side.[231] Two
of these ancient cities are supposed to have been built by
Aineias when he was fleeing to Italy and the wind carried
him into this gulf: the story is that Etias was his daughter and
they say the third city was called after Danaos's daughter
Side. [12] So the people from these cities had left home and
were trying to discover where they had to settle; there was a
prophecy that Artemis would show them where to live, and
when they touched land a hare appeared, so they took the
hare for a guide, and where he disappeared under a myrtle-
bush they decided to build a city. They still worship that very
tree, and give Artemis the title of Saviour. [13] There is a
shrine of Apollo in the market-place at Boiai; elsewhere there
are shrines of Asklepios and Sarapis and Isis. The RUINS OF

229. This is now an island called ELAPHONISI. At the end of the seventeenth
century you could still wade across to it; it was still very shallow in 1806, but
by 1839 there was a clear fathom of water running in the straits. Leake landed
here to shoot quail and believed he had found traces of the antiquities a little
way inland (Morea, 1, p. 508). Kinados's grave appears to have been a small
pyramid of big rectangular stones, like the one at Ligourio in the Argolid.
Kinados is a very obscure figure; in the Odyssey Menelaos's steersman is called
Phrontis, but Aineias in one story it seems had a steersman called Kinaithos
(Dionysios of Halikarnassos, 1, 50). Perhaps he died in the same way as Vergil's
Palinurus, who was murdered by a god. Dionysios of Halikarnassos says simply
that he died between Kythera and the Peloponnese, and that the cape where they
buried him was called Kynaithion. Phrontis was killed by Apollo off the cape
of Sounion and was buried there (Nestor's story in Odyssey, 3, 278–85). It is
not impossible that the large unexplained and unexcavated mound in the north-
west corner of the sanctuary of Athene at Sounion was believed to be the tomb
of Phrontis. A British underwater survey at Elaphonisi two or three years ago
produced inconclusive results.

230. Boiai is north of the modern NEAPOLIS (once called VATIKA), the port
opposite Kythera (B.S.A., 14, pp. 168–72).

231. These three sites are conjectural. Thukydides connects Aphrodisias
with Kotyrta (4, 56), and Skylax says that Side was on the other side of Cape
Malea; perhaps it was at VELANIDIA (B.S.A., 14, p. 174).

ETIS are not as much as a mile from Boiai, on the way a stone statue of Hermes stands on the left, and in the ruins is a considerable sanctuary of Asklepios and Health.

[1] KYTHERA lies opposite Boiai, but to the Plane-trees 23 where the crossing to the island is shortest, that is to the cape called the Plane-trees from the cape on the mainland coast called the Donkey's Jaw, is a distance of five miles sailing. The people of Kythera have the port of Skandeia on the coast,[232] but the city of Kythera itself is about a mile and a quarter inland from Skandeia. The sanctuary of the Heavenly goddess is most sacred and the most ancient of all the sanctuaries of Aphrodite in Greece. The goddess is an armed wooden idol.[233]

[2] If you sail from Boiai under Cape Malea you come to a harbour called NYMPHAION and a standing statue of Poseidon and a cave very close to the sea with a spring of fresh water; the district has a large population.[234] But if you sail on round Cape Malea, twelve miles farther on there is a sanctuary of Apollo on the coast at the boundaries of Boiai; the place is called EPIDELION, [3] because the image of Apollo which is there now once stood in Delos.[235] In those days Delos was a trading station for Greece, and it was believed that the

232. Skandeia was at KASTRI, in the bay of AVLEMONA on the south-east of the island, facing towards Crete (not marked on modern maps). A recent British excavation of the much earlier Minoan colony on the KASTRI promontory (discovered by Miss Sylvia Benton in 1932) has confirmed that classical Skandeia was roughly in this area, but the centre of the classical town has not been identified.

233. The last trace of the inland city and the sanctuary of Aphrodite has survived in the magnificent fourteenth-century church of HAGIOS KOSMAS, which has bits and pieces of the ruins of another sanctuary built into it. In July 1437 Cyriaco of Ancona drew the temple ruins *in summa civitatis arce*, and his drawing has survived.

234. The spring in the cave was discovered by the French survey at HAGIA MARINA, facing east on the southernmost bulge of this whole tongue of the Peloponnese, just west of Malea.

235. The site has not been found, and Pausanias's distances are strangely long (twelve miles from Malea to Epidelion, and above thirty more to Epidauros harbour (cf. Note 237 below)). No site suggested is convincing, but the underwater ruins of HAGIOS PHOKAS cannot I suppose be excluded (*B.S.A.*, 14, p. 175).

presence of the god made it safe to do business there: but Mithridates' general Menophanes either out of his own wickedness or by Mithridates' command, because when a man has his eyes on money his own advantage comes before the gods' – [4] this Menophanes sailed in with warships: Delos was unfortified, the people had no arms in their possession, and he massacred the foreigners and the islanders together.[236] He looted an enormous wealth from the merchants, and the entire mass of consecrated treasures. he sold the women and the children into slavery, and demolished Delos to its foundations. During the looting and the destruction some insulting barbarian threw this idol into the sea: but the waves took it, and carried it away to the coast of Boiai, to this place; and that is why they call it Epidelion. [5] Neither Menophanes nor Mithridates himself escaped the curse of the god: Menophanes was immediately ambushed at sea by the merchants who escaped, and sank on his way home from desolating Delos, and later the empire of Mithridates was annihilated, he was driven from place to place by the Romans, and the god forced him to take his own life, though there are some say he begged his own murder as a favour from one of his mercenaries. [6] That was the punishment of those men's sacrilege.

Boiai has a border in common with EPIDAUROS HARBOUR, which is about thirty miles from Epidelion.[237] The people say

236. The details of the attack and the name of Menophanes are known only from Pausanias. (There is a shorter and less likely story in Appian, *De Bell. Mith.* 28.) Delos fell in 88; it had taken its position in the war against Mithridates under the influence of an organized and flourishing Italian community (cf. Homolle in *B.C.H.*, 1, pp. 113f., and Hatzfeld in *B.C.H.*, 36, pp. 5f.). The antiquities of Delos are published by the French School of Archaeology in Athens in an authoritative series which has now reached its twenty-sixth volume; they have been working there since 1873. The best general account of its history is by P. Roussel (1916). The Italian market-place naturally suffered badly in 88 B.C., although it was rebuilt and reused until Italians stopped calling at Delos, about 50 B.C. As a monument to Roman capitalism it is unique in Greece.

237. This thirty miles may be a mistake; it may refer to the distance from Epidauros to Boiai by sea. The mistake may be due to the vagaries of a ship's

they are not Lakonians but Epidaurians from the Argolid; they were sailing to Kos on a public mission from the sanctuary of Asklepios,[238] and put in here on Lakonian territory, and stayed and settled here because of visions in their sleep. [7] And they say they had a snake from home that they brought from Epidauros, which escaped from the ship and not far away went into the sea, and so because of the vision in their dreams and the omen of the snake, they decided to stay and live here. Where the snake went into the sea there are altars of Asklepios with olive-trees growing round them. [8] About a quarter of a mile farther on to the right is INO'S WATER, as they call it,[239] the size of a small lake only that it goes deeper; they throw loaves of barley bread into this water at Ino's festival. When the water accepts the loaves and keeps them it means a good omen for whoever threw them in, but if it sends them up to

chart or a coastal *itinerarium* that Pausanias was consulting. At any rate Epidauros harbour is just north of the great Byzantine fortress of MONEMVASIA, where one of its inscriptions was found built into HAGIA SOPHIA. The remains of EPIDAUROS are substantial. They were first recorded by Cyriaco of Ancona in July 1437. The list of identifications of ancient sites with modern places which he used for this whole area has survived as annotations to manuscripts both of Ptolemy and of Pausanias (on whom it is based) and as a separate document (now lost, but printed by Sambucus in an edition of Stobaeus and a work of Gemistus Plethon, Plantin. Antwerp 1575, pp. 230-1). It is on these annotations that I base the view that Plethon working at Mistra was the first scholar to realize the archaeological usefulness of the text of Pausanias. This view is confirmed by Cyriaco's and his copyist's annotations in the Eton MS. of Strabo.

238. The SANCTUARIES OF ASKLEPIOS were the equivalent of hospitals. The enormous and very rich Asklepieion at Epidauros in the Argolid and the almost equally elaborate sanctuary on the island of Kos were the two most important centres of Asklepios's worship in Greece. Epidauros harbour is certainly not on a direct route from the Argolid to Kos; perhaps there was a storm, or possibly they were sailing by way of Crete. There was a prehistoric occupation of Epidauros harbour; I am not clear about the date of its classical refoundation: it certainly existed by the fifth century.

239. Ino's water is probably the small pool over a hundred foot deep a quarter of a mile north-east of the akropolis. It was discovered by the French Survey. Ino was very popular on this coast (cf. Bk III, 24 (4)). She was a tragic heroine who suffered a long saga of troubles and finally jumped into the sea and became a goddess.

the surface again, this is accepted to be a terribly bad sign.
[9] The craters of Etna give the same omens;[240] people throw
in things made of gold and silver, and even sacred animals of
every kind, and if the fire accepts them and takes them in the
people are happy with their stroke of good luck, but when it
flings out what was thrown in they believe trouble will come
to the man concerned. [10] On the road leading from Boiai
to Epidauros Harbour in Epidaurian territory there is a SANC-
TUARY OF ARTEMIS of the Lake.[241] The city is not far from
the sea, but built in mid-air;[242] the sanctuary of Aphrodite,
and that of Asklepios and his upright stone statue, the shrine
of Athene in the upper city, and of Zeus the Saviour in front
of the harbour, are all worth seeing. [11] There is a cape
projecting out to sea opposite the city called Minoa; the gulf
is no different from other inlets of the sea in Lakonia, but the
beach here produces pebbles of a finer shape and all kinds of
colours.[243]

24    [1] Twelve miles from Epidauros is ZARAX, a place with a
fine natural harbour, but the most damaged of all the Free
Lakonian towns: this was the only Lakonian town that
Kleonymos uprooted.[244] Kleonymos was Kleomenes' son and
Agesipolis's grandson; I have already told his story else-

240. This dangerous and active volcano was much visited by Romans as a
natural wonder. According to the poet of the *Aetna*, a somewhat prosy Latin
poem written a hundred years before Pausanias, people burnt placatory incense
on the top (358–9).

241. This has never been found.

242. That is the akropolis of Epidauros harbour.

243. Cape LIMENARIA surely, as Pausanias was moving north, and not the
rock fortress of Monemvasia (which at that time admittedly was a cape and not
an island). Pausanias is speaking about the coloured marble sea-pebbles which,
before I had read this passage, were my most vivid recollection of the coast
hereabouts.

244. Zarax is the fishermen's harbour of HIERAX (or HIERAKA). It is a
peaceful deep anchorage protected by cliffs; you enter it by a narrow neck of
water. The ruins were first surveyed by Wace and Hasluck (*B.S.A.*, 15, pp.
167f.); it is very seldom visited. Wace and Hasluck call it 'ill-watered and
fever-haunted', and the nearest villages 'backward and cut off from the
world'.

where.[245] There is nothing at Zarax, except for a SHRINE OF
APOLLO and his statue with a stringed instrument at the edge
of the harbour.

[2] If you go on from Zarax beside the sea for about twelve
miles and then turn away from the sea and proceed inland
for a mile or so, you come to the ruins of KYPHANTA, and
among them is a sacred CAVE OF ASKLEPIOS with a stone
statue.[246] There is a stream of cold water running out of the
rock: they say Atalante came hunting here and when she was
drooping with thirst she hit the rock with her javelin and the
water ran out.

[3] BRASIAI marks the end of the Free Lakonians in this
direction along the coast, twenty-five miles by sea from
Kyphanta.[247] The people here tell a story that conflicts with
all the rest of Greece, of how Semele bore her son by Zeus,
how Kadmos found out and put her and Dionysos into a
chest; and they say the waves washed up the chest here, and
as they found Semele dead they buried her with honour and
brought up Dionysos:[248] [4] and this was why they changed
the name of their city, which used to be called Oreiatai, to
Brasiai because of the chest being washed up, because to this

245. Cf. Bk III, 6 (2f.). He was Agesipolis's great-nephew, not his grandson,
but, as Frazer remarks, 'Pausanias may well have made a slip in the dreary
genealogies of the Spartan kings.'

246. The twelve miles depend on a textual emendation by Boblaye of the
French survey (*Recherches*, pp. 101f.). What Pausanias's manuscripts say is
three quarters of a mile. If you allow Boblaye his twelve miles, Kyphanta is
inland from the KYPARISSI lighthouse and the harbour there. Some perfectly
plausible traces of the Asklepieion have been found (rock-cuttings, and a
spring in the rock; cf. *B.S.A.*, 15, p. 173). The difficulty is that this is a wild
coast, and it has never been adequately surveyed; admitting that three quarters
of a mile is an unlikely distance, it will be impossible to correct the mileage
until Kyphanta has been definitely placed, and hard to place Kyphanta without
knowing the mileage.

247. Brasiai or Prasiai seems to be the rather well preserved ancient site
south-east of LEONIDION, at the port of PLAKA. The old name has been confirmed by an early third-century verse epitaph found at Sparta (*I.G.*, V (1),
723).

248. Cf. Note 239 above. The story that Ino nursed Dionysos is widespread,
but the details vary.

day the vulgar word for the waves throwing things up on the coast is *ekbebrasthai*. The people of Brasiai tell a further story, that Ino in her wanderings came to their country, and wanted to be Dionysos's nurse, and they show you the GROTTO where Ino brought up Dionysos, and the level ground there is called Dionysos's garden. [5] They have SANCTUARIES OF ASKLEPIOS AND ACHILLES, and they hold an annual festival for Achilles. There are small capes at Brasiai, projecting gently

*3. Herakles of Las*

into the sea, and there are bronzes standing on them not more than a foot or so high, with caps on their heads; I am not sure whether they think of them as Dioskouroi or as Korybantes, but anyway there are three of them and the fourth is a statue of Athene.[249]

[6] Turning right from Gythion you come to LAS,[250] a mile

249. They sound like the Kabeiroi, the strange, tiny earth-gods of Lemnos, Imbros, and Samothrake. In general, cf. B. Hemberg, *Die Kabiren* (Uppsala, 1950); he prints an invaluable map of sites.

250. Having worked round the coast eastwards from Gythion as far as LEONIDION, Pausanias goes back to Gythion and sets out in the opposite direction, down the east coast of the Mani towards Cape MATAPAN. The akropolis of LAS was refortified by the French Marshal of Achaia as the castle PASSAVA (*Passe en avant*) in 1254; it was finally reduced to picturesque ruins by the

and a quarter from the sea and five from Gythion. The present city is built over the land between three mountains, Ilion, Asia, and Knakadion,[251] though it used to stand on the crest of Asia, and there are still ruins of the ancient city to this day, with a statue of Herakles in front of the walls and a battle-trophy for a victory against Macedonia: the battle was with a detachment of Philip's army when he invaded Lakonia, which had left the main army to devastate the coast.[252] [7] In the ruins is a TEMPLE OF ASIAN ATHENE, which they say Polydeukes and Kastor made when they got safely home from Kolchoi: the Kolchians have a sanctuary of Asian Athene as well.[253] I knew Tyndareos's sons took part in Jason's expedition, but the Kolchian cult of Asian Athene is something I heard about in Lakonia. There is a water-spring near the contemporary city which they call the Milk-woman because of the colour of the water, and beside this spring is a training-ground where an ancient statue of Hermes stands.[254] [8] There are temples on the mountains: one of Dionysos on Ilion and one of Asklepios on the very top, and one of Karneian Apollo by Knakadion. Four miles from this temple at a place called HYPSOI, which is already on the borders of Spartan territory,

---

Venetians in 1685, who thought it badly planned. Mr Papahadzis in his commentary on Pausanias produces splendid drawings of it as it was in 1650.

251. The plain between three hills is south of Passava; it is thickly seeded with miscellaneous antiquities.

252. Philip V looted Lakonia to its southern extremities in 218 B.C.

253. Athene figures on the coinage of Las. 'Asian' because the hill was called Asia. The suggestion about the Kolchians is a fantasy; so is the attempt made by some scholars to connect Asia and Philip's defeat at Las with Polybios's account of his defeat at *Asina* (5, 19). This Lakonian Asine is not mentioned by Pausanias (cf. Note 255 below). For the site of the Messenian Asine, cf. Bk IV, 34 (12).

254. Galako (the Milkwoman) seems to be a nymph's name. The Christian apologist Tatian in a phrase which might be taken from Aischylos speaks of the everlasting breasts of the rock-springs. A spring and what may be a gymnasion do exist in the area called HOSIARI. in the plain south of Passava (*B.S.A.*, 13, pp. 232–3). The water is not milky, but the cloudiness of spring-water may be due to an underground disturbance and will not last for ever.

there is a sanctuary of Asklepios and Artemis of the Bay-tree.[255] [9] By the sea there is a TEMPLE OF ARTEMIS Diktynna on a cape, where they hold a festival every year.[256] On the left of this cape the river Smenos drops into the sea; if ever river-water was fresh to drink, this is it. Its springs are on Mount Taygetos, but the river is not much more than half a mile from the city. [10] At the place called ARAINON is the grave of Las, with a statue standing on the tumulus.[257] The people here say this Las was their founder, and that he was killed by Achilles, who landed in this country to ask Tyndareos if he could marry Helen. But the truth is it was Patroklos who killed Las, and it was Patroklos who was wooing Helen. The fact that Achilles is not one of Helen's wooers in the *List of Women* is no evidence that he never asked for her, [11] but Homer in the very beginning of his poem writes that Achilles came to Troy to please the sons of Atreus, not because he was obliged by Tyndareos's oath, and in the games Homer makes Antilochos say Odysseus is older than he is, yet, when Odysseus tells Alkinous about Hades and all the rest, he says he wanted to see Theseus and Peirithous who were men of an earlier generation than his own: but we know that Theseus carried off Helen. So it is utterly inadmissible that Achilles was Helen's wooer.[258]

255. These temples have never been found. There is an *embarras de richesses* of antiquities in this area: for example a site above SKUTARI where an early classical temple of Violet-crowned Aphrodite and a considerable settlement have been identified by Mr Angelos Delivorias, Inspector of Antiquities for Lakonia, to which no name has yet been put. (Can it really be Asine? Cf. *B.S.A.*, 13, p. 235.)

256. Perhaps one of the unexcavated sites discussed by E. S. Forster (*B.S.A.*, as Note 255 above) and noticed in every survey since Leake's *Travels in the Morea.*

257. The name may have survived in the modern AYERANOS (the alternative name for Cape *Vathy*). An analogous conjecture about Cape TYROU in north-east Lakonia turned out to be justified. (Cf. *I.G.*, V (1), p. 305.) I am not sure about the river Smenos.

258. The references are to the *Iliad* (1, 158, and 23, 790) and to the *Odyssey* (11, 630). The best edition of the Catalogue of Women, or the *Eoiai*, is now in

[1] Beyond the memorial a river runs out into the sea; this 25 river is called Skyras, because before it had a name Pyrros son of Achilles put in here with his ships, when he was sailing from Skyros to the marriage of Hermione. Across the river is an antique SANCTUARY ... from Zeus's altar.[259] PYRRICHOS lies inland, five miles from the river.[260] They say the city was named after Achilles' son Pyrros, [2] though some say Pyrrichos is a god, one of the Kouretes, and there are some who say Silenos came here and built it from Malea. There is this quotation from a song by Pindar which goes to prove Silenos was brought up at Malea:[261]

> The strong one, the stamping-footed dancer,
> mountain-bred Malean Silenos,
> husband of Nais.

Pindar does not say that Pyrrichos was also his name, but the people round Malea say it was. [3] There is a well in the market-place at Pyrrichos, which they believe Silenos gave them; if this well ever dried up, they would be short of water. They have sanctuaries in their territory of Unwarlike Artemis,

---

the Fragmenta Hesiodea, edited by Merkelbach and West (1967). Pausanias is talking about a stray passage in that long and loosely structured poem, which has fortunately been recovered from a papyrus (Fr. 204, 87f.).

> Cheiron of forested Pelion brought up
> Achilles the fine man, the good runner.
> He was a boy: fighting Menelaos
> Or any other human on the earth
> Would have lost in the wooing of Helen
> If Achilles had met that virgin girl.

259. The river south of Cape Vathy. There are some important Roman ruins, perhaps of a great country-house, at KAMARES, north of the river-mouth.

260. In the pass between KROTONES and AREOPOLIS, the only practicable road across the spine of the Mani. The village of KAVALOS where the site is has now been renamed PYRRICHOS.

261. This fragment (142) is preserved only by Pausanias. The fragments of Pindar's Dionysiac poems, from one of which this probably comes, contain some splendidly wild verses (cf. Bowra, Pindar, pp. 62-4). Silenos-Pyrrichos seems to have been a god or daemon of the water-sources in these very stony mountain villages. Malean Pan may have come from a different Malea (cf. Anth. Pal. 9, 341; Kal. fr. 412; Wilamowitz, Glaub. Hell., 1, p. 388).

because the Amazon expedition stopped its advance here, and and Amazonian Apollo: both the cult-statues are wooden idols, and they say they were dedicated by the women of Thermodon.[262]

[4] If you go down from Pyrrichos to the sea you come to TEUTHRONE, where the people show you the founder TEUTH-RAS, who was an Athenian; the god they worship most is Issorian Artemis, and they have a water-spring called Naia.[263] Fourteen miles from Teuthrone, Cape Tainaron sticks out into the sea with Achilles's harbour and Sandy harbour, and on the cape itself a shrine shaped like a cave, with a statue of Poseidon in front of it.[264] [5] Some of the Greek poets have written that at this place Herakles brought up the hound of Hades, yet no road leads underground through the cave, nor is it credible that the gods should have an underground house where they collect the souls of the dead. But Hekataios of Miletos thought of a likely story: he says that a terrible serpent was bred at Tainaron, and called the Hound of Hades because anyone it bit was bound to die immediately from the poison, and he says Herakles took this serpent to Eurys-theus.[265] [6] But Homer, who first named the Hound of

262. The legendary site of the Amazons somewhere in Russia.

263. On the promontory at KOTRONES. We are still going down the east coast of the MANI. Issorian Artemis seems to be named after the hilltop of Issorion; cf. Bk III, 14 (2).

264. Cape MATAPAN, the southernmost point of mainland Greece and a formidable crag. It is at its most impressive from the deck of a small ship. If you go by land you must travel on foot or by mule and should carry water. SANDY HARBOUR is the old PORTO QUAGLIO east of the point, and ACHILLES' HARBOUR is the old PORTO MARINARI on the west. Cyriaco of Ancona landed here in the fifteenth century and copied inscriptions; so did the eighteenth-century French doctor Pouqueville. The TEMPLE and cave of Poseidon were in the ravine east of the ruins of the chapel of HAGIOI ASOMATOI. In 1856 seventy bronze statuettes were found there. Now there is very little left of the temple except a cutting in the rock (cf. *B.S.A.*, 56, pp. 123–4). It was an asylum for criminals and an oracle of the dead, and a place where mercenary soldiers waited to be recruited.

265. The local belief that this was an entrance to the kingdom of death survived into the nineteenth century. Hekataios wrote in the generation before

Hades that Herakles took, gave it no name and put together no such description as he gave of the Chimaira; later they gave it the name of Kerberos and made it like a dog except that it had three heads: Homer having no more called it a domestic dog than if he called a serpent the hound of Hades.[266]

[7] Among other dedications at Tainaron is Arion the musician in bronze on a dolphin. Herodotos told the story of Arion and the dolphin from hearsay in his records of Lydia; and I have seen the dolphin at Poroselene showing its gratitude to a boy who cured it when it was wounded by fishermen; I saw it come when he called it and carry him when he wanted to ride on it.[267] [8] There is also a water-spring at Tainaron which works no miracles nowadays, but once (so they say) if you looked into the water it would show you the harbours and the ships. A woman stopped the water from ever showing such sights again by washing dirty clothes in it.

[9] About five miles sailing from Cape Tainaron is KAINE-

---

Herodotos the same kind of mixture of geography, history and mythology of which Pausanias is a fuller example. He made Herodotos possible; his prose was admired by Strabo. Some fragments of his works have been collected by Jacoby (*Fragments of the Greek Historians* I; this is Fr. 27). Eurystheus was the king who set Herakles his tasks. When Herakles brought him the serpent-headed hound of hell he hid in a pot; this pregnant moment is represented on a late sixth-century hydria from Cervetri (Etruscan Caere), now in the Louvre, and also on the Villa Giulia hydria. The motif of Eurystheus peeping out of his pot is very popular in archaic and classical art, but what Herakles frightens him with is usually a boar. The vase-painters of Caere had not read Hekataios, but they do preserve the popular story he was trying to explain away.

266. *Iliad*, 8, 368, *Odyssey*, 11, 623; for the Chimaira, which is a composite monster, cf. *Iliad*, 6, 181. The name Kerberos occurs first in Hesiod's *Theogony* (311; cf. also 769f.). Hesiod calls him 'savage Kerberos, the fifty-headed bronze-voiced dog of Hades'. He was a brother of the Lernaian monster (cf. Bk II, 37 (4)).

267. Herodotos, 1, 24. This dolphin was trained like a circus animal and you had to pay to see it (Aelian, *On the Characteristics of Animals*, 2, 6). POROSE-LENE, originally Pordoselene, is a small island between Lesbos and the Asian coast, now called MOSCHONISI (cf. E. Kirsten in Pauly-Wissowa, see under 'Pordoselene'). On the behaviour of dolphins, cf. R. Stenuit, *The Dolphin, Cousin to Man* (1969).

POLIS, which was also called Tainaron at one time.[268] There is a barn of Demeter there and a shrine of Aphrodite on the sea-shore with a standing stone statue. Four miles from here lies Thyrides, a promontory of Tainaron, with the ruins of the city of HIPPOLA: in the ruins is a sanctuary of Athene of Hippola. A little farther on are the city and harbour of MESSA.[269] [10] Something like twenty miles from this harbour is OITYLON; the divine hero from whom the city took its name was an Argive by blood, the son of Antimachos's son Amphianax. The sanctuary of Sarapis and the wooden idol of Karneian Apollo in the market-place are worth seeing at Oitylon.[270]

26    [1] The road from Oitylon to THALAMAI is almost ten miles, with a sanctuary and an oracle of Ino on the way.[271] The

268. Roman ruins north of VATHEIA but still in country which is inhospitably wild. Kainepolis means New City. An inscription to C. J. Eurykles has been found there.

269. ANO POULA, at a point west of KIPOULA, perched on the rocky heights north of YEROLIMENA, is probably the ancient Hippola. Thurides means the Windows; this huge cape (CAPO GROSSO) has a lot of sea-caves in it. The temple seems to have been north of the KASTRO TIS HORAIAS. It is inaccessible and not often visited by archaeologists. Messa seems to be MEZAPOS, north of the cliffs, sheltered by the fortified peninsula of TIGANI (the frying-pan). The impressive ruins there are the medieval CASTLE OF THE MANI, but there are also traces of an ancient settlement (B.S.A., 56, pp. 122–3) if not of any Homeric city (Iliad, 2, 582). There is no real harbour now, though there used to be one.

270. It survived as PORTO VITYLO north of AREOPOLIS (the old TSIMOVA). The upper town is now renamed by its ancient name. The anchorage at LIMANI the ruinous lair of the MAVROMICHALIS family, is the first negotiable harbour north of the small modern one at Yerolimena; it was here that the Russian fleet landed Count Orlov's expedition to disturb the Turks in Greece in the mid eighteenth century. Modern OITYLON has numerous traces of antiquity, but the area has not been systematically surveyed or excavated. The classical site was on the southern slopes of the hill below the town.

271. The sacred spring which was the centre of Ino's sanctuary (cf. Bk III, Note 239) was probably the one in the dark Hellenistic well-house at SVINA near KOUTIPHARI (now renamed THALAMAI) next to the ordinary village spring which is still in use. The ordinary spring has a spectacular series of inscribed and ornamented stones built into it like trophies. The well-house is called the Jews' spring, I suppose because the only ancient world known to a Byzantine peasant was that of the Old Testament: ruins are sometimes called Jews' Castles in the same way in England. There are also traces of a temple at KAMPINARI, between Platsa and Koutiphari.

oracles are given in sleep: whatever people ask to be told the goddess reveals it to them in dreams. There are bronze statues in the sanctuary in the open air, one of Pasiphae, the other of the Sun. It was impossible to get a clear look at the statue in the temple itself because of the wreaths, but they say it is made of bronze like the others. Fresh drinking water runs from a sacred water-spring; Pasiphae is a title of the Moon, not a local divinity of Thalamai.[272] [2] On the coast two and a half miles from Thalamai is PEPHNOS. There is a little isle offshore no bigger than a big rock, which is also called Pephnos.[273] The people of Thalamai say this is where the Dioskouroi were born, and I know Alkman says the same thing in a song. They say they were not brought up on Pephnos, but Hermes took them to Pellana.[274] [3] On this little island there are bronze statues of the Dioskouroi a foot high standing on the island in the open air. When the sea sweeps over the rock in winter it never moves them. This is a wonderful thing, and also the ants here have a whiter colour than is usual. The Messenians say that this countryside was theirs in ancient times, so they believe the Dioskouroi belong really to them, not to the Lakonians.

[4] LEUKTRA is two and a half miles from Pephnos. Why the city is called Leuktra I have no idea, but, if it was named after Leukippos son of Perieres as the Messenians say, I suppose that is why the people here worship Asklepios most

272. Plutarch (*Agis*, 9 ) says it was Pasiphae's sanctuary and Pasiphae's oracle. An inscription recording a dedication to her was found by British archaeologists in the 1900s built into the schoolhouse where it acted as a window-sill. (Doors and windows were once very precious in the Mani. As late as the 1830s Lord Carnarvon records that the Maniotes raided Kalamata in force and looted nothing but doors, windows and nails.) For the Thalamai excavation, cf. *B.S.A.*, 11, p. 124. For the inscription, cf. *B.S.A.*, 10, p. 188.

273. This rock was first identified, I suppose correctly, by W. S. Morrit of Rokeby, a friend of Sir Walter Scott. The classical site must therefore have been the site at CHRISTEIKA at the mouth of the river Milia.

274. Alkman's song has not survived. 'Thalamai' means Bridechambers. Pellana was on the Eurotas north of Sparta. The Dioskouroi were ship-gods as well as land-gods. According to the Homeric hymns they were conceived and born in the caves below the heights of Taygetos.

of the gods, believing he was the son of Leukippos's daughter Arsinoe.[275] There is a stone statue of Asklepios and elsewhere of Ino. [5] There is also a shrine and statue of Priam's daughter Kassandra, locally called Alexandra; and there are wooden idols of Karneian Apollo exactly according to the traditions of the Lakonians of Sparta. On the akropolis is a sanctuary of Athene with a statue, and there are a shrine and a sacred wood of Love at Leuktra; in the winter water runs through the wood, but even if it flooded it could never clear away all the leaves that drop from those trees in early spring. [6] I will describe something that I know happened on the ground near the sea at Leuktra in my own time. A wind carried fire into the wood and destroyed most of the trees; when the place was stripped bare they found a statue put up there to Zeus of Ithome. The Messenians say this is a proof that Leuktra belonged to Messenia in ancient times, but it is possible that, even if the Lakonians lived at Leuktra from the beginning, they could still worship Zeus of Ithome.

[7] KARDAMYLE, which Homer mentions in Agamemnon's promises of presents, is subject to the Lakonians of Sparta: Emperor Augustus cut it off from Messenia.[276] Kardamyle is a mile from the sea, and five from Leuktra. Not far from the

275. The name of LEUKTRA survived as LEFTRO, now changed to LEUK-TRON, which is what Strabo calls it. The akropolis is a hill commanding wide prospects above the small port of STOUPA. In 1970 it was for sale, the land is cultivated. For Leukippos, cf. Bk IV, 2 (4). He was the legendary king whose daughters the Dioskouroi carried off. Rich Messenia had very possibly once penetrated the poor and rocky Mani, but all these inaccessible Maniote towns must always have been more or less independent. (The once fine but now ruined coastal mule-track which looks like an ancient road was built only in the early nineteenth century by the Mavromichalis family.)

276. *Iliad*, 9, 149f. Its name survived as SKARDAMOULA, but has now been reclassicized. (There is still another *Skardamoula* in Chios.) Most of its visible antiquities are on the akropolis, which is a high, rough hill below Taygetos. Part of the western brow of this crag has been trimmed to a sheer face with an elaborate rock-cut gateway and rock steps. There was once an extensive Roman hill-town on lower ground, but it has not been excavated. Until recently there was a small harbour, but now no ships call. Most of the casual finds from Kardamyle as from other sites in the Mani are now in the Kalamata museum.

beach here stands a sacred enclosure of Nereus's daughters. They are supposed to have come up out of the sea to this place to catch sight of Achilles' son Pyrros, when he was on his way to Sparta to marry Hermione.[277] In the town is a SANCTUARY OF ATHENE, and a Karneian Apollo in the local Dorian style.

[8] There is a city that Homer in his epic calls Enope, which is Messenian but belongs to the Free Lakonian league, and which is now called GERENIA.[278] Some people say Nestor was brought up in this city, others think he came here for refuge, when Pylos was taken by Herakles. [9] At Gerenia is the memorial of Asklepios's son Machaon; there is a holy sanctuary, and people ask Machaon to cure their diseases. They call the sacred place the Rose, and they have a standing statue of Machaon in bronze: he has a wreath on his head which the Messenians in their local dialect call *kiphos*. The poet of the *Little Iliad* says Machaon was killed by Telephos's son Eurypylos.[279] [10] This is the reason for what I know takes place in the Asklepieion at Pergamon: they begin their hymns with Telephos, but then they sing nothing to Eury-

277. The *Odyssey* says Menelaos sent her to him. Hyginus (*Fab.* 123) tells the same story as Pausanias. He must have been sailing round Matapan and the Nereids climbed on to rocks to see him go by? Or is there some hint of a later complication? When the Nereids surfaced to watch the Argo go by, *nutricum tenus extantes e gurgite cano.* Peleus fell in love with Thetis.

278. *Iliad* 9, 150 and 292. A classical fortress stood on the hill of ZARNATA, the ragged little castle of the village of KAMPOS south-east of KALAMATA. We know from Ptolemy's geography that Gerenia was an inland city, but there are also minimal traces of antiquity at KITRIES on the coast. The only certain Gerenian inscription (from the sanctuary of Machaon) was found at LEUKTRO built into a house (*B.S.A.*, 10, pp. 175–7). Strabo says some people identified Homer's Enope with Gerenia, but others with Pellana, north of Sparta. The only trace of a Mycenaean settlement at Zarnata is a great domed tomb, excavated by Tsountas in 1891 (*B.S.A.*, 52, pp. 236–8); there is no prehistoric pottery and the supposedly prehistoric walls are all classical.

279. Strabo says this sanctuary was founded from one at Trikka (the modern Trikkala) in Thessaly. The *Little Iliad* is the story of the last stages of the Trojan War; not more than a few words of the poem have survived. Asklepios's son Machaon is a Homeric hero as well as a religious figure, in the same way as the Dioskouroi.

pylos; they never even mention him inside the temple, since they know he was Machaon's murderer. Nestor is supposed to have rescued Machaon's bones; but when they came home from the sack of Troy, they say Podaleirios went astray, landed up at Syrnos on the Karian mainland, and settled down there.[280]

[11] Mount Kalathion belongs to the territory of Gerenia; KLAIA'S SANCTUARY is on it, with the sacred cave beside it, narrow at the entrance but with interesting things inside.[281] About four miles inland from Gerenia is ALAGONIA, which is another Free Lakonian town I have already counted; there are interesting sanctuaries there of Dionysos and of Artemis.[282]

280. The ASKLEPIEION at Pergamon was found by the German excavators in the 1870s. It was a rich and important sanctuary, connected to the city by a covered and colonnaded street stretching nearly half a mile. The snake-god Asklepios at Pergamon has the unenviable distinction of a mention in the Book of Revelations (2, 13). For the cult of Telephos, cf. Bk V, 13 (3). Podaleirios was Asklepios's son and Machaon's brother; he was a healer with supernatural powers like the rest of the family. Apart from legends, nothing whatever seems to be known about Syrnos.

281. There are plenty of caves and plenty of mountains near enough to Zarnata, but this sanctuary has not been discovered; Klaia sounds like a nymph, but nothing at all is known about her.

282. Its site is lost somewhere in the hills south of Kalamata, perhaps in one of the passes over Taygetos. But there is an important classical site 5 km. northeast of Kampos, among the GAITZES villages, where inscriptions to Apollo and Caracalla have been found; Valmin (*Messénie ancienne*, pp. 187–91) identified the akropolis. This place was certainly a flourishing hill town and close to the Messenian frontier, the deep ravine on the main road crossed by a medieval and a modern bridge. It may be Alagonia.

# BOOK IV
# MESSENIA

[1] Towards Gerenia, the boundary between Messenia and **1**
the piece of Messenian territory which the emperor awarded
to Lakonia is what is now called Pig Valley.¹ The first settlers
are supposed to have taken it over when it was wild country.
Then after the death of Lelex who was king of the modern
Lakonia – or Lelegia as it used to be called in those days, being
named after him – Lelex's elder son Myles succeeded;
Polykaon was a younger son and only a private citizen, until
he married Triopas's daughter and Phorbas's grand-daughter
Messene, from Argos.²

[2] Messene's father was the grandest and most powerful
figure in Greece at that time, so she had ideas, and felt it was
below her husband to live a private life. They collected forces
from Argos and Lakonia, and arrived in this territory, and the
whole country was named Messene after Polykaon's wife.
Among the cities they founded was Andania, the royal capi-

---

1. Messenia is the south-west corner of the Peloponnese. This boundary is
either the wild, wooded ravine of the SANDAVA or the NEDON which runs
down from TAYGETOS north-east of KALAMATA (cf. also Bk IV, Notes 27 and
129). Boundary inscriptions have been found high up on Taygetos, and
Pausanias's boundary can be connected with other landmarks through a
description found inscribed on stone at Messene (*I.G.*, V (1), 1431).

2. All these persons are of course legendary; this kind of prehistory is an
elaborate series of rationalizations of tribal mythology, poetry, the chronology of legendary generations, place-names and religious beliefs. The Pausanian
prehistory ot Messenia does not emerge from this kind of unreality until a very
late stage. The exile that ended with the restoration of the Messenians in the
fourth century B.C. made such a break in traditions and in physical antiquities
that their early history is still most obscure. The best source may one day be
the results of the University of Minnesota's archaeological survey of Messenia
under Dr W. McDonald, which is still in progress. The text ot Pausanias is the
earliest continuous account of Messenian history that we have. In general, cf.
Pearson in *Historia*, 1962, pp. 397–426.

tal.[3] Down to the battle between the Thebans and Lakonians at Leuktra, and the settling of modern Messene under Mount Ithome, I do not believe any city called Messene ever existed; I rest this opinion largely on Homeric epic. In Homer's list of the Greek army against Troy he mentions Pylos and Arene and other cities, but he never calls any of them Messene; and there is a line in the *Odyssey* which shows the Messenians were a nation and not a city:

> *Messenians sheep-raiding in Ithaka.*

The point is made even more clearly over the bow of Iphitos:

> *the two met in Messene,*
> *in Ortilochos's house . . .*

By Ortilochos's house in Messene he means the town of Pherai, as he explains in Peisistratos's visit to Menelaos:

> *they came to Pherai, house of Diokles*
> *son of Ortilochos.*[4]

So the first king and queen in this area were Lelex's son Polykaon and Polykaon's wife Messene. It was to this same Messene that Kaukon brought the mysteries of the Great goddesses from Eleusis. Kaukon was the son of Kelainos and the grandson of Phlyos; according to the Athenians Phlyos was a son of Earth, and the hymn to Demeter that Mousaios wrote for the Lykomidai agrees with them.[5] [6] But it was Lykos son of Pandion many years after Kaukon's time who

3. The site was traditionally identified with DESYLLA near SANDANI (now renamed ANDANIA) in the upper Messenian plain, south-south-east of DIA-BOLITSI and north-north-west of Kalamata. But Valmin places it more securely farther west at POLICHNE on the evidence of an inscription (*I.G.*, V (1), 1390); cf. also Bk IV, 33 (6). (Valmin, *Messénie ancienne*, pp. 89f.)

4. *Iliad*, 2, 591f. *Odyssey*, 21, 18 and 15f.; and 3, 488f. Leuktra was fought in 371.

5. Kaukon was usually thought of as a Peloponnesian hero; Poseidon was his father, and he was worshipped in Messenia and at Lepreos in Elis (cf. Bk IV, 27 (6), and Bk V, 5 (5)). A long series of ritual instructions for the Andanian mysteries inscribed on stone in 93 B.C. was discovered at KEPHALOBRYSI near Konstantinoi in 1858; it has since been broken and built into the wall of a church. For the hymn of the Lykomidai, cf. Bk I, 22 (7).

brought the initiations of the Great goddesses to a higher eminence, and the place where he purified the initiates is still called Lykos's oak-wood.[6] The existence of an oak-wood in this country called Lykos's oaks is confirmed in a poem by Rianos the Cretan,[7]

*beside rough Elaios over Lykos's oaks;*

[7] and Lykos being the son of Pandion is proved by the verses inscribed on the portrait of Methapos, who also added certain touches to the solemnity of the initiations. He was an Athenian by blood, a priest of initiations and in fact a composer of religious celebrations of every kind; it was he who established the initiations of the Kabeiroi at Thebes.[8] Methapos dedicated his portrait at the shrine of the Lykomidai with an inscription which includes among other things a confirmation of my argument.

[8]    *I sanctified the houses of Hermes,*
       *the highways of holy Demeter*
       *and the first-born Maid, the place appointed*
       *by Messene for the assembly of the Great goddesses*
       *so taught by Kaukon son of famous Phlyos.*
       *I marvelled how Lykos son of Pandion*
       *newly created in Andania*
       *the complete holy rites of Attika.*

6. For Lykos, cf. Bk I, 9 (3).

7. A long literary epic by the Cretan Rianos of Bene is one of Pausanias's principal sources in this book. We know very little about him except that he wrote a series of poems in the third century B.C. about Achaia, Elis, Thessaly and Messenia (cf. Jacoby, *Fragments of the Greek Historians*, III A, n. 265). He is supposed to have been an ex-slave who was once doorman in a wrestling school. There is a recent discussion of the problem of Rianos with a full bibliography by L. Pearson in *Historia*, 1962, pp. 397-426.

8. Methapos would appear to be a Hellenistic priest; no doubt he was one of the Lykomidai and was responsible for the Attic and Eleusinian elements in the Messenian mysteries. For the Kabeiroi at Thebes, cf. Bk IX, 25 (5f.). We know from the 93-B.C. inscription that they or the Dioskouroi were worshipped as the Great gods (at least in 93 B.C.) in the Messenian mysteries; presumably Methapos introduced them. If he lived in the fourth century Methapos did not found the worship of the Kabeiroi at Thebes; he was perhaps a liturgical reformer. On titles like 'Great gods' cf. H. J. Rose in *Harvard Theological Review*, 51, 1958.

[9] This inscription shows that Kaukon was a descendant of Phlyos who came and met Messene, and it also shows the story of Lykos, including the fact that originally the initiation was at Andania; and in fact it seemed likely enough to me that Messene should establish the mysteries where she and Polykaon were living and not in a completely different place.

2 [1] I was extremely anxious to discover what sons Polykaon had by Messene, so I read through the *Eoiai* and the epic *Naupaktia*, and also the genealogies of Asios and Kinaithon, but none of them say anything about this; I know the great *Eoiai* say Euaichme the daughter of Herakles' son Hyllos married Polykaon, son of Boutas, but they leave out the question of Messene's husband and Messene herself.[9] [2] At a later period when all Polykaon's descendants had died out, as I reckon they did within five generations, they introduce Perieres son of Aiolos as king. It was he who received Melaneus, so the Messenians say. Melaneus was a good archer and was therefore believed to be Apollo's son; Perieres granted him the region called the Karnasion to live in, which in those days was called Oichalia; the city is supposed to have been named Oichalia after Melaneus's wife.[10] [3] But as most things in Greece are controversial, the Thessalians and Euboians disagree; the Thessalians claim Eurytion, which in modern times is a deserted place, was once a city called Oichalia; the poet Kreophylos in his *Herakleia* agrees with the

9. That is, 'Messene' is not a genuine mythological figure, but a simple projection of the city of Messene who would hardly occur in an archaic epic poem. The mention of Euaichme in the *Eoiai* has been preserved on a fragment of papyrus (*Frag. Hesiod.* 251). The papyrus reads Polykreion, not Polykaon.

10. Homeric Oichalia belonged to the archer Eurytos, who challenged Apollo to a shooting-match and was killed (*Iliad*, 2, 596, and *Odyssey*, 8, 224–8). His bow was the one with which Odysseus killed the suitors. Strabo says it was Herakles who killed Eurytos and stormed Oichalia (which Strabo identifies with Andania), and the *Odyssey* couples Eurytos and Herakles as great archers. Surely Melaneus and Eurytos are identical? The Karnasion and Pausanias's Oichalia, which was already in ruins in the fourth century B.C., were about a mile away from Andania (cf. Bk IV, 26 (6), and 33 (4)). The name Oichalia has now been given to the village of ALI TCHELEBI south-east of Andania (Sandani), to which it can hardly belong.

Euboian version, and Hekataios of Miletos wrote of Oichalia in Skios, a region in the territory of Eretria; but I think in general the Messenians make the most convincing case, particularly when you consider the bones of Eurytos, which I shall come to later in this book.[11]

[4] Perieres had two sons by Perseus's daughter Gorgophone, called Aphareus and Leukippos, who reigned over the Messenians after his death. Aphareus was the more important; in his reign he founded the city of ARENE, which he named after Oibalos's daughter: she was his wife and his sister, his own mother's daughter.[12] Gorgophone had been married to Oibalos as well as Perieres. I have told her story twice already, once in my treatise on the Argolid and once in my account of Lakonia.[13] [5] Anyway, Aphareus founded a city in Messenia which was Arene, and received and entertained his cousin Neleus, the son of Aiolos's son Kretheus, and called a son of Poseidon, a fugitive from Iolkos because of Pelias; Aphareus gave Neleus the sea-coast and its cities, including Pylos, where Neleus settled and built his palace.[14] [6] Pandion's son Lykos also came to Arene; he was a fugitive from Athens because of his brother Aigeus. He revealed to Aphar-

11. The *Iliad* has one Oichalia in Thessaly and another in Messenia. To make matters worse there seems to have been one Oichalia known to Strabo on the Peneios between Trikka and Pelinna, one in Euboia, another in Trachis and another in Aitolia. The area of Skios in Euboia cannot be pinpointed; perhaps the Euboian Oichalia was a village in the Lelantine plain, between Eretria and Chalkis. (Cf. the survey of Euboian sites in *B.S.A.*, 61, p. 33, for instance p. 62, *Kamarion*.) For the lost poem of Kreophylos of Samos on the fall of Oichalia, cf. Kinkel, *Epic. Graec. Frag.*, pp. 60–2. For the bones of Eurytos, cf. Bk IV, 33 (5).

12. ARENE was a Homeric city in Nestor's kingdom. Pausanias mentions Messenian Arene several times, but he knows nothing about its site. We know both from Pausanias and from Strabo that there was an Arene in Triphylia (at KATO SAMIKO south of PYRGOS). Pausanias may be confusing Arene with Erana (which was probably at DIALISKARI on the coast between PYLOS and KYPARISSIA) perhaps because of some mythological or genealogical assumption. There is a lucid analysis of the probabilities in M. N. Valmin's brilliant *Études topographiques sur la Messénie ancienne* (Lund, 1930), p. 136 and pp. 140f.

13. Bk III, 1 (4), and Bk II, 21 (7).

14. For Pylos, cf. Bk IV, 36 (1–5).

eus and his wife and children the mysteries of the Great goddesses; he showed them these things at Andania because it was there that Kaukon initiated Messene.[15] [7] Aphareus's elder and stronger son was Idas, and the younger was Lynkeus, of whom Pindar (and one should trust Pindar) says his sight was so sharp he could see through the trunk of an oak-tree.[16] We know nothing about any son of Lynkeus, but Idas had a daughter Kleopatra, who was born from Marpesse and who married Meleager. The epic poet of the *Kypria* says that Meleager son of Oineus had a daughter called Polydora, who married Protesilaos, the man who had the courage to be first to land when the Greeks reached Trojan soil.[17] If this is true, then all three of these wives, starting with Marpesse, died by suicide for their husbands.

3    [1] When Aphareus's sons fought their cousins the Dioskouroi about the cattle, and Polydeukes killed Lynkeus and Idas met his death from a thunderbolt,[18] the house of Aphareus was annihilated in the male line and the government of the Messenians passed to Nestor son of Neleus, including those who had been Idas's people, except for the subjects of the sons of Asklepios. [2] They claim Asklepios's sons were Messenians in the Trojan War, Asklepios's mother not being Koronis but Leukippos's daughter Arsinoe, and there is a deserted place in Messenia they call Trikka; they quote from Homer the verses where Nestor looks after Machaon's arrow-wound with

15. Pausanias has just said Aphareus lived at Arene, wherever that was. He is also committed to the view that the legendary Athenian Pandion instructed Aphareus in the mysteries, yet he knows that these mysteries took place at Andania.

16. Homer says Idas was the strongest of all human beings (*Iliad*, 9, 558). The reference to Pindar is a misinterpretation of the tenth Nemean ode (61–2). Pindar says Lynkeus looked down from Taygetos and saw the Dioskouroi sitting in the trunk of an oak-tree: they were hiding in a hollow tree and peering out, I suppose.

17. The *Kypria* was an epic poem known to Herodotos (2, 116f.) It dealt with the complicated opening stages of the Trojan War, ending more or less where the *Iliad* began. Protesilaos was killed in it by Hektor (Kinkel, *Epic. Gr. Fr.*, pp. 15f.).

18. Idas had killed Kastor.

kindly care; they reckon he would not have taken such great trouble except for a neighbour and the king of a brother-people. But their principal foundation for what they believe about Asklepios's sons is Machaon's tomb which they show you at Gerenia, and the sanctuary of Machaon's sons at Pharai.[19]

[3] After the Trojan War had been fought to its conclusion and Nestor had come home and had died, the Dorian invasion with the return of the sons of Herakles, which occurred two generations after those events, expelled the descendants of Neleus from Messenia. I have already added an account of this to the story of Tisamenos, but I will just say this much: when the Dorians left Tisamenos in possession of Argos, Kresphontes asked them for Messenia, since he as well as Tisamenos was older than Aristodemos.[20] [4] Aristodemos of course was already dead, and Theras was in flat opposition to Kresphontes: Theras was Theban by ancestry, and fourth in line from Oedipus's son Polyneikes, and at this time he was regent for Aristodemos's children, since he was their maternal uncle, as Aristodemos had married Autesion's daughter Argeia. So Kresphontes, who particularly wanted Messenia for his share of the inheritance, asked Temenos for it, and when he had worked on Temenos he supposedly left the question to the luck of the draw. [5] Temenos put lots into a water-jar with water in it for Aristodemos's sons and for Kresphontes, on the agreement that whosoever's lot came up first should have the first choice of territory; Temenos made the lots for both sides out of clay, only the one for Aristo-demos's sons was dried in the sun, but the one for Kresphontes was fire-baked. So the lot for Aristodemos's sons was dis-

19. The kingdom of the two sons of Asklepios was Trikka and Ithome and Oichalia (*Iliad*, 2, 729–33). But these are Thessalian cities, and Protesilaos (cf. Note 17 above), who comes close to Asklepios's sons in the *Iliad*, was also a northerner. Messenia had its own Ithome and its own Oichalia, but not its own Trikka. Strabo says there was a sanctuary of Trikkaian Asklepios at Gerenia, but that is another matter. For Gerenia and Pharai, cf. Bk III, 26 (8), and 30 (2). For Nestor and Machaon, cf. *Iliad*, 11, 505–20.

20. Cf. Bk II, 18 (7f.).

solved, and Kresphontes won and chose Messenia. [6] The ancient Messenian people were not uprooted by the Dorians; they agreed to be ruled by Kresphontes and to divide their territory with the Dorians. They were able to give in over this through their reserved, hostile view of their own royal family, because the house of Neleus came originally from Iolkos. Kresphontes married Merope, daughter of Kypselos who was then the king of Arkadia. The youngest of his sons by her was Aipytos. [7] He built the palace where he and his sons were to live at Stenykleros.[21] In ancient times Perieres and the other kings had lived at Andania, then when Aphareus built Arene he and his sons lived in it; in the time of Nestor and his descendants the palace was at Pylos; Kresphontes established that the king should live at Stenykleros. He was arranging things mostly for the pleasure of the people, and the rich rebelled and murdered Kresphontes and all his sons but one. [8] Aipytos was still a child being brought up by Kypselos; he was the only one of his family to survive, and when he grew to be a man, the Arkadians brought him home to Messene. Aristodemos's sons and Temenos's son Isthmios and all the other Dorian kings helped to bring him back. When Aipytos became king, he took vengeance on his father's murderers and all their accomplices; he won over the governing men in Messenia by courtesies and the people by presents, and became so respected that his descendants were called the clan of the children of Aipytos rather than of Herakles.

[9] Glaukos son of Aipytos reigned after Aipytos, and in his public policies and private actions he was content with his father's example, but in religion he went beyond it. The sacred place of Zeus on the summit of Ith'ome dedicated by Polykaon and Messene had never received any honours from

---

21. Stenykleros was the upper, that is the northern part of the Messenian plain; its modern name is the MELIGALA plain: *Meligala* is the name of a town – it means Honeymilk; it was perhaps the name of a medieval nymph or nereid or powerful fairy. No ancient city or palace of Stenykleros has ever been identified.

the Dorians, and it was Glaukos who brought in the Dorians to its worship.[22] He was the first to sacrifice to Machaon son of Asklepios at Gerenia,[23] and he recognized Messene daughter of Triopas with all the religious offerings due to divine heroes. [10] Glaukos's son Isthmios built the sanctuary at Pharai to Gorgasos and Nikomachos, and Isthmios's son was Dotadas who built the harbour at Mothone, and added it to the other Messenian harbours.[24] Dotadas's son Sybotas

*4. Harbour of Mothone*

founded the royal sacrifices once a year to the river Pamisos and the incineration of victims to Eurytos son of Melaneus at Oichalia before the mystery of the Great goddesses which was still held at Andania.[25]

22. For the cult of Zeus on the summit of Ithome, cf. Bk IV, 33 (2).

23. Cf. Bk III, 26 (8).

24. For Gorgasos and Nikomachos, cf. Bk IV, 30 (3). The harbour at Mothone, which later became the Venetian fortress of MODON, was on the south-west tip of Messenia, north of one of the few Greek islands still called by its Venetian name, SAPIENZA. The harbour in Pausanias's time was apparently a colonnaded circle of quays. It is represented on the imperial coinage of Mothone. The immense and desolate ruins of Modon still exist; they contain an impressive quantity of Roman Mothone, and some traces of Greek Mothone, most of which is deeply buried under it.

25. The Pamisos runs from north to south through the whole Messenian plain; the upper plain was once a lake; below the upper plain between SKALA

4    [1] It was under Sybotas's son Phintas that the Messenians
first sent a sacrifice to Apollo at Delos with a chorus of men.
Their song was a processional hymn to the god, and they were
taught by Eumelos; this is supposed to be Eumelos's only
authentic poem.[26] The first quarrel with the Lakonians was
also in Phintas's reign; the origin of the quarrel is itself a
matter of controversy, but this is what is supposed to have
happened. [2] On the borders of Messenia there is a sanctuary
of Artemis of the Lake,[27] and the only Dorians who took part

and HAGIOS FLOROS there are marshes and springs, which in the classical
period were believed to be the springs of the Pamisos. In this area in 1820 Sir
William Gell spotted a ruined temple, which was afterwards pulled to pieces
by peasants. Its remnants were rediscovered in 1929 by Valmin and excavated
in 1933 by the Swedish Messenian Expedition. It was a small temple to the
river Pamisos, with inscribed dedications, standing between two cold springs
and a warm spring on the river-bank. It was in continuous use from the late
archaic to the Roman period. Cf. also Bk IV, 31 (4).

26. Pausanias quotes two lines later (Bk IV, 33 (2)). Eumelos is a lost epic
poet, who was believed in the classical period to have lived in the mid eighth
century B.C. If that is true he was more or less a contemporary of Hesiod and
Homer and of the greatest 'ripe geometric' vase-painters. The sanctuaries of
Delos certainly existed at this time (cf. Gallet de Santerre, *Délos primitive et
archaïque*, 1958).

27. We know from Tacitus (*Annals*, 4, 43) that this was a border sanctuary
and its possession was disputed. It belonged to the Denthelians, and stood in the
*ager Dentheleatis*. (Alkman is said to have mentioned a delicious Denthian wine
which came from a fortress.) We know from a definition of Messenian boundaries
inscribed in 78 B.C. (*I.G.*, V (1), 1431, l. 38) that it stood 'above Pig Valley',
though the interpretation of this inscription is not absolutely clear (cf. Bk IV,
Note 1); the sanctuary has in fact been identified by Ross at what is now the
ruined chapel of PANAGIA VOLIMNIOTISSA (Artemis was called LIMNIOTIS)
on a terrace about three hundred feet up the hillside at the southern foot of
GOMOVOUNO above the valley of the NEDON on the western slopes of
Taygetos. (Gomovouno seems also to be called GOUPATA RACHI.) Valmin
in his *Messénie ancienne* (pp. 186–94) insists that the goddess had several sanctuaries, and that this is the wrong one. He places the border at the Sandava
gorge (cf. Bk IV, Note 129) and then identifies the lost sanctuary with the
Artemis's temple at ALAGONIA (Bk III, 26, (11) and Note 282) which fortress
he believes he has found on the hill of Hagios Elias at BRINDA. His arguments
are reasonable, but unconfirmed by any inscription, and they depend on
assumptions which have not been verified. Pausanias evidently believes the
border was near Abia (Bk IV, 30 (1), and Note 129), but he certainly does not

in its worship were the Messenians and the Lakonians. The Lakonians claim that Messenians raped some virgin girls of theirs who were there at the festival, and killed the Lakonian king when he tried to stop them: that is Teleklos, son of Archelaos and sixth in line from Agis. Even worse, they say the raped girls then did away with themselves from shame. [3] But the Messenian story is that because of the high quality of the Messenian territory Teleklos plotted against the Messenians who went to this sanctuary, that is the most important men in Messene. The plot was to pick all the Spartans who were still beardless, and dress them up like virgins with virgins' ornaments, and bring them in armed with daggers to the Messenians while they were resting, but the Messenians fought off these beardless adolescents and even killed Teleklos; so the Lakonians, knowing they had committed the first crime, demanded no vengeance for Teleklos's death, because the king's plan was a public matter. Those are the stories: believe one or the other according to which side you want to be on.

[4] A generation later when Teleklos's son Alkamenes was king of Lakonia, and the king of the other family was Theopompos, the sixth in line from Eurypon, when Messenia was under Antiochos and Androkles the sons of Phintas, the mutual hatred of the Lakonians and Messenians came to a head. The Lakonians opened the fighting; they were already deliberately hostile and extremely ready for a fight, and they were given an occasion which was not only sufficient but perfectly decent-looking, although in a more pacific frame of

---

think the Alagonia temple was the famous Artemis of the Lake, or he would say so. Admittedly he gives no evidence of having visited either Artemis of the Lake or Alagonia, and also admittedly the boundary inscription does put the sanctuary above what is surely the SANDAVA. It is certain there were temples of Artemis both at Ross's site and at Valmin's; Tacitus and the boundary inscription support Valmin. If Alagonia was once in or nearly in Messenia and if Ross's temple was a substitute in undisputed Messenian territory, the anomaly would be explained. It is significant that Pausanias in his tour of Messenia never comes to the famous sanctuary; it is anchored in his text only by what to him were ancient stories.

mind it could have been settled by the decision of a court of justice. These are the facts. [5] Polychares of Messenia, who was in general a not undistinguished man and an Olympic winner when Elis held the fourth games, when running was the only contest, owned a herd of cattle.[28] He did not possess enough private land to give grazing to his herd, and so he handed the cattle over to a Spartan called Euaiphnos to graze them on his own land and take a share of the produce. [6] Euaiphnos was the kind of man to take an unjust profit and not keep an honest bargain, and in general he was a scoundrel. When some merchants put in on the Lakonian coast he let them have Polychares' cattle, and went himself to see Polychares and said pirates had landed and overpowered him, and run away with the herd and the herdsmen. Just as he was convincing Polychares of this story, one of the herdsmen got away from the merchants and arrived in time to catch Euaiphnos with his master, and accused him to Polychares. [7] Euaiphnos was caught and unable to deny it, but he begged and beseeched Polychares and Polychares' son to forgive him; for of all the elements in human nature that force us into dishonesty, avarice is the most irresistible. He told them the price he had taken for the cattle, and asked Polychares' son to come with him and fetch it. But when they reached Lakonian territory Euaiphnos committed a second crime even more wicked than the first: he murdered Polychares' son. [5] When Polychares discovered what had been done to him, he hung about Lakonia besieging the kings and the governors with long lamentations for his son, and a catalogue of the injuries Euaiphnos had done him, a man he had befriended and

28. 776 is the traditional and conventional date of the first Olympic games; it is from this year that the dating system of Olympic periods begins; it became fashionable at the end of the fourth century, and Pausanias may well have these dates from a fourth-century source; but Polychares and his Olympic victory should have been recorded on the lists at Elis, which we know Pausanias had seen and consulted. One should be suspicious, but the whole story of Polychares, through whatever epic tradition it may have passed, has a solid note of authenticity about it. It is told with a further twist by Diodoros (*Fragments of the Greek Historians* II B, 106, Fr. 8).

trusted more than any other Lakonian. When he had been continually to the magistrates and still no vengeance was granted, Polychares went out of his mind; he gave way to his anger, and as he had no more thought for himself he committed murder on every Lakonian he could catch.

[1] So the Lakonians say they went to war because Poly- 5 chares was not handed over, because of the killing of Teleklos and because of their bad feelings even earlier over Kresphontes' malpractice about the lots. About Teleklos the Messenians reply as I have already said, and they point out that Aristodemos's sons helped to restore Kresphontes' son Aipytos, which they would never have done if they had quarrelled with Kresphontes. [2] They claim they refused to hand over Polychares to the Lakonians for vengeance, because the Lakonians refused to give up Euaiphnos, but that they wanted the case tried in the League by the Argives, who were related to both sides, and also submitted to the court at Athens called the Areopagos, since that court appeared to have been trying murder cases since ancient times.[29] [3] They argue that this was not why the Lakonians went to war, but the whole thing was an avaricious plot to take territory, and they instance what happened to Arkadia and what happened to Argos, how the Lakonians have continually cut away land from one or the other and have never been satisfied. Kroisos sent presents to Lakonia and Lakonia was the first to be the friend of a barbarian, and this after Kroisos had enslaved the Greeks of Asia including every Dorian on the Karian mainland.[30] [4] They point out that when the lords of Phokis captured the Delphic sanctuary, the kings of Sparta and every important individual took privately, and the court of governors and the council of elders took publicly, from the wealth of the god.

29. This Argive League is never mentioned except here and once by Plutarch; it seems a probable enough conception. The Areopagos court in Athens is supposed to have tried Orestes.

30. He was the last king of Lydia and reigned in the sixth century B.C. He sent a number of rich presents to Greek sanctuaries including Delphi. A century later his story was told by Herodotos, whom it reached in a highly popular form. On his friendship with Lakonia, cf. Bk III, 10 (8).

But above all, to show the Lakonians will stop at absolutely nothing for material advantage, they insult them about their alliance with Apollodoros the dictator of Kassandreia. [5] I cannot bring the reason why the Messenians feel this to be so bitter an insult into the present discussion, because, although the high courage the Messenians fought with and their long endurance of the war are different from the story of Apollodoros's dictatorship, the calamities the Kassandreans suffered were not much less than the tragedy of Messenia.[31]

[6] Those are the origins of the war that each side gives. So then a Lakonian embassy came to demand Polychares. The Messenian kings answered the ambassadors that after consulting the people they would send the decision to Sparta, and when the embassy had gone they called the people to an assembly. The opinions given were sharply divided: Androkles wanted to give Polychares up because of his wicked and outrageous crimes, Antiochos replied with many arguments including the most pitiful of all, in which he supposed Polychares had to suffer before the eyes of Euaiphnos, and enumerated in detail what his sufferings must certainly be.[32] [7] In the end Androkles' party and Antiochos's party both became so excited that they took to weapons. The battle did not last long: Antiochos's side were far superior in numbers; they killed Androkles and his most important supporters. Antiochos was now the only king and he sent to Sparta saying he wished to submit the case to the courts I have already mentioned. The Lakonians are not supposed to have answered the messengers who brought this letter.

31. Kassandreia was a Hellenistic city built on the site of Potidaia in the north-east corner of mainland Greece, near Mount Athos. The barbarous tyranny of Apollodoros was so horrifying and so detestable that is is only in modern times he has found his equals. He was executed by Antigonos Gonatas Cf. *Potidaea, Its History and Remains* (1963) by J. A. Alexander. Kassandreia was an amalgamated resettlement of the survivors of many towns. It was destroyed by the Huns in the sixth century A.D.

32. Pausanias's source, which he will name below, is Myron of Priene, a Hellenistic historian who did not despise this rebarbative kind of rhetoric; it is fundamentally an imitation of bad tragic poetry; cf. Note 35 below.

[8] A few months afterwards Antiochos died and his son Euphaes succeeded him. The Lakonians sent no herald to declare war on Messenia, and without revocation of friendship prepared on the quiet and as far as possible in absolute secrecy, and then first swore an oath that neither the length of the war if it should not be short, nor its calamities if they should be great, would deter them until they had taken possession of the Messenian territory by force of arms. [9] When they had sworn this oath they made a night march on AMPHEIA, with Alkamenes the son of Teleklos in command of the army.[33] Ampheia was a town in Messenia towards the Lakonian border; it was of no great size, but it stood on a high hill and had an abundance of water-springs, and in general they felt Ampheia would be a useful starting-point for the entire war. They took the town with open gates and no garrison, and murdered the Messenians they caught in it, some still in their beds, and others who realized what had happened crouching in formal supplication at the temples and altars of the gods; there were a few who escaped. [10] That was the first Lakonian march on the Messenians, in the second year after the ninth Olympic games, when Xenodokos the Messenian won the running, at a time before there were any annual governors at Athens chosen by lot; first of all the descendants of Melanthos who were called Medon's children had most of their powers taken away by the people, then Athens moved from monarchy to answerable government, and later they fixed the limit of ten years in office. At this time when Ampheia fell Aisimides son of Aischylos was governor of Athens in his fifth year.[34]

[1] Before I write the history of the war and of everything  6

33. No one knows where Ampheia was, though naturally suggestions have been made. It was a fortress town somewhere on the west of Taygetos. Valmin may be right in suggesting DESYLLA, in the far north-east corner of the upper Messenian plain, north-west of Taygetos.

34. That is in 743. The digression about Athens is an explanation of the impossibility of dating so early an event by the name of the annual Athenian magistrate. According to the Hellenistic dating system recorded on the *marmor Parium*, the first annual magistrate at Athens sat in 683–682 B.C.

the daemonic powers had in store to be done or suffered by both sides, I want to decide the question of the date of a certain Messenian. This war between the Lakonians with their Allies and the Messenians with the aid they had is not named after the attacking nation like the Persian War and the Peloponnesian War, but it was named the Messenian War because of the Messenian calamities, just as the war against Troy came in the end to be called the Trojan and not the Greek war. Rianos of Bene in his epic has written about the Messenian War, and so has Myron of Priene,[35] whose history is in prose, [2] but neither of them goes through the whole war continuously from start to finish; they each choose a part, Myron takes the fall of Ampheia with what followed it but not beyond the death of Aristodemos, while Rianos has not even touched this early part of the fighting, and even in the later period of the Messenian revolt from Lakonia, he has not recorded everything, but only events after the battle at the Great Trench, as it was called.[36] [3] Well then, a Messenian called Aristomenes – and it is because of him I give this whole account of Rianos and Myron – Aristomenes, who first and very effectively made the name of Messene important and respected, occurs in Myron's history, and Rianos in his epic makes him as glorious as Achilles in Homer's *Iliad*. Such a difference in the texts meant that I must follow one story or the other, but could hardly follow both, and Rianos's version seems to me more probable about the date of Aristomenes;[37] [4] whereas Myron in general and by no means least in his Messenian history can be convicted of indifference to truth

35. For Rianos and for the general problem of these writers, cf. Bk IV, Note 7. Myron may well be contemporary with Rianos and have written in the mid third century B.C. He is quoted twice by Athenaios and twice by a late Roman writer on rhetorical devices. Apart from his Messenia, he wrote a book on the praises of Rhodes (*Fragments of the Greek Historians*, II B, 106).

36. Cf. Bk IV, 17 (2). Pausanias dates the first Messenian War from 743 to 724 B.C. The battle of the Great Trench was in the third year of the second war, which Pausanias dated from 685 to 668.

37. That is, Myron treats the first war and Rianos treats the second war, yet both stories feature Aristomenes. Cf. Note 36 above.

and to probability. In his version Aristomenes killed Theopompos, king of Lakonia, a short time before the death of Aristodemos, but we know that Theopompos did not die either in battle or in any other way before the war had been fought and finished. [5] It was Theopompos who put an end to the war, as I can prove from the verses of Tyrtaios where he says

> Through Theopompos king that the gods loved
> we took Messene, a broad floor for dancing.[38]

So in my view Aristomenes lived during the later war, and when this book has reached the right point, I shall tell you his story.

[6] When the Messenians heard about Ampheia from the survivors of its fall, they gathered from their cities at Stenykleros. They met in an assembly, and men of authority and last of all the king beseeched them not to be overwhelmed by the sack of Ampheia as if it had decided the whole war already, and not to fear the prepared Lakonian force as if it were better than theirs; Messenia had concerned herself with military things for a longer time, they were under a stronger necessity to be true men, and the gods would be kinder to them because they were defending their own and not committing a first injustice.

[1] With this speech Euphaes dismissed the assembly, and 7

---

38. Tyrtaios, *Fr.* 4. We have not two but eight consecutive lines of Tyrtaios's poem at this point. Pausanias is the only source for the first two lines, but he also quotes lines four to six in one place (Bk IV, 15 (2)) and lines seven and eight in another (Bk IV, 13 (6)). It is another geographer, Strabo, who preserves the last five lines consecutively. The only authority for line three is an ancient commentary on Plato's Laws (629a). The whole fragment together should run:

> Through Theopompos king that the gods loved
> we took Messene, a broad floor for dancing,
> Messene good for ploughing, good for growing:
> for nineteen years they fought over it:
> pitilessly and with patient rage:
> our fathers' fathers with their spears;
> and after twenty years deserting the rich fields
> they fled from the tall Ithomaian mountains.

from this moment he kept the whole of Messenia under arms; he forced anyone ignorant of the business of war to learn it and anyone who knew it to practise its exercises more vigorously. The Lakonians made raids on Messenia, but without injuring the land which they thought of as their own, and without cutting trees or knocking down buildings: they simply carried off any loot they could lay their hands on, and took the wheat and the crops. [2] They attacked the cities but took none of them, because they were fortified with walls and attentively garrisoned; the Lakonians suffered casualties and retreated without success, and in the end they left the cities alone. The Messenians in their turn savaged the Lakonian coast and the farms around Taygetos.

[3] The fourth year after the fall of Ampheia Euphaes was longing to let loose the full blast of Messenian anger, which at that moment was at its height; and as he reckoned the Messenians were by now well enough exercised, he gave orders for an expedition to march, and for the serfs to march with it to carry timber and all the materials for stockades. The Lakonians found out through their garrison at Ampheia that the Messenians were marching, and Lakonia sent out an army at the same time. [4] There was a place in Messenia with a fine strategic position but there was a deep ravine in front of it. It was here that Euphaes positioned the Messenian army, under the command of Kleonnis; the cavalry and the light infantry, which taken together were less than five hundred men, were under Pytharatos and Antandros. [5] When the two forces met, in spite of their extreme recklessness born of hatred, the regimental infantry were prevented by the chasm from getting at each other, but the cavalry and the light infantry did come to grips higher up the ravine; they were evenly matched in numbers and in training, so the battle was even.

[6] During this engagement, Euphaes told the serfs to fortify first of all the back of his camp and then both his flanks with stakes. At nightfall, when the fighting broke up, they also fortified the front of the camp above the ravine; so that at

daybreak the Lakonians suddenly understood Euphaes' far-sightedness: they had no way of provoking battle unless the Messenians left their stockade, and being unprepared in all departments they knew they were incapable of besieging it.

[7] So for the time being they went home, but a year later, when they had been taunted by the old men with accusations of cowardice and of forgetting the oath, they mounted their second open campaign against Messenia. Both kings, Theopompos son of Nikander and Polydoros son of Alkamenes, were in command; Alkamenes had died. The Messenians mounted a force against them, and when the Spartans offered battle the Messenians went to meet them. [8] Polydoros was on the Lakonian left wing and Theopompos was on the right, with the centre under Euryleon, who was a Lakonian citizen descended from Kadmos of Thebes: he was fourth in line from Aigeus son of Oiolykos, the son of Autesion's son Theras. The Messenians opposite the Lakonian right were under Antandros and Euphaes, with Pytharatos on the other wing to face Polydoros, and Kleonnis taking the centre. [9] When they were just about to meet, the kings spoke to encourage their men: Theopompos made a short appeal to the Lakonians in the tradition of his country, reminding them of the oath against Messenia, and saying what a fine act of pride it would be to do more glorious actions than their fathers, who had enslaved the peoples of the Spartan provinces, while they were to conquer a wealthier territory; Euphaes spoke at more length than the Spartan though for no longer than he could see that the time allowed. [10] He showed they were not fighting just for land and possessions, but he was absolutely certain what would happen if they lost: the women and children carried off into slavery, and the grown men lucky if they were massacred without being tortured, their holy places plundered and their towns and cities destroyed with fire; and this was not guessing, the proof was obvious to everybody – it was the fate of the captives at Ampheia; [11] a noble death was preferable to such dreadful suffering, and it

was much easier unbeaten as they were and confronting danger on equal terms to overcome the enemy by their courage than it would be to put their losses right if they lost their present frame of mind.

8    [1] That was the speech Euphaes made; the leaders on both sides gave the signal, and the Messenians ran charging at the Lakonians reckless of their lives like men in search of death in their anger, every one of them longing to strike the first blow. The Lakonians came at them eagerly, but they were careful not to break rank. [2] As they closed they shouted out threats and brandished their weapons and glared at each other: the Lakonians were jeering that the Messenians were nothing but their slaves and no freer than the serfs, and the Messenians that Lakonia was committing a crime attacking its own kindred out of greed, and a sin against the ancestral Dorian gods, and above all against Herakles. [3] And still yelling insults they came into action, the mass of the Lakonians pressing man to man into the mass of the Messenians. Lakonia was far superior in military skill and training, and in numbers as well. They already commanded the men of the subject provinces, and the Dryopians from Asine who were thrown out of their own country by the Argives a generation before and were refugees in Lakonia were also forced to join this expedition;[39] against the Messenian light infantry they brought a mercenary force of archers from Crete. Only in its desperation and acceptance of death was Messenia a match for them. [4] The Messenians thought nothing they suffered was dreadful, but simply inescapable to genuine patriots, that everything they did was greater than it was and that things were going worse for Lakonia than they really were. Some of them leapt forward out of rank and did glorious deeds of courage, and others with serious wounds hardly paused before desperation drove them back fresh into the battle. [5] They shouted out encouragements, and unhurt men drove on the wounded to do some deed before they dropped that might enable them to meet their destiny with satisfaction; when

39. Cf. Bk II, 36 (5), and Bk III, 7 (4).

wounded men felt strength deserting them and life ebbing away, they yelled to the unhurt to do as well as they had, and not to let their death be useless to their country. [6] The Lakonians did not call out to each other, nor did they rival the Messenians in acts of spectacular courage, but knowledge of war was something they had been brought up to, they kept a deeper formation, expecting the Messenians not to hold a line against them for as long as their own would hold, and to be tired by the fighting before they were, and to give in to their wounds before they did. [7] These were the special characters of the two forces in their behaviour and in their frame of mind, but otherwise they were the same: they were slaughtered without asking for mercy and without offering ransom, and this was perhaps in some cases because in the face of such bitter hostility they knew it would be useless, but mostly they disdained it because up to that moment they had not been cowards; while the killers neither boasted nor insulted, because up to that moment neither side was sure of winning. The strangest death was of those who tried to despoil the dead; either they left some part of themselves uncovered and were speared and stabbed while they were too busy to see what was coming, or they were killed by the men they stripped who were still breathing. [8] The kings fought memorably; Theopompos made a wild charge to kill Euphaes; Euphaes saw him coming. He said to Antandros that Theopompos was doing just the same as Polyneikes his ancestor. Polyneikes brought an army from Argos against his own country, killed his brother with his own hands, and was killed by him, and Theopompos wanted to bring a bloodstain on the children of Herakles like the curse on the children of Laios and of Oedipus:[40] but at any rate Theopompos was not going to get out of the battle smiling. With these words he counter-charged; [9] and now, tired as they were, the entire battle flared up again to the utmost point of vigour, strength came back into their bodies and both sides became more

40. Oedipus's children were cursed; his two sons killed each other in the battle of the Seven against Thebes.

careless of death: you would have thought the action was just beginning. Finally Euphaes' men through a desperation that was close to madness and through sheer courage – all the men around the king were the Messenian elite – forced their enemies back; they fought off Theopompos and drove back the Lakonians opposite them. The other Messenian wing was in trouble. [10] The commander Pytharatos was dead, and they were fighting in confusion for lack of orders, but not in poor spirits. Polydoros did not pursue the Messenian retreat, nor did Euphaes' men follow up the Lakonians; Euphaes and his men preferred to help their own beaten men, though without engaging Polydoros and his troops as by this time it was dark, [11] and ignorance of the lie of the land contributed a good deal to stop the Lakonians following up the retreat. Anyway it was their tradition to be rather unhasty in pursuit, and to be more interested in keeping rank than in killing an occasional fugitive. In the centre, where the Lakonians were under Euryleon and the Messenians under Kleonnis, the fighting was even, but here too the fall of the darkness broke it up.

[12] This battle was fought exclusively or chiefly by regimental infantry on both sides. There were not many mounted men, and they did nothing worth recording; in those days the Peloponnesians were not good horsemen. The Messenian light infantry and the Lakonian Cretans never even met, as both sides were in support positions in the ancient style. [13] The day after this battle neither side thought to begin fighting again, or to put up the first trophy, but as the day went on they sent heralds for the recovery of the dead, and when both sides had agreed they buried them there and then.

9 [1] But on the Messenian side frightful things began to happen after this battle. The Messenians were exhausted by the expense of the garrisons in their cities, their slaves ran away to the Lakonians, and some of them contracted a sickness that disturbed the people as if it had been plague, although it did not spread everywhere. For the present they decided to abandon all their multitude of inland towns, and move to

Mount Ithome. [2] There did exist a little town there which they claim is in Homer's list,

*rock-laddered Ithome.* [41]

They moved to this town, extending its ancient circuit until it gave enough protection for all of them. It was a strongly sited place to start with; Ithome is as high as any mountain in the peninsula, and this part of it was a particularly tough terrain.[42] [3] They also decided to send a sacred ambassador to Delphi, and they chose Tisis the son of Alkis, one of the most important citizens, and one who was believed to have talent in matters of prophecy. Tisis was ambushed on his way home from Delphi by some Lakonians from the Ampheia garrison; he refused to be taken prisoner and defended himself, and was wounded fighting until suddenly a voice from nowhere cried out: Let the oracle-bearer go! [4] Tisis got away to Ithome and brought back the prophecy to the king, and not long afterwards he died of his wounds. Euphaes gathered the Messenians together and revealed the oracle:

> You are to sacrifice in night slaughter
> a spotless girl to the underworld gods
> chosen by lot from Aipytos's blood.
> If you fail, then sacrifice a girl
> of other blood, willing to be slaughtered. [43]

41. *Iliad*, 2, 729. MOUNT ITHOME is west of SKALA, that is on the west side of the neck between the upper and the lower Messenian plain. The nearest big village is MAVROMMATION. Homeric Ithome may not have been in classical Messenia at all (cf. Bk IV, Note 19), and there is in fact no trace of any prehistoric occupation of Ithome.

42. It is only 800 m. high and the whole range to which it belongs does not rise above 1151 m. Mount Kyllene rises to twice that height (2376 m.), and Taygetos even higher (2404 m.). Pausanias's remark (surely inherited from Myron) has not even the status of a wild guess: it is simply a rhetorical flourish.

43. There were stories about the part played by Delphi in the quarrels of Lakonia and Messenia at least as early as the time of Isokrates, though perhaps the oracles that belong to the war narrative are later. Another version of this particular oracle also exists from a source contemporary with Pausanias: It consists of a single hexameter couplet (Parke and Wormell, *The Delphic Oracle*, n. 361): 'The lot calls the virgin daughter of Aipys: give her to the gods

[5] When the god made this revelation all the virgin girls of Aipytos's clan immediately drew lots; the lot came to Lykiskos's daughter, but Epebolos the prophet forbade her to be sacrificed because Lykiskos was not really her father; Lykiskos's wife was incapable of child-bearing, and the girl was not genuine. While the prophet was telling her story Lykiskos ran away to Sparta and took the girl with him. [6] The Messenians found out Lykiskos had gone, and were in low spirits, when Aristodemos, who also belonged to the clan of Aipytos's children, and who was a more distinguished man, particularly as a soldier, freely offered his own daughter for the sacrifice. But destiny obscures human purposes like everything else human, just as if it were a muddy river-bottom swallowing pebbles, and now when Aristodemos was struggling to save Messene it brought in this obstacle. [7] A Messenian whose name is not known was in love with Aristodemos's daughter, and at this moment due to marry her. He began by arguing that having engaged his daughter Aristodemos was not her master, and being engaged to her he was more her master than her father was. When he saw this was not going to succeed, he shamelessly declared they had slept together and she was pregnant by him. [8] In the end he had Aristodemos in such a state that Aristodemos went crazy with rage and killed his daughter, and then cut her up and showed people she had nothing in her womb. But Epebolos came and said someone else must give a daughter because Aristodemos's child's death got them no further forward; she was murdered by her father and not sacrificed to the gods that the Pythian priestess had designated. [9] When the prophet spoke like this, the Messenian people rushed at the girl's lover

---

below and save Ithome.' Pausanias's longer version allowing for the willing victim evidently depends on an involved romantic elaboration of a simpler story. Unfortunately we cannot exclude the influence of conventional romantic narrative on historiography even in the third century B.C.; it is interesting that there were two versions. One should remember the existence of variants of other parts of Pausanias's Messenian history preserved by Diodoros (*Fragments of the Greek Historians*, II B, n. 106, Myron, Frs. 8–15).

and wanted to kill him for putting a meaningless blood-stain on Aristodemos and making their hope to be saved an uncertain one. But this man was a great friend of Euphaes, and Euphaes convinced the Messenians that the oracle had been fulfilled by the girl's death and what Aristodemos had done was enough. [10] As he made his speech the whole clan of Aipytos's children backed him up; each of them was terrified for his own daughter, and they were anxious to be relieved of that terror. So they accepted the king's advice, and breaking up the assembly they turned their attention to divine sacrifices and holy celebration.

[1] When the Lakonians heard about the Messenian oracle 10 they and their kings were dispirited and frightened to fight a battle. But the sixth year after Lykiskos ran away from Ithome the Lakonians got good omens from their sacred observations, and they marched on Ithome; the Cretans were not with them any longer. The Messenian allies had also failed to arrive – the Spartans were suspect by this time elsewhere in the Peloponnese, particularly in Argos and Arkadia – the Argives were going to come without Lakonia knowing, and as private individuals rather than by any public decision; and the Arkadians had declared war, but not turned up. But belief in the oracle induced Messenia to put herself in danger even without allies. [2] In general things were the same as in the first battle, and once again the sun went down on the fighting before it was over; there is no record of either wing or even a detachment crumpling, as they say ranks were not kept as they originally formed, but the best men on both sides met right in the middle and bore the brunt of the whole battle.[44] [3] Euphaes was keener than a king should have been; he fell recklessly on Theopompos's men and was repeatedly and

44. The alternation in these battles of *phalanx* fighting (the tactics of exact drill, regular massive formation and heavy arms) and conventionally heroic individual duelling is reminiscent of the same mixture in Homeric poetry. *Phalanx* fighting and its arms and tactics were gradually introduced and perfected in Greece from the early seventh century onwards. (The conventions of epic narrative were first formed in a more individualistic period.)

fatally wounded; as he fainted and fell and lay just slightly breathing, the Lakonians made an effort to drag him to their side, but the Messenians were roused by their old love for Euphaes, and by the disgrace that faced them: it seemed better then to lay down their lives and be massacred for the king than to lose him and any of them escape. [4] When Euphaes fell he prolonged the battle and intensified courageous behaviour on both sides. Later he revived, and heard Messenia had not had the worst of the action; in a matter of days he died, after a reign of thirteen years; throughout his reign Messenia had been at war with Lakonia.

[5] Euphaes had no children, so the crown went to whoever was chosen by the people; Kleonnis and Damis were thought better men particularly in a war, and quarrelled with Aristodemos over the succession; Antandros had already died in battle, killed by the enemy fighting for Euphaes. Both the prophets Epebolos and Ophioneus held the same opinion, that the special honour of Aipytos's descendants ought not to be given to a man under a curse, stained with his daughter's blood. Still, it was Aristodemos who was chosen and became king. [6] This Messenian prophet Ophioneus was blind from birth, and he had a kind of prophetic gift that was like this: he found out what was happening to everyone, in private and in public, and in this way he predicted the future. That was how he prophesied, as I have said; Aristodemos when he was king continued in the wish to satisfy everyone as he should, and respected the governing class, particularly Kleonnis and Damis; he also took trouble with the allies, and sent presents to the powerful men in Arkadia and to Argos and to Sikyon. [7] In his reign the war was carried on with continual small-scale banditry and seasonal raids on each other's territory, and Arkadia sent men to join the Messenians invading Lakonia; Argos did not want to open hostilities against Lakonia, but when fighting had broken out they prepared to take part in it.

11    [1] In the fifth year of Aristodemos's reign, when they agreed to meet and fight a pitched battle, because both sides were exhausted by the length of the war and by all its ex-

penses, these were their allies: from the whole Peloponnese the Lakonians had only Corinth, and the Messenians had the whole Arkadian army and picked detachments from Argos and Sikyon. Lakonia gave the centre to Corinth and the serfs and the men from the provinces who were serving with them, while the Lakonians with their kings took wing positions, in deeper, denser formation than ever before. [2] Aristodemos and his men were placed for battle like this: those Arkadians and those Messenians who were courageous and physically tough but were not strongly armed were given the pick of the most effective arms, and as the action was imminent he put them in with the Argives and Sikyonians, and drew the lines thinner so as not to be surrounded by the enemy, and took care to position his men with Mount Ithome standing at their backs. He put Kleonnis in command, [3] and he and Damis took the light infantry, a few slingers or archers but the great majority physically fit for charges and withdrawals and lightly armed: not everyone had a breast-plate or a shield; those who were without wore goat-skins or sheep-skins, some wore the hides of wild animals, particularly the Arkadian mountaineers, who wore wolf-skins and bear-skins. [4] Each of them had a lot of javelins and some had heavy spears as well; they went to ground on the slope of Ithome where they were likeliest not to be seen. The Messenian and allied regimental infantry met the first Lakonian charge, and then and later they behaved like men, but the enemy were in superior numbers: still, they were elite troops fighting against the mass of a people, not against the best men, so that by a mixture of enthusiasm and experience they held out for a long time. [5] And now the Messenian light army when they got the signal charged at the Lakonians and closed around them throwing javelins on the flanks, and those who were even more daring ran right in, stabbing hand to hand. Still, the Lakonians were not confused by the sight of this second and unexpected danger suddenly dropping down on them; they turned on the light infantry and tried to fight them off; the lightness and ease with which they escaped left the Lakonians helpless, and helplessness left them enraged. [6] It is part of human nature that indignity is the most intolerable thing of all; and so now the wounded Spartans and those the spaces left by falling men had now brought nearest to the assault of the light infantry went rushing out whenever they saw them coming near, and followed up their retreat for long distances in sheer rage. The Messenian light troops went on as before, spearing and stabbing them where they stood their ground, escaping when they pursued, and attacking them again when they turned back. [7] These tactics were carried out by small handfuls of men against different points in the enemy formation, and meanwhile the Messenian and allied regimental infantry assaulted the troops that faced them more fiercely than ever. In the end, worn down by long hours and by wounds and puzzled and confused by the light infantry, the Lakonians broke rank, and when they were turned, the light infantry did them worse damage than before. [8] It was not possible to get the exact number of Lakonians who perished in that battle, but personally I too am convinced they were numerous. The Lakonian line of retreat was secure, but the Corinthian retreat cannot but have been difficult: whether they went by Sikyon or through Argos their escape road led through enemy territory.[45]

12 [1] The Lakonians grieved over this disaster, the list of those killed in battle being a long one and the names important, and the whole prospect of the war filled them with depression; so they sent a sacred embassy to Delphi. When they arrived the Pythian priestess gave them this oracle:

> Phoibos commands work not only at war:
> the people hold Messene by a trick;
> it shall be captured by the same cunning.[46]

45. The road from Ithome to Corinth passes either through Arkadia, reaching the coast at Sikyon near Corinth, or over the passes of Parnon to the Argolid and then north.

46. Quoted by two other sources, always in the same version. The trick was the baked and the unbaked lumps of clay (cf. Bk IV, 3 (5)). It seems to have been told fully in the Little Iliad.

[2] So the kings and the governors tried hard to think of a trick, but they could not think of one; and then like Odysseus at Troy they sent a hundred apparent fugitives into Ithome to find out what the Messenians were up to.[47] The Lakonians publicly pronounced a sentence of exile on these men. But Aristodemos just sent them away, saying Lakonia invented new crimes but it used old tricks. [3] When this failed the Lakonians tried to break up the Messenian alliance. The ambassadors went to Arkadia first, and the Arkadians refused, so the embassy went on to Argos. When Aristodemos discovered what the Lakonians were doing, he sent to ask the god about it, and the Pythian priestess gave him this oracle:

[4]     *The god gives you war glory:*
*beware the trickery of the Spartan ambush,*
*in case it overcomes you by cunning.*
*Then the War-god shall occupy strong walls,*
*a bitter people settle in the stone wreath of dances,*
*when two together leap from their ambush.*
*But sacred day shall not see this fulfilled*
*before what changes nature shall have met destiny.*[48]

For the time being Aristodemos and his prophets were unable to unravel what this meant, but not many years afterwards the god was to reveal it and fulfil it.

[5] Another thing happened to the Messenians at this same time. While Lykiskos was living in Sparta, death came to the daughter he brought with him when he fled from Messene. He was going as he often did to visit the tomb of his child, when he was ambushed and captured by Arkadian horsemen. He was taken to Ithome and brought before the assembly; and his defence was that he had not committed treason by escaping, because he believed what the prophet said about the

47. This story is not told by Homer, though Homer knows it (*Odyssey*, 4, 249f.).
48. Parke (writing in *Hermathena*, 27, 1938, pp. 66f.) believes this oracle, which we know only from Pausanias, was invented later than the others. He thinks of it as obscurer and clumsier; it seems to me more powerful and sinister, but there is no doubt that it is different.

child not being his. [6] No one thought this defence was the truth until a woman who was now the priestess of Hera came into the theatre; she confessed that the child was hers, and it was she who gave it to Lykiskos's wife. And now, she said, I have come here to explain this mystery and to put an end to my priesthood. She said this because the Messenian tradition was that if the child of a priestess or a priest died before him, the priesthood passed to someone else. So they believed she was telling the truth and chose another woman to be priestess to the goddess, and Lykiskos was forgiven.

[7] After that they decided, as the war was now reaching its twentieth year, to send to Delphi once again to ask about winning it. The Pythian priestess answered with this oracle:

> They who shall stand twice five times ten tripods
> to Ithomaian Zeus at his altar,
> the god gives them the land of Messene
> and the glory of war; Zeus decrees this.
> Treachery advances you, and vengeance follows you;
> you would deceive gods; act your destiny.
> The curse falls on some men before others.[49]

[8] When they heard it they thought the prophecy was on their side, and gave them victory in the war: as they had the sanctuary of Zeus of Ithome inside their fortress, the Lakonians could hardly be first to dedicate there. Since they had no money for bronze, they were going to make wooden tripods, but someone from Delphi had reported this oracle at Sparta. When the Spartans heard about it they could think of no public plan, [9] but Oibalos, who was not a distinguished man but a wise one as things turned out, happened to have made a hundred terracotta tripods,[50] and brought them hidden in a game-bag, with some nets like a professional huntsman. Since not many people knew him even in Lakonia, it was all the easier to get past the Messenians. He mingled with the

49. We have the oracle only from Pausanias.

50. These tripods must have been small dedicatory terracottas; I can find no record of such a thing except in relief representations, but there is no difficulty about admitting their real existence.

country people and went into Ithome with them, and then as soon as darkness fell he dedicated his terracotta tripods to the god and went back to Sparta with the news. [10] When the Messenians saw what had happened they were profoundly disturbed, guessing that the tripods came from Lakonia, as of course they did; still, Aristodemos comforted them with the kind of speech you might expect, and stood the wooden tripods, which by now were finished, round the altar of Ithomaian Zeus. And it happened that Ophioneus the prophet, who was born blind, recovered his sight in the most extraordinary way that has ever been recorded; he got a fearful headache, and from that moment he could see.

[1] And now, when destiny had decided on the fall of 13 Messenia, the god gave signs of what was to come. The statue of Artemis, which was bronze with weapons of bronze, dropped its shield; and when Aristodemos went to sacrifice to Zeus of Ithome, the rams smashed their own horns against the altar and killed themselves; and a third thing happened: the dogs gathered and howled all night, and finally ran away in a pack to the Lakonian camp. [2] Aristodemos was even further disturbed by a dream that came to him. He thought he was going out to fight and had his armour on, and his weapons, and the entrails of the victims lay on a table, and then his daughter appeared in black clothes and showed him her breast and stomach cut open, threw everything off the table, took away his armour and weapons, and crowned him with a golden wreath and dressed him in a white cloak. [3] While Aristodemos was in low spirits and thinking this dream foretold his death, as the Messenians used to bury their great men crowned with wreaths and dressed in white cloaks, someone told him the prophet Ophioneus had lost his sight and suddenly gone blind again, just as he was in the beginning. Then they understood the oracle; by the two who came out of ambush and then met their destiny the Pythian priestess had meant Ophioneus's two eyes. [4] So Aristodemos considered his personal record: he had murdered his daughter to no purpose, and he could see no more hope for his country:

he slaughtered himself on his daughter's grave. By human reckoning he saved Messenia, but fortune brought his energies and his devices to nothing. When he died he had reigned for six years and a few months.

[5] The Messenians were in such despair they wanted to send an embassy to Lakonia to beg for peace: Aristodemos's death had put them into a complete panic. Bitterness prevented them from doing it, but they met in their assembly and instead of choosing someone to be king they made Damis commander in chief and dictator. Damis co-opted Kleonnis and Phyleus to act with him and got ready even as things were to fight a battle. He was forced into this by the siege, and as much as anything else by starvation and by the fear it engendered that they might perish anyway from want. [6] There was no lack of courage or daring even at this point of Messenian history; but all the generals and all the great were killed: they held out after that for about another five months, and then at the turn of the year they abandoned Ithome, after fighting for twenty full years, as Tyrtaios says in his poem:

> and after twenty years deserting the rich fields
> they took flight from the tall hills of Ithome.[51]

[7] The war finished in the first year after the fourteenth Olympics, when Dasmon of Corinth won the running: the Medontidai were still governing Athens in ten-year terms. Hippomenes had just finished his fourth year in office.[52]

14   [1] All the Messenians who happened to have guest-privileges at Sikyon or at Argos or anywhere in Arkadia simply migrated there, and the priestly family who celebrated the mysteries of the Great goddesses went to Eleusis, but the mass of the people all scattered to their old home towns. [2] The Lakonians first of all destroyed Ithome to its foundations, and then went on to take the other cities. They dedicated bronze tripods from the spoils to Amyklaian Apollo, with a figure of Aphrodite standing under the first tripod, Artemis under the second, and Demeter or the Maid under the third.[53]

51. Cf. Note 38 above.   52. It was 724 B.C.   53. Cf. Bk III, 18 (7).

[3] They dedicated these at Amyklai; and they granted to the people of Asine, whom the Argives had turned out, the Messenian coastal territory which they still occupy today.[54] They granted Hyamia to Androkles' descendants: he had a daughter and the daughter had sons, who fled when he was killed, and went to Sparta.[55] [4] What the Lakonians did to the Messenians was this: first they imposed an oath never to rebel against Sparta and never to introduce any political change at all; secondly they imposed no fixed tribute, but the Messenians had to bring half of all the produce of their farms to Sparta. It was decreed that at the burial of Spartan kings and governors men must come from Messenia with their women dressed in black: [5] and there was a penalty for failure. Tyrtaios speaks of the outrages they punished the Messenians with in his poem.

> Like asses exhausted under great loads:
> painful necessity to bring their masters
> full half the fruit their ploughed land produced.

And in these lines he shows they were forced to take part in Spartan mourning:

> man and wife together lamented their masters,
> when the dreadful destiny of death took them.[56]

[6] Given that the Messenians were caught in this situation, with no future prospect at all of mercy from Lakonia, they thought it would be preferable to die fighting or to clear out of the Peloponnese altogether; so in spite of everything they

54. Cf. Bk II, 36 (4–5), and Bk III, 7 (4), and Bk IV, 34 (6f.). They are supposed to have settled at what is now KORONI, a fortified harbour town in the south-east corner of Messenia, south-south-west of Kalamata. Ancient Korone was farther north at PETALIDION; when it fell to the Turks refugees moved south to a small Byzantine castle on the site of the Messenian Asine, and renamed it Koroni (cf. K. Andrews, *Castles of the Morea*, 1953, Chapter 1).

55. Strabo says Hyamia is one of the five subdivisions of Messenia as it was organized by Kresphontes. But no one knows exactly where Hyamia was: there is not even enough evidence on which to base a sensible conjecture.

56. We have these two fragments of Tyrtaios only from Pausanias.

decided to rebel. It was the younger men who were at the bottom of it; they had no experience of war and a certain nobility of mind, and preferred to die free in their own country than to be slaves even if they could have been happy in all other respects. [7] These youths were bred up in various parts of Messenia, but most of them and the best of them came from around Andania: [57] one of these was Aristomenes, whom the Messenians worship to this day as a divine hero. And there are those who even believe there was something extraordinary about his birth: they say his mother Nikoteleia slept with a daemonic spirit or a god in the likeness of a serpent. I know the Macedonians say this kind of thing about Olympias and the Sikyonians about Aristodama, but there was this difference: [8] the Messenians do not foist Aristomenes on Herakles or on Zeus, as the Macedonians do Alexander on Ammon and the Sikyonians Aratos on Asklepios; [58] most of Greece says Aristomenes' father was Pyrros, but I know myself that when they pour the ritual wine the Messenians call Aristomenes the son of Nikomedes. He was at the height of his youth and enterprise, and he and some other leaders stimulated the revolt: it was not done in an immediate, public way, but they sent secretly to Argos and Arkadia to ask if the people there were willing to fight for them without hesitations and with the same strength as they had in the earlier war.

15    [1] With everything ready for war and the help from the allies even more eager than the Messenians expected, because Argos and Arkadia were already on fire with enmity against Lakonia, Messenia rebelled thirty-eight years after the fall of Ithome, in the fourth year after the twenty-third Olympics, when Ikaros of Hyperesia won the running; by now at Athens

57. For the site of Andania, cf. Bk IV, Note 3.

58. Olympias was the mother of Alexander the Great, Aristodama was the mother of the great Hellenistic statesman Aratos (cf. Bk IV, 8 (1f.)). For the story of Alexander's magic birth, which by this time existed in more than one version, cf. for example Plutarch, *Alexander*, 2, and the first pages of Pseudo-Kallisthenes, *Historia Alexandri Magni*. For Aratos's divine birth, cf. Bk IV, 10 (3).

there was a yearly governorship, and in that year Tlesias was governor.[59] [2] Tyrtaios has not recorded the names of the kings of Lakonia at this time, but Rianos in his epic writes that Leotychides was king in this war. I simply cannot agree with Rianos about this; even though Tyrtaios says nothing one might suppose he had in a way said something in the following verses, his poem being about the earlier war:

> *for nineteen years they fought over it:*
> *pitilessly and with patient rage:*
> *our fathers' fathers with their spears.*[60]

[3] So obviously the Messenians fought this war in the second generation, and the progression of time shows us that the kings of Sparta in those days were Anaxander the son of Polydoros's son Eurykrates, and in the other family Anaxidamos son of Zeuxidamos, the son of Theopompos's son Archidamos. Theopompos's great-grandson had succeeded because Archidamos died before his father, and Zeuxidamos inherited the throne of Theopompos as a little boy. It is clear that Leotychides was king after Ariston's son Demaratos, and Ariston came sixth in line of descent from Theopompos.[61]

[4] So now the Messenians fought the Lakonians at DERAI in Messenia:[62] it was in the first year of the revolt and neither side had their allies. Neither side won outright, but they say Aristomenes did more than was credible for a single individ-

59. That is in 685 B.C. He believed the war ended in 668 B.C. That makes seventeen years, but Pausanias covers only fourteen of them. Perhaps the lost three years have something to do with Rianos's narrative starting in the third year of the war (cf. Note 36 above).

60. Cf. Note 38 above.

61. Herodotos (8, 131) has another king called Leotychides in an earlier generation, who is no doubt the cause of this uninteresting and insoluble confusion. There is a full discussion by Hitzig and Blümner in their commentary on Pausanias.

62. That is, not at the Lakonian Dereion (Bk III, 20 (7)). One would expect Derai to mean a small hill. The place-name Dera occurs in a fragmentary late second-century Messenian inscription, which appears to have been a definition of the Messenian borders with Arkadia (*I.G.,* V (1), 1429, l. 2). We know nothing more about it.

ual, so after the battle they chose him as king, as he came from the clan of the children of Aipytos; but he refused, so they made him commander in chief and dictator. [5] Aristomenes could rely on everyone being ready to suffer in the pursuit of war and the execution of memorable action, and for himself he believed it was the most important thing in the world to strike panic into the Lakonians from the very beginning of the war, to terrorize them more and more for the future. In this frame of mind he went into Sparta at night and dedicated his shield at the temple of Bronzehouse Athene, with an inscription saying Aristomenes gave it to the goddess from the spoils of the Spartans.[63]

[6] The Lakonians were told by an oracle from Delphi to consult the Athenian, so they sent to Athens to announce this prophecy and to ask for the man who was to advise them as they needed. The Athenians were in a dilemma: the Lakonians without great risk would obtain the richest part of the Peloponnese, or else Athens would disobey the god; so they thought of a device. There was Tyrtaios, a teacher of writing who was not thought at all clever, and was lame in one foot, so it was him they sent to Sparta. When he arrived there he chatted privately to the great men and wherever he could gather people together recited his poems in couplets and his anapaestic verses.[64] [7] A year after the fighting at Derai, the two sides and their allies met and prepared for a battle at a place called the BOAR'S GRAVE.[65] The Messenians had help from Elis and Arkadia, and also from Argos and from Sikyon; all the Messenians who had previously gone into voluntary exile came back, so did the family from Eleusis who traditionally celebrated the mysteries of the Great goddesses, and so did Androkles' descendants: in fact they were the most enthusias-

63. Pausanias did not see this shield himself (cf. Bk III, 17 (3)). This is one of the repertory of Aristomenes' adventures which are also told by Polyainos (2, 31, 2-4).

64. One would like to know the origin of this ridiculous tale. It has been suggested that since Diodoros also mentions it (8, 27, 1) it comes from Ephoros.

65. We only know that it was somewhere in upper Messenia.

tic supporters of the revolt. [8] The Lakonians had allies from Corinth and some from Lepreos[66] who came because they hated Elis. The men of Asine had sworn an alliance with both sides. The place called Boar's Grave is in Stenykleros which belongs to Messenia, and it was here that they say Herakles swore an oath with the sons of Neleus over the pieces of a dismembered boar.[67]

[1] The prophets on both sides offered sacrifices: for Lakonia it was Hekas, a descendant of the other Hekas who came to Sparta with Aristodemos's sons, and for Messenia it was Theoklos, the son of Eumantis of Elis, who was brought to Messene by Kresphontes and who belonged to the Iamidai.[68] And now inspired by the presence of their prophets both sides went into battle. [2] Every man had the eagerness of his youth or his strength, Anaxander the Lakonian king and the Spartans around him more than anyone, and on the Messenian side the descendants of the first Androkles, Phintas and Androkles with their company, put their manhood and their courage to the test. Tyrtaios and the hierophants of the Great goddesses stayed out of action, but spurred on the rear of their armies. [3] Here is what happened to Aristomenes himself. He had eighty picked Messenians around him, all of his own age, and each one thinking it a tremendous honour to be picked for Aristomenes' company. Aristomenes and his elite were hard worked from the start, as they were ranked

16

66. For Lepreos, cf. Bk V, 5 (3–6). It was in southern Triphylia, a few miles inland and just north of the Neda, which reaches the sea north of Kyparissia. For the pro-Lakonian position of Lepreos against Elis, cf. Thukydides 5, 31, of which this passage may well be a projection.

67. Neleus had twelve sons including Nestor. Their only known connexion with Herakles is that when Herakles killed Iphitos he went to Neleus to be purified, but Neleus refused because Iphitos was the son of a friend of his (Diodoros, 4, 31). So Herakles fought and killed all Neleus's sons except Nestor (Iliad, 11, 690). There was surely another version of the story in which he made peace with them at this place.

68. A prophetic clan in which inspired powers were hereditary. Iamos the legendary founder of the family is probably the bearded prophet among the east pediment figures from the temple of Zeus at Olympia. There were still Iamidai (children of Iamos) at Olympia in the third century A.D.

opposite Anaxander and the bravest Lakonians; in their complete carelessness of the wounds they received, and in their utter recklessness, with time and daring they broke Anaxander's men. [4] Aristomenes ordered another Messenian company to pursue them as they fled, and once having assaulted and beaten his enemy where the resistance was strongest he turned against another point. He soon shifted the Lakonians here as well, so he attacked those who stood with all the more vigour, until he had crumpled up the entire Lakonian and allied line. By now they were running without shame and happy to abandon each other, but he pressed into them like a thing of dread more terrible than any individual rage. [5] And here at a wild pear-tree growing somewhere on the plain, the prophet Theoklos told Aristomenes not to run past, because the Dioskouroi were sitting in the tree.[69] But Aristomenes gave rein to his anger and did not listen to the prophet at all; and when he came to the tree he lost his shield, and his mistake gave the Lakonians a chance for some of their men to escape from the rout, as he used up time trying to find his shield.

[6] The Lakonians were dispirited after the disaster and wanted to finish with the war, but Tyrtaios chanted his couplets and won them over, and he chose men from the serfs to serve in the companies in place of the dead. As for Aristomenes, when he came home to Andania the women flung him ribbons and blossoming flowers and sang the song which is still sung to this day:

> Into the mid Stenyklerian plain, into the high mountains
> Aristomenes hunted Lakonians.[70]

[7] He even rescued the shield: he came to Delphi, and as

69. The Dioskouroi have a tree between them on the coinage of Gythion. When Lynkeus spotted Kastor from Taygetos, Kastor was sitting in a hollow oak.

70. Flower-throwing and leaf-throwing was the traditional way to celebrate a triumph. The singing of impromptu couplets on this or any kind of occasion survived until recently all over Greece; in Cretan villages it still survives.

the Pythian priestess commanded he went down into the holy inner sanctuary of Trophonios at Lebadeia. Later he brought the shield to Lebadeia and dedicated it: I myself have seen it there consecrated. The device on it is an eagle stretching its wings on both sides right to the edge.[71] When Aristomenes came home from Boiotia after finding his shield through Trophonios and then taking it to Lebadeia, he immediately set about action on a bigger scale. [8] He chose some Messenians and took his own picked men, and when he had waited for nightfall he marched on a Lakonian city which in Homer's list had the ancient name Pharis, though the Spartans and the local people called it PHARAI.[72] He reached the city, annihilated the attempted defence, took loot there and carried it away to Messene. Lakonian heavy infantry under King Anaxander attacked him on the road, but he broke them as well, and wanted to pursue Anaxander, but he was hit in the buttock by a javelin and stopped the pursuit, without of course letting go the loot he was driving home. [9] He allowed time for the wound to heal, and then made a night march on Sparta itself, but he was turned back by visions of Helen and the Dioskouroi. Still, when day broke he ambushed the virgin girls who dance for Artemis at Karyai, and took away the ones who were rich or had important fathers.[73] He brought them into a Messenian village and rested there for the night, leaving some men from his company to guard the girls. [10] It was then that these youths who were drunk in my opinion, and generally wild in their moral attitude, began to rape the girls; Aristomenes forbade this behaviour, which was against the accepted decencies of Greece, but they took no notice so that he was forced to kill the drunkest ones. He released his captives for a sizeable ransom, virgin as they were when he captured them.

[1] There is a place in Lakonia called AIGILA, where there is    17

71. For the oracle of Trophonios at Lebadeia, cf. Bk IX, 39 (5–14). For the shield cf. Bk IX, 39 (14).

72. Cf. Bk III, 20 (3).

73. Cf. Bk III, 10 (7).

a sanctuary sacred to Demeter.[74] Aristomenes and his men knew that the women were holding a festival there: but by some power from the goddess the women were inspired to defend themselves and most of the Messenians were wounded, either with knives the women had been using to slaughter victims or with spits they used for spitting the meat to roast it; Aristomenes was beaten with burning torches and taken alive, but the same night he escaped to Messenia. Demeter's priestess Archidameia was responsible for letting him go; it was not a bribe, but even before all this happened she was in love with him; she explained it by saying Aristomenes burnt through his own cords and got away.[75]

[2] The third year of the war, when a battle was about to be fought at the Great Trench, with every city in Arkadia helping the Messenians, the Lakonians bribed Hiketas's son Aristokrates of Trapezous, king of the Arkadians and at this time their commander in chief.[76] The Lakonians are the first people known to history to have bribed an enemy in war and the first to have set up victory in battle as a saleable commodity. [3] Before this Lakonian crime in the Messenian War and the treachery of Aristokrates the Arkadian, fighting was decided by courage and by whatever fortune the god sent. Later as well, you find the Lakonians buying Athenian generals, including Adeimantos, when they attacked the Athenian fleet at Goat Rivers.[77] [4] Still, the vengeance of

74. The Andanian inscription about the mysteries mentions the position the priestess of Demeter at Aigila should take in the procession. Aigila can hardly be the same as Aigilia (sometimes Aigila) the ancient name for the island of Antikythera; or if it does mean an island then Pausanias does not grasp the fact. Nor can it be Karyai, about which Pausanias has just told a quite different story. I doubt if Pausanias had any idea where it was, but we do know that Pliny mentions a *sinus Aigilodes* on the east coast of the Mani. For a reasonable but unconfirmed guess, cf. B.S.A., 13, p. 253.

75. Pausanias's version is more romantic than Polyainos's more soldierly and condensed story (cf. Note 63 above).

76. For Trapezous, cf. Bk VIII, 5 (4), and 27 (4–6). The site is near MAVRIA in the hills above Megalopolis.

77. After the battle of Aigospotamoi (Goat rivers) in 405 he was the only Athenian commander not to be executed by the Spartans because he had not

Neoptolemos as they call it came round in time to the Lakonians themselves. Achilles' son Neoptolemos killed Priam at the hearth of the Courtyard god, and then he was murdered himself at Delphi at Apollo's altar; this is why they call it the vengeance of Neoptolemos when what a man did is done to him.[78] [5] When Lakonia had reached its highest point, when it had destroyed the Athenian fleet and when Agesilaos had already mastered most of Asia, the Spartans failed to conquer the whole Persian empire, and the barbarians bested them with their own invention, by sending round presents to Argos and Corinth and Athens and Thebes: and that money started what was called the Corinthian war, which forced Agesilaos to abandon his Asian campaign.[79]

[6] A divine agency was to make the trick they used against Messenia calamitous for the Lakonians. Aristokrates accepted the Lakonian money, and for the time being he hid his plans from the Arkadians, but when the two armies were on the point of meeting, he terrified his men by telling them they were caught in difficult country with no way to retreat if they were beaten, and the omens of their sacrifices were unpromising. He ordered everyone to run when he gave the signal. [7] When the Lakonians came into action with the Messenians against them, just as the battle began Aristokrates withdrew the Arkadians, and the Messenian centre and left were deserted: Arkadia had taken both because Elis and Argos and Sikyon were not in the battle. And Aristokrates did another thing: he sent his men running through the Messenian ranks. [8] The Messenians were stupefied by the unexpectedness of what happened, and confused by the Arkadians passing through them, so that they almost forgot what they were

---

been a party to cutting off the right hands of Spartan prisoners. He was later accused of cowardice or treachery at Athens, and Konon impeached him.

78. This story is not Homeric. On Neoptolemos's death, cf. Bk I, 39 (9). The murder of Priam by the son of Achilles, Achilles being of course already dead, is described by Vergil (*Aeneid*, 2, 506–58).

79. He was recalled in 394. The war lasted from 395 to 386. Foreign money was not its only motive.

doing; instead of watching the Lakonian attack they were watching the fleeing Arkadians, and begging them to stop, insulting them and calling them villains and traitors. [9] With the Messenians isolated it was easy enough for the Lakonians to surround them, and they won the quickest of victories at the lightest of costs. Aristomenes and his men stood their ground, and tried to fight off the Lakonians where they pressed hardest: but they were only a few and could not do much good. Such a number of the common Messenian people was wiped out that from having believed they were going to be the masters of the Spartans instead of their slaves, from that moment they lost all hope of survival. Among the chief men who died were Androkles and Phintas, and also Phanas, who fought very memorably; before all this he had won the long-distance running at Olympia.

[10] After the battle Aristomenes gathered those of the Messenians who had fled and escaped, and persuaded them to abandon Andania and all their midland towns, and settle on Mount EIRA.[80] Huddled together in this place they were besieged by the Lakonians, who thought they could take it at once. But the Messenians held out even after the disaster at the trench, and defended themselves for eleven years. [11] There are some verses of Rianos about the Lakonians which prove that the siege was as long as this.

> . . . *fought in the folds of the glittering white mountain*
> *through twenty-two seasons, winter and shooting green.*

Winter includes autumn, and shooting green means the green corn or a little before the reaping.

18    [1] When the Messenians settled at Eira they were cut off from all Messenia except what the people of Pylos and

---

80. This may or may not be the Homeric *Ira*, which Strabo believed was on the mountain road from Megalopolis to Andania (8, 4, 5). The site is usually identified by scholars of Pausanias with the ruins on the hill south of KAKA-LETRI due west of MEGALOPOLIS on the river Neda (cf. 20, 3), but if we follow Strabo this identification is not only unconvincing, but impossible, since KAKALETRI is not on the right road.

Mothon held for them on the coast; they robbed from Lakonia and their own countryside, which by now they thought of as enemy territory; there were others who took part in these raids according to occasion, but Aristomenes had increased the number of his picked men to three hundred. [2] They collected from the Spartans and took away what they could carry, taking corn and cattle and wine for consumption, and people and furniture for sale. In the end the Lakonians passed a resolution, since they seemed to be farming more for the people on Eira than for themselves, to leave the land in Messenia and on the Lakonian borders unsown for as long as the war went on. [3] This caused a corn shortage at Sparta, and with the shortage of corn came revolution, as the people who had land in that area would not put up with seeing it lie idle. This quarrel was settled by Tyrtaios, but Aristomenes marched out in the late dusk, took the road to Amyklai at speed, arrived there before dawn broke, took and looted Amyklai town, and had already withdrawn before help came from Sparta. [4] He went on raiding in the countryside until one day he met more than half the Lakonian army under both the kings, and one of the wounds he got in the fighting was a hit on the head with a stone that knocked him out. When he fell a mass of Lakonians rushed at him and took him alive; and fifty of his men were taken with him. The Lakonians decided to throw them all into KEADAS, where they throw people by the worst penalty of the law.[81] [5] The other Messenians were thrown down and killed immediately, but now as always, and now more than ever, some god was looking after Aristomenes. Those who romanticize his story maintain that when Aristomenes was thrown into Keadas

---

81. No one knows the whereabouts of this fearful-sounding cavern. It was deep enough for a dead body to lie and rot innocuously. It could possibly be the TRYPI cavern west of Sparta. The tradition of throwing persons tainted by terrible guilt from a high place or into the sea so that the gods could be thought personally to execute them goes back to remote prehistory; cf. N. K. Sandars, *Prehistoric Art in Europe*, pp. 85–6, on an engraved rock at Addaura in Sicily (about 8000 B.C.).

an eagle spread its wings below him and held him up so that he got to the bottom without breaking a bone or receiving a scratch. And even from here the divine agency was to show him a way out. [6] When he got to the bottom of the ravine he lay down, drew his cloak over his head, and awaited the death which was obviously his destiny. On the third day he heard a noise and uncovering his head – by now he could see through the darkness – he saw a vixen nosing at the corpses. He realized this animal must have got in from somewhere, so he waited until she came close and then seized hold of her, using his other hand whenever she turned at him to hold his cloak for her to bite. Mostly he ran along with the vixen, but in the very difficult places she dragged him up. Finally he saw an opening big enough for a fox to get into, and the light shining through it. [7] When Aristomenes let the vixen go, she must have gone into her own hole, but as the opening was not big enough for him, Aristomenes made it bigger with his hands and escaped home to Eira. He was captured by an extraordinary chance, as his cleverness and his daring were both so great that no one could hope to take him prisoner; but his escape from Keadas was even more extraordinary and in fact absolutely obviously due to a god.

19   [1] The Lakonians heard at once through runaways that Aristomenes had got safely home. They thought it as incredible as if a dead man was supposed to have come to life, but Aristomenes himself gave them proof. Corinth sent a force to help the Lakonians capture Eira. [2] Aristomenes found out through watchers in the hills that they were rather disorganized on the march and careless in camp, so he attacked them at night. He slaughtered most of them in their sleep and killed the commanders, Hypermenides, Achladaios, Lysistratos and Sidektos. He looted the command tent, and proved only too clearly to Sparta that this was the work of Aristomenes and no one else. He also slaughtered to Ithomaian Zeus the sacrifice called the hundred deaths. This sacrifice is a most ancient tradition: the belief is that any Messenian who kills a

hundred enemies has offered it.[82] [3] He had offered it first after the battle at the Boar's Grave, and now the massacre of the Corinthians at night gave him the chance to offer it again. Later, during his raids he is supposed to have offered it a third time. [4] Now the Hyakinthia were coming on, and Lakonia made a forty days' truce with Eira, so the Lakonians went home and celebrated the festival, while the Cretan bowmen, who were mercenaries from Lyktos and some other cities, roamed around Messenia.[83] As there was a truce, Aristomenes was some distance from Eira, and was travelling carelessly when seven of these bowmen ambushed him, and tied him up with the thongs from their quivers as night was coming on. [5] Two of them went to Sparta to give the Lakonians the good news that Aristomenes was taken, while the rest went off to a farmhouse somewhere in Messenia. There was a girl who was virgin living there with her mother; her father was dead. On the night before this girl had seen a vision: some wolves brought a tied up lion with no claws into the farmhouse, and she let the lion loose and found his claws for him, and then it seemed the lion tore the wolves to pieces. [6] So when the Cretans brought in Aristomenes, she realized her vision had come true, and asked her mother who he was. When she found out the knowledge strengthened her and as she watched him she understood what she had to do. She poured out plenty of wine for the Cretans, so that they got drunk, and then she stole a sword from the one who was deepest asleep. The young girl cut Aristomenes free, and he took the sword from her and killed them. Aristomenes' son Gorgos married this girl; Aristomenes gave his son to pay his debt to her: Gorgos was only seventeen when he married.

82. This is mentioned twice by Plutarch and once by Polyainos, always in connexion with Aristomenes.

83. For the festival of Hyakinthos at Amyklai, cf. Bk III, 10 (1) and 19 (3). Lyktos or Lyttos was an island city in eastern Crete; the site is east of KASTEL-LION and south-east of HERAKLEION. Aristotle (*Politics*, 2, 7, 1) says it was a Spartan colony. It was destroyed by Knossos in 220 B.C., but the unexcavated ruins are still conspicuously visible. (Cf. *Insc. Creticae*, vol. I, pp. 179f.)

20    [1] In the eleventh year of the siege Eira was destined to fall
and the Messenians to be rooted out of their country; and in
fact the god fulfilled something prophesied to Aristomenes
and Theoklos. When they went to Delphi after the disaster
at the trench and asked if they could be saved, the Pythian
priestess said,

> When the he-goat drinks Neda's swirling water,
> I have abandoned Messene: destruction comes.[84]

[2] The springs of the Neda are on mount Lykaion; the river
passes through Arkadia, turns back into Messenia, and divides
the coastal territories of Messenia and Elis. At the time they
were terrified of male goats drinking from the Neda, but
what the god meant was this: in some parts of Greece they
call the wild fig-tree olynthe, but the Messenians call it the he-
goat. At this time a wild fig-tree sprouted beside the Neda,
and did not grow straight up, but bent over into the stream
and stroked the water with its topmost leaves. [3] The prophet
Theoklos noticed it, and realized that when she foretold the
he-goat drinking from the Neda the Pythian priestess meant
this tree, and that the Messenians were doomed. He kept it
secret from everyone, but he took Aristomenes to the wild
fig-tree and instructed him that the time for being saved had
run out. Aristomenes was convinced, and understood that the
end could not any longer be put off; but even in these
circumstances he took care to act for the best. [4] There was
something the Messenians kept hidden; if it was lost it would
make Messene disappear for ever, but if it was kept the oracles
of Lykos son of Pandion declared that one day in the course
of time the Messenians would recover their country. Aristomenes knew the oracles and went and got this thing during
the night. When he was in the loneliest part of Mount Ithome,
he dug a hole in the mountainside, and asked Zeus of Ithome
and the gods who had saved the Messenians to guard what he

84. The story of this oracle occurs only here. The trick seems to be copied
from a very early oracle which used the same pun (Parke and Wormell, *The
Delphic Oracle*, n. 46).

left there, and not to put the one Messenian hope of a return home into Lakonian hands.[85]

[5] After this trouble came to the Messenians just as it did to the Trojans from lust. They controlled the mountain itself and the land towards Eira as far as the Neda, and some of them had houses outside the gates. No runaways came to them from Lakonia, except a slave who was Emperamos's herdsman driving his master's cattle; Emperamos was a man of reputation in Sparta. [6] This herdsman was grazing his beasts not far from the Neda, when he saw the wife of one of the Messenians who lived outside the walls, coming down to the river; he fell in love and dared to talk to her, and gave her presents so that he could sleep with her. From this moment he watched for the times her husband went on guard duty; the Messenian guard was stationed at a certain part of the fortress rock, where they were most frightened the enemy might climb into the city. Whenever the husband went on duty, the herdsman visited the wife. [7] One night the husband happened to be one of the men on guard when it came on to rain heavily, and the Messenian guards deserted their post: the water was pouring down on them in streams out of heaven, and there were no battlements or towers because the walls had been built in such a rush; and anyway they did not expect the Spartans to stir on a moonless night when it was so stormy. [8] Not many days before this Aristomenes had been wounded while he was rescuing a Kephallenian merchant with his load, a guest of his who was bringing necessities into Eira and got caught by Lakonians and bowmen from Aptera under Euryalos of Sparta;[86] so Aristomenes was unable to visit the watch as he usually did. This was the chief reason why they deserted the top of the

85. It was the ritual of the mysteries; cf. Bk IV, 26 (8).
86. That is, Eira was being supplied from the islands off the west coast of Greece. The archers were Cretans (cf. Book X, 5 (10)). Aptera once stood at PALAIOKASTRO, above the south shore of SOUDA BAY in north-west Crete. It was first identified by Robert Pashley in 1834. (Cf. *Insc. Creticae*, vol. 2, pp. 9f.)

fortress rock; [9] they all left their watch, including the husband of the woman the herdsman made love to. She had the herdsman in her room, and she heard her husband coming, so she hid the man as quickly as she possibly could. When her husband came in she looked after him as never before, and asked him why he had come home. He had no idea she had a lover or that the herdsman was in the room, so he told the truth, and said every one of them had deserted the watch because of the heavy rain. [10] The herdsman heard what he said, and when he had grasped all the details, became a double runaway and went over again to the Lakonians. The Lakonian kings were not in camp, but the general then in command of the siege of Eira was Emperamos, the herdsman's master. He went to Emperamos and first of all asked to be forgiven for running away, and then gave information that they could take Eira that very moment: and he explained everything he had heard from the Messenian.

21  [1] They thought he was telling the truth and he guided Emperamos and the Spartans; the march was difficult as it was dark and the rain never slackened, but they finished it eagerly, and when they reached the fortress rock of Eira they climbed with ladders or however they could. The Messenians knew of the trouble they were in chiefly from the dogs, which were not baying as usual but howling loudly and continuously. They realized that the last and inevitable battle had come, and so without complete armour, snatching whatever weapon came to hand, they fought for that city, which was all they had left of the whole of Messenia. [2] The first to know the enemy had entered and to counter-attack were Aristomenes' son Gorgos, Aristomenes himself, Theoklos the prophet, and Theoklos's son Mantiklos, and with them Euegetidas, a man of honoured position in Messene who had become even more important through his wife, as he was married to Aristomenes' sister Hagnagora. And now the others knew they were caught in a net though they still took some sort of hope from circumstances, [3] but Aristomenes and the prophet knew that the destruction of the Messenians

must follow without any let-up: because they understood the Pythian priestess's prophecy and its word-play about the he-goat, but still they kept it secret, and the others had not been told. They rushed through the city and its population, telling everyone they met, if they saw they were Messenians, to be good and true men, and calling those who were still left from their houses. [4] During the night nothing worth talking about was achieved by either side. The Spartans were held up by ignorance of the ground and by Aristomenes' daring, and the Messenians had no password from their generals, and the rain from heaven put out the torches and every other light that anyone lit. [5] When the dawn came and they could see each other, Aristomenes and Theoklos tried to spur on the Messenians to utter recklessness, telling them what you might have expected, and particularly recalling the brave behaviour of the people of Smyrna; they were Ionians, and when Gyges son of Daskylos and his Lydians occupied their city, they threw them out by sheer courage and spirit.[87] [6] When the Messenians heard this they were filled with reckless courage, and they formed up in whatever numbers it might be and attacked the Lakonians. All the women wanted to pelt the enemy with tiles and whatever else they could, but the heavy force of the rain stopped them from doing it and kept them from the roofs; but they had the courage to take up weapons, and enflamed their husbands' daring even more; the men could see their wives choosing to die with their country, rather than be taken as slaves to Lakonia, so that they might almost have escaped from the decree of destiny. [7] But heaven poured down a deluge of rain with powerful crashes of thunder and they were dazzled by lightning flashing in their eyes. All this gave the Lakonians confidence, and they said the god was fighting on their side. The lightning flashed on their right,

87. Herodotos refers to this war (1, 14). From a passage where Pausanias mentions it again (Bk IX, 29(4)) it is evident that his source was a poem on the history of Smyrna by Mimnermos of Kolophon, of which a few fragments have survived (*Fr.* 12–14, and cf. Strabo, 14, 1, 4). Gyges and Aristomenes are supposed to have been more or less contemporaries.

and Hekas the prophet declared it was a favourable omen.
[8] And it was Hekas who thought of the following tactics.
The Lakonians had far superior numbers, but as the battle
was not in ranks in an open space, but a matter of different
people fighting in different parts of the city, the rear men in
every formation were useless. He told them to go away to
camp and get food and sleep and then come back again
before dusk to take over the work. [9] So resting and fighting
by divisions they held out well, but the Messenians had no
resources of any kind; the same men fought all day and night
continuously through to the third night. Now it was dawn
again, and they were suffering from lack of sleep, from the
rain and the cold, and attacked by hunger and thirst. The
women in particular were exhausted with unaccustomed
fighting and continuous wretchedness. [10] Theoklos the
prophet was standing by Aristomenes and said: 'Why are
you taking this useless trouble? Messene is certainly predes-
tined to fall, and the tragedy we can see was foretold by the
Pythian priestess, and not long ago the fig-tree made it clear.
The god is bringing me my death with my country's death,
but you must save what Messenians you can see, and save
yourself.' When he had spoken he ran at the enemy, and as
he went in among the Lakonians he cried out: 'You will not
be happy always reaping Messenian earth.' [11] After this he
leapt on his opponents, killed them and was struck down, and
then with his anger glutted by the slaughter of his enemies,
he breathed his last. Aristomenes called the Messenians back
from battle, all but the brave men who fought in the front
rank; he let those hold their ground, and ordered the rest to
form up with the women and children inside the column and
follow him wherever he created a way through. [12] He put
Gorgos and Mantiklos in command of the rearguard, and ran
back to the front ranks where he could be seen by the movement of his head and his spear to be asking for a way through,
and determined to leave the city. Emperamos and the Spartans
who were there preferred to let the Messenians pass, and not to
enrage men already crazy with fury and at the last stage of

recklessness any further; and the orders of Hekas the prophet confirmed this decision.

[1] The Arkadians heard at once that Eira had been taken 22 and at once ordered Aristokrates to lead them to save the Messenians or to perish with them. But as he was bribed by Lakonia he was unwilling to lead such an expedition, and said he knew there were no Messenians left to fight for. [2] Then when they knew more definitely that men had survived and been forced to abandon Eira, they waited on Mount Lykaion to receive them, with clothing and food ready, and sent some powerful men to comfort the Messenians and to guide their march.[88] When they got safely to Lykaion, the Arkadians took them in and treated them kindly, and wanted to distribute them between cities and divide land for them. [3] But Aristomenes' sorrow over the sack of Eira and his hatred of the Lakonians produced the following plan. He picked five hundred Messenians from the crowd, who he really knew would not spare themselves, and questioned them in the hearing of Aristokrates and the Arkadians, not knowing Aristokrates was a traitor; Aristomenes supposed Aristokrates had fled from the battle out of cowardliness and unmanliness and not from wickedness of any kind, so it was in his presence too that he questioned the five hundred men. He asked them if they were willing to die with him to avenge their country. [4] When they answered that they were, he unfolded everything: he promised to lead them against Sparta the next sunset. At that moment most of the Lakonians were away at Eira and others were making journeys there to take Messenian plunder. 'And if we can take and occupy Sparta', said Aristomenes, 'we can give the Lakonians back what they own in exchange for what we own. If we fail we shall still die having done something worth remembering in the future.' [5] When he had spoken about three hundred Arkadians wanted to join the adventure. They did not march at once as the omens of the sacrifices were not favourable, and the next day they realized that the Lakonians had found out their

88. The Arkadians waited in the mountains north of the Neda.

secret and they they had been betrayed for the second time by Aristokrates. He had written down Aristomenes' plans at once in a book, given the book to a slave who he knew was very faithful to him, and sent him off to Anaxander at Sparta. [6] Some Arkadians who were already opposed to Aristokrates, and had a certain suspicion of him now, ambushed this slave on his way home. They brought him before the Arkadian assembly, and showed the people what had been sent from Lakonia: Anaxander had sent to say that the retreat at the Great Trench had not been left unpaid by Lakonia, and further thanks would be coming to him for his present warning. [7] When everyone heard this, the Arkadians stoned Aristokrates and encouraged the Messenians to join in: but the Messenians looked at Aristomenes, and Aristomenes looked at the ground and wept. The Arkadians stoned Aristokrates to death and threw out his body unburied outside their boundaries. And they dedicated a stone tablet in the sacred enclosure of the Lykaian god, saying:

> Time has brought justice to the wicked king:
> Time and Zeus brought easily to light
> the betrayer of Messene: O how hard
> for a perjured man to escape a god.
> Hail Zeus, king, save Arkadia.[89]

23  [1] All the Messenians who were caught around Eira or anywhere else in Messenia were enrolled as Lakonian serfs. At the fall of Eira the people of Pylos and Mothone and the coast took ship to Kyllene, the port of Elis.[90] From there they sent to the Messenians in Arkadia, saying they wanted to

89. This inscription really existed; Polybios saw it beside the altar of Lykaian Zeus (4, 33). For Lykaian Zeus and his sanctuary, cf. Bk VIII, 38 (2–8).

90. For Kyllene, cf. Bk VI, 26 (4). It lies on the north-west coast of the Peloponnese somewhere between the modern Cape Kyllene, with its great castle of KLARENTZA, and the old estuary of the Peneios, which is now south of Klarentza but in the classical period was somewhere to the north of that point. There are very few classical relics at Klarentza, but some, and a very little pottery.

mount a combined expedition to look for a country to live in, and they appointed Aristomenes to lead them to found a settlement. [2] Aristomenes replied that for as long as he lived he was going to fight the Lakonians, and he knew for certain that there would always be something evil brewing for Sparta through him; and he gave them Gorgos and Mantiklos for leaders. One of the Messenians who retreated to Lykaion was Euegetidas; when he saw Aristomenes' plan to capture Sparta had fallen through, he persuaded about fifty Messenians to join him and went back to attack the Lakonians at Eira; [3] he found them still fumbling among the spoils of victory and did them considerable damage. He met his fate there, but Aristomenes met his fate after he had appointed commanders for the Messenians at Kyllene and sent away everyone who wanted to go; and they all joined that migration, except anyone prevented by age or lack of means, who stayed where they were with the Arkadians.

[4] Eira fell and the second Lakonian–Messenian war ended when Autosthenes was governor of Athens, the first year after the twenty-eighth Olympics, when Chionis the Lakonian won.[91]

[5] When the Messenians gathered at Kyllene they decided to last out the winter there, and Elis granted them a market and money. The plan was to set off in spring wherever they had to go. Gorgos's idea was to take over Zakynthos beyond Kephallenia[92] and become islanders instead of mainlanders, and raid the Lakonian sea-coast in their ships and harm the

91. In 668 B.C. The epic narrative was sprinkled with these scientific-looking dates probably in the fourth century B.C., very likely by Ephoros. It is highly unlikely that they reached Pausanias through the hexameter verses of Rianos of Bene.

92. ZAKYNTHOS (the old Zante) is so plainly visible from Kyllene that you can see its lights at night. It is not 'beyond Kephallenia' unless you think of all the Ionian islands as dependencies of northern Greece. This is probably how Pausanias did think of it, as it came under the Roman province of Epirus, not the province of Achaia. (It is interesting that the boundaries of the Greece which Pausanias describes correspond more or less exactly to those of Roman Achaia.)

countryside. Mantiklos said they ought to forget Messene and the feud with Lakonia and sail to occupy Sardinia, that enormous and most desirable of islands.[93] [6] Meanwhile Anaxilas sent to invite the Messenians to Italy. He was the lord of Region, third in line of descent from Alkidamidas, who migrated from Messene to Region after the death of King Aristodemos and the fall of Ithome: and now Anaxilas sent for the Messenians, and when they came he said the people of Zankle were quarrelling with him: they had a well-endowed territory and city in a fine part of Sicily, which Anaxilas would help the Messenians to conquer and was willing to give them. They accepted these conditions, and Anaxilas took them across to Sicily.[94]

[7] ZANKLE was originally occupied by pirates, who fortified nothing but their harbour, as a base for brigandage and sea-raiding. Their captains were Krataimenes of Samos and Perieres of Chalkis. Later Perieres and Krataimenes decided to bring in other Greeks as settlers. [8] And now Anaxilas defeated Zankle at sea and the Messenians defeated it in a pitched battle. So the Zanklaians were besieged by the Messenians on land and blockaded by Region at sea, the fortress fell, and they fled to the altars of the gods and the sanctuaries. Anaxilas told the Messenians to kill the Zanklaians though they were formally begging for mercy, and to send the rest into slavery with their women and children. [9] But Gorgos and Mantiklos beseeched Anaxilas not to force them to do to Greeks the same wicked things their own brothers had done to them. Then they took the Zanklaians from the altars and exchanged oaths with them, and both sides lived together: only they changed the name of the city from Zankle to Messene.[95] [10] This was in the period of the twenty-ninth Olympics when Chionis the Lakonian won the second time,

93. Pausanias is very keen on Sardinia; cf. Bk X, 17.

94. Region stood on the point of the toe of Italy at Reggio, and Zankle just across the straits on the Sicilian coast, between the river BOCCETTA and the PORTALEGNI.

95. The modern MESSANA.

and Miltiades was governor of Athens.[96] And Mantiklos made the Messenian sanctuary of Herakles; the god is installed outside the walls and called Herakles Mantiklos, like the Ammon in Libya named after the shepherd who founded it, and the Bel at Babylon, which is named after an Egyptian called Bel, the son of Libya.[97]

[1] So the Messenian fugitives came to the end of their 24 wanderings, and when Aristomenes had refused the command of the settlement expedition, he married off his first and second daughters and his sister Hagnagora: the eldest to Theopompos of Heraia, the second to Damothoidas of Lepreon, and Hagnagora to Tharyx at Phigalia; then he went to Delphi and consulted the god. What the oracle said to Aristomenes is not recorded, [2] but the Pythian priestess prophesied to Damagetos of Rhodes the king of Ialysos,[98] who had come to Apollo to ask where he should get a wife, that he should take the daughter of the best man in Greece; Aristomenes had a third daughter, so Damagetos married her, as he was convinced that Aristomenes was by far the best man in Greece in that age. So Aristomenes went to Rhodes with his daughter, and from there he thought of going up to Sardis, to Ardys the son of Gyges, and to Persian Ekbatana,

96. The twenty-ninth Olympic period was 664–661 B.C. But Anaxilas really captured Region more than 150 years later; the details of the story are no more reliable than the date. The best analysis of the conflicting literary traditions about the foundation of Messene (the modern Messana) is in Pauly-Wissowa (XV (1), 1214–21).

97. This sanctuary of Herakles has not been identified. Zeus Ammon is really the Libyan god Amun, who was worshipped as Zeus Ammon at the Siwah Oasis (cf. Oric Bates, *The Eastern Libyans*, pp. 189–200, and Bk V, Note 149.). Pausanias's etymology is quite wrong about Ammon and Bel: it may well be equally so about Herakles Mantiklos (*Mantiklos*, prophetic Herakles?).

98. Lepreos was in Triphylia a few miles north of the Neda and a few miles inland (on the road to Kato Phigalia). Heraia was an Arkadian town on the north bank of the Alpheios a few miles above the point where the Ladon joins it, near the village of HAGIOS IOANNIS. Ialysos stood on Mount PHILERIMOS, above TRIANDA, a few miles south-west of the city of Rhodes itself, but still in the north-east corner of the island. After the foundation of Rhodes in the late fifth century, Ialysos dwindled and declined to the status of a village.

to the king, Phraortes.[99] [3] But in fact before that he sickened and died: fate had no more disasters coming to the Lakonians from Aristomenes. When he died Damagetos and the Rhodians made him a glorious tomb, and worshipped him from that day onwards. I have left out the story of the Diagoridai of Rhodes, the descendants of Diagoros son of Damagetos and grandson of Dorieus, who was the son of Damagetos and Aristomenes' daughter, as it might seem an unwarranted digression.[100] [4] Now that the Lakonians controlled the whole of Messenia they took possession of it all except for the Asine territory, and the grant of Mothone to the Nauplians, who had just been expelled from their own country by Argos.[101]

[5] The Messenians who were caught in the countryside and forcibly enrolled as serfs were fated to rebel against Lakonia again in the period of the seventy-ninth Olympics, when Xenophon of Corinth was a winner and Archimedes was governor of Athens.[102] The opportunity they took for a revolt was this: there were Lakonians condemned to death on some charge or other who took sanctuary at Tainaron, and the government authority tore them away from the altars there and killed them. [6] The curse of Poseidon came on the Spartans for not paying attention to ritual supplication, and the god shook down their entire city to its foundations. At this calamity the serfs of Messenian origin raised a rebellion on Mount Ithome. The Lakonians raised allied troops against them, including Miltiades' son Kimon, who had Spartan privileges, with a force of Athenians. When the Athenians arrived Sparta seems to have suspected they might well be

99. For Sardis, cf. Bk III, 9 (5). Ekbatana was a great and legendary city in Media, south of the Caspian sea: it was the summer capital of the Persian kings. It is described by Herodotos (1, 104) and in the *Book of Judith* (1, 1–5). Judith's king should probably be identified with Phraortes.

100. The tomb has never been found. For the digression, cf. Bk VI, 7 (1–7).

101. The Lakonians took for themselves everything but the southernmost and most inaccessible tip of Messenia (cf. Bk IV, 14, (3) and 35 (2)).

102. In 464 B.C. We know this war from Thukydides (1, 101–3), but nothing is known about Archimedes.

revolutionaries, and they were soon sent home from Ithome on suspicion. [7] The Athenians understood that the Lakonians suspected them, so they made friends with Argos, and when the Messenians besieged on Ithome were driven out under truce, the Athenians gave them Naupaktos, which they captured from the Lokrians on the Aitolian border, the so-called Stinking Lokrians.[103] The Messenians were able to get out of Ithome because of the strength of the place, and because the Pythian priestess warned the Lakonians they would certainly suffer for sins against any formal suppliant of Zeus of Ithome.

[1] So they were allowed out of the Peloponnese under a 25 truce. When they had occupied Naupaktos, they were not satisfied with obtaining a city and territory from Athens; they were longing to make some memorable conquest with their own hands, and as they knew Oiniadai in Akarnania possessed good land and had been opposed to the Athenians, all through history, they went to war with Oiniadai.[104] They were not more numerous but their fighting spirit was far greater, and they won, and shut their enemies inside the walls and besieged them. [2] But at that time the Messenians had none of the siege-engines history has elaborated, so they placed ladders and attempted to climb into the city and dug tunnels under the walls, and brought up the kind of machines that took no time to construct; and bit by bit the destruction proceeded. The defenders were terrified that when the city

103. Naupaktos was on the north side of the Corinthian gulf just inside the gulf proper, north-east of Patrai. For the Stinking Lokrians and how they got their name, cf. Bk X, 38 (1-3).

104. OINIADAI was a coastal city on the south-west corner of the main mass of continental Greece, in the very fertile country around the river Acheloos, which was disputed for a long time between Aitolia and Akarnania. Oiniadai was on the northern, Akarnanian side of the river, but it seems to have been dominated by its Aitolian neighbours, since all the other Akarnanians were pro-Athenian and the Aitolians were anti-Athenian. The ruins of Oiniadai now stand on a small crag overlooking a marshy and desolate lake; its local name is TRIKARDOKASTRO. The ruins are partly overgrown but very well preserved. (Cf. Heuzey, Le Mont Olympe et l'Acarnanie, 1860, pp. 435f., and American Journal of Archaeology, VIII, 1904, pp. 137-237.)

fell they would perish and their wives and children be sold as slaves, so they chose to withdraw under a truce.

[3] For more or less a year the Messenians held that city, and occupied its territory. But the next year the Akarnanians gathered a force from all their cities and planned a campaign against Naupaktos. They decided against this when they realized the line of march was going to be right through the Aitolians, who had always been their enemies, and also they suspected the Naupaktians had a fleet, which in fact they did have, and not much harm could be done to them even with an army while they commanded the sea. [4] So they changed their minds and turned on the Messenians at Oiniadai. They prepared for a siege, as they never conceived that so few men could ever be reckless enough to fight the entire Akarnanian army. The Messenians got ready food supplies and everything you might expect, expecting a long siege, [5] but there was a chance before the coming siege of fighting an open battle, and being Messenians, who were worsted by Lakonian luck, not by Lakonian valour, they were not put into any panic by the advancing multitudes of Akarnania. They recalled what the Athenians had done at Marathon, where three hundred thousand Persians were destroyed by not ten thousand men. [6] They engaged the Akarnanians in battle; the tactics are supposed to have been as follows. As the Akarnanians had far greater numbers they easily surrounded the Messenians, except where the gates were behind their backs and there was a vigorous defence from the walls. At this point the noose could not be closed, but the Akarnanians contained them from both flanks and threw javelins from every direction. [7] The Messenians were massed together and when they charged in a body they threw the opposition into confusion and massacred and wounded large numbers of them, but they were unable to break them completely, because wherever the Akarnanians felt their ranks were being mauled by the Messenians they reinforced the men under pressure, and kept the Messenians back by overwhelming numbers. [8] Whenever the Messenians were beaten back,

they tried to cut through the Akarnanian formation in another direction, and the same thing happened: wherever they attacked they shook the enemy and broke him on a small scale, but the Akarnanians came pouring back at them from the same point and they were forced to retreat again. The fighting was even until nightfall, and under cover of darkness new forces arrived from the Akarnanian cities, so the Messenians were besieged. [9] They had no fear of the fortifications being stormed by the Akarnanians climbing in or anything forcing them to desert their guard posts, but after eight months all their provisions had run out. They jeered at the Akarnanians from the walls, that their food would never give out even if the siege went on for ten years, [10] but in the first sleep of that night they left Oiniadai; the Akarnanians discovered they were running away and forced them to a battle: they lost about three hundred men and killed more than that number of the enemy, but most of them broke through and took the road through Aitolia, and the Aitolians being their friends they escaped to Naupaktos.

[1] They were always obsessed by bitterness with the 26 Spartans, and after this time they really showed how they hated them when the Peloponnesian War broke out with Athens. They offered Naupaktos as a base against the Peloponnese, and Messenian slingers from Naupaktos helped to take the Spartans who were captured at Sphakteria. [2] After the Athenian disaster at Aigospotamoi, the victorious Lakonian fleet threw the Messenians out of Naupaktos: some went to their brothers in Sicily or to Region, but most of them went to Libya, to Euhesperides,[105] where the people had been worsted fighting their barbarous neighbours, and were inviting any Greek whatsoever to come and join them. Most

105. Very little has been recovered from the site of Euhesperides; it was certainly a great city, but it has been swallowed by what were once salt-marshes on the eastern side of Benghazi near the Wavell Barracks. Its site is some scrubby-looking ground on your left as you drive in from Cyrenaica. Antiquities from Euhesperides are badly corroded, and it is hard to make much of them.

of the Messenians went there, under the command of Komon who was also their general at Sphakteria.

[3] A year before the Theban success at Leuktra the god prophesied to the Messenians their return to the Peloponnese. They say the priest of Herakles at Messene on the straits saw a vision in his sleep; it seemed that Herakles Mantiklos was invited to feast with Zeus at Ithome. At the same time in Euhesperides Komon dreamed he was sleeping with his mother's corpse, and when they slept together his mother came back to life. Komon was hoping for a return to Naupaktos with Athenian naval power, but the dream showed him the salvation of Messene. [4] Not long afterwards the disaster due for so long hit the Lakonians at Leuktra.[106] In the oracle given to King Aristodemos of Messenia about his death there was a line,

> *act your destiny,*
> *the curse falls on some men before others;*

it meant that at the present time he and the Messenians were fated to misfortune, but in later time the curse would come to Lakonia. [5] So now after the Theban victory at Leuktra they sent messengers to Italy and Sicily and Euhesperides, and invited all Messenians wherever they might be to the Peloponnese. They gathered faster than all expectation, longing for their land and country, and still nursing their bitterness against Lakonia. [6] Epaminondas was in difficulties about founding a city that would be a match for the fighting strength of Lakonia, and unable to discover whereabouts in the territory he ought to build it. The Messenians refused to resettle Andania or Oichalia because of their tragic history. They say that, when he was in despair, an old man in the likeness of a hierophant came to him at night and said: 'My gift to you is victory wherever you arm yourself and go, and although your birth is human, man of Thebes, I shall make your name and your glory live for ever. Give the Messenians back their land

---

106. In 371 (cf. Bk IX, 13 (3f.)). Epaminondas founded or refounded the Messenian state as a permanent threat and check to Sparta.

and country and cities, because the curse of the Dioskouroi has left them.' [7] He spoke to Epaminondas, and made a revelation to Epiteles son of Aischines,[107] who was chosen by Argos as commander to rebuild Messene. The dream commanded him to find where a yew and a myrtle grew together on Mount Ithome, and to dig between them and rescue the old woman, because she was tired out and fainting away shut in her brazen chamber. Next morning Epiteles came to the place that was described, and when he dug there he found a bronze jar, [8] which he took to Epaminondas at once, explained his vision and told him to take off the lid and see what was inside. Epaminondas offered sacrifice and prayed to the vision he had dreamed and then he opened the jar. Inside he found a leaf of tin beaten to extreme fineness and rolled up like a scroll, and inscribed with the mystery of the Great goddesses: this was the thing Aristomenes had hidden. They say it was Kaukon that had come to Epiteles and Epaminondas in their sleep: the same Kaukon who came to Andania from Athens and visited Triopas's daughter Messene.[108]

[1] The curse of the Dioskouroi on Messenia had begun 27 before the battle at Stenykleros, and I imagine it arose in the following way. There were two adolescent lads from Andania, Panormos and Gonippos, who had a close friendship and marched together to battles and made raids together in Lakonia. [2] When the Lakonians were keeping the feast of the Dioskouroi in their camp, and were drinking and joking after dinner, Gonippos and Panormos put on white tunics and crimson cloaks, and with spears in their hands, riding on

107. This Epiteles is not mentioned by anyone but Pausanias, but we are now in a realm of ascertainable facts and he is likely to have existed. The entire restoration story as Pausanias tells it seems to come from Andania. The Freudian or matriarchal dream is the same as Julius Caesar's dream in the temple of Hercules at Cadiz when he was a young man (Suetonius, *The Life of Julius Caesar*, 7).

108. The mystery inscribed on thin metal recalls certain Orphic verse inscriptions about how to become immortal after your death, which have been found inscribed on very thin gold and were buried with the dead. There is at least one of these in the British Museum, but it is not exhibited.

magnificent horses and wearing wide-brimmed hats, they suddenly appeared to the Lakonians. At the sight of them the Lakonians bowed down and prayed, thinking the Dioskouroi had come to their sacrifice. [3] Once the two youths were in among them, they galloped right through them stabbing with spears, and leaving numbers of dead they withdrew to Andania, having outraged the sacrifice of the Dioskouroi. I think this is what brought their hatred on the Messenians; but now, as the dream showed to Epaminondas, the return of the Messenians was not against their will. [4] Epaminondas's principal reason for making the settlement was Bakis's prophecies. Bakis was maddened by the Nymphs and prophesied about the return of the Messenians, and about other Greek peoples as well.[109]

> Then the strong-coloured flower of Sparta will wither,
> Messene will be peopled once again and for always.

And I have rummaged out the fact that Bakis also spoke of the way in which Eira would fall; this also comes from among his prophecies:

> men from Messene thunder-broken, rain-broken.

[5] When the mystery was found the men of priestly race wrote it into books, and Epaminondas, as the place where the Messenians now in fact have their city seemed to him right for the settlement, ordered an inquiry by the prophets, whether the divine powers would wish to come there. The prophets said the sacrificial omens were favourable, so he got ready to build. He ordered stone to be fetched, and sent for craftsmen who knew how to lay out streets and build houses

109. A man who encountered a nymph would be possessed, frenzied by the nymphs, but might also receive uncanny power. It is still believed in the remote country that this kind of thing happens if you break certain rustic rituals or sleep under certain trees. The splendid grotto of the nymphs at Vari near Athens is a cave-sanctuary founded by someone the nymphs had taken over (he was *nympholeptos*). He was a local prophet who never achieved national or literary status, perhaps the kind of country figure who still exists, whom religion, loneliness, and the conditions of his life have driven into a prophetic role. Bakis was a generic name for prophets of this kind in the archaic period,

and sanctuaries, and draw the circle of fortifications.[110] [6]
When everything was ready then the Arkadians produced
victims, and Epaminondas and his Thebans sacrificed to
Dionysos and Ismenian Apollo in their traditional style, and
the Argives to Hera of Argos and Nemean Zeus, the Messenians to Zeus of Ithome and the Dioskouroi, and their priests
to the Great goddesses and to Kaukon. Then they called out
together to the divine heroes to return and live with them,
particularly to Triopas's daughter Messene, and Eurytos and
Aphareus and their children, and to Kresphontes and Aipytos
of the children of Herakles. But the greatest and most universal cry was to Aristomenes. [7] They spent that day in
sacrifices and prayers, and on the following days they erected
the encircling wall and built houses and sanctuaries inside it.
They worked with no other music but Boiotian and Argive
flutes; at that time the tunes of Sakadas and Pronomos were
at the height of their rivalry. They called the city itself
Messene, but they built other towns as well. [8] They did not
shift the Nauplians from Mothone, and they allowed the
people of Asine to keep to the ground they were on; the
Messenians recalled the kindness of the Asinaians who had
been unwilling to fight against them on the Spartan side, and
the Nauplians had given what they could raise to bring the
Messenians back to the Peloponnese, had prayed continuously
to heaven for their return, and continually requested the
Messenians to come and save them.[111]

---

though Herodotos (8, 20) thought Bakis was an individual, and prophecies
attributed to him were particularly popular in the Peloponnesian War. He was
much mocked by Aristophanes.

110. The site of Messene is on Mount Ithome well north of the modern
town of MESSINI, with the village of MAVROMMATION at the spring more or
less in the middle of the ruins. The fortifications and gateways, which are
sophisticated and strangely well preserved, are those of the great city as
Epaminondas ordered it to be built in 369 B.C. In 1447 the travelling scholar
Cyriaco of Ancona had reidentified it and copied two inscriptions, one of
which he later recopied into the margin of his Strabo, which is now at Eton.
He was probably sent there by Gemistos Plethon from Mistra (near Sparta).

111. For Mothone, cf. Bk IV, 24 (4). For the Asinaiani, cf. Bk IV, 14 (3) and
15 (8).

[9] The Messenians returned to the Peloponnese and recovered their inheritance two hundred and eighty-seven years after the fall of Eira, when Dyskinetos was governor of Athens, in the third year after the hundred and second Olympics, when Damon of Thourioi won for the second time.[112] The Plataians were in exile for a considerable time, and so were the Delians, when the Athenians threw them out and they lived in Adramyttion;[113] [10] the Minyans were expelled from Orchomenos by the Thebans after the battle of Leuktra, and they and the Plataians were brought back to Boiotia by Philip son of Amyntas; Thebes itself was devastated by Alexander, and Antipater's son Kassander built it again not many years afterwards. The Plataian exile appears to be the longest in this list, but even that lasted not more than two generations. [11] But the Messenians were wandering outside the Peloponnese for roughly three hundred years, during which they can be seen to have changed none of their home customs and not even unlearnt their Doric dialect, but even to this day they preserve it in its purity better than anywhere else in the Peloponnese.

28  [1] When the Messenians first came home the Lakonians did nothing very dreadful; the Lakonians were restrained by fear of Thebes, and they did not interfere with the building of Messene or the assembly of all the Arkadians into one city.[114] But when the Phokian war, which was also called the Sacred war, drew the Thebans away from the Peloponnese, the Lakonians perked up again and were unable to keep their

112. Pausanias puts the exile of the Messenians in 668 and their restoration in 370, which gives more or less 300 years of exile. But Isokrates gives a 400-year exile (*Archidamus*, 27) and Lykourgos a 500-year exile (*Against Leokrates*, 62); none of the early dates is to be taken literally.

113. For the Plataian exile after the fall of Plataia in the Peloponnesian War, cf. Bk IX, 1 (4f.). The Athenians turned the whole island of Delos into a sanctuary in 426 and turned out the inhabitants in 422. ADRAMYTTION, which Thukydides calls Atramyttion, is still called EDREMID to this day. It is a small harbour on the Turkish coast opposite Lesbos. It was granted to the Delians by the Persian satrap of the Hellespont (Thukydides, 5, 1).

114. Megalopolis (Great City); cf. Bk VIII, 27 (1f.).

hands off the Messenians. [2] The Messenians with Argos and Arkadia resisted in arms and asked the Athenians to come and fight for them; the Athenians said they would never invade Lakonia with them, but they promised to come if Lakonia started the war and attacked Messenia. In the end the Messenians made an alliance with Philip and the Macedonians, and they say this is what prevented them from taking part in the battle the rest of Greece fought at Chaironeia: and of course they certainly had no intention of bearing arms on the opposite side to Greece.[115] [3] When Alexander died and Greece raised its second war against the Macedonians, the Messenians took part in it, as I showed before in my Athenian treatise.[116] They did not fight against the Gauls with the rest of Greece because Kleonymos and the Lakonians refused to make a truce with them.

[4] Not long afterwards, by a combination of cleverness and daring the Messenians occupied Elis.[117] In the most ancient times there was no one else in the Peloponnese so peacefully law-abiding as the people of Elis, but among the injuries it was said that Philip son of Amyntas did to Greece was his corruption of powerful men in Elis with bribes; they say it was the first revolution Elis had ever known and the first time the Eleians bore arms.[118] [5] From then on they would feud with each other still more easily, since they quarrelled over this Lakonian policy, and in fact they reached the point of civil war. When the Lakonians heard of this they got ready to fight for their own party in Elis. They marshalled divisions and formed companies, but a thousand picked Messenians reached Elis first, with Lakonian emblems on their shields.[119]

115. Philip defeated the Greeks at Chaironeia in 338.    116. Bk I, 25 (4).

117. When? After Pyrros's death in 272? So far as I can see we have no way of knowing. For the site of Elis, cf. Bk VI, 23 (1).

118. Polybios (4, 73f.) and Strabo (8, 3, 33) say the same thing about the peaceful and prosperous Eleans. There were prosperous farming families in Elis that had never seen the sea for three generations.

119. The painted letter L instead of the letter M. The Sikyonians had an S and the Mantineans had a trident. These national shield-emblems seem to have begun in the Peloponnese. The Greek L is simply half of an M.

[6] When the pro-Spartan party at Elis saw the shields, they hoped an allied force had arrived, and let the men inside the fortifications. Once they had got in as I have said, the Messenians chased out the pro-Spartans, and handed over the city to their own side. [7] The trick comes from Homer, and it appears the Messenians copied it when it was needed: Homer makes Patroklos wear the arms of Achilles in the *Iliad*, and he says the impression sprang up in the barbarians that Achilles was attacking them, and it broke up their front rank.[120] There are other tactical devices in Homer, for example the two Greek spies instead of one who come to the Trojans at night, and the man later who enters Troy claiming to be a runaway, but really in order to sniff out their secrets. [8] And he puts Trojans too young or too old to fight on guard on the wall, while the men of fighting age are in camp against the Greeks; and the wounded Greeks help the fighting men put on their armour, so that they are not utterly idle. Homer's works are useful to the human race in every way.[121]

29   [1] Not long after the success at Elis the Macedonians and Demetrios son of Philip son of Demetrios captured Messene. I have already described most of what Perseus dared to do against Philip and his son Demetrios in my treatment of Sikyon;[122] the capture of Messene happened like this. [2] Philip was short of money, and as he had to get it in one way or another he sent off Demetrios with a fleet to the Peloponnese. Demetrios put in somewhere in the Argolid at one of the lonelier harbours, and straight from there by the shortest route he led his army against Messene.[123] He put all his light weapons and everyone who knew the way to Ithome in front, and as dawn was just about breaking he climbed the walls without being noticed, at a point between the city and the peak of Ithome. [3] When the sun had risen and the people

120. *Iliad*, 16, 278f.
121. *Iliad*, 10, 222f., and 8, 517f.
122. Bk II, 9 (4f.).
123. From PARALION ASTROUS by the passes south of Tripolis and south of Megalopolis?

inside saw the danger they were in, first of all they imagined armed Lakonians had broken into the city, so they rushed to attack them with an abandon that came from their ancient bitterness. But when they recognized the Macedonians and Demetrios son of Philip by their arms and voices, they were terribly frightened by the thought of the Macedonian war training and the universal Macedonian luck. [4] Still the scale of the trouble gave them a certain manly courage and induced them to go beyond their own capability, and at the same time it opened the possibility of hoping for better things: their return to the Peloponnese after so long had not happened independently of divine power. So the Messenians from the city charged the Macedonians with their full fury, and the guard from the upper fortress assaulted them from above. [5] All the same, to begin with, by courage and experience the Macedonians defended themselves vigorously, but they were exhausted from their journey and worn down by the attacks of the men and the shower of tiles and stones from the women, and they fled in complete disorder. Most of them died by being pushed over the cliffs, as Ithome is precipitous at this point; but a few threw away their weapons and escaped.

[6] I think the original reason the Messenians did not join the Achaian League is this.[124] They came self-invited to help the Lakonians when Pyrros son of Aiakides was fighting a war against them, and from the time of that kindness they had friendlier relations with Sparta. They did not want to re-awaken the enmity by joining the League, who were openly the special enemies of Lakonia. [7] But what I have not forgotten, and nor did it escape the Messenians, is that even without their membership the Achaian policy would be anti-Lakonian: Arkadia and Argos were not the smallest members of the league. In time they did join the Achaians; but not long afterwards Kleomenes the son of Leonidas and grandson of Kleonymos took the Great City of Arkadia (*Megalopolis*)

124. The history of the Achaian league is given in detail in Pausanias's *Achaia* (Bk VII, 6 (1f.)). We are now on the verge of the Roman conquest of Greece.

during a truce.[125] [8] Some of the Arkadians who were caught there perished in the fall, but Philopoimen son of Kraugis[126] and the people who withdrew under him – and they say the refugees were over two thirds of the citizens – were taken in by the Messenians for the sake of the old behaviour of the Arkadians in Aristomenes' day, and later at the building of Messene, to pay them like for like. [9] It must be in the nature of human affairs to turn completely upside down, if the divine power allowed the Messenians in their turn to rescue the Arkadians, and even more unexpected than that, to capture Sparta. They fought against Kleomenes at Sellasia and with Aratos and the Achaians they captured Sparta.[127] [10] When the Lakonians were rid of Kleomenes the dictator Machanidas arose, and when he died Nabis appeared, yet another dictator. As he not only robbed human beings but looted sanctuaries, it did not take long for Nabis to collect plenty of money and therefore also an army. Nabis took Messene, but Philopoimen and his people arrived the same night; [11] the dictator of Sparta withdrew under a truce, but later the Achaians found some fault with the Messenians, and went to war against them with their entire apparatus: and cut the crops over most of their territory. And when the corn was ripe they assembled again for another invasion of Messenia; but Deinokrates the people's leader was chosen at that time as Messenian commander, and he occupied the passes between Messenia and Arkadia with the city Messenians and everyone from the provinces who was fighting on their side, and made it impossible for Lykortas and his army to retreat. [12] Philopoimen arrived with a few cavalry long after Lykortas's army and knew nothing about this opposition; the Messenians fought from higher ground and beat him, and they took Philopoimen

125. Perhaps misguidedly I have usually translated 'Megalopolis', the Hellenistic capital of Arkadia, as Great City, since Pausanias usually spells it out *he megale polis*. There is a modern MEGALOPOLIS on the site, which is at more or less the navel of the Peloponnese, in the plain north of the Taygetos range. Kleomenes took it in 222 B.C.

126. Cf. Bk VIII, 49–51.

127. The battle of Sellasia was fought in 222 or 221, and Sparta fell.

alive. My account of Arkadia will explain later how Philopoimen was captured and how he died; but those Messenians responsible for Philopoimen's death paid the penalty and Messene contributed once again to the Achaian League.[128]

[13] So far my account has dealt with the numerous Messenian tragedies, and how the divine power scattered them to the ends of the earth and the farthest distances from the Peloponnese, and then at a later time brought them safely home to their own country; from now on let us turn to the description of the land and the cities.

[1] In modern Messenia two or three miles from Pig valley there lies the coastal city of ABIA.[129] They say it used to be called Ire and was one of the seven cities Homer makes Agamemnon promise to Achilles.[130] When Hyllos and the Dorians were beaten in battle by the Achaians, Herakles' nurse Glenos's daughter Abia is supposed to have withdrawn to Ire and settled down there, and founded a sanctuary to Herakles; because of this she was afterwards honoured by Kresphontes, and he renamed the city after her. There was a glorious HERAKLEION there and an ASKLEPIEION.[131]

128. Cf. Bk VIII, 51f. For the punishment of the murderers, cf. Polybios (24, 12).

129. The site of Abia is at PALAIOCHORA, just north of the outfall of the SANDAVA river in the northern Mani south-east of Kalamata. This identification is certain because of the inscriptions found there (I.G., V (1), 1351-8).

130. Mr R. Hope-Simpson has published two studies (B.S.A., 52 and 61) of these seven cities (Iliad, 9, 149f. and 291f.) He is convinced that Homer was writing more or less literally about Mycenaean Greece. Even one who by no means accepts this view cannot deny that the topography of Homeric Greece (that is the Greece of the Iliad) at least approached to being coherent. (For the site of Abia, cf. B.S.A., 16, pp. 164-5, and B.S.A., 52, p. 240.) But Homer's Greece could well be the Greece of the eighth century. The Pylos tablets (from Ano Engliani) hardly support the equivalence of Homer's description with the reality of the Mycenaean period. I had intended to publish a specialized study of these questions, but cf. now A. Giovannini, Origines du Catalogue des Vaisseaux (1969), and Hope-Simpson and Lazenby, Catalogue of Ships (1970), which I have not yet digested.

131. Not identified with the least certainty.

[2] PHARAI is eight or nine miles from Abia, and there is a salt-water-spring on the road; the emperor Augustus decreed that the Messenians of Pharai should belong to Lakonia.[132] They say Pharis the founder was the son of Hermes and Phylodameia, daughter of Danaos; he is supposed to have had no sons, only a daughter Telegone, and Homer in the *Iliad* traces this family tree: Diokles was the son of Ortilochos and the grandson of Alpheios, and he had twin sons, Krethon and Ortilochos.[133] He has left out Telegone, but the Messenian account of this is that Telegone bore Ortilochos for Alpheios. [3] And there was something else I heard at Pharai, that Diokles had a daughter Antikleia as well as his twin sons; Antikleia's children were Nikomachos and Gorgasos, and their father was Asklepios's son Machaon. They stayed at home, and when Diokles died they succeeded to his kingdom. To this day they still have the power of curing the lame and the sick, and so the people they cure bring sacrifices and dedications to their sanctuary. Pharai also has a TEMPLE OF FORTUNE with an ancient statue. [4] Homer is the first poet I know of who mentions Fortune in his poetry: he mentions her in the *Hymn to Demeter*, where he goes through a number of other daughters of Okeanos who were playing with Demeter's daughter the Maid, and he makes Fortune one of them. This is how the verses go:

132. The salt spring was the one at HALMYRON north of Abia. Pharai was where *Kalamata* now is. There seem to be some traces of a prehistoric akropolis and there are certainly reconstructed classical towers embedded in Kalamata Castle, which is a weak early Byzantine fortification enormously strengthened in the thirteenth century. Mr Hope-Simpson found considerable traces of the latest prehistoric and of classical pottery on the sandy hill about a mile north-east of the castle. There are other ancient sites in the neighbourhood; the identification of Pharai has never been confirmed by coins or inscriptions, but it is more or less certain. Some small bronzes and the foundations of buildings at AKOBITIKA, by the Nedon at the south-west of modern Kalamata, have turned out to be an important sanctuary of Poseidon; cf. Themelis in *Athens Annals of Archaeology*, 1969, p. 352. It belonged to Thouria.

133. *Iliad*, 5, 541f.

*We were together in the fine meadows,*
*Ianthe with Leukippe and Phaino,*
*Elektra, Melobosis, Fortune,*
*Okyroe with eyes as round as buds.*[134]

[5] But he tells you nothing more: nothing of how this goddess is the greatest of all divine powers in human affairs and has the most strength; so in the *Iliad* he gives Athene and Enyo the leadership of war, he makes Artemis terrify women in childbirth and puts Aphrodite in charge of the operations of marriage, yet he says nothing more about Fortune. [6] But Boupalos, a fine animal sculptor and builder of temples, who was working for Smyrna, became the first person we know of to create a statue of Fortune, holding the sphere on her head and what the Greeks call Amaltheia's horn in her other hand. That was as much as he showed of the operations of this goddess; and later Pindar sang to Fortune in his songs, and called her 'City-carrying'.[135]

[1] A little way out from Pharai is a sacred grove of Kar- 31 neian Apollo, with a water-spring in it; Pharai is about three quarters of a mile from the sea.[136] Ten miles from here into inner Messenia is the city of THOURIA, which they say Homer called Antheia in his poetry; Augustus granted Thouria to the

134. Homeric *Hymn to Demeter*, 417–20. Hesiod (*Theogony*, 349f.) gives a longer series of the same names with certain variations, but Fortune appears in both. The list of names in the hymn ends with Pallas and Artemis; Hesiod ends with Styx. Alkman calls Fortune the sister of Law and Persuasion and the daughter of Forethought (*Fr.* 64). She never occurs in the *Iliad* or the *Odyssey*. In the Hellenistic period there was a religious cult of the Fortune of cities (cf. for example Bk II, 2 (8)). I do not know when she was first worshipped; her only known Greek festival was at Lampsakos, but she had an important cult at Antioch.

135. Boupalos came from Chios. He lived in the second half of the sixth century B.C. and was the enemy and the victim of the satiric iambic poet Hipponax. Amaltheia's horn is the Horn of Plenty, the *cornucopia*. The horn is a goat's horn; Amaltheia is a nymph who was Dionysos's nurse; sometimes Amaltheia is a nanny-goat. Pindar's epithet comes from a lost poem (though cf. *Olympian Odes*, 12, 2); Plutarch also mentions it.

136. Maybe the grove was at PERA KALAMITSI, where stray antiquities have come to light recently and where a tiny spring still exists.

Spartan Lakonians.[137] When Augustus was emperor of Rome, Antony, who was also a Roman by blood, fought a war with him: Messenia and the rest of Greece attacked with him, because the Lakonians were on Augustus's side. [2] Because of this, Augustus struck at Messenia, and at the others who served against him, some heavily and some lightly. The Thourians came down from their city, which in the old days was built high in the air and settled on the plain. Still, they have not abandoned the upper city altogether; the ruins of the fortress-wall are there, and there is a sanctuary with the title of the Syrian goddess; the river Aris flows past the city in the plain.

[3] In the inland region there is a village called the REEDS and a place called the LAKES where there is a sanctuary of Artemis of the Lake where they say King Teleklos of Sparta met his end.[138] [4] On the way to Arkadia from Thouria, you come to the SPRINGS OF THE PAMISOS; little children are cured there.[139]

Five miles away on your left as you leave the springs the Messenians have a city below Ithome. Not only Ithome shuts it in, but also Mount Eua towards the Pamisos: they say this mountain got its name from the Bacchic cry of 'Euoi!' that Dionysos and his women first uttered in this place. [5] The walls of MESSENE are a complete circle built in stone, with towers and fortifications built into them.[140] I have never seen the walls of Babylon or Memnon's walls at Sousa in Persia,

137. Thouria must be the site north of the railway near MIKROMANI west of the modern THOURIA, and the akropolis at the village once called Beïsaga and now renamed ANTHEIA, which has yielded a number of inscriptions. The reference to the *Iliad* is to Book 9 (the cities offered to Achilles), 151 and 293. For Poseidon's temple, cf. Note 132 above.

138. KALAMAI, the Reeds, was some kind of fortress in Polybios's time (5, 92). An inscription found there (*I.G.*, V, (1), 1369) makes it clear that Kalamai was the site at JANITZA, a few miles north-east of the modern Kalamata, on the edge of the mountains, commanding the pass to Lakonia, which used often to be taken for Pharai. For Artemis of the Lake, cf. Bk IV, Note 27.

139. Well inland between SKALA and HAGIOS FLOROS; cf. Bk IV, Note 25.

140. Cf. Bk IV, Note 110.

nor have I ever heard them described by an eye-witness; but if you take the walls at Ambrossos in Phokis and at Byzantion and at Rhodes, which are extremely well-walled places, the Messenian walls are stronger still.[141] [6] In the market-place the Messenians have a statue of Zeus Saviour, and a water-fountain of Arsinoe; the name comes from Leukippos's daughter, but the water comes from the spring called Klep-saydra.[142] There are divine SANCTUARIES of POSEIDON and APHRODITE, and the most memorable thing of all is a statue of the Mother of the gods in Parian stone by Damophon; it was Damophon who refitted the Zeus at Olympia perfectly when its ivory was breaking away, and Elis granted him honours. [7] It was also Damophon who made the Messenian Laphria, the tradition of whose worship arose as follows.[143]

141. Pausanias gets his idea of the walls of Babylon from Herodotos's amazing description (1, 178f.). Babylon was first excavated by Layard; perhaps the most dramatic discoveries were made by the German Orientgesellschaft expedition of 1899. The walls have been swallowed by time and the Euphrates; they were made of clay-brick. The Homeric or sub-Homeric hero Memnon was supposed to have built the walls of Sousa: Strabo says they were fifteen miles round. The French archaeologist Dieulafoy has described the remnants of these walls; they were made of clay-brick faced with unbaked clay. The sites of these cities, in Mesopotamia and beyond, were remote from Pausanias's world. The walls of Ambrossos (Bk X, 36, (1f.)) survived into the early nineteenth century to be seen by Dodwell, who tells us only that 'the few visible remains are of regular masonry'. The magnificent surviving walls of Byzantion at Istanbul are (alas) far later than whatever walls of Byzantion Pausanias knew. To look at, the present walls are not unlike the walls of Rome. The famous walls of Rhodes are not older than the early fourteenth century, though they follow the same circuit as the Byzantine walls, but a few fragments of the ancient (that is pre-Christian) walls do exist.

142. The market-place seems to have been between the theatre and the stadium, in the western part of the city where the ground is level. Pausanias's spring is surely the abundant spring that still exists.

143. Damophon's name is never mentioned by anyone but Pausanias, who mentions him several times, but enough of his original work has been recovered (by Kabbadias at Lykosoura in 1889) to make him one of the clearer landmarks in the history of Hellenistic art. There have been wild and slippery controversies about the date when he worked; almost certainly he worked at the last moment before the age of Hadrian when an original and monumental art could flourish in the Peloponnese, that is in the early second century B.C. (Cf. G. Dickins in

Artemis was called Laphria by the Kalydonians, who worshipped her more than any other god, and the Messenians who took over Naupaktos from Athens found themselves living extremely close to Aitolia, and took over the title from Kalydon. I shall explain the specific appearance of Laphria elsewhere. So the name of Laphria travelled only as far as the Messenians and Patrai in Achaia, [8] but every city recognizes Ephesian Artemis, and people individually honour her above all the gods. I think the reason is the glory of the Amazons who have the reputation of having established the statue, and also the fact that the sanctuary was built so very long ago. Three other things have contributed to make it famous: the size of the temple which overtops every other human construction, the flourishing strength of the city of Ephesos, and the glittering position of the goddess in the city.[144]

[9] The Messenians also have a SHRINE OF EILEITHUIA with a stone statue, near the HALL OF THE KOURETAI where all kinds of animals are burnt as offerings together.[145] They begin with cattle and goats, and they end up by throwing birds into the fire. The Messenians also have a sanctuary consecrated to Demeter, and statues of the Dioskouroi carrying Leukippos's daughters. I have already explained in earlier discussions how the Messenians claim Tyndareos's sons belong to them and

B.S.A., 12, pp. 109f.) For Laphrian Artemis, cf. Bk VII, 18 (11–13). The Laphrion at Kalydon stood just outside the city gate on a spur of the same hill. It was excavated and fully published by the Danish archaeologist Ejnar Dyggve (Copenhagen, 1948). The site yielded some splendid architectural ornaments in painted terracotta.

144. 'Great is Diana of the Ephesians' (Acts, 19, 21–40). She had breasts all over her body like boiled eggs. They may in fact quite possibly be meant for eggs rather than breasts. There is an extremely odd wall-painting in the Naples museum in which Dionysos has sprouted grapes in the same way. The temple was discovered after a lot of digging by an engineer called Mr Wood, and finally excavated to its lowest level by D. G. Hogarth, who discovered a very rich foundation deposit of gold.

145. Eileithuia is the birth goddess. The Kouretai are the daemonic creatures who looked after the infant Zeus in his cave in Crete. They were also worshipped in Elis and Arkadia. A hymn to the Great Kouros which throws light on them has survived. (Cf. Journal of Hellenic Studies, 85, pp. 149–59.)

not to the Lakonians.[146] [10] Most of their statues and the ones most worth seeing are to be found in the SANCTUARY OF ASKLEPIOS: there are other statues there apart from the god and his sons, and apart from Apollo and the Muses and Herakles: there are the City of Thebes and Epaminondas the son of Kleommis, and Fortune and Light-carrying Artemis; Damophon made some of them in stone – I know of no other Messenian sculptor whose work is worth recording – but the portrait of Epaminondas is in iron, and someone else's work,

5. Messene

not his.[147] [11] There is also a temple of Triopas's daughter Messene, with a statue in gold and Parian stone; the paintings behind the temple are the kings of Messene, Aphareus and his sons before the Dorian expedition to the Peloponnese, and after the return of the children of Herakles there is Kresphontes, who was a Dorian commander himself, and also Nestor and Thrasymedes and Antilochos who all lived at

146. Bk III, 26 (3).

147. Iron statues are rarely mentioned but not unheard of. Pausanias knew and tells us twice that Epaminondas was the son of Polymnis, not Kleommis; Kleommis is unexplained, unless Pausanias mistook the inscribed name of the sculptor. What seems to be a statue of the City of Messene appears on Messenian coins.

Pylos; Thrasymedes and Antilochos were picked out among Nestor's sons because they were the eldest and went to the Trojan War. [12] Aphareus's brother Leukippos is there, Hilaeira and Phoibe are there, and Arsinoe with them. Asklepios is also painted; in the Messenian version he was Arsinoe's son. Machaon and Podaleirios are there, because they also took part in the victory at Troy.[148] These paintings are by Omphalion, a pupil of Nikias the son of Nikomedes; some people even say he was Nikias's slave and his boy-friend.[149]

32    [1] What the Messenians call the ALTAR OF SACRIFICE has statues of all the gods the Greeks believe in and a bronze portrait statue of Epaminondas. Some ancient tripods are kept there that Homer calls flameless.[150] The statues in the TRAINING-GROUND are Egyptian work: Hermes and Herakles and Theseus, whom all the Greeks and by now many barbarians traditionally honour in training-grounds and wrestling schools.[151] [2] But I discovered there was someone called Aithidas, older than I am, who became substantially wealthy and so the Messenians give him the honours of a divine hero. Certain Messenians admitted Aithidas was in fact rich, but they claimed this person named on the inscribed tablet was not the same man; it was an ancestor, another Aithidas. They say the first Aithidas commanded the Messenians when Philip's son Demetrios and his army got secretly and unexpectedly into the city at night.[152]

[3] Aristomenes also has a monument here. They say this is not an empty memorial, but when I asked how they brought home Aristomenes' bones and where from, they claimed to

148. Asklepios's sons. All these mythical figures and their relationships have been discussed earlier in the book.

149. No one else mentions Omphalion at all. He would probably be an early third-century painter. (For Nikias, cf. Bk III, 19 (4).)

150. *Iliad*, 9, 122. He means unused.

151. The gymnasion (training-ground) has not been accurately identified.

152. Could this Aithidas possibly be the Tiberius Claudius Saithidas Caelianus, the priest who appears on an inscription first copied by Cyriaco of Ancona and later found here by Leake? Probably not.

have fetched them from Rhodes and to have done so on the orders of the god at Delphi. Further, they instructed me in the ceremonies they perform at the grave. They bring the bull they are going to sacrifice up to the monument, and tie it to the pillar that stands on the grave. Being wild and not used to a halter the bull will not want to stop there. If his fretting and curvetting stirs the pillar, it is a good omen to the Messenians, but if not the omen points to something unfavourable. [4] They insist that Aristomenes was present even at the battle of Leuktra when he was no longer on the face of the earth; they claim he fought for the Thebans and was chiefly responsible for the Lakonian disaster. The Chaldaians and the Indian wizards are the first people to my knowledge who ever said the soul of man is immortal, and one of the most important Greeks they convinced was Plato; and if everyone has decided to accept it, then it becomes impossible to maintain that Aristomenes could not have clung to his bitterness against Lakonia through all the ages. [5] But what I heard myself at Thebes, although it gives a certain backing to the Messenian story, is certainly not in complete agreement with it. The Thebans say that when the battle of Leuktra was looming they sent questions to various oracles including the god at Lebadeia. They tell you the prophecies from the Ismenian and the Ptoan god, and the prophecies at Abai and at Delphi; Trophonios they say spoke in hexameters:[153]

> Before the spears whizz raise your trophy:
> take my shield; raging Messenian
> Aristomenes leaned it on my walls.
> I tell you I shall destroy this army
> of wicked-willing men in their shell of shields.

[6] When this oracle arrived they say Epaminondas put the request to Xenokrates, who sent for Aristomenes' shield and

153. Ismenian Apollo at Thebes, Apollo at the Ptoon in upper Boiotia, and Apollo at Abai in Phokis and at Delphi; Trophonios at Lebadeia. There is a useful comparative study of all these oracles by a Canadian scholar A. Schachter ('A Boeotian Cult Type') in the *Bulletin of the London Institute of Classical Studies* (no. 14, 1967, pp. 1–16).

decorated a trophy with it where the Lakonians would be able to see it. The people of Lebadeia knew Aristomenes' shield, having seen it in peace-time, and everyone had heard of it. When the Thebans won they gave the dedication back again to Trophonios.[154] There is also a bronze statue of Aristomenes in the Messenian stadium, and not far from the THEATRE stands a SANCTUARY OF SARAPIS AND ISIS.[155]

33 [I] On the way to the peak of Ithome, which is the Messenian upper fortress, you come to the water-spring of Klepsydra. It would be impossible even for a man who had

*6. Zeus of Ageladas*

the appetite to number all the people who insist that Zeus was born and reared in their countries, but the Messenians claim their part in the story: like the others they say the god was reared in their country, they say Ithome and Neda nursed him, the river was named after Neda, and Ithome gave her name to the mountain. They say the two of them washed Zeus here when he was stolen by the Kouretai for fear of his father, and the water was named after that theft; and every day they take water from this spring to the sanctuary of Zeus

154. For the dedication of this famous relic, cf. Bk IV, 16 (7). An inscription about the incident has been found on a statue-base at Thebes.
155. The stadium is in the south-west corner of the ruins.

of Ithome.[156] [2] The statue of Zeus is by Ageladas, and it was originally made for the Naupaktos Messenians; a priest chosen every year keeps the statue in his house.[157] They keep an annual feast of the Ithomaia, and in the old times there was a contest in music: among the proofs of that there are Eumelos's verses. This comes from his processional hymn to Delos:

> Zeus of Ithome whose heart the muse pleased:
> with her pure strings: with her free sandals.

I think when he wrote these verses he knew they held a music contest.[158]

[3] As you leave on the road for Arkadia heading for the Great City, there is a Hermes of Athenian workmanship in the gates; the four-square style in Hermes figures comes from Athens, and that was where other people learnt it.[159] Four miles down from these gates you come to the streams of the Lyrethrow (*Balyra*): the story is that the river got its name when Thamyris threw away his harp there when he was blinded: he was the son of Philammon and the nymph Argiope. Argiope used to live around Parnassos, but when she was pregnant with Thamyris she went to the Odrysians, as Philammon did not want to take her home. This is why they call Thamyris Odrysian and Thracian. The Leukasia and the Amphitos mingle their streams in one.[160]

156. The big village spring. *Klepsydra* means 'Water-theft'.

157. This statue is represented on coins. Ageladas was an early-fifth-century sculptor who worked mainly in bronze. Pheidias and Myron were his pupils. The Zeus must have been like a less humanistic version of the great bronze Poseidon from Cape Artemision which is in the National Museum at Athens. Cf. Lullies and Hirmer, *Greek Sculpture*, pls. 128–31.

158. Cf. Bk IV, Note 26.

159. The gate towards Megalopolis, the Arkadian gate, has survived.

160. The Balyra is really the upper Pamisos. Its modern local name is MAVROZOUMAINA. Pausanias derives Balyra from *Bal-* and *lyra* ('throw' and 'harp'). Thamyris was blinded for challenging the Muses at music; Parnassos is the mountain above Delphi, but the Odrysians lived in Thrace, so that the pregnant nymph must have withdrawn into the wildest parts of the Pindos range. Philammon was a mythical poet and musician who used to sing his verses at Delphi. The Leukasia and the Amphitos are unidentified.

[4] When you have crossed over them you are in the Stenyklerian plain; they say Stenykleros is a divine hero. Directly opposite this plain is what in ancient times was called OICHALIA; this is now the Karnasian grove, and is particularly full of cypresses.[161] There are statues of the gods, Karneian Apollo, the Pure One, and Hermes carrying a ram. The Pure One is a title of Demeter's daughter, the Maid; water comes up from the spring right beside her statue. [5] As for the story of the Great goddesses, whose mystery is also celebrated in Karnasion, let me not speak of it: I judge them for their awful holiness to be second only to the Eleusinians. But the dream has not forbidden me to tell everybody that the bronze jar the Argive commander found and the bones of Eurytos son of Melaneus were kept here.[162] The river Torrent runs past the Karnasian grove, [6] and about a mile farther to the left lie the RUINS OF ANDANIA.[163] The sacred guides agree that the city got its name from a woman called Andania, but I have no way of saying anything about her parents or whom she married. On the way towards Kyparissia from Andania you come to Polichne and the streams of the two rivers Elektra and Koios; they might tell some story about Atlas's daughter Elektra and Leto's father Koios, or maybe Elektra and Koios might be local divine heroes.[164]

[7] If you cross Elektra you come to a water-spring called Achaia and the ruins of the city of DORION.[165] Homer makes

161. The Stenyklerian plain is the whole upper Messenian plain. Oichalia has not been securely identified. Cf. Bk IV, Note 10.

162. The dream came to him when he wanted to speak about Eleusis (Bk I, 14 (3), and 38 (7)). For the bronze jar, cf. Bk IV, 26 (6f.).

163. Cf. Bk IV, Note 3.

164. Pausanias has turned west; Kyparissia was a coastal city. No one knows where Polichne is. (The modern Polichne has hardly even the status of a guess.) Mr Papahadzis in his commentary on Pausanias, and Valmin in his *Messénie ancienne*, discuss a number of interesting sites in north-west Messenia, and no doubt there are still others to be found, in this as in every part of Greece. Mr Hope-Simpson lists a number of new places which are possible candidates in the right area in his *Gazetteer of Mycenaean Sites*.

165. The same difficulties arise as in the previous note. Strabo says it may have been a mountain, it may have been a plain, and it may have been a little town.

Thamyris's tragedy happen at Dorion, because he declared he could beat the Muses themselves at singing; but Prodikos the Phokaian, if in fact he was the poet of the Minyad, says Thamyris pays the penalty in Hades for his boast against the Muses.[166] In my view Thamyris lost his eyesight from an eye disease, and the same thing happened later to Homer; but Homer went on to the very end as a poet, without yielding an inch to his tragedy, and Thamyris lost even his singing because of that trouble.

[1] The road from Messene to the mouth of the Pamisos is 34 ten miles, but the Pamisos flows through ploughed land, the water is pure, and ships sail up it from the sea about a mile and a quarter inland; sea-living fish run up it as well, around the spring season. The fish do the same in the Rhine and the Maiander, and particularly swimming upstream in the Acheloos which discharges into the sea opposite the islands of the Echinades.[167] [2] But fish of a quite different kind run up the Pamisos, because of the water being pure and not oozy like the other rivers I have mentioned. Grey mullet, being mud-living fish, like the coarser-textured rivers.[168] Greek rivers by their nature do not produce man-murdering monsters like the Indus and the Egyptian Nile and even the Rhine and the Danube, the Euphrates and the Phasis, which fatten monsters as man-eating as any in existence; to look at they are like the Catfish in the Hermos and the Maiander, but blacker and stronger: the catfish is not so black or strong.[169]

166. *Iliad*, 2, 594–600. The *Minyad* is a lost epic about how Herakles fought the Minyans and conquered Orchomenos. Pausanias is virtually the only witness even to the existence of this poem. He often refers to it and at one point quotes two lines (Bk X, 28 (2)).

167. The road west has petered out. Now we are heading south again. The Echinades were very close to the shore of Akarnania.

168. Grey mullet do as a matter of fact chew mud in the way that one might chew tobacco. The cleaner the water the better they taste.

169. The Phasis runs into the Euxine; it was supposed to be the barrier of Europe and Asia. The Hermos and the Maiander run down to the eastern Mediterranean from Asia Minor. There are a number of sizes and kinds of catfish. The monstrous one is the Sheatfish, or great European Catfish, *silurus glanis*. Ailian (14, 25) says they fished for it with lumps of beef in the Danube,

[3] The Indus and the Nile both produce crocodiles, and the Nile has hippopotamus as well, which are quite as troublesome to human beings as crocodiles. Greek rivers are quite unterrifying as far as monsters are concerned; even the sharks in the Aoos which flows through Thesprotis in mainland Greece are not river creatures, but visitors from the sea.[170]

[4] KORONE is a city on the right of the Pamisos by the sea below Mount Mathia.[171] Along that road there is a place on the coast which they believe is sacred to Ino: they say she came up from the sea when she was already recognized as a goddess and called Leukothea.[172] Not far beyond here the river Bias runs into the sea; they say it was named after Bias son of Amythaon. Two and a half miles farther along the road is the water-spring called the Plane spring, where the water runs out from a huge hollow plane-tree. The girth of the tree makes it more or less like a small cave, and the water they drink in Korone runs out from it.[173] [5] The ancient name of the place was Aipeia,[174] but when the Thebans brought home the Messenians, they say Epimelides who was sent as founder called it Koroneia, as he came from Koroneia in Boiotia, but the Messenians never got the name right from the beginning, and in the course of time the mistake held the field. There is

---

and it had to be dragged out by a team of oxen or a team of horses, like Patroklos's corpse. There is a monstrous fish in the Thames above King's Lock which has bitten a hole in a wooden boat and is believed to be a giant pike; it could be a sheatfish.

170. The Aoos is the Albanian river Vijosë. I do not know if it still has sharks.

171. The ancient Korone was at PETALIDION on the west side of the Messenian gulf. The ruins are substantial, and the mountain confirms the identification, although unfortunately the inscriptions found there do not mention the name of the city. Cf. also Bk IV, Note 54.

172. She had other sacred places in the western Mani on the opposite coast. The modern Petalidion is in fact a Maniote settlement.

173. I drank from a spring like this in Crete, in the White Mountains above Chania. Sir James Frazer drank from one between Andritsaina and Krestena. Huge plane-trees very often grow above springs all over Greece. Bias was the brother and protégé of the prophet Melampous (Bk II, 6 (18)).

174. *Iliad*, 9, 152 and 294.

also another story they tell about finding a bronze crow when they were digging the foundations of the walls.[175]

[6] There is a TEMPLE there of Nursing Artemis and Dionysos and Asklepios. Dionysos and Asklepios have stone statues, and Zeus the Saviour has a bronze statue in the market-place. The statue of Athene holding a crow which stands in the open air in the upper city is also bronze. I saw Epimelides' monument, but why they call the HARBOUR the Achaian harbour I have no idea.[176]

[7] Ten miles beyond Korone you reach a SANCTUARY OF APOLLO by the sea where worship takes place: the Messenian account of it makes it most ancient, and the god curses diseases; they call him Apollo Korythos. He is a wooden figure, but the statue of Argeotas is in bronze; they say it was dedicated by the crew of the Argo.[177] [8] The city of Korone has a common border with KOLONIDES, where the people claim not to be Messenians but Athenians brought by Kolainos, whose expedition was guided by a crested lark, according to the prophecies of an oracle.[178] But in the course of time their dialect and their customs were going to become Dorian. The town of Kolonides is high up, a little way back from the sea.

[9] The Asinaians originally lived around Parnassos next to Lykorea, and their name, which they preserved and brought to the Peloponnese, was the Dryopes, after their founder.[179]

175. That is, a *korone*.

176. The remains of the jetty are still visible in the sea. This was probably a naval base of the Achaian league.

177. Apollo Korythos means Apollo of the Head of the Crest. This sanctuary was excavated and identified through inscriptions by Mr Versakis and later by Valmin. Among the dedications there was an archaic miniature bronze figure or a soldier 'dedicated by the Messenians to Athene from the spoils'. The site is near LONGA, almost opposite KARDAMYLE across the gulf.

178. Perhaps the site noted by Mr Hope-Simpson at CHARAKOPEION, north-west of the modern Koroni? Or a site nearer LONGA, of which there appear to be several? (Cf. Valmin, *Messénie ancienne*, pp. 171f.) A crested lark is a *korydos* (cf. Apollo *Korythos*). Kolainos was a mythical king even older than Kekrops (Bk I, 31 (3)).

179. Lykorea is a lost prehistoric city on Mount Parnassos in which Pausanias says the Delphians used to live.

But the third generation afterwards under King Phylas, the Dryopes were beaten in battle by Herakles, and taken to Delphi and dedicated to Apollo. But the god's oracle to Herakles brought them to the Peloponnese; first they occupied ASINE near Hermione, then when the Argives expelled them from there they settled in Messenia by a Lakonian grant, and when in the course of time the Messenians came home their city was allowed to stay.[180] [10] But the Asinaians tell their own story as follows: they agree they were beaten in battle by Herakles and their city on Parnassos fell, but they deny they were prisoners and taken to Apollo: they say that when Herakles captured the walls they abandoned their city and fled up to the peaks of Parnassos, and then later they crossed to the Peloponnese in ships and begged help from Eurystheus who was angry with Herakles and gave them Asine in the Argolid. [11] The Asinaians are the only people of the race of the Dryopes who are still proud of that name to this day, quite unlike the Euboians of Styra.[181] The people of Styra were originally Dryopes who took no part in the battle with Herakles as their houses were some way from the city. They loathe being called Dryopes just as the Delphians try not to be called Phokians, but the Asinaians are happiest when you call them Dryopes, and in their holiest sanctuaries they clearly recall the sanctuaries they once had on Parnassos: I mean their TEMPLE OF APOLLO, and their SANCTUARY OF DRYOPS and its ancient statue. Every year they celebrate a mystery for Dryops, and they say he is Apollo's son. [12] Their city lies beside the sea in the same way as Asine in the Argolid. The road here from Kolonides is five miles, and as much again

180. For the Asine 'near Hermione', which is actually just east of Nauplion, cf. Bk II, 28 (2), and Bk III, 7 (4). For the Messenian Asine, cf. Bk IV, 24 (4). It was the modern KORONI, where the ruins of a powerful and elaborate Venetian fortification are still standing with a few courses of reused ancient blocks still embedded in them, and there are some other classical bits and pieces. (Cf. Kevin Andrews, *Castles of the Morea*, Chapter 1 and n. 54.)

181. Herodotos talks about them (8, 46). Styra was on the west coast of southern Euboia north-west of Marathon. The site seems to be at the south of NEA STYRA bay. (Cf. *B.S.A.*, 61, 78–80, site no. 88 of the Euboian survey.)

from Asine to AKRITAS. Akritas juts out into the sea, with the
desert island of Theganoussa lying offshore; beyond Akritas
is the harbour of Phoinikous, and the islands opposite are the
OINOUSSAI.[182]

[1] Before the army gathered against Troy and during the 35
Trojan War MOTHONE was called Pedasos,[183] but the Mothon-
aians say it was renamed after Oineus's daughter; they say
Oineus son of Porthaon came back to the Peloponnese after
the fall of Troy to live with Diomedes and had a daughter
Mothone by a concubine; but my view is that the place got
its name from the rock Mothon, which is also what creates
the harbour there: it runs below the surface leaving a narrow
entrance for ships and makes a barrier against deep sea-
waves.[184] [2] I have explained in earlier discussions that when
the Nauplians were exiled as pro-Spartans under King
Damokratidas of Argos the Lakonians gave them Mothone,
and that they were left undisturbed even when the Messenians
returned.[185] In my opinion the Nauplians were Egyptians at
an earlier period who arrived in the Argolid with Danaos's
fleet and were settled three generations later by Amymone's
son Nauplios in Nauplia. [3] The emperor Trajan granted

182. The island off Cape Akritas is now called BENETIKO (Venice island).
The tiny island even farther south is called AVGO, the egg. The harbour of
Phoinikous, a name which is as likely to refer to palm-trees as it is to Phoeni-
cians, has been renamed with its old name. There are some Roman ruins. The
Islands are SAPIENZA, SCHIZA, HAGIA, MARIANE, the Bomb, and the Two
Brothers. Akritas is Cape GALLO, but it has now been renamed AKRITAS on
Greek maps.

183. North of the island of SAPIENZA on the south-west tip of Greece. It
was another of the cities Agamemnon offered to Achilles (*Iliad*, 9, 152 and
294). Its history as the Venetian fort of Modon has not obliterated its earlier
antiquity (cf. Bk IV, Note 24).

184. The *Mediterranean Pilot* calls this rock Sukuli point. It stands fifty-three
feet out of the sea; it has been joined to the fortress and has a round Venetian
tower on it (recently restored) which Leake described at the end of the
eighteenth century (*Morea*, 1, pp. 429f.). The classical mole was used by the
Venetians and still exists in a dilapidated state, though the harbour has silted
and has rocks in it, like most of the Venetian harbours in Greece, and in the
seventeenth century even the Piraeus.

185. Cf. Bk IV, 24 (4).

Mothone freedom and self-government. But at an earlier time they were the only coastal Messenians to suffer the following disaster: Thesprotian Epeiros had been ruined by lack of authority, as Pyrros's daughter Deidameia had no sons, and when she came to die she handed over everything to the people. She was the daughter of Pyrros and the grand-daughter of Ptolemy son of Alexander son of Pyrros.[186] [4] I have already explained the story of Pyrros son of Aiakides in my discussion of the Athenians; Prokles of Carthage gave higher marks for good luck and glittering successes to Philip's son Alexander, but for infantry and cavalry tactics and for inventive generalship he reckoned Pyrros was the better man.[187] [5] When the Epirotes abolished kings the people went out of control and disdained to listen to authority; so the Illyrians from the coast of the Ionian sea above Epeiros overran them. We have no record of anyone but the Athenians ever growing fat on democracy, though Athens made great progress on it: they overwhelmed Greece with their cleverness without the least disobedience to established law. [6] But the Illyrians, having tasted political power and longing for more and more of it, constructed ships and made pirate raids whenever occasion offered, and they put into Mothone and made a show of friendship. They sent a messenger into the city and asked for wine to be brought to the ships. When

186. The story of an Egyptian fleet in this area is told by Herodotos at the beginning of his history. For Danaos's fleet, cf. Bk II, 38 (4). Pyrros's daughter Deidameia died about the year 232. Pausanias is almost always democratic, an anti-tyrant and anti-monarchist, and even his occasional eulogies of Roman emperors are the merest formalities (with the same formula used for different emperors); but here he seems to have got hold of an anti-democratic tradition. Polyainos (8, 52) takes a similar view, and Ovid (*Ibis*, 307f.) uses members of the Molossian royal family as examples of a gruesome fate. No doubt the Molossians were a rough and wild people; their organization was still tribal in the fourth century, and the country where they lived was inaccessible, as indeed most of it still is. (Cf. J. K. Campbell, *Honour, Family and Patronage*, 1964.)

187. Bk I, 11 (1f.). Prokles of Carthage may have been a travel writer like Pausanias and not a historian. (This seems to be Jacoby's view, since he does not appear in *Fragments of the Greek Historians*.) Pausanias quotes him twice, here and at Bk II, 21 (6); otherwise he is completely unknown.

a few men came with the wine they bought it at the price it was offered for, and sold some of their own cargo. [7] The next day more people came from the city and they were allowed to make their profit as well. In the end men and women went on to the ships to give them wine and to get things in exchange. And now the Illyrians had the effrontery to carry away many men and even more women; they stored them into the ships and sailed for the Ionian sea, leaving the city of Mothone stripped.

[8] There is a SHRINE at Mothone of ATHENE of Winds; they say it was Diomedes who dedicated the statue and named the goddess. The countryside was being ravaged by violent, unseasonable winds, so he prayed to Athene, and from that time on no further calamities ever touched that earth so far as the winds were concerned.[188] There is also a SANCTUARY OF ARTEMIS here, and a well of water mixed with pitch: it looks just like the sweet ointment from Kyzikos: water can be any colour or smell.[189] [9] The bluest water I have ever seen was at Thermopylai: not all of it, but the water running into the swimming bath the local people call the Women's Pots. Water as red as blood is to be found in the country of the Hebrews, near the city of Joppe: this water is very close to the sea and the people there have a story about the spring, that when Perseus slaughtered the sea-monster to which Kepheus's daughter was offered, this is where he washed off the blood.[190]

188. It is still extremely windy and can be stormy. Philippson the geographer saw breaking waves here throwing up spray 150 feet into the air.

189. It was made of orris root, from a certain kind of iris.

190. Leake found the blue springs at Thermopylai, which are still running and now supply a small and squalid-looking bathing establishment. The swimming-bath was built by Herodes Atticus (Philostratos, *Lives of the Sophists*, 2, 1, 9). Perhaps Perseus washed off the monster's blood at Joppe because this is where Andromeda was chained to the rock (Pliny, *Natural History*, 5, 69, and Strabo, 16, 2, 28). Frazer found a well much farther north, near the village of *Sour*, on the promontory where *Tyre* is, with very good water that ran red in the month of September; but this is nowhere near the right place. Joppe is the same as Jaffa, which is now Tel Aviv. It is extremely rich in Hellenistic antiquities. Pausanias must surely have landed there to visit Jerusalem, where we know he went at some time.

[10] I myself have seen black water coming up from springs at Astyra, which is the name of the hot baths at Atarneus opposite Lesbos. The place called Atarneus is the wages paid to the Chians by the Persians for handing over a man who was formally begging for mercy: Paktyes the Lydian.[191] That water is black, and the Romans have white water: it is beyond their own city, across the river Anio, and if you go into it the immediate effect is cold and you shiver, but if you stay in for a little it heats you like the most feverish drug.[192] [11] These are the water-springs I have actually seen which genuinely amazed me: I know some that are marvellous only not so wonderful as these, but I will leave them out. Salt, brackish water is not a very extraordinary thing to discover. But there are two other kinds: in the White plain in Karia beside the village of Daskylos there is hot water which is sweeter than milk to drink, [12] and I know Herodotos says a spring of bitter water discharges into the river Hypanis. And how can we fail to accept the truth of what he says, when in our own time at Dikaiarchia in Campania they discovered some hot water so acid that in a few years it consumed the lead pipes it ran through?[193]

36   [1] To Cape Koryphasion from Mothone the road is about twelve or thirteen miles; that is where PYLOS is.[194] It was built

191. Atarneus was a deserted site when Pausanias visited it (Bk VII, 2 (11)). There are still abundant hot springs near the site, which is at DIKILI, east of Mytilene. The story of Paktyes comes from Herodotos (1, 160).

192. A small milky lake called SOLFATARA about fifteen miles from Rome towards Tivoli. It empties into a stream that discharges into the Anio. The Romans called it *Aquae albulae*.

193. Athenaios says the water at Daskylos was very oily; no one knows where Daskylos is, but it seems to have been somewhere near Ephesos. For the Hypanis, cf. Herodotos, 4, 52. The Hypanis is the Bug (in the Middle Ages it was the Bagossola or the Bogu). It runs out into the Black Sea at Nikolayev, near the ancient Olbia. The phenomenon of the salt springs was famous in the Roman period. Ovid (*Metamorphoses*, 15, 285) brings it into a list of paradoxical changes in the behaviour of rivers. Dikaiarchia was the Greek name for PUTEOLI, the port of Cumae, west of Naples. The ground is volcanic.

194. He is moving up the west coast of Greece. Koryphasion is the north point of NAVARINO bay, north of the northernmost of the two channels which

by Pylos son of Kleson, who brought the Lelegai from the Megarid which they occupied then. But he never enjoyed it, because Neleus and the Pelasgians from Iolkos threw him out; so he withdrew to the next place and occupied the Pylos in Eleia.[195] Neleus as king made Pylos so important that even Homer in his epic calls it city of Neleus.[196] [2] There is a SANCTUARY OF ATHENE there with the title Koryphasian Athene, and what they call NESTOR'S HOUSE, which has a painting of Nestor in it. Nestor's monument is inside the city, the one a little distance from Pylos is said to belong to Thrasymedes. There is also a CAVE inside the city, where they say Nestor and even before him Neleus used to herd their cattle.[197] [3] These cattle would have been Thessalian, and once would

---

make Sphakteria an island. There was certainly a prehistoric as well as a classical and a Hellenistic occupation of this site. The north part of Pylos bay seems to have silted up since Mycenaean times to form the lagoon protected by a sand-bar and flanked by marshes which it now is. (This used to be called the Osman Aga lagoon and is now called DIBARI.) Remains of prehistoric pottery have been found in several places in the lagoon. Presumably they represent the harbour area of prehistoric Pylos, which was no doubt identified as Nestor's Pylos in Pausanias's time because the Homeric epithet 'sandy' applied to it so conspicuously. But the important and sophisticated but provincial Mycenaean palace now called 'Nestor's palace' is further inland. It was found by American and Greek archaeologists, and Pausanias had never heard of its existence. It is extremely dubious whether 'Nestor' ever existed, but there was certainly a Mycenaean kingdom in this area. There is a castle on the crest of Koryphasion called AVARINOS, later called Old Navarino, built by the Frankish Marshal of Achaia about 1278. The late classical town stood below it on the north slopes, but at several points including two of the towers, the medieval castle still embodies powerful relics of classical fortifications.

195. Cf. Bk VI, 22 (5f.).

196. *Iliad*, 11, 682; *Odyssey*, 3, 4.

197. The Athene appears on the coins of Pylos, and a poem dedicating some captured weapons to Koryphasian Athene by Leonidas of Tarentum has survived in the *Palatine Anthology* (6, 129). The cave is not far below the castle on the northern slopes. Nestor's son's tomb must be the small Mycenaean *tholos* tomb nearby, above the tiny harbour called *Boïdokoilia*, where traces of worship in the classical period were found. He had a statue at Messene (Bk IV, 31 (11)) and occurred in genealogies (Bk II, 18 (8)). He occurs in both the *Iliad* and the *Odyssey* (in Book 3, home at Pylos after the Trojan War).

have belonged to Iphiklos the father of Protesilaos. Neleus demanded these heifers as a bride price from his daughter's lovers, and that was why Melampous went to Thessaly to please his brother Bias and was tied up by Iphiklos's herdsmen, and then got the cattle as wages for agreeing to prophesy when he was asked.[198] In those days they must have been mad about assembling wealth of this kind – herds of horses and cattle: when you think how Neleus longed for Iphiklos's heifers, and how because of the reputation of the Iberian cattle Eurystheus ordered Herakles to rustle Geryon's herd. [4] And Eryx who was a lord in Sicily at that period appears to have had such a powerful passion for the Erytheian heifers[199] that he wrestled against Herakles with those cattle and his kingdom for the prizes. And Homer in the *Iliad* has written how Antenor's son Iphidamas gave his father-in-law a hundred cattle for the beginning of his bride-price. It all confirms what I say, that in those days people were really fond of cattle. [5] In my opinion Neleus's cattle mostly grazed outside the borders, because the countryside at Pylos is all rather sandy and incapable of producing enough grass for that herd. I can bring Homer as my witness; he always calls Nestor king of sandy Pylos.[200]

[6] The island of SPHAKTERIA lies opposite the harbour, just as Reneia lies opposite the anchorage at Delos. Human fortunes seem to make places famous which were hitherto quite unknown; for example Kaphareus in Euboia where a storm hit Agamemnon and the Greeks on the journey home from Troy, and Psyttaleia at Salamis, which we know only because the Persians perished on it. In the same way the Lakonian disaster made Sphakteria universally familiar. The Athenians

198. Bias married Neleus's daughter Pero. Melampous's gift of prophecy consisted of understanding the voices of birds and listening to what they said. It was a reward for cleaning the ears of snakes with their tongues while they were asleep.

199. Erytheia is the same as Gades, which is the same as Cadiz, where Geryon lived.

200. For example, *Iliad*, 11, 244.

dedicated a bronze statue of Victory in the akropolis, in memory of what happened at Sphakteria.[201]

[7] When you reach KYPARISSIAI from Pylos, you see a water-spring near the sea below the city; they say this water first flowed when Dionysos struck the ground with his thyrsos, and because of that they call the spring Dionysias. There is also a SANCTUARY OF APOLLO at Kyparissiai and one of Athene under the title Kyparissian.[202] In what they call Aulon is a SHRINE OF ASKLEPIOS with a statue of Asklepios of Aulon and this is where the river Neda runs between Messenia and Eleia.[203]

201. For Kaphareus, cf. Bk II, 23 (1). It was the south-east tip of Euboia. The story of Agamemnon's storm is not in the Homeric poems, although Homer leaves room for it where Nestor in the *Odyssey* speaks of the separation of the fleets (3, 130–200; cf. Aischylos *Agamemnon*, 626). There is more than one allusion to it in Euripides. The story was presumably told at length in a lost epic poem. The small island in the straits of Salamis was touched by history in the famous sea-battle in 480 B.C. Sphakteria fell in 424.

202. Pausanias seems to be travelling by ship. The site of Kyparissiai, which is the modern town of KYPARISSIA, is guaranteed by an inscription copied there towards the end of the nineteenth century by a local priest, Father Eustathios Floros. Antiquities have often been found in the rather marshy ground between the castle and the sea; the remains of Apollo's TEMPLE are in this area, and in 1963 there were a few fragments of statuary kept in a small chapel. The spring called Dionysias may be the spring of HAGIA LOUGOUDIS, south-east of the harbour, which still has its ancient stones.

203. Aulon means the Hollow. It sounds more like a place than a town, and this is the sense in which Strabo and perhaps Pausanias refer to it. But we know from Pliny (*Natural History*, 4, 5, 14) and Valerius Flaccus (*Argonautica*, 1, 389) that this was the name of a town on the coast. Valmin seems to have found it, on a hill which is a spur of Mount KOUTRA where the mountains come close to the sea, between Kyparissia and the Neda, about 4 km. north of KALO NERO railway station and 1½ km. south of HAGIANNAKIS (*Messénie ancienne*, pp. 107–11). The ruins are now impenetrably overgrown.

# BOOK V
# ELEIA I

[1] Those Greeks who say there are only five divisions of the 1
Peloponnese must necessarily admit that both the Eleans and
Arkadians live in Arkadia, the second division must be
Achaian, and the Dorians must have three more.[1] The aboriginal races in the Peloponnese are the Arkadians and the
Achaians, and of these the Achaians were turned out by the
Dorians, though not right out of the Peloponnese because
they expelled the Ionians and cultivate ancient Aigialos, which
is now named after them,[2] [2] but from the beginning to this
day the Arkadians have continued in possession of their own
country. All the rest belongs to immigrants. The modern
Corinthians are the youngest Peloponnesians: in my day they
had held their territory by the emperor's grant for 217 years.[3]
The Dryopes and the Dorians arrived in the Peloponnese from
Parnassos and from Oite respectively.[4]

[3] We know the Eleians crossed over from Kalydon and
from all over Aitolia, and I discovered something about their
history even before that. They say the first king in this

1. The three Dorian divisions would be Lakonia, Messenia, and the Argolid.
The division of the Peloponnese into five may be a mistranslation of Thukydides, who says (1, 10, 2) that the Lakonians owned two parts out of five,
meaning simply two fifths. But Messenia did not exist in Thukydides' time, or
for some time afterwards, and a schematic division of the Peloponnese into five
could easily have arisen in that period. These tidy divisions do not correspond
exactly to the realities of any period; there were always independence and loose
organization on the edges of the map.

2. This is discussed in Book VII.

3. Corinth stood in ruins for a century after the Roman conquest. It was
restored as a Roman colony by Julius Caesar in 44 B.C. Pausanias is writing this
in A.D. 174 under Marcus Aurelius.

4. The story of all these migrations is an unwieldy mass of myths which had
been formalized by Hellenistic synthetic historians. Mount Oite is above
Thermopylai; Parnassos is above Delphi.

197

territory was Aethlios, who was a son of Zeus by Deukalion's daughter Protogeneia, and Endymion was his son: [4] the Moon was in love with Endymion and bore him fifty daughters.[5] But there exists a rather more likely story that Endymion married Asterodia – though some say it was Chromia, the daughter of Amphiktyon's son Itonos, and some say it was Arkas's daughter Hyperippe – and Endymion's children were Paion and Epeios and Aitolos and a daughter Eurykyda. Endymion held a race for the throne between his sons at Olympia, and Epeios won it and became king; it was then that the people were first called Epeians. [5] Of Epeios's brothers Aitolos stayed with him, but Paion was infuriated by losing and went as far away as possible: the country beyond the river Axios got its name Paionia from Paion.[6] The Eleians and the Herakleians near Miletos tell different stories about Endymion's death: the Eleians show you Endymion's tomb, but the Herakleians say he went away to Mount Latmos, where they honour him and have a holy place of Endymion.[7] [6] Epeios married Koronos's daughter Anaxiroe, and by her he had a daughter Hyrmina but no male offspring. Another thing that happened in Epeios's reign was this: Oinomaos son

5. Fifty has not only the status of a round number; it is the number of the children of Priam, of Aigyptos, of Danaos and of several other heroic broods.

6. Paionia lay north and north-east of Macedonia. The Axios, which in the Middle Ages was called the Bardari but which the Greeks have now renamed Axios, is the big river that runs down to the coast just west of Saloniki; its sources are in Yugoslavia, where it is still called Vardar. The international railway follows its valley northwards for a long way towards Belgrade.

7. For Endymion's grave in Eleia, cf. Bk VI, 20 (9). Herakleia near Miletos was an inland city south-west of Samos on the eastern shore of Lake BAFA at the foot of Latmos (Besparmak Dagi). There is a strange building at Herakleia, half the shrine of a divine hero and half a sanctuary of natural rock, which might belong to Endymion. The story about his going to Mount Latmos is that Zeus punished or rewarded him with perpetual youth and perpetual sleep; or else that the moon saw him asleep and loved him and kept him asleep for ever. Certain Christian fathers have maintained that Endymion was a saint, a mystic who tried to discover the name of God through the moon; his coffin was opened once a year in their time and the bones hummed melodiously.

of Alxion (though according to poets and in most people's version he is the son of Ares) was lord of Pisaia and lost his throne when Pelops son of Lydos crossed over from Asia.[8] [7] When Oinomaos died, Pelops occupied Pisaia and Olympia which bordered on Pisaia and which he annexed from Epeios's territory. The Eleians say Pelops was the first to found a temple of Hermes in the Peloponnese and to offer him sacrifice, to turn away the curse of the god because of the death of Myrtilos.[9]

[8] Aitolos, who reigned after Epeios, underwent exile from the Peloponnese, when the sons of Apis convicted him of manslaughter: Apis was a son of Jason from Pallantion in Arkadia, and Aitolos had run him over driving a chariot at the funeral games for Azan. Endymion's son Aitolos gave his name to the people living around the Acheloos;[10] he went into exile in that part of mainland Greece, and Eleios, who was the son of Endymion's daughter Eurykyda and (if you like to believe it) of Poseidon, took over the Epeian monarchy, and that people are now renamed Eleans instead of Epeians.

[9] Eleios's son was Augeas; the romanticizers of his story have twisted Eleios's name to claim that Augeas was a son of the Sun.[11] It was Augeas who had so many cattle and goats that most of his territory was lying idle under the dung of his beasts, so he persuaded Herakles either for part of his kingdom or for some other payment to clean the dung off the ground. [10] Herakles managed it by turning the streams of the Menios on to the dung,[12] but because the job was done without hard

8. Pisaia was an ancient territory near Olympia, which Elis had overrun long before Pausanias's time (cf. Bk VI, 21, (3) f.).

9. The story of Pelops and Oinomaos is told later (cf. Note 90 below).

10. For Pallantion, which lay south-west of Tripolis by Lake Taka, cf. Bk VIII, 43 (1f.) and 44 (5f.). Aitolos founded Aitolia on the mainland north of the north-west Peloponnese. The Acheloos reaches the sea at the south-west tip of mainland Greece.

11. The sun is *Helios*.

12. The Menios was a little river at Elis which must have flowed into the Peneios. The site of Elis is so wet as to require pumping but the Menios is not now distinguishable.

work but more by cleverness Augeas refused to pay him, and when his own elder son Phyleus complained he was repaying a kindness with an injury, he threw Phyleus out. Augeas was getting ready to fight in case Herakles marched on Elis, so he made friends with Amarynkeus and the sons of Aktor: [11] Amarynkeus was a good soldier whose father Pyttios was a Thessalian by origin who had come to Elis from Thessaly. Augeas gave Amarynkeus a share in the government of Elis, but Aktor and his sons were a local family with hereditary rights; Aktor's father was Phorbas son of Lapithos, and his mother was Epeios's daughter Hyrmina: Aktor founded a city named after her in Eleia.[13]

2   [1] Herakles did nothing to boast about in his war against Augeas: Aktor's sons were at the peak of their youth and daring, and always routed Herakles' allies until Corinth announced the peace of the Isthmian games; Aktor's sons were going to the games when Herakles ambushed and murdered them at Kleonai.[14] No one knew who the murderer was, so Moline took great care to find out who had assassinated her children, [2] and when she did discover, Elis demanded the murder penalty from Argos, where Herakles, who was at Tiryns, happened to be living.[15] Argos refused, so Elis demanded that Corinth should put the whole Argolid outside the peace of the Isthmian games. When they failed in this as well, the story is that Moline put a curse on her people unless they kept away from the Isthmian games. Moline's curse has been preserved to this day, and Elean athletes keep

13. This was a Homeric city (*Iliad*, 2, 616). It had already died out before the time of Strabo (8, 3, 10), bequeathing the name Yrmina or Ormina to some part of what is now Cape Kyllene.

14. South-west of Corinth (cf. Bk II, 15 (1)). Their route would have been through Arkadia and then by Phlious and Nemea from Lake Stymphalos.

15. Tiryns is a prehistoric fortress in the Argolid, south-west of Argos. Tiryns and Mycenae are not certain to have been subject to Argos in the Mycenaean period, but later poets imposed their own political geography. In Aischylos's *Agamemnon* when Agamemnon comes home from Troy he prays first to the gods of Argos.

the tradition of never entering for the Isthmian games. [3] But there are two other legends about it differing from this. One is that Kypselos the dictator of Corinth dedicated a gold statue to Zeus at Olympia, and when he died before inscribing his own name on it Corinth asked Elis to inscribe it as a public dedication from the city of Corinth: when this was refused the Corinthians were furious and excluded Elis from the Isthmian games. But how could the Corinthians go to the games at Olympia, if they kept the Eleans away from the Isthmian games against their will? [4] The other legend is that a distinguished Eleian called Prolaos and his wife Lysippe had two sons Philanthos and Lampos who were on their way to the Isthmian games for the boys' all-in fighting, and one of them was wrestling with the other boys before the games started when he was throttled or (however it happened) he was killed, so that the curse of Lysippe came on the Eleians unless they agreed to keep away from the Isthmian games. But this can be shown to be a stupid story too, [5] because Timon of Elis won the pentathlon more than once in Greece, and he has a portrait statue at Olympia with a verse inscription, saying how many wreaths Timon won, and also why it was he never won at the Isthmian games; what the verses say about it is this:

> but the dreadful death of Molione's sons
> kept him from the country of Sisyphos.[16]

[1] That is enough of these discussions. Afterwards Herakles 3 captured and looted Elis, with an army he collected from Argos and Thebes and Arkadia; the people of Pylos in Eleia and the Pisaians fought for Elis.[17] Herakles took vengeance

16. For Timon, cf. Bk VI, 16 (2). The two murdered boys are usually called sons of Molione (not Moline). They are a legendary pair of mighty twins or Siamese twins. The country of Sisyphos is Corinth.

17. The Pylos in Eleia (as opposed to the famous Pylos in Messenia where Nestor is supposed to have lived) was between Olympia and the city of Elis (cf. Bk VI, 22 (5)).

on Pylos but a prophetic command from Delphi stopped him marching on Pisaia:

*Pise to my father: Pytho to me in the mountain hollows.*[18]

That oracle saved the Pisaians, and Herakles handed over the Elean territory and the other things to Phyleus, not so much from his own will but out of respect for Phyleus: he let him have the prisoners and let Augeas go unpunished. [2] They say the Elean women prayed to Athene to make them conceive as soon as they slept with their men, because the country was stripped bare of its youth; and their prayer was granted, so they founded a SANCTUARY OF ATHENE under the title of the Mother. And as both the women and the men experienced extreme pleasures in that first coming together, they named the place Sweet and they named the river that flows past it in their local speech Sweetwater.[19]

[3] As soon as things in Elis were settled Phyleus went away to Doulichion,[20] Augeas met his death in old age, and Augeas's son Agasthenes held the throne of Elis, with Amphimachos and Thalpios: Aktor's sons had brought home the twin daughters of Dexamenos of Olenos, Amphimachos was the son of Kteatos by Theronike, and Thalpios was the son of Eurytos by Theraiphone. [4] But neither Amarynkeus himself nor his son Diores remained a commoner; and Homer has confirmed this in his Elean list, where he makes their whole fleet forty ships, with half under Amphimachos and Thalpios, ten of the other twenty under Diores son of Amarynkeus, and

18. That is, Pise (Pisaia is its territory) belongs to Zeus, just as Delphi belongs to Apollo. For the circumstances under which oracles like this were invented, cf. Parke and Wormell, *The Delphic Oracle*, 1, p. 342.

19. Bady (Vathy). It is apparently a dialect form of *hady*, the Greek word for sweet. An ancient commentary on Plato (*Phaido*, 89c) says it was somewhere between Elis and Dyme in Achaia, which must mean that it was north of the Peneios. Cf. Jacoby, *F.G.H.*, 3 fr. 79 (a).

20. Doulichion was either Kephallenia or one of the islands opposite the Acheloos estuary, north of the gulf of Patras. Phyleus went there first when his father threw him out of Elis.

ten under Agasthenes' son Polyxenos.[21] When Polyxenos came safely home from Troy he had a son Amphimachos – I suppose Polyxenos named him after his friend Amphimachos son of Kteatos who died at Troy – and Amphimachos's son was Eleios, [5] who was king of Elis when the Dorian expedition and the sons of Aristomachos gathered for the return to the Peloponnese. The kings received a prophetic command to take the three-eyed man for their guide. While they were in despair about what the oracle meant, a man happened past driving a mule that had lost one eye: [6] Kresphontes realized this was the man the prophecy referred to, so the Dorians made friends with him. He told them to enter the Peloponnese by ship, and not to attempt the isthmus with a land army. He not only gave them this advice but guided them on the voyage from Naupaktos to Molykrion,[22] and when he asked for the Eleian territory in return they agreed to give it to him. This man was Oxylos son of Haimon son of the same Thoas who helped the sons of Atreus to destroy the kingdom of Priam, and there are five generations from Thoas to Endymion's son Aitolos. [7] The children of Herakles were related to the kings of Aitolia, and, for example, the mothers of Thoas son of Andraimon and of Hyllos son of Herakles were sisters. And by coincidence Oxylos was an exile from Aitolia, as they say he threw wide with the discus and committed a manslaughter: it was his brother Thermios he killed with the discus, or some say it was Alkidokos son of Skopios.

[1] There is another story told about Oxylos, that he 4 suspected the sons of Aristomachos might refuse to give him Eleia when they saw how good the land was and how it was all under cultivation, so he guided the Dorians through Arkadia instead of Eleia.[23] Oxylos was anxious to take over

21. *Iliad*, 2, 615f.

22. Molykrion was not in the Peloponnese, but very close to Antirrion, on the north side of the straits at the entry to the gulf of Corinth. What he showed them was the narrow crossing.

23. Eleia is still one of the most highly cultivated areas in Greece; according to the latest reliable statistics between forty-five and seventy per cent of land

as sovereign of Eleia without a fight, but Dios would not give it up, and invited him to choose one soldier from each side to fight it out instead of risking a full-scale engagement. [2] Both sides liked the idea, and the men chosen to fight were Degmenos the Eleian bowman and Pyraichmes the Aitolian slinger. Pyraichmes won and Oxylos became king; he allowed the original Epeians to stay in their places, but he brought in Aitolians as their fellow-settlers with a new land distribution. He gave Dios rights and honours, and kept the ancient worship of divine heroes including the incinerations to Augeas, which are still going on in our own times. [3] They say he persuaded people from the villages that were not far outside his circuit wall to come into the city, and left Elis both stronger in population and richer in general. An oracle came to him from Delphi, telling him to bring in the son of Pelops as a fellow settler, so Oxylos made a careful search and discovered Agorios son of Damasios and grandson of Orestes' son Penthilos, and brought him in from Helike in Achaia, with a small following of Achaians.[24] [4] They say Oxylos's wife was called Peiria, but nothing else about her is recorded. They say Oxylos had two sons, Aitolos and Laias: Aitolos died first and his parents buried him and made his tomb right in the gateway towards Olympia and Zeus's sanctuary; they buried him there by the command of an oracle that his dead body should not lie inside or outside the city. Even in my time the head of the training-grounds still incinerates offerings to Aitolos every year.[25]

[5] After Oxylos his son Laias came to power, but I did not

is under cultivation; this figure is unrivalled in mainland Greece except in Macedonia and Thessaly. Eleia produces some of the best Greek wine.

24. Helike was one of the drowned cities of the southern side of the Corinthian gulf (cf. Bk II, 24 (5f.)). Orestes' father Agamemnon was the son of Atreus, and Atreus was the son of Pelops.

25. The gate of Elis leading south towards Olympia was near the great Elean *gymnasion*; the worship of divine heroes, divine heroic athletes and ancestors, is closely bound up with the routine of the *gymnasion*. The head of the training-grounds (*gymnasiarches*) was a public official.

discover that Laias's descendants were kings, so although I know who they were I am leaving them out, since I do not want my story to extend to private individuals. Later on Iphitos, who was descended from Oxylos and a contemporary of Lykourgos who wrote the laws of Lakonia, arranged the games at Olympia and re-established the Olympic festival and the Olympic truce all over again, which had died out for however many years it was; I shall explain why the Olympics were abandoned when I come to the part of this treatise which deals with Olympia.[26] [6] At this time Greece was being ruined by civil war and by plague; it was Iphitos who asked the god at Delphi for a cure for these troubles, and they say the Pythian priestess gave orders that Iphitos himself and the Eleans were to restore the Olympic games. Iphitos persuaded the Eleans to sacrifice to Herakles as well: until then the Eleans had thought of Herakles as an enemy. The inscription at Olympia[27] claims Iphitos was a son of Haimon, but most say he was Praxonides' son, not Haimon's; the ancient Elean records trace Iphitos to a father with the same name as himself.

[7] Elis took part in the Trojan War and served against the Persian invasion of Greece. When the dangers of their conflict with Pisaians and Arkadians over the management of the games at Olympia were over, they unwillingly joined the Lakonian invasion of Attica, and not long afterwards the Mantinean and Argive rebellion against Lakonia, and took Athens into the same alliance.[28]

26. The conventional first Olympics were in 776 B.C. Records were kept that went back to this date (at whatever date they were actually composed). The list of winners which made it possible to use the Olympic games as a dating system seems to have been diffused at the end of the fifth century by the savant Hippias of Elis who figures in the dialogue of Plato. For the legendary interruption of the Olympics, cf. Bk V, 8 (5).

27. The inscription on the discus (cf. Bk V, 20 (1)).

28. The Eleans were internally disorganized allies of the Spartans until they quarrelled over Lepreos in 420 B.C. The Elean dialect suggests they originally came from Aitolia. The city of Elis was apparently not built until about 470 B.C. There is no archaeological evidence about this since the site has not yet been thoroughly excavated, and the akropolis not at all.

[8] At the time of Agis's march on Eleia and Xenias's treachery, the Eleans won a battle at Olympia: they routed the Lakonians and drove them out of the sanctuary precinct.[29] Later on the war was finished by a treaty which I have already explained in my treatise on Lakonia.[30] [9] When Philip son of Amyntas refused to leave Greece alone, the Eleans were devastated by internal quarrels and they joined the Macedonian alliance, but they could not tolerate fighting on the anti-Greek side at Chaironeia, though they did take part in Philip's attack on Lakonia, because of ancient bitterness. When Alexander died they fought on the Greek side in the war against Antipater and the Macedonians.

5    [1] Later on Aristotimos son of Damaretos and grandson of Etymon turned Eleia into a dictatorship; he was helped to make the coup by king Antigonos of Macedon, Demetrios's son.[31] Aristotimos's dictatorship had lasted six months when it was put an end to by the rebellion of Chilon and Hellanikos and Lampis and Kylon; it was Kylon who assassinated the dictator when he fled to the altar of Zeus Saviour and begged for mercy.

That is the history of the wars of Elis, so far as I could give a reasonably short account of it for the present; [2] the surprising natural features of Eleia are firstly the linen flax, which grows only here and nowhere else in Greece, and secondly the fact that Elean mares are impregnated by donkeys outside the territory of Elis, but not inside it: the origin of this is supposed to be some curse. For its fineness Elean linen flax is just as good as Jewish, though not so tawny.[32]

[3] On the way from . . . in Eleia is a place that comes down to the sea called SAMIKON; inland of this on the right is what

29. Cf. Bk V, 20 (4f.).                    30. Bk III, 8 (5).

31. About 272 B.C. A few of his coins have been found. Plutarch discusses his atrocities in *De Mulierum Virtute* 15, in the story of Mikka and Megisto.

32. Almost certainly cultivated flax, *linum usitatissium*, though it is just possible that Pausanias could mean cotton. Wild flax (*linum bienne*) was fairly common in Europe from the neolithic period; it was cultivated for its seeds (linseed) and oil (as it still is in central Asia) before it was used for cloth. Colonel Leake is

is called Triphylia, and in Triphylia is a city called LEPREOS.[33]
The Lepreans claim to belong to Arkadia, but they appear to
have been Elean subjects from the beginning, and when they
have won at Olympia the herald has called them Eleans of
Lepreos. Aristophanes writes that Lepreos is an Elean town.[34]
There is a road to Lepreos from Samikon that leaves the river
Anigros on its left, another from Olympia and a third from
Elis: the longest is a day's journey.[35] [4] The city is supposed
to have got its name from its founder Lepreos son of Pyrgeus.
Lepreos was said to have taken on Herakles in an eating
match, each of them slaughtered an ox at the same time and
served it up for dinner, and Lepreos just as he said was as
powerful an eater as Herakles, and afterwards he dared to
challenge him with weapons: the legend is that Lepreos was
beaten and killed in the fight, and buried in the territory of
Phigaleia, though the Phigaleans are unable to show you
Lepreos's memorial.[36] [5] I have in the past heard people
attributing the foundation of Lepreos to Pyrgeus's daughter
Leprea, but there are some who say the first settlers in this

---

patronizing about the flax growing in Eleia around 1800, which he says was
coarse, but nineteenth-century Greek bed-linen is extremely comfortable. For
the birth of mules, cf. Note 77 below.

33. On the way north from the Neda, from Messenia? SAMIKON is the
coastal plain north of the Neda, so far as ZACHARO and Lake KAIAPHA. LEP-
REOS or Lepreon is the fine akropolis at HAGIOS DEMETRIOS north of the
modern LEPREON (which used to be called Strovitsi) on the road to Phigalia
from the coast. In 1891 the people of Strovitsi were gradually demolishing the
ruins for building materials; Dr Dorpfeld put a temporary stop to this, but the
older descriptions are fuller than anything which can now be written. Frazer in
his commentary on Pausanias is good about Lepreos, which he liked.

34. In the *Birds* (149-51) in 414 B.C. when Elis was an Athenian ally.

35. Frazer says it would take two days to walk from Lepreos to Elis: it is
about forty-five miles by a roundabout route over easy country; it is not much
farther than the walk from Athens to Thebes over Mount Parnes and considerably easier. Olympia is a hilly walk away but much closer. Samikon is an
afternoon walk. Frazer has a bulky appearance even in his youthful photographs, and confesses to a dislike of heat and steepness.

36. Phigalia is a little farther inland east-south-east of Lepreos, above the
gorges of the *Neda*. It belonged to Arkadia (cf. Bk VIII, 39 (1)).

territory contracted leprosy and the city took its name from that tragedy. The Lepreans said they used to have in their city a temple of Zeus of White Poplars and a grave of Lykourgos son of Aleos and a grave of Kaukon, with a figure of a man standing on it holding a harp;[37] [6] but in my time they had no distinguished monument or sanctuary of any god except Demeter: and even that was made of mud-brick and had no statue. Not far from the city of Lepreos is a water-spring called Arene, which they say took its name from Aphareus's wife.

[7] If you turn back to Samikon and pass right through it, you come to where the river Anigros runs out into the sea. Violent blasts of wind often push back the streams of this river, carrying up silt into it from the sea and damming back its water. When this sand has been thoroughly soaked by the sea on one side and the river on the other, there is the danger that a beast or even an athletic man can sink into it.[38] [8] This river Anigros runs down from Arkadia, from Mount Lapithos, and even right at the springs its water is not pleasant to smell but horribly displeasing. Before the Akidas runs into it, it is certainly quite unable to breed fish, and below this meeting-point the fishes that enter it with the Akidas water are not eatable, though if you catch them in the Akidas you

37. Probably Kaukon of the Andanian mysteries (cf. Bk IV, 1 (5), etc.). But there had once been a tribe called the Kaukonians here (Herodotos 4, 148), and there was a Kaukon who was supposed to be Lepreus's father. Zeus of the White Poplar (unless we should alter the Greek by one letter to read Zeus of Lykaion) would be an underworld Zeus; white poplar was burnt on Zeus's altar at Olympia, but most of the associations of white and still more so of black poplars in Greek religion are with the underworld. It was the shivering and fruitless tree that Herakles brought back from Hades. Perhaps the underworld character of these trees is to do with water and pot-holes. An experienced cave-club could do useful service in Greece, though it is at present illegal for civilians to enter Greek caves.

38. The marsh is Lake KAIAPHA, but continuous silting has altered the lie of the land here, and at some time in the nineteenth century the outlet of the lake became choked and it ceased to communicate with the sea. Colonel Leake calls the river that runs into it Mavropotamo. I am doubtful about the identification of any river easily visible in 1967 with the Anigros of Pausanias. (Cf. also Strabo, 8, 3, 19.)

can eat them.[39] [9] Nothing I know would have led me personally to suppose that the ancient name of the Akidas was Jardanos, but I have in fact heard this from an Ephesian, and I am saying what he said.[40] I am convinced that the peculiar smell of the Anigros comes from the earth in which the water rises, just as the breath of certain waters beyond Ionia is fatal to human beings for the same reason:[41] [10] though some of the Greeks say Chiron and others say that when the centaur Pylenor was shot by Herakles he ran away and washed his wound in this water, and the dragon's poison on the arrow gave a filthy smell to the Anigros; and there are some who trace what happened to the river to Melampous son of Amythaon and the things infected at the purification of Proitos's daughters which were thrown in here.[42]

[11] There is a CAVE not far from the river at Samikon belonging to Anigros's daughters the nymphs. The traditional law is that anyone who enters it with any kind of leprosy first prays to the nymphs and promises whatever sacrifice it may be, and then wipes the diseased parts of his body, and when he swims across the river he leaves his disgrace in its water, and comes out healthy and clear-skinned.[43]

[1] Across the Anigros along the straight road towards 6 Olympia, not very far and on the right of the road, is a high place with the city of SAMIA built on top of it. An Aitolian

39. The Akidas has not been identified with any certainty. Mount Lapithos seems to be the mountain immediately above the lake.

40. This is really a problem of Homeric geography (*Iliad*, 7, 135). Strabo speaks of Jardanos's grave and Jardanos's meadow between the marshes and the mountain.

41. Perhaps he means Strabo's hot springs at Hierapolis; the steam would kill you if you breathed it.

42. Herakles took the venom from the Hydra. For a substantial fee the holy man Melampous caught and cured two of Proitos's three daughters whom the gods had driven mad, and he and his brother married them.

43. There are two of these caves; Strabo says the other one belonged to Atlas's daughters. They are in the south face of Mount Kaiapha on the lake; they contain sulphur springs even more nauseous than the springs at Bath. Frazer says 'they emit foul mephitic vapours and inflammable gas', and this is putting it mildly. They are still in use as a bathing establishment.

called Polysperchon is said to have used it as a fortress against Arkadia.[44]

[2] No one in Messenia and no one in Eleia could show me exactly where the ruins of Arene are; a variety of mutually contradictory positions are open to anyone who feels inclined to make a conjecture, but it seemed to me that the most convincing story was that Samikon at an even earlier period than the heroic age was called Arene. The supporters of this view quote the *Iliad*:

> there is a river Minyeïos
> running into the sea close to Arene.[45]

[3] These ruins are extremely close to the Anigros, and although you might doubt that Samikon was called Arene, the Arkadians in fact agree that Minyeïos was the ancient name of the Anigros. One might well believe that the Elean coastal boundary with Messenia at the Neda belongs to the period of the return of the children of Herakles to the Peloponnese.[46]

44. At KATO SAMIKO. The akropolis is high up on a steep and slippery hill, and probably for that reason extremely well preserved. It is evident even from the visible remains that this site had a richer and more complicated history than Pausanias suggests. There are some traces of a massive prehistoric road or causeway in a field near the foot of the hill. There are traces of the lower city in the woods and under water south-west of the akropolis; antiquities are turned up by tractors. Both the buried ruins and the fragments of pottery extend well beyond the akropolis in several directions; there is at least one unexcavated rectangular bump on the hillside with the top of a column lying beside it. Strabo says there was a temple of Samian Poseidon nearer the sea. Dorpfeld's site for Pylos is not far away; it is a small Mycenaean akropolis just above the road; it is overgrown with flowers and bushes, and there is no visible trace of later reoccupation although just south of it (at KOLONES) there is a Roman site, perhaps a big villa. The last of the columns after which Kolones (a small farm) was named has been sawn in half for the grinding of salt; it was a small, undistinguished Roman pillar.

45. *Iliad*, 11, 723, cf. 2, 591.

46. And that originally Kato Samiko was in Messenia, or perhaps that the Minyeïos was the border, because Homer couples Arene with Pylos, and Nestor and the Messenian cavalry mustered at dawn by the Minyeïos for an expedition to raise the siege of Thryoessa, apparently a city subject to Pylos as far north as the Alpheios (*Iliad*, 11, 711–12).

[4] After the Anigros if you travel quite a long way through country which mostly has a sandy subsoil and is wooded with wild pines, you will see the ruins of SKILLOUS back on the left.[47] Skillous was one of the cities in Triphylia; in the war between the Pisaians and the Eleans Skillous supported the Pisaians and openly quarrelled with Elis, and so the Eleans rooted out the entire people from Skillous, [5] though later the Lakonians annexed it from Eleia and gave it to Xenophon son of Gryllos, who was by this time in exile from Athens.[48] Xenophon was exiled by the Athenians for serving with Cyrus, one of their worst public enemies, in a campaign against the king of Persia who was their friend; when Cyrus was at Sardis he gave money for the fleet to Lysander son of Aristokritos and the Lakonians. So Xenophon was exiled, and he settled at Skillous and built a sacred enclosure and a sanctuary and temple to Ephesian Artemis. [6] Skillous is stocked with wild pig and deer for hunting, and the river Selinous runs through this countryside.[49] The Elean officials

47. Probably at MAZI, an inland hill-village where antiquities are sometimes found, east of Lake *Agoulinitsi*, which is on the coast south of the Alpheios. I suppose this detour inland (through a landscape that has not altered much since Pausanias described it) was in order to reach the Alpheios, which even in summer is a dangerously powerful, tawny-looking, fast-running river, at a point where it could be crossed. A little way out of Mazi an early Christian basilica has been found on the foundations of a fourth-century Doric temple. (There are some sculptures from it in the Patrai museum.)

48. The war between Elis and Pise was in the early sixth century. Xenophon is of course Xenophon the historian and writer of pamphlets. He was a conservative, very religious squire and ex-soldier with his head full of notions, who liked riding and hunting and improved his estate and wrote his memoirs. There is an excellent account of his improvements at Skillous in the *Anabasis* (5, 3, 7–13). The site is said to have been found a year or two ago, but I have not visited it since.

49. The river Selinous runs into the Alpheios below Olympia. There are no deer in the Peloponnese now, and I do not think there are any wild pig; the wild boar one eats in Athens in winter comes from north Greece. Every kind of game has become scarce: fifty years ago quail and woodcock were abundant but now it is incredible that even an occasional thrush should survive the massive and indiscriminate slaughter of everything with feathers that takes place annually.

claimed that Elis took Skillous back, and that when Xenophon got the land from Lakonia he was tried by the Olympic council and lived freely in Skillous only because he was pardoned by Elis. And in fact a little way from the sanctuary they showed you a monument with a portrait on the grave in stone from the Pentelic quarry;[50] the local people say this is Xenophon's grave.

[7] On the way to Olympia before you cross the Alpheios as you come from Skillous there is a precipitous mountain with high rocks; the mountain is called Typaion. This is where the laws of Elis hurl down any woman detected entering the Olympic assembly or even crossing the Alpheios during the forbidden days; though they say not one has ever been caught with the single exception of Kallipateira: there are some people who call her Pherenike, not Kallipateira, but they mean the same woman. [8] Her husband died before her, so she completely disguised herself as a trainer and took her son to Olympia to fight; but when Peisirodos won, Kallipateira leapt over the fence where they shut in the trainers, and as she leapt over she showed herself. They detected she was a woman, but let her off scot-free out of respect for her father and her brothers and her son all of whom were Olympic winners, but they passed a law about trainers for the future, that they had to enter the arena naked.[51]

7   [1] As you arrive at Olympia you are already at the water of the Alpheios, the greatest of rivers in its volume of water, and the most pleasure-giving to the sight, because there are seven important rivers among the streams that run into it.[52] The Helisson that passes through Great City discharges into the Alpheios, the Brentheates from the same territory, the Gortynios that flows past Gortys and Asklepios's sanctuary,

50. From the mountain just north of Athens.

51. She was a daughter of Diagoras of Rhodes (Bk 7 (2)) who won at Olympia in 464 B.C.

52. Even in August the Alpheios at this point is the strongest river I have ever been into in Europe.

the Bouphagos from Melaineai between the Great City
territory and Heraian territory, the Ladon from Kleitor and
the river from Mount Erymanthos which takes its name from
the mountain: all these come down from Arkadia and run
into the Alpheios, and the Kladeios comes from Eleia and
mingles its streams in the same river, but the water-springs of
Alpheios itself are in Arkadia and not in Eleia.[53] And there are
other legends about Alpheios: how he was a huntsman and
fell in love with Arethousa who also hunted hounds, but
Arethousa did not want to marry, and so they say she crossed
over to an island opposite Syracuse called Ortygia; there she
turned into a water-spring, and Alpheios changed into a river
for love.[54] [3] That is the legend of Alpheios and Ortygia; but
the fact that the river passes through the sea to mingle its
water in the water of the spring is something I cannot dis-
believe, because I know the god at Delphi has confirmed it
when he sent Archias of Corinth to found Syracuse and spoke
these verses:

53. The Helisson which passes through Megalopolis (Great City) is called
the DABIA or the BARBUTSANA. The Brentheates is either the LANGADIA or
one of its near neighbours; which one depends on the site of Brenthe, which is
uncertain (Bk VIII, 28 (7)). The Gortynios is the DEMITSANA; it joins the
Alpheios north of Megalopolis, not far from Karytaina. It is also called the
Lousios (cf. Bk VIII, 28 (2)). The Bouphagos rose from a spring close to the
Alpheios near the site of Bouphagion west of the Lousios. (The site of Heraia
lies farther north-west, on a spur of the mountains above the place where the
Ladon and the Alpheios meet.) Melaineai was five miles from Bouphagion
(cf. Bk VIII, 26 (8)) near the modern villages of KOKKORAS and KAKOURAI-
IKA north of the Alpheios, a little east of due north of ANDRITSAINA. The
Ladon and the Erymanthos are the two big rivers that join the Alpheios from
the north eleven and ten miles east of Olympia.
54. Ortygia means 'quail island'. Syracuse was originally founded on
the island, which was always the akropolis of Syracuse. But by the fifth
century B.C. it was already joined to the mainland. Later in that century
or the next it was artificially reseparated. It was sacred to Artemis. The
fabulous spring is on the western shore near the southern point of the
island. Cicero, in his attack on Verres for looting Syracuse, calls it 'incredibili
magnitudine, plenissimus piscium'. He says the sea was prevented from overwhelming it only by artificial constructions. It now has a more domestic
look.

> *Somewhere in the misty field of the sea*
> *where Ortygia lies by Thrinakia*
> *Alpheios's bubbling mouth intermingles*
> *with Arethousa's streaming water-springs.*[55]

So I am sure it was because of this mingling of Alpheios's water with Arethousa that the river became fabulous for love. [4] Those Greeks or Egyptians who have been up to Aithiopia beyond Syene and the Aithiopian city of Meroe say that the Nile enters a lake and flows right through it and out again as if it were dry land, and then runs down through lower Aithiopia and into Egypt to flow out to Pharos and discharge into the sea there.[56] And I myself know a river Jordan in the Jewish country that travels through a lake called Tiberias and into another lake called the Dead Sea, where it enters and is swallowed up. [5] The Dead Sea behaves in the opposite way to all other water: living creatures are carried on the surface without swimming, and dead ones drop to the bottom. The lake produces no fishes, they rush back from it to their own water as if it gave the clearest danger signals. There is another river in Ionia that behaves like the Alpheios: its springs are on Mount Mykale, it crosses the sea between, and

55. Thrinakia means Sicily. This pleasant piece of oracle looks like part of a longer poem. Ibykos (Page, *Poetae Melici Graeci*, 323) and Pindar (*Nemean Odes*, I, I) knew a simple form of the same legend. The name Arethousa seems to have belonged first to a famous spring in Eubois near Chalkis which like the spring at Syracuse had fish in it. Professor Parke believes this oracle is genuine, in which case (since Syracuse was founded in 733 B.C.) it would have been written by a contemporary of Hesiod and of Homer. No one quotes it but Pausanias.

56. Syene was Assuan in upper Egypt. The kingdom of Meroe was over 400 miles farther south; it was the territory between the Nile, the Atbara and the Blue Nile above Khartoum. The site of the city of Meroe is on the east bank of the Nile near Bakarawiya. It has over 200 pyramids. Some reliefs from Meroe are in the British Museum. But it is possible that Pausanias says Aithiopian Meroe because he means Napata, the ancient capital of Aithiopia at the foot of Jebel Barkal, for which (probably by confusion) Meroe seems to have been an alternative name. Napata was farther north near Merawi. The capital city moved from Napata to Bakarawiya, apparently before the time of Herodotos. (In general, cf. P. L. Shinnie, *Meroe*, 1967.)

comes up again at Branchidai beside the harbour called Panormos.[57]

[6] All this is as I have said. The historians of the earliest Elean antiquity say of the Olympic games that Kronos was the first king in heaven, and the people of that time, who were called the people of the golden age, made a shrine to Kronos at Olympia; when Zeus was born Rea gave the child to the Daktyloi of Ida to guard; they were also called the Kouretes, and they came from Ida in Crete: Herakles, Paionaios, Epimedes, Iasios and Idas.[58] [7] Herakles who was the eldest set his brothers a race for a game and crowned the winner with a branch of wild olive. They had plenty of this wild olive: so much so that they piled up the foliage of it fresh to sleep on. The story is that Herakles brought the wild olive to Greece from the country beyond the North wind.[59] [8] Olen

57. Panormos was the port for Apollo's temple at Didyma (the Branchidai properly speaking are the early priests of Didyma who surrendered the sanctuary treasures to the Persians in the fifth century B.C. and fled to Persia, but Branchidai is sometimes used as a place-name). The temple was south of Miletos in Asia Minor; Miletos is south-east of Samos. There was a sacred road between Panormos and the temple (cf. Bk VII, 2 (6)). Richard Chandler, who was sent out to explore classical Asia Minor by the Dilettanti Society in the 1760s, found the port of Panormos 'over-run with thickets of myrtle, mastic and ever-greens' and found and traced this spring: 'I traced it to the gulf, which it enters at the head, after a very short course, full and slow' (Travels, 1817 edition, vol. I, p. 173).

58. Cf. Bk III, 25 (2), and the note there. The cave on Mount Ida where they kept the child Zeus is near Anoyia in central Crete on Mount PSILORITI (at 1,538 m., but the height of the mountain is 12,456 m.). It was recognized as a treasure-house of antiquities by a shepherd in the summer of 1884, dug by local people haphazardly for a year and then officially stripped by learned men (cf. American Journal of Archaeology, 1888, pp. 431f.). To understand the significance of the cave and the cult it is essential to digest Paul Faure's Fonctions des cavernes crétoises (1964), which cannot be distilled into a footnote.

59. Pindar in his third Olympian Ode says Herakles pursued the golden hind (does he mean a reindeer?) from Taygetos to the springs of the Danube, where Artemis welcomed him among the fine trees, and he persuaded Apollo's servants, the people beyond the North wind, to give him the wild olive to shade the end of the race-track at Olympia. It is interesting that a recent pollen analysis of the Mycenaean levels of a small but in the Mycenaean period populated and cultivated area of Messenia has indicated that the introduction of

the Lykian in his hymn to Achaiia was the first to write that Achaiia came to Delos from that country; and then Melanopos of Kyme sang in his ode to Opis and Hekaerge how they came to Delos from the North country even before Achaiia, and [9] Aristeas of Prokonnesos who also mentioned that country may perhaps have known more about them through the Issedones, for he says in his epic that he visited their country.[60] The Idaian Herakles has the glory of first arranging the games of that time and calling them Olympic; he decided they should be held in every fifth year because he and his brothers numbered five. [10] Some say Zeus wrestled there with Kronos himself for the throne of heaven, but some say he held the games as a celebration of his triumph. Among the winners they say Apollo raced Hermes and outran him, and beat Ares at boxing. This is why they say the Pythian flute tune was introduced for the jumping in the pentathlon, because that tune is sacred to Apollo and Apollo won matches at Olympia.

8    [1] Later on the legends say that Klymenos son of Kardys came from Crete in about the fiftieth year after Greece was flooded in Deukalion's time; he was descended from the Idaian Herakles, and held games at Olympia and founded an altar to his ancestor Herakles and all the Kouretes, giving

---

olive-farming on any significant scale was post-Mycenaean: like the Homeric poems it was apparently a product of the so-called Dark Ages after the Mycenaean collapse. But the Mycenaeans certainly had olives, since carbonized olives have been found on Mycenaean palace sites.

60. The land of the Hyperboreans beyond the North wind was Apollo's fairyland in the far north; he spent half the year there. Offerings arrived annually at Delos from a mysterious source in the remote north which was identified with that country. They travelled by what we now know were the trade-routes for amber. Olen is a legendary religious poet Pausanias was particularly fond of; Melanopos is a similar poet; the works of neither of them have survived. The poems he mentions were addressed to Delian divine heroines and were presumably hymns in use at Delos; they are hardly likely to have been genuinely ancient poems. Aristeas and his shamanistic magic journey were already known to Herodotos; unfortunately his poem too has perished (he is discussed in Boulton's *Aristeas*, 1965). The Issedones were the remotest central Asian tribe that the Greeks knew. Herodotos tells stories about them.

Herakles the title of the Helper. But Endymion son of Aethlios drove Klymenos from the throne and offered it as a prize to his sons for a race run at Olympia. [2] Pelops a generation later held the games for Olympian Zeus in the most memorable style the world had then seen, but his sons were scattered from Elis all over the rest of the Peloponnese, and Kretheus's son Amythaon, who through Kretheus was Endymion's cousin – as they say Aethlios was a son of Aiolos, which is a title of Zeus – Amythaon held the Olympics, and after him Pelias and Neleus together held them. [3] Augeas also held them, and so did Herakles son of Amphitryon when he took Elis: and one of the winners crowned by Herakles was Iolaos driving Herakles' mares. It was an ancient tradition to compete with someone else's mares: Homer writes of Menelaos using Agamemnon's Aithe at the funeral games for Patroklos, while the other horse was his own.[61] [4] Iolaos generally drove Herakles' mares; Iolaos won in the chariot race, and an Arkadian called Iasios won the horse race on a riding horse; and Tyndareos's sons won, Polydeukes at boxing and his brother in the foot race.[62] The story is that Herakles himself won the wrestling and the all-in fighting.

[5] After the reign of Oxylos, who also held the games, the Olympics died out until Iphitos. When Iphitos (as I have already said) restored the games, people had still forgotten the old days; little by little they remembered, and whenever they remembered something else they added it on.[63] [6] You can prove it: in the period when the Olympic games have been continuously remembered, the prize was first of all for a foot race, and Koroibos of Elis won it. There is no portrait of Koroibos at Olympia, but his grave is on the boundaries of Eleia. At the fourteenth Olympics they added the two-lap

61. *Iliad*, 23, 293f.        62. Kastor and Polydeukes, the Dioskouroi.

63. Cf. Bk V, 4 (5). We have now reached the beginning, or at least the conventional beginning, of the fourth-century Olympic records, which claimed to start with the first recorded Olympic games outside legends and fables, in 776 B.C. The legendary games in which the gods took part could not be disregarded, nor could they be given an exact date, and a divine example was claimed for every major change in the games as it was introduced.

race, and a Pisaian called Hypenos won the wild olive for it, and next time Akanthos the Lakonian won the long distance race.[64] [7] At the eighteenth Olympics they remembered the pentathlon and the wrestling: and two more Lakonians won, Lampis in the pentathlon and Eurybatos in the wrestling.[65] At the twenty-third Olympics they gave prizes for boxing: the winner was Onomastos of Smyrna, which by this time was already part of Ionia.[66] At the twenty-fifth they accepted the race for fully-grown horses, and Pagondas of Thebes and his team were proclaimed winners. [8] In the seventh games after those they took in men's all-in fighting and ridden horses: Krauxidas of Krannon's horse came in first, and Lygdamis of Syracuse beat the others who entered for the all-in fighting.[67] His monument is beside the quarries at Syracuse: whether Lygdamis rivalled Theban Herakles for his physical development I have no idea, but the Syracusans say so.[68] [9] There is no ancient record of the boys' contests, and the Eleans have simply established them as they wished. The boys' running and wrestling prizes were first offered at the thirty-seventh Olympics; Hipposthenes of Lakonia won the wrestling and Polyneikes of Elis won the running. Boy boxers were invited to the forty-first Olympics, and Philytas

64. For the site of Koroibos's grave, cf. Bk VIII, 26 (3). The fifteenth Olympics were in 720.

65. The pentathlon was running, jumping, javelin, discus and wrestling.

66. Smyrna was an Aiolian, not an Ionian city (Herodotos 1, 150). The city was taken over by Ionian refugees from Kolophon. This change of allegiance has been confirmed by the evidence of pottery. The city fell before 688, in the reign of Gyges of Lydia who had taken Kolophon and created the Kolophonian refugees.

67. Racing on ridden horses started with the thirty-third Olympics, in 648. Horses were driven in harness long before they were ridden. Homeric and Olympic chariot-horses ran without traces, like nineteenth-century fire-engine horses, but the art of riding is post-Homeric in Greece. Chariot-horses in traces are often represented in archaic and classical art. The earliest representations of riders in Greek art so far as I know are on the ripe geometric painted vases of the Argolid which are a century earlier than 648.

68. He is supposed to have been not only strong but physically enormous; he had particularly large feet. Nothing is known about his tomb at Syracuse, though the quarries still exist.

of Sybaris beat the other boys who entered.[69] [10] The race in armour was tried at the sixty-fifth Olympics, I suppose for the sake of military training. The first winner among the runners racing with shields was Damaretos of Heraia.[70] The race for couples of fully-grown horses called the Pair was held at the ninety-third Olympics, and Evagoras of Elis won it. At the ninety-ninth Olympics they decided on a race for teams of foals, and the wreath went to a Lakonian called Sybariades with his chariot and his foals.[71] [11] Later they added a pair of foals and a ridden foal: they say Belistiche, a woman from the coast of Macedonia, won with the pair, and Tlepolemos the Lykian was proclaimed for the ridden foal, Tlepolemos at the hundred and thirty-first Olympics and Belistiche two games before.[72] At the hundred and forty-fifth games they held all-in fighting for boys, and Phaidimos won it: he was an Aiolian from the city of Troas.[73]

[1] Contests at Olympia have also been abolished, when the 9 Eleans decided to stop holding them. For example, there was a boys' pentathlon at the thirty-eighth Olympics; Eutelidas of Lakonia won the wild olive at it, and the Eleans felt it was better from then on for boys not to enter for the pentathlon.[74] The race for carts and the trotting race were instituted, one at the seventieth and the other at the seventy-first Olympics, and Elis made a proclamation about them both at the eighty-fourth

69. Running and wrestling in 632, and boxing in 616.

70. In 520.

71. Pairs of horses in 408 B.C., and full teams of foals in 384 B.C.

72. Belistiche in 264 B.C. (there is a controversy about the spelling of her name), and Tlepolemos in 256.

73. In the year 200. In every age the new sports were more violent and more spectacular, except that the only novelties introduced between 520 and 200 were various new kinds of horse-races.

74. In 628: that is, in 632 B.C. boys ran and wrestled, and in 628 they tried the pentathlon. It was not a success, but from 616 onwards they were allowed to box. All-in fighting was never open to boys until the late Hellenistic age. It seems clear from the evidence of art and of Olympic age-groups that adolescence occurred later in classical Greece than it does now in England: it occurs now in England up to two years earlier than it did in 1939, presumably because of better food. The boys at Olympia seem to have been sixteen or so.

Olympics that in future there would be no carts and no trotting.[75] When these races were first held Thersios of Thessaly
won with his cart, and Pataikos, an Achaian from Dyme, won
the trotting. [2] The beasts in this race were mares, and on
the last lap the mounters jumped off and ran with the mares,
holding their bridles just as the mounters (as they are called)
still do in my time.[76] The difference between the mounters
and the trotting race is their insignia, and the fact that they
use colts and not mares. There was no ancient origin or beauty
attaching to the carts, and Elis was under an ancient curse if
the beast was even born in their country: the carts had a
couple of mules instead of horses.[77]

[3] The ordering of the games in our own time, with the
victims sacrificed to the god after the pentathlon and the
horse racing but before the other contests, was instituted at
the seventy-seventh Olympics;[78] until then men and horses
alike competed on the same day, but on that occasion the all-in
fighters fought on into the darkness, not having been called
in time because of the horses, and still more because of the
pentathlon. Kallias of Athens in fact beat the other all-in
fighters, and for the future the pentathlon and the horses
would never again hold up the all-in fighting.

[4] The arrangements nowadays for presidents of the games
is not the same as the ancient tradition: Iphitos held them on
his own and so did those who followed Oxylos, but at the
fiftieth Olympics[79] two men chosen by lot from all Elis were
given charge of the games, and after that double presidency
lasted a very long time. [5] At the ninety-fifth Olympics[80]

75. The proclamation was in 444, and the races ceased from 440. These two
races had lasted under sixty years.

76. The mounters had to jump on and off their moving chariots; the effect
must have been something like Cossack acrobatics. There is a stone relief
representation of this event in the colonnade of the Agora museum at Athens.

77. For the ancient curse, cf. Bk V, 5 (2). In the Mani until well within
living memory all the male donkeys were kept in villages on one side of the
mountains and all the females on the other. They were allowed to meet only
once a year in a particular village about which there are a lot of jokes.

78. In 472 B.C.          79. In 580.          80. In 400.

they appointed the nine Greek Arbiters, three were put in charge of the horse racing, three were inspectors of the pentathlon, and the rest took care of the other contests. At the next Olympics after this they added a tenth judge. At the hundred and third, ône man from each of the twelve Elean tribes became a Greek Arbiter.[81] [6] But Elis was put under pressure by Arkadia: they lost a part of their land and the population of the annexed territory, so at the hundred and fourth Olympics they were reduced to eight tribes, and

7. *Olympia*

they chose the corresponding number of Greek Arbiters. At the hundred and eighth Olympics they went back to having ten men and that arrangement has survived to this day.[82]

[1] There are a lot of truly wonderful things you can see 10 and hear about in Greece, but there is a unique divinity of

81. In 368.
82. There was trouble in 364 B.C., but in 348 arrangements were regularized. (There is a textual problem about this whole passage.) After Leuktra (in 371) Lakonia abandoned Triphylia, which then applied for membership of the Arkadian federation, and was granted it in 368. Elis had owned Triphylia until 402 and regarded this as an annexation by Arkadia.

disposition about the mysteries at Eleusis and the games at Olympia.[83]

From antiquity by an alteration of the common name, they have called the sacred grove of Zeus by the name ALTIS; this place was called Altis by Pindar in a song he composed for an Olympic winner.[84] [2] The TEMPLE and the statue to ZEUS were built from spoils when Elis and the local people who joined the rebellion captured Pisa.[85] It was Pheidias who made the statue, as an inscription written below Zeus's feet bears witness:

*Pheidias the son of Charmides from Athens has made me.*

The style of workmanship of the temple is Doric, with a pillared portico around it; it is made of local stone. [3] Its height up to the pediment is sixty-eight feet, its width is ninety-five, and its length is two hundred and thirty; the architect was a local man called Libon. The roof-tiles are not terracotta, but Pentelic stone worked like tiles; they say this was invented by a Naxian called Byzes, whose son they say made the statues in Naxos that have this inscription:

83. OLYMPIA is inland on the Alpheios near PYRGOS in an unusually gentle but grand landscape which to classical sensibility was extremely beautiful. It was a sanctuary on the flat sandy ground by the Alpheios. In 1723 the great antiquarian Montfaucon tried unsuccessfully to persuade Cardinal Quirini, the Latin Archbishop of Corfu, to explore it. Winckelmann himself projected an Olympian expedition in the mid-century. It was in fact found by Richard Chandler in 1766. It has been the scene of the greatest triumphs of German archaeology in Greece.

84. Altis is a form of the word *alsos*, which means a wood; Pindar's song is the eleventh Olympic ode (55).

85. That is in 471, when sovereignty was formally transferred to the new democratic city of Elis. The destruction of Pisa by Elis and the looting of the Pisaian territory are highly problematic events. But the claim of the new Elis which emerged from the Persian Wars to control Olympia is reflected in the coinage of Elis from exactly this period onwards. From 470 sacred building enterprises in Altis ceased to be piecemeal and were controlled by the Eleans. The temple of Zeus seems to have been started in 468 and finished in nine years.

*Euergos of Naxos, son of Byzes the first maker
of tiles of stone, made me for Leto's children.*[86]

This Byzes lived in the time of Alyattes the Lydian, when
Astyages the son of Kyaxares was King of Persia.[87] [4] There
is a gilded basin at Olympia at either edge of the temple roof
and a Victory which is also gilded standing just about the
centre of the pediment. A gold shield with the Gorgon
Medusa worked on it has been dedicated at the foot of the
statue of Victory. The inscription on the shield shows who
dedicated it and why; what it says is this:

> *The temple keeps the golden circle:
> Lakonians and allies dedicated the gift
> from Tanagra:
> the tithe of Argos, of Athens, of Ionia,
> for victory in war.*

I mentioned this battle in my treatise on Athens, when I was
going through the Athenian monuments.[88] [5] On the outside
of the band that runs above the pillars of the temple at
Olympia there are twenty-one gilded shields dedicated by the
Roman general Mummius when he won the war against
Achaia and took Corinth and rooted out the Corinthian and
Dorian people.[89] [6] On the front pediment Pelops's horse-
race with Oinomaos is just going to start and they are both
getting ready. Zeus's statue is just in the middle of the gable,

86. That is, for Apollo and Artemis. Measurements like these were available
in guide-books to Olympia at least as early as the third century B.C. They appear
to be more or less accuate. Kallimachos (*Iamb.* 6 = fr. 196) had already
described the statue and given the measurements in verse. The geologist
Lepsius (*Griechische Marmorstudien*, 1890) has identified Naxian marble roof
tiles from several early temples. Some Pentelic marble tiles have been found
at Olympia, but they represent repair; the original roof seems to have been
Parian marble, which is so fine-grained as to be nearly translucent.

87. Byzes lived in the seventh century.

88. Cf. Bk I, 29 (9). The battle was in 457 B.C.; this is where we get the
*terminus ante quem* for the completion of the temple. Some fragments of this
inscription have been recovered: the verses were not on the shield itself but on
a block of marble the shield rested on. Still, Pausanias can hardly be blamed for
not scrambling about the pediment.

89. Cf. Bk VII, 15 (1) to 16 (10).

Oinomaos is on Zeus's right putting his helmet on his head,
with his wife Sterope who was one of Atlas's daughters beside
him, and Myrtilos who drove Oinomaos's chariot sitting in
front of the horses, of which there are four. Behind him there
are two men, who have no names, but Oinomaos must have
given the job of looking after his horses to them as well.[90]
[7] Kladeos is lying down at the very edge: Kladeos receives
in general more honours in Elis than any other river except of
course Alpheios.[91] Left of Zeus are Pelops and Hippodameia
and Pelops's driver and horses, and two men who must be
Pelops's grooms. Just here where the pediment narrows
towards its point, Alpheios is represented. The Troizenian
legend is that the man driving for Pelops is called Sphairos,
but the sacred guide at Olympia said it was Killas.[92] [8] The

90. The front of most Greek temples is the eastern end, and the cult-statues
regularly face east. (The shrines of divine heroes are not bound by this law.)
The impressive series of the east and west pediment sculptures from the temple
of Zeus at Olympia have been recovered and reconstituted by German archaeologists over a hundred years; the mass of this work was done by Georg Treu.
The exact arrangement of the figures is still controversial (cf. Ashmole and
Yalouris, *Olympia*, 1967). Pelops wanted to marry Oinomaos's daughter
Hippodameia, but Oinomaos loved his own daughter, so he proposed a race
in which Pelops was to win and have the daughter or be killed. Pelops bribed
the charioteer Myrtilos to wreck Oinomaos's chariot. Later Pelops murdered
Myrtilos for claiming a share in the girl: Myrtilos cursed him, and the curse
descended to his children. Pausanias is wrong about the two grooms. The old
man crouching on the ground behind Oinomaos's horses is certainly a prophet,
almost certainly Iamos who foresees disaster; the kneeling figure beside him is
not a man, it is a girl in a long plain dress like a chariot-driver's. Professor
Ashmole believes Pausanias is wrong again about Myrtilos: the boy crouching
in front of the horses has a young-looking body and no pubic hair and is therefore too young to drive them, so he cannot be Myrtilos, and Pelops must have
won the race simply by using Poseidon's horses. I find this unconvincing; the
boy looks old enough and strong enough to be Myrtilos. (Cf. Note 74 above.)

91. The Kladeos is the rather depressed stream that runs along the west side
of Altis to join the Alpheios not far beyond the south-west corner of the
excavations. The Kladeos comes to life in winter; one can measure its power
by the ground it has eaten away. Kladeos and Alpheios are the earliest representations of Greek rivers in sculpture.

92. Pelops's grooms are another mistake; one of them is an old prophet
crouching on the ground who foresees victory, probably Klytios. Klytios and
Iamos were the fabulous founders of the two resident prophetic families of the

front pediment is by Paionios, who came by descent from Mende in Thrace, but the rear pediment is by Alkamenes, a contemporary of Pheidias, and second only to Pheidias in his genius as a sculptor.[93] His subject for the pediment is the battle of Lapiths and Centaurs at Peirithous's marriage. In the centre of the pediment stands Peirithous; beside him on one side is Eurytion carrying off Peirithous's wife and Kaineus fighting for Peirithous; on the other Theseus is fighting the centaurs with an axe, one of them has carried off a fine young girl and another a fine young boy. I believe Alkamenes made these pieces because he was taught in Homer's poetry that Peirithous was a son of Zeus and he knew that Theseus was Pelops's great-grandson.[94]

[9] Most of the labours of Herakles are represented at

---

Olympic sanctuary. For Sphairos, cf. Bk II, 33 (1). Killas (Killos) was a divine hero whose bones were worshipped at a mound beside the sanctuary of Killaian Apollo in Lesbos; he was supposed to have died there and asked Pelops in a dream to bury him.

93. The east pediment sculptures are almost certainly not by Paionios of Mende, whose work we know from a statue he carved soon after 425 B.C. and whose style was different. What he certainly did carve was the akroteria, the figures on the points of the roof (cf. Bk V, Note 253). There are also ponderable but less easily verified objections to Alkamenes. We know he was still working as late as 403 B.C. and the pediment sculptures are surely not the work of an apprentice? Yet Alkamenes was Pheidias's apprentice, and if you think of the work of the young Michelangelo, you may choose at least not to exclude the possibility that the sculptures of both pediments were the work of a young man.

94. Iliad, 2, 741. The king of the Lapiths invited Theseus and all the centaurs to his wedding: the centaurs got drunk and tried to rape the women, but Theseus and the Lapiths killed them or drove them away. Most scholars agree that the central figure is Apollo (since it had a long bow in its left hand) and not Peirithous. This problem is a matter of intuitions and imponderables. It is very hard to believe so commanding a presence is not that of a god; if it is a god it is certainly Apollo. Once again there is a problem of arrangement; Theseus and Peirithous should stand one on each side of the god and back to back. (They may one day be moved to the new Olympia museum but in 1968 they were still wrongly placed.) Pausanias's Kaineus is really Peirithous. There are clear evidences that a restorer has worked on certain figures in the west pediment, probably after an earthquake in the Hellenistic period. (Was it Damophon?)

Olympia: above the temple doors you see the hunting of the Arkadian boar, the labour with Diomedes the Thracian, the labour with Geryon at Erytheia, and Herakles on the point of taking over Atlas's burden, and clearing the ground of dung for the Eleans; over the rear doors he is taking the Amazon's belt, and you see the story of the hind and the bull of Knossos and the Stymphalian birds and the many-headed dragon and the lion of the Argolid.[95] [10] As you go in through the bronze doors it is Iphitos crowned with a wreath by a woman called Truce who is standing in front of the pillar on your right, as the couplet tells you. There are columns inside the temple as well, with upper galleries by which you can approach the statue, and a way up to the roof by a spiral staircase.[96]

11      [1] The god is sitting on a throne;[97] he is made of gold and

95. These fine sculptures have been recovered. S. Stucchi, writing in the *Annuario* of the Italian School of Archaeology at Athens (1952-4, pp. 75f.), has shown that the twelve labours of Herakles were not in their original positions when Pausanias saw them. (Cf. also Ashmole and Yalouris, *Olympia*, pp. 24-5.) The boar came down from Mount Erymanthos in the north-west of Arkadia; Herakles chased it through deep snow until it was tired, netted it, and carried it home to King Eurystheus of Tiryns who hid from it in a pot. He satisfied the man-eating horses of Diomedes by feeding them their master. He stole Geryon's cattle from Cadiz; Geryon had three bodies and Herakles killed all three. He held up the world for Atlas and cleaned the accumulated dung from Augeias's farmyard by damming and turning a river (Athene shows him where to break the dam). He killed an Amazon to get her belt, captured Artemis's hind alive, and caught the great bull of Knossos with a rope. He wrestled with the lion and cauterized the stumps of the many-headed dragon of Lerna (the Hydra) to prevent regrowth. He brought home the dead birds of the Stymphalian marshes to Athene. Pausanias has left out the dog of Hades, which we know existed since it was recovered by the French who dug here in 1829, and was taken to Paris; those fragments are now in the Louvre.

96. Iphitos the restorer of the games, crowned by the Olympic truce. These internal staircases leading to the attic seem to have been particularly common in early-fifth-century temples in the Western Greek overseas settlements. The dedications at Olympia also how a strong connexion with *Magna Graecia*.

97. The famous masterpiece is represented on the coinage of Elis. Pausanias's glittering description is closer to Paul the Silentiary on Hagia Sophia than it is to the white classical marbles we are used to. Quintilian says this statue added something to human religion. Paulus Aemilius when he saw it said it was the Zeus of Homer. It perished in a burning palace in the fifth century A.D. in Constantinople.

ivory. There is a wreath on his head like twigs and leaves of
olive; in his right hand he is holding a Victory of gold and
ivory with a ribbon and a wreath on her head; in the god's
left hand is a staff in blossom with every kind of precious
metal, and the bird perching on this staff is Zeus's eagle. The
god's sandals are gold and so is his cloak, and the cloak is
inlaid with animals and flowering lilies. [2] The throne is
finely worked with gold and gems, and with ebony and with

8. Olympian Zeus

ivory. There are animals painted on it and figures worked on
it: and four Victories dancing on the four feet of the throne,
with two more at the bottom of each of the four feet. On the
two forward feet the Theban children are being carried off
by sphinxes and under the sphinxes Apollo and Artemis are
shooting down Niobe's children.[98] [3] Between the feet of the
throne there are four bars stretching right across from one
foot to another; the first begins with seven figures, but the
eighth, no one knows how, has become indecipherable: they
could be representations of the contests of antiquity, as in
Pheidias's time the boys' contests had not been instituted.
They say the one tying the ribbon round his head looks like

98. Niobe boasted her children were more beautiful than Artemis and
Apollo.

Pantarkes, an Elean adolescent who was Pheidias's boy-friend, and who in fact won the boys' wrestling at the eighty-sixth Olympics.[99] [4] On the other bars is Herakles' regiment fighting the Amazons. The number of figures on both sides is twenty-nine, and Theseus is serving with Herakles' allies. The throne rests not only on the feet but also on four columns standing between them. It is impossible to get underneath the throne in the way that we got inside the throne at Amyklai;[100] at Olympia there are barriers like walls to keep you out. [5] The part of these barriers facing the doors is only coloured blue, but the rest of them have paintings by Panainos.[101] One of them is Atlas holding up heaven and earth, with Herakles standing by ready to take over the weight; Theseus and Peirithous are there, and Greece and Salamis with the decorations of a ship's prow in her hand, also Herakles' struggle with the Nemean lion and [6] Ajax's crime against Kassandra.[102] Oinomaos's daughter Hippodameia is there too with her mother, and Prometheus is still held in his chains with Herakles coming through the air towards him; this is another legend about Herakles: that he killed the eagle who was torturing Prometheus in the Caucasus, and took Prometheus out of his chains. Finally in these paintings Penthesileia is breathing her last breath and Achilles is holding her up, and there are two Hesperides carrying the apples which legend says they were set to guard. Panainos was Pheidias's brother, and the battle of Marathon in the Painted Colonnade at Athens is also by him. [7] On the topmost part of the throne above the statue's head Pheidias has carved three Graces and three Seasons. Epic poetry tell us they were among Zeus's daughters, and Homer

99. Cf. Bk VI, 10 (6).     100. Cf. Bk III, 18 (9f.).

101. Panainos was Pheidias's nephew or perhaps his brother. His painting style, particularly in these simple two-figure compositions, cannot have been very different from that of contemporary vase-painters.

102. Sacrilege (because she was a formal suppliant) and perhaps rape in the temple of Athene at the fall of Troy. The goddess very properly drowned him or thunderblasted him on the way home to Greece. He was a Lokrian, and at the time this picture was painted the Lokrians were still sending young girls to the temple of Athene on the site of Troy, to pay for the crime of Ajax.

has written in the *Iliad* that the Seasons were given charge of
heaven like some kind of royal palace guards.[103] The stool
under Zeus's feet, which in Attica they call a *thranion*, has
golden lions worked on it and Theseus fighting the Amazons,
the first Athenian act of valour outside civil war. [8] On the
platform that holds up Zeus and all the decoration that goes
with him there are golden figures of the Sun mounting his
chariot, and Zeus and Hera and . . . with a Grace, followed
by Hermes,[104] who in turn is followed by the Hearth goddess,
and then Eros welcoming Aphrodite as she rises from the sea,
and Persuasion crowning Aphrodite with a wreath; Apollo
with Artemis is worked on it, Athene and Herakles, and right
at the end of the platform Amphitrite and Poseidon, and the
Moon who I think is driving a horse; some people have said
the goddess rides on a mule and not a horse and they tell some
silly story about the mule.[105]

[9] I know the recorded measurements of the height and
breadth of Zeus at Olympia, but I find myself unable to
commend the measurers since the measurements they give
fall a long way short of the impression this statue has created
in those who see it, who say even the god himself bore witness
to the art of Pheidias: when the statue was completely
finished, Pheidias prayed to the god to make a sign if the work
pleased him, and immediately a flash of lightning struck the
pavement at the place where the bronze urn was still standing
in my time.[106]

103. *Iliad*, 5, 749f. The gates of heaven and heaven itself and the peak of
Mount Olympos belonged to the Seasons, who could open and shut the barriers of clouds.

104. Could the missing word be Hephaistos, who was married to a Grace, or
could it be Dionysos? or Ares?     .

105. The two horses left on the east pediment of the Parthenon are the last
of the moon's tired team of horses and the sun's eager team of horses. Frazer
produces what he considers a silly story from Festus, that the moon and the
mule are both barren, but I doubt if this is silly enough to be the right one,
particularly in view of the Elean prejudice against mule-breeding.

106. Already in the third century B.C. Kallimachos in his sixth iambic poem,
which was dedicated to an intending tourist, gives minutely detailed measurements of the Zeus of Olympia, and we have them from several later sources.

[10] The paving in front of the statue is not made of white stone but black, with a rimmed circle of Parian stone running round it to stop the oil poured out there, as oil is good for the statue at Olympia, and oil is what keeps the ivory from taking harm in the marshy atmosphere of the Altis. What the ivory needs in the statue called the Parthenon in the upper city at Athens is not oil but water, the upper city being dry because of its extreme height, so that the ivory statue is longing for water and dampness. [11] At Epidauros when I asked why neither oil nor water was poured out for Asklepios, the sanctuary people explained that the god's statue and throne are constructed on top of a well.[107]

12   [1] Those people who believe what sticks out through elephants' mouths is teeth and not horns ought to consider the elk, the Celtic animal, and also Aithiopion bulls: male elks have horns on their eyebrows whereas the female has none at all, the Aithiopian bulls grow horns on their noses, so who would be greatly surprised if an animal grew horns out through its mouth?[108] [2] And there is another way of seeing that this is true: year by year animals lose their horns and grow them again: it happens to deer and to gazelles, and in just the same way it happens to elephants. But no tooth ever grows a second time for any adult animal, so if it were teeth that came out from the mouth and not horns, how could they grow again? And anyway teeth are not subject to fire, but

107. Pieces of the water-basin from the Athenian akropolis have in fact been found. Asklepios at Epidauros stood in a closed white marble rotunda which later, like the west end of the temple of Zeus at Olympia, became the tower of a Byzantine fortress. Its foundations are very deep concentric stone walls. Most of the rotunda, including its black and white marble floor, is now in the museum of the Asklepieion, though there are bits and pieces built into local churches as far afield as LIGOURIO. The ivory of Olympian Zeus did in fact crack; it was repaired by Damophon of Messene (cf. Bk IV, 31 (6)). The trouble was probably not so much in the ivory as in the wooden core of the statue. The oil that was used was probably flower-scented (cf. Bk IX, 41 (7)) and fed the wooden core through an internal network of tiny tubes (Pliny, Natural History, 16, 213f.).

108. The Aithiopian bull is the rhinoceros. For these animals, cf. Bk IX, 21 (2f.).

using fire you can straighten out the curved horns of oxen and elephants, and make other shapes of them. Admittedly the hippopotamus and pig carry tusks in their lower jaw, and you never see horns growing out of their jaws; [3] but I assure you that the elephant's horn comes right down from the dome of his head and then turns outwards. I am not writing this from hearsay: I have seen an elephant's skull in Campania at a sanctuary of Artemis, about four miles from Capua, which is the Campanian capital city.[109] One of the differences between elephants and other animals is the way they grow their horns, and their size and shape are nothing like any other beast. My own view is that the Greeks are extremely ambitious of honour and generous with money in the worship of the gods, since they brought ivory from India and Aithiopia to make statues.

[4] There is a woollen curtain at Olympia decorated by Assyrian weavers and dyed with Phoenician crimson, dedicated by Antiochos, who dedicated the golden skin with the Gorgon on it above the theatre at Athens. This curtain is not hung up from the roof like the one in the temple of Ephesian Artemis but suspended on cords and let down to the pavement.[110] [5] As to the dedications inside the temple or in the porch, there is the throne of Arimnestos, the king of the Etruscans who was the first barbarian ever to give a dedication to Zeus at Olympia, and Kyniska's bronze horses, the symbols

109. The temple of Diana on the western slope of TIFATA ridge, the mountain above CAPUA on the borders of Campania and Samnium. It was already an important and ancient sanctuary of Diana when Sulla dedicated an estate to the goddess after a victory near here in 83 B.C. The columns of this temple were built into the tenth-century church of S. ANGELO IN FORMIS which still stands on the site, about two miles north-east of Capua; Pausanias seems to have the distance wrong. The elephant's skull was probably a trophy from Sulla's battle.

110. For the Gorgon, cf. Bk I, 21 (3). Antiochos must surely be the philhellene Antiochos IV Epiphanes (c. 215–163 B.C.) who looted and defiled the TEMPLE OF GOD at Jerusalem. We know that he carried off the veil of the temple which was fine linen and scarlet, and attempted to rededicate the building to Olympian Zeus. Can it have been the Veil of the Temple that Pausanias saw at Olympia?

of Olympic victory.[111] These are not so big as real horses, and stand on the right as you go into the porch. There is a bronze-plated tripod dedicated there where before the table was made they used to put out the wreaths for the winners. [6] There are royal statues: one of Hadrian dedicated by the Achaian cities made of Parian stone, and one of Trajan dedicated by the whole of Greece. Trajan conquered the Getai north of Thrace, and fought against the Parthians and Osroes the descendant of Arsakes; his most important constructions are the baths named after him and the great circular theatre, and the building a quarter of a mile long for horse-racing, and his Roman forum which is worth a visit for all its decorations but more than anything for its bronze roof.[112] [7] The portraits in niches in the curved structures are the Roman emperor Augustus in amber, and King Nikomedes of Bithynia, so I was told, in ivory: the biggest city in Bithynia, previously called Astakos, was renamed after him, though its original founder was Zypoites, who must (to guess from his name) have been a Thracian by blood.[113] The kind of amber

111. Arimnestos is otherwise utterly unknown. The white marble base for Kyniska's bronze horses has been found. The horses were by Apelles. For Kyniska, cf. Bk III, 8 (1) etc. She was the daughter of Archidamos II, a fifth-century king of Sparta; her dedication at Olympia was in the early fourth century.

112. The ruins of Trajan's baths were still a formidable monument in the sixteenth century, though there was not much left by 1800. They lie south-east of S. Pietro in Vincoli. Apart from open courts and all the usual rooms, they included a theatre. Trajan's theatre stood in the Campus Martius, but Hadrian pulled it down. Perhaps Pausanias means the *amphitheatrum castrense*, which Trajan also seems to have built and of which massive traces still exist near S. Croce in Gerusalemme. The building for races is surely the old *circus maximus*, so often damaged and so expensively rebuilt, which reached under Trajan the height of its magnificence and the farthest extent of its enormous size. The *forum Trajani* was the last and greatest Roman forum; it was probably planned by Domitian, but Trajan finished it; the architect was called Apollodoros. The bronze roof was the roof of the *basilica Ulpia*, a huge hall of yellow or white marble columns with *giallo antico* steps on the north-west side of Trajan's forum. It was finished in A.D. 112.

113. Nikomedes the first founded Nikomedeia in 264 B.C. Zypoites was his father; Astakos (which means a lobster) was a Megarian colony that had been

or electrum they used for Augustus's portrait, which is found as a natural product in the sands of the Eridanos, is extremely rare and for many reasons precious to humanity, but the other kind of electrum is a compound of silver and gold.[114] [8] In the temple at Olympia there are three wreaths copied from the foliage of wild olive, dedicated by Nero, with a fourth copied from oak-leaves. Twenty-five bronze shields are also kept there, which they use for the race in armour. Among the stone tablets that stand there is the one with the Elean oath of alliance for a hundred years with Athens, Argos and Mantinea.[115]

[1] Inside Altis Pelops has his own separate enclosure: 13 Pelops is worshipped by the Eleans as much more than the other divine heroes at Olympia as Zeus is worshipped more than the other gods. The PELOPION is towards the north-east, on your right as you stand at the entrance to Zeus's temple, and far enough away from it for statues and other dedications to stand between them; it begins about level with the middle of the temple and stretches as far as the rear porch.[116] It is enclosed

---

badly damaged by King Lysimachos of Thrace. The site is at IZMIT south-east of Istanbul on the Sea of Marmara. Arrian was born there. We know that King Zypoites (Ziboites) did found a city called Zypoition and that he fought a war against Astakos; the site of Zypoition is quite unknown but it may well have been a stage in the creation of Nikomedeia.

114. 'Electrum' can mean an alloy or it can mean amber. Eridanos can mean either the Po or the Rhine. The ancient trade-routes for amber were considered mysterious and perhaps magical by the classical historians. Amber is really fossilized resin which occurs in lumps and drops in certain kinds of marine sand, notably on the shores of the Baltic and the North Sea, particularly in Lithuania. The Greeks in Sicily seem to have used imported northern amber for a long time without realizing that local Mediterranean amber existed in their beaches, just as the Chinese used Persian cobalt for blue glazes before they discovered their own.

115. In 420 B.C. A large part of the text of the treaty of alliance has been recovered from an Athenian inscription (M. N. Tod, *Greek Historical Inscriptions*, n. 72), and all its provisions were recorded by Thukydides (5, 47).

116. This SANCTUARY is an odd pentagonal shape with a protruding porch, south of the Heraion and north of the west end of the massive ruins of the temple of Zeus. The porch was rebuilt in the early fourth century B.C. and

with a stone wall and has trees growing inside it, and there are statues there; [2] the entry faces the setting sun. They say it was Herakles son of Amphitryon who assigned it to Pelops, since he was one of Pelops's great-grandsons, and he is supposed to have sacrificed to Pelops at the pit. And the officials of every year still sacrifice to him at present; the victim is a black ram. From this sacrifice the prophet takes no share: the tradition is to give only the ram's neck to the woodman, as they call him. [3] The woodman is one of Zeus's servants, whose job is to provide timber at a fixed price to cities and private individuals for their sacrifices. All the timber has to be white poplar and no other tree. Anyone, Elean or foreigner, who eats meat from the victim sacrificed to Pelops is not allowed entry to Zeus. The same thing happens when you sacrifice to Telephos at Pergamon on the river Kaikos: you are not allowed up to Asklepios without a bath.[117] [4] There is this story too: when the Trojan War was dragging on, the prophets announced Greece would never capture the city until they brought Herakles' bow and a bone of Pelops, so they sent for Philoktetes to come to the camp,[118] and for a shoulder blade from the bones of Pelops to be fetched from Pisa. As they were on the way home the ship carrying Pelops's bone was wrecked by a storm off the coast of Euboia: and [5] many years later than the fall of Troy a fisherman from Eretria called Damarmenos let down his net at sea and hauled in this bone. He was staggered at its size and kept it hidden under the sand, but in the end he went to Delphi, to ask whose bone it was and what he should do with it. [6] Now by some kind of divine foresight an Elean embassy was there at the same time to ask for a cure for the plague, so the Pythian

---

stuccoed by the Romans. The sanctuary itself was a mound where Pelops was worshipped as a divine hero. This site has yielded a mass of archaic dedications of different kinds. The pit for sacrifices seems to have been at the south-east.

117. For the Asklepieion at Pergamon, cf Bk II, 26 (8), and Bk III, 26 (10). It was a wealthy inland city opposite Lesbos.

118. Philoktetes had the bow; the others had marooned him at Lemnos because he had a poisoned snake-bite that stank and made him howl.

priestess told the Eleans to rescue Pelops's bones, and Damarmenos to give them his discovery. He did so, and among other rewards the Eleans made Damarmenos and his descendants the guardians of the bone. In my time Pelops's shoulder-blade had already vanished, in my opinion because it was hidden for so long on the sea-floor, and the sea and the other processes of time wore it away.[119] [7] Some traces of the life of Pelops and of Tantalos are still left in our country today: the lake of Tantalos named after him and his by no means inglorious grave, and Pelops's throne, on the mountain-top at Sipylos, over the sanctuary of Plastene the mother, also a statue of Aphrodite at Temnos across the river Hermos, carved in living myrtle, which traditional memory records that Pelops dedicated to propitiate the goddess and to obtain a marriage with Hippodameia.[120]

[8] The ALTAR of Olympian Zeus is just about equidistant from the Pelopion and the sanctuary of Hera, but it lies

119. When Pelops was a baby his father Tantalos chopped him up and served him to the gods at dinner for a practical joke; the gods put him together again, but regrettably Demeter had absent-mindedly eaten a piece, so he had to be given an ivory shoulder.

120. Pausanias comes from somewhere near Magnesia, south-east of Ephesos, under Mount Sipylos (Manisa Dagi). Pausanias is quite right about the abundant local interest in Tantalos; he may well be a legendary version of a Hittite king. Tantalos's lake is possibly a small, deep lake called KARAGÖL in a pine forest high up on YAMANLAR DAGI. Tantalos's tomb is probably a very ancient stepped, rock-cut chamber-tomb which used until recently to be called the tomb of HAGIOS CHARALAMPOS, about a mile east of TAS SURET at the foot of Sipylos. Pelops's throne on the mountain-top is probably a massive, simple throne cut in rock on a steep slope which opens out 900 feet up the west face of the crack in the same mountainside called YARIKKAYA; it cannot be reached now except by determined rock-climbing. The sanctuary of Mother Plastene lay in the plain, under a mile from TAS SURET and about an hour east of MANISA; it was securely identified on the evidence of inscriptions by the Greek and French archaeologists of the 1880s. Plastene was Kybele; a new temple seems to have been built in Pausanias's time. Temnos lay in the high ground north of Hermos not far from Magnesia across the river. It was pinpointed as the akropolis visible across the river from EMIR AALEM railway station (seventeen miles from Magnesia) by Sir William Ramsay as a young man (*Journal of Hellenic Studies*, 1881, pp. 286–92).

farther forward than either of them. Some say it was constructed by the Idaian Herakles, and some say by local divine heroes two generations later. It is built from the ash of the thighs of victims sacrificed to Zeus, just the same as at Pergamos; there is in fact also an ash altar to Samian Hera not a bit more glorious than what Athenians call the impromptu hearths in the Attic countryside.[121] [9] But in the altar at Olympia the first step, which is called the outer circle, is a hundred and twenty-five feet round, and the circumference of the next step above it is thirty-two feet: the entire height of the altar is as high as twenty-two feet. The tradition is to sacrifice victims in the lower area, the outer circle, then they take up the thighs to the topmost point of the altar, and burn them there. [10] Flights of stone steps lead up to the outer circle from both sides, and even virgin girls, and in the same way women, are allowed up to the outer circle, at times when they are not excluded from Olympia: but only men may climb up from here to the top of the altar. There are private sacrifices to Zeus and daily Elean sacrifices even outside the time of festival, [11] and every year, observing the nineteenth day of the month Elaphios, the prophets bring the ash from the council-house, puddle it with Alpheios water and plaster the altar with it.[122] And the ash must never be muddied with any other water; this is why they think Alpheios is the most delightful of all rivers to Olympian Zeus. There is another altar at Didyma in the territory of Miletos, built by Theban Herakles so the Miletos people say, out of the blood of

121. Traces of the altar at Olympia have been found. The ash altar at Pergamon rested on a massive marble construction elaborately and heavily carved with scenes of violence and effort. This expensive technical tour-de-force has been reassembled in Berlin; it is a long roofed colonnade crowned with statuary, with two projecting wings and an enormous flight of steps. The modest hearths of Samos and the Attic countryside are naturally very hard to identify; something of this kind has been found on Mount Parnes, associated with ancient dedications of iron knives, but the excavation has never been fully published. Porphyry (De antro nympharum, 6) says the Olympic gods had their temples, and the underworld gods their dark places, but these hearths belonged to the earth-gods and divine heroes.

122. In March.

victims: but since then the blood of sacrifices has not swollen it to overwhelming size.[123]

[1] There is another marvellous feature of the altar at 14 Olympia: the kites, which are naturally the most rapacious of birds, do no harm to the sacrifices at Olympia, so if ever a kite does snatch some offal or some meat, it is believed to be a bad omen for the sacrificer. They say that when Herakles son of Alkmene was sacrificing at Olympia he was badly pestered by flies, so he invented or was taught by someone the sacrifice to Zeus of Flies, and so the flies were turned away across the Alpheios. The Eleans are said to sacrifice to Zeus of Flies in the same way, to drive away flies from Olympia.

[2] The Elean practice is to use only the timber of white poplar for sacrificing to Zeus, and no other tree: I think they have no reason for preferring white poplar except the fact that Herakles brought it to Greece from the Thesprotian country. It appeared to me that when Herakles himself sacrificed to Zeus at Olympia he burnt the thighs of the victims on logs of white poplar. Herakles had found it growing beside the river Acheron in Thesprotia, which they say is why Homer calls it *Acherois*.[124] [3] Rivers have always been different from each other and are so to this day in the trees and grasses they naturally produce: the Maiander breeds huge tamarisks in great numbers, the Boiotian Asopos has the deepest reed-beds, and the avocado-tree likes no other waters except the Nile. So one need not be amazed that the white

123. For the sanctuary of Apollo at Didyma, cf. Bk V, Note 57, and Bk VIII, 2 (6). From at least as early as the third century B.C. there was a great athletic festival at Didyma on the lines of the Olympic games. I do not think that any trace of the great altar of Apollo has been found. It is unlikely to have been built earlier than the revival of Didyma under Seleukos in the early third century.

124. *Iliad*, 13, 389. Acherois probably means simply river-tree; Acheron seems to be like Achelous, a very common Greek river-name meaning simply river, like Avon in English. The white poplar is a very distinctive landmark in Greece; it plays an important part in the directions a shepherd will give for finding a path. A slightly less interesting Canadian variety is common now, but you still see the native Greek white poplar beside streams and ditches particularly in the Peloponnese. I suppose it was from the underworld Acheron and not from northern Greece that Herakles brought it.

poplar first grew on the Acheron, and the wild olive on the Alpheios, and the black poplar was nursed in the Celtic country, on the Celtic river Po.[125]

[4] Well now: as we have talked about the greatest altar, let us go round all the ALTARS at Olympia. In this discussion I shall take them in the same order in which Elean sacred practice dictates that sacrifice should be offered to them. They sacrifice first to the Hearth goddess,[126] then to Olympian Zeus at the altar inside the temple, thirdly ... on a single altar.[127] [5] The fifth sacrifice is to Artemis and Athene of spoils, and the sixth is to the Worker. This is where Pheidias's descendants who are called the polishers, who were granted by Elis the office of cleaning dust and dirt from Zeus's statue, offer sacrifice before they begin to polish it. There is another altar of Athene near the temple, with a four-square altar of Artemis beside it rising gradually to a height. [6] After the altars I have listed they sacrifice to Alpheios and Artemis on one altar. Pindar has thrown light on the reason for this in an ode, and I write about it in my Letrinaian chapter.[128] Not far from this stands another altar of Alpheios, beside which is one of Hephaistos, though there are some Eleans who call

125. I believe that there are still tamarisks near the Maiander (the MEN-DERES) though I have never been there. The Asopos is less reedy than it was, but Pausanias is not above deriving its reediness from Homer (*Iliad*, 4, 385). The poplars in the Po valley make it one of the most sharply characterized landscapes in the world. The question of identifying the Greek *persea* is not simple. The late-eighteenth-century German botanist Schreber thought it was *Cordia myxa* (*Cordia officinalis*) but the received modern identification is with the *lebbach* (*Mimusops Schimperi*). The avocado (*Aztec ahuacatt*) is a West Indian discovery; it grows well in Israel and could grow in Egypt, but its Latin name is *Persea gratissima*.

126. Mr Kondis in his *Hieron tis Olympias* (1958) has argued that this sacrifice took place in a very ancient sanctuary at the south-east corner of the sacred area, near the entrance to the race-course and Nero's house.

127. Herakles was supposed to have founded six altars for twelve gods by the grave of Pelops (*Olympian Odes*, 5, 5, and 10, 24). Apart from traces of one altar between the Heraion and the Pelopion, the altars have not been found, though cf. Note 132 below; they were probably used as building materials for the Byzantine castle.

128. Bk VI, 22 (8–10). Pindar's poem is the *First Nemean ode*.

Hephaistos's altar the altar of Zeus of War, and who say Oinomaos sacrificed to Zeus of War at this altar whenever he was going to have a horse-race with one of Hippodameia's lovers.[129] [7] Beyond this stands an altar to Herakles with the title of Helper, and to Herakles' brothers Epimedes and Idas and Paionaios and Iasos: though I know there are others who call Idas's altar the altar of Akeidas.[130] This is where the foundations of Oinomaos's house are, with two altars, one of Courtyard Zeus which Oinomaos would appear to have built himself, and one to Zeus of the Thunderbolt which I suppose they built later, when the thunderbolt struck down Oinomaos's house.[131] [8] I discussed the great altar just now: it is called the altar of Olympian Zeus. Near it is an altar of the Unknown gods, and beyond that of Purifying Zeus and of Victory and another of Underworld Zeus. And there are altars of all the gods including Hera with the title Olympian Hera, which is also made of ash: they say it was dedicated by Klymenos.[132] Beyond this is an altar of Apollo and Hermes together, because the Greek legend about them is that Hermes invented the lyre and Apollo the viol. [9] Next in order comes an altar of Concord, next Athene, then the Mother of gods.[133] Very close to the entrance to the race-track there are two altars, one of Hermes of the Games and one of Opportunity. I know a hymn to Opportunity by Ion of Chios, where he traces Opportunity's ancestry as the youngest son of Zeus.[134] Near the Sikyonian treasury is an altar of Herakles, either Herakles of the Kouretes or Alkmene's son: both

129. Because he wanted to overtake them and kill them and recapture his daughter. Zeus of War was worshipped in Molossia and in Karia.

130. The Daktyloi of Mount Ida; cf. Bk V, 7 (6) and Bk VIII, 31 (3).

131. Cf. Bk V, 20 (6).

132. This at least has been identified. There are the local stone foundations of a big altar and another smaller one just east of the east front of the temple of Hera.

133. There are traces of an altar to the west of the sanctuary of the Mother of the gods: that is, not far from the two altars in front of Hera's temple, but farther east. It is not at all certain that this is the right one; all we know is that Pausanias is not moving regularly round a circle of altars.

134. Ion of Chios was a fifth-century poet and intellectual. This hymn is lost, alas.

accounts are given.[135] [10] At what they call the Earth-sanctuary, there is an altar of Earth, and this also is made of ash: they say that in even more ancient times there was an oracle of Earth here. The altar to Themis is built at what they call the Mouth.[136] The altar of Descending Zeus is fenced off in every direction by a barrier that masks it, but it stands near the great altar of ashes. You must remember I have not numbered over the altars in line as they stand; my description has wandered around in the order in which the Eleians sacrifice. By the enclosure of Pelops is an altar of Dionysos and the Graces together,[137] with one of the Muses between

135. There are a dozen national TREASURIES, that is small shrines for the national dedications to Zeus, more or less in line along the north side of the sacred area of Altis, from the temple of Hera in the north-west to the entry to the stadium in the north-east. The Sikyon treasury was the farthest west, nearest to the altars in front of the temple of Hera; it has been identified by an inscription. Traces of what could possibly be the right altar have been found behind the semi-circular wall of an elegant ornamental building erected by Herod of Athens, Pausanias's contemporary.

136. Probably the Earth-sanctuary was outside the sacred area; very likely on the slopes of Kronion, the conical pine-covered hill north of Altis. It has not been found. The Earth-oracle and Law and the chasm at what had later become an oracular sanctuary of Zeus correspond closely to the relations of Earth, Law, the chasm and Apollo at Delphi; this is probably a deliberate assimilation dating from perhaps the late fourth century. The chasm need not have been very deep. (Cf. Parke, Oracles of Zeus, pp. 180f.) There was once a Mycenaean settlement at and above the junction of the Kladeos and Alpheios; it is not completely impossible that there was more or less continuous occupation of the area until the classical period, though very little of the latest Mycenaean pottery and very little protogeometric pottery has been found; nor is there apart from one Cretan figurine any archaeological evidence at all that Olympia or the oracle of Earth could have been a Mycenaean sanctuary.

137. Plutarch in his Quaestiones Graecae (36) quotes an Elean women's hymn to Dionysos:

> Come heroic Dionysos
> to the pure temple of Elis
> with the Graces
> to the temple
> cattle-footed
> spotless bull, spotless bull.

the altar and the enclosure, and after those two an altar of the nymphs.

[1] There is a building outside Altis called Pheidias's 15 workshop, where Pheidias worked detail by detail at the statue, and there is an altar in the building to all the gods together.[138] If you turn straight back to Altis, opposite the Leonidaion [2] (of course the LEONIDAION is outside the sanctuary enclosure, but stands by the entrance to Altis where the Processional road goes in, which is the only road for processions, and it was dedicated by a local man named Leonidas, though in my time the Roman governors of Greece lived in it, separated from the processional entrance by a highway, as what the Athenians call alleys the Eleians call highways [3]) – in the Altis as you are going to pass to the left of the Leonidaion there is an altar of Aphrodite, and one of the Seasons beyond it.[139] At the back porch of the temple,

138. PHEIDIAS'S WORKSHOP has been found, in the ruins of a Byzantine church just west of the sacred area; the identification was confirmed by the spectacular find of a black-glazed jug with Pheidias's name scratched on it in a fine lettering. It was here that the great Zeus was made for the temple; the excavators have found traces of the processes Pheidias used, including the moulds for Zeus's cloak.

139. To deal first with the long parenthesis: the LEONIDAION is the strong and sophisticated building outside the south-west corner of the sacred area; it was built in the third century B.C. by a certain Leonidas of Naxos, as a residence for distinguished guests; it was twice rebuilt, once around 174 (by the Roman governor?) and after Pausanias's time in the third century A.D. It was identified through an inscription. There is a confusion about the processional entrance: the boundaries of Altis had been extended southwards and new walls built on the south and west round the new wedge in the Roman period, perhaps under Nero, to take in a line of Roman statues which until then had been outside the sacred area. Pausanias's processional entrance is a triple entrance in the western wall of Altis just opposite the Leonidaion, the southernmost of the three entrances in the western wall (the northernmost is also a triple entrance, but the middle entrance is simpler). The difficulty is that there was a triumphal arch and a main entrance to which Pausanias more than once refers, not at the south-west but the south-east corner of Altis at the thin end of the new wedge. The old processional road still ran through the Roman extension of Altis which had originally been outside the sanctuary, along the line of the old southern wall and the Roman statues, to enter the old Altis at the south-east, but since the Roman extension this road was considered as being inside Altis, and since the

just to the right grows a wild olive-tree, called the CROWN OLIVE, from which tradition dictates that Olympic winners should be given their wreaths.[140] Near this wild olive is an altar to the Nymphs, and they call them the Wreath-crowned Nymphs. [4] Outside Altis there is an altar of Market Artemis to the right of the Leonidaion and an altar to the Mistresses – I shall give information about the goddess they call Mistress in my work on Arkadia – and beyond that an altar of Market Zeus, and in front of the PRESIDENCY (as they call it) one of Pythian Apollo, and beyond that one of Dionysos, which they say is quite recent and dedicated by private individuals.[141] [5] There is an altar on the way to the starting-place for horses, inscribed to the Leader of Fates: this is obviously a title of Zeus, who knows everything that happens to humanity, what the Fates grant and what they determine shall not be.[142] Near it is a long altar of the Fates, beyond that one of Hermes, and then two of Zeus the Highest. At the starting-place for horses there are two altars just in the middle in the open air, to Poseidon of Horses and Hera of Horses, and one

---

Greeks refused to alter their processional route the comparatively undistinguished gate opposite the Leonidaion became the formal processional entrance to Olympia. This solution, which has stood up to all later criticisms, was proposed by R. Heberdey in *Eranos Vindobonensis* (1893, pp. 34–47). The road was narrow because the new walls cut into it. One of the two altars has been found inside the gate. Passing to the left means turning north, which as a matter of fact is the only way you can turn.

140. South-west of the temple of Zeus. This is the very old wild olive supposed to have come from the country beyond the north wind. The wreaths were cut by a boy with a golden pruning-hook. The area where it grew was called the Pantheon.

141. Cf. Bk VIII, 37 (9). No one knows exactly what or exactly where the Presidency (*proedria*) was. Could it be the great marble platform in front of the colonnade of Echo at the east end of the sacred area? Frazer calls it the grandstand, perhaps rightly.

142. At the south-east corner. This title of Zeus is known not only from Pausanias (in several passages) but now also from an inscribed stone altar of the Roman period which in 1967 was lying beside the path leading to the mountains of Hagios Elias and Theokafta from the Asklepieion at Epidauros (since published by Peek).

of the Dioskouroi by the pillar. [6] On one side of the entrance to the BEAK, as they call it, is an altar of Ares of Horses, and on the other of Athene of Horses, and just inside the Beak is an altar of Good Fortune, one of Pan, and one of Aphrodite, and right inside, one of the Nymphs they call Nymphs of the Fine Point.[143] On the way back from the colonnade the Eleans have named after its architect and call AGNAPTOS'S COLONNADE, there is an altar of Artemis on the right.[144] [7] When you go into Altis again by the processional road,[145] there are altars behind the sanctuary of Hera to the river Kladeos and to Artemis, beyond them of Apollo, and fourthly of Artemis Kokkoka and fifthly of Thermian Apollo. Even I can guess that the Eleian word Thermian would in the Attic dialect be Thesmian: Apollo of Right; but I was not able to discover why Artemis is called Kokkoka.[146] [8] There is a building in front of what they call the PRESBYTERY, in one corner of which is an altar of Pan.[147] The Elean COUNCIL-HOUSE is inside Altis, by the exit opposite the training ground, where the running-tracks and wrestling-schools are for the athletes.[148] In front of the Council-house doors is an altar of Huntress Artemis, [9] and inside as you enter the building

143. For the Beak, the fine point, and the entrance to the race-course, cf. Bk VI, 20 (10f.).

144. For the colonnade, cf. Bk VI, 20 (10f.). The inscribed altar of Artemis has been found south of the entrance to the race-course near what in the Middle Ages became the bed of the Alpheios, at the south-east corner of the excavations.

145. That is when you enter from the Leonidaion at the south-west corner and turn north following the inside of the west wall, parallel with the river Kladeos.

146. It means 'Artemis of Seed'; *kokkos* means a pomegranate seed; it can also mean a man's or a woman's private parts. There was a very ancient sanctuary of Apollo at Thermon in Aitolia, but no doubt Pausanias is right.

147. *Theokoleion* is an unusual word meaning priests' house; I have translated it Presbytery. This building was probably the one just west of Altis, north of Pheidias's workshop and the Leonidaion, and south of the wrestling-ground.

148. The Council-house was in the far north-west corner of Altis, north-west of Hera's temple. The entry was from the south. The gymnasion stretched north from the wrestling-grounds, beside the Kladeos; it extends under what is now the car-park.

where the hearth is there is an altar of Pan on the right of the entrance. This hearth as well is made of ashes, and fire burns on it throughout the day and the night. It is from this hearth they carry out the ash as I have already said to the altar of the Olympian, and what they bring from this hearth makes a considerable contribution to the altar.

[10] Once a month the Eleans offer sacrifice at every altar in this list. They sacrifice in an antique style; they burn frankincense with honey-kneaded wheaten cakes on the altars, and lay branches of olive on them and pour wine. It is only to the Nymphs and the Mistresses and on the common altar of all the gods that the practice is to pour no wine. The performance of the sacrifices is under a priest who holds that honour for a month, also prophets and wine-carriers, a sacred guide and a flute-player and the woodman. [11] It would not be proper to clutter up this treatise with the form of words that tradition dictates they should follow at the wine-pouring in the Council-house, or with the hymns they sing, but they pour wine not only to Greek gods, but the Libyan god and Ammonian Hera and Ammon's friend, which is a title of Hermes.[149] They appear to have used the Libyan oracle from a very early period, and there are altars in Ammon's sanctuary which are Elean dedications, inscribed with the Elean questions and the god's prophetic replies, and the names of the men from Elis who visited Ammon. That is in Ammon's sanctuary.[150] [12] The Eleans also pour wine to the divine heroes worshipped in Elean territory and in Aitolia, and to the wives of the heroes.[151] The language in which they sing in the Council-house is Doric, but they do not say who

149. Ammon really was the Libyan oracular god of the Siwah oasis; the Egyptians identified him with Amon Ra, and the Greeks from Kyrene with Zeus. His cult-object was a stone representation of a draped mummy bent into a curved, upward shape like a banana on a pedestal and smothered with every kind of precious stone. (Cf. Oric Bates. *The Eastern Libyans*, pp. 189-200.)

150. There were also bronze dolphins on pillars dedicated by Kyrene. The site ought to be properly excavated.

151. The national heroes Pausanias talks about in the early chapters of this book.

composed the songs. The Eleans have a BANQUET-HOUSE as well, which is also inside the Council-house, opposite the building where the hearth is; they give a banquet in it for the Olympic winners.[152]

[1] After this it remains for me to describe the TEMPLE OF 16 HERA and its notable contents. The Eleans say it was the people of Skillous, one of the cities in Triphylia, who constructed the temple just about eight years after Oxylos became king of Elis.[153] The style of its workmanship is Doric, and there are columns all round it. Its length is a hundred and sixty-nine feet, its width is sixty-three, and its height not less than fifty; the name of the architect is not recorded.[154] [2] Every four years the sixteen women weave a robe for Hera, and the same women hold Hera's games. The games are a running match between virgin girls; [3] they run with their hair let down and their tunics rather above their knees, and the right breast and shoulder bared.[155] The course for the race is the Olympic track, less about a sixth. They give the winners crowns made of olive-branches and a share of the ox they slaughter to Hera; and the girls can dedicate painted portraits. The servants who wait on the committee of sixteen who hold the games are also women. [4] They trace the girls' games to antiquity as well as the men's: they say Hippodameia first gathered the sixteen women to give thanks to Hera for her marriage to Pelops, and first celebrated Hera's games with them, and they also record that the winner was Chloris, the

152. In the back rooms of the Council-house.

153. This entails a date of legendary antiquity in the early eleventh century B.C., smack in the middle of the Dark Ages. Dorpfeld at one time believed this and so did Frazer, but the excavation by Dorpfeld and Buschor showed the temple had been built in the seventh century B.C., which is still very early for a Doric temple, and that it had predecessors for perhaps a hundred years.

154. The unit of measurement is the Greek, not the English foot; Pausanias's figures for the length seem a little too low; there may be some outer part he is not counting.

155. Pausanias has seen a statue dedicated for this race; it must have been like the small sixth-century Lakonian bronze of a girl athlete from Albania now in the British Museum. (Cf. W. Lamb, *Greek and Roman Bronzes*, pl. 33, and pp. 97–8.)

only surviving daughter of Amphion. They say there was
also one boy who survived with her: but I have explained
in my discussion of Argos all that I personally was able to
conclude about Niobe's children.[156]  [5] There is a second
legend as well as the first about the sixteen women. They say
when Damophon was dictator of Pisa he did a lot of dreadful
things to the Eleans,[157] and when he died, as the Pisaian people
had not been willing to join in the dictator's crimes and Elis
had resolved to dismiss the charges against them, the Eleans
chose a woman of the most venerable age and the most
distinguished position and reputation from each of the inhabited cities of Eleia at that time to settle their quarrels for
them. [6] The cities the women were chosen from were Elis
... ;[158] the women from these cities reconciled the Pisaians
and the Eleans, and afterwards they were put in charge of
holding Hera's games and weaving Hera's robe. The sixteen
women also arrange two dances, one of which they call
Physkoa's dance and the other Hippodameia's; they say
Physkoa was from the Valley of Elis and the town she lived
in was called Orthia: [7] The story is that Dionysos slept with
Physkoa and she bore his son Narkaios, who as he grew rose
to great power through provincial wars, and even founded a
SANCTUARY OF ATHENE with the title Narkaian Athene; and
they say Narkaios and Physkoa were the first to worship
Dionysos.[159] One of the honours Physkoa receives is the dances
named after her that the sixteen women provide; and the
Eleans still keep them up as well as ever even though some

156. Cf. Bk II, 21 (9).          157. Cf. Bk VI, 22 (3).
158. Strabo says there were eight Pisaian cities.
159. Physkos was a son of Aitolos. There is a poem about a cold and windy
swimming-place in the *Palatine Anthology* (9, 617) which says 'this place belongs
to Phrixos and Narke' (Shivering and Numbness). Presumably the Bacchic
etymology of Physkoa and Narkaian Athene referred to girth and drunkenness.
The sanctuary of Narkaian Athene has not been found. A recent emergency
survey of the Peneios barrage area revealed an extraordinary number of
unexcavated and uncharted sites, although there was probably no exceptional
richness in the area to be flooded. For a map of this survey, cf. *Athens Annals of
Archaeology*, 1968, p. 46.

of the cities have perished; they divide into eight tribes, so they take two women from every tribe. [8] No ceremony that tradition dictates the sixteen women or the Greek arbiters of Eleia are to perform is ever carried out until they have purified themselves with a pig which is right for purification, and with water. They purify at the fountain of Piera, which is a water-spring on the level road from Olympia to Elis.[160]

[1] All this is as I have explained it. In Hera's temple there 17 is a statue of Zeus, and Hera's statue is seated on a throne: he stands beside her, bearded and helmeted. These are works of a simple art; the Seasons enthroned next to them are by Smilis of Aigina, and beside them again stands a statue of Themis as mother of the Seasons, by Dorykleidas, a Lakonian apprentice of Dipoinos and Skyllis.[161] [2] The five daughters of Hesperos are by another Lakonian, Theokles the son of Hegylos, who is also supposed to have been taught by Skyllis and Dipoinos.[162] The helmeted Athene with spear and shield is said to be by Medon of Lakonia, Dorykleidas's brother, who was taught by the same masters.[163] [3] Demeter and the Maid are enthroned opposite each other, and a standing Apollo faces a standing Artemis. Leto is dedicated here, and Fortune and Dionysos and winged Victory: I am not able to say who made them all, but they appear to me to be extremely ancient. Those I have listed are ivory and gold, but at a later period other dedications were made at this sanctuary: a stone Hermes

160. The road has not been traced, and the spring has not been found.

161. Before the temple of Zeus was built this was the temple of Zeus and Hera. The archaic limestone head of Hera's statue was found in 1878: there were traces of colour on it. She has a flat, smiling, majestic face and heavy curling hair; she was carved about 600 B.C. For a photograph cf. Lullies and Hirmer, *Greek Sculpture*, pl. 10. For Smilis, cf. Bk VII, 4 (4). He made the Hera at the Heraion of Samos. For Dipoinos and Skyllis, cf. Bk II, 15 (1), and 22 (5), etc. Nothing is known about Dorykleidas.

162. Nothing is known about Theokles, but for these statues, cf. Bk VI, 19 (8).

163. For this Athene, cf. Bk VI, 19 (12); for Medon, cf. Bk VI, 19 (14). Was the statue from a group?

carrying a baby Dionysos by Praxiteles,[164] and a bronze Aphrodite by Kleon of Sikyon, [4] whose master was Antiphanes, who studied with Periklytos, who was in his turn a student of Polykleitos of Argos.[165] A little gilded boy stark naked is sitting in front of Aphrodite; he was made by Boethos of Chalkedon. The gold and ivory statues of Aridaios's wife Eurydike and Philip's wife Olympias have been transferred here from what was called the SHRINE OF PHILIP.[166]

[5] There is a cedar-wood CHEST with figures on it in ivory and gold, and carvings in the cedar-wood itself. In this chest Kypselos the dictator of Corinth was hidden by his mother when he was a baby and the Bacchiadai were searching for him. In return for Kypselos's escape then his descendants who are called the Kypselidai dedicated the chest at Olympia: in those days Corinthians called their chests kypselai, and they say that was how the boy came to be called Kypselos.[167] [6]

164. The famously smooth and skilful 'Hermes of Praxiteles' in the Olympia museum. Its pedestal is Hellenistic or Roman, the legs except for the right foot are modern; the conception is that of Praxiteles working about 325 B.C., and the finish is glittering, but this is not the original statue; it is a fine Hellenistic copy. This sad but important truth is argued irrefutably by Sheila Adam in *The Technique of Greek Sculpture* (1966), pp. 124–8.

165. This might be thought to put Kleon at the end of the fourth century but Pausanias associates him at Bk V, 21 (3), with two statues dated 388 B.C. These lists of who taught whom are no more than rather sketchy and often conjectural tables of influences.

166. There is no way of knowing for certain whether Boethos came from Chalkedon or Carthage. The shrine of Philip stood south-west of the temple of Hera; cf. Bk V, 20 (9).

167. Kypselos was dictator of Corinth in the second half of the seventh century; the Bacchiadai had previously been the ruling family. This chest, like the throne at Amyklai, recalls the rich, crowded narrative compositions of early-sixth-century vase-painters; but if this was really the chest in which Kypselos hid, it would be Corinthian work of a hundred years earlier. A deep golden bowl rather like half a pomegranate inscribed and dedicated by Kypselos's family from the spoils of Herakleia was found at Olympia in 1917, somewhere east of Altis between the stadium and the river; it can be dated between 625 and 550 B.C. but not more accurately; it seems to have been made and inscribed at Corinth. It was found by a peasant and bought by the Boston Museum of Fine Arts in 1922. Its weight exactly fits a Babylonian standard measure.

Most of the figures on the chest have inscriptions in ancient lettering, some of which read straight, though others are in the style called in Greek cattle-track, which is like this: from the end of the line the next line follows backwards like a two-lap race-track. And in general the inscriptions on the chest are written in twisting lines which are difficult to make out.[168] Beginning from the bottom the first area of the chest has the following decorative scheme. [7] Oinomaos is chasing Pelops who has Hippodameia; each of them has a pair of horses, but Pelops's horses have wings growing on them.[169] Next comes the house of Amphiaraos with some old woman carrying the baby Amphilochos; Eriphyle stands in front of the house holding the necklace, with her daughters Eurydike and Demonassa beside her, and the naked boy Alkmaion.[170] [8] Asios in his epic writes that Alkmene was another daughter of Amphiaraos and Eriphyle.[171] Baton, who drives for Amphiaraos, holds the horses' reins in one hand and a spear in the other. One of Amphiaraos's feet has already mounted the chariot, but his sword is naked and he turns towards Eriphyle in the stress of anger, and can hardly keep his hands off her. [9] Beyond Amphiaraos's house are Pelias's funeral games, the watchers and the contenders.[172] Herakles is sitting

168. Cattle-track (*boustrophedon*) like a team ploughing. This style persists until the archaic period, and could still be used for religious inscriptions even in early fifth-century Athens.

169. Pelops had borrowed Poseidon's horses.

170. Amphiaraos was going to fight in the war of the Seven against Thebes. He was a prophet and foresaw catastrophe, but Eriphyle was bribed with a necklace to trick him into promising to go. Amphiaraos was killed, and his son Alkmaion in time murdered his mother and commanded a second expedition of seven which took Thebes. Amphilochos the younger son helped Alkmaion, fought at Troy, and was a prophet and founder of cities in Asia Minor. Exactly the scene Pausanias describes also occurred on a late-Corinthian column krater found in Italy in 1872 and destroyed in Berlin (n. 1471) in an air-raid during the Second World War. Cf. Note 172.

171. Asios was the putative author of a genealogical epic to which Pausanias often refers; cf. Bk IV, 2 (1).

172. Pelias's funeral games were on the back of the same vase in Berlin which had the Amphiaraos scene. The same two subjects are combined on one or two vases made or found in Italy. The coincidence is not so surprising that one can

on a throne with his wife behind him: the inscription to say who she was is missing, but she plays Phrygian flutes, not Greek ones. The drivers of racing pairs are Pisos son of Perieres and Asterion son of Kometes, who is said to have sailed in the Argo, Polydeukes and Admetos, and Euphemos, who poets say was a son of Poseidon, and who took part in Jason's voyage to Kolchoi. He is also the winner with his racing pair. [10] Those daring to box are Admetos and Mopsos son of Ampyx; a man stands between them playing the flute, just as in our time the practice is to play it in the jumping for the pentathlon. Jason and Peleus are wrestling, and the contest is even. Someone or other famous for the discus called Eurybotas is letting go a discus. The runners in the foot-race are Melanion and Neitheus and Phalareus, fourthly Argeios and fifthly Iphiklos. Iphiklos is winning, and Akastos is stretching out with the wreath: that must be the father of Protesilaos who fought against Troy. [11] There are tripods as prizes for the winners, and Pelias's daughters are there, though only Alkestis has her name written in. Iolaos, the voluntary partner of the labours of Herakles, is winning the chariot race, and Pelias's funeral games end at this point. Athene stands beside Herakles who shoots the many-headed dragon, the monster of the river Amymone.[173] Herakles is recognizable by the labour and by his style of dress, so his name is not written in. Phineus the Thracian is there, and the sons of the north-east wind are chasing the Harpies away from him.[174]

---

draw exact conclusions about it, but it does tend to bring down the date of the chest of Kypselos to the sixth century. Taken together, the most striking analogies to the composition of the chest of Kypselos are not on a Corinthian but an Attic vase, the François (Francesi) vase in the Archaeological Museum at Florence. (Cf. Arias Hirmer and Shefton, *History of Greek Vase-painting*, n. 40–6.) But it must be admitted that the style of Kleinias on the François vase is more vigorous and sharply conceived than most Corinthian work of its date.

173. The Lernaian hydra; cf. Bk II, 37 (4).

174. The harpies used to steal Phineus's dinner or drop their droppings all over it.

[1] In the second area on the chest we shall go round from 18
the left. There is a woman carrying a white boy asleep in her
right arm, and a black boy in her left who seems to be asleep,
facing in different directions; the inscription proves, but you
could guess without any inscription, that the children are
Death and Sleep, and Night is the nurse of both of them.[175]
[2] A beautiful woman punishing an ugly woman, throttling
her with one hand and beating her with a stick with the
other, is Justice doing this to Injustice. Two other women are
pounding in crushing-bowls with pounders and are believed
to have the knowledge of herbs, since they have no inscription.[176] The hexameter verses explain the man with the woman
following him as follows:

> Idas brings home Marpessa with the fine ankles
> daughter of Euanos, she is not unwilling,
> Apollo had dragged her away from him.[177]

[3] There is a man in a tunic, with a cup in his right hand and
a necklace in his left, and Alkmene is taking hold of them; this
refers to the Greek legend that Zeus lay with Alkmene in the
likeness of Amphitryon.[178] Menelaos in a breast-plate with a
sword is coming at Helen to murder her, obviously at the fall
of Troy. Medea is enthroned with Jason on her right and
Aphrodite on her left; there is an inscription on them:

> Aphrodite commands: Jason marries Medeia.

175. This genealogy is conventional (Hesiod, Theogony 212), and even the
image has probably a literary ancestry (cf. Hesiod, Theogony, 748–61).

176. Pindar in an unregarded fragment (cf. D. S. Robertson in Classical
Review, 72, pp. 11–12) says Quiet was the child of Justice, and Disturbance was
the child of Injustice. But the only known personification of Justice fighting
Injustice is a picture of this scene with the names inscribed, on the handle of a
very early red-figure Attic neck-amphora now in Vienna (n. 3722). If I am
right about the date of the chest of Kypselos the vase was made within the same
generation.

177. Idas was a strong man; he and Apollo fought over Marpessa (Iliad, 9,
557). Zeus told Marpessa to choose, and she chose Idas.

178. Amphitryon was her husband. This was how she begot Herakles.

[4] The Muses are singing with Apollo leading the song, and the inscription written on them says:

> Lato's son, the lord, the worker in the distance: Apollo,
> Muses around him, a lovely troop, and he leads them.

Atlas holds up heaven and earth on his shoulders as the legend says, and carries the apples of the Hesperides. Nothing is individually inscribed on the man holding the sword and coming to Atlas to say who he is, but it is completely obvious that this is Herakles; the general inscription is:

> Look, Atlas holds heaven and will drop the apples.[179]

[5] Ares fully armed is leading Aphrodite; his inscription calls him Enyalios. Thetis is a virgin, and Peleus has hold of her, and a snake from Thetis's hand is attacking him. Medusa's sisters with wings are chasing Perseus in flight, but only Perseus has his name written in.[180]

[6] The third area of the chest is military: most of the men are infantry but there are some in chariots with pairs of horses. One can guess the soldiers are coming into battle, yet at the same time they are going to recognize and greet each other. The sacred guides take two sides: some say this is the Aitolians under Oxylos, and the ancient Eleans, meeting in the consciousness of their ancient relationship and showing kindness to each other; others say that these are armies meeting in conflict, and the Pylians and Arkadians are going to fight by the city of Pheia and the river Jordanos.[181] [7] But

179. Herakles held up the universe in return for the apples. One version of this story is that Atlas went to fetch the apples.

180. Being a sea-creature Thetis had magic powers and could produce monsters or turn into one. Peleus had to keep tight hold of her. Frazer in his commentary on Pausanias quotes a story of the same kind from nineteenth-century Crete. Medusa's sisters are the Gorgons; Perseus has cut her head off and the others are after him. The scene is very commonly represented in vase-painting.

181. A battle from Nestor's reminiscences in the Iliad (7, 133f.) and therefore of local interest like Oxylos and the Aitolians. Anonymous rows of soldiers are an extremely common feature of Corinthian vase-painting.

it is quite unacceptable that Kypselos's Corinthian ancestor who made himself this chest as a valuable thing should be happy to pass over local Corinthian history and to work foreign and otherwise obscure stories onto his chest. My own guess is this: Kypselos and his ancestors came originally and by blood from Gonoussa above Sikyon, and Melas the son of Antasos was their ancestor; [8] now (as I have already said in my Corinthian history) Aletes was unwilling to accept Melas and his followers as fellow settlers, being suspicious through a prophecy from the Delphic oracle, and then after every kind of subservience from Melas, and when as often as he was driven off Melas returned with entreaties, in the end Aletes did accept them against his will. One might argue that this was the military scene on the chest.[182]

[1] Going round the fourth area on the chest from the left, 19 the north-east wind has snatched away Oreithuia – he has serpent tails instead of feet – and there is the contest of Herakles with Geryon, who consists of three men joined together.[183] Theseus has a lyre, and Ariadne beside him holds a wreath. Achilles and Memnon are fighting with their mothers standing by, [2] and Melanion has Atalante beside him holding a fawn. Hektor is fighting a duel with Ajax by invitation, and Conflict stands between them, extremely ugly to look at. Kalliphon of Samos made Conflict like this, in his painting of the battle at the Greek ships, in the sanctuary of Ephesian Artemis.[184] The Dioskouroi are also on the chest, one of them still with no beard, and Helen is between them;

182. Cf. Bk II, 4 (4).

183. Boreas (the north-east wind) stole Oreithuia from near the river Ilissos and married her. Herakles killed Geryon to get his cattle. Daimonic figures like Geryon often have two or three bodies in archaic art.

184. Theseus had Ariadne and abandoned her before Dionysos found her. For Achilles and Memnon, cf. Bk III, 18 (12). Melanion obtained Atalante by beating her at running; he won by dropping the golden apples of Aphrodite for her to pick up. Is it the same Melanion who hated women and lived alone in the mountains hunting hares (like Hippolytos)? Cf. Aristophanes, *Lysistrata*, 781f. For Hektor and Ajax, cf. *Iliad*, 7, 225f. For Kalliphon cf. Bk X, 26 (6). He could well have been a sixth-century painter.

[3] Pittheus's daughter Aithra is dressed in black and has been thrown down on the ground under Helen's feet; the inscription on them is a single hexameter verse with one name left over.

> The sons of Tyndareos take Helen and drag Aithra
> from Athens.[185]

[4] That is how the verse goes; Antenor's son Iphidamas has fallen and Koon is fighting over him with Agamemnon: Fear, which has a lion's head, is on Agamemnon's shield; there is an inscription over the corpse of Iphidamas,

> Look: Iphidamas: Koon is fighting for him,

and on Agamemnon's shield,

> This is human Fear; Agamemnon holds it.[186]

[5] Hermes brings the goddesses to Priam's son Alexander, to be judged for beauty; here is the inscription:

> Hermes shows for Alexander's choice the beauty
> of Hera, of Athene, of Aphrodite.

Artemis – for I have no idea what reason – has wings on her shoulders, and holds a leopard in one hand and a lion in the other. Ajax is dragging Kassandra away from Athene's statue, with an inscription on him:

> Lokrian Ajax drags Kassandra from Athene.

[6] There are the sons of Oedipus: Polyneikes has fallen on

185. On the fine black-figure amphora by Exekias in the Vatican, painted about the thirties of the sixth century, Kastor seems to have a beard and Polydeukes has none, but the difference may be only a difference of hair-style; on a roughly contemporary statue-base in the National Museum at Athens four youths playing together have four quite different hair-styles. In Exekias's painting Kastor has a horse, a cloak and a spear, but Polydeukes is naked and playing with a dog. (Cf. Arias Hirmer and Shefton, *Greek Vase-painting*, pl. 63.) Aithra was Theseus's mother and became Helen's slave; cf. Bk X, 25 (3).

186. Iphidamas and his brother Koon were killed by Agamemnon (*Iliad*, 11, 248–63). For the shield of Agamemnon, cf. *Iliad*, 11, 36–7.

one knee and Eteokles is coming at him. Behind Eteokles stands a woman with ferocious teeth like a wild beast and curved nails on her fingers; the inscription calls her Doom, as Polyneikes is being carried off by destiny, and Eteokles is dying as he deserves.[187] Dionysos, bearded and dressed in an ankle-length tunic, is lying in a grotto holding a golden drinking-cup: there are vines around him and apple-trees and pomegranates.

[7] The uppermost area of the five that there are has no inscriptions at all, but one can guess about what has been worked on it. There is a woman sleeping in a cave with a man on a bed: I think they are Odysseus and Circe, because of the number of slave-women in front of the cave and what they are doing: there are four of these women, and they are doing the work Homer spoke of in his epic.[188] There is a centaur with only two hooves, as his front feet are human. [8] Next in line come pairs of horses and women standing in the chariots: the horses have golden wings and a man gives arms to one of the women. They argue that this refers to Patroklos's death, with Nereus's daughters in the chariots and Thetis taking the arms from Hephaistos. And in fact the figure handing over the arms is not strong in the feet, and a slave follows behind him holding a pair of tongs. [9] They say of the centaur that Cheiron, when he was free from humanity and permitted to live with the gods, came to give Achilles some relief in his grief.[189] They think the young girls in a mule-cart, one holding the reins and the other with her head

187. Oedipus's sons were doomed to quarrel after his death; they killed each other like Balin and Balan in the war of the Seven against Thebes.

188. *Odyssey*, 10, 348f. They were setting chairs and tables, mixing wine and fetching water; they were river-nymphs. Loeschke offered in 1880 the excellent suggestion that the real subject here was the wedding of Peleus and Thetis with the armour being brought for a wedding present (*Iliad*, 16, 194f.). The centaur Cheiron figures in the same scene on the Francois vase (cf. Note 172 above).

189. Cheiron had educated the boy Achilles on Mount Pelion. As ideas of education altered, people's idea of Cheiron's wisdom and the way he trained Achilles also developed. At first Cheiron must have trained him to live wild, to outrun the animals, and to kill.

veiled, are Nausikaa, the daughter of Alkinoos, and her servant, driving to the washing-place.[190] As for the man shooting centaurs, who has in fact already killed some of them, it is obviously Herakles shooting and Herakles' doing.[191]

[10] I was quite unable to make out who it was that worked on this chest; someone else of course could possibly have composed the inscriptions, and Eumelos of Corinth came most to mind, because of his processional for Delos among other reasons.[192]

20 [1] There are other dedications here: a bed not of any great size but mostly decorated in ivory, and Iphitos's discus, and the table where they put out the wreaths for the winners. They say the bed was Hippodameia's toy; Iphitos's discus has the truce which the Eleans proclaim for the Olympic games, not written out straight but with the writing going round the discus in a circle;[193] [2] the table was made in ivory and gold by Kolotes, who they say came from Herakleia, though the real specialists in the history of sculpture make him out to be a Parian, an apprentice of Pasiteles, who was an apprentice of . . .[194] There is a Hera and a Zeus and a Mother of gods and Hermes and an Apollo with Artemis; and on the back is the management of the games. [3] On one side is Asklepios with one of his daughters, Health, and Ares is there

190. *Odyssey*, 6, 72. It seems an unlikely guess, but no better suggestion has been made.

191. Cf. Bk V, 17 (7). This scene occurred also on the Corinthian column krater in Berlin; cf. Notes 170 and 172 above.

192. There is obviously a hint here about the stark narrative style and the mythological content of Eumelos's Delian hymn. It sounds to have been more like Hesiod's *Theogony* than any of the Homeric hymns. Cf. also Bk IV, 4 (1), and 33 (2). For the fragments of other works attributed to Eumelos, cf. Kinkel, *Epic. Graec. Frag.*, pp. 185f.

193. Aristotle knew this disk, which was not necessarily an athletic discus, but probably the text used for the ritual proclamation of the Olympic truce. There are a number of inscribed bronze disks in museums; Iphitos's disk has not survived; it also named Lykourgos. It is unlikely to have been as old as the eighth century; cf. Jeffery, *Archaic Scripts*, p. 217; and for inscribed disks in general, cf. Jacobsthal, *Diskoi* (Winkelmannsprogramm 93, 1933).

194. Pliny says he was a pupil of Pheidias. Pasiteles is otherwise unknown.

with Contest beside him; on the other side you have Plouton and Dionysos and Persephone and two Nymphs, one of whom is carrying a ball: what they say about the key which Plouton is holding is that Plouton has locked up Hades and that no one ever returns from there.[195]

[4] But it would be wrong for me to pass over the story that Aristarchos used to tell; he was a sacred guide to the Olympian sanctuaries.[196] He said that in his own lifetime, when the Eleans were repairing the dilapidated roof of the temple of Hera, the corpse of a man-at-arms was found with the wounds on it between the ceiling and the tiled roof; he must have fought in the battle in Altis between Elis and Lakonia, [5] when the Eleans climbed up on to the temples of the gods and on to every high point they could find to defend themselves. The man seems to have lost consciousness from his wounds and slipped into this crevice, and when he breathed his last, neither the violence of the summer heat nor the freezing winter could hurt his dead body, because it was perfectly sheltered. And Aristarchos said they took the dead body outside Altis, and buried it with its armour on.[197]

[6] What the Eleans call OINOMAOS'S PILLAR is on the way to Zeus's sanctuary from the great altar; there are four columns on the left with a roof on them, to protect a wooden pillar dilapidated by the processes of time and almost covered with

195. More probably Aiakos: Plouton is supposed to have trusted him with the keys of Hades.

196. Nothing is known about Aristarchos except what Pausanias tells us. It is not impossible that Pausanias took the story from a literary source. We know that Hadrian's ex-slave Phlegon of Tralles wrote a chronicle of the Olympics (*Fragments of the Greek Historians*, II B 3, n. 257, Fr. 1–34), and there were certainly accounts of the Olympic sanctuary: unfortunately they have not survived.

197. Gurlitt (*Über Pausanias*, 1890, p. 405) believed with other German scholars that Aristarchos was wrong about the war, and that the man was really killed in the Arkadian War in 364. The war with Lakonia lasted from 401 to 399, and Eleia was looted, but there was no battle in Altis so far as we know; we do on the other hand know of a battle in Altis in 364 (Xenophon, *Hellenika*, 7, 4, 28).

chains.[198] The legend is that this pillar stood in Oinomaos's house, and when the god's thunderbolt struck, the rest of the house perished in the fire, and only this one pillar was left from the whole house. [7] There is a small bronze sheet in front of it inscribed with couplets:

> *I am what is left of the famous house, traveller,*
> *I have been a pillar in the halls of Oinomaos;*
> *am now with Zeus, son of Kronos, holding chains,*
> *and am venerable: dreadful flaming fire*
> *has not destroyed me.*

[8] And there was something else that also happened in my time. A Roman senator won at Olympia, and wanted to leave a bronze portrait statue with an inscription in memory of his victory; so he dug down to make a foundation trench: when the digging had got very close to Oinomaos's pillar, the diggers found fragments of arms and horse-bits and curb-chains. [9] I myself saw them excavated.[199] There is a small Doric temple which they still in my day call the MOTHER'S SANCTUARY, preserving its ancient name. There is no statue of the Mother of gods in it, but figures of the Roman kings stand there. The Mother's sanctuary is inside Altis, and so is the round building called the SANCTUARY OF PHILIP, on the pinnacle of which is a bronze poppy that ties together the roof beams.[200] [10] This building is on the left by the exit

198. It has never been found.

199. Mr Papahadzis in his commentary on Pausanias tells a story of bronze armour that was found when one of the enormous pine-trees planted in the Altis a hundred years ago by order of Queen Amalia, who disliked the heat at Olympia, was blown down in a gale in December 1963.

200. The fourth-century SANCTUARY OF THE MOTHER lies east of the Heraion, just south of the terrace of the treasuries which is the northern limit of Altis. PHILIP'S SANCTUARY was a fine rotunda with external pillars in the north-west corner of Altis not far from the west end of the Heraion. Pausanias is raising an eyebrow that the 'sanctuaries' of dead kings should be inside the sacred area. It was not unheard of for the Romans in Greece to take over an existing sanctuary, but one would expect a smoother story: an emperor would be identified with the existing god or worshipped in an annexe. Perhaps the sanctuary of the Mother became the family shrine of the imperial family.

by the Council-house, built in fired brick with columns standing round it; Philip built it after the fall of Greece at Chaironeia. Philip and Alexander are there, and Philip's father Amyntas, all by Leochares in ivory and gold like the portraits of Olympias and Eurydike.[201]

[1] I shall now move on to explain the statues and dedications; but I preferred not to give an indiscriminate account of them. In the upper city at Athens the statues like everything else are all dedications, while in Altis some things are kept for divine reverence, but the statues of winners are granted as a kind of prize.[202] I shall mention these statues again later, but first of all I want to consider the dedications and go through the most important ones.

[2] On the way to the racing-track from the Mother's sanctuary, on the left at the edge of Mount Kronion, there is a stone platform against the mount itself, with steps that go up through the platform; bronze statues of Zeus have been dedicated against this platform, made from the money paid in penalties by athletes fined for dishonouring the games; the local people call them ZANS.[203] [3] The first six were set up at the ninety-eighth Olympics, when Eupolos of Thessaly bribed the boxers who entered, Agetor of Arkadia and Prytanis of Kyzikos, and also Phormion of Halikarnassos, who won the boxing at the previous Olympics. This is said to have been the first crime that athletes ever committed in the games, and Eupolos and the men he bribed were the first to be fined by Elis. Two of the statues are by Kleon of Sikyon, but we

201. They employed probably the most graceful of all late-fourth-century sculptors. Olympias was Alexander's mother, Eurydike was Philip's, the battle of Chaironeia was in 338.

202. The analogy with Athens comes to his mind because in both places a commentator in the age of Hadrian would be appalled by the task of finding his way through the marble forests of statuary.

203. Sixteen bases from these statues have been found in front of the terrace where the treasuries are, between the METROON (the sanctuary of the Mother) and the stadium. From the position of the feet one may reasonably conjecture that a *Zan* (dialect word for Zeus) was a naked Zeus advancing and hurling his thunderbolt.

have no way of knowing who made the other four.[204] [4] Apart from the third and fourth of these statues, they all have couplets inscribed on them. The first couplet is meant to show that you win at Olympia with the speed of your feet and the strength in your body, and not with money; the one on the second statue says it was put up out of respect for religion and by the pious practice of the Eleans, and to frighten crooked athletes. The sense of the inscription on the fifth is to praise Elis, and particularly for fining the boxers, and on the last one that these statues are a lesson to the whole of Greece not to give bribes to win at the Olympics.

[5] They say the next offender after Eupolos was Kallippos of Athens, who bought off his opponents with bribes when he was competing in the pentathlon: it happened in the hundred and twelfth Olympics. Kallippos and his opponents were fined by Elis, and Athens sent Hypereides to persuade the Eleans to let him off.[205] Elis refused this favour, and the Athenians were so contemptuous as neither to pay the money nor to attend the games, until the god at Delphi refused to give them any more oracles about anything until they paid the Eleans first: [6] so they paid and the statues were made for Zeus, six of them, and inscribed with couplets quite as ham-handedly composed as the ones about Eupolos's fine. The sense of them is this: first that these statues were dedicated by command of the god who honoured the Elean decree about the pentathlon competitors, on the second and third the Eleans are lauded for the pentathlon fine, [7] the fourth means to say that the Olympics are a contest for a man's quality and not for money, and of the inscriptions on the fifth and sixth, one explains why the statues were put up and the other records the Delphic oracle's message to Athens.

[8] There are two more statues next to those I have listed,

204. In 388 B.C. Kleon's signature has been found.

205. In 332. Unfortunately we have only two stray words from Hypereides' speech, and the fact that he mentioned a prize given at the Eleusinian games. It sounds as if he was defending professionalism in athletics. His potted biography in the *Vitae decem oratorum* says he won his case; perhaps there was some dispute about the decision, which was taken to Delphi for arbitration.

dedicated from a fine imposed on wrestlers. Either their names have escaped the Elean sacred guides, or the mistake is mine. There are inscriptions on these statues too, the first saying that Rhodes paid a fine to Olympian Zeus for the crime of a wrestler, the second that the statue was made from fines imposed on corrupt wrestlers. [9] The Elean guides explain the rest of the story of these athletes by saying that in the hundred and seventy-eighth Olympics Eudelos took a bribe from Philostratos who was a Rhodian.[206] But I have found that this story differs from the Elean records of Olympic winners: in the records for the hundred and seventy-eighth Olympics Strato of Alexandria won the wrestling and the all-in fighting on the same day.[207] Alexandria on the Kanopic mouth of the Nile was founded by Alexander son of Philip: there is supposed to have been a small earlier Egyptian town there called Rakotis.[208] [19] There are three men before Strato and three more after him who certainly won the wild olive both for all-in fighting and for wrestling : Kapros of Elis, and two Greeks from across the Aegean, Aristomenes of Rhodes and Protophanes from Lethaian Magnesia, and then after Straton Mario from the same city, and Aristeas of Stratonike, which used to be called Goldensword, both city and territory;[209] the seventh man was Nikostratos, from the Kilikian coast, though he had nothing to do with Kilikia except for the word. [11] Nikostratos came from a dis-

206. In 68 B.C.

207. Strato was a particularly great and famous athlete; cf. Bk VII, 23 (5). Philostratos could have bribed Eudelos and still not have won.

208. Rakotis survived as the name of the district behind the docks. Alexandria has never ceased to be partly a Greek city. The first man ever to win both was Kapros in 212 B.C.; after A.D. 37 no one was allowed even to enter for both.

209. Lethaian Magnesia means Magnesia on the Lethaios, a tributary of the Maiandros. Is Pausanias not going out of his way to commemorate someone from his own city? Stratonike was a Macedonian city founded by Antiochos Soter in Karia and named after his wife, near the sanctuary of Goldensword Zeus (Chysaoris), which was the centre of a confederation of towns. Chandler discovered the ruins in 1760 at ESKIHISSAR and confirmed the identification from inscriptions; they have never been properly excavated. Hadrian changed the name to Hadrianopolis (cf. Real–Encyclopädie, Suppl. VII).

tinguished family and was stolen by Phrygian pirates from Prymnessos as a little baby;[210] they took him to Aigiai where he was bought by someone or other, and some time later this man had a dream in which he thought there was a lion cub crouching under the mattress where Nikostratos was sleeping. And when Nikostratos grew up, among his other victories he was Olympic champion in the all-in fighting and in the wrestling.

[12] There were other men afterwards who were fined by Elis, one of whom was an Alexandrian boxer fined in the two hundred and eighteenth Olympics;[211] his name was Apollonios but his nickname was Sprinkler: nicknames are a sort of local tradition in Alexandria. This man was the first Egyptian tried and convicted by Elis, not for giving or taking a bribe, but for dishonouring the games in the following way. [13] He failed to arrive at the stated time and as a result the Eleans followed the law and barred him from the games; Herakleides, who was another Alexandrian, proved that his excuse, that contrary winds had held him up in the Cyclades, was a lie: he was really late through collecting prizes from the games in Ionia. [14] So the Eleans expelled Apollonios and any other boxer who failed to turn up on the agreed day from the games, and awarded Herakleides the wreath without a fight. At this point Apollonios tied up his hands in leather thongs for boxing, and ran in and hit Herakleides, who was already wearing the wild olive and had then taken refuge with the Greek arbiters. Apollonios's lack of common sense was very expensive to him. [15] There are two other statues of modern workmanship: at the two hundred and twenty-sixth Olympics some boxers who fought then were discovered to have made a money agreement and were fined for it; from the money statues were made of Zeus, one to stand on the

210. He came from Phrygia not Kilikia, but he was bought from the Kilikian coast. Aigiai is in Lakonia (cf. Bk VII, 21 (5)). Prymnessos was an inland town between KONIA and ESKISHEHR, near KARAHISSAR (cf. Ramsay, *Cities and Bishoprics of Phrygia*, p. 27).

211. In A.D. 93.

left and one on the right of the entrance to the stadium. The
boxer who gave the bribe was called Sarapammon and the
other was called Deidas; they came from the same district,
Arsinoites, the newest district in Egypt.[212] [16] It is surely a
staggering thing that people should so despise the god at
Olympia as to give or take a bribe, but it seems even more
extraordinary that any Elean can have perpetrated such an
outrage. Yet they say this of Damonikos of Elis, at the hundred
and ninety-second Olympics, when Damonikos's son Polyktor met Sosander son of Sosander of Smyrna in the wrestling.[213]
Damonikos terribly wanted his son to win, and gave money
to Sosander's father. [17] When the transaction leaked out,
the Greek arbiters imposed a fine, but not on the boys; they
visited their anger on the fathers, because the fathers committed the crime. Statues were made from this fine, one of
which is dedicated at the Elean training-ground, and the
other in Altis in front of what they call the PAINTED COLON-
NADE, because in ancient times there were paintings on its
walls; though some people call it Echo's colonnade, because if
you shout in it the echo of your voice comes back seven times,
and sometimes even more.[214]

[18] They say that an Alexandrian all-in fighter called Sarapion at the two hundred and first Olympics was so terrified
of his opponents that he ran away the day before the all-in
fight was due.[215] He is recorded to be the only Egyptian and
in fact the only man ever to be fined for cowardice.

I have discovered that those were the reasons for the
casting of the statues I have listed;

212. They were fined in A.D. 125; Arsinoites was the very rich region south-
west of Memphis on the west bank of the Nile. As a settled area it was extremely
old; but its Ptolemaic name was comparatively modern. The Greeks called it
Crocodile City because of the superstitions of its inhabitants.

213. In 12 B.C.

214. This runs from north to south down the eastern boundary of Altis,
from the stadium to Nero's house. It appears to be a late-fourth-century construction perhaps by the same architect as the Philippeion. The remains of a
dismantled fifth-century colonnade lay behind it, and there was a line of statues
in front of it.

215. In A.D. 25.

22   [1] but there are also some statues of Zeus which were public and private dedications. There is an altar in Altis near the entrance into the stadium, on which the Eleans never sacrifice to any god, but tradition dictates that competing trumpeters and heralds should stand on it. Beside this altar a bronze platform has been installed with a statue of Zeus on it about eight feet high, with a thunderbolt in each hand, dedicated by the Kynaithaians. The Zeus as a boy wearing a necklace was dedicated by a Phliasian called Kleolas.[216]

[2] Beside the SANCTUARY OF HIPPODAMEIA there is a SEMI-CIRCULAR STONE PLATFORM with statues on it of Thetis and Dawn begging Zeus for mercy for their children.[217] Those are in the centre of the platform, and Achilles and Memnon like soldiers already in action are at either end of it. In just the same way, man against man, barbarian against Greek, Odysseus stands against Helenos, because they had the highest reputation for cleverness in the two armies, Paris against Menelaos because of the original feud, Aineias against Diomedes, and Deiphobos against Ajax son of Telamon. [3] These are by Lykios son of Myron, and they were dedicated by the Apollonians on the Ionian sea, and in fact there are some couplets in ancient lettering below Zeus's feet.

> Apollonia has dedicated these monuments:
> long-haired Phoibos built it on the Ionian sea:
> conquerors of Abantis and its boundaries
> through the gods we set these statues up:
> this is the tithe of the spoils of Thronion.[218]

216. Kynaitha is in Arkadia (cf. Bk VIII, 19 (1)). Phlious is in the hills west of Corinth (cf. Bk II, 13 (3–8)). The tortuous poet Lykophron calls Zeus 'the Kynaithean'.

217. Fragments of this platform with the name Memnon have been found, but the sanctuary of Hippodameia has never been identified. The story is epic but non-Homeric; it was told by Arktinos (cf. Bk III, 18 (16)). Hammond (*Epirus*, p. 384) suggests that all the figures had a special local significance at Apollonia.

218. APOLLONIA was an early-sixth-century Corinthian settlement which had Illyrian cooperation and support. The site lies west of FIER near the coast of southern Albania just north of the river Vijosë (Aous). Thronion is twenty

The region called Abantis and its town of Thronion were
part of the Thesprotion mainland by the Thundering mountains. [4] When the Greek ships scattered on the way home
from Troy, the Lokrians from Thronion on the banks of the
Boagrios river and the Abantes from Euboia with eight ships
each were driven on the Thundering mountains. They settled
there and built the city of Thronion, and agreed together to
name as much of the country as they occupied Abantis: but
later on the Apollonians who bordered on it defeated them
in war and expelled them. APOLLONIA is said to be a colony
founded from Corfu, but some people say the Corinthians
shared the spoils.[219]

[5] A little farther on you come to a Zeus facing east with
an eagle on one hand and a thunderbolt in the other; he has
a wreath of spring flowers on his head. He was dedicated by the
Metapontines and made by Aristonos of Aigina. We have no
knowledge of who taught Aristonos or what his period was.[220]
[6] The Phliasians dedicated another Zeus and Asopos with
his daughters; the grouping is like this: Nemea is the first
sister, and then comes Zeus taking hold of Aigina, with
Harpina standing beside her, who in the Elean and Phliasian
legend slept with Ares, and became the mother of Oinomaos
who reigned over Pise; then comes Korkyra, and after her

---

miles south near the port of Amantia (Vlorë) between the river Shushicë
(Polyanthos) and the sea. This verse inscription has now been found, and can
be dated between 475 and 450 B.C. Lykos was working in his father's lifetime;
cf. Kunze, *Bericht* 5 (1956, pp. 149f.). Thronion had controlled an important
asphalt mine, and presumably also an important trade-route.

219. There is something wrong with the manuscripts here: or did the
Corinthians share the spoils of Thronion? The coincidence of the place names
Thronion and Abantis with the Lokrian Thronion at PIKRAKI opposite north
Euboia and the Homeric Abantes of Euboia makes it very likely that Thronion
was a combined Lokrian and Euboian settlement. The Trojan story has of
course no historical authority at all.

220. Metaponton was an Achaian settlement in southern Italy; it was a
coastal city on the gulf of Tarentum. It was a successful early-seventh-century
foundation; it was one of the first Greek cities in Italy to strike its own coins
(before the mid sixth century), and it had a fine sixth-century temple. This
dedication may have been an early one.

Thebe, and last of all Asopos. Legend says of Korkyra that Poseidon made love with her, and Pindar in his songs has said the same about Thebe and Zeus.[221]

[7] Some Leontinians have erected a Zeus privately and not by public decree; the statue is ten feet high, and has in its hands an eagle and the weapon of Zeus that poets speak of. It was dedicated by Hippagoras and Phrymon and Ainesidemos, who (I think) was some other Ainesidemos and not the Leontinian dictator.[222]

23    [1] Past the entry to the SENATE you come to a Zeus with no inscription and then as you turn north there is a statue of Zeus that faces east, dedicated by all the Greeks who fought at Plataia against Mardonios and the Persians.[223] The cities who took part in the action are inscribed on the right of the base, Lakonians first, then Athenians, third and fourth Corinthians and Sikyonians, fifth Aiginetans, [2] then Megarians and Epidaurians, Tegeans and Orchomenians from Arkadia, people from Phlious, Troizen, Hermione, men from Tiryns in the Argolid, the Plataians alone from Boiotia, Mycenaeans alone of all the Argives, islanders from Keos and Melos, Ambrakiotes from the Thesprotian mainland, Tenians and Lepreans, the Lepreans being the only men from Triphylia, but from the Aegean sea and the Cyclades there were not only Tenians, but Naxians and Kythnians as well; Styrians from Euboia, Eleans, Potidaians, Anaktorians, and

221. Korkyra is the modern Greek Kerkyra (Corfu). Pindar on Thebe and Zeus has not survived. The Asopos was the Phliasian river; for Asopos's daughters, cf. Bk II, 5 (1), and 12 (3). The Phliasians had also dedicated a Zeus and an Aigina at Delphi (Bk X, 13 (6)).

222. Leontinoi was in Sicily between Syracuse and Catana; the site is on a hill above a shallow lake eight miles from the coast. Who was the Ainesidemos who was dictator there? Gelon's contemporary the son of Pataikos? (cf. Herodotos, 7, 154). A fragment of what might possibly be the inscribed base of this statue has been found to the south-east of Altis. The inscription seems to me to be early fifth-century, on Parian marble.

223. The senate-house (bouleuterion) was on the south of the sacred area (cf. Bk V, 24 (1) and (8), and Xenophon, Hellenika, 7, 4, 31) outside Altis. The Plataian Zeus was a bronze statue fifteen foot high (Herodotos, 9, 81).

finally men of Chalkis on the Euripos.[224] [3] Of those cities the following are deserted in our time: Mycenae and Tiryns were rooted out by Argos after the Persian wars; the Roman emperor brought in the Ambrakiotes and the Anaktorians, who were Corinthian colonists, to the combined settlement of Nikopolis at Aktion;[225] the Potidaians were fated to be twice expelled from their country, by Philip, son of Amyntas, and even before that by Athens, but later on Kassander restored the Potidaians to their rights, though the city was not called by its ancient name, but KASSANDREIA after its founder. The statue the Greeks dedicated at Olympia is by Anaxagoras of Aigina: the historians of Plataia have passed him over in their histories.[226]

224. The cities were also inscribed at Delphi on the column of twisted bronze serpents which has in fact survived at Istanbul. Cf. Bk X, 13 (9). Herodotos gives a slightly different list (9, 28–30 and 77).

225. Mycenae and Tiryns are powerful prehistoric fortresses, Tiryns in the very rich plain north of the gulf of Nauplion, and Mycenae in a stronger position farther north on the edge of the mountains. They are both clearly visible from the akropolis of Argos a few miles away across the river. Anaktorion was the chief trading city of Akarnania; the site is at HAGIOS PETROS on a peninsula west of Aktion, north of LEVKAS at the entrance to the Ambrakian gulf. For the harbours of Anaktorion, cf. L. Robert, *Hellenica*, XI–XII, 1960, pp. 263–6. Colonel W. M. Leake found it, but by 1860 there was very little of it left (cf. Heuzey, *Le mont Olympe et l'Acarnanie*, pp. 383–6). Professor Hammond (*Epirus* p. 62) observed that a good deal of it is now under water. The port of Ambrakia (Ambrakos) on the north side of the gulf has all but disappeared in the same way: it is now called PHIDOKASTRO (Snakes' castle), and you can reach it by wading through the lagoon from Salaora or in summer on foot across the mud-flats from Neochori (Hammond, *Epirus*, p. 137). The site of Nikopolis is on the PREVEZA peninsula which is the northern lip of the gulf. It is the ruins of a vast Byzantine and Roman settlement; relatively to its importance it must be the most neglected archaeological site in Greece. Augustus built it to commemorate the defeat of Antony and Cleopatra in the sea-battle off Aktion (Actium) in 31 B.C., and devastated Akarnania and Aitolia to people it. Like Roman Patrai it was a creation not only of strategic but of mercantile policy, and it flourished.

226. The Athenians threw them out in 430 or 429 and Philip threw them out in 356. Potidaia was the city on the neck of land joining the western prong of Chalkidike to the mainland south-east of SALONIKI. Kassander restored Thebes as well as Potidaia (in 316) and founded Thessalonike (Saloniki). The sculptor is mentioned by Diogenes Laertius, and Anakreon wrote a dedicatory couplet for one of his works (*Palatine Anthology*, 6, 139).

[4] In front of this Zeus is a bronze tablet with the terms of thirty years' peace between Lakonia and Athens, made by Athens after the second conquest of Euboia, in the second year after the eighty-third Olympics, when Krison of Himera won the running.[227] One of the written conditions is that the city of Argos should be outside the peace between Lakonians and Athenians, but that Athens and Argos may if they so wish behave with mutual friendship. That is what the terms say.

9. Hyblaia

[5] There is another statue of Zeus beside Kleisthenes' chariot, which I shall mention again later;[228] the statue was dedicated by the Megarians, and is the work of the brothers Psylakos and Onaithos, and of their sons. I have no way of knowing when or where they lived or who they studied under. [6] By Gelon's chariot stands an ancient Zeus holding a staff, which they say was a dedication from Hybla. The cities of HYBLA were in Sicily, one called Hybla Gereatis, and the other Greater Hybla, which in fact it was. They still keep their names even in my day in the territory of Catana: but Greater

227. That is, in 445 B.C.; Himera was on the north coast of Sicily.
228. Cf. Bk VI, 10 (6).

Hybla is utterly deserted, and Gereatis is a village with a sanctuary of a goddess Hyblaia where the Sicilians still worship.[229] I imagine it was from these people that the statue was brought to Olympia: Philistos son of Archimenides speaks of them as interpreters of omens and dreams, and of all the barbarous peoples of Sicily the most inclined to religious piety.[230] [7] Near the Hybla dedication is a bronze base with a Zeus on it; I reckon it to be about eighteen feet high. Some couplets say who gave it to the god and who made it:

> Kleitor dedicated this statue: the god's tithe:
> their hands having forced many cities:
> Ariston and Telestas have made it:
> full brothers and Lakonians.

I do not believe they were famous all over Greece, as in that case the Eleans would at least have had something to tell us about them, and the Lakonians would have had a great deal more.[231]

[1] By the altar of Zeus Laoitas and Poseidon Laoitas,[232] there is a Zeus on a bronze base given by the people of Corinth, the work of Mousos, whoever Mousos was. On the way from the senate to the great temple there is a statue on the left of Zeus crowned apparently with a wreath of flowers, with a thunderbolt in his right hand by Askaros of Thebes, who was taught by Kanachos of Sikyon; the inscription on

229. Greater Hybla was a pre-Greek city on the southern slopes of Etna, near the Greek city of Aitna. Little Hybla or Hybla Gereatis (or Geleatis) seems to have been the same as Hyblaian Megara (Megara Hyblaia); it was on the coast near Syracuse (Thukydides, 6, 49) at the mouth of the Cantaro. Pausanias's account of the two places is confused; Thukydides calls Greater Hybla 'Geleatis'. The goddess Hyblaia figures on the coinage of Hybla.

230. Cicero (De divinatione, 1, 20) reports Philistos, whom he calls a learned and industrious writer, at greater length: the story is that the mother of Dionysios the future dictator of Syracuse dreamed when she was pregnant that her son would be a young satyr, and the Galeotae of Hybla told her the dream meant the boy would be great and fortunate.

231. Kleitor was an east Arkadian city; cf. Bk VIII, 21.

232. Cf. Bk V, Note 127.

it says it was a tithe from the war between Phokis and Thessaly, [2] but if Thessaly did fight a war with Phokis and this dedication is from Phokian spoils, it would not be the Sacred War, but the one they fought before the King of Persia invaded Greece.[233] Not far from this is a Zeus which the verse inscribed on it proves was dedicated by Psophis for a military success.[234]

[3] On the right of the great temple is a Zeus facing east twelve feet high, which they say the Lakonians dedicated when they went to war the second time against the Messenian rebellion. A couplet is inscribed on it:

> *Zeus Lord son of Kronos Olympian*
> *accept this good statue: bless the Lakonians.*[235]

[4] We have no knowledge of any Roman before Mummius dedicating at any Greek sanctuary, neither a private citizen nor a senator; Mummius dedicated a bronze Zeus at Olympia from the spoils of Achaia. It stands to the left of the Lakonian dedication, by the first pillar on this side of the temple.[236] The biggest bronze statue of Zeus in Altis was dedicated by the Eleans themselves from the war with

233. The first holy war, which Thessaly won. was about 590 B.C. Phokis and Thessaly often fought. Askaros was evidently a sculptor of the 490s, but we know that at Hyampolis about 500 B.C. it was Phokis who won (Bk X, 1 (3f.)). All this is a mystery.

234. Psophis was in north-west Arkadia on the borders of Eleia (Bk VIII, 24 (7)).

235. This couplet has been found (Curtius and Adler, *Olympia*, vol. 5, *Inschriften von Olympia*, n. 252). It can be dated between 500 and 492, which is not the date of any Messenian War known to Pausanias, but is at least a period when we know the Lakonians were having trouble from their subject populations. (Cf. Jeffery, *Local Scripts of Archaic Greece*, p. 196.) The inscription is on a round base of bluish grey Peloponnesian marble.

236. Several inscriptions from Mummius's dedications and statues have been found at Olympia: cf. also Section 8 of this chapter. This one, which has not turned up, must date from the Roman conquest of Greece in 146 B.C. We know from fragments of an inscription that Mummius and the ten legates who administered Greece under him were honoured with statues a full century later. They seem to have stood at the triumphal arch on the south-east of Altis.

Arkadia; it is twenty-seven feet high.[237] [5] There is a small
column by Pelops's sanctuary with a little statue of Zeus on
it stretching out one hand. Opposite to this is a line of other
dedications, and statues of Zeus and Ganymede. Homer has
written how Ganymede was carried off by the gods to be
Zeus's wine-pourer, and how Zeus gave Tros a gift of horses
in exchange. This was dedicated by Gnathis of Thessaly, and
made by Aristokles, Kleoitas's apprentice and his son.[238] [6]
There is also a Zeus before his beard has grown, kept among
Mikythos's dedications. I shall explain the story of Mikythos
as I go on: what his ancestry was and why he gave so many
dedications to Olympia.[239] A little way straight on beyond this
statue I have mentioned is another Zeus which is also beardless, dedicated by the people of Elaia, who are the first Aiolian
people as you come down to the sea from the Kaikos plain.[240]
[7] Next to this is yet another statue of Zeus, the inscription
of which says the Chersonesians of Knidos dedicated it from
the spoils of their enemies: beside the Zeus they also dedicated
Pelops on one side and the river Alpheios on the other. Most
of the city of KNIDOS is built on the Karian mainland, and the
Knidian things most worth talking about are there, but the
Chersonesos is an island lying offshore, and you can get across

237. The inscribed piece of a statue-base often associated with this statue is
probably not the right one. It is inscribed 'The Eleans, for Concord' in a script
which seems to me probably earlier than 364 B.C. (*Inschriften von Olympia*, n. 260).

238. The reference to Homer is to the *Iliad* (5, 265f., and 20, 231f.). Pausanias speaks of statues not of a statue; the magnificently vigorous Corinthian
painted terracotta statue of Zeus carrying away Ganymede now in the Olympia
museum appears to be an architectural ornament rather than an independent
dedication; it can be dated about 470 B.C. But Kleoitas's father was called
Aristokles as well as his son (Bk VI, 20 (14)), and we also know that the fine
archaic gravestone of Aristion in the National Museum at Athens was by a
sculptor called Aristokles; on the other hand for Kleoitas, cf. Bk VI, 20 (14);
it is impossible to be certain about the generations of this family.

239. Cf. Bk V, 26 (2).

240. Near the mouth of the Kaikos (BAKIR CAYI) east of the river and due
east of the southern tip of Lesbos. The river has silted and the ruins of the
harbour now lie among mud-flats. This city has never been thoroughly excavated; so far as I can discover the visible ruins have been casually dismembered, but cf. now G. Bean, *Aegean Turkey*, pp. 112f.

to it by a bridge. [8] The people who live there have dedicated
to Zeus at Olympia, just as if the inhabitants of what they
call Koresos in the city of Ephesos were to dedicate on their
own, apart from the Ephesian people.[241] By the Altis wall is
a Zeus facing west without any inscription: this one as well
was said to come from Mummius and the Achaian war.[242]
[9] Of all the statues of Zeus, the one in the senate is most
calculated to unnerve criminals; its title is Zeus of Oaths, and
it has a thunderbolt in one hand. The tradition dictates that
the athletes and their fathers and brothers and even their
trainers should take before this statue an oath over a dismembered boar to do no wrong to the Olympic games. The
actual athletes have to swear further that they have been in
full training for ten months, [10] and the entry examiners of
the boys and the colts swear to make their judgement rightly
and without bribes, and to keep secret all information about
passes and failures. I forgot to ask what tradition dictates they
should do with the boar after the athletes' oath, as at least in
ancient times there was a traditional observance about victims;
that if you took an oath on one, no human being was allowed to
eat it. Homer proves this as well as anyone: [11] he says the dismembered boar on which Agamemnon swore that Briseis had
never been to his bed was thrown into the sea by the herald.

> He spoke, and his harsh bronze opened the boar's throat,
> then Talthybios whirled it round and threw it far out
> into the deep places of the grey sea to feed fishes.[243]

241. Knidos is the point of Turkey just south-east of Kos. Its ruins were
spectacular and discovered early; they were one of the first enthusiasms of the
Dilettanti Society (*Antiquities of Ionia*, pt 3, 1840, from drawings made in June
1812), and there is an important Demeter from Knidos in the British Museum.
The island is now joined to the mainland. Koresos at Ephesos was a harbour
suburb to the north of the city near the stadium (cf. Bk VII, 5 (10)). There is in
fact an early-third-century honorary decree of the community of Koresos in
the Smyrna museum, and there are several dedications by the community at
Ephesos. (Cf. Louis Robert, *Hellenica*, XI–XII, 1960, pp. 132f.)

242. Cf. Note 236 above.

243. *Iliad*, 19, 266f. There is a better translation of this by Christopher
Logue in *Pax* (1967).

That was the practice of antiquity in this matter. There is a small bronze sheet in front of Zeus of Oaths inscribed with couplets meant to terrify oath-breakers.

[1] I have given a most accurate survey of the statues of 25 Zeus that are inside Altis. But the dedication placed beside the great temple by a Corinthian, not by a citizen of ancient Corinth but one of the people who hold that city by the emperor's grant, is of Alexander, son of Philip, apparently in the likeness of Zeus.[244] I must also touch on the statues which are neither Zeus nor an imitation of Zeus, but I shall include those images people have erected not out of divine reference but to please themselves in my treatment of the athletes.

[2] The Messenians on the straits had an ancient custom of sending to Region a troop of thirty-five boy-dancers with a master and a flute-player to some local Region festival, and they once suffered a disaster when not one member of the expedition escaped: the ship the boys were in simply disappeared into the depths of the sea. The sea in those straits is the stormiest of all seas; [3] the winds disturb it and stir up the waves from the Adriatic on one side and what they call the Etruscan sea on the other, and even if not a blast of wind is blowing, the water in the straits moves with extreme violence on its own, the currents are powerful, and so many sea-monsters gather there that their smell hangs thick in the air over the straits; so for a shipwrecked man in that neck of water there is not a hope of surviving. And if it was there that Odysseus's ship was wrecked one would not have believed he could reach Italy alive by swimming: but the favour of the gods can bring relief in any conditions. [4] The Messenians went into mourning for the loss of their sons, and among the ways they thought of to pay honours to them they dedicated their images in bronze at Olympia, with the master and the flute-player. The ancient inscription showed they were dedications from the Messenians on the straits, but later on

244. Apparently a statue of Alexander the Great as Zeus erected by a Corinthian of the Roman period; I am unable to offer any explanation. Perhaps it stood on a Roman pedestal found at the north-east corner of the temple.

Hippias the legendary Greek wise man composed the couplets on them. The statues were cast by Kallon of Elis.[245]

[5] Near the Sicilian headland that faces Libya and the south which is called Pachynon, is the city of MOTYE, with a population of Libyans and Phoenicians. The people of Akragas went to war with these barbarous Motyans, took loot and spoils of war from them, and then dedicated at Olympia the bronze boys with their right hands held out like men praying to the god. They stand on the wall of Altis; I conjectured they were by Kalamis, and that is in fact who they are supposed to be by.[246] [6] Sicily is populated by these nations: Sikanians and Sicilians and Phrygians, the Sikanians having crossed over from Italy and the Phrygians from the river Skamander and the Troad; the Phoenicians and Libyans arrived in the island in a combined expedition as a Carthaginian colony, and so much for the barbarous peoples of Sicily, but there are also Dorian and Ionian Greeks, a small offshoot of the people of Phokis, and a small offshoot of the people of Attica.

[7] There are two naked figures of Herakles as a boy on the same wall as the dedications from Akragas; in one he is represented shooting the Nemean lion. This Herakles and the

245. The children were drowned in the straits between Italy and Sicily in the late fifth century. Hippias was a philosopher and a literary man. Frazer says he sailed through three times in calm weather and smelt nothing; I have to admit that nor did I, and the only monster was a big butterfly. But there is no doubt at all about the storms, and the movement of sharks in the Mediterranean alters even more quickly than the coastline. There used in the nineteenth century to be few or none around Greece, where they are now a menace. Perhaps whatever created the smell had also attracted the sharks.

246. Motye ceased to be inhabited in the very early fourth century B.C., and it was not at the southern point of Sicily (Pachynon) but the western point. It is now being excavated. Kalamis was one of the great archaic sculptors of what one might call the last preclassical generation. He worked in the early fifth century. He was famous for his horses, and one might be forgiven for imagining that the latest of the archaic riders and horses in the Akropolis Museum at Athens might be by him. What seems to be the inscribed base of a statue of Aphrodite by Kalamis was found in 1937 in the agora (Raubitschek, *Dedications from the Athenian Akropolis*, no. 136).

lion with him are by Nikodamos of Mainalos; they were dedicated by Hippotion the Tarantine. The other statue was a dedication of Anaxippos of Mende, which was brought here by the Eleans; it used to stand at the edge of the road from Elis to Olympia, which they call the SACRED ROAD.[247] [8] There are combined dedications from the Achaian people, of all the men who drew lots for the duel when Hektor challenged any Greek to fight him man to man.[248] They stand close to the great temple with their spears and their shields, and opposite them on a different base stands Nestor, with all the lots thrown together in a helmet. There are eight men who drew to fight Hektor – they say the ninth, a portrait of Odysseus, was taken away to Rome by Nero – [9] but of all the eight only Agamemnon's name is inscribed, and even that is written from right to left. But the one with the cock on his shield is Idomeneus whose ancestor was Minos: they say Idomeneus was descended from the Sun, through the Sun's daughter Pasiphae, and the cock is the sacred bird of the Sun, and cries out just before sunrise. [10] There is an inscription on the base:

> The Achaians consecrated these figures to Zeus:
> the seed of godlike Pelops, son of Tantalos.

That is what is written there, and the name of the sculptor is written on Idomeneus's shield:

> The genius of Onatas of Aigina son of Mikon
> flowered in many works of art, and this is one.

[11] Not far from the Achaian dedication is a Herakles

247. For the Arkadian Nikodamos, cf. Bk VI, 6 (3). He worked for Mikythos in the mid fifth century (cf. Bk V, 26 (6)). It is interesting that so many of the dedications at Olympia come from the western Greek settlements and almost none from Athens though Athenian artists worked here. Mende was a Euboian colony on the south-west of the western prong of Chalkidike (but cf. also Note 265 below). The inscribed marble base of Hippotion's statue was found in the Leonidaion in 1954–5; so far as I can discover it has not yet been properly published.

248. *Iliad*, 7, 161f. The semi-circular platform for these statues was found south-east of the temple of Zeus. They seem to have been very late archaic or early classical bronzes.

fighting for the belt with a mounted Amazon, by Aristokles of Kydonia, dedicated by Euagoras of Zankle. Aristokles must be numbered with the most ancient artists: no one can say for certain in what generation he lived, but obviously it was before Zankle got its modern name of Messene.[249]

[12] The Thasians, who were originally Phoenicians and sailed from Tyre in Phoenicia with Agenor's son Thasos in search of Europa, dedicated a Herakles at Olympia, with the base and the statue both in bronze. The statue is fifteen feet high, with a club in its right hand and a bow in its left.[250] I heard in Thasos that they worshipped the same Herakles as the Tyrians, and then later when they became part of Greece they adopted the practice of paying honours to Herakles son of Amphitryon as well.[251] [13] There is a couplet on the Thasian dedication at Olympia:

> Onatas son of Mikon has made me
> whose house is in Aigina.

We should rank this Onatas, whose style in sculpture is as Aiginetan as he is, not a step below Daidalos's apprentices and the school of Athens.[252]

249. Part of what may be the right pedestal was found in the temple of Zeus in 1876 (*Inschriften von Olympia*, n. 836). Kydonia is CHANIA in Crete. Zankle became Messene in the first ten years of the fifth century.

250. The surviving antiquities of THASOS are some of the most wonderful in Greece. The story about the Phoenician origin of Thasos may just possibly reflect some real but remote and prehistoric relationship; at any rate a similar myth about Thebes was commonly thought to have been strangely confirmed a few years ago by the discovery among the remains of Mycenaean Thebes of Syro–Hittite and Babylonian cylinder seals (*Illustrated London News*, 28 November 1964).

251. On the Tyrian Herakles, cf. Bk IX, 27 (8).

252. The principal sculptures which have survived from AIGINA are the pediment figures dug up and stolen in 1811 by C. R. Cockerell, the architect who designed the Ashmolean Museum at Oxford and the large ball and cross on top of Wren's St Paul's, and by his colleague Haller von Hallerstein. They were offered to the British, who haggled over the price, and then sold at auction to Crown Prince Louis of Bavaria. The Prince's new sculptures were restored rather thoroughly by the contemporary sculptor Thorwaldsen; the result is that we are even more uncertain than we need have been about the

[1] The Messenian Dorians who once obtained Naupaktos 26 from the Athenians have dedicated a statue at Olympia of VICTORY ON THE PILLAR, by Paionios of Mende: it was made from enemy spoils, I believe during the war with Akarnania and Oiniadai. But the Messenian story is that this dedication comes from the action on Sphakteria where they were Athenian allies, and that the name of the enemy was not inscribed for fear of Lakonia: they were not at all frightened of Oiniadai and the Akarnanians.[253]

[2] I found a great number of dedications of Mikythos not grouped together; next to Iphitos of Elis and Truce crowning Iphitos with a wreath, there are three dedications of Mikythos: Amphitrite and Poseidon and the Hearth goddess, by Glaukos of Argos. By the left side of the great temple he has dedicated some other figures: Demeter's daughter the Maid and Aphrodite, Ganymede and Artemis, the poets Homer and Hesiod, and the gods Asklepios and Health. [3] Contest carrying jumping-weights is another of Mikythos's dedications; the weights are like this: elongated, not perfectly curved semi-circles, made so that your fingers fit round them like the grip of a shield, that is the shape of them. Beside the image of Contest are Dionysos and Thracian Orpheus and a statue of Zeus that I mentioned just now, all by Dionysios of Argos.

---

Aiginetan style. (But cf. in general Ashmole's *Classical Ideal in Greek Sculpture*, Cincinatti, 1964.) Bavarian neoclassic taste is embodied to this day in the architecture of nineteenth-century Athens. I hope it is not overnationalistic to say that after Athens the British neoclassic palace by Whitmore at Corfu (1816) comes as a relief, but British guilt in the spoliation of Greek national monuments (in Corfu even after the foundation of a Greek museum) is too deep to be whitewashed. At Aigina for example it was commercial.

253. Among the strictly classical dedications that have been recovered in the Olympia excavations this statue surely holds the first place. It was found four days before Christmas in 1875 and is now in the Olympia museum. It stands a little over seven feet high ($9\frac{1}{2}$ to the wing-tips) and it stood on a pillar about thirty feet high. Victory is coming down from the sky; she is arrested in dramatic movement with her dress blowing back and her left arm in the air. The marble is Parian. It must have been carved soon after 421 B.C. The inscription says that Paionios won the competition for the akroteria of the temple of Zeus.

They say there were others like them dedicated by Mikythos, but they were part of what Nero took away. [4] No master is spoken of as having taught Dionysos and Glaukos of Argos who made them, but the fact that Mikythos dedicated their works at Olympia indicates their date. Herodotos says in his history that Mikythos was a slave of Anaxilas the dictator of Region and was Anaxilas's treasurer, and then later on when Anaxilas died he absconded to Tegea.[254] [5] The inscriptions on the dedications give Mikythos's father as Choiros and his country as the Greek cities of Region and Messene on the straits; and they say he lived in Tegea and consecrated the dedications at Olympia to fulfil a vow on the recovery of his son, who was sick with a deadly disease.

[6] Near his bigger dedications which are by Glaukos of Argos stands a statue of Athene in a helmet and wearing the goat-skin, by Nikodamos of Mainalos, dedicated by Elis.[255] There is a Victory beside the Athene, dedicated by the Mantineans, though from which war is not stated in the inscription. Kalamis is said to have made it wingless in imitation of the wooden idol of the Wingless Victory at Athens. [7] By Mikythos's smaller dedications, which Dionysios made, there are Herakles' labours with the Nemean lion and the many-headed dragon and the dog of Hades and the boar by the river Erymanthos. The Herakleans brought these to Olympia after overrunning the territory of the barbarous Mariandynians on their borders. HERAKLEIA is a city built on the Euxine sea as a Megarian colony, though the Boiotians of Tanagra helped to found it.[256]

254. Herodotos (7, 170) says he was Anaxilas's slave and regent of Region for Anaxilas's children; he was banished from Region and went to Tegea, and dedicated numerous offerings at Olympia. He was apparently regent from 476 to 467. Some of his inscribed pedestals have been found; they are acknowledgements of a cure by the power of prayer at Olympia after paying doctors a lot of money with no result. This form of acknowledgement is not unlike what was demanded if one was miraculously cured at Epidauros. We know nothing about Glaukos of Argos.

255. Cf. Bk VI, 6 (3).

256. The site of Herakleia is what is now EREGLI in Turkey, south-west of Zonguldak, on the southern shore of the Black Sea.

[1] Opposite all these statues I have mentioned there are 27 some other dedications in a row, facing south very close to Pelops's sacred enclosure. Among these are the dedications of Phormis of Mainalos, who crossed over to Sicily to Gelon son of Deinomenes, and gave glorious service in Gelon's campaigns and later in his brother Hieron's, and became so rich as to make these dedications at Olympia, and others to Apollo at Delphi.[257] [2] At Olympia there are two horses and two drivers, a driver standing by each horse. The first horse and man are by Dionysios of Argos, the second by Simon of Aigina. The first horse has an inscription on its side the beginning of which is unmetrical; it goes like this:

> Dedicated by Phormis the Arkadian
> of Mainalos and now of Syracuse.

[3] This is the mare that the Eleans say is the subject of the famous horse-madness; and what happens to this mare is in fact obviously the work of some skilful magician. It is not nearly the biggest or the most beautiful of the Altis horses, and its tail has been docked which makes it look even worse: yet stallions go wild for it, not only in spring but every day in the year. [4] They break their halters and escape from their grooms and come galloping into Altis and leap up on it much more madly than they would on the finest living mare that was used to being mounted. Their hooves slip on it, but they go on and on whinnying all the more and leaping up on it more and more strongly until you manage to drag them away with whips and main force: until you do so nothing can release them from that bronze. [5] And I remember another wonderful thing I saw in Lydia, a different kind of thing from Phormis's horse and yet it surely involves magical skill. The Lydians who are called Persian have two sanctuaries, one at

257. Pausanias never mentions this interesting Arkadian at Delphi; perhaps his dedications had been plundered. Since he employed Dionysios who was also employed by Mikythos (Bk V, 26 (3) above), he must have been making his dedications in the mid fifth century or a little earlier.

the city of HIEROKAISAREIA and one at HYPAIPA:[258] in each
one is a building, and in each building is an altar with ash on it,
just the same colour as any other ash. [6] A magician comes
into the building and piles up some dry wood on the altar:
and first he puts a crown on his head and then he chants the
cult-title of some god in barbarous words quite incompre-
hensible to any Greek, reading what he chants out of a scroll,
and it is absolutely certain the wood will take fire and strong,
clear flame will break out.[259]

[7] That is enough of this explanation. Among these
dedications is Phormis himself meeting an enemy in battle,
and next to that he is fighting another one, and next to that
again a third. They are inscribed that the soldier fighting is
Phormis of Mainalos and the dedicator was Lykortas of
Syracuse, who obviously dedicated them out of friendship
with Phormis, though the Greeks call Lykortas's dedications
Phormis's dedications as well. [8] Hermes in a tunic and a
cloak with a peasant's cap on his head and carrying a ram

258. Hierokaisareia was under thirty miles from Magnesia and Mount
Sipylos, and seven or eight miles south of Thyateira (AKHISSAR); it was
identified by M. Frontier of Smyrna (B.C.H., 1887, pp. 79f., and pl. 14).
Persian Artemis was worshipped here in a temple founded by Cyrus (Tacitus,
Annals, 3, 62); her head is on coins. Hypaipa was somewhere near ODEMIS,
on the route from Ephesos to Sardis, where the road strikes north at the
southern opening of the pass over Tmolos, east of IZMIR (Ramsay, Historical
Geography of Asia Minor, 1890, pp. 128 and 167).

259. The dedication of almost every Greek hilltop to the Prophet Elias is
connected with Elias's famous miracle when he competed with the priests of
Baal to make fire spring out of an altar in this way. On medieval Greek
miraculous fires, cf. Dawkins, Chronicle of Makhairas, vol. 2, p. 214. Archbishop Arethas, from whose lost manuscript of Pausanias all the surviving
manuscripts remotely descend, is credited with a marginal note at this point
that there used to be a Saracen at Region in Sicily who could draw a black crow
in charcoal on the wall, and make it burst into flames when he muttered some
gibberish. But not all the marginalia of Pausanias manuscripts are by Arethas,
nor is this (alas) his usual style. Still, it would be pleasing if it were by Gemistos
Plethon. (If so, or even if not, these annotations also contain the only proof we
have that Gemistos Plethon visited Rimini in his lifetime. Supposing as does
seem very likely that he wrote the note about Rimini, we have at least a solid
biographical basis for the difficult problem of the Tempio Malatesta, which was
dedicated to him after his death.)

under his arm is not another of Phormis's dedications: it was given to the god by the Arkadians of Pheneus, and the inscription says it was made by Onatas of Aigina and Kalliteles, who I suppose was Onatas's son or his apprentice. Not far from the Phenean dedication is another statue of Hermes with his herald's wand; an inscription says it was by Kallon of Elis, dedicated by Glaukias of Region.[260] [9] The two bronze oxen are one of them from Corfu and the other Eretrian, by Phlesios of Eretria.[261] I shall explain why the people of Corfu dedicated one ox at Olympia and another at Delphi when I come to discuss Phokis, but this is something I was told about that happened in connexion with their Olympian dedication.[262] [10] There was a little boy playing bending down under this ox, who suddenly raised his head and cracked it on the bronze, and a few days afterwards he died of the injury. The Eleans wanted to take the ox out of Altis because it had incurred blood-guilt, but the god at Delphi told them to leave it where it was and perform those purifications over it which the Greeks observe for manslaughter.

[11] Under the plane-trees in Altis more or less in the centre of the enclosure is a bronze TROPHY with an inscription on the shield of the trophy saying that the Eleans erected it from the spoils of the Lakonians.[263] This was the battle in which that man died who was found in the roof of Hera's temple when it was restored in my time, lying there with his weapons around him. [12] The dedication from the Thracians of MENDE very nearly fooled me into supposing it was a portrait of a pentathlon athlete: its position is next to Anauchidas of

260. The inscribed base was found in the wrestling-ground west of Altis. Half of the inscription is in Chalkidian and half in Elean. It was probably written between 420 and 410 B.C. (*Inschriften von Olympia*, n. 271).

261. The pedestal of the Eretrian bull was found well east of the temple of Zeus; it has been dated to the early fifth century. One of the ears and one of the horns of the bull were found with it; the ear weighs six pounds, and the horn, which is incomplete, twenty.

262. Bk X, 9 (3f.).

263. At the end of the fifth century, but cf. Bk V, Note 197.

Elis,[264] and it has antique jumping-weights, but there is a couplet engraved on its thigh.

> *The Mendaians have beaten down Sipte:*
> *I am first fruits to Zeus king of gods.*

It seems that SIPTE must have been a fortress and a city in Thrace: the Mendaians are Greeks by descent from Ionia, and they live up country from the coastal city of AINOS.[265]

264. Cf. Bk VI, 14 (11).

265. There are two cities of Mende, one in Chalkidike and the other in Thrace. The whereabouts of Thracian Mende and of Sipte are unknown; all we know is that Ainos (ENEZ) was at the mouth of the Hebros (the Meric) in eastern Thrace, just inside Turkey. For a cult of Hermes at Ainos, cf. Kallimachos, *Iambi* 7 (= fr. 197). Servius (*Aeneid* 3, 16) says he believed Ainos, a companion of Odysseus, was buried there.

# BOOK VI
# ELEIA II

[1] I shall proceed from this point in the discussion of the
dedications to mention the race-horses and the athletes and the
private individuals. Not all Olympic winners have their
statues standing at Olympia; some men who achieved glory
in the games, and some of them in other fields as well, have
never had statues.[1] [2] The method of this discussion has
forced me to leave them out, as I am not writing a list of all
the Olympic winners, but only a description of the portraits
and the other dedications. I shall not even cover all those
whose statues are actually standing there, as I am well aware
who obtained the wild-olive by drawing a bye and not by
bodily strength. Those I shall mention are the ones with some
genuine distinction, or whose statues were better as sculpture.

[3] On the right of the temple of Hera is a statue of a
wrestler of Elean descent called Symmachos son of Aischylos;
beside him stands Neolaidas son of Proxenos from Pheneus
in Arkadia, who won the boys' boxing; then Archedamos son
of Xenios, another unbeaten boy wrestler and another Elean.
All their statues are by Alypos of Sikyon, a pupil of Naukydes
of Argos.[2] [4] The inscription on Kleogenes son of Silenos

1. Pliny in a sentence too rhetorical to be authoritative says all the winners
had figures dedicated and triple champions the portraits of their bodies.
Probably most of them gave the inexpensive miniature statues of which so
many have been recovered from the excavations. Girls seem to have offered
painted reliefs (cf. in general Hyde's *Olympic Victor Monuments and Greek
Athletic Art*, pp. 27–9). Pausanias treats Eleia in two books, not only because
of the richness of Olympia but because ten books make a classic number.

2. They all won some time between 404 and 364. We know of Alypos only
from Pausanias. Naukydes is supposed to have been master to Polykleitos
junior. The positions of all these statues, even supposing they were never
moved in antiquity (an unlikely supposition on the analogy of Delphi), cannot
be accurately traced, although here and there a group or a series in Pausanias
can be related to a particular area.

says he was a local man who was successful with a ridden race-horse from his own breeding stable.[3] Near Kleogenes there are Deinolochos son of Pyrros and Troilos son of Alkinos, two more Eleans by birth, but not winners in the same event: Troilos was a Greek arbiter at the same games as his horses won in the races for fully-grown pairs and for teams of colts. It was the hundred and second Olympics, [5] and from then onwards Elis brought in a law that no horse belonging to a Greek arbiter could ever compete. His statue was made by Lysippos. Deinolochos's mother had a vision in her dreams that the child she held in her arms was crowned with a wreath, which is how it happened that Deinolochos was trained for the games and won the boys' running; his portrait is by Kleon of Sikyon.[4] [6] I have already given an account of Archidamos's daughter Kyniska, her family and her Olympic victories, in my discussion of the Lakonian kings: at Olympia beside the statue of Troilos is a stone ledge with a chariot and team and a driver and a portrait of Kyniska herself by Apelles, and there are inscriptions about Kyniska.[5] [7] And next to

3. The horse was by his own stallion out of his own mare, and we know that he won twice, as the bronze plate from the pedestal has been found (*Inschriften von Olympia*, n. 166). The year 372 was presumably his first win; the lettering on the bronze appears to be later, but even so this must be an early work of Lysippos, who was still working at the end of the century. He was a popular bronze-caster who had many great commissions; he was famous for precision of detail and slim bodily proportions, and for moments of action. The nearest we can come to his original work is the bronze praying boy in Berlin (whose arms are an eighteenth-century restoration – he should be crowning himself) and the reliefs from the statue-base of Poulydamas, which were probably by his pupils (cf. Bk VI, Note 37).

4. Cf. Bk V, 21 (3).

5. Cf. Bk III, 8 (1). Her inscription has been found in early-fourth-century lettering on a piece of black, round stone pedestal; the poem was already known since it was in the *Palatine Anthology* (13, 16):

> My fathers and brothers were Spartan kings,
> I won with a team of fast-footed horses,
> and put up this statue: I am Kyniska:
> I say I am the first woman in Greece
> to win this wreath.

Kyniska some Lakonians have been dedicated, all winners of horse-races. Anaxander came first in the chariot race, though the inscription on him says his father's father had already won the wreath for the pentathlon. He is represented praying to the god. Polykles, who was called Bronze Polykles, was another chariot-and-team winner; his portrait has a ribbon in the right hand, and there are two boys beside him, one holding a hoop, and the other asking for the ribbon. Polykles' horses, as the inscription says, won races at the Pythian and Isthmian and Nemean games as well.

[1] There is a figure of an all-in fighter by Lysippos; he 2 was the first Akarnanian and the first man from Stratos to win the all-in fighting, and his name was Xenarkes son of Philandridas.[6] After the Persian invasion the Lakonians took up horse-breeding more ambitiously than anyone else in Greece. Apart from those I have mentioned already, there are these other Spartan horse-breeders dedicated beyond the portrait of the Akarnanian athlete: Xenarkes and Lykinos and Arkesilaos and Arkesilaos's son Lichas. [2] Xenarkes won at Delphi and at Argos and at Corinth as well; Lykinos brought colts to Olympia, and as one of them failed to qualify he entered his colts in the race for fully-grown horses, and they won. He dedicated two statues at Olympia by Myron of Athens.[7] Arkesilaos won twice at Olympia, and his son

---

We know rather little about Apelles except that his father was called Kallikles. Pliny says Apelles made statues of people praying, and this is a common motif for athletic statues (cf. Hyde, *Olympic Victor Monuments*, pp. 130-1). But the crucial word in Pliny may be either 'adoring' or 'adorning', (Cf. also an elaborate suggestion by Dr Alfred Emerson, discussed by W. Hyde in *Olympic Victor Monuments*, p. 267.)

6. For Lysippos cf. Note 3 above. Stratos is north-west of Agrinion on the main road between ARTA and MESOLONGION, overlooking the Acheloos. Its fifth-century fortifications have survived; the great gate, the temple of Zeus, the agora and the theatre have been identified. There is an excellent survey of this important and virtually unexcavated site by F. Courby and C. Picard (*Recherches archéologiques à Stratos d'Acarnanie*, 1924).

7. This race was first run in 384, and Myron was a mid-fifth-century sculptor. Perhaps the statues were for Arkesilaos, or there was another Myron.

Lichas, as Lakonia was excluded from the games at the time, entered his chariot in the name of the people of Thebes, and when his driver won Lichas crowned him with a ribbon. The Greek arbiters whipped him for it, [3] and it was because of Lichas that the Lakonian campaign against Elis was mounted under King Agis, and the battle was fought inside Altis.[8] When the war was over he stood his portrait here, but the Elean records of Olympic winners do not give Lichas as the winner: they give the people of Thebes.

[4] Near Lichas stands the Elean prophet Thrasyboulos son of Aineias from the clan of Iamidai; he prophesied for the Mantineans against the Lakonians under King Agis son of Eudamidas: I shall explain all this more fully in my treatise on the Arkadians.[9] There is a gecko lizard crawling up the right shoulder of Thrasyboulos's statue, and a dog which must be a sacrificial victim, lying beside him cut right open to show its liver. [5] Prophecy through kids and lambs and calves is clearly an ancient tradition of mankind, and the Cypriots discovered a kind of prophecy through pigs, but no people exist who believe in prophesying anything through dogs, so it appears that Thrasyboulos instituted a kind of prophecy from the offal of dogs which was all his own. The clan of the Iamidai are prophets descended from Iamos; Pindar says in one of his songs that he was Apollo's son who received the art of prophecy.[10]

[6] By the portrait of Thrasyboulos stand Timosthenes of Elis who won the boys' running and Antipater of Miletos, son of Kleinopater, who won the boys' boxing. Some Syracusans

8. It happened in 420, when Lichas was an old man.

9. Cf. Bk VIII, 10 (5f.).

10. *Olympian Odes*, 6, 58f. The Iamidai prophesied by tearing or by burning the hides of the victims. The Greeks appear to have performed divination by the movements of the gecko lizard, and very commonly by the scrutiny of livers. Frazer in his commentary on Pausanias tells a good story about a British Colonel in India and a pig's liver. There is a fascinating Etruscan bronze dedication of a liver marked into elaborate divisions each inscribed with a god's name, in the Museo Civico at Piacenza, and similar dedications in terracotta have been found at Babylon and at Bogazköy.

on the way to Olympia with a sacrifice from Dionysios bribed
Antipater's father to have his boy proclaimed as a Syracusan,
but Antipater despised the dictator's presents and said he was
from Miletos, and wrote on his portrait statue that he was a
Milesian by birth and the first Ionian to dedicate a portrait
statue at Olympia. [7] The statue was by Polykleitos, and
Timosthenes' statue was by Lysippos's apprentice Eutychides
of Sikyon; it was Eutychides who made a statue of Fortune
for the Syrians on the Orontes, which is very much venerated
by the local people.[11]

10. *Fortune of Antioch*

[8] Beside Timosthenes' statue in Altis is a dedication of
Timon and his son Aisypos, a little boy sitting a horse. The
boy won with a race-horse, and Timon won with a team of
horses. The portrait statues of Timon and the boy are by
Daidalos of Sikyon, who also made the trophy in Altis for

11. Dionysios the First reigned from the beginning of the fourth century
until 367, and Dionysios the Second for another nine years. The Fortune of the
Syrians on the Orontes was a gilded bronze goddess in the act of being crowned
by Seleukos and Antiochos; she sits enthroned with her feet on a river-god.
The statue (assuming it is the same one) is known from the coins of Antioch,
from a marble copy in the Vatican, and from the Byzantine chronicler John
Malalas.

the Eleans for the victory over Lakonia.[12] [9] The inscription
on the Samian boxer says the boy who dedicated it was
trained by Mykon, and the Samians are the best and bravest
athletes and sea-fighters in Ionia: it says all that, but it tells you
nothing at all about the boxer. [10] Next to that is Damiskos
the Messenian, who won at Olympia when he was twelve
years old. This is one of the most extraordinary things I have
ever heard: when the Messenians left the Peloponnese they
lost their luck at the Olympic games. Apart from Leontiskos
and Symmachos from Messene on the straits, it is clear that
no other Messenian either from Sicily or from Naupaktos
ever won at Olympia: and the Sicilians say even Leontiskos
and Symmachos came from the ancient Zanklaians and not
the Messenians. [11] Yet when the Messenians came back
to the Peloponnese, their luck at the Olympic games came
back with them, and when Elis held the games the year after
the foundation of Messene this Damiskos won the boys'
running, and later he went on to win the pentathlon at
Nemea and the Isthmus.[13]

3  [1] Very close to Damiskos stands a man whose name is not
recorded, dedicated by Ptolemy son of Lagos: in the inscription Ptolemy calls him a Macedonian, though Ptolemy was
king of Egypt.[14] There is an inscription on the boy boxer
Chaireas of Sikyon that he won as a young boy and his father
was Chairemon, and the sculptor's name is also inscribed:
Asterion son of Aischylos. [2] After Chaireas come a Messen-

12. So he was an important sculptor in 399 B.C. We know of other works
of his in 396 and in 388, and one in 369 (Bk X, 9 (5f.)). His signature on
pedestals has been found twice at Olympia and once in Ephesos. His statues
seem to have been old-fashioned naked athletes standing still. Not only pupils
like Naukydes and Daidalos, but the master Polykleitos himself who had
published a technical work on his own new style in the mid fifth century could
sometimes work in the earlier convention.

13. Messene was restored in 369, and he won in 368.

14. Ptolemy son of Lagos was Ptolemy the First; he was a Macedonian
general who took Egypt in the general carve-up after Alexander's death (cf.
also Bk X, 7 (8)). King Antiochos was still calling himself Macedonian in an
inscription at Delos a hundred years and two generations later.

ian boy Sophios, and an Eleian man Stomios; Sophios was the best boy runner, and Stomios won the pentathlon at Olympia and three times at Nemea. The inscription about him also says that as commander of the Elean cavalry he erected trophies and killed an enemy general in single combat by personal challenge. [3] The Eleans say the general was from Sikyon and a Sikyonian commander; Elis being at war with Sikyon as an ally of Thebes serving with a Theban force. This Elean and Theban campaign against Sikyon would appear to have taken place after the Lakonian disaster at Leuktra.[15]

[4] Next in order come a boxer from Lepreos in Eleia called Labax son of Euphron, and a man called Aristodemos son of Thrasis, who was a wrestler from Elis itself; he also won twice at the Pythian games, and his portrait is by Daidalos of Sikyon, the apprentice and the son of Patrokles.[16] [5] Hippos the Elean who won the boys' boxing is by Damokritos of Sikyon, who can be traced through four generations of pupil and master to Kritias of Athens: Ptolichos of Corfu who was Kritias's apprentice taught Amphion, who taught Pison of Poros, and Damokritos was taught by

15. No one knows anything about the sculptor Asterion: the name Aischylos is relatively common but not always Athenian, and there was an Eleian Aischylos who was an Olympic official in the time of Alexander the Great. We have an inscribed piece of Sophios's pedestal with a fragment of verse on it (*Inschriften von Olympia*, n. 172). Stomios seems to have won his fight in the 60s of the fourth century.

16. We know from Eusebios, who preserved a list of Olympic winners compiled by the early-third-century Christian historian Julius Africanus, that Aristodemos won in 388 B.C., and we know from Hephaistion's treatise on Greek metre the couplet on his statue:

*I won and was crowned twice at the Isthmos twice at Nemea, once at Olympia, not by my breadth of body but by art.*

Perhaps the word should be Pythian and not Isthmian, but Pausanias may be wrong. The verses survived under the name of Simonides, who was certainly not their author; a mass of anonymous epigrams was fathered on him in compilations from the fourth century onwards. (Cf. the similar epigram on Diophon, *Palatine Anthology*, 16, 3.)

Pison.[17] [6] In his own time Kratinos of Aigeira in Achaia had the most beautiful body in his generation and the most skill as a wrestler; when he won the boys' wrestling Elis granted the erection of a statue of his trainer as well. The statue was by Kantharos of Sikyon, son of Alexis and pupil of Eutychides.[18]

[7] The statue of Eupolemos of Elis is by Daidalos of Sikyon, and the inscription announces that Eupolemos won the men's running at Olympia, two wreaths for the pentathlon at the Pythian games, and another at Nemea. It is also said of Eupolemos that, out of three Greek arbiters standing at the end of the track, two declared Eupolemos the winner, but the third voted for Leo of Ambrakia, and Leo had the two arbiters who declared for Eupolemos fined by the Olympic Council.[19]

[8] The Achaians dedicated the statue of Oibotas by command of Apollo at Delphi in the eightieth Olympics; Oibotas won the running in the sixth Olympics. Then how could Oibotas have fought for Greece at the battle of Plataia? The defeat of Mardonios and the Persians at Plataia took place in the period of the seventy-fifth Olympics. I am bound to tell the stories that are told by the Greeks, but I am not bound to believe them all. I shall include the rest of the history of Oibotas in my description of Achaia.[20]

17. Damokritos must have worked in the first half of the fourth century: Kritios worked in the early fifth (cf. Bk I, 8 (5)). Damokritos carved portraits of philosophers; we also know from a pedestal that was once in the Villa Matthaei at Rome (where it was copied by the seventeenth-century French traveller Dr Spon) that he carved a girl called Lysis of Miletos.

18. In the early third century. Surely the compliment reflects the terms of the inscription, which sounds likely enough for a contemporary of Theokritos. Kantharos's signature has survived on a pedestal at Thebes.

19. Eupolemos won in 396 B.C. (Bk VIII, 45 (4)). The Greek arbiters, who were the umpires of the games, would have been Eleans, and Elis I suppose controlled the putting-up of statues; for Daidalos, cf. Note 12 above.

20. Cf. Bk VII, 17 (6f.). Pausanias says he won in 756; the statue was put up in 460. That is, in 460 the Delphic oracle announced the need to propitiate a very early Olympic winner. Plataia was fought in 479; was Oibotas supposed to have fought as a divine hero? Was it the Delphic oracle or was it a later religious confusion that identified the Oibotas of Plataia with an almost prehistoric champion?

[9] The statue of Antiochos is by Nikodamos, who was by birth a Leprean, and won the men's all-in fighting once at Olympia and the pentathlon twice at the Isthmus and twice at Nemea. The Lepreans are not terrified of the Isthmian games as the Eleans are; for example Hysmon the Elean who stands near Antiochos won the pentathlon at Olympia, and again at Nemea and was obviously barred from the Isthmian games like all other Eleans; [10] they say when Hysmon was only a boy he contracted a muscular disease and that was why he took up the pentathlon, to become a sound, healthy man by hard work: a discipline which was to bring him glittering prizes. His statue is by Kleon, and it has old-fashioned jumping-weights.[21] [11] The dedication beyond Hysmon is a boy wrestler from Heraja, Nikostratos son of Xenokleides, by Pantias who comes sixth in the succession of master and apprentice from Aristokles of Sikyon.[22]

Dikon son of Kallibrotos won five running prizes at the Pythian games, three at the Isthmian, four at Nemea, and one in the boys' running and two in the men's at Olympia; and he has as many statues at Olympia as he won races. As a boy he was proclaimed as a Kaulonian, which is what he was, but later he announced himself for money as a Syracusan.[23] [12] Kaulonia was an Achaian settlement in Italy founded by

21. For Lepreos, which is in Triphylia, between Messenia and Eleia proper, cf. Bk V, 5 (3). The career of Antiochos touched recorded history in 367 when he went on an embassy to Persia (Xenophon, *Hellenika*, 7, 1, 33f.). He went as an Arkadian, not as an Elean. For the Eleans and the Isthmos, cf. Bk V, 2 (2–5). For Kleon of Sikyon, cf. Bk V, 17 (3), etc.

22. Pantias was a Chian (cf. also Bk VI, 14 (12)). From what can be pieced together of the supposed line of masters and pupils from Aristokles of Sikyon it seems he could have worked in the early fourth century.

23. Probably after Kaulonia (on the south coast of Calabria) was taken by Dionysios of Syracuse in 389; Julius Africanus makes Dikon a Syracusan in 384. The inscription which Pausanias evidently saw exists without an attribution in the *Palatine Anthology* (13, 15).

> I am Dikon son of Kallimbrotos:
> I won four times at Nemea, twice at Olympia,
> five times at Delphi, three at the Isthmus:
> I put a crown on the city of Syracuse.

Typhon of Aigiai. In the war of Pyrros son of Aiakides and the Tarantines against Rome, some of the cities in Italy were uprooted by the Romans and some by the Epirots, but the fate of Kaulonia was to be captured and utterly devastated by the Campanians, the biggest partners in the allied Roman armies.[24]

[13] Xenophon son of Menephylos, an adult all-in fighter from Aigion in Achaia, is dedicated next to Dikon, with the distance-runner Pyrilampes of Ephesos; Xenophon is by Olympos, and Pyrilampes is by a sculptor of the same name as himself, not a Sikyonian by birth but from Messene below Mount Ithome.[25]

[14] Lysander son of Aristokritos of Sparta was dedicated at Olympia by the Samians, and their first inscription is this:

> In the amazing woods of Zeus king of the sky
> I stand by dedication of the people of Samos;

so far it tells you who dedicated the offering, and the rest of it is in praise of Lysander:

> Lysander has achieved everlasting glory for Aristokritos
> and for his country: is famous for courage.[26]

[15] The Samians and all the Ionians were obviously to use their own expression putting plaster on both walls. When Alkibiades and the Athenian warships were in strength around Ionia, most of the Ionians paid court to him, and there is a bronze portrait-statue of Alkibiades in Hera's sanctuary on Samos; but when the Athenian fleet was taken at Aigospotamoi, the Samians dedicated Lysander at Olympia and the Ephesians dedicated in the sanctuary of Artemis not only Lysander but Eteonikos and Pharax and other Spartans that hardly any Greek has ever heard of. [16] Yet when the balance

24. It happened in 277. Strabo (6, 1, 10) says it was deserted in his time, that is in the age of Augustus, and a new Kaulonia had been built in Sicily.

25. Nothing else is known about Olympos. There does exist a statue-base by a Messenian Pyrilampos son of Agias (Inschriften von Olympia, n. 400).

26. Lysander commanded the Lakonian navy (at the end of the Peloponnesian War) and restored oligarchic government wherever he went. Aristokritos was his father.

tipped again, and Konon won the sea-battle off Knidos and Mount Dorion, the Ionians changed sides, and you can see a bronze Konon and Timotheos dedicated to Hera on Samos and the same at Ephesos to the Ephesian goddess. Things go on in the same way throughout the ages, and all mankind are like the Ionians: they pay court to the strongest.

[1] Just next to Lysander's portrait come an Ephesian boy 4 boxing champion who was called Athenaios, and an adult all-in fighter called Sostratos of Sikyon, who was nicknamed Fingertips, because he used to catch hold of his opponents' fingertips and bend them back, and never let go until they surrendered.[27] [2] Between the Nemean and the Isthmian games he won twelve times, and twice at the Pythian games and three times at Olympia. The Eleians do not record the hundred and fourth Olympics, when Sostratos first won, because the games were held by the Pisaians and the Arkadians instead of by Elis.[28] [3] Beside Sostratos is an adult wrestler called Leontiskos, a Sicilian by birth from Messene on the straits. He won a wreath from the League, and two from the Eleans; his style of wrestling is said to have been just like Sostratos of Sikyon's all-in fighting: they say Leontiskos like Sostratos was unbeatable, and always won by bending fingers. [4] His statue is by Pythagoras of Region, who was as good a sculptor as there has ever been. He is supposed to have been taught by Klearchos, who was also from Region, and was an apprentice of Eucheiros of Corinth, who studied under Syadras and Chartas of Sparta.[29]

[5] For the sake of Pheidias and his genius as a sculptor I must introduce here the boy tying a ribbon round his head,

27. Athenaios's statue-base has been found.

28. The hundred and fourth Olympics were in 364. Sostratos's victories were recorded in these terms in a verse inscription that has been found at Delphi (*B.C.H.*, 1882, p. 446). Probably there was a duplicate at Olympia.

29. The wreath from the League means a win at Delphi. Pythagoras of Region was one of the most important of all early classical sculptors. It has been argued though without any substantial evidence that it was Pythagoras who cast the life-size bronze charioteer at Delphi. No one knows anything at all about Eucheiros or Syadras or Chartas.

although we have no idea whose portrait Pheidias's statue is. Satyros of Elis son of Lysianax of the clan of the Iamidai won the boxing five times at Nemea, twice at Delphi and twice at Olympia; his statue is by Silanion of Athens. Another Athenian sculptor Polykles, an apprentice of Stadieus of Athens, made the Ephesian boy all-in fighter, Amyntas son of Hellanikos.[30]

[6] Chilon an Achaian from Patrai won twice at Olympia in the men's wrestling, once at Delphi, four times at the Isthmus and three times in the Nemean games. The Achaians gave him a public burial; he met his death in a war. My evidence for this is the Olympic inscription:

> Wrestling champion twice at Olympia
> twice at Delphi, three times at Nemea
> and four times at the Isthmus on the beach:
> Chilon son of Chilon of Patrai: perished in war:
> buried for my courage by the Achaian people.

[7] That is as much as the inscription tells you; but if I may argue to the war in which Chilon fell from the date of Lysippos who made his statue, it appears to me that he either fought with all the Achaians at Chaironeia or as a private individual had the courage and daring to be the only Achaian who fought at Lamia in Thessaly against Antipater and the Macedonians.[31]

[8] After Chilon there are two other dedications: one is called Molpion, who the inscription says won an Elean wreath, and the other, who has no inscription, is recorded to

30. Pliny dates the peak of Silanion's career at 328 B.C. He is supposed to have been a self-taught portrait-sculptor, which probably means only that he was left out of the lists of master and pupil. There is an enormous profusion of evidence about a number of sculptors called Polykles and Timarchides, all different but all related; the same name can crop up twice in one generation. Frazer in his commentary on Pausanias gives a family tree. Our Polykles was working about 156 B.C.; this event was first fought at Olympia in 200 B.C. It is ordinary for Greek names to alternate in succeeding generations; when a man has two sons a third name is introduced, but those two sons may easily each name a son after his grandfather.

31. At Patrai they believed he fought at Lamia in 323–322 (Bk VII, 6 (6)).

be Aristotle of Stageira in Thrace, dedicated by some disciple or some military man, as he was influential with Antipater, and with Alexander before him.[32] [9] Sodamas of Assos below Mount Ida in the Trojan country was the first Aiolian of that people to win the boys' running at Olympia. Beside Sodamas stands Archidamos king of Lakonia, son of Agesilaos. I have discovered no king's portrait dedicated abroad by Lakonia until this one of Archidamos.[33] Among other reasons I think they sent Archidamos's statue to Olympia because of his death, as he met his fate among barbarians, and was certainly the only king of Sparta who had no grave. [10] I have already explained this more fully in my Spartan treatise. Euanthes of Kyzikos was a boxing champion, once in the men's boxing at Olympia, and at Nemea and the Isthmus as a boy. Beside Euanthes is a horse-breeder with a chariot, and a young girl mounted in it. The man is called Lampos, and he came from the youngest city in Macedonia, which was named after its founder Philip son of Amyntas.[34] [11] The portrait of Kyniskos of Mantinea the boy boxer is by Polykleitos.[35] Ergoteles

32. As far as the literary sources go, Aristotle was a short, bald, physically sensitive, fat man with small eyes and an odd hair-cut. He died in 322 in exile from Athens. In A.D. 500 there was a bronze statue of Aristotle at Constantinople (*Palatine Anthology*, 2, 16f.); portraits of him had become common at one time as Roman garden ornaments, but this bronze is likely to have been a choice piece of imperial loot, and it may have come from Olympia. A number of stone heads of him have survived (cf. Richter, *Portraits of the Greeks*, vol. 2, p. 170, and figs. 976–1014).

33. He died in Italy in 338 (cf. Bk III, 10 (5)). Assos is on the Turkish coast north of Lesbos.

34. The ruins of Kyzikos are on the east side of the isthmus of the large peninsula on the southern side of the sea of Marmara. Philippi is on the road inland from Kavalla north of Thasos towards Drama. It was an important point on the Roman road from Italy to Asia, which is why it was a battlefield. Considerable ruins of Roman Philippi have been excavated.

35. Part of the inscribed base of this statue was found in the church built on Pheidias's workshop: 'Kyniskos of Mantinea the boxer put this here: he took his name from a glorious father.' He won in about 460. The statue was not of a boy boxing but standing in an easy position. For Polykleitos, cf. Bk VI, Note 12. He was probably the greatest single influence in the naturalistic development of Greek athletic sculpture. It is all very well to deplore this development,

son of Philanor won the long-distance running twice at Olympia, and twice at Delphi and the Isthmus and Nemea; he was not originally from Himera as the inscription says he was, but they say he was a Cretan from Knossos; he was expelled from Knossos by a revolution, and went to Himera where he was made a citizen and received all kinds of honours: probably because he was going to have himself proclaimed a Himeraian in the games.[36]

5　[1] The figure on the high pedestal is by Lysippos; he was the biggest and tallest of all human beings except for the heroes as they are called, and whatever race of mortals may have existed before the heroic age of the human beings of this age this man, Poulydamas son of Nikias, was the biggest and tallest.[37] [2] In our own time Poulydamas's native city Skotoussa is uninhabited: Alexander the dictator of Pherai captured Skotoussa during a truce. There happened to be an assembly going on, and Alexander surrounded the people massed in the theatre with a ring of slingers and archers and then shot down the entire crowd; of the rest he massacred the men and boys of fighting age, and gave the women and children as wages to his mercenaries. [3] This disaster at Skotoussa occurred when Phrasikleides was governor of Athens, the next year after the hundred and second Olympics, when Damon the Thourian won for the second time.[38] The

but one should remember that no original work by Polykleitos now exists: even his theoretic writings are available only through the opaque medium of Pliny.

36. Pindar's twelfth Olympic ode was written for Ergoteles in 472 for the first of his two Olympic championships; at that time he had already won twice at Delphi and twice at the Isthmus, and was in exile.

37. For Lysippos, cf. Bk VI, Note 3. Poulydamas won in 408. He was a professional strong man, and various sources say he killed lions in front of the king of Persia, outran a chariot, and fought unarmed against armed men. His statue at Olympia was believed to have a magical power to cure fever (Lucian, *Deorum Concilium*, 12). Some badly preserved fragments of a fine series of relief carvings of the deeds of Poulydamas have been found between the south-east corner of the temple of Zeus and the Echo colonnade.

38. In 371 B.C.; but Diodoros (15, 75) says it was in 367, and historians follow him. Skotoussa lies west of VOLOS, between Pherai and Pharsalos, near the modern village of Soupli.

Skotoussans who escaped stayed on a little while, but they were not strong enough and soon even they abandoned the city, at the time when the daemonic power was preparing a second catastrophe for the whole of Greece in the Macedonian War.

[4] There have been other outstanding winners at all-in fighting, but beyond the wreaths he won for all-in fighting there are things of another kind to Poulydamas's credit. The Thracian mountains up country from the river Nestos which runs through the territory of Abdera are stocked with wild beasts, including lions; they attacked Xerxes' army and preyed on the camels that carried his provisions.[39] [5] These lions often range into the country round Olympos: one side of Mount Olympos is towards Macedonia, and the other faces Thessaly and the river Peneios. It was here that Poulydamas, completely unarmed, killed a strong, wild lion of considerable size on Mount Olympos. He was led into this adventure by an ambitious envy of the labours of Herakles, because the story goes that Herakles killed the lion at Nemea. [6] And Poulydamas left another amazing thing to be remembered by: he went into a herd of cattle and took the biggest and most savage bull by one of its hind legs and held it by the hoof. It pulled and plunged but he never let go until finally after a long time the bull summoned all the force it had and escaped, leaving its hoof in Poulydamas's hands. And they say he held back a chariot from behind with the driver driving furiously: he took hold of the car from behind with one hand, and held the driver and the curvetting mares. [7] Artaxerxes' bastard son Darius who led the Persian people and took the throne from his legitimate son Sogdios, when he became king sent messengers to Poulydamas because he knew of his wonderful deeds, and persuaded him with promises of presents to come

39. The Nestos runs down from Bulgaria to enter the sea north of Thasos. Abdera was a coastal city a little farther east. Herodotos talks about these lions (7, 125), and Aristotle, who was brought up in north Greece, mentions them twice. Xenophon on hunting (*Kynegetikos*, 11) speaks of lions, leopards, lynxes, panthers and bears. Lynxes (very rare) and of course jackals and bears still exist in Greece. Folk-songs refer (less reliably) to lions in the Turkish period.

to Sousa for Darius to see him. At Sousa Poulydamas challenged three of those Persians who were called the Immortals, and fought alone against the three of them together and killed them. Some of the deeds I have mentioned are on the pedestal of his statue at Olympia, and others are explained in the inscription.[40] [8] But what Homer foretold was coming to Poulydamas as it has come to other men proud of their physical vigour; like them he was going to be destroyed by his own strength.[41] Poulydamas went into a cave in the summer season with his drinking companions, and by some evil providence the roof of the cave broke open; it was obviously due to fall in, and it was not going to hold for long. [9] They realized what was happening and the others turned and ran, but Poulydamas stayed and put out his hands as if he could fight off the falling cave and not be overwhelmed by the mountain. That was how he died.

6   [1] Beside Poulydamas's statue at Olympia there are two Arkadian athletes and one Athenian. Protolaos son of Dialkes of Mantinea who won the boys' boxing is by Pythagoras of Region; Narykidas son of Damaretos from Phigalia who won the men's wrestling is by Daidalos Sikyon; the figure of Kallias of Athens the all-in fighter is by Mikon of Athens the painter.[42] Nikodamos of Mainalos carved an all-in fighter from Mainalos who won twice as an adult, Androsthenes son of Lochaios.[43] [2] Next comes the dedication of Eukles son of

40. It was Darius the Second. The Immortals were the ten thousand guardsmen of the kings of Persia.

41. *Iliad*, 6, 407. Andromache said to Hektor: 'O my dear, your strength will destroy you, and you have no pity for your infant child or for me.'

42. For Pythagoras, cf. Bk VI, Note 29; for Daidalos, Note 12. Part of Narykidas's base and inscription have been recovered. Mikon was not only a famous fifth-century painter (Bk I, 17 (3)) but a well-known athletic sculptor (Pliny, *Natural History*, 34, 88). We know from the inscribed base, that this was a larger than life-size bronze man standing easily (*Inschriften von Olympia*, n. 146). The house of a sculptor Mikion has recently been found at Athens with a bone tool scratched with his name (*Hesperia*, 1969, p. 383). Kallias was a very successful athlete: a list of his triumphs has been found inscribed at Athens (*I.G.*, I, 419). He won at Olympia in 472.

43. He won once in 420. Nikodamos was still working twenty years later.

Kallianax, a Rhodian by birth from the family of the Diagoridai: his mother was Diagoras's daughter, and he won the men's boxing at Olympia. His portrait is by Naukydes.[44] Polykleitos of Argos, not the one who made Hera's statue but Naukydes' pupil, made the boy wrestler Agenor of Thebes; the portrait was erected by the Phokian community; his father Theopompos had public privileges with the Phokian people. [3] The sculptor Nikodamos of Mainalos made an adult boxer called Damoxenidas from Mainalos.[45] A portrait of the Eleian boy Lastratidas who won a wreath for wrestling also stands here. He also won as a boy at Nemea and again as an adolescent. Lastratidas's father Paraballon won the two-lap running, and left an ambition to later generations by inscribing the names of the Olympia winners in the training-ground at Olympia.[46]

[4] That was the story of these men; but it would not be right for me to leave out the story of Euthymos the boxer, his victories at the games and his glorious reputation outside them.[47] By birth Euthymos came from the Lokrians in Italy,

44. Eukles' base has been recovered; the lettering of the inscription does not seem very much later than the early fourth century, which might be right for a grandson of Diagoras of Rhodes (*Inschriften von Olympia*, n. 159). For Naukydes, cf. Bk II, 22 (7). The inscription says he was the son of Patrokles, which ought to make him the brother of Daidalos of Sikyon: yet Naukydes and Polykleitos (who are certainly brothers or close relations) are always called Argives. To make matters worse Daidalos's fragmentary inscription for Narykidas (Note 42 above) calls him '. . . sios', while another Daidalos inscription (*Inschriften von Olympia*, 635) agrees with Pausanias. The confusion then is not original to Pausanias but is in the Olympic inscriptions.

45. The pedestal of this has been found. The boxer seems to have been hitting out with his left foot well forward and all his weight on it. The signature and title are in different hands (*Inschriften von Olympia*, n. 158).

46. Regrettably we know nothing about Paraballon: one may suspect him of being later than Hippias of Elis. Cf. also Bk VI, 8 (1).

47. The inscription for Euthymos's statue has been discovered; the statue was by Pythagoras of Samos (*Inschriften von Olympia*, n. 144). It was two metres east of the Eretrian bull (Bk V, 27 (9)). Pliny says this statue and one at Euthymos's home city were struck by lightning on the same day during his lifetime; the Delphic oracle when consulted said he must be worshipped even before his death. He won first in 484. Pythagoras of Samos is surely the same as Pytha-

who occupy the country round Cape Zephyr; he was called the son of Astykles, though the local people say he was not Astykles' son but the son of the river Kaikines, which divides the Lokrian and the Region territory and produces the miracle of the cicadas.[48] The cicadas on Lokrian ground sing just the same as all other cicadas, but across the Kaikines the cicadas in the territory of Region never utter a sound. [5] This is the river they say was Euthymos's father; he won the boxing at Olympia in the seventy-fourth Olympics, but at the next games things were not going to go in the same way:[49] Theagenes of Thasos wanted to win the boxing and the all-in fighting at the same games, and he beat Euthymos at boxing though even so not even Theagenes was able to win the wild olive for the all-in fighting, because he was already done up by the fight with Euthymos. [6] So the Greek arbiters made Theagenes pay a sacred fine of a talent to the god and a talent in damages to Euthymos because they believed he had taken the boxing prize from malice against Euthymos: this was why they condemned Theagenes to pay the private penalty to Euthymos. At the seventy-sixth Olympics, Theagenes paid the part of the money due to the god . . . and did not enter for the boxing; at these Olympics and the next as well Euthymos won the wreath for boxing. His statue is by Pythagoras and is very

goras of Region, since Samians were brought over to take Zankle (Messene) for Anaxilas of Region in the 490s (cf. Note 29 above).

48. Cape Zephyr is a rather common name for promontories; it was the ancient name for the Capo di Bruzzano, some miles north of Spartivento which is nearly the southernmost point of the toe of Italy. The site of LOKROI itself is near GERACE SUPERIORE, which was founded by Lokrian refugees in the ninth century and still has a Byzantine look. A circuit of four or five miles of fortifications has been traced, and the ruins of the city extend over two miles inland. The best general descriptions of this enormous site are by Petersen in *Tempel in Lokri* (*Römische Mitteilung*, 1890, pp. 161f.), with a miserable but invaluable map, and a popular article by Dr de Franciscis in *Archaeology* (September 1958, pp. 206f.). The river Kaikines, which Thukydides also mentions (3, 103), has never been identified. Aristotle tells the same odd but possible story about cicadas, but he says it happened in Kephalenia (*Historia Animalium*, 8, 2, 1).

49. He won in 484, and again in 476 and 472.

well worth seeing. [7] When Euthymos had gone back to Italy, he fought the Hero: this is the story of the Hero. When Odysseus was wandering after the fall of Troy they say he was carried by winds to some of the cities in Italy and Sicily, and he and his ships arrived at Temesa; one of the sailors got drunk there and violated a virgin girl, and was stoned to death for his crime by the local people.⁵⁰ [8] Odysseus completely disregarded this man's death and sailed away, but the daemonic spirit of the man they stoned to death never stopped committing murders against Temesans and attacking old and young alike, until they wanted to abandon Temesa and leave Italy altogether, but the Pythian priestess would not let them give it up: she ordered them to placate the Hero: to enclose an area of holy ground and build a temple, and give him the most beautiful virgin girl in Temesa for a wife every year. [9] They did what the god commanded and the daemonic spirit terrified them no further. But Euthymos happened to come to Temesa at the time when the rituals of this daemonic presence were being observed, and when he discovered what the situation was he decided to go inside the temple to see the girl. When he saw her at first he was moved to pity and then he fell in love with her; the girl swore to marry him if he saved her, and Euthymos got ready and waited for the spirit to approach. [10] He fought it and won, and it was driven out of the land; the Hero dived down under the sea and disappeared, Euthymos got a glorious wedding, and the people of the place were free of this daemonic being for the rest of time. And I have even heard it said of Euthymos that he reached the farthest point of age and escaped death and departed from the world of mankind in a different way.⁵¹

50. Temesa was probably at a site two and a half miles west of NOURA. At about this time it was under Lokrian control. The sailor's name was Polites. Kallimachos tells the story of Euthymos and the hero of Temesa (*Aitia*, fr. 98–9).

51. Ailian (*V.H.*, 8, 18) says Euthymos vanished into the same river which Pausanias says was his father. Ailian's version contains no reference to the girl; he says Euthymos stopped the hero from imposing unjust taxes and made him pay back his winnings with interest. The prose version of Kallimachos says

And I have heard from a man who sailed there as a merchant that Temesa is still inhabited in my own time. [11] That is what I have heard, and I know more from a painting I happened on which was a copy of an ancient painting: there is a young lad Sybaris and a river Kalabros and a water-spring Lyka, with a hero's shrine beside it and the city of Temesa: and between them is the daemonic spirit that Euthymos expelled: his colour is terribly dark, and he is absolutely terrifying to look at, he wears a wolf-skin tied round him; the writing on the picture gives him the name Lykas.

7   [1] That is enough said about that. Beyond the statue of Euthymos stand Pytharchos of Mantinea the runner and Charmides of Elis the boxer, who both won as boys.[52] When you have looked at these you come to the portraits of the Rhodian athletes, Diagoras and his family; the dedications are in a continuous series arranged like this: Akousilaos who took the wreath for men's boxing, then Dorieus the youngest who won the all-in fighting at three Olympic games in succession. Even before Dorieus Damagetos was champion of all-in fighting: [2] they were brothers, the sons of Diagoras, and their father Diagoras who won the men's boxing is with them. His portrait is by Kallikles of Megara son of Theokosmos who made the Megarian statue of Zeus. The sons of Diagoras's daughters were Olympic boxing champions: Eukles the son of Kallianax and Kallipateira, who won as a man, and Peisirodos as a boy; Peisirodos's mother dressed up as a trainer and brought him to the Olympic games herself.

---

*dasmon apelusen.* This must surely have something to do with the Lokrian conquest of Temesa? Strabo knew the hero's shrine, which was apparently not closed; it was overshadowed by wild olives, the tree Herakles brought to Olympia.

52. We have a fragment of the inscribed base for Charmides. It was found where Pausanias saw it next to Euthymos's base (Note 47 above); they were thirty-two metres east of the north-east corner of the temple of Zeus. It was a simple life-size bronze (*Inschriften von Olympia*, n. 156).

[3] Peisirodos stands in Altis beside his mother's father. They say Diagoras came to Olympia with his sons Akousilaos and Damagetos, and when the young lads had won they carried their father through the festival crowd, while all Greece pelted him with flowers and called him happy in his sons.[53] Diagoras was originally Messenian by birth on his mother's side, as his mother was Aristomenes' daughter. [4] Besides Olympic wins Diagoras's son Dorieus won eight times at the Isthmus and one less than eight at Nemea, and they say he won without fighting at Delphi. He and Peisirodos were proclaimed as Thourians as the opposite party had expelled them from Rhodes, and they went to join the Thourians in Italy.[54] Later on Dorieus came home to Rhodes, and he certainly seems to have been pro-Lakonian *par excellence*, so much so that he even fought the Athenians at sea with his own ships, until he was taken by Athenian warships and brought to Athens alive. [5] Before Dorieus was brought to them the Athenians were threatening and furious with him, but when they met in their assembly and saw a man so big and tall and so extremely famous presented as a prisoner they changed their minds about him and let him go without doing him the least ungracious action, though they could have done many, and

53. Kallikles' father Theokosmos was still working in 404; for his Megarian Zeus, cf. Bk I, 40 (4). Diagoras won the boxing at Olympia in 464, and Pindar's seventh Olympic was written for him. He had the poem engraved in golden letters and dedicated it to Athene at Lindos. The Hellenistic learned commentary on Pindar which tells us this, and which seems to be borrowing from a lost work of Aristotle, goes on to describe the family statues at Olympia. Diagoras's statue was a boxer over life-size; his two younger sons were smaller; Akousilaos the elder son held a boxing strap in one hand and his other was raised in prayer. The grandsons were not part of the group. Bits of the inscriptions have been found and were published in 1896 in *Inschriften von Olympia*, which is the fifth volume of *Olympia* (the formal publication of the German excavations of the last century). For the story of Peisirodos, cf. Bk V, 6 (8).

54. Thourioi was founded in the 440s on the gulf of Taranto not far from the site of Sybaris (which had been demolished by Kroton). It was partly an Athenian settlement.

with justice.[55] [6] The story of Dorieus's death is told by Androtion in his history of Athens;[56] the king's fleet was at Kaunos at that time, and Konon was in command of it: Konon had persuaded the people of Rhodes to change sides, leave the Lakonians, and become allies of the king and of Athens, and Dorieus was out of Rhodes at this time in the interior of the Peloponnese, where he was arrested by Lakonians, brought to Sparta, and condemned to death by Lakonia. [7] If what Androtion says is true, he appears to me to want to put Lakonia on equal terms with Athens, because Athens can be accused of rashness over Thrasyllos and his fellow-commanders at Arginousai.[57]

That was how famous Diagoras and his family became. [8] Alkainetos son of Theantos of Lepreos and his sons also won at Olympia. Alkainetos won as an adult boxer, and had already won before as a boy. His sons Hellanikos and Theantos were proclaimed in the boys' boxing, Hellanikos in the eighty-ninth Olympics and Theantos in the next; they all have statues at Olympia.[58] [9] With Alkainetos's sons stand Gnathon the Dipaian from the region of Mainalos and Lykinos of Elis, who also both won the boys' boxing at Olympia. The inscription on Gnathon says in addition that he was extremely young when he won it; his statue is by Kallikles of

55. This was in 407.

56. Androtion was a fourth-century politician; he wrote a history of Athens to which Pausanias refers again (Bk X, 8 (1)). The rather meagre fragments of his work have been collected by Jacoby in *Fragments of the Greek Historians*, n. 324, with a valuable introduction and commentary (*Supp.* vol. 1). Androtion took a conservative and somewhat futile line in politics; he had the virtues and vices of his upper-bourgeois background: in politics the vices, but in literature perhaps the virtues, predominated. Demosthenes wrote two savage tirades against him.

57. They were executed, like Dorieus, for dereliction of duty and *pour encourager les autres*.

58. The sons won in 424 and in 420. Hellanikos's inscribed base has been found (*Inscriften von Olympia*, n. 155). The base seems to have been reinscribed in the late Hellenistic period in order to call Hellanikos 'an Elean from Lepreos'. In the fifth and fourth centuries such an inscription would be politically impossible (cf. Bk V, 5 (3-6)).

Megara.[59] [10] There is a man from Stymphalos called Dromeus who was so successful as a long-distance runner that he won twice at Olympia, twice at the Pythian games, three times at the Isthmian and five at the Nemean. Meat-eating is supposed to have been his idea: until then the food for athletes was cheese straight out of the basket.[60] His portrait is by Pythagoras, and the next one, Pythokles of Elis of the pentathlon, is a work of Polykleitos.[61]

[1] Sokrates of Pellene won the boys' running, and Amertes 8 of Elis was boys' wrestling champion at Olympia and men's champion at Delphi: Sokrates' sculptor is not recorded, but Amertos's portrait is by Phradmon of Argos.[62] Euanoridas of Elis won the boys' wrestling both at Olympia and at Nemea; he grew up to be a Greek arbiter and he too inscribed the names of the winners at Olympia.[63]

[2] Apart from the fact that he won at Olympia, I find myself unable to accept the kind of thing romanticizing charlatans have written about the Arkadian boxer Damarchos of Parrasia, about his metamorphosis into a wolf at the sacrifice to Zeus of Wolves, and how he changed back into a

59. He was an Arkadian boy. Mainalos is not only a mountain but an Arkadian district.

60. They used to eat pheta, the commonest Greek cheese, freshly made; it was hung in baskets to strain. The change must have been about 500 or earlier (cf. Note 89 below). Dromeus was another Arkadian.

61. For Pythagoras, cf. Bk VI, Note 29. This was perhaps not the great Polykleitos but a son or nephew of the same name (cf. Bk II, 17 (4)). For the great Polykleitos, cf. Note 35 above. We have the base of the statue; it was found between the temple of Hera and the sanctuary of Pelops. It was inscribed in the late fifth century and then reinscribed in the late Hellenistic period (Inschriften von Olympia, 162-3). It is clear from the base that the original statue was removed from it and a different statue substituted, perhaps at the same time; and the inscribed base for a copy or more probably for the stolen original has been found in Rome. The weight of the statue was on its right foot, which was forward; only the ball of the left foot was on the ground; the figure was not in violent action as the feet were quite close. It was standing in the characteristic stance of a relaxed athlete which we know from many copies, and which Polykleitos first petrified.

62. Not much is known about Phradmon except his later fifth-century date.

63. Cf. Bk VI, 6 (3), and Note 46 above.

man again nine years later.[64] It appears to me that even the Arkadians tell no such story about him, or it would have been written in his inscription at Olympia, which goes like this:

> *Damarchos son of Dinytas Arkadian*
> *from Parrasia dedicates this image.*

[3] That is as far as it goes. Eubotas of Kyrene knew before-hand from the Libyan oracle he was going to win the running at Olympia and had his portrait made in advance; he dedicated it on the actual day he was proclaimed winner. He is said to have won the chariot race at the Olympic meeting which the Eleans say was invalid because it was held by Arkadia.[65]

[4] Timanthes of Kleonai who won the wreath for the men's all-in fighting and Baukis of Troizen the men's wrest-ling champion are by Myron of Athens and by Naukydes respectively.[66] They say Timanthes met his death in this way: he had given up competitive athletics but he went on trying his strength by bending an enormous bow every day, and then for a time he was away from home and at that time gave up the exercise with the bow: when he came home and found he was incapable of bending the bow, he kindled a great fire and threw himself on to it alive. All the actions of this kind that the history of the human race records or ever will should in my opinion be considered to be madness, not manliness.

[5] Beyond Baukis there are portraits of Arkadian athletes: Euthymenes from Mainalos itself who won first the boys' and then the men's wrestling, Philip the Azanian from Pellana the boys' boxing champion, and Kritodamos of Kleitor, another

64. Pliny tells the story; he says it comes from a book by Skopas about Olympic champions. The superstition about the effects of cannibalism that gives rise to it is alluded to in Plato's *Republic* (565d). For this sacrifice, cf. Bk VIII, 38 (7).

65. In 364 B.C. (cf. Bk 4 (2)). But he won the running in 408. Even if he won it at sixteen, he was eighty-eight when his horses won the chariot race. Could that not have been won by his nephew or his grandson?

66. Naukydes was one of the sons of Polykleitos (cf. Note 44 above) and worked in the late fifth century. For Myron, cf. Note 7 above. Timanthes won in 456.

boy boxer. The statue of the boy Euthymenes is by Alypos, Damokritos is by Kleon, and Philip the Azanian is by Myron.[67] The story of Promachos son of Dryon the all-in fighter from Pellene is another of the things I shall include in my treatise on Achaia.[68] [6] Not far from Promachos is the dedication of Timasitheos the Delphian, by Ageladas of Argos;[69] he won the all-in fighting twice at Olympia and three times at the Pythian games, and his war record is one of glorious daring with good luck to match it, all except for the last story of all, the adventure that brought him to his death. Isagoras the Athenian had occupied the upper city of Athens as dictator, and Timasitheos had taken part in the action, and as he was one of those who were caught in the upper city the Athenians condemned him to death.[70]

[1] Theognetos of Aigina won the wreath for the boys' 9 wrestling, and his statue was made by Ptolichos of Aigina, whose master was his own father Synnoon, a pupil of Aristokles of Sikyon, Kanachos's brother, and almost as distinguished an artist as Kanachos. I was unable to deduce why

67. For Alypos, cf. Bk VI, Note 2, and for Kleon cf. Bk V, 17 (3). Kleitodamos's inscription exists, in early-fourth-century lettering (*Inschriften von Olympia*, 167). Some verses from Philip's statue were found in the wrestling-ground outside Altis engraved on a bronze plaque.

> *Once like this the Pelasgian boxer stood*
> *beside Alpheios when he was champion:*
> *father Zeus give Arkadia glory*
> *and honour Philip again, who knocked down*
> *four boys from the islands in a straight fight.*

He probably won between 304 and 280. The lettering of these verses (*Inschriften von Olympia*, n. 174) is middle or late Hellenistic; until the late fourth century Pellana was in Lakonia, but the great Myron worked in the mid fifth century. Unless there are two Myrons (cf. Bk VI, Note 7), there is a confusion we have no means of explaining with any certainty (though cf. Note 102 below).

68. Bk VII, 27 (5f.).

69. Ageladas made a famous Zeus for the Messenians while they were at Naupaktos (Bk IV, 33 (2)).

70. Herodotos mentions this (5, 72). Isagoras was an anti-democratic Athenian politician of the late sixth century; he was finally defeated by Kleisthenes.

it is that Theognetos carries a sweet pine-cone and a pomegranate, but there may possibly be some local story about
them in Aigina.[71] [2] Over beyond the portrait of the man
who the Eleans say is not inscribed with the others, because
what he won was a trotting-race, stand the boy wrestling
champion Xenokles of Mainalos, and the boy boxing champion Alketos son of Alkinoos, another Arkadian from Kleitor:
Alketos's statue is by Kleon and Xenokles' statue is by
Polykleitos.[72] [3] Aristeus of Argos won the long-distance
running, and his father Cheimon won the wrestling: they
stand close together, Aristeus is by Pantias of Chios, the son
and pupil of Sostratos, and Cheimon's portraits are in my
opinion among the finest works of Naukydes: I mean both
the one at Olympia and the one that was taken to Rome from
Argos and installed in the temple of Peace.[73] There is a story

71. There has been an attempt to date Theognetos by some verses Simonides
is supposed to have written for him (*Palatine Anthology*, 16, 2), but I doubt if
they are really by Simonides. Still, we do know he was the uncle of Aristomenes
of Aigina, whom Pindar celebrated in his *eighth Pythian ode* in 446 B.C.; this
dates the sculptors more or less. Kanachos was one of the great late archaic
masters.

72. Xenokles' statue-base has been found inscribed with lettering of the
early fourth century; no one knows which Polykleitos is involved (cf. Note
61 above), but the perfectly preserved footprints show that Xenokles had his
weight on his right leg with his left advanced and flat on the ground, well out,
poised for a grip.

73. Cheimon won in 448. The bases of statues by Sostratos have been found
in Athens and at the Piraeus. Pantias of Chios is not well known, but cf. Bk VI,
Note 22. For the great Naukydes, cf. Bk VI, Note 44. The temple of Peace at
Rome was Vespasian's commemoration of his conquest of the Jews, and of the
opening of his reign as emperor. It had a library crammed with loot from all
over the world. It was one of the most magnificent buildings in Rome; it was
dedicated in A.D. 75 and burnt down probably in A.D. 191, but it seems to have
been restored. It was finally struck by lightning, though even in the sixth
century A.D. its ruins were surrounded by works of art (Prokopios, *B.G.*, 4,
21). The space where it stood was called the *forum pacis*; the monumental
passage which once led into this space from the *via sacra* is now the church
of saints Cosmas and Damian, in the crypt of which and on the stairs down
to them there is a lot left. Apart from this all that survive of the temple
and its forum are some pieces of pavement made of *giallo antico* and *pavon-
azzetto*.

that Cheimon beat Taurosthenes of Aigina in a wrestling match, and when Taurosthenes won the wrestling in the next Olympic games a vision in the shape of Taurosthenes appeared at Argos the same day to tell them he had won.[74] [4] The boy wrestling champion Philles of Elis is by Kratinos of Sparta.[75]

As to Gelon's chariot I do not find myself able to share the view of those who have written about it before me, who claim that this chariot was dedicated by Gelon the Sicilian dictator. Its inscription in fact says it was dedicated by Gelon son of Deinomenes of Gela, and this Gelon won his race in the seventy-third Olympics, [5] but Gelon the dictator of Sicily occupied Syracuse when Hybrilides was governor of Athens, the year after the seventy-second Olympics, when Tisikrates of Kroton won the running, so he would obviously proclaim himself as a citizen of Syracuse and not Gela by this time; this Gelon must be some private individual, with the same name and the same father's name as the dictator. Glaukias of Aigina made the chariot and Gelo's portrait.[76]

[6] In the previous Olympic games they say Kleomedes of Astypalaia killed a man called Hikkos of Epidauros in a boxing match; he was condemned by the Greek arbiters and lost his victory, and went out of his mind from grief: he went home to Astypalaia and attacked a school there where there were sixty boys: he overturned the pillar that held up the roof, [7] and the roof fell in on them: the people stoned him and he took refuge in Athene's sanctuary, where he climbed inside a chest that was kept there and pulled down the lid. The Astypalaians laboured uselessly to open it; in the end they broke open its wooden walls, but they found no trace of Kleomedes either alive or dead. So they sent to Delphi to ask what had happened

74. Ailian says Taurosthenes sent a pigeon with a purple flag.

75. Nothing is known about him.

76. Three Parian marble blocks still showing a fragment of this inscription have been found (*Inschriften von Olympia*, 143). Gelon won in 488. He took over Gela in 491 and Syracuse only in 485, so this dedication does belong to Gelon the dictator. Pausanias thinks he took over Syracuse in 491. (Why?)

to Kleomedes [8] and they say the Pythian priestess gave them this oracle:

> Astypalaian Kleomedes is the last hero:
> worship him: he is no longer mortal.

Ever since then the Astypalaians have paid honours to Kleo-medes as a divine hero.[77] [9] Beside Gelon's chariot is the dedication of Philon by Glaukias of Aigina. Simonides son of Leoprepes made a very clever couplet about Philon:

> I am Philo from Corfu, son of Glaukos,
> the boxing champion of two Olympic games.

Agametor of Mantinea who won the boys' boxing is also dedicated.[78]

10   [1] After all of these comes Glaukos of Karystos; they say that by descent he came from Anthedon in Boiotia from Glaukos the daemonic spirit in the sea.[79] But his father was called Demylos, and they say he began as a labourer on the land; when the ploughshare fell out of the plough he stuck it in again using his hand for a hammer. [2] Demylos happened to see what the boy had done, so he took him along to Olympia to box. Glaukos had no experience as a boxer and his opponents hurt him, and when he was boxing with the last one, people thought he was too badly hurt to carry on: and then they say his father shouted out to him 'Come on

77. He won in 484. Astypalaia is an island due east of the south-east tip of the Peloponnese and due north of the eastern tip of Crete. Pausanias has at this point abandoned the inscriptions to consult an Olympic chronicle about Gelon's dates, and has found this story under the next Olympics. Kleomedes had no statue at Olympia.

78. The great Simonides the lyric poet who wrote the epitaphs for the dead after the Persian wars.

79. For the legend and the cult of Glaukos at Anthedon, cf. Bk IX, 22 (6–7), and Bk X, 4, (7). Dikaiarchos (23–4) says all the people of Anthedon were fishermen, they were red-eyed and broken-nailed from diving and fishing; they grew old among foreshores and seaweed and fishermen's huts, and they said they were all Glaukos's descendants. Anthedon was on the east Boiotian coast opposite Euboia. Glaukos of Karystos (a sea-port in south Euboia) probably won in 520.

son, the one for the plough', and he hit his opponent a harder punch and suddenly found he had won. [3] They say he won other wreaths as well, twice at the Pythian games, and eight times each at Nemea and the Isthmus. Glaukos's portrait was dedicated by his son and made by Glaukias of Aigina: the figure is a man shadow-boxing, because Glaukos had the best natural hand movement in his generation. The Karystians say when he died they buried him in the island which is called Glaukos's island to this day.[80]

[4] Damaretos of Heraia and his son and his grandson all won twice at Olympia. Damaretos won in the sixty-fifth Olympics, when the race in armour was first accepted, and again in the next; his statue is the figure of a man holding a shield just like the modern shields, but also with a helmet on his head and guards on his legs, which in the course of time have been dropped from this race by the Eleans and by the whole of Greece. Damaretos's son Theopompos and Theopompos's son another Theopompos won the pentathlon and the wrestling respectively.[81] [5] We have no record of the name of the artist who carved Theopompos the wrestler, but the inscription says his father and his grandfather are by Eutelidas and Chrysothemis of Argos. Nothing is said about whose pupils they were; it goes like this:

> Eutelidas of Argos: Chrysothemis of Argos:
> learning the art from men before them made these works.[82]

80. We know nothing about Glaukias of Aigina except that he worked in the early fifth century. The possibility of a late archaic statue of an athlete in vigorous action being made by an Aiginetan can be confirmed from the pediment figures of the Aphaia temple (Lullies and Hirmer, *Greek Sculpture*, pls. 79–83). Glaukos's island has not been identified; so far as I know no one has ever looked for it. It might if it were near Karystos be the island of MANDILOU off the south point of Euboia, but more likely one of the PETALIOI. It is not uncommon to find graves, sometimes those of very poor people on offshore islands.

81. Damaretos ran in armour in 520 and in 516. For Heraia, an Arkadian city on the Alpheios, cf. Bk VIII, 26 (1f.). Theopompos the father probably won in 504 and 500.

82. In the early fifth century I suppose. W. Hyde suggests 'men before them' included Polymedes of Argos, who carved the massive twin youths Kleobis and Biton at Delphi.

Ikkos son of Nikolaidas the Tarantine took the Olympic wreath for the pentathlon, and later he is said to have become the best trainer of his age;[83] [6] beyond Ikkos stands the boys' wrestling champion Pantarkes of Elis whom Pheidias loved.[84] Beyond Pantarkes is Kleosthenes' chariot: Kleosthenes came from Epidamnos, and this is by Agelades. It stands behind the Zeus dedicated by the Greeks from the spoils of the battle of Plataia. Kleosthenes won at the sixty-sixth Olympics, and he dedicated not only a team of horses but his own portrait and the driver.[85] [7] The horses are inscribed with the names Phoinix and Korax, while the outer pair are Knakias on the right and Samos on the left, and there is this couplet on the car itself:

> I am consecrated by Kleosthenes
> a Pontian from Epidamnos winning
> with horses at the fine games of Zeus.

[8] This Kleosthenes was the first Greek horse-breeder to dedicate a portrait at Olympia: the dedication of Euagoras of Lakonia is a chariot, but Euagoras is not riding in it, and with the dedication Miltiades of Athens consecrated at Olympia I shall deal elsewhere.[86] The Epidamnians of today still occupy their original territory, but not their ancient city: the modern city, which is a short distance away, is called DYRRACHION after its founder.[87]

83. Plato says he was a proverbially strict trainer (*Laws*, 839e). His career was just after the Persian wars.

84. He won the boys' wrestling in 436. Pheidias is supposed to have written Pantarkes' name on the finger of the great Zeus, but the story calls him Pantarkes of Argos. (Cf. Bk V, 11 (3).)

85. Agelades made the Zeus of Ithome (Bk IV, 33, (2)); Kleosthenes won in 516. For the Plataian Zeus, cf. Bk V, 23 (1).

86. Later in this book (19 (6)).

87. Dyrrachion became Durazzo and then DURRËS on the coast of Albania. It was an important Roman harbour and the starting-point of a system of roads. No one knows why or exactly when Epidamnos became Dyrrachion; Pausanias is thinking of a myth about Dyrrachos the son of Poseidon by Melissa the daughter of Epidamnos's daughter. (Appian, *Civil Wars*, 2, 39; Dio Cassius, 41, 49.)

[9] Lykinos of Heraia and Epikradios the Mantinean, Tellon the Oresthasian and Agiadas the Elean won boys' championships, Lykinos at running and the others at boxing. Epikradios is by Ptolichos of Aigina, and Agiadas is by Serambos of Aigina; Lykinos's statue is by Kleon, and the artist of Tellon's statue is not recorded.[88]

[1] Next to these there are some Elean dedications: Philip 11 son of Amyntas and Alexander son of Philip and Seleukos and Antigonos; they are on horseback, except that the portrait of Antigonos is the figure of a man on foot.

[2] Not far from these kings stands the Thasian Theagenes son of Timosthenes, though the Thasians say that Theagenes was not Timosthenes' son, but Timosthenes was a priest of Thasian Herakles and the spirit of Herakles appeared in the form of Timosthenes and lay with Theagenes' mother.[89] They say that when the boy was nine years old he was on his way home from school one day and pulled up a bronze statue that he liked of some god that was dedicated in the market-place, and carried it home with him over one shoulder. [3] The people were furious at this behaviour, but there was some distinguished citizen of advanced age who would not let them put the boy to death, but ordered him to carry the statue back to the market-place from his house. The boy carried it, and became very famous for his strength, and what he had done was gossiped about all over Greece. [4] I have already discussed the most notable of those of the deeds of Theagenes that concern the Olympic games, earlier in this treatise: how he fought and beat Euthymos the boxer and how he was fined by the Eleans.[90] On that occasion a man from Mantineia called Dromeus became the first recorded winner of the all-in

88. Some inscribed fragments which may belong to the base of Agiadas's statue have been found (*Inschriften von Olympia*, 150), and Tellon's base has certainly been found (*Inschriften von Olympia*, 147-8). It has a fragmentary fifth-century inscription, and a couplet which may well be early, inscribed in very late Hellenistic lettering. We know little about these sculptors.

89. Theagenes was Olympic boxing champion in 480. He is supposed to have eaten an entire bull for a bet.

90. Bk VI, 6 (5f.).

fighting to win without getting dirty, but Theagenes won the all-in fighting at the next Olympics. [5] He won three times in the Pythian games as a boxer, and between boxing and all-in fighting he won nine times at the Nemean and ten at the Isthmian games. At Phthia in Thessaly he gave up concentrating on those two events and took it into his head to become a distinguished Greek runner, and he won the long-distance running. I think it was ambitious envy of Achilles, to win a race in the native town of the fastest runner among all the heroes, as they are called. Altogether he won one thousand four hundred wreaths.[91] [6] When he died, someone who hated him in his lifetime came every night to Theagenes' statue to flog the bronze as if he were beating up Theagenes himself: the statue fell on him and put an end to his impertinence, but as he was killed his sons prosecuted the statue for murder, and the Thasians took the opinion of Drakon, who rules in the Athenian murder laws that even inanimate objects which fall on a man and kill him must be taken outside the boundaries, and they drowned Theagenes' statue in the sea.[92] [7] In the course of time the earth of Thasos ceased to give fruit, so they sent ambassadors to Delphi and the god in his oracle commanded them to take back the exiles. Yet the men they took back because of this brought no remedy to the earth's barrenness, and they went to the Pythian priestess a second time to say the curse of the gods was still on them even

91. Plutarch says 1200, 'and he regarded most of them as rubbish.' In a career of thirty years he must have won a prize almost once a week. If we take this claim seriously we must suppose there were an enormous number of small local festivals we know nothing about. This is certainly true of dramatic festivals in the Hellenistic period, and it is not at all impossible. I suppose they were country gatherings like village fairs.

92. Eusebios tells this story (De Praeparatio Evangelica, 5, 34) and says that ever afterwards the Thasians wore long hair in honour of Demeter. Aristotle (Poetics, 9, 12) and Theokritos (23, 60) both tell stories about statues falling to take their revenge. There is another version of the oracle:

> You forget Theagenes, he lies in sand,
> he was ten thousand times a champion.

though they had done what the oracle commanded. [8] Then the Pythian priestess replied to them:

*You leave great Theagenes unremembered.*

They say that while they were in despair of how to rescue Theagenes' statue some fishermen let down nets into the sea for a catch of fish; the statue was entangled in their net and they brought it back to land. The Thasians dedicated it again where it had first stood, and they offer customary sacrifices to it as a god. [9] And I know of statues of Theagenes erected in many other places by Greeks and by barbarians, where he cures diseases and receives local worship. The portrait figure of Theagenes is in Altis; it is by Glaukias of Aigina.[93]

[1] Near by there is a bronze chariot with a man mounted 12 in it, with race-horses standing beside the chariot one on either side, and boys sitting on the horses. These are memorials of the Olympic victories of Hieron son of Deinomenes, the dictator of Syracuse after his brother Gelon. It was not Hieron who sent the dedications, but Hieron's son Deinomenes gave them to the god; the chariot is by Onatas of Aigina, and the horses on either side and the boys riding them are by Kalamis.[94]

93. Lucian says it cured fevers like the statue of Poulydamas. There are a number of recorded monuments to Olympic champions outside Olympia (cf. Hyde, *Olympic Victor Monuments*, pp. 361f.). Kallimachos (*Aitia*, fr. 84–5) tells the story of the Lokrian Euthykles, an Olympic champion whose statue at home was mutilated because he was accused of accepting a bribe on an embassy; Apollo sent a plague and in the end his statue was honoured like the statue of Zeus. Not much can be said about Glaukias.

94. Onatas and the Athenian Kalamis were perhaps the most famous and admired of the sculptors of their generation. We have no original work by either of them, though Kalamis's bronze Apollo at Apollonia in Asia Minor does appear on coins. Kalamis was famous for his horses. Onatas could possibly be the sculptor of the east pediment figures from the temple of Aphaia at Aigina. Hiero died in 467, and we know that his son Deinomenes survived him only from several passages in Pausanias. Hiero's brother attempted to succeed as dictator of Syracuse, but after a year of troubles the people took over in 466. Deinomenes could have dedicated this magnificent and expensive group in exile, just as the Alkmaionidai in exile rebuilt the temple of Apollo at Delphi, but after 466 seems late for Kalamis and Onatas: several solutions of this pro-

[2] Beside Hieron's chariot is a different Hieron who was also dictator of Syracuse, Hieron son of Hierokles. After the death of the earlier dictator Agathokles, dictatorship at Syracuse sprouted again in Hieron son of Hierokles, who took over control the year after the hundred and twenty-sixth Olympics when Idaios of Kyrene won the running.[95] [3] This Hieron was on terms of friendship with Pyrros son of Aiakides and allied to him by marriage: he married his son Gelon to Pyrros's daughter Nereis. When Rome went to war with Carthage over Sicily the Carthaginians held more than half the island, and at the very beginning of the war Hieron took the Carthaginian side, but he soon decided that Rome was more powerful and Roman friendship more reliable, so he changed over. [4] He met his death from Deinomenes, a Syracusan who deeply detested dictatorship; it happened later when Hippokrates the brother of Epikydes from Erbessos had just arrived in Syracuse and began to make a speech to the people; Deinomenes attacked Hippokrates and tried to kill him, so Hippokrates fought back and some of the bodyguard overcame Deinomenes and murdered him. Hieron's statues at Olympia, one on horseback and the other on foot, were dedicated by his sons, and executed by Mikon son of Nikeratos of Syracuse.[96]

[5] Beyond Hieron's portraits stand Areus son of Akrotatos,

---

blem are possible, none certain. There is a fine dedicated bronze helmet that was picked up at Olympia by an English tourist, I think Sir Thomas Cartwright of Aynho, and given to a friend in Naples, where it was first studied by scholars. Morritt of Rokeby found another in the bed of the Alpheios in 1795, and wrote home in a letter that he saw nothing at Olympia worth writing about. Cartwright's helmet was given by George IV to the British Museum; it has been worn in battle, and was dedicated to Zeus from the spoils of the Etruscan navy at Cumae in 474 by Hiero.

95. In 276.

96. It was Hiero the Second's grandson Hieronymos the son of Gelon and Nereis who died in this way (Livy, 24, 7). Hieros died in 215; Gelon was already dead, and Hieronymos succeeded. Erbessos was a native anti-Syracusan city in east Sicily. Mikon of Syracuse is known only from this commission and from one desultory mention by Pliny.

king of Lakonia, and Aratos son of Kleinias, and then Areus again, riding on a horse. Aratos was dedicated by Corinth and Areus by Elis. Neither Areus nor Aratos has passed unnoticed in the earlier part of my work, but in addition to that [6] Aratos was an Olympic chariot winner.[97] Timon son of Aisypos of Elis entered horses at Olympia . . . this is in bronze, with a virgin girl mounted in it, Victory I imagine. Kallon son of Harmodios and Hippomachos son of Moschion were Elean boy boxing champions; Kallon is by Daippos, and the sculptor of Hippomachos's statue is unknown, but they say he fought and beat three opponents without being hit once and without getting a mark on his body.[98] [7] Theochrestos of Kyrene was a horse-breeder in the local tradition of Libya, and he and his grandfather before him who had the same name both won racing victories at Olympia, but Theochrestos's father won at the Isthmus as the inscription on the chariot tells you. [8] Agesarchos son of Haimostratos the Tritaian won the men's boxing at Olympia and Nemea and Delphi and the Isthmus as the couplet indicates, but I have discovered the couplet is mistaken in calling the Tritaians Arkadians. For the Arkadian cities that became famous we have the stories of their founders, but were even those cities whose original weakness kept them obscure, and which were therefore resettled at Megalopolis, not included in the resolution passed by the Arkadian community on that occasion?[99] [9] Nor is there any city of Tritaia to be found in Greece other than the one in Achaia. So one might suppose that the Tritaians belonged to Arkadia in the sense in which some of the Arkadians today belong to the Argive League. Agesarchos's portrait is by the sons of Polykles, of whom we shall have more to record later on.[100]

97. Cf. Bk II, 8f., and Bk III, 6 (4f.). Areus reigned from 309 to 265 B.C.
98. Cf. p. 330, n. 137.
99. For Tritaia, cf. Bk VII, 22 (6f.). Dikaiarchos in the third century B.C. thought of it as Arkadian, but the sons of Polykles who made this statue belong to the mid second century.
100. Cf. Bk X, 34 (6), also Bk VI, Note 30.

13   [1] Astylos of Kroton is by Pythagoras; he won the running at Olympia three times in succession and scored victories in the two-lap race as well. Because in his two last victories he proclaimed himself as a Syracusan to please Hieron son of Deinomenes, the people of Kroton decreed that his house be turned into a prison and they destroyed his portrait in the sanctuary of Lakinian Hera.[101]

[2] There is a tablet dedicated at Olympia which gives the victories of Chionis the Lakonian. Those who believe it was Chionis himself and not the Lakonian people who dedicated this tablet are being idiotic: given what the tablet says, that the race in armour had not been introduced yet, how on earth would Chionis know that the Eleans ever would pass the law to introduce it? Those who say the man's statue standing beside the tablet is a portrait of Chionis are even stupider, as it is by Myron of Athens.[102]

[3] There was a Lykian called Hermogenes the Xanthian who won the same kind of distinctions as Chionis; he carried off the wild olive eight times in three Olympics, and the Greeks nicknamed him 'the Horse'. Polites is another man you might well be really staggered by. Polites came from Keramos in Karia, and at Olympia he proved himself a master of running of every kind. He could switch within the shortest period of time from the longest slog to the shortest sprint: on the same day he won the long-distance and the ordinary running and the two laps as well. [4] Polites . . . so that each of them is subject to the draw, and they are not all

101. Astylos won in 488, in 484, and in 480. We have three lines of a poem by Simonides about Astylos: *Who else has tied so many victories with myrtle leaves and wreaths of roses?* For Pythagoras, cf. Bk VI, Note 29. KROTON was between Taranto and Reggio; from the eleventh century to 1929 it was called COTRONE (now CROTONE). The great Doric temple of Lakinian Hera was at CAPO COLONNA. In 173 B.C. Q. Fulvius Flaccus pulled off its roof-tiles and took them to Rome, but the senate made him put them back. The temple was not pulled down until the sixteenth century, when it was vandalized to build a bishop's palace. There is one column still standing.

102. Chionis won in 668 B.C. and in the next three Olympic meetings. There are a number of cases of statues dedicated long after the event (cf. W. Hyde, *Olympic Victor Monuments*, p. 32).

allowed to race together; then the winners of each heat run again in the actual race for the prize, so the man who wins the wreath has won two races. The most distinguished of all running records belongs to Leonidas of Rhodes. He held out at the height of his speed for four Olympic cycles, and won twelve times.[103]

[5] Not far from Chionis's tablet at Olympia stands Skaios the son of Douris from Samos, who was a boy boxing champion; his portrait is by Hippias son of . . . and the inscription on it shows that Skaios won while the Samian people were in exile from the island, and at the time . . . the people to its rights.[104] [6] Beside the dictator is the dedication of Diallos son of Pollis, who was born at Smyrna, the first Ionian so this Diallos says to win the boys' wreath for all-in fighting.[105] Thersilochos of Corfu who won his wreath as a boy boxer and Aristion son of Theophiles of Epidauros who won the adult boxing are by Polykleitos of Argos, and [7] Bykelos, the first boy boxer from Sikyon to be champion, is by Kanachos of Sikyon who was Polykleitos of Argos's pupil.[106] Beside Bykelos stands a man at arms nicknamed the Libyan, Mnaseas of Kyrene; the portrait is by Pythagoras of Re-

103. He won for the first time in 164 B.C. and for the last in 152 B.C. Xanthos was the greatest Lykian city. In the wars after Caesar's death Brutus took Xanthos after fierce fighting; most of the city was burnt, and it never recovered. Its rich ruins were stripped by Sir C. Fellows for the British Museum; the site is east of Rhodes. KERAMOS was on the south side of the gulf of BOUDROUN between Knidos and Halikarnassos.

104. Douris was dictator of Samos in the late fourth century, in the lifetime of Theophrastos. The exile means the Athenian occupation (365–322). No one knows who Hippias was.

105. Not before the second century B.C.

106. Aristion's pedestal has been found inscribed in mid-fourth-century lettering (*Inschriften von Olympia*, 165), but there exists a papyrus fragment (cf. C. Robert in *Hermes*, 30, pp. 141f.) which gives a list of Olympic champions between 480 and 448, so that we know Aristion won in 452. For Polykleitos, cf. Bk VI, Note 35. If Kanachos was Polykleitos's pupil, this is not the great late archaic sculptor who made the Apollo that the Persians looted from Miletos, and whose work Cicero thought rather too stiff, but another Kanachos working at the end of the fifth century, probably a grandson (Bk X, 9 (10)).

gion.[107] Agemachos of Kyzikos from the Asian mainland . . .
his inscription announces he was born in Argos. [8] Naxos
was once a settlement in Sicily founded by Chalkis on the
Euripos; today there are not even any ruins of that city left,
and Tisander son of Kleokritos should be given the chief
credit for the memory of its name in later generations:
Tisander fought and won four times in the men's boxing at
Olympia, and just as often at Delphi, but in those days
Corinth and Argos still kept no complete memorials of
Nemean and Isthmian champions.[108]

[9] The mare of Pheidolas of Corinth is called Breeze
according to the Corinthian records, and just as the race
started she threw her rider; yet she ran just as perfectly, turned
round the post, and when she heard the trumpet quickened
her pace and got to the umpires first; she realized she had won
and stood still. The Eleans proclaimed Pheidolas the winner
and allowed him to dedicate this mare. [10] Pheidolas's sons
also won with a race-horse, and the horse is carved in relief
on a tablet, with this inscription:

> Fast-running Wolf has crowned Pheidolas's sons
> with one wreath at the Isthmus, two in this place.

But the Elean records of Olympic winners do not agree with
this inscription. There is a win for Pheidolas's sons in the
Elean records for the sixty-eighth Olympics and nothing
else.[109] You may accept that this is the case. [11] The Eleans,
Agathinos, Thrasyboulos and Telemachos all have statues:
Telemachos got his portrait for winning with horses,

107. Cf. Bk VI, Notes 29 and 149. Mnaseas won in 456.

108. Agesamachos is supposed to have won the running in 192. One of
Tisander's championships was celebrated in a lost poem by Pindar (*Fr.* 23,
Snell). The Sicilian city of Naxos was destroyed by the Syracusans at the end
of the fifth century B.C. The Euripos is the narrow strip of sea with a violent
tide between Euboia and the mainland. The Venetian name for Chalkis,
NEGROPONTE, is a corruption of Evripounta (ston Evripounta).

109. The sixty-eighth Olympics were in 508. The *Palatine Anthology*
contains a similar couplet for Pheidolas himself (6, 135):

> Pheidolas's horse from Corinth the broad dancing-ground
> dedicated to Zeus for the courage he ran with.

Agathinos was dedicated by the Achaians of Pellene. The Athenian people dedicated Aristophon son of Lysinos, the adult all-in champion at the Olympic games.[110]

[1] Pherias of Aigina, whose statue is dedicated beside **14** Aristophon of Athens, was judged to be too young at the seventy-eighth Olympics and not up to wrestling, and was barred from the games, but the next time when he was accepted with the boys he won the wrestling.[111] Nikasylos of Rhodes had a quite different kind of luck from Pherias at Olympia: [2] as he was eighteen he was barred by the Eleans from wrestling with the boys, but he was proclaimed winner of the men's wrestling. Later on he won at Nemea and the Isthmus. He met his destiny at the age of twenty, before he got home to Rhodes. But in my opinion Artemidoros of Tralles surpassed the Rhodian wrestler's adventure at Olympia. Artemidoros happened to fail in the Olympics as a boy all-in fighter, the reason being that he was too young, [3] but when the time came for the Ionian games at Smyrna his physique had so improved that on one day he fought and beat his own Olympic opponents in the all-in fighting, then the adolescents as they call them as well, and best of all, the men. They say he went in for the adolescent competition because of a trainer's encouraging him, and went in for the men's because an adult all-in fighter taunted him. Artemidoros was men's champion at Olympia in the two hundred and twelfth games.[112] [4] Next to Nikasylos's portrait comes a smallish

110. Telemachos's base was found at the south edge of the terrace of the temple of Zeus; his statue was by Philonides, who is otherwise unknown. The inscription is early Hellenistic, and the statue seems to have been a naked bronze man standing evenly. A fragment of Aristophon's base has also been found (*Inschriften von Olympia*, 177 and 169).

111. He was too young in 468, although he was already a good wrestler, and in 464 he was champion.

112. In A.D. 67; Tralles was an inland city due east of Magnesia and of Samos. There was a bad earthquake there in the reign of Augustus, and the emperor had paid for the restorations. There is a fine marble statue of a boy boxer from Tralles wrapped in his cloak before fighting, in the Istanbul museum (cf. Metzger, *Anatolia* II, pl. III, or Boardman, *Greek Art*, pl. 198). It is usually dated in the first century B.C., but I wonder if it may not be later.

bronze horse dedicated by Krokon the Eretrian who won the wreath for his race-horse; near the horse is the boy boxing champion Telestas of Messenia by Silanion.[113]

[5] Milo son of Diotimos is by Dameas; they were both from Kroton. Milo won six times in the wrestling at Olympia, one of them as a boy, and six times as a man and once as a boy at Delphi.[114] He came to wrestle at Olympia a seventh time, but he was not able to out-wrestle his fellow-citizen Timasitheos who was still young, and unwilling to stand close up to him. [6] Milo is supposed to have carried his own statue into Altis, and there are other stories about Milo and the pomegranate and Milo and the discus. He could hold a pomegranate so that no one could force him to release it, and yet the pressure of his hand did it no damage; and he could stand on an oiled discus and laugh at people flinging themselves at him and trying to shove him off. And there were other spectacular things he did. [7] He tied a string round his brows like a ribbon or a wreath, and by holding his breath and filling the veins of his head with blood, he snapped the string with the power of his veins. He is supposed to have kept his right elbow by his side and held out his forearm straight to the front with the hand turned thumb uppermost and fingers flat: yet no one could shift his little finger. [8] They say he was killed by wild beasts. Somewhere in the Krotonian territory he came across a tree of dry wood split open and held with wedges. It came into Milo's head to put his hands inside the tree; the wedges slipped and Milo was held in the tree and the wolves found him. These beasts are particularly abundant in the territory of Kroton.[115]

113. For Silanion, cf. Bk VI, Note 30.
114. One of his wins seems to have been in 532. There is an epigram for his statue attributed to Simonides (*Patatine Anthology*, 16, 24):

> Milo: the fine statue of a fine man:
> he won seven times at Pise
> and never dropped to his knees.

115. In Calabria. In 1956 Italian wolves ate a postman near Florence and chased a bus into Rome.

[9] That was the death Milo died. Pyrros son of Aiakides, who was king in the Thesprotian mainland and did many memorable deeds (as I have explained in my discussion of the Athenians), was dedicated in Altis by Thrasyboulos of Elis.[116] Beside Pyrros is a little man with pipes in relief on a tablet; he was the next Pythian winner after Sakadas of Argos, [10] who won at the games held by the League before wreaths were awarded, and twice won the wreath afterwards.[117] Pythokritos of Sikyon won at the next six Pythian games; he was the only flute-player ever to do such a thing. It is clear that he also played six times for the pentathlon at the Olympic games. Pythokritos got a tablet at Olympia in return for this with an inscription:

*Monument of Pythokritos son of Kallinikos.*

[11] The Aitolian community dedicated Kylon, who freed Elis from the dictatorship of Aristotimos.[118] Gorgos son of Eukles the Messenian pentathlon winner and another Messenian, Damaretos the boy boxing champion, are by Theron of Boiotia, who made Gorgos, and Silanion of Athens, who made the portrait of Damaretos.[119] Anauchidas son of Philys the Elean took the boys' wrestling prize, and later the men's. We have no record of the sculptor of his portrait, but Anochos son of Adamatas the Tarantine is by Ageladas of Argos.[120] [12] The inscription says the boy on horseback and the man standing beside the horse are Xenombrotos of Meropian Kos, who took the prize for a horse-race, and Xenodikos, a winner in the boys' boxing. Xenombrotos is by Philotimos of Aigina,

116. Cf. Bk I, 11 (1f.). He was king of Epeiros.

117. Sakadas was a famous sixth-century musician; cf. Bk IV, 27, and Bk X, 7 (4).

118. Cf. Bk V, 5 (1).

119. Gorgos won after the rebuilding of Messene and after 368 (cf. Bk VI, 2 (10)), and in fact Polybios (7, 10) speaks of him in a context of the late third century. Theron seems from the evidence of an inscribed base from Asia Minor to have been at work after 200 B.C. For Silanion, cf. Bk VI, Note 30.

120. Ageladas made the Zeus of Ithome which appears on fourth-century Messenian coins and the boy Zeus of Aigion; he was at work by 520 B.C.

Xenodikos is by Pantias.[121] Pythes son of Andromachos was born an Abderan and is by Lysippos, and his soldiers dedicated two portraits of him: he seems to have been a commander of mercenaries or at any rate some kind of successful military man.[122]

[13] Then there are the boy running champions Meneptolemos of Apollonia on the Ionic gulf and Philo of Corfu, and next to them comes Hieronymos of Andros who wrestled and beat Tisamenos of Elis in the pentathlon at Olympia: later on Tisamenos was a prophet for the Greeks against Mardonios and the Persians at Plataia. Hieronymos is dedicated here with another Andrian beside him, a boy wrestler called Prokles son of Lykastidas. The sculptor of Hieronymos's figure was called Stomios, and Prokles is by Somis. Aischines of Elis won the pentathlon twice and has two portraits for the two victories.[123]

15 [1] The Mytileneans credit Archippos of Mytilene the men's boxing champion with the further honour of having won the four wreaths at Olympia, Delphi, Nemea and the Isthmus before he was more than twenty years old.[124] The boy sprinter Xenon son of Kalliteles from Lepreos in Triphylia is by Pyrilampes of Messenia; Kleinomachos of Elis the pentathlon winner is by a sculptor whose name is un-

121. Fragments of this inscription have been recovered, and the verses can be reconstituted. They are in mid-fourth-century lettering, though Xenombrotos is believed to have won in the mid fifth century (*Inschriften von Olympia*, 170). Meropian Kos is the island of Kos north of Rhodes; its founder was supposed to be a king Merops. Philotimos's cooperation with Pantias ties their dates together at the end of the fifth century (cf. Bk VI, 3 (1), and 9 (1)).

122. For Lysippos, cf. Bk VI, Note 3. No one knows anything about Pythes of Abdera. Abdera was a city on the coast of Thrace, east of the Nestos. He sounds like a Macedonian commander, perhaps a descendant of the Pythes Herodotos mentions (7, 137).

123. For Philo, cf. also Bk VI, 7 (8). For the prophet Tisamenos, cf. Bk III, 11 (6f.). Apollonia is in Albania; these are late archaic dedications, and it was a very strong city at that time. Nothing is known about Stomios or Somis.

124. A round inscribed base of dark grey marble for this statue was found south of the temple of Zeus. The lettering is early Hellenistic; the upper part of the pedestal is broken.

known.[125] [2] Pantarkes of Elis was dedicated by the Achaians according to the inscription: he negotiated a peace between Achaia and Elis and the release of prisoners on both sides. Pantarkes also won a race with his race-horse, and there is a monument at Olympia to his victory. Olidas of Elis was dedicated by the Aitolian people, and Charinos of Elis was dedicated for winning the two-lap race and the race in armour; beside Charinos stands Ageles of Chios champion boy boxer, by Theomnestos of Sardis.[126]

[3] The portrait of Kleitomachos of Thebes was dedicated by his father Hermokrates, and his achievements were as follows. At the Isthmus he became men's wrestling champion and boxing champion and all-in fighting champion all on the same day: he won three championships at Delphi, all for all-in fighting, and at Olympia he was the next man after Theagenes to win the all-in fighting and the boxing as well. [4] He won the all-in fighting at the hundred and forty-first Olympics, and at the next games Kleitomachos went in for the all-in fighting and the boxing as well, and at the same games Kapros of Elis wanted to wrestle and fight all-in on the same day. [5] When Kapros had won the wrestling, Kleitomachos suggested to the Greek arbiters it would be fair if they brought forward the all-in fighting so that he could fight before getting cut up in the boxing. That was reasonable, so the all-in fighting was brought forward and he was beaten all-in by Kapros, and yet he went on to fight vigorously and indomitably in the boxing.[127]

125. Pyrilampes of Messenia is another unknown Hellenistic sculptor.

126. Pantarkes' peace was probably in the third century (Polybios, 4, 5, etc.). Elis was loyal to the Aitolian league against the Achaian league. The base of a statue by Theomnestos has been found in Chios, but nothing much is known about him.

127. Kleitomachos won the all-in fighting in 216 B.C. Boxing was always thought of as tougher and more damaging than the all-in fighting, probably because it was always fought to a knock-out and with hard gloves, while the all-in fighters could win without doing so much damage. In 212 Kleitomachos won the boxing against Aristonikos of Egypt. Polybios (27, 9) says the crowd was very excited and enthusiastic.

[6] The Ionians of Erythrai dedicated Epitherses son of Metrodoros for two Olympic boxing victories and winning twice at Delphi, and at Nemea and the Isthmus as well; the Syracusan people dedicated two portraits of Hieron and Hieron's sons added a third: I explained just now that this Hieron was another man of the same name as the son of Dinomenes, and also like him was dictator of Syracuse.[128] [7] Timoptolis son of Lampis the Elean was dedicated by the Paleans, who are the fourth subdivision of the Kephallenians and in older times used to be called Doulichians. There are dedications of Archidamos son of Agesilaos and someone as a huntsman. You should realize that Demetrios who led his army against Seleukos and was captured in battle and his son Antigonos are Byzantian dedications.[129] [8] Eutelidas of Sparta was a double boys' champion at wrestling and the pentathlon in the thirty-eighth Olympics; it was the first and last time a boys' pentathlon was held. The portrait of Eutelidas is ancient, and the letters on its pedestal are dim with age.[130] [9] Beyond Eutelidas comes Areus king of Lakonia with Gorgos of Elis next to him.

128. Part of Epitherses' statue-base has been found; his statue was by Pythokritos, who seems from two other statue-bases at Rhodes to have worked around 200 B.C. (*Inschriften von Olympia*, n. 186, and Loewy, *Inschriften griechischer Bildhauer*, n. 176). For Hiero the second, cf. Bk VI, Note 94.

129. Kephallenia north-west of the Elean coast was identified with the Homeric island of DOULICHION. Its four cities seem to have been very wealthy in the Roman period. Pale was at PALIKI, opposite the big fortifications of Krane (beside the modern ARGOSTOLI). But 'Paleans' here is very probably a mistake: the archaic spelling of the people of Elis and of Pale (Baleioi and Paleioi) is almost the same: they were in fact confused by Herodotos (9, 28). The walls of Pale survived into the seventeenth century. Archidamos III reigned from 359 to 338. Demetrios's final hopeless expedition against Asia ended in his being trapped and captured by Seleukos in 285. For his story, cf. Bk I, 10 (2), and Bk I, 16 (1). Parts of the statue-bases have been found (*Inschriften von Olympia*, 304–5). The statues were probably put up to commemorate a battle Antigonos won against the Gauls in Thrace in 276. Frazer thinks the Antigonos of the statue was Demetrios's father not his son.

130. He must have won in 628; this is the oldest athletic monument that Pausanias saw at Olympia; such a statue would be contemporary with the oldest *kouroi*, the statues of Richter's Sounion group.

Down to my time Gorgos was the only man to have won the Olympic pentathlon four times, and he also won the two-lap race and the race in armour once each.[131]

[10] They say the man with the boys standing beside him is Ptolemy son of Lagos. Next to him comes a man, Kapros son of Pythagoras of Elis, who won the wrestling and the all-in fighting on the same day, and was the first man to win both. I have already explained whom he beat at the all-in fighting, and in the wrestling he fought and beat Paianios of Elis, who carried off the wrestling in the previous Olympics and the Pythian boys' boxing, and then the Pythian men's wrestling and boxing on the same day.[132]

[1] Kapros did not win his victories without extremely hard 16 work, and toil and trouble. There are also portraits at Olympia of Anauchidas and Pherenikos, Elean boy wrestling champions. Pleistainos son of Eurydamos, Aitolian commander against the Gauls, was dedicated by the Thespians. [2] Tydeus of Elis dedicated Seleukos, and Demetrios's father Antigonos. Seleukos's name is world-famous, and particularly for the capture of Demetrios.[133] Timon won the pentathlon everywhere in Greece except the Isthmus, where like all other Eleans he was not allowed to enter, and his inscription adds that he took part in an Aitolian campaign against Thessaly, and as a friend of Aitolia he commanded the garrison at Naupaktos. [3] Not far from Timon's portrait stands Greece with Elis beside her; Greece is crowning Antigonos the regent for Philip son of Demetrios with one hand, and Philip himself

131. For Areus and his other statue, cf. Bk VI, 12 (5), and the note there. Gorgos's dates are unknown.

132. Ptolemy is the king of Egypt, Ptolemy the First. Kapros beat Kleitomachos in 212; Paianios won the wrestling in 216 when Kleitomachos won the all-in fighting.

133. Anauchidas has been mentioned already (Bk VI, 14 (11); cf. also Bk V, 27 (12)). I suppose the Aitolian statue was put up at the time of the Gaulish raid on Delphi, but at Delphi itself they erected the father not the son (cf. Bk X, 16 (4)). Statues of Seleukos and Antigonos have already been mentioned (Bk VI, 11 (1)). There is something very odd about this whole passage.

with the other, and Elis is crowning the Demetrios who fought Seleukos and Ptolemy son of Lagos.[134]

[4] The inscription on Aristeides of Elis tells you he won the race in armour at Olympia and the two-lap race at Delphi and the boys' race on the riding-track at Nemea. The length of the riding-track is twice the two-lap race; the event died out at Nemea and the Isthmus but the emperor Hadrian restored it to Argos for the Nemean winter games.[135]

[5] Very close to Aristeides stand Menalkes of Elis who won the Olympic pentathlon and Philonides son of Zotes, from Cretan Chersonesos, who was a dispatch runner for Alexander son of Philip.[136] Beyond him comes Brimias of Elis, adult boxing champion, and then Leonidas from Naxos in the Aegean, dedicated by Psophis in Arkadia, and a portrait of Asamon the men's boxing champion and one of Nikander, who won two two-lap championships at Olympia, and six other running championships between Nemea and the Isthmus. Asamon and Nikander were Eleans; Nikander's portrait is by Daippos and Asamon is by Pyrilampes the Messenian.[137] [6] Eualkidas of Elis won championships as a

134. Timon fought against Macedonia for the Aitolian League soon after 239 B.C., when Antigonos Gonatas had died and Demetrios the Second had come to the throne; the Aitolians were trying to annex Akarnania. Timon led the Aitolian defence of Naupaktos. In the late 220s Demetrios was dead and Antigonos was regent; Demetrios's son Philip the Fifth reigned from 221 to 179. These statues go more or less together, but Elis is crowning the elder Demetrios (336–283 B.C.) and Ptolemy the First, who both belong to a much earlier generation. The Elean gesture of gratitude to these two rival princes must have been about the year 301, when they were allies for three or four years.

135. For these games, cf. Bk II, 15 (3).

136. The base of Philonides' statue was found in the south-west corner of Altis, and another copy of the same inscription was found to the west of the sacred area, in the Byzantine church (*Inschriften von Olympia*, 276 and 277). The stone and the lettering of the two inscriptions are quite different; I am unable to judge the difference of date. Philonides must have been a very steady runner as he was used not only for dispatches but for pacing out the stages of roads. Cretan Chersonesos was on the north coast of the island thirteen or fourteen miles east of HERAKLEION.

137. The base for Leonidas of Naxos has been found; the lettering is late-fourth-century. This was the Leonidas who built the Leonidaion (Bk V, 15 (1));

boy boxer, Seleadas of Lakonia as an adult wrestler. There is also a smallish chariot dedicated here by Polypeithes of Lakonia and on the same tablet his father Kalliteles, who was a wrestler; Polypeithes won with a team of horses, Kalliteles in the men's wrestling. [7] Lampos son of Arniskos and ... son of Aristarchos were private individuals dedicated by Psophis either because they had a diplomatic connexion there or for some blood relationship. Between them stands Lysippos of Elis, who fought and beat the other boys in the boys' wrestling; his portrait is by Andreas of Argos.[138]

[8] Deinosthenes the Lakonian won the men's running at Olympia and he dedicated a tablet in Altis beside his statue, saying that the distance by road from here at Olympia to another tablet at Sparta is eighty-two and a half miles.[139] You may wish to know that Theodoros who won the pentathlon and Pyttalos son of Lampis the boys' boxing champion and

---

he was not an athletic champion but a benefactor of the Arkadians at Psophis (*Inschriften von Olympia*, 294). We know little about Daippos and Pyrilampes, except that Daippos was Lysippos's son and must have been working around the year 300.

138. Almost nothing can be said about all these except that it seems reasonable to associate the benefactors of Psophis with Leonidas of Naxos and the late fourth century (cf. Note 137 above), and that a statue-base has been found which might possibly be by Andreas of Argos; more solidly we can date Andreas of Argos by his statue of Q. Marcius Philippus (*Inschriften von Olympia*, 318) to the early second century B.C.

139. This stone has been found; Pausanias says 660 furlongs, but what the stone says is 630 to Sparta and another 30 to 'the first stone', which was possibly in the sanctuary at Amyklai (cf. Thukydides, 5, 18, 9). The French surveyors of the Peloponnese in the early nineteenth century reckoned the distance at sixty-five or -six miles. Throughout this translation I have taken an English furlong as equivalent to a Greek 'stade': this is roughly accurate, but the equivalence is not exact; a more exact equivalent to what Pausanias says here would be about seventy miles, but I have preferred to make a uniform error. Pausanias himself almost always gives numbers of furlongs only to the nearest multiple of five. The route would be up the Alpheios gorges to KARYTAINA, then straight down to Sparta through MEGALOPOLIS and LONGANIKOS. Deinosthenes must have been a professional measurer like Philonides (Note 136 above). He was an Olympic champion probably in 316 but there is some confusion about the spelling of his name.

Neolaidas who won the sprint and the race in armour were all Eleans; and there is a further story told about Pyttalos, that when Elis and Arkadia were quarrelling about the boundaries of their territory, it was Pyttalos who gave judgement. His statue is by Sthennis of Olynthos.[140] [9] Next you come to Ptolemy mounted on a horse with the Elean athlete Paianios son of Damatrios beside him, who won the Olympic wrestling and won twice at Delphi. Then there is Kleuretos of Elis who took the pentathlon wreath, and the chariot of an Athenian called Glaukos son of Eteokles who won the full team chariot race.[141]

17 [1] Those are the most interesting objects that present themselves to a man approaching Altis, as I have said. But if you should choose to turn right from the Leonidaion and make for the great altar, here are some of the memorable things you will see. Demokrates of Tenedos who won the men's wrestling and Kriannios of Elis who won the race in armour are by Diomysikles of Miletos and Lysos of Macedonia.[142] [2] Hero-

140. Olynthos was destroyed by Philip of Macedon in 348 and the survivors later joined the new city of Kassandreia with the Potidaians. Olynthos lay at the head of a gulf south-east of SALONIKI. We have scattered pieces of evidence about one or more sculptors called Sthennis: there was a Sthennis who made a statue of Lysimachos after 306 B.C., and a Sthennis who was Athenian (possible for an Olynthian after 348). It is not at all impossible they were the same person. Pliny knew three of his statues in the temple of Concord at Rome, and Lucullus carried away another from Sinope, but we have no idea what they were like (Plutarch, Lucullus, 23; Pliny, Natural History, 34, 90).

141. Paianios's base has been found; he won in 216 B.C.; the statue had its weight forward on the right foot (Inschriften von Olympia, 179). He won three times at Delphi, the third perhaps too late to be included in the list of titles which is here Pausanias's source (cf. Bk VI, 15 (10)). The base of Glaukon's chariot has been found with a third-century inscription (Inschriften von Olympia, 178).

142. No satisfactory explanation of Pausanias's new route has been offered. Things are all the worse because there have been doubts about the whereabouts of the altar of Zeus (cf. Hyde, Olympic Victor Monuments, pp. 348f.). Is it possible that he enters Altis through the north gate in the west wall, turning right from the narrow road and along the west wall of Altis? I dislike this solution but I know of no better. For the altar of Zeus, cf. Bk V, 13 (8). A bronze tablet has been found recording an Elean grant of honours to Demokrates of

dotos the Klazomenian and Philinos son of Hegepolis the
Koan had their portraits dedicated by their cities: the Klazo-
menians because Herodotos, who won the boys' running, was
the first Klazomenian to win at Olympia, and the Koans
because of Philinos's famous reputation for winning the
running five times at Olympia, four at Delphi and Nemea,
and eleven times at the Isthmus.[143] [3] Ptolemy son of
Ptolemy son of Lagos was dedicated by a Macedonian called
Aristolaos. There is the dedication of Boutas son of Polyneikes
of Miletos, boys' boxing champion, and a portrait statue by
Lysippos of Kallikrates from Magnesia on the Lethaios, who
won two prizes for the race in armour.[144] [4] Then there are
Enation the boy runner and Alexibios the pentathlon champion from Heraia in Arkadia by Akestor; the inscription does
not tell you where Enation came from, only that he was an
Arkadian. The Kolophonians Hermesianax son of Agoneos
and Eikasios the son of Lykinos and Hermesianax's daughter
were both boy wrestling champions; Hermesianax had his
portrait dedicated by the Kolophonian community.

[5] Near these stand the Eleian boy boxing champions,
Choirilos by Sthennis of Olynthos and Theotimos by
Daitondas of Sikyon. Theotimos was a son of Moschion who
took part in Alexander son of Philip's campaign against
Darius of Persia.[145] There are two more from Elis: Archi-
damos who won with a team of horses [6] and Eperastos son

---

Tenedos; the lettering is Hellenistic (*Inschriften von Olympia*, 39). Tenedos is an
island off the Turkish coast near Troy and the Dardanelles. We know nothing
about the two sculptors.

143. KOS lies north-west of Rhodes, and KLAZOMENAI on the coast west of
Izmir. Philinos won the sprint in 264 and 260.

144. Ptolemy the Second, the Sister-lover (285–264). For Lysippos, cf.
Bk VI, Note 3. Magnesia on the Lethaios is not Pausanias's home town, but an
Ionian city at the place where the Lethaios flowed into the Maiander: MANISA,
north-east of IZMIR.

145. Kolophon is another of the great Ionian cities; it lay south of IZMIR.
For Sthennis, cf. Note 140 above. The base of a statue by Daitondas with an
early Hellenistic inscription has been found at Delphi. If Theotimos fought
under Alexander the Great in Asia, it must be the same man.

of Theogonos who won the race in armour. The end of Eperastos's inscription says he was a prophet of the clan of the Klytidai,

> born to the Klytidai with holy tongues:
> prophet of the blood of Melampous's godlike children.

Mantios was a son of Melampous son of Amythaon, Mantios's son was Oikles, and Klytios was the son of Alkmaion, grandson of Amphiaraos and great-grandson of Oikles. Klytios was Alkmaion's son by Phegeus's daughter, and he migrated to Elis because of not wanting to live with his mother's brothers, who he knew were responsible for Alkmaion's murder.[146]

[7] Among some undistinguished dedications stand the figures of Alexinikos of Elis the boy wrestling champion by Kantharos of Sikyon, and Gorgias the Leontinian, whose Olympic portrait Eumolpos the grandson of Deikrates who married Gorgias's daughter says he dedicated.[147] [8] Gorgias was the son of Charmantides, and he is said to have been the first restorer of the study of language, which was utterly neglected and so forgotten that it had nearly vanished from mankind. They say Gorgias was famous for his speeches both at the Olympic festival and when he went on an embassy to Athens with Tisias. Among Tisias's contributions to language was the speech he wrote (the most convincing of his time) in a money quarrel for a Syracusan woman: [9] but Gorgias won even more respect than Tisias at Athens, and Jason the dictator of Thessaly put Gorgias before Polykrates, a considerable orator of the school of Athens. Gorgias is said to have lived to be a hundred and five. In my day the city of

146. This sudden spurt of mythology is an explanation of the respectably prophetic origins of this particular family of prophets. Phegeus's daughter was Alphesiboia, and her brothers killed Alkmaion because Alkmaion tricked Phegeus into giving him a fatal necklace (cf. Bk VIII, 24 (4)).

147. Kantharos of Sikyon seems to be an early Hellenistic sculptor (cf. Bk VI, Note 18). Gorgias's base has been found with eight lines of verse on it (*Inschriften von Olympia*, 293). Pausanias is repeating the terms in which the inscription praises the old man.

LEONTINOI which was at one time wiped out by Syracuse was in fact inhabited.[148]

[1] There is also Kratisthenes of Kyrene's bronze chariot, 18 with Victory and Kratisthenes himself riding in it. Obviously his victory was in a chariot race; they say that Kratisthenes was a son of Mnaseas the runner, who was known in Greece as the Libyan: his dedications at Olympia are by Pythagoras of Region.[149]

[2] I discovered a portrait of Anaximenes here, who wrote the whole ancient history of Greece and the history of Philip son of Amyntas and of Alexander; he got his honours at Olympia from the people of Lampsakos. These are the stories recorded of Anaximenes. There was a device he used to get the better of Philip's son Alexander, a monarch who was not always a kindly man, and in fact was extremely irascible. [3] Lampsakos had been or was thought to have been on the side of the king of Persia; Alexander was blazing with anger about it and threatening the most frightful visitations. So out of consideration for the women and children and their native town itself they sent Anaximenes to beg for mercy, because he knew Alexander and had known his father. Anaximenes then approached Alexander, and Alexander who knew what he had come for swore by all the gods of Greece to do the opposite to whatever he asked. [4] So Anaximenes said:

148. Gorgias came to Athens in 427 B.C.; he was a theorist and teacher of spoken language; his influence is so vast as to be immeasurable. He schematized the sounds and rhythms and all the traditional resources of language into what we call rhetoric. Some fragments of his own writings including his Olympic speech have survived; they are pleasant and interesting, like the noise of rococo silver sheep-bells, but not powerful. We have none of the works of Tisias or Polykrates. Leontinoi broke free of Syracuse at the beginning of the Peloponnesian War and was destroyed in 403 B.C., but it was refounded as a Syracusan satellite. Leontinoi was unimportant in the Roman period, and utterly overshadowed by Syracuse, but it survived long enough to fall to the Saracens in A.D. 848. It was finally ruined by an earthquake in 1693, though there are said to be traces of the akropolis at the *castellaccio* of LENTINI between Catania and Syracuse.

149. For Pythagoras, cf. Bk VI, Note 29; for Mnaseas, cf. Bk VI, 13 (7). Mnaseas himself was by the same artist as his son.

'Grant me this favour, O king, make slaves of the women and children of Lampsakos, destroy the entire city to its foundations, and burn down the sanctuaries of the gods there.' When he spoke like that Alexander could find no way of countering the trick and as he was forcibly obliged by his oath he forgave Lampsakos against his will. [5] Anaximenes appears to have taken revenge on an enemy with a certain brilliance but also with a high degree of malice. He was a talented rhetorician and a talented imitator of rhetorical styles, and because he had a quarrel with Theopompos son of Damasistratos he wrote an insulting historical book about Athens, Lakonia and Thebes: it was a perfect imitation of Theopompos's manner, and he signed it Theopompos and spread it around among the cities. He had written it himself but it swelled people's hatred of Theopompos all over Greece. [6] Moreover, no one before Anaximenes had discovered the art of impromptu speech. But I am not able to believe it was Anaximenes who wrote the epic poem about Alexander.[150]

Sotades was proclaimed as a Cretan, which he was, for his long-distance running victory in the ninety-ninth Olympics, but by the next time he had taken money from the Ephesian community and claimed to be an Ephesian; because of this he was exiled from Crete.[151]

[7] The first athletes' portraits dedicated at Olympia were of Praxidamas of Aigina who won the boxing at the fifty-ninth Olympics and Rexibios of Opous the all-in champion

150. Anaximenes was a philosopher as well as a royal historian and seems to have been one of Alexander's teachers. He was a Cynic and should have been no respecter of persons. The fragments of his works have been collected by Jacoby (*Fragments of the Greek Historians*, II A, n. 72). There is an ancient collection of snappy sayings (*Gnomologium Vaticanum*) which records that Alexander once said to Anaximenes: 'Good heavens, I would sooner be Thersites in Homer's poetry than Achilles in yours.' The poem, whoever it was by, has (perhaps fortunately) not survived. Lampsakos was a great but unfortified city on the Asian shore of the Dardanelles (the Hellespont). It was the home city of the garden fertility god Priapos.

151. He won as a Cretan in 384. Sotades is a very common Cretan name.

at the sixty-first Olympics. These dedications are not far from Oinomaos's pillar; they are made of wood, Rexibios in fig-wood and the Aiginetan in cypress, but less elaborately carved.[152]

[1] There is a TERRACE of conglomerate stone in Altis to the 19 north of Hera's sanctuary, and at the back of this platform is KRONION. On this terrace stand the TREASURIES: in the same way as some of the Greeks have made treasuries for Apollo at Delphi. There is a treasury at Olympia called the SIKYONIAN TREASURY, [2] dedicated by Myron the dictator of Sikyon; he built it when he won the chariot race at the thirty-third Olympics.[153] He made two chambers in this treasury, one Doric and the other Ionic. I could see they were made of bronze, but whether the bronze is Tartessian as the Eleans say I have no idea. [3] They say Tartessos is a river in Spain that runs down into the sea by two mouths with the city of TARTESSOS in the middle, in between the two outfalls of the river. This river is the biggest in Spain and it runs a tide; later generations have called it the Baitis. There are some people who believe the Spanish city of KARPIA was called Tartessos

152. Pindar (*Nemean Odes*, 6, 27f.) says Praxidamas was the first winner from his family and his island; he won five times at the Isthmus and three at Nemea. Praxidamas won in 544 and Rexibios in 536. Why does he say they were the first athletes' statues at Olympia when he has already mentioned Eutelidas (Bk VI, 15 (8))? Eutelidas's statue could well have been later than the date of his championship (628), even assuming that date to be correct, but we know Pausanias thought it a genuine seventh-century dedication. Probably it was a stiff, massive, primitive Pharaoh-like figure, and Pausanias was instinctively not thinking of it as an athletic portrait. In the mid sixth century *kouros* statues were strong slim-looking stone youths of great charm and some beginnings of individuality (Richter's Tenea-Volomandra group).

153. KRONION is the conical hill north of the sacred area. The Sikyon treasury is the farthest west; it was identified through an inscription found on the building itself. It is the latest of the archaic treasuries. Whatever building Myron dedicated in 648 has not survived; if it really existed it was probably wooden; it would have stood very close to the temple of Zeus and Hera, which had been built by 700 B.C. It may well be that the growth of these treasuries marks the emergence of the cult of Zeus, who was at this time taking over the functions of the earth-oracle and was at first no more than the equal partner of Hera.

in older times.[154] [4] But to return to Olympia, there are inscriptions on the smaller of these chambers saying the weight of the bronze is five hundred talents, and it was dedicated by Myron and the people of Sikyon.[155] There are three discuses dedicated in this treasury, that they use for the pentathlon contest, and a bronze shield decorated with some lettering on the inside, with a helmet and leg-guards; an inscription on the armour says they were first-fruits dedicated to Zeus from the Myanian spoils. Not everyone is equally able to conjecture who the Myanians were, [5] but I happen to remember that in the writings of Thukydides he puts some Myoneans among the Lokrian cities on the borders of Phokis; so in my opinion the Myanians on the shield are the same people as the Myoneans on the Lokrian mainland. The lettering on the shield is rather a jumble, but that is because of the

154. The existing remains are of a pure Doric treasury with no trace of bronze at all. The two bronze chambers must have been dedicated bronze models, like the miniature houses and temples modelled in pottery which have been recovered, only much bigger. 648 would be an early but not an impossible date for an early version of an Ionic pillar in Greece, and perfectly acceptable for an early version of Doric. Tartessos bronze means bronze from south-west Spain that reached the sea at the Guadalquivir (Wad-el-Kebir, the great river). The river is navigable a long way inland. The city of Tartessos is probably the biblical city of TARSHISH, which was rich in iron and tin as well as silver and lead (Ezechiel, 27, 12). This region became an important source of metal for the eastern Mediterranean at a very early period. The ruins of Karpia or Karteia are on the hill called EL ROCADILLO about four miles from Gibraltar (Mount Kalpe) towards ALGECIRAS. It is nowhere near the Guadalquivir: the city between its two branches is probably lost in the marshes through which it runs before it reaches Jerez and the sea.

155. There were a number of different weight standards, and a talent may mean either a weight or a price; in Homeric poetry it is used only of gold. The golden bowl of the Kypselidai was exactly calculated by a Babylonian weight standard. It is very hard to know what these bronze chambers weighed. If a talent meant more or less a hundredweight, as it sometimes does, then the smaller of these objects weighed twenty-five tons. (A Centurion tank weighs fifty.) Either Pausanias or the manuscripts have the number wrong, or it refers perhaps to the weight and equivalent value in gold. I do not know enough about ancient weight standards to make any other suggestion, but I cannot believe that Myron dedicated twenty-five tons of bronze.

antiquity of the dedication.[156] [6] There are some other things worth recording which are kept here: Pelops's gold-handled dagger and Amaltheia's horn worked in ivory dedicated by Miltiades son of Kimon, who was the first of his family to govern the Thracian Chersonese. The inscription on the horn is in ancient Athenian lettering:

> Consecrated to the delight of Olympian Zeus
> by Chersonesians who took the fortress
> of Aratos; Miltiades commanded.

Then there is a box-wood statue of Apollo with a gilded head, which says it was dedicated by the Lokrians of Cape Zephyr and made by Patrokles son of Katillos of Kroton.[157]

[7] Next to the Sikyonian treasury comes the Carthaginian, which is by Pothaios and Antiphilos and Megakles. There are dedications in it of a large-scale Zeus and three linen breast-plates which Gelon and the Syracusans dedicated for a victory with warships or perhaps in a land battle against the Phoenicians.[158]

156. Later on Pausanias visited Myania (Bk X, 38 (8)). It was south-west of Amphissa not far from Delphi. For the Myoneans, cf. Thukydides, 3, 101, 2. Myaneans is the Doric form of Myoneans.

157. Miltiades son of Kimon commanded the Athenians at Marathon; it was another Miltiades who began the annexation of the Thracian Chersonese (south-east of Saloniki) in the sixth century: Miltiades son of Kypselos, a collateral relation not a member of the same family. Miltiades son of Kimon was all but an independent monarch in Thrace at the end of the sixth century, but he had been sent out by Hippias dictator of Athens, and it was to Athens he returned after the failure of the rebellion of the Ionian cities against Persia. A helmet dedicated by Miltiades was found at Olympia in the 1950s. Amaltheia was the nanny-goat who suckled Dionysos; her horn was the horn of plenty. Nothing is known about the fortress of Aratos or about Patrokles of Kroton. (For the Lokrians, cf. Bk VI, Note 48; and for Kroton cf. Bk VI, Note 101.)

158. There are twelve treasuries, and all the foundations have been recovered, but the second and third (moving from west to east, that is from left to right) had apparently already been pulled down in Pausanias's time, in order to make room for a new road towards Kronion. It is tempting to connect this development with the construction of a finely designed, nine-spouted water-fountain and the water-conduits that supplied it, which was built by Herod of Athens (Herodes Atticus) who died in A.D. 177; Pausanias does not describe it, so it may

[8] The third of the treasuries and the fourth dedication are Epidamnian ...[159] with Atlas holding up the universe and with Herakles and the apple-tree of the Hesperides with the serpent twisting round the apple-tree, all in cedar by Theokles son of Hegylos, who (the lettering on the universe says) helped his son to make it. The Hesperides were shifted by the Eleans and were still to be seen in my day in the temple of Hera. The Epidamnian treasury was made by Pyrros and his sons Lakrates and Hermon.[160]

[9] The Sybarites have also built a treasury next to the Byzantines. Those who have busied themselves about Italy and its cities say that the ancient Sybaris has changed its name and become Lupiae, which lies between Brindisi and Hydrous. The anchorage there is artificial and was made by the emperor Hadrian.[161]

---

seem to have been unbuilt or at least unfinished when he visited Olympia: but the evidence of the inscribed dedications of its statues suggests that it was built as early as the 50s. Pausanias was writing in A.D. 174 (Bk V, 1 (2)). No one knows to whom the two demolished treasuries belonged. The Carthaginian treasury was Syracusan; it contained the Carthaginian spoils probably of the battle of Himera in 480. There are certain Sicilian characteristics about its architecture which confirm its identification (cf. Dinsmoor, *Architecture of Ancient Greece*, p. 116), but it appears to be twenty years earlier than the reign of Gelon, who took over Syracuse only in 485 B.C.

159. The manuscripts have left out the Byzantine treasury, which fortunately gets named again later; the Epidamnians ornamented theirs with a painted stone horse and rider, the horse with a red and blue striped mane; the Byzantines had a cock, a hen and a wild waterfowl. Epidamnos became Dyrrachion (cf. Bk VI, Note 87); and Byzantion became Constantinople (the second Rome) and then Istanbul (*Eis tin polin*). The Byzantine treasury had a cedar-wood triton with a silver cup.

160. For the Hesperides, cf. Bk V, 17 (2). Theokles was a mid-sixth-century Lakonian. (For a full discussion and bibliography, cf. Pauly-Wissowa, *Supp.* VIII, 853.)

161. The seventh from the west. Sybaris, a city famous for its luxury and for the arts of living, was destroyed in 510 and has never been excavated. Scattered traces of it have been discovered deep in the alluvial mud of the CRATI (Krathis), south-west of Taranto. Hydrous or Hydrountinos became OTRANTO on the heel of Italy; Brindisi is a better harbour, but Otranto is the nearest Italian harbour to Greece: you can see the Illyrian (Albanian) coast. Rather little is

[10] Beside the Sybarite treasury is that of the Libyans of Kyrene, in which they keep Roman kings. The people of Selinous in Sicily were uprooted by the Carthaginians in a war; but before the catastrophe they built a treasury to Olympian Zeus. There is a Dionysos there with his face and feet and hands worked in ivory.[162]

[11] In the Metapontine treasury, which is right next to the Selinountian, is a representation of Endymion, all in ivory except for the clothes. I am not at all sure how the Metapontines came to perish, but in my day there was nothing at all left of Metapontion but its theatre and the circuit of its fortification.[163]

[12] The Megarians from the borders of Attica have built a treasury and consecrated offerings in it: little cedar figures inlaid with gold, of Herakles' fight with Acheloos. There are

---

known about its early history and material culture, whereas Brindisi is not only well documented but has a rich and exceptionally efficient museum. The Roman Lupiae became LECCE, between the two, but it has nothing whatever to do with Sybaris, which is on the instep of the foot of Italy; Brindisi is the spur and Otranto is on the heel. The mistake may come from some kind of confusion with Thourioi, which did replace Sybaris, or it may represent the misreading of names written on a formalized map, or a wrong position in a list of harbours and landmarks. The treasury of Sybaris had a stone flower on it.

162. The Libyan treasury was early-sixth-century; the identification is confirmed by an inscription. It was ornamented with a stone girl carrying a little lion being pursued by Apollo, and some big cocks and hens. The girl is the nymph Kyrene. The story was told in the *Great Eoiai* (*Fragmenta Hesiodea*, 215–16) and later by Pindar in a poem of astonishing brilliance (*Pythian Odes*, 9, 25f.). There were more Roman kings in the Metroon (cf. Bk V, 20 (9)). The people of Selinous were massacred and the city destroyed by Carthaginians in 409 B.C. The site of Selinous (SELINUNTE), which has some of the finest of all Doric temples, is near the western point of the south coast of Sicily, east-south-east of MAZZARA DEL VALLO and south of CASTELVETRANO. There is a fine archaic inscription from a temple at Selinous naming Zeus first and last among the gods who give help in war.

163. Metapontion was twenty-four miles from Taranto along the coast of the gulf. It still existed in Cicero's time (*De Fin.*, 5, 2), but it died soon afterwards, probably from malaria. The only surviving fragment of ornament from this treasury is part of the quarters and sex of a stone mule or a stallion, painted in red and bluish green. The treasury once held 132 silver and 3 gold cups, 3 silver wine-jugs and a silver dish.

Zeus and Deianeira, Acheloos and Herakles, and Ares helping Acheloos, and there used to be a statue of Athene standing there because she was Herakles' ally; this is now beside the Hesperides in the temple of Hera.[164] [13] On the pediment of the treasury is the war of gods and giants, and there is a shield dedicated above the pediment saying the Megarians dedicated this treasury from the spoils of the Corinthians. I think this Megarian victory was when Phorbas was governor of Athens; he governed for his whole lifetime, because annual magistracies had not then been instituted at Athens, nor were there even any Elean records of Olympic games. [14] Argos is said to have played some part in the Megarian success against Corinth. The Megarians made their treasury at Olympia years after the battle, but they probably kept the dedications from an early date, since they are by Dontas the Lakonian, the apprentice of Dipoinos and Skyllis.[165] [15] The last of the treasuries is right beside the stadium; the inscription on it says the treasury and statues were dedicated by the Gelans, though there are no statues kept there now.[166]

164. Fortunately most of this treasury was built into the Byzantine fortress, and the pieces were recovered by the excavators. The identification is confirmed by an inscription. For the Hesperides, see Bk V, 17 (2). Zeus may really have been not Zeus but Deianeira's father. Acheloos was a river-god, a man-faced bull with a dripping beard from whom Herakles took Deianeira.

165. Almost all the pediment figures have been found; they were patiently and most dexterously pieced together by Georg Treu. The reliefs were carved in the local limestone when the blocks were already built into the temple, the figures were painted red against blue, with paler colours for bodies. The treasury cannot be much earlier than 550 B.C. The war of Megara with Corfu cannot be dated, and no one knows the date of Dontas; C. Robert suggested we should substitute the name of Medon (Bk V, 17 (2)), but it seems to me not strictly necessary and therefore not advisable. So-called apprentices of Dipoinos and Skyllis mean simply archaic sculptors; the definition cannot usefully be narrowed.

166. This was built about 540 B.C., and a portico was added fifty years later. The cornices were sheathed in slabs of brightly painted terracotta, which was produced in Gela itself (in southern Sicily), and the architects were Sicilian. The entire construction is characterized by Dinsmoor as 'of nondescript character and of more imposing size than usual' (*Architecture of Ancient Greece*, pp. 115–16).

[1] MOUNT KRONION runs along the line of the terrace and 20
the treasuries, as I have already said. The peak of this mountain
is where the Kings as they call them offer sacrifice to Kronos
at the spring equinox, which falls in the Elean month of the
deer.[167] [2] On the edge of Kronion, to the north of Altis
between the mountain and the treasuries, is a sanctuary of
Eileithuia in which the local Elean daemonic spirit called the
City Saviour receives worship.[168] They call Eileithuia by the
title Olympian and choose a priestess for the goddess every
year. The old woman who ministers to the City Saviour is
bound by Elean law to observe chastity, and she herself brings
in the god's bathing water and leaves him barley-cakes
kneaded with honey. [3] In the front part of the temple,
which is a double one, stands Eileithuia's altar, and the people
can go in to her, but the City Saviour's worship takes place
right inside, and no one can go in there except the god's
minister with her head and face muffled in a white veil. The
virgin girls waiting in Eileithuia's room and the women sing
a hymn, and they incinerate every kind of sweet-burning
things to him, but the practice is to pour out no wine. And
there is a traditional oath by the City Saviour on the greatest
occasions. [4] They say that when the Arkadian army invaded

167. The asphalt road between the perimeter fence of the archaeological site
and the conical hill called Kronion north of the sacred area was made in 1930.
The hill must certainly have been badly eroded and its skirts have fallen round
its ankles, so the road across this collapsed hemline may not have done much
damage. The peak is flat, sandy and dusty; there are no traces of an altar. The
Kings were a local priesthood of Pise. The Archon basileus at Athens was a kind
of priest and a survivor of a royal priesthood; the Pisaian 'kings' are probably
survivors of what had once been ruling families.

168. Carl Robert has showed from an analogous cult mentioned by Strabo
(14, 1, 41) that the city Saviour (Sosipolis) was the child Zeus (*Ath. Mitt.*, 18,
1893, pp. 37f.). The significance of this secret male child-god in close association with the birth-goddess Eileithuia and the earth for the development of the
religion of Zeus from an oracle of the Earth hardly needs stressing. Zeus's
father Kronos was worshipped on the hilltop where at a later date one would
expect Zeus himself to be worshipped as a fully-grown, bearded sky-god and
father of gods. But at Olympia the earlier stages of Greek religion coexisted
with the later. The sanctuary has never been found. The top of Kronion is flat
but there is nothing left on it.

Eleia, and the Eleians counter-attacked, an Elean woman
came to the commanders with a baby boy at her breast and
said she had borne the child and was commanded by dreams
to hand him over to fight for Elis. The authorities believed
she was trustworthy, and put the little boy naked in the front
of the army. [5] The Arkadians charged, and suddenly the
little boy had turned into a serpent. This spectacle threw the
Arkadians into confusion, they turned and ran, and the
Eleans laid into them and won a most outstanding victory:
and they called the god the City Saviour. They built his
sanctuary in the place where they thought the serpent
disappeared underground when the battle was over, and they
decided to worship Eileithuia with him, because the goddess
herself had brought that child into the world. [6] The monument to the Arkadians who died in the battle is on the hill the
other side of the KLADEOS towards the west. Near Eileithuia's
temple, the RUINS of Heavenly APHRODITE'S SANCTUARY
still survive, and they offer sacrifices on the altars there.[169]

[7] Inside Altis by the processional entry is what they call
the HIPPODAMEION: an area of about a quarter of an acre
enclosed with a wall, where the women go in once every
year to perform ceremonies in honour of Hippodameia, and
to offer her sacrifices.[170] They say Hippodameia went away
to Midea in the Argolid, because Pelops was very angry with
her over Chrysippos's death, but they say they brought back
Hippodameia's bones to Olympia by the command of an
oracle.[171] [8] At the end of the statues erected from athletes'

169. The monument to the Arkadians was probably a tumulus; the battle
may well never have happened. It is not uncommon either in ancient or in
medieval Greece to find a number of different natural features or unexplained
ruins in the same area named after different parts of the one story (cf. Bk III,
Note 1). The sanctuary of Heavenly Aphrodite is also lost.

170. The processional entrance probably means the south-east (cf. Bk V, 15
(1f.), and Note 139 there). Hippodameia was Oinomaos's daughter whom
Pelops raced to win.

171. For the great Mycenaean fortress called DENDRA on the east of the plain
of Argos which Pausanias knew as the ruins of Midea, cf. Bk II, 25 (9). Proitos
was supposed to have lived there. Long after Hippodameia had married Pelops,
she egged on their two doomed sons, Atreus and Thyestes, to murder their

penalties is what they call the HIDDEN ENTRANCE, through which the Greek arbiters and the competitors enter the stadium. The STADIUM is a mound of earth, but it has a seat built for the presidents. Opposite the Greek arbiters is a white stone ALTAR, [9] and on this altar a woman sits and watches the Olympic games, the priestess of Demeter of the Ground, an office awarded by Elis to different women at different times. Virgin girls of course are not barred from watching. By the end of the stadium where they have made the starting-place for the sprinters is the grave of Endymion, so the Eleans say.[172]

[10] If you climb over out of the stadium near where the Greek arbiters sit, you come to an area where the ground has been levelled for horse-racing and to the STARTING-PLACE for horses.[173] The starting-place is shaped like the prow of a ship, with the beak pointed towards the race-course. At the point where the prow touches Agnaptos's colonnade it broadens out, and there is a bronze dolphin on a road at the farthest tip of the beak.[174] [11] Each of the sides is more than four hundred feet long, and there are buildings incorporated in them; the competitors in horse-races draw lots for these build-ings. Instead of an automatic cable they use a rope stretched in front of the chariots or the race-horses, and for every Olympic games they have a mud-brick altar which they plaster with ash just in the middle of the prow, [12] and a bronze eagle on the altar with its wings stretched right out. The clerk of the course operates the machinery on the altar; when he works it

half-brother Chrysippos who was Pelops's bastard son. Why did she choose Midea? Probably the truth is simple: she had a tomb and a cult there and the oracle directed her bones to be brought home to Olympia.

172. The Hidden entrance is still standing; it is an arched stone tunnel leading east from the north-east corner of Altis. For the athletes' penalties, cf. Bk V, 21 (2f.). For Endymion, cf. Bk V, 1 (3f.), and 8 (1f.). The earth banks of the stadium collapsed in the heavy winter rain of early 1970, but have been repaired.

173. The race-track for horses lay south of the stadium. It remains un-excavated.

174. Agnaptos built the Echo colonnade; cf. Bk V, 15 (6).

the eagle flies right up so that the spectators·can see it, and the dolphin leaps down to the ground. [13] The first cables to give are the ones on both sides by Agnaptos's colonnade, and the horses in those positions gallop out first, and as they gallop past the horses in the second position the cables give in the second position as well, and the same thing happens with all the horses until they are even at the beak of the prow, and from then on it is all a matter of the expertise of the drivers and the speed of the horses.[175] [14] The original engineer of the starting machinery was Kleoitas, and he appears to have been proud of his invention, as the inscriptions on his statue at Athens says:

> the first inventor of the Olympic racing start
> made me; Kleoitas son of Aristokles.

They say that after Kleoitas Aristeides introduced some further refinement of the mechanism.[176]

[15] One side of the race-course is longer than the other, and on the longer side, which is a mound, beside the way out which cuts through it, is the terror of horses, the HORSE-SCARER. The shape is like a circular altar, and as horses gallop past it they suffer extreme panic from no visible cause, the panic puts them into confusion, the chariots are smashed up and the drivers are injured. Because of all this the drivers offer

175. The problem was how to contrive for a number of full teams of horses to start even, when there was no room for them to start abreast. The ropes were flung down one by one in a staggered start; the farthest horses from the eagle and the altar started first. The starting area was triangular: the base of the triangle was the colonnade. Beyond this it is impossible to be certain.

176. There was a Kleoitas who was a fifth-century sculptor (Bk V, 24 (5)), and Pausanias is clear that this is the same man. Aristeides perhaps added the machine for the eagle and the dolphin. At the Scoppio del Carro outside the Cathedral at Florence in the 1950s on Holy Saturday at midnight they were still using a mechanism that shot a mechanical dove on a line right up the nave; I think it was to carry the new fire. The dove has (or used to have) fireworks in its tail and connects with a cart of fireworks outside the Cathedral. It was not a very good machine, and whether it worked or not gave the people an important omen for the harvest. No doubt the eagle at Olympia glittered more and wobbled less.

sacrifices and pray to the Horse-scarer to be kind to them.
[16] There are different Greek beliefs about the Horse-scarer;
some say it is the grave of a local man who was good with
horses, and they call him Olenios and say the Olenian rock in
Eleia is named after the same man, and some say Dameon
son of Phlious, who took part in Herakles' campaign against
Augeas and the Eleans, was killed with the horse he rode on
by Kteatos son of Aktor, and Dameon and his horse shared
the same grave.[177] [17] And they tell the story that Pelops
made an empty tumulus here for Myrtilos and offered him
sacrifice to be rid of the curse of his murder, and called him
the Horse-scarer because his skill scared Oinomaos's mares,
though some say it is Oinomaos himself who hurts riders on
this race-course. I have even heard a story that puts the blame
on Alkathous son of Porthaon: that he got his ration of earth
here when he was killed by Oinomaos for wanting to marry
Hippodameia: and because he was unlucky on the race-course
he became a malicious daemonic spirit, jealous of the riders
on it.[178] [18] There was an Egyptian who said Pelops was
told to dig for something here by Theban Amphion, and
Oinomaos was scared by what he dug up, and all mares have
been scared of it ever since. This Egyptian believed that
Amphion and Thracian Orpheus were dark and brilliant
magicians, and the wild beasts came to Orpheus and the rocks
built themselves into a wall for Amphion at the singing of
their spells. But in my view the most convincing story is that
Horse-scarer is a title of Poseidon of Horses. [19] Glaukos son
of Sisyphos at the Isthmus is also a Horse-scarer: they say he
was killed by horses when Akastos held the games for his

177. Olenios and Damion are local divine heroes. The Olenian rock comes
into Nestor's story-telling in the *Iliad* (11, 757), and later generations had tried
to identify it (e.g. Strabo 8, 3, 9 and 11). A fragment or two of the Hesiodic
*Eoiai* refer to Olenos and his rock (*Fragmenta Hesiodea*, ed. Merkelbach and
West, 12–13). Olenios is surely a projection of Olenos. Damion is an obscure
epic hero; it is probable that this was at some period really thought of as his
grave, that Olenios was more famous, at least locally, and took it over, and then
Pelops took over from them both.

178. For the myth of Pelops, cf. Bk V, 10 (6), and the note there.

father's funeral.[179] At Nemea in the Argive country there was
no divine hero who hurt the horses, but there were red-
coloured rocks that reared up above the turn of the race-
course, and the light on them panicked the horses just as if it
were fire. Still, the Horse-scarer at Olympia is a much worse
panicker of horses. On one of the turning-posts is a bronze
portrait of Hippodameia holding a ribbon to tie on Pelops's
head as the winner.

21   [1] The other side of the race-course is not a mound of earth
but a small mountain. At the edge of the mountain is a SANC-
TUARY OF DEMETER of the Ground; some believe this is an
ancient name because this is where the earth gaped open for
Hades' chariot and closed its mouth on him, but others say
there was a Pisaian called Chamynos who opposed Omphalion's son Pantaleon the dictator and planned a revolt
against Elis, and Pantaleon killed him and built Demeter's
temple out of his possessions.[180] [2] Herod of Athens has
dedicated statues of Demeter and the Maid in Pentelic stone
in place of the ancient ones.

Training for the pentathlon and for running takes place in
the TRAINING-GROUND at Olympia; there is a stone platform
there in the open air where originally a trophy for a victory
over Arkadia used to stand. There is another smaller enclosure
on the left of the entrance to the training-ground, where the
competitors have their WRESTLING-PITS. The athletes' houses

179. Dio Chrysostom believed it was really Poseidon, so the explanation is
probably not original. Akastos's father was Pelias, and Pelias's funeral games
were the origin of the Isthmian games (though cf. Bk I, 44 (8)). For the
Isthmus sanctuary, cf. Bk II, 1 (7f.). Glaukos is Glaukos of Potniai (Bk II, 4 (3)).
According to Aischylos (*Fr.* 38–9) he was killed in a driving smash and eaten
by his own horses at Pelias's funeral games. According to the *Etymologicum
Magnum* this smash was at Olympia with Azeus the father of Aktor. This last
is surely an attempt to have the same disaster happen twice in successive generations: Glaukos killed by Azeus and Dameon by his grandson.

180. I have translated Demeter *Chamyne* as Demeter of the Ground. Her
sanctuary has recently been traced (*Olympia Bericht*, 8, p. 69). The old bumps
and tumuli of Olympia did not survive the floods of the Alpheios in their
original shape. Pantaleon is a legendary figure; he is supposed to have fought
against Sparta in the Second Messenian War.

face south-west by the wall of the east colonnade of the training-ground.[181] [3] On the other side of Kladeos is OINOMAOS'S GRAVE: a mound of earth encased in a stone construction with RUINED BUILDINGS above the monument where the story is that Oinomaos used to stable his horses.[182]

What are now the boundaries between Eleia and Arkadian territory were originally Arkadian–Pisaian boundaries; they go like this. Across the river Erymanthos by what they call Sauros's ridge lies SAUROS'S MONUMENT and a TEMPLE OF HERAKLES which nowadays is in ruins.[183] They say Sauros used to commit crimes on travellers and neighbours, until he got what he was asking for from Herakles. [4] By the ridge named after this bandit there is a river running down from the south into the Alpheios more or less opposite the Erymanthos, which forms the boundary of Pisaian and Arkadian territory: this river is called Diagon.[184] Five miles beyond Sauros's ridge

181. We are now on the west of Altis. The wrestling-ground (*palaistra*) is a square of pleasantly unimposing colonnades, west of the temple of Hera. The training-grounds (*gymnasion*) stretch away north and have been traced and planned but not fully excavated; they are partly under the car-park. The *gymnasion* was about 220 metres by a hundred. All these buildings are middle or late Hellenistic. The houses have not been excavated. For the *palaistra*, cf. *Olympia Bericht*, 4 (1944).

182. Oinomaos's grave sounds as if it were of prehistoric antiquity but it has never been identified. If it was on the same hill as the hotel and the old museum, every trace of it was long ago obliterated, but a mass of bronzes and even some Mycenaean pottery were found when the foundations of the new museum were dug, so that it looks as if the site attached to Altis stretches a long way west.

183. Pausanias is entering Eleia from Heraia, crossing the Erymanthos at the point he will reach at Bk VIII, 26 (3), in his description of Arkadia. He is moving west down the north bank of the Alpheios towards Olympia; the Erymanthos is a tributary west of the Ladon, it has been renamed with its ancient name. Sauros's ridge seems to be the ridge west of ASPRA SPITIA, but the temple of Herakles has not been found. Dio Chrysostom speaks of coming across it when he was lost in this area; he describes it as a very modest, rustic place (*Or.* 1).

184. That is, the river runs north, being a tributary of the Alpheios on its south side. It runs down a small valley east of TRYPITI and joins the Alpheios from the south just west of where the Erymanthos joins it from the north. Its name now is the TSEMBEROULA.

is a TEMPLE OF ASKLEPIOS that takes its title from its founder
Demainetos, but that also is in ruins. It was built on a height
beside the Alpheios. [5] Not far from here is a SANCTUARY OF
DIONYSOS the Leukyanian with the river Leukyania flowing
beside it: it comes down from Mount Pholoe and runs into
the Alpheios. If you cross the Alpheios from here you will be
in Pisaian territory.[185]

[6] There is a sharply pointed hill in this area on which lie
the ruins of the city of PHRIXA and a TEMPLE of Kydonian
Athene, which is not completely preserved though there was
still an altar there in my time. Klymenos the descendant of
Idaian Herakles is supposed to have come from Kydonia in
Crete and the river Jardanos and founded the goddess's
sanctuary. The Eleans have a further story that Pelops offered
sacrifice to Kydonian Athene before his contest with Oinomaos.[186] [7] If you go on from here you come to the streams
of Virginal River, with the grave of Marmax's horses by the
riverside. The legend is that Marmax was the first of all

185. The sanctuary of Asklepios ought to be somewhere near Louvro north
of the river, but it has not been pinpointed. The stream below Kamena may
have watered it. The river Leukyania must be the stream that joins the Alpheios
south-east of MOURIA (still on the north bank and moving west), but the
sanctuary of Dionysos has not been found. There is still what looks like a ford
of the Alpheios near this point, above PALIO PHANARI (Phrixa) on the
southern bank.

186. The sharp hill is called PHANARI or PALIO PHANARI; it commands a
loop of the Alpheios from the south: it was a medieval signalling station to the
castle of Klarentza and to Zante (Zakynthos). It is also called the Robber's hole
(TRYPI TON KLEFTON) because of an ancient cistern of enormous depth
opening from the summit. The crest of the hill has no other antiquities but this
cistern and the remains of the phanari, and the hillsides are disturbed by land-
slides, but the evidence of fragments of pottery in the sloping fields west and
south of the look-out post suggests there was already a settlement here in the
protogeometric period (cf. Herodotos, 4, 148). An old woman gathering
salad recently found a bronze deer probably of the classical period, I think on
the ridge to the south-west towards KALYBAKIA. It seems likely that the main
settlement area of ancient Phrixa was away from the river. The classical
Kydonia in Crete is CHANIA, but Pausanias is thinking of Homer's 'Kydonians
by the streams of Iardanos' (Odyssey, 3, 292). No sanctuary of Kydonian
Athene has ever been found at Phrixa.

Hippodameia's wooers to come and be killed by Oinomaos, and his mares were called Virginal and Kid: Oinomaos slaughtered Marmax's mares but granted them burial, and the river took the name of Virginal from Marmax's mare.[187] [8] There is another river called the Harpinian: the city of HARPINA is not far away with altars among its ruins. Oinomaos is supposed to have founded this city and named it after his mother Harpina.[188]

[9] Not far on from here is a tall MOUND OF EARTH which is the grave of Hippodameia's wooers. They say Oinomaos covered them over with earth all close together and without much ceremony, but later on Pelops raised their common monument high out of respect for them and to please Hippodameia, and I suppose as a reminder to later generations of the number and greatness of the victims of the man he beat.[189] [10] According to the verses of the Great Eoiai those who were killed by Oinomaos were Alkathous son of Porthaon, who came after Marmax, then Euryalos, Eurymachos and Krotalos, whose ancestry and native towns I have been unable to discover, though one could find grounds to argue that Akrias who died after them was a Lakonian and the founder of Akriai.[190] They say the next to be murdered by Oinomaos

187. Having dealt with Phrixa Pausanias retreats across the river at the same point (probably the lowest ford on the Alpheios) and continues his progress downstream along the north bank. The Virginal (*Parthenias*) might be the BAKIREIKA stream. The connexion of glorious horses, murdered heroes, and the names of rivers in this myth points to Poseidon, the earthquake-maker and lord of horses and of water.

188. The river may be the BYLIZEIKO near MIRAKA. The ruins were plausibly identified by Boblaye and the French surveyors near VILITZA (*Recherches*, pp. 128–9). Some faint-witted chauvinist has now renamed Vilitza as PEVKAI. There were once some rival ruins north of Miraka, but only a careful archaeological survey of the whole Alpheios valley will solve questions of this kind.

189. Guidebooks used to identify this, but one eminence is like another, and cf. Bk VI, Note 169.

190. A tiny shred of a papyrus text of this part of the Great Eoiai does exist but it tells us almost nothing. Pindar refers to the story of the suitors (*Olympian Odes* 1, 114 and 127), and an ancient learned commentary on Pindar gives a list of names; it says Hesiod and Epimenides agreed the number was thirteen. Since Pausanias's list does not quite agree with the commentator's, and the

after Akrias was Kapetos, and then Lykourgos, Lasios,
Chalkodon and Trikolonos who, the Arkadians say, was
descended from his namesake Trikolonos the son of Lykaon.
[11] The next after Trikolonos to meet their fate on the race-
course were Aristomachos and Prias, and then Pelagon,
Aiolios and Kronios. Some people add to this list Erythras son
of Leukon son of Athamos, after whom the Boiotian town
of Erythrai was named,[191] and Eioneus son of Magnes son of
Aiolos. This is where their monument is, and they say that
when Pelops reigned at Pisa he incinerated offerings to them
every year.

22     [1] About a furlong from the grave there are traces of the
SANCTUARY OF ARTEMIS KORDAX, because Pelops's followers held their victory celebration to the goddess here and they
danced the local dance of the people of Sipylos, the kordax.
Not far from the sanctuary is a smallish building in which there
is a bronze chest, in which they keep the bones of Pelops. There
was no town wall or any other construction to be seen, and
vines grow over the entire area where PISA used to be.[192] [2]
They say its founder was Pisos son of Perieres son of Aiolos;
the Pisaians brought disaster on their own heads by their
hostility to Elis and by their anxiety to take over the Olympic
festival from the Eleans. At the eighth Olympics they
brought in Pheidon of Argos, the most outrageous dictator

fragment of papyrus as far as it goes is on Pausanias's side, we must assume
Pausanias has the Hesiodic version and the commentary on Pindar draws on a
lost epic by 'Epimenides the Cretan' (*Fragmenta Hesiodea*, 259). For Akriai, cf.
Bk III, 22 (4f.). It was a coastal town at the north-east corner of the Lakonian
gulf.

   191. For Erythrai, cf. Bk IX, 2 (1). It lay south of Thebes on the edge of the
mountains.

   192. The kordax was a country dance with a cheerful and vigorous erotic
content. Pausanias was apparently brought up on it, since he came from Sipylos
(in Asia Minor). Pausanias is now somewhere in the fields east of Olympia.
There are still vines and they make extremely good wine. Pisa was swallowed
up by the ground or by the Olympian sanctuary (the modern place-name of
course has nothing to do with it). Kallimachos says *Pisa* where Pausanias would
say *Altis*, and *Pisa* occurs on Olympian inscriptions.

in Greece, and they and Pheidon held the games together; at the thirty-fourth Olympics the Pisaians under King Panteleon son of Omphalion collected a local army and arranged the Olympic games instead of the Eleans.[193] [3] But the Eleans call those two Olympic periods and the hundred and fourth when the Arkadians held the games Non-Olympic, and exclude them from the written Olympic lists. At the forty-eighth Olympics Pantaleon's son Damophon made the Eleans suspect he was up to something and they invaded Pisa in arms, but with entreaties and solemn oaths he managed to get them to withdraw with no damage done.[194] [4] In the reign of Pantaleon's other son, Damophon's brother Pyrros, the Pisaians declared a deliberate war on Elis, and the Makistians and Skillountians from Triphylia joined the rebellion, and so did the Dyspontians, another provincial people who had particularly close ties with Pisa and recorded that their founder was Oinomaos's son Dysponteus.[195] The Pisaians and everyone who joined them were devastated and uprooted by Elis. [5] The ruins of PYLOS in Eleia are easy to see ten miles from Elis on the mountain road to Elis from Olympia. As I have already said this Pylos was founded by a Megarian called Pylon son of Kleson. Herakles uprooted it and the Eleans refounded it, but a time was to come when it would be uninhabited. The river Ladon runs down beside it to meet the Peneios. [6] The

193. The eighth Olympics were in 748 B.C. It used to be said of Pheidon of Argos that his appeal to historians lay in the fact that he could be put in three separate centuries. Professor Huxley accepts Pausanias's date (*Ancient Sparta*, pp. 28–30). Professor Hammond rejects it, I think assuming an emendation in the text of Pausanias. While reluctant to do that, I am by no means competent to discuss the problem of the real date of Pheidon of Argos. The thirty-fourth Olympics were in 644 B.C. Strabo (8, 3, 30, relying on Ephoros) says it was after 676 that Pisa first took control; Eusebios says it was only for the years 668 and 660. Whatever else is true, obviously there was some kind of disturbance in the seventh century.

194. The Arkadian take-over was in 364; the forty-eighth Olympics were in 588 B.C.

195. For Makistos, cf. Bk V, 6 (1). For Skillous, cf. Bk V, 6 (4f.). Dyspontion was a deserted city in the coastal plain somewhere north of the Alpheios.

Eleans say there is a verse of Homer which refers to this
Pylos:

> born of the river Alpheios
> who runs through the broad earth of the Pylians.

I accept what they say, because the Alpheios does run through
that country, and this verse cannot be referred to the other
Pylos, since the Alpheios simply does not travel through the
territory of the Pylians opposite the isle of Sphakteria, and in
fact even in Arkadia we have no knowledge of any city which
was called Pylos at that period.[196]

[7] The Elean village of HERAKLEIA is six miles or so from
Olympia on the banks of the river Kytheros; there is a water-
spring that runs into the river with a SANCTUARY OF THE
NYMPHS at the spring. These nymphs have the personal names
of Kalliphaeia and Synallasis and Pegaia and Iasis, and their
general title is the Ionides. If you wash in the spring you can
be cured of all kinds of aches and pains; they say the nymphs

196. The uninhabited ruins of Elean Pylos represent an attempt to point to
real places that would correspond to the sometimes flighty geography of the
Homeric poems (*Iliad*, 5, 544f.). For Pylon (or Pylos), cf. Bk IV, 36 (1).
Pausanias identified the Homeric city with a ruined city on the Ladon where the
Ladon runs into the Peneios: the little Ladon, not the great Alpheios tributary.
We have the double problem of explaining Homer and following Pausanias.
Assume that the lesser Ladon has been rightly identified: Frazer had a site below
AGRAPIDOCHORI near where the rivers meet (something over twenty miles
east of Cape Kyllene), but Leake found what is far more likely to be Pausanias's
deserted fortress five miles or so farther south, near the modern EPHYRA
(*Morea*, 2, pp. 227–31). Since his time Mr Themelis and Mr Yalouris have
surveyed Agrapidochori more thoroughly and established it as certainly a
classical site, though this does not mean it was 'Pylos'. Strabo identified
Homeric Pylos elsewhere, and to find Strabo's Homeric Pylos is outside the
scope of these notes. To return to Homer's text, surely all he says is that the
Pylians controlled the Alpheios valley: he never suggests that there was a Pylos
in Eleia; he extends the boundaries of Nestor's kingdom perhaps because there
was no other great legendary kingdom in the area; we know that there were
pre-Homeric sagas about Nestor's battles in this part of Greece. For the
'Pylos' site at ARMATOVA, now inundated, cf. J. Coleman in *Athens Annals of
Archaeology*, 1968, p. 285 (the pottery was archaic). For a new discussion of all
the 'Pylos' sites cf. M. Pantelides in *Athens Annals of Archaeology*, 1969, pp.
309f.

are named after Ion son of Gargettos, who migrated here from Athens.[197]

[8] If you wanted to travel to Elis by the plain, it would take you fifteen miles to LETRINOI and twenty-two and a half from Letrinoi to Elis.[198] Letrinoi was originally a town founded by Letreus son of Pelops, but in my time all that was left was a few buildings and a statue of Alpheian Artemis in a TEMPLE. [9] This is how they say the goddess got her title: Alpheios fell in love with Artemis, and as he knew she would never marry him for prayers and persuasions he found the courage to try to violate the goddess: he came to a night festival at Letrinoi which the goddess was holding with the nymphs who played with her. Artemis suspected what Alpheios was planning, and covered her face and all the nymphs' faces who were there with mud; when Alpheios arrived there was no way for him to tell Artemis from the others, and not being able to recognize her he went away with his purpose unfulfilled. [10] So the Letrinaians called the goddess Alpheian because Alpheios loved her. But the Eleans who were always friendly with the Letrinaians introduced the traditional worship they paid to Artemis of deer to Letrinoi and observed its practices for Alpheian Artemis, and so in the course of time the title of Artemis of Deer for the Alpheian goddess prevailed. [11] The Eleans called Artemis the Deer-goddess: I suppose because of deer-hunting, though what they say is that there was a local woman called the Deergirl by whom Artemis was reared. About three quarters of a mile from Letrinoi is a perpetual lake something under half a mile across.[199]

[1] One of the things worth recording at ELIS is the ancient 23

197. Perhaps at BROUMA, north-west of Olympia, now renamed HERA-KLEIA. I am not sure about the spring, but Hesychios knew of these nymphs and so did Athenaios (15, 683a).

198. Letrinoi was probably near HAGIOS IOANNIS, west of Pyrgos, where antiquities sometimes turn up. (Cf. also Note 199 below.)

199. The big salty expanse of MOURIA has swallowed it up, if we have the right site for Letrinoi. The two Greek words for the titles of Artemis are extremely similar: Elaphiaia and Alpheiaia.

TRAINING-GROUND.[200] The tradition is that all the ceremonies the athletes observe before they arrive at Olympia
should be carried out in this training-ground. There are tall
plane-trees growing up and down the tracks inside the walls;
this whole enclosure is called the Grubground because it was
part of Herakles the son of Amphitryon's training to grub up
all the thorns that grew here every day. [2] There is a separate
track specially for running contests, which the local people call
the sacred track, and another where runners in training and
pentathlon competitors do their running. What they call the
Hundred Feet is also in the training-ground: this is where the
Greek arbiters make matches by age and ability: they make
the matches for wrestling. [3] There are altars of the gods in
the training-ground, to Idaian Herakles with the title of the
Helper, to Love and to the god the Eleians and Athenians both
call Love Repaid, and to Demeter and her daughter.[201] There
is no altar to Achilles, but an empty MONUMENT by command
of an oracle. At the beginning of the festival on a special day
as the sun declines to its setting the Eleian women perform
ceremonies in honour of Achilles, and observe the rites of
lamentation for him.

[4] There is another training-ground enclosure which is
smaller and which adjoins the big one; they call it the SQUARE

200. The site of Elis is on the Peneios on the road east from GASTOUNI to
HAGIOS DEMETRIOS. The main site is between the road (which is south of the
river) and the river itself, but there are evident traces of several unexcavated
buildings on the slopes of the small hill with the chapel of HAGIOS IOANNIS,
which appears to stand more or less on the site of a temple. The site of Elis
seems to have been known to Chandler in the 1760s; his account is incoherent
and he may not have visited it – he was suffering from fatigue, sun, damp,
vermin, and 'fruits not easily eaten with moderation' – but Poucqueville in
the 1790s and Dodwell took its whereabouts for granted. It may have been
identified by some Renaissance geographer, perhaps a Venetian? Its medieval
name is PALAIOPOLIS (for the village) and KALISKOPI or BELVEDERE (a hill
above the ruins). For the state of the ruins on Belvedere in the nineteenth
century, cf. Stanhope's Olympia (1824, pages unnumbered); these have mostly
disappeared now. The gymnasion of Elis and the baths connected with it are
on both sides of the modern road but mostly south of the road.

201. For Idaian Herakles, cf. Bk V, 7 (6). For Love Repaid, cf. Bk I, 30 (1).

because of its shape. The athletes have their wrestling-pits here, and this is where they match athletes who have finished their wrestling with soft boxing thongs; one of the statues made for Zeus from the fine imposed on Sosander of Smyrna and Polyktor of Elis is dedicated here.[202] [5] There is also a third training-ground enclosure called the SOFT GROUND because of the softness of the surface, which is open to the boys of fighting age throughout the festival. In a corner of the Soft ground stands a bust of Herakles, and in a corner of the wrestling-pits is a relief of Love and Love Repaid: Love has a palm-branch, and Love Repaid is trying to take it from him. [6] On either side of the entrance to the Soft ground stands a portrait of a boy boxer; the Elean official said it was someone from Alexandria opposite the island of Pharos, called Sarapion, who came to Elis during a wheat shortage and gave them supplies, and in return they honoured him here. The date of his wreath at Olympia and his generosity to Elis was the two hundred and seventeenth Olympics.[203] [7] The Eleans also have a COUNCIL-HOUSE in this training-ground where they hold performances of impromptu speech and literature of every kind. They call it the Lalichmion after the man who dedicated it. There are shields dedicated round it which were made to be looked at, not to be used in war.

[8] The route from the training-ground to the BATHS by the lane is SILENCE STREET, beside which lies the SANCTUARY OF ARTEMIS the Lad-lover. The goddess got the title because she lived so close to the training-ground.[204] They say the lane

202. For this fine, cf. Bk V, 21 (16f.). The penalty was to pay for a statue of Zeus. Soft leather thongs were not to deaden the blow but to protect the fist. They were used in the great games to the end of the fifth century and went on being used for training in the fourth. They were driven out of competitive boxing by thick, formidable leather mittens like a cross between a knuckle-duster and the heel of a boot.

203. A.D. 87.

204. This may be a temple that has been excavated. The excavations at Elis started before the First World War under Austrian archaeologists; there is a tiny but invaluable plan of the excavations in *Jahrshefte des Österreichischen Archäologischen Instituts* 27, 1932, *Beiblatt*, pp. 145f., Otto Walter; the temple is Gebaude C p. 147. For photographs of the small-scale renewed excavations

got the name of Silence street from when some men in Oxylos's army were sent to spy on Elis, and agreed on the way that when they got close to the walls they ought not to utter another sound, but listen in case they could hear anything from inside, and they got right into the city by this lane without being noticed and listened to everything they wanted and then got back to the Aitolian lines; so the lane took its name from the silence of the spies.[205]

24   [1] There is another way out of the training-ground leading to the market-place and the COURT of the Greek Arbiters; it lies above the grave of Achilles, and this is the route traditionally established for the Greek arbiters to proceed to the training-ground. They arrive before sunrise to match runners, and about noon they move to the pentathlon and what they call the heavy events.[206]

[2] The Elean MARKET-PLACE is not like an Ionian market-place or those of any of the Greek cities around Ionia.[207] It was constructed in the older manner with separate colonnades and lanes between them. The modern name for the market-place is the Horse-track, and the local people do in fact school their horses there. The southernmost COLONNADE is in the Doric style, and the columns divide it into three divisions. This is where the Greek arbiters mostly pass the day. [3] They have altars to Zeus built by the columns, and there are a small number of altars in the open air of the market-place; they are rather easily ruined as they are casually built. By this colonnade as you go into the market-place on the left at the end of the colonnade is the Court of the Greek Arbiters, separated from the market-place by a lane. Those elected to be arbiters live here for the next ten months learning their duties for the games from the law guardians.

---

cf. *Jahrshefte des O.A.I.*, 46, 1961–3, *Beiblatt*, pp. 31f. The Greek archaeological service has been working at Elis recently.

205. For Oxylos and his legendary war, cf. Bk V, 3 (5f.), and 18 (6).

206. Wrestling, boxing, discus, and all-in fighting.

207. This market-place was partly excavated by the Austrians before the war (cf. Note 204 above).

[4] There is another colonnade close to the one where the Greek arbiters spend the day, with a lane between them which the Eleans call Corfu Lane, because Corfu sent an invasion fleet ... took all kinds of things as their share of the Corfu booty and built this colonnade from a tenth of the spoils.[208] [5] The construction of the colonnade is Doric and built double, with columns facing the market-place in one direction and facing away from it in the other; there are no columns down the middle but a wall that holds up the roof, with portraits dedicated up against the wall on either side. In the market facing part of this colonnade stands a portrait of Pyrro son of Pistokrates, a professional intellectual and a man who never definitely came down on the side of any proposition whatever. Pyrron's grave is not far from the city of Elis: the place is called the ROCK, and they say that in antiquity the Rock was an inhabited settlement.[209] [6] The greatest glories in the open air of the Elean market-place are a SHRINE and statue of APOLLO of Healing: the title would mean nothing different from the Athenian title Turner-away-of-evil.[210] Elsewhere there are stone statues of the Sun and Moon: she with horns on her head, and he with rays on his. There is a SANCTUARY OF THE GRACES that has wooden idols with gilded clothes, and faces, hands and feet of white stone. The first one has a rose, the middle one has a knuckle-bone, and the third has a smallish branch of myrtle: [7] one may reasonably conjecture this is because the rose and myrtle are sacred to Aphrodite and linked with the legend of Adonis, and the Graces belong more with Aphrodite than with any other goddess, and the knuckle-bone is the play-thing of young lads and virgin girls whose graces are still uncontaminated by age.

208. Since the city of Elis was founded only in about 471, I suppose these spoils were won in the Peloponnesian War, while Elis was a Spartan ally.

209. The sceptical philosopher Pyrro started life as a mediocre painter; there was a painting by him at Elis of a torch-race. He was very popular and respected in the city during his lifetime (from the late fourth to the early third century). He was preoccupied with problems of knowledge and their relation to peace of mind. I do not know where the Rock was.

210. Cf. Bk I, 3 (4).

On the right of the Graces is a statue of Love that stands on the same pedestal. [8] There is a SHRINE OF SILENOS here too that belongs to Silenos alone without Dionysos: Drunkenness is giving him some wine in a cup. One can argue that Silenos was born mortal particularly from his graves: Silenos has a monument in the Jewish territory, and another Silenos has one at Pergamos.[211] [9] There was another thing I saw in the market-place of Elis: it was shaped like a temple but not very high, it had no walls and its roof was held up by oak-pillars. The local people agree this is a monument, but they have no record of whose monument it is: but if the old man I asked gave me the right answer, this would be the monument of Oxylos.[212] [10] The sixteen women as they call them also have a building in the market-place, where they weave the robe for Hera.[213]

Adjoining the market-place is an ancient TEMPLE set in a circle of colonnades, but its roof had fallen in and there was no statue left in it: it belongs to the Roman emperors.

25 [1] Behind the colonnade built from the spoils of Corfu is a TEMPLE OF APHRODITE with an open-air precinct not far away from it. She is called Heavenly Aphrodite in the temple, and the cult-image is gold and ivory, by Pheidias; one of her feet is treading on a tortoise. Her precinct is enclosed with a wall; inside this precinct is a platform, and on the platform is a bronze statue of Aphrodite sitting on a bronze billy-goat; she is by Skopas and they call her Popular Aphrodite. As for the

211. Neither of these graves is otherwise known. Certain very restricted kinds of Dionysiac imagery fitted easily into Jewish religion at this time, as has been shown by Goodenough in his studies of Jewish and Christian religious imagery in Palestine in the time of Christ or recently by the discovery of a plate with David dancing naked like a Greek satyr. Further there was some temptation to identify Iahweh with a Zeus-like or sun-like nature-god as Iao (Cook, *Zeus*, vol. 1, pp. 232f.). Dionysos's nurse Nysa was supposed to be buried in the Syrian decapolis (Pliny, *Natural History*, 5, 74). Silenos was a figure so Greek and so pagan it is certain his grave was in a Greek city. It may be that his grave was an oracle. Whatever it was, it remains undiscovered and unexplained.

212. Cf. Bk V, 3 (5f.).

213. Cf. Bk V, 16 (2). It was presented at the Heraion in Olympia.

tortoise and the goat, if you want to make a conjecture I leave it to you.[214]

[2] The sacred precinct and TEMPLE OF HADES – for Elis has a precinct and temple of Hades – are opened only once in the year, and even then no one but the priest is allowed in. The only people we know of in the world who worship Hades

*11. Aphrodite on a Goat*

are the Eleans and this is why: when Herakles led his army against Pylos in Eleia they say Athene came to help him, and so Hades who hated Herakles came to fight for the Pylians,

214. Cicero had seen Aphrodite's temple at Elis (*De Natura Deorum*, 3, 23, 59); he says the Elean Aphrodite was *coelo et die nata*, the daughter of the Sky and the Dawn. Some ancient representations of Aphrodite with a tortoise exist, but they seem to have little relation to Pheidias. There is a naked boy standing in a gymnastic pose on a tortoise from an Etruscan bronze jar in the British Museum; no doubt Pheidias's conception was more informal but also more solemn. Skopas's Aphrodite on the bronze goat is represented on Elean coins; goddesses and heroines riding sidesaddle on birds and animals are rather a common motif of Greek art: the subject retains the dignity of the archaic period. Versions of Aphrodite on a goat have been collected by P. E. Arias in his *Skopas* (1952, pp. 125–6). In particular, there are two splendid red-figured Attic hydriai in the Louvre and in the Berlin Museum that seem to be by a painter conscious of Skopas (*Jahrbuch des deutschen Archäologischen Instituts*, 4, 1889, p. 208; Beazley, *A.R.F.*, p. 1485).

who were worshippers of Hades. [3] They confirm this from what Homer wrote in the *Iliad*:

> *At Pylos, huge Hades took the stab of a swift arrow*
> *when the same son of Zeus of the goat-skin*
> *shot him and made him suffer with the dead.*[215]

And given that according to Homer Poseidon assisted the Greeks in the expedition of Agamemnon and Menelaos against Troy, then the same poet might very possibly think of Hades fighting for the Pylians. So the Eleans made the god a sanctuary because he was their friend and Herakles' enemy; I suppose that they observe the opening once a year because human beings go down to Hades only once. [4] The Eleans also have a sanctuary of Fortune; there is a statue of some size in a colonnade in this sanctuary, made of gilded wood except for the hands and face and feet, which are white stone. The City Saviour is also worshipped here on the left of Fortune in a small building; the god is represented according to a vision seen in a dream as a boy wrapped in a cloak embroidered with stars and holding Amaltheia's horn in his other hand.[216]

[5] In the most densely crowded part of the city of Elis, there is a smallish bronze figure of a man who has not yet grown a beard, with one leg crossed over the other, leaning on a spear with both hands. They dress him in wool, and also in coarse linen and in the finest linen. [6] This statue was supposed to be of Poseidon and to have been worshipped in ancient times at Samikon in Triphylia; but now that it has been brought to Elis it has reached an even higher position of honour, though they call it Satrapes and not Poseidon: they heard of the name Satrapes, which is a title of Korybas, after the extension of Patrai.[217]

---

215. *Iliad*, 5, 395f. The goat-skin is the *aigis*.
216. This is the child Zeus; cf. Bk VI, 20 (2f.) and the Note there.
217. For the strong prehistoric akropolis of Samikon, cf. Bk V, 5 (3f.). The god Satrapes is known from an inscription of 8 B.C. at Byblos, one of A.D. 54–5 at Palmyra, and at least two other first-century oriental inscriptions (*Real-Encyclopädie*, *Supp*. VIII, 705). The word Satrap may be an approximation to an unknown oriental divine name, or it may mean prince or viceroy; our

[1] There is an ancient THEATRE: it lies between the market-  26
place and the river Menios with the SANCTUARY OF
DIONYSOS. The statue of Dionysos is by Praxiteles.[218] The
worship of Dionysos is one of the principal Elean cults, and
they say the god himself visits them at the feast of Thuia. They
hold the feast they call Thuia about a mile away from the city.

*12. Dionysos*

The priests take three empty basins in the presence of the citizens and of any foreigners there may be and deposit them in a

only firm information is that Satrapes was the same as Korybas, who was a
mystery-god (or gods) closely related to the great mother-goddess Kybele. After
the extension of Patrai under Augustus, the Mother was worshipped there
(Bk VII, 20 (3), and cf. 17, 9). The invasion of the Roman empire by eastern
religions at this time is a commonplace of history, but Frazer records an excellent suggestion by Lobeck that the eastern cults in this particular corner of the
Peloponnese may have been introduced by the retired pirates from the Asian
coast who were settled here by Pompey.

218. The Menios is supposed to be the small tributary of the Peneios to the
east of the site: but this is almost incredible, since pseudo-Theokritos (25, 15)
calls it 'the great mere of Menios'. Perhaps it was once a big stretch of water
and finally choked itself in its own mud. The theatre has now been cleared by
Mr Yalouris. The sanctuary of Dionysos has not yet been identified so far as I
know, but the statue appears on Elean coins under Hadrian. For his cult at
Elis, cf. also Bk V, 16 (2) and the Note there.

building. The priests themselves and anyone else who wants put seals on the doors of the building; [2] the seals can be inspected the next day, and then when they go inside they find the basins full of wine. The most distinguished men in Elis and foreigners as well have sworn that this happens as I have said, though I myself was not there at the moment of the feast. The Andrians say that every second year on the feast of Dionysos their sanctuary runs with wine of its own accord.[219] If these Greek stories are to be believed then by the same reckoning one should accept what the Aithiopians above Syene say about the table of the sun.[220]

[3] In the upper city of Elis is a SANCTUARY OF ATHENE with a statue of gold and ivory. They claim this is by Pheidias; it has a cock carved on its helmet because cocks are extremely ready for a fight, though it could be thought of as the sacred bird of Athene the Worker.[221]

[4] KYLLENE is fifteen miles from Elis on a site facing Sicily, and it gives a good anchorage for shipping. This is the sea-port of Elis, and it was named after an Arkadian. Homer makes no mention of Kyllene in his Elean list, but in later verses he proved that he knew there was a town of Kyllene:

[5]     *Poulydamas killed and stripped Otos of Kyllene,*
        *Phyleideus's friend, lord of great-hearted Epeians.*[222]

219. ANDROS is the big island just south-east of Euboia. The ancient city at PALAIOUPOLIS is at present being excavated by Australian archaeologists. Pliny says the miracle on Andros happened every year on the fifth of January, but if you took the wine away from the temple it turned back to water (Pliny, *Natural History*, 2, 231 and 31, 16).

220. On the shores of the Indian Occan. The miracle was a god-given public feast which in fact was put out in the fields overnight by the governors (cf. Herodotos 3, 17f.).

221. Pliny says it was by Pheidias's pupil Kolotes; the shield was painted by Pheidias's brother Panainos (*Natural History*, 35, 54).

222. *Iliad*, 15, 518f. Kyllene is lost. In antiquity the Peneios reached the sea somewhere north of the modern Cape Kyllene, and we know the port of Kyllene was north of the river; it is probably now under water or silt or both. There is a big Roman bath complex at LOUTRA KYLLENIS west of Gastouni, and there are possible traces of classical as well as of prehistoric occupation at CHLEMOUTSI or KLARENTZA, the powerful ruined fortress that dominates

There are divine sanctuaries at Kyllene of Asklepios and Aphrodite, but the statue of Hermes which the people there worship so very devoutly is just an erect penis on a pedestal.

[6] The Elean territory is productive and fruitful and among other crops particularly good for fine flax.[223] People whose soil is right for it sow hemp and flax and fine flax, but the threads the Silk people use for their cloth do not come from a bark or stem of any kind: they are produced in quite another way, like this.[224] There is an insect in their country which in Greek is called the silk-worm though the Silk people themselves have some other name for it of their own. [7] Its size is about twice the biggest kind of beetle, but otherwise it is like the spiders that weave their webs in the trees, and just like a spider it has eight feet. The Silk people look after these creatures and make them the right kind of houses for winter and for summer, and the work of these creatures is found as a fine mass of thread twisted up in their feet. [8] They look after the creatures for four years giving them millet to eat, but in the fifth year they know the creatures will die and they feed them green rushes: this is the most delicious food there is for these creatures, and they stuff themselves on rushes

the cape, the last castle of the last of the Palaiologoi in Greece; neither of these two sites is far enough north to have any relation to the port of Kyllene, which should be looked for in the area of the KOTYCHI lagoon.

223. Cf. Bk V, 5 (2), and the Note there.

224. The Silk people (Seres) are the Chinese. There were overland routes as well as a sea-route to China at this time (cf. in general Heyd, *Histoire du commerce du Levant*), and we know from Chinese literary sources that an embassy arrived in China from Marcus Aurelius. But the principal silk route avoided Parthia by crossing the Hindu Kush from the Oxus to reach the Indus and the sea. (Cf. Map 5, p. 144 of Miller's *Spice Trade of the Roman Empire*.) The silk-worm was known to Aristotle, and raw silk was woven on the island of Kos under the Roman empire. One could be forgiven for wondering if there is not an element of Hadrianic influence in Khmer architecture; classical motifs were commonplace in Gandhara and in Afghanistan, and a little later Hellenistic terracottas had a vogue in Tang China. The word Pausanias uses for a silk-worm (*ser*) appears to come not from Chinese but from Korean, which (if it is true) would point to a coastal not an overland route. (Again, cf. Miller's discussion.)

until they burst open and die, and you find the greater part of the yarn inside them. There is a well known Silk Island in a bay of the Red Sea, [9] but I have heard it said that this island is not created by the Red Sea but by the Silk river as they call it, just as the Egyptian Delta is a creation of the Nile and not surrounded by the sea and nothing but the sea: the Silk Island is another like it. These Silk people and the people of the neighbouring islands of Abasa and Sakaia belong to the Aithiopian race, though some people claim they are not Aithiopians but Skythians mixed up with Indians.[225]

[10] So much for that. For a man travelling from Elis into Achaia, the river Larisos is nearly twenty miles from Elis, and the river Larisos is in our time the border of the Elean and Achaian territories, but in older times the border was Cape Araxos on the coast.[226]

225. It is difficult to be exact about these places, since 'the Red Sea' includes the Indian Ocean and the Persian Gulf. Can the Silk river possibly be the Indus? The Skythians had certainly penetrated northern India by this period. For the ramifications of the word Seres, cf. Tarn's *The Greeks in Bactria and India*, pp. 109f.

226. The Larisos is now called the RIOLITIKO or the MANA. The cape has been renamed ARAXOS, but its old name, Cape PAPAS, is still used. It is the north-west point of the Peloponnese. Pausanias has gone right round the coast from Corinth through Lakonia, Messenia and Eleia. His next book is Achaia, and he leaves Arkadia which has no coast until last. In this edition I have altered the arrangement in order to include south Greece in one volume and central Greece in the other, putting Achaia with Corinth and the Argolid into central Greece.

# BOOK VIII
# ARKADIA

[1] The Arkadians on the borders of the Argive country are  1
the Tegeans and Mantineans, and these peoples with the other
Arkadians occupy the inland region of the Peloponnese.[1] First
come the Corinthians who live at the isthmus, whose neighbours along the coast are the Epidaurians: Epidauros and
Troizen and Hermione make up the Argolic gulf and the
coastal territories of the Argive country; next to that come
the provincial Lakonians, who share a border with Messenia
which comes right down to the sea at Mothone and Pylos and
as far as Kyparissiai. [2] On the Lechaion side of Corinth live
the Sikyonians, who are the most distant people in this direction to belong to the Argolid; beyond Sikyon come the
Achaians who live along the coast; and the other end of the
Peloponnese opposite the Echinades is occupied by the Eleans,
the frontiers of whose territory meet Messenia near Olympia
and the Alpheios estuary and Achaia at the boundaries of
Dyme.[2] [3] All these peoples reach to the sea, but the Arkadians
occupy the territory in the centre of them all, cut off from the

1. Pausanias has already worked clockwise round the outside of the Peloponnese leaving Arkadia, the wildest and innermost part of the Peloponnese,
until he has covered Achaia; but he starts his Arkadian book at the frontier as
if he were coming straight from the Argolid, by a pass he described in Book II,
Chapter 25 (cf. Chapter 6, Section 4, of this book). Each book is in principle
a journey, which begins from a frontier and ends at one (or at more than one).
Even the first book begins with an arrival off Sounion by sea from an unspeci-
fied port, and apart from the appendix on the Lokrians with its tail-piece like a
dedication to Asklepois, the last book ends at a harbour where the road dies
out (Bk X, 27 (4f.)).

2. He thinks of Triphylia here as part of Messenia, although he includes it
in Book V as part of Eleia. Perhaps he has Nestor's Homeric kingdom at the
back of his mind. Elis had a privileged position under the Roman empire, but it
had no effective control of Triphylia (cf. Bk V, 5 (3)). All the other places
mentioned here are treated in their order in the different books.

sea in every direction: so that Homer says when they went to Troy they got ships from Agamemnon rather than sail in their own fleet.[3]

[4] The Arkadians say the first inhabitant of this country was Pelasgos. But it seems likelier that there were other people with him and not just Pelasgos by himself, or else who could Pelasgos have ruled over? But Pelasgos was taller and stronger and more beautiful and cleverer than the others, and in my opinion that was why they picked him to be king. Asios has written this about him:

> And black earth produced god-equalling Pelasgos
> in mountains with long hair of tall trees
> that a mortal race might come to be.[4]

[5] When Pelasgos was king he thought of making huts, so that the people should not be shivering with cold or dripping with rain or suffering in the heat, and it was Pelasgos who invented sheep-skin tunics, which poor people still wear now around Euboia and in Phokis. And it was Pelasgos who stopped the people eating fresh leaves and grasses and inedible roots some of which were poisonous, [5] and he discovered that the fruit of oak-trees was a food, not of all oak-trees but only the acorn of Dodona oaks, and that same diet has

---

3. *Iliad*, 2, 603–14.

4. Asios of Samos wrote a long genealogical poem which Pausanias often uses; he wrote in the seventh or very possibly the sixth century B.C. Pelasgos was supposed to be autochthonous, born from the ground; he was the first father of the Pelasgian race, who were believed to be the first inhabitants at the beginning of the prehistory of Greece. The belief in autochthonous ancestors is a projection of nationalism and constitutes a claim to racial purity. In Germany in the 1890s it was believed that the first Germans were a special fruit of evolution that arose autochthonously from the Pripet marshes. There is no helpful sense in which the Pelasgians ever really existed; but it appears to be true on the evidence of dialect that some very early inhabitants of Greece retreated into the Arkadian mountains during or soon after the late Mycenaean period, and survived there much as the Welsh have survived. A survey of the early material culture of Arkadia was recently carried out by Mr Roger Howell; it will be published in the *Annual of the British School of Archaeology* (64, 1969).

survived in some places from the time of Pelasgos to this day; so that when the Pythian priestess forbade the Lakonians to lay hands on Arkadian land, these verses were part of what she said:

> There are many acorn-fed Arkadians
> to stop you: though I do not grudge it to you.[5]

And they say in the reign of Pelasgos the country came to be called Pelasgia.

[1] Pelasgos's son Lykaon made as many inventions even 2 cleverer than his father's. He founded the city of Lykosoura on Mount Lykaion and named Lykaian Zeus and instituted the Lykaian games.[6] My considered judgement is that the Panathenian games at Athens had not been instituted at this date: they were called the Athenian games, and they got the name Panathenian only under Theseus, because he held the games after he had collected all the Athenians into one city. [2] They trace back the Olympic games to before the beginning of the human race, with the legend that Kronos and Zeus wrestled there and the Kouretes ran the first race, so of course I am excluding the Olympics from this argument.[7] But I believe Kekrops king of Athens and Lykaon were contemporaries, though they were not equally gifted with religious

5. One of Vergil's peasants is *uvus de glande*; he has been giving his pigs acorns steeped in water, as recommended in Ministry of Agriculture pamphlets during the Second World War. Acorns were not eaten by human beings in Pausanias's time, although they were eaten again in medieval Europe; it was believed under the Roman empire that acorns had been the food of the Golden Age (cf. Ovid, *Metamorphoses*, 1, 101, and Page, *Poetae Melici Graeci* 986 (b)), or even that edible acorns died out when the Golden Age ended (Vergil, *Georgics*, 1, 145–9). Appian (*B.C.* 1, 50) speaks of acorns as a starvation diet; he is describing the fate of a defeated army in Albania in mid-winter, but it is not quite certain whether he says they died eating acorns or that some ate acorns and others died. The Arkadians were famous acorn-eaters from before the time of Herodotos, who quotes the whole of this oracle (1, 66). The first line was 'You want Arkadia? You want a lot; I won't give it'; but the Lakonians were allowed to take Tegea. The acorn occurs on Arkadian coins.

6. Cf. Bk VIII, 38.

7. Cf. Bk V, 7 (6f.).

wisdom. [3] Kekrops first named Zeus the Supreme, and decided to offer him no slaughtered sacrifices but to incinerate on the altar those local honey-cakes the Athenians today still call oatmeals, but Lykaon brought a human child to the altar of Lykaian Zeus, slaughtered it and poured its blood on the altar, and they say at that sacrifice he was suddenly turned into a wolf.[8] [4] And I believe this legend, which has been told in Arkadia from ancient times and has likelihood on its side. Because of their justice and their religion the people of that time entertained gods and sat at table with them, and the gods visibly rewarded their goodness with favour and their wickedness with wrath: and in those days certain human beings were turned into gods and are still honoured, like Aristaios and Britomartis of Crete, Herakles son of Alkmene and Amphiaraos son of Oikles, and Polydeukes and Kastor as well. [5] So one may well believe that Lykaon was turned into a wild beast and Tantalos's daughter Niobe was turned to stone.[9] But in my time when wickedness has increased to the last degree, and populates the whole world and all its cities, no human being ever becomes a god, except by a verbal convention and to flatter authority, and the curse of the gods is a long time falling on the wicked, and is stored away for those who have departed from the world. [6] Those who have added so many constructions of lies on to truthful foundations

8. There are a number of versions of this story, but no one else relates it so directly to religion. Of all the observances and myths of the Greeks in his time this is the only one by which Pausanias is really horribly shocked. The myth has arisen from the cult of a mountain wolf-god, and from the human sacrifices offered on Mount Lykaon. At first a child was murdered to placate the god of wolves and mountains, and later when Zeus had taken over the peak and an element of guilt attached to the sacrificing priest, the myth and no doubt the observance itself became more complicated. For learned references, cf. Immerwahr, *Die Kulte und Mythen Arkadiens* (1891), the first chapter, cf. also Herodotos on the Neuroi (4, 105).

9. Tantalos murdered his son Pelops and served him to the gods to eat, but they brought the child back to life. Niobe boasted she had more children than Leto, and her children were murdered by the gods; they lay nine days unburied, on the tenth the gods buried them and Niobe was turned to stone among the rocks where goddesses give birth: at Mount Sipylos (*Iliad*, 24, 603–17).

have made a lot of things in the history of the world, things
that happened in antiquity and things that still happen now,
seem incredible to the majority of mankind. For example, they
say that after Lykaon someone was always turned into a wolf
at the sacrifice of Lykaian Zeus, but not for his whole life, because if he kept off human meat when he was a wolf he
turned back into a man after nine years, though if he tasted
man he stayed a wild beast for ever.[10] [7] And they say Niobe
on Mount Sipylos weeps in the summer.[11] And there are other
stories I have heard told: that griffins have spots like leopards
and tritons speak in human voices, and some people say they
blow through a pierced conch. People who enjoy listening to
mythical stories are inclined to add even more wonders of
their own, and in this way they have done injuries to the truth
which they have mixed up with a lot of rubbish.

[1] In the second generation after Pelasgos the country 3
increased its number of cities and its human population.
Nyktimos was the eldest son and all power was in his hands,
but Lykaon's other sons founded cities wherever each of them
preferred. Pallas and Orestheus and Phigalos founded Pallantion and Oresthasion and Phigalia; [2] Pallantion is mentioned
by Stesichoros of Himera in his *Geryonis*, but in the course of
time Phigalia and Oresthasion changed their names, and came
to be called Oresteion after Orestes the son of Agamemnon

10. The nine years may be the period of the man's priesthood or the ten
years after he commits the murder. They begin at a certain pool (perhaps
Hagno; cf. 38, 3) where he must leave all his clothes on an oak-tree and swim
away naked, *atque abire in deserta transfigurarique in lupum*; after nine years he
swims back across the same pool, and takes his clothes again. (Pliny, *Natural
History*, 8, 81.) There is also the story Pausanias refuses to credit at Bk VI, 8 (2),
and which Pliny, who also disbelieves it, says comes from Skopas's book on
Olympic champions. Petronius (62) has a powerful story about a *versipellis* who
could turn into a wolf, but the superstitious belief that this power exists, which
was common in Europe until recently, need not have anything to do with
cults like that of Lykaian Zeus.

11. Pausanias has seen the stone Niobe, and in fact must have lived in the
area; he was probably brought up there; cf. Bk I, 21 (3), and Bk V, 13 (7). It
was evidently dry in his time, and I think must always have been so.
(Cf. pl. 2 of G. E. Bean, *Aegean Turkey*.)

and Phialia after Boukolion's son Phialos.[12] Trapezeus and Daseatas and Makareus and Helisson and Akakos and Thoknos founded cities: Thoknos Thoknia and Akakos Akakesion, it being from his name so the Arkadians say that Homer made a title for Hermes. [3] Helisson gave his name to the city and the river Helisson, and Makaria and Dasea and Trapezous were named after Lykaon's sons in the same way.[13] Orchomenos founded Methydrion and Orchomenos which Homer in his poetry calls the home of many flocks, and Hypsous and ... founded Melaineai and Hypsous, with Thyraion and Haimoniai. The Arkadians believe Thyrea in the Argolid and the Thyreatic gulf were named after this same Thyraios.[14]

12. Orestes was ordered to Arkadia and promised the name of Oresthasion by the Dioskouroi after his revenge and acquittal (Euripides, *Elektra*, 1273–5, and cf. Denniston's references). For Pallantion, cf. Bk VIII, 43 (1); Oresthasion 44 (2); Phigalia 39 (1). Stesichoros was one of the greatest Greek poets of the archaic age, and even the miserable fragments we have of his poem about Herakles and Geryon leave the same impression of strength and brilliance as fragments of archaic sculpture. There seems to be a particularly close relationship between Stesichoros's poetry and the metope reliefs from the Heraion at *foce del Sele* (cf. the publication by P. Zancani Montuoro and V. Zanotti-Bianco (vol. 2, 1954, pp. 106f.)) which include the big centaur Pholos (pp. 111f. and pl. 52) who we know in Stesichoros's *Geryonis* offered Herakles a cup of wine, the smell of which drew every centaur out of the mountains for miles around; they attacked Herakles with rocks but he beat them off into the southernmost mountains in Greece, around Cape Malea (?). Stesichoros possibly mentioned Pallantion because he believed Pholos's cave was there or because the centaurs retreated that way; but Pholos's cave is more likely to have been on Mount Pholoe north of the Alpheios at the western limits of Arkadia (cf. Bk VIII, 24 (4)), and Pallantion is on the other side of the country, between Megalopolis and Tegea. For the other Malea or Malaia near Psophis, cf. Bk VIII, 27 (4), and Bk III, note 261.

13. For Trapezous, cf. Bk VIII, 29 (1); Dasea and Makaria 36 (9); Helisson (where the river rises) 30 (1); Thoknia 29 (5); Akakesion and Akakesian Hermes 36 (10). The allusion to Homer is to the *Iliad* (16, 185). Pausanias's source for this account of Lykaon's sons must be earlier than the foundation of Megalopolis in 370 B.C., when they lost their importance. In general this division of Arkadian cities into generations of founders is anomalous, nor does it include all the cities in Arkadia.

14. For Orchomenos, cf. Bk VIII, 12 (9), and for Methydrion 36 (1–3); the quotation from Homer is from the *Iliad* (2, 605). For Hypsous, cf. Bk VIII, 35 (7); Melaineai 26 (8); Thyraion 35 (7); Haimoniai 44 (1). For Thyrea cf. Bk II, 38 (5), and Bk III, 7 (5); it was either the very rich coastal plain below Astros, or the fertile valley where the railway climbs inland south of Lerna (Myloi).

[4] Mantineus and Tegeates and Mainalos founded what in antiquity was the most famous city in Arkadia, Mainalos, and Tegea and Mantineia. Kromoi was named after Kromos, Charisia after its founder Charisios, Trikolonoi after Trikolonos, Peraitheis after Peraithos, Asea after Aseatas, Lykoa after Lykeus, and Soumatia after Soumateus, and both Alipheros and Heraieus had cities named after them.[15] [5] Lykaon's youngest son Oinotros asked his brother Nyktimos for money and men and crossed over by ship to Italy where the country of Oinotria was named after King Oinotros. By the most accurate calculation, this was the first colonizing expedition ever sent out from Greece, nor were there any barbarians who had ever settled abroad earlier than Oinotros.[16]

[6] In addition to all these boys Lykaon had a daughter Kallisto with whom, according to the Greek legend, which I am simply repeating, Zeus fell in love; Hera caught him as he lay with her and turned Kallisto into a bear, and then Artemis shot her dead to please Hera, but Zeus sent Hermes with orders to save his son, who was in Kallisto's belly. [7] He turned Kallisto into the constellation of stars called the Great Bear, which Homer mentions in Odysseus's voyage from the Island of Kalypso:

> He saw the Pleiades and the Waggoner who sets late,
> he saw the Bear they also call the Waggon.

And apart from this these stars are perhaps named in honour of Kallisto, whose grave the Arkadians can show you.[17]

15. For Mainalos, cf. Bk VIII, 36 (8); Tegea 45 (1f.); Mantinea 8 (4f.); Kromoi 34 (6); Charisia 35 (5); Trikolonoi 35 (6f.); Peraitheis 36 (7); Asea 44 (3); Lykoa 36 (7); Soumatia 36 (8); Aliphera 26 (5); Heraia 26 (1).

16. Oinotria was more or less the shoe of Italy; the name was used for the people whom the historical Greeks found in possession there when they arrived. The story of Oinotros is of course nonsense.

17. *Odyssey*, 5, 272–3. The name of Kallisto's son Arkas means 'the Bear'. For her grave not far from a spring in central Arkadia, cf. Bk VIII, 35 (8). Ariaithos of Tegea says she was called Megisto and that these dire events, of which he has a more romantic version with the mother bear and the bear-cub taking refuge in the temple of Lykaian Zeus, took place *in Nonacri monte*

4    [1] After the death of Nyktimos, Arkas son of Kallisto came
to power: he introduced cultivated crops which Triptolemos
taught him, and he showed people how to make bread and
weave cloth and so on; he learnt wool-spinning from Adris-
tas.[18] It was his reign that gave the people their name of
Arkadians instead of Pelasgians. [2] He was supposed to have
married no mortal woman, but the nymph Dryas. The
Dryads were also called Nymphs of the Flocks, and some of
them were called Naiads, and Homer in his poetry particularly mentions Naiads.[19] Arkas's nymph was called Erato, and
they say she bore Arkas's children – Azan and Apheidas and
Elatos. He already had a bastard called Autolaos. [3] When the
boys grew up Arkas divided the country into three, and one
division was called Azania after Azan: it was from here they
say the colonizing expedition was sent out that settled by the
cave in Phrygia called Steunos and the river Penkalas.[20]
Apheidas received Tegea and the territory around it, and the
poets call it the lot of Apheidas. [4] Elatos received Mount
Kyllene which in those days was still unnamed, but later he

---

*Arcadiae* near the falls of the Styx on Mount Chelmos (cf. Bk VIII, 17 (6)), in
northern Arkadia a long way from the grave. Probably the cult of Kallisto or
Megisto was localized in many places: perhaps she was also Hagno (38 (3)).
The Bear-nymph is closely connected and in the end identified with Artemis.

18. This otherwise unknown hero evidently gets his name from the verb
*atrizomai*, which means to wind wool.

19. Homeric naiads are water-goddesses (*Iliad*, 6, 22; *Odyssey*, 13, 104, etc.),
even though you sometimes meet them wandering in the countryside.

20. The city was called Azanoi; its ruins were discovered and identified in
1824 by Viscount St Asaph at TCHAVDOUR in central Phrygia, due east of
Mytilene on Lesbos and due south of Bashna on the Black Sea. The river which
has its head-springs in this area is called the Ryndakos; the Penkalas must be one
arm of it. The Steunos cave was sacred to Kybele (Bk X, 32 (3)). It was
identified in 1898 by J. G. Anderson and J. W. Crowfoot (*B.S.A.*, 4, pp. 52–7)
at the KESSIK MEGARA cave. The cult was the same as at TAS SURET below
Sipylos (Bk III, 22 (4)), which has proved to be a Hittite shrine of the Mother.
We know from an inscription that the Steunian mother of the gods was
worshipped as far away as Cadiz in the Hellenistic period, but antiquities like
the rock cuttings at the Steunos cave are common in Anatolia and not easy to
date.

migrated to what is now called Phokis where he fought for the Phokians who were under military pressure from the Phlegyans, and he founded the city of Elateia.[21] They say Azan's son was Kleitor, Apheidas's son was Aleos, and Elatos had five sons, Aipytos, Pereus, Kyllen, Ischys and Stymphelos. [5] The first funeral games were held for Azan son of Arkas: there was a horse-race but there were other games. I know nothing about them.[22] Azan's son Kleitor lived at Lykosoura and was the most powerful of the kings; he founded and named the city of Kleitor after himself.[23] Aleos succeeded to his father's inheritance, [6] and as for Elatos's sons Mount Kyllene was named after Kyllen, and the water-spring of Stymphelos and the city beside it were named after Stymphelos,[24] and I have already told in my treatise on the Argolid the story of the death of Ischys son of Elatos; they say Pereus had no son but a daughter Neaira: she married Autolykos who lived on Mount Parnassos and was said to be a son of Hermes, though really his father was Daidalion.

[7] Azan's son Kleitor had no children, so the Arkadian crown passed to Aipytos son of Elatos. Aipytos was killed out hunting, but not by any of the tougher kinds of wild beasts: he was killed by an unnoticed adder. I saw this serpent once myself: it was a tiny ashen-looking snake with irregular spotted markings, with a broad head, a thin neck, a biggish belly and a short tail; this and the crested snake move sideways as crabs do.[25] [8] Aleos succeeded Aipytos as sovereign, as

21. For Elateia, which was north-west of Thebes and the Kopaic lake but still in Phokis, cf. Bk X, 34 (1-6).

22. Pausanias knew there was a chariot-race only because Apis was killed in it (Bk V, 1 (8)).

23. For Lykosoura; cf. Bk VII, 27 (4f.); Kleitor 21 (1f.).

24. For Stymphelos, cf. Bk VIII, 22 (1f.).

25. I believe this is or used to be classified as *coluber ammodytes*, up to fifteen or eighteen inches long. It is the south European viper. It was identified somewhere near Lykosoura by the Expédition scientifique de la Morée in 1829, and I saw one among the rocks in the Neda gorge at Stomio below Phigalia in 1963 but I have forgotten the local name for it; it looked more undernourished than vicious, though I was told it was extremely dangerous. I am not sure what

Stymphelos's sons Agamedes and Gortys were in the third generation from Arkas, and Apheidas's son Aleos was in the second. Aleos built the ancient sanctuary to Athene Alea at Tegea, and Tegea was the capital city of his kingdom. Gortys son of Stymphelos founded the city of Gortys on the river, which is in fact called the Gortynian river.[26] Aleos's sons were Lykourgos and Amphidamas and Kepheus and a daughter Auge; [9] according to Heketaios Herakles lay with Auge when he came to Tegea, and in the end she was caught with Herakles' child, and Aleos shut her and the boy into a chest and sent them out to sea: she landed and met Teuthras, who was a powerful man in the Kaikos plain, and he loved and married her: and today Auge's monument is at Pergamos on the Kaikos, a tumulus of earth surrounded by a stone platform and surmounted by a naked woman in bronze.[27] [10] When Aleos died, his son Lykourgos inherited the throne by right of seniority. Lykourgos is recorded to have killed an enemy Areithoos by treachery and unfairly. He had two sons, Anchaios and Epochos; Epochos met his death by sickness, but Anchaios took part in Jason's voyage to Kolchoi, and later he joined Meleager in the hunt for the Kalydonian monster and the boar killed him.

5    [1] Lykourgos reached extreme old age and saw both his sons dead, but when he died the sovereignty of Arkadia passed to Echemos, the son of Kepheus's son and Aleus's grandson Aeropos. In his days the Dorians returned to the Peloponnese under Hyllos son of Herakles and were beaten

---

Pausanias means about his snake moving sideways like a crab; so far as I know all groundsnakes weave sideways, perhaps he thought they weave up and down; mine was weaving sideways very fast.

26. For Alean Athene cf. Bk VIII, 45 (4); for Gortys 28 (1).

27. Heketaios of Miletos is the first geographer and historian about whom we know anything worth knowing; he wrote at the beginning of the fifth century, and without him Herodotos could hardly have existed. It is symbolically just that the fragments of Hekataios are the first item in Jacoby's *Fragments of the Greek Historians*. This story (Fr. 29a) comes from a book about Herakles and his children. Pergamos and the Kaikos are in Asia Minor, more or less east of the southern tip of Lesbos. Auge means 'the dawn'.

in battle by the Achaians at the Corinthian isthmus: Echemos killed Hyllos in formal single combat. This appears to me more probable than the version I gave before about Orestes being king of Achaia at that time and Hyllos attempting a return to the Peloponnese when Orestes was king.[28] In the version I am giving now Tyndareos's daughter Timandra would seem to have been married to Echemos who killed Hyllos. [2] The king after Echemos was Agapenor son of Ankaios son of Lykourgos; Agapenor commanded the Arkadians at Troy. After the fall of Troy the storm that broke on the Greeks as they sailed home carried Agapenor and the Arkadian fleet to Cyprus, where Agapenor founded PAPHOS and built Aphrodite's sanctuary at Old Paphos; the goddess already had a cult in Cyprus at a place called GOLGOI.[29]

28. Bk I, 42 (2).
29. Aphrodite's sanctuary at Old Paphos in south-west Cyprus is the place where she came ashore when she was born from the blood of the dismembered Titans and the waves of the sea. Pausanias knew (Bk I, 14 (7)) that her worship came to Cyprus from the east. Homer mentions this sanctuary in the *Odyssey* (8, 362), and Aischylos and Aristophanes knew about it; it was very famous in the Augustan age, and we know its appearance at several different periods from coins and gems (Head, *Catalogue of the Coins of Cyprus*, pp. 121f.). It was rebuilt by one of the Flavian emperors. The site, which is at KOUKLIA, was probably known to Cyriaco of Ancona, who went to Cyprus as an agent for the Contarini family between 1412 and 1414; it was mentioned even in the fourteenth century. St Jerome, whose sensibility to caves and ruined antiquities was highly developed and movingly expressed, spoke about the ruins of Paphos in his life of Hilarion. The first detailed survey was by an Austrian, Josef van Hammer, in 1811; the principal excavation was carried out while Cyprus was still Turkish in 1887-8 by the students of the British School at Athens in its first year of existence, including the young M. R. James, who appears from the publication to have been particularly anxious to replace the excavated bones in their old graves (*Journal of Hellenic Studies*, 9, pp. 190-271). Unfortunately the excavators seem to have misinterpreted their results (cf. *Swedish Cyprus Expedition*, vol. 4, pt 3, 1956, pp. 7-8). The site appears to have been occupied continuously (it would be rash to say in what strength) from the late Bronze Age until the classical period, but in spite of recent excavations we still know far too little about the most important aspects of this crucial site (cf. *Antiquaries' Journal*, 31, 1951, p. 51, and Desborough, *Last Myceneans and Their Successors*, 1964, pp. 198-202). The best evidence for a real connexion between Arkadia and Cyprus is a common ancient dialect. It was surely old Paphos,

[3] Sometime after this Agapenor's daughter Laodike sent a robe to Alean Athene at Tegea, with an inscription on the dedication which also showed where she was born:

> The robe of Laodike dedicated
> to Athene in her own vast country:
> sent from holy Cyprus.[30]

[4] Agapenor never got home from Troy, and the throne passed to Hippothous son of Kerkyon son of Agamedes son of Stymphelos. They say nothing outstanding occurred in his lifetime except that he reigned from Trapezous and not Tegea. After Hippothous his son Aipytos succeeded, and Orestes son of Agamemnon moved to Arkadia from Mycenae by the command of the Delphic oracle.[31] [5] Aipytos dared to enter POSEIDON'S SANCTUARY at MANTINEIA, where no human being was permitted to enter then any more than now, and he was blinded, and not long after this catastrophe met his death.[32]

[6] In the reign of Aipytos's son Kypselos, who inherited his father's throne, the Dorian expedition returned to the Peloponnese, not through the Corinthian isthmus as they had done three generations before, but by sea by way of Rion.[33] When Kypselos heard about them, he gave his daughter to the only son of Aristomachos who he discovered was still unmarried, and because of this marriage alliance with Kresphontes Kypselos and the Arkadians had nothing more to fear. [7] Kypselos's son Holaias with the clan of Herakles from

---

which is a pre-Persian and prehistoric city, that Agapenor was supposed to have founded, not (as Dr Platon suggests) New Paphos, which was probably a fourth-century foundation and became the Roman capital of the island; New Paphos is ten miles north-west. Golgoi was for a long time dubiously and controversially identified, but the site found by the American consul Cesnola in the last century near ATHIAINOU north-north-west of Larnaka seems now to be generally accepted. The excavations have been piecemeal.

30. Cf. Bk VIII, 53 (7).

31. Cf. Note 12 above.

32. Cf. Bk VIII, 10 (2f.).

33. The twin fortresses of Rion and Antirion guard the straits at the mouth of the Corinthian gulf.

Sparta and Argos installed his sister's son Aipytos at Messene. His son was Boukolion, and Boukolion's son was Phialos, who stole the honours of Lykaon's son Phigalos the true founder by renaming his city Phialia after himself, though the new name never completely drove out the old.³⁴ [8] In the reign of Phialos's son Simos the ancient wooden Phigalean idol of Black Demeter was consumed by fire; and it was an omen that not long afterwards Simos was to come to the end of his life.³⁵ Pompos succeeded, and in his day Aiginetans used to sail into Kyllene to trade, and brought their goods up to Arkadia with pack-animals. Pompos gave them high honours in return for this service, and he even named his son Aiginetes as a mark of his friendship.³⁶ [9] After Aiginetes his son Polymestor became king of Arkadia, and that was when the Lakonian army first invaded Tegea under Charillos, but the Tegean men and women together put on armour, beat them in battle and took Charillos alive with the rest. I shall give a fuller record of Charillos and his expedition when I deal with Tegea.³⁷ [10] Polymestor died childless, and Aichnis succeeded to the throne: he was the son of Briakas and Polymestor's nephew, since Briakas was another son of Aiginetes only younger than Polymestor. The Lakonian war against Messenia took place in the reign of Aichmis; the Arkadians had always been friends of the Messenians, and now they fought openly against Lakonia with King Aristodemos at Messene.³⁸ [11] Aichmis's son Aristokrates perhaps committed other outrages against Lakonia, but I will now tell the

34. The difference between Phialia and Phigalia is just a question of how carefully the name was pronounced.

35. For the Black Demeter, who was worshipped in a cave below Phigalia in the Neda gorge, cf. Bk VIII, 42 (3f.).

36. The story about islanders from north-east of the Peloponnese sailing right round to Kyllene (Bk VI, 26 (4)) is an attempt to explain the name Aiginetes; it is possible that there was really such a trade-route, but more probably Pausanias or his source is arguing from some lost fragment of epic poetry.

37. Bk VIII, 48 (4 and 5).

38. For this legendary hero and his epic battles, cf. the earlier part of Bk IV.

story of the wickedest sacrilege I know of his having committed. There is a SANCTUARY OF SINGING ARTEMIS: it lies inside the Orchomenian borders near the frontier of Mantineia, and the worship of Singing Artemis is universal in Arkadia and very ancient; in those days the priestess of this goddess used to be a young virgin girl.[39] [12] Aristokrates had designs on this girl's virginity but she continually resisted, and in the end she took refuge with Artemis in the sanctuary and he raped her there. When everyone heard what he had dared to do the Arkadians stoned him to death, and because of him they altered the law, and now instead of a virgin priestess they give Artemis a mature woman who has had enough of intercourse with men. [13] Aristokrates' son was Hiketas, and Hiketas's son was another Aristokrates who had the same name and who died the same death as his ancestor. The Arkadians stoned him to death when they found he had been taking bribes from Lakonia and was responsible for the Messenian disaster at the Great Ditch: and that crime was the end of the royal authority of the whole house of Kypselos.[40]

6 [1] This genealogical series is what the Arkadians produced to satisfy my curiosity about the history of their kings. The glories that the Arkadians in common have given to history are first of all the Trojan War, and then the war they fought for Messenia against Lakonia; they also took part in the successful action at Plataia against the Persians.[41] [2] Rather because they had no alternative and not because they liked the Lakonians, they fought for Lakonia against Athens and crossed over to Asia with Agesilaos, and even followed the

39. For this sanctuary and the laws of its clergy, cf. Bk VIII, 13 (1). Nothing much is known about the goddess's cult or her festival. Her title *Hymnia* might mean not that she sang but that hymns were sung to her. Artemis is sometimes represented with a stringed instrument; she may be one of the figures usually taken as muses on the pedestal of Apollo's statue at Mantineia; cf. Note 64 below.

40. This is another part of the legendary history of Messenia (Bk VI, 17 (1f.), and 22 (7)).

41. In 479 when the Persians were chased out of Greece. This is the first non-fabulous event Pausanias knows in the history of Arkadia.

Lakonians to Boiotian Leuktra. But they showed their distrust of Lakonia in various ways: most of all when the Lakonians were defeated by Thebes at Leuktra and Arkadia immediately deserted them. They neither fought on the Greek side nor of course against Greece with Philip of Macedon at Chaironeia or later with Antipater in Thessaly. [3] They say it was because of the Lakonians that they took no part in the risks of Thermopylai against the Gauls, in case the Lakonians should injure their territories while the strong and young were away. But they took a readier part in the Achaian League than anyone else in Greece. As for the part of their history which is not communal, I shall reserve each of the events I have discovered in the histories of particular cities to its proper place in this treatise.

[4] There are ways into Arkadia from the territory of Argos near HYSIAI across Mount Parthenion into the territory of Tegea, and a second and third by Mantineia through what they call PRINOS and by the LADDER.[42] This last is wider, and

42. Cf. Note 1 above and Bk II, 25. There are three passes south-west from the Argolid into Arkadia. The route from HYSIAI (Bk II, 24 (7)) to Tegea is more or less that of the modern main road from Athens to Tripolis by ACHLA-DOKAMPO, and this is the farthest south; it turns away from the sea into the mountains south of Lerna (Myloi). Mantineia is farther north than Tegea; the two passes that lead to it from Argos were until recently called PORTES and SKALES. They are routes 60B and 60C in the old (1916?) British Admiralty *Handbook to Greece*, vol. 1, which is effectively a guide to the then existing principal footpaths and mule-tracks of mainland Greece. The best pass is SKALES; it can be approached either from KEPHALARI (where some interesting antiquities now in the Argos Museum were found) and KRUONERION, or more directly up the XERIAS valley north of Argos, and then by either of two paths from KARYA. I have not been to the top of this pass and am uncertain which is the ordinary ancient road. Stepped mule-paths are extremely common in Greece, as they were once in Wales. The PORTES pass is farther north again and involves a more roundabout route up the river Inachos to KAPARELION. (The Inachos used to be the PANITSA.) The pass itself has been cut through the ridge; there is abundant evidence of the ancient route near the top of the pass. Prinos means an oak, probably here a small bushy holly-oak; the crest of the mountain is saw-toothed, but it seems very unlikely a tree could ever have grown there (though they do grow on the Skales route); if it did so, it would be strange enough to have a pass named after it. But it is much likelier that the

the road down once had steps made in it. When you get across the Steps the place you come to is called Black Pots: the Mantinean drinking-water runs down from here into the city.[43] [5] Beyond Black Pots about a mile from the city you come to a spring called the FOUNTAIN OF THE MELIASTAI. These Meliastai perform the mysteries of Dionysos, and a HALL OF DIONYSOS and a SANCTUARY OF DARK APHRODITE stand by the spring. The goddess has this title for no other reason than the fact that human copulations do not always take place in daylight like those of cattle but mostly at night.[44] [6] The other road is narrower and goes by ARTEMISION; I mentioned that this mountain has a shrine and a statue of Artemis, and the head-springs of the Inachos. As long as it runs beside the mountain road, the Inachos is the frontier of Argos and Mantineia, but when it turns away from the road it runs through Argive country from then on; this is why Aischylos and others call the Inachos an Argive river.[45]

7    [1] When you cross by Mount Artemision into Mantinean

---

northern pass, PORTES, is the ancient route called the Ladder, and the southern pass, SKALES, is the ancient Prinos. The fact that SKALES also means 'steps' is only a misleading coincidence.

43. Black Pots (Melangeia) may be at PIKERNI, where L. Ross in the early nineteenth century found ancient water-works which no subsequent traveller has been able to trace. If Portes is the Ladder this is acceptable, though Leake (*Peloponnesiaca*, pp. 372–3) found an alternative site.

44. The spring of the Meliastai was at TRYPI-GI about a mile north-east of Mantineia. This confirms that the Portes route is really the Ladder. Some traces of the temple have been found. The standard work on this area is by G. Fougères, *Mantinée et l'Arcadie Orientale*, 1898, with misleadingly lucid maps. Pausanias's explanation of Dark Aphrodite carries an undertone of Aphrodite's night-festival, the *pervigilium Veneris*. Athenaios (13, 588) says the Aphrodite at Corinth was another Dark Aphrodite; I do not know the real origin of the title.

45. For the shrine of Artemis, cf. Bk II, 25 (3). I take it Pausanias is talking about the modern Skales route. The Inachos rises near Karya below XEROBOUNI (dry mountain) and runs north for some time before it swings away to the east towards Argos. (Fougères' map is not accurate.) The reference to Aischylos is to a fragment of the *Xantriai* quoted by Plato (Aischylos, *Fr.* 168).

territory you will find yourself in a plain called the Waste, which it is, because the rain of heaven runs down on it from the mountains and makes this land a waste: in fact nothing could prevent it from flooding altogether if it were not that the water disappears into a crack in the earth.[46] [2] It disappears here and reappears at DINE near the Birthplace in the Argolid, where a fresh-water stream rises in the sea.[47] In antiquity the Argives used to send down bitted and bridled horses to Poseidon at Dine. There is certainly fresh water that rises in the sea both at this spot in the Argolid and in Thesprotis at a place called CHEIMERION. [3] An even more amazing thing is the boiling water in the Maiander that comes out of a rock in mid-stream and also out of the river-bed. Off Etruscan DIKAIARCHIA there is a spring of boiling water in the sea, with an artificial island, so that the water there is not waste but provides them with warm baths.[48]

[4] On the left of the Mantinean Waste is a mountain with the ruins of Philip's camp and of the village of NESTANE. They say Philip encamped beside Nestane, and the water-spring there is called after him PHILIP'S SPRING. Philip had come to Arkadia to make friends with the Arkadians and separate them

46. When you cross the Skales pass (the ancient Prinos) you come to the plain above NESTANI which at the end of the nineteenth century was a marsh but has now been properly drained. The river disappears near TSIPIANA, now renamed NESTANI (cf. 7 (4) below).

47. Cf. Bk II, 38 (4). There are two spectacular fresh-water springs off KYBERI (anabolos tou Kyberiou) and farther south. Someone is at present (1968) trying to capture fresh water from the smaller, more accessible spring and pipe it across the gulf to ASINE to water a market-garden. Ancient beliefs about the interconnexions of disappearing streams are of course unscientific but right in principle.

48. Poseidon was the god of horses and the sea and of disturbances of the earth. Frazer has collected an entertaining series of ancient and modern stories about horse sacrifices (vol. 4, p. 197, of his commentary). Cheimerion is at HAGIOS IOANNIS on the coast south-west of Ioannina; the spring was identified by a Mr Skene of the British Ionian Islands community in the 1840s; the bay where it rises is an hour and a half on foot north of the mouth of the Acheron (cf. Hammond, Epirus, p. 76). I am unable to trace the hot springs in the Maiander. For the hot springs at Dikaiarchia, cf. Bk IV, 35 (12), and the Note there.

from the Greek alliance.[49] [5] One might well take the view that of all the Macedonian kings before or after him it was Philip whose achievements were the most illustrious: but no one could reasonably call him a good commander, since he continually trampled solemn oaths underfoot, broke sworn truces on every occasion, and showed less respect for the obligations of good faith than any man in the world: [6] and the curse of the god fell on him quickly enough, before any other case known to history. Before Philip had lived beyond forty-six years he fulfilled the Delphic prophecy, which they say was given when he asked the oracle about the Persians:

> The bull is wreathed, he is perfect,
> he who shall slaughter him is here.[50]

And this soon turned out not to refer to the Persians but to Philip himself: [7] and when he died Olympias took his baby son, the child of Attalos's niece Kleopatra, and murdered the child and the mother together by dragging them on to a bronze oven filled with fire, and later she killed Aridaios. But the daemonic power was to make a terrible harvest of Kassander's family as well: the mother of Kassander's sons was

49. It was the autumn of 338 B.C.; Philip had won the battle of Chaironeia and was engaged in strong-arm diplomacy against Sparta. He must have crossed over the Skales pass. The ruins of Nestane are on a hill near the modern village of NESTANI (the old Tsipiana); the town-walls look like fourth-century masonry; Philip's spring was presumably a water-source he fitted up with marbles and probably inscribed. The spring was last reconstructed in 1840, and has an inscription built into it dated by the local priesthood of Poseidon. It is close to the entrance to the akropolis.

50. The punishment followed not the crime but the oracle very fast. The oracle was given in July 336 when Philip was marrying his daughter to Alexander of Epeiros and planning to invade Persia; he was assassinated during the wedding (Parke and Wormell, *The Delphic Oracle*, vol. 1, pp. 238f.). The same single line is quoted by Diodoros (16, 91); it is usually accepted as genuine and probably is so, but there is a suspicious reminiscence of the language of tragedy (Euripides, *Elektra*, 1142–4), and we know at least one other case of an oracle about Philip's death which seems to be no more than a popular legend. It is a story about a sword with a chariot on the hilt that Philip was killed with; Parke believes the sword was shown at Delphi, but evidently not so in Pausanias's time.

Philip's daughter Thessalonike, whose own mother like Aridaios's mother was Thessalian.[51] As for the story of Alexander and his death, everyone knows it. [8] If Philip had paid attention to Glaukos of Sparta and remembered that verse at each of his actions,

> *and the seed of a man who keeps his oath*
> *grows stronger after him,*

I do not believe that a god would so unreasonably have extinguished at a single stroke Alexander's life and with it the power of Macedonia.[52]

[1] That is all by way of parenthesis. Beyond the ruins of 8 Nestane is a sacred SANCTUARY OF DEMETER to whom the Mantineans hold a festival every year.[53] And just under Nestane lies ... a division of the Waste called Maira's dancing-ground. The road across the Waste is one and a quarter miles, and not far beyond it you come down to another plain where beside the high-road is the fountain called the LAMB-SPRING.[54] [2] There is an Arkadian legend that when Rea gave birth to Poseidon she left him in a sheepfold to live with the lambs, and that was how this spring got its name, because this is where the lambs were penned. And she told Kronos her baby was a horse, and gave him a foal to swallow

51. Olympias was Alexander's mother; Kleopatra was another of Philip's wives; it is not certain although probable that the disgusting story is untrue. Aridaios was Philip's son by a dancing-girl, Philinna of Larissa. For Kassander's family, cf. Bk IX, 7 (2f.), where the gory tale is told.

52. Glaukos of Sparta received a long oracle which Herodotos quotes as already legendary (6, 86). Oath has a child with no name and no hands and no feet, very fast to pursue and utterly to destroy the family of an oath-breaker.

53. Conjecturally identified by Conze and Michaelis in 1860 (*Annali dell' Istituto Archeologico*, Rome, 1861, p. 27), with the remains of a big building oriented east–west and not far from the hill of Nestane and exactly on what was in 1860 the existing road. These remains are believed to have disappeared by the end of the century.

54. There is no way of pinpointing the right spring, although travellers have offered their guesses. Maira had a grave at Tegea (Bk VIII, 48 (6)), and she may have been Atlas's daughter or she may have been a daughter of Proitos (Bk X, 30 (6)).

instead of her son, just as later on she gave him a stone wrapped in baby-clothes instead of Zeus. [3] When I began to write my history I thought these Greek stories were rather silly, but now that I have reached Arkadia I have decided to treat them from the point of view that the famous Greek wise men told their stories in riddles and not out of stupidity, and I conjectured that what was said of Kronos was a piece of Greek wisdom. So in religious matters this is the principle we shall follow. [4] The city of MANTINEIA is roughly a mile and a half from this spring: Lykaon's son Mantineus appears to have built his city elsewhere, and the Arkadians still call it the City to this day, but Aleus's granddaughter, Kepheus's daughter Antinoe took away the people by the command of an oracle, and brought them to this place, guided by a snake, though what kind of snake is not recorded. Because of this the river that flows past the modern city is called the Snake.[55] [5] If one can draw conclusions from Homeric poetry, I am sure this snake was a dragon: when Homer writes of Philoktetes in the list of ships that the Greeks deserted him in Lemnos suffering from the snake-bite, he does not give the water-serpent the title of snake, but he does call the dragon the eagle dropped on the Trojans a snake: and so the probabilities are that Antinoe was guided by a dragon.[56]

55. The ruins of Mantineia are a few miles north of TRIPOLITSA or TRIPOLIS. which was the Turkish capital and is now a big modern town. For what Pausanias calls the City, that is the old akropolis of Mantineia, cf. Bk VIII, 12 (4). It was north of the Hellenistic city, at the hill called GOURTSOULI, where substantial traces of a sanctuary and a settlement from late geometric to early classical times and of a Hellenistic reoccupation have been found (cf. Hope-Simpson, *Gazeteer and Atlas of Mycenean Sites*, site no. 87). The river is now called the PHEIDIAS; *phidi* means a snake. From the akropolis of Nestane you see it snaking this way and that through flat marshy ground that floods in winter.

56. Homer says Philoktetes was bitten by a *hydros* (*Iliad*, 2, 723), and an eagle dropped a crimson *drakon* on the Greek army (*Iliad*, 12, 202). The river was called the Ophis. It is impossible to catch these distinctions exactly in English, but Homer uses all three words for different kinds of real snake. The English 'dragon' is more than half-Chinese in its resonance, I suppose; Pausanias seems to feel a *drakon* is a huge snake with magical powers and perhaps wings.

[6] The Mantineans were not in the battle at Dipaia against Lakonia with the rest of the Arkadians, but in the Peloponnesian War they joined the Eleans in a revolt against Lakonia, and with an allied detachment from Athens they met and fought the Lakonians. Also as friends of Athens they took part in the Sicilian expedition. [7] Later on a Lakonian army invaded their country under King Agesipolis son of Pausanias. Agesipolis won the battle and shut the Mantineans inside their fortifications, and soon afterwards he captured the city; he took it without an assault where it was strong, by turning the river Snake against the walls which were built with clay-brick. [8] Bricks give more security than stone against engines of assault, as stone shatters and is dislodged from its joins: brick suffers less under artillery, but it melts in water like wax in the sun.[57] [9] Agesipolis was not the inventor of the device he used against Mantineia; Kimon son of Miltiades invented it when he was besieging Boges and his Persians in Eion on the Strymon.[58] Agesipolis was simply imitating a traditional, proverbial Greek invention. When he had taken Mantineia he left a little of it inhabited, but destroyed most of it to its foundations, and sent the people to live in villages. [10] The Thebans were to bring back the Mantineans from the villages into their native city after the battle of Leuktra. They did not behave with absolute integrity after this return: they were caught negotiating with Lakonia and arranging a private peace separately from the Arkadian community, and so for fear of Thebes they moved into an open Lakonian alliance, and at the battle of Mantineia between the Lakonians and Epaminondas of Thebes the

57. For Dipaia, cf. Bk III, 11 (7); it was fought in the mid fifth century. Arkadia was loosely organized, and Mantineia was particularly independent. Agesipolis broke down its walls by turning the river in 385 B.C. (Xenophon, *Hellenika*, 5, 2, 4–7). Until then the river flowed right through the city.

58. Kimon took Eion in the 470s; no one else says how he did it. Eion was on the Strymon on the coast north of Mount Athos, and presumably Kimon altered the course of the river.

Mantineans served on the Lakonian side.[59] [11] After this
Mantineia and Lakonia quarrelled, and the Mantineans joined
the Achaian League; they beat King Agis son of Eudamidas
of Sparta fighting over their own land: they won this victory
with the help of an Achaian army under the command of
Aratos.[60] They took part in the Achaian victory over Kleomenes and the destruction of the strength of Sparta.[61] When
Antigonos was regent in Macedonia for the boy Philip, that
is for Perseus's father, since Antigonos had most particular ties
with the Achaians, he was honoured in several ways by the
Mantineans, and they changed the name of their city to
Antigoneia.[62] [12] At a later time when Augustus was going
to fight his naval battle off the cape of Aktian Apollo,[63] the
Mantineans fought on the Roman side, though the other
Arkadians served with Antony, I think simply because the
Lakonians liked Augustus. Ten generations later, when
Hadrian became emperor, he took away the adventitious
Macedonian name from the Mantineans and gave the city
back its name of Mantineia.

9    [1] The Mantineans have a DOUBLE TEMPLE divided pretty
well at the middle with a wall. One part of the temple has a
statue of Asklepios by Alkamenes, and the other part is a
sanctuary of Leto and her children: the statues are by Praxiteles two generations after Alkamenes, with the Muses and
Marsyas piping carved on the pedestal. There is a man
engraved on a tablet here called Polybios son of Lykortas, [2]
whom we shall have to mention again later.[64] The Mantineans

59. The fortifications excavated by Fougères, traces of which survive, are
contemporary with the walls of Messene and were probably planned by the
same Theban architect. The circuit of the walls is oval. The battle was in
362; Epaminondas was killed.

    60. Cf. Bk VIII, 10 (5–10).        61. Bk III, 10 (7).

    62. What really happened is that once again Mantineia had turned pro-
Spartan, and Antigonos captured it for the Achaian League in 222 B.C.

    63. The battle of Actium in which Augustus broke Antony and Cleopatra
in 31 B.C. just north of LEVKAS.

    64. Alkamenes was a late-fifth-century sculptor, perhaps a pupil of Pheidias;
he may be the sculptor of the Karyatids of the Erechtheion. Praxiteles worked
in the mid fourth century; he carved the original of the famous Hermes at

have other SANCTUARIES of Zeus Saviour and of the Generous god as they call him, as he gives generously to human beings. There is also a sanctuary of the Dioskouroi and elsewhere a sanctuary of Demeter and the Maid, where they keep a fire burning and take great care never to let it out.[65] And I saw a TEMPLE OF HERA by the THEATRE, [3] with statues by Praxiteles of Hera enthroned with Athene and Hera's child Youth.[66] Beside Hera's altar is the grave of Kallisto's son Arkas: they brought his bones here from Mainalos because of a prophecy from Delphi:

[4]  *In stormy Mainalos Arkas lies:*
 *and all of them are called by his name*
 *where the three roads meet and the four and the five roads:*
 *I command you to go there and cheerfully*
 *bring Arkas home to the loved city,*
 *give him a holy place with sacrifices.*

They call this place where Arkas's grave is the ALTARS OF THE

---

Olympia. Polybios is the famous and great Hellenistic historian, a substantial part of whose work has survived. As a young man he carried home the ashes of Philopoimen, he was cavalry general of the Achaian League and was taken to Italy as a hostage after the débâcle, became a friend of Scipio, and saw Gaul, Spain and Africa. He died aged about eighty-two. Pausanias mentions him often. Not a proper portrait but a rather formal relief of Polybios as a cavalry soldier has survived (cf. *I.G.*, V 2, 370, and *Praktika* for 1920). The pedestal reliefs mentioned here were found by Fougères, face downwards, acting as flagstones in the ruins of a Byzantine church at the south of the city but some way inside the walls. There are three reliefs each with three figures; the main scene is Apollo and Marsyas with a Phrygian holding a knife, and the other two are said to be sets of muses, one of whom is playing an instrument like a lute. They are now in the National Museum at Athens.

65. Frazer copied down an inscription to Zeus of Counsel on the site of the agora ('market-square'), and Dioskouroi appear on Mantinean coins behind what looks like an altar. The Generous god is a Lakonian title of Zeus (Bk III, 17 (9)). There are two interesting Mantinean inscriptions about the cult of Demeter and the Maid, about the arrangements for the Mysteries and for a festival called the Maid-fetching at Mantineia (*I.G.*, V (2), 265–6).

66. The theatre has been excavated, and the temple of Hera identified close in front of it.

SUN.[67] [5] Not far from the theatre there are some famous monuments of the dead: the one called the PUBLIC HEARTH, which is circular, where they said Antinoe daughter of Kepheus was buried, and another with a stone tablet engraved with a man on horseback, Grylos son of Xenophon.[68] [6] Behind the theatre there was a statue left in the ruins of a TEMPLE OF APHRODITE of Alliance; the inscription on the base said it was dedicated by Nikippe the daughter of Paseas. The Mantineans built this sanctuary for a memorial to future ages of the sea-battle at Aktion where they served with the Romans.[69] They worship ALEAN ATHENE too, and they have a SANCTUARY and a statue of her.[70] [7] They have accepted ANTINOUS as a god: his shrine is the newest in Mantineia. The emperor Hadrian was extraordinarily enthusiastic about him: personally I never saw him in his lifetime, but I have seen him in statues and in paintings. He has formal honours elsewhere as well as at Mantineia, and there is a city in Egypt on the Nile named after Antinous. He received his honours at Mantineia in the following way: Antinous was born at Bithynion above the Sangarios river, and by ancestry the Bithynians are Arkadians

67. Can this oracle have something to do with the Mantinean attempt to unite Arkadia in the late 420s B.C.? It is impossible to date on internal evidence, and no one but Pausanias quotes it. 'Three Roads' is the place where Arkas's bones were (Bk VIII, 36 (8)). Pausanias does mention five roads out of Mantineia; two of them lead to Orchomenos, but there is also the road from Argos. The four roads may be the four that meet at Tegea.

68. Antinoe was the legendary foundress of the city; Grylos son of the historian Xenophon was killed with his brother in battle as a cavalry soldier near Mantineia (Bk VIII, 11 (5f.)). Before his death he was believed to have killed Epaminondas. The base of his statue at the entrance to the Athenian akropolis still exists. The glorious death of Grylos was a common theme of short poems and prose panegyrics.

69. This Nikippe must be the same Nikippa daughter of Pasias who was thanked and honoured in one of the two inscriptions about the cult of Demeter (cf. Note 65 above). The ruins behind the theatre have not been found; it is interesting that a temple put up after 31 B.C. (cf. Note 63) should have fallen down inside 150 years and not been repaired.

70. Fougères found an archaic inscription (I.G., V (2), 262) in a church near the market-place, apparently dealing with the settlement by fines of a massacre of men, women and children in this sanctuary.

and in fact Mantineans. [8] So the king instituted a cult to him
in Mantineia as well, with a sacrifice to him every year, and
games in his honour every four years.[71] There is a house in
the Mantinean TRAINING-GROUND with statues of Antinous,
worth seeing for the stone of its decoration and for its paintings, most of which present Antinous as Dionysos, even apart
from the statues. There is also a copy here of the Kerameikos
painting of the Athenian victory at Mantineia.[72] [9] In the
Mantinean MARKET-PLACE there is a bronze portrait of a
woman whom the Arkadians call Diomeneia daughter of
Arkas, and a divine HERO'S SHRINE to Podares, who they say
died in the battle against Epaminondas of Thebes. Three
generations before my time they changed the inscription on
the grave to refer it to a descendant of Podares who shared his
ancestor's name, born in a period when he could hold Roman
citizenship; [10] but in my day the Mantineans still worshipped
the ancient Podares: they said the best men of all the Mantineans and allies in that battle was Xenophon's son Grylos, and
after him Kephisodoros of Marathon, who commanded the
Athenian cavalry, and the third bravest and best man was
Podares.[73]

[1] From Mantineia there are roads into the rest of Arkadia,   10
and I shall go through the most interesting things on each of

71. No civilized city and no great international sanctuary seems to have been
without its statue of Antinous; an enormous number of them have survived,
and they convey strongly the sense of a particular kind of ripe or overripe male
bodily charm. Antinous died mysteriously: he probably drowned himself in
the Nile: Hadrian founded Antinoupolis to mark the spot. His head is on the
coins of Mantineia sometimes as Antinous Pan. There were regular games in
his honour at a number of cities. The votive inscription of a colonnade dedicated
to him has been found at Mantineia. The city of Bithynion was in inner
Bithynia; it has not been found, and nothing else is known about its connexion
with Arkadia, whether real or (more likely) mythical.

72. For the Kerameikos painting at Athens, cf. Bk I, 3 (4). The *gymnasion*
(training-ground) of Mantineia has never been found.

73. For the battle, cf. Bk VIII, 11 (5f.); what was probably the shrine of
Podares survived for some time as a church, and the French excavators of the
1880s found the remains of it, in front of the north half of the theatre. The
name Podares was stamped on its tiles. Grylos and Kephisodoros commanded
the cavalry.

them. On the way to Tegea on the left of the highway beside
the walls of Mantineia there is a place for racing horses and
no distance from it a STADIUM where they hold the games for
Antinous. The mountain above the stadium is Alesion, which
they say is named after the wanderings of Rea; there is a
sacred wood of Demeter on this mountain.[74] [2] By the very
edges of the mountain is the SANCTUARY OF HORSE POSEI-
DON, which is not far from the Mantinean stadium.[75] I am
writing the story of this sanctuary by hearsay and out of other
people's books. It was built in our time by Hadrian, who put
inspectors over the workmen to see that no one looked inside the ancient sanctuary or shifted a stone of its ruins: he
ordered them to build the new temple all round it. They say
this sanctuary of Poseidon was originally built by Trophonios
and Agamedes by working and joining logs of oak, and they
kept people out without building any barrier round the entrance, [3] just by stretching a woollen thread across it, perhaps
in the belief that since the people of those days respected
religion, a thread would be enough to frighten them away, or
perhaps there may have been some kind of strength in the
thread. But Aipytos son of Hippothous appears to have not
jumped over the thread or ducked under it but just cut it and
entered the sanctuary: he was blinded for the sacrilege by the
waves breaking over his eyes and he suddenly dropped dead.[76]

74. Alesion (*aletes* is a wanderer) is the mountain now called BARBERI or
ALOGOBRACHOS, which protects the site of Mantineia from the north-east
and the east. Tegea is south of Tripolis near Lake TAKA, so Pausanias is moving
south past the southern tail of Alesion.

75. Polybios (11, 8, 11) says it was on flat ground about a mile from Mantineia,
and Fougères found it at KALYBIA TIS MILEAS. He reported odd bits and
pieces of marble, two flagstones which at that time were still in place, a relief
carving of Poseidon, and an inscription recording an enfranchisement dated by
a priest of Poseidon. These pieces have been dispersed, and I think the site is
now built over, as the village of MILEA has spread. Poseidon was the patron of
Mantineia; its shield emblem was a trident and dating by the priests of Poseidon
became conventional.

76. Aipytos is a legendary king who was killed by a snake (cf. Bk VIII, 16
(2), and Note 25). Trophonios and Agamedes were more than half-divine
builders who were supposed to have built the Delphic sanctuary and other
great buildings (Bk IX, 3, 7, 5, and Bk X, 5 (13)).

[4] There is an ancient story that the waves of the sea appear in this sanctuary like the Athenian story about the waves on the akropolis and the story the Karians of Mylasa tell about the sanctuary of the god whose name in the local language is Osogoas. At Athens the sea at Phaleron is two and a half miles from the city, just as the port of Mylasa is ten miles from the city, but at Mantineia the sea rises at the farthest distance inland and most manifestly by the god's will.[77]

[5] Beyond Poseidon's sanctuary is a stone TROPHY of victory over the Lakonians under Agis, and the details of the battle are recorded. The Mantineans had the right wing, with an army of every age and Podares in command, the grandson of the Podares who fought against Thebes; there was a prophet with them from Elis, Thrasyboulos son of Aineias of the Iamidai, who predicted the Mantinean victory and took part in the action himself.[78] [6] All the other Arkadian forces were on the left, under their city commanders, with the Great City contingent under Lydiades and Leokydes; Aratos with the Sikyonians and Achaians took the centre. The Lakonians under Agis extended their close formation to meet the whole enemy forces, with King Agis and his company in the centre. [7] By agreement with the Arkadians, Aratos and his force

77. Was it a brackish spring? For the story of the sea in the Erechtheion at Athens, cf. Bk I, 26 (5). I have somewhere a note of an inland tidal well in Yorkshire, but I do not know what causes the phenomenon. The port for Mylasa Pausanias is talking about was Physkos. Mylasa was the principle city in Karia. It was rich and was notoriously crammed with temples. The ruins were visited by nearly all the classic English travellers between 1750 and 1850. They have deteriorated since the days of the Dilettanti, but there is still an extensive site near MILAS, some way inland due east of Patmos. We know from inscriptions and from Strabo that the god's full title was Zeus Osogos; it is interesting that Pausanias does not call him Zeus, perhaps because of the sea-water miracle. The head of Zeus from Mylasa in the Boston Museum which used to be thought of as Zeus Osogos is more likely to be Zeus Labraundos, as it seems to have been wearing a sort of miniature bronze top-hat (*polos*) which belongs to that god. The salt spring must have been well known; it is mentioned by Theophrastos and Pliny. It has not been found.

78. He was a prophet, and he came from a family of prophets (cf. Bk VI, 2 (5), etc.). For the date of the battle, cf. Note 79 below.

fell back as if the Lakonians were pressing them, and as he retreated the line quietly re-formed into a crescent. Agis and the Lakonians smelt victory, and they pressed more and more massively into Aratos's company, with the men from their two wings closing in beside them thinking it was a wonderful fighting success to make Aratos and his army withdraw: [8] the Arkadians got behind their backs unnoticed, they were surrounded and lost most of their army, and King Agis son of Eudamidas fell.[79]  The Mantineans said that Poseidon had appeared and fought for them, and that was why they built a trophy consecrated to Poseidon. [9] Those who have composed the tragic histories of the heroes at Troy have written that the gods were present at war and the murdering of men, and it is proverbial at Athens that gods fought on the Athenian side at Marathon and at Salamis; and the most obvious case of all is when the Gaulish army was destroyed by the god at Delphi: openly, visibly destroyed by daemonic powers.[80] So the Mantineans can claim that Poseidon had a hand in this victory. [10] The Arkadians say that Leokydes who commanded the Great City contingent with Lydiades was the ancestor in the eighth generation of Arkesilaos who lived at Lykosoura, and that Arkesilaos saw the Mistress's holy deer in a state of extreme age: the deer had a collar round her neck with writing on it:

> Caught as a fawn when Agapenor was at Troy.

That story shows a deer is a much longer-lived beast even than an elephant.[81]

79. This whole battle is not mentioned by anyone else, and Plutarch (*Agis*, 19f.) says that this Agis was killed at Sparta after a revolution. If the battle really happened it was in the 240s B.C. It is possible that Agis was simply wounded.

80. Cf. Bk X, 23 (2).

81. Arkesilaos seems to have lived a little after Augustus. Agapenor was the Arkadian commander at Troy (Bk VIII, 5 (2)). A deer lives twenty years and an elephant can live a hundred, but it was widely believed in antiquity that deer lived the longest of all animals. This has certainly something to do with their being sacred to Artemis; the belief may date from a time when the deer of the

[1] Beyond Poseidon's sanctuary you will find yourself in 11 an area full of oak-trees, which they call the Sea, and the road from Mantineia to Tegea passes among the oaks. The boundary of Mantineia and Tegea is the CIRCULAR ALTAR on the highway. But if you decided to turn off to the left from Poseidon's sanctuary you would go for about half a mile and come on the graves of Pelias's daughters. The Mantineans say they migrated here to get away from the disgrace of their father's death. [2] When Medea arrived at Iolkos she started to plot against Pelias at once in actual cooperation with Jason, although he pretended to be horrified. Pelias's daughters were told that if they wanted to they could turn their ageing father into a young man. She slaughtered a ram and boiled up the meat with magic drugs in a basin, and through these magic drugs she brought the boiled ram out of the pot again alive as a young lamb. [3] Then she took Pelias and cut him up for boiling, and his daughters did not even give him a decent burial. This business forced the women to migrate to Arkadia, and when they died their monuments were dug in this place. No poet has given them names so far as my reading goes, but Mikon the painter wrote on their portraits that they were Asteropeia and Antinoe.[82]

[4] About two and a half miles farther on from these graves there is a place called PHOIZON: Phoizon is a monument not very high out of the ground, surrounded by a stone platform. The road is extremely narrow here, and the

---

great European forests, or even earlier the reindeer of the European tundra, were more important to human beings than any other animal, and may be connected with their reappearance after winter migration. In northwestern Europe mysterious beliefs about deer survived into the Middle Ages. Cf. Aristotle, *De Mirabilibus*, 110.

82. This may have been in his painting of the Argonauts in the Anakeion at Athens; it is possible (although a most hazardous conjecture) that his treatment of the scene may be reflected in the conventions of certain Attic red-figure *stamnoi*. The two names sound more like local divine heroines than epic persons, so far as any such distinction exists.

monument is called the grave of Areithous, surnamed the Clubman because of his weapon.[83] [5] About four miles along the road to Pallantion from Mantineia the oak-wood called the Sea stretches right to the highway, and this is where the Athenian and Mantineian cavalry battle was fought against the Boiotian horse.[84] The Mantineans say Epaminondas was killed by a Mantinean called Machairion; the Lakonians say it was a Spartan who killed him, and they give him the same name, Machairion. [6] But the Athenian story, which the Thebans confirm, is that Epaminondas was wounded by Grylos: and the painting of the battle at Mantineia shows the same. The Mantineans appear to have given Grylos a public burial and dedicated his portrait in relief at the spot where he fell, as the best and bravest of the allies: and although they and the Lakonians talk about Machairion, there is not really any Machairion at Sparta, or at Mantineia either, whom they honour as a true and good man. [7] When Epaminondas was wounded, they carried him out of the battle alive; he kept his hand on his wound, suffering and watching the fighting – the place he looked from was later named the Look-out – and then when the fighting ended evenly he took away his hand from his wound; he breathed his last and they buried him on the battle-field itself. [8] A pillar stood over his grave with a shield on it engraved with a serpent. The serpent means that Epaminondas belonged to the clan of the dragon's teeth. There are stone tablets at this monument, one of them ancient with a Boiotian inscription, the other dedicated by the emperor Hadrian, who composed the inscription on it

83. Areithous comes into the *Iliad* (7, 8f. and 137f.). He was killed by Lykourgos of Arkadia (Bk VIII, 4 (10)). Attempts to identify Phoizon have been unconvincing.

84. The road to Tegea and to Pallantion would not be the same; Pallantion is several miles west-south-west of Tegea. The two roads south would at this point have had a river between them. The battle (Xenophon, *Hellenika*, 7, 5, 14f.) was in 362. There is a simple geographic reason why there were so many battles south of Mantineia. The huge plain of Eastern Arkadia is like a figure of eight hemmed in by mountains, with Mantineia in the upper loop and Tegea in the lower. (Modern Tripolis is in the centre.)

himself.[85] [9] Among all the famous Greek commanders one might well give the highest praise to Epaminondas, or at any rate rank him as equal to the highest. The Lakonian and Athenian commanders could rely on the ancient importance of their cities and fairly confident soldiers, but Epaminondas found the Thebans dispirited and accustomed to taking second place, yet in a short time he made them supreme.

[10] Epaminondas had once been given an oracle from Delphi warning him to beware of the sea, and he was terrified to go on board a warship or even travel in a merchant ship, yet it was not the ocean, it was the oak-wood called the Sea that the daemonic spirit had foretold. Two places with the same name had tricked the Athenians in the past and tricked Hannibal of Carthage later. [11] Hannibal received a prophecy from Ammon that when he died the Libyssan earth would cover him, so he hoped to destroy the Roman empire and then go home to Libya to die of old age: but when Flaminius the Roman was anxious to capture him alive, he came to ask for mercy from Prousias and when Prousias refused to have him he leapt on to his horse and cut his fingers with his naked sword. Not many miles on he took a fever from the wound and on the third day he died: and the Nikomedeans call the place where he died Libyssa. [12] The Athenians received an oracle from Dodona telling them to colonize Sicily, which in fact is a little hill not far from the city, but without considering what was meant they felt encouraged to overseas campaigning and the war with Syracuse. And you could find plenty of examples like these.[86]

85. The Look-out must surely have been the shoulder of the hill MYTIKA where there was a fourth-century watch tower. The clan of the dragon's teeth was the military aristocracy, supposed to be descended from the first Theban fighters magically seeded in the earth from the teeth of a dead dragon (Bk XI, 5 (3)). Hadrian's poem for this memoria has not survived, though several other of his poems have done, including a dedicatory epigram for a monument at Troy.

86. For example, that Philip should beware of chariots, and there was a chariot on the hilt of the sword that killed him; the Messenians (in Bk IV) were warned in just such deliberately ambiguous terms. Hannibal really was

12    [1] Two hundred yards or so from Epaminondas's grave
stands a SANCTUARY OF ZEUS of Joy. The Arkadians have
different kinds of oaks in their oak forest, some of which they call
broad-leaved oak and some true oak. The third kind has a
spongy bark which is so light they make sea-markers out of it
for anchors and nets. Some of the Ionians, including the
elegiac poet Hermesianax, call it the cork-oak.[87]

[2] There is a road from Mantineia to METHYDRION, which
is no longer a city but a village that belongs to the Great City
league.[88] After four miles you come to a plain called Alkimedon, and above this plain is Mount Ostrakina which has a
cave on it where Alkimedon lived; he was one of the heroes,
as they were called. [3] The Phigaleans say Herakles lay with
Alkimedon's daughter Phialo, and when Alkimedon noticed
she was pregnant he threw her out to die on the mountain
with the boy she gave birth to, whom the Arkadians call
Aichmagoras. As the child lay crying the jay heard it scream
and imitated the wails; [4] Herakles happened to be coming

buried at Libyssa, and Plutarch and Appian both tell the same story of the
oracle. Libyssa was a town in Bithynia; there was nothing left of it but Hannibal's grave by the time of Pliny. Prousias was king from about 228 to about
180. Hannibal is usually said to have died by suicide under the threat of extradi-
tion. Sicily at Athens seems to be one of the small hills above SYNGROU street
on the way to the Piraeus. There is epigraphic evidence for its existence, as well
as mentions in Suidas, Dio Chrysostom, and a topographic papyrus. I suppose
these are none of them real oracles, but popular stories.

87. The sanctuary has not been found. Cork-oaks are still used for making
bottle-corks. I suppose the *Phegos* oak is the Valonia oak, which produces more
or less edible acorns, and still grows in open forests in the eastern Mediterranean
and in Italy. The broad-leaved oak is probably the ilex. For a modern summary
list of Greek oaks, cf. Polunin and Huxley, *Flowers of the Mediterranean* (1965),
p. 55, but this invaluable handbook does not list all existing still less all past
species. There is a crying need for a glossary of ancient trees and flowers like
D'Arcy Thompson's glossaries of ancient fish and birds.

88. This road goes west from Mantineia into the mountains of central
Arkadia. I have translated *he megale polis* as Great City, although it is generally
called MEGALOPOLIS, which is also its modern Greek name. It was founded
only in 370, and by Strabo's time (the age of Augustus) it was mostly ruins.
For Methydrion, cf. Bk VIII, 36 (1-3).

along the road and heard the jay, and thinking it was a child crying and not a bird, he turned off at once and followed the voice. He recognized the girl, untied her and rescued the boy. Ever since then the water-spring near by has been called the JAY'S SPRING after the bird. Ten miles from the spring is a place called PETROSAKA which is the boundary of the Great City and Mantineia.[89]

[5] As well as these roads there are two others to Orchomenos, on one of which is LADAS'S STADIUM in which Ladas trained as a runner;[90] there is a SANCTUARY OF ARTEMIS beside it and a tall tumulus on the right of the road which they say is Penelope's grave, though [6] the poem called the *Thesprotis* tells a different story about her. In the poem Penelope bears Odysseus a child (Ptoliporthes) after he comes home from Troy, but the Mantinean legend about her says that Odysseus condemned Penelope for bringing plunderers into his house, and sent her away; she went to Sparta first and then later on moved from there to Mantineia where she finished her life.[91]

89. The plain is evidently the valley near KARDARA, and the mountain is presumably the great northern dome of Mainalos (modern MAINALON) that rears above it. I am not sure where the Jay's spring is, but it may have been near the cave, which sounds like a cult-place. I have seen jays in Arkadia, and Sibthorp, the first important naturalist to travel in Greece (in 1795), 'frequently heard the hoarse screams of the Jay' in the Arkadian oak-forests. Petrosaka must have been a fortress in wild country on the pass west of ALONISTAINA; it has never been found, but Fougères argues effectively about it (*Mantinée*, pp. 115–17).

90. Orchomenos lay north-west of Mantineia; there is still a choice of an A road and a B road. Ladas was buried near SPARTA (Bk III, 21 (1)), and he had a statue in Apollo's temple at Argos (Bk II, 19 (7)). There was another Ladas from Aigion at Achaia who won in 278 (Bk X, 23 (9)). Neither of them seems to have had a statue at Olympia itself. We know Pausanias checked the Achaian Ladas in the Olympic records, but is there not something peculiar about Ladas the Lakonian?

91. This tumulus has ceased to exist, and the sanctuary of Artemis has not been found. The Thesprotis is never mentioned except here, but Homeric Thesprotia seems to have stretched far enough south to be closely related to the Ithaca (ITHAKI) of Odysseus. It is odd at first sight that Odysseus and Penelope should be local figures in Arkadia so far from the sea; perhaps it was here Odysseus was to make his last journey, in a country where they mistook an

[7] The grave looks on to a smallish plain, and in the plain is a mountain with the ruins of the ancient Mantineia: and that area is still called the CITY today.[92] Not far along the road north from here is Alalkomeneia's spring, and four miles from the City there are the ruins of a village called MAIRA, with Maira's grave, if in fact she was buried here and not on Tegean ground, since probability favours the Tegean story and not the Mantinean: I mean the story that Atlas's daughter Maira was buried among them. But perhaps Atlas's daughter Maira had a descendant also called Maira who came to the Mantinean country.[93]

[8] There is another road left that goes to Orchomenos by Mount Anchisia with the monument of Anchises at the foot of the mountain. When Aineias was travelling to Sicily, his ships put in on the Lakonian coast and he founded the cities of Aphrodisias and Etis, and his father Anchises was here for some reason when his death overtook him, so Aineias buried him here, and the mountain is named Anchisia after Anchises. [9] The Aiolians who occupy Troy in our own time confirm this, because they have no tomb of Anchises to show you in their territory. By Anchises' grave stand the ruins of a SANCTUARY OF APHRODITE, and the Mantinean border with Orchomenos runs across Anchisia.[94]

---

oar for a winnowing-fan (*Odyssey*, 23, 264f.). There is a fascinating though by no means convincing study of *Ulysse chez les Arcadiens* by the numismatist J. N. Svoronos (Paris and Athens, 1889) which stirs up essential questions about this problem and accumulates some most useful material.

92. Cf. Bk III, Note 55; the hill called GOURTSOULI.

93. The spring is the big spring called KARYDA below KAKOURI (now renamed ARTEMISION). The French surveyors in the early nineteenth century travelled along this road in a carriage; they claim to have observed substantial ruins which certainly sound like Maira not far from the spring, *sur un petit mamelon qui traverse la route*. Fougères failed to find any such vestiges, but Mr Roger Howell has now convincingly identified Maira at the southern tip of a rocky spur west of Kakouri, but east of what used to be called KHANI BILAI.

94. The second Orchomenos road would be through LEBIDION, and the mountain must be the small one just south of the village. The grave of Anchises and the sanctuary were perhaps at KHANI BILAI at the foot of the hill. There is another unidentified and unexcavated sanctuary at the ANALEPSIS chapel on

[1] In the territory of Orchomenos on the left of the road 13 from Anchisia there is a SANCTUARY OF SINGING ARTEMIS on the mountainside, which Mantineia and Orchomenos share . . .[95] a priestess as well as a priest, who tradition dictates must preserve a perfect purity, not only sexual purity, all their lives long: they bathe and live their whole lives differently from other people, and they never enter a private house. I know of a similar thing that lasts a year and no more, in the case of the Ephesians who serve as guest-masters to Ephesian Artemis: the Ephesians call them the King bees.[96] There is an annual festival of Singing Artemis.

[2] The old city of ORCHOMENOS was on the topmost crest of a mountain, and the ruins of the walls and the market-place are still there. The modern city is below the circuit of the ancient fortifications.[97] There is an interesting spring they take

---

top of the hill, completely buried. For Aphrodisias and Etis, cf. Bk III, 22 (11). They were near Cape Malea; Etis was named after his daughter; there must have been a story about a storm. But how did Anchises, father of the Trojan founder of Rome, come to wander up here to die? This Aineias was not a Homeric Trojan, still less a Vergilian Roman, but an Arkadian shepherd whom Aphrodite loved, just as there was an Arkadian Endymion. Is Pausanias in these sentences betraying an implicit consciousness of Vergil's *Aeneid*?

95. Probably near LEBIDION; Leake saw pieces of some handsome Doric columns in a church below this village. The old opinion that Lebidion was Xenophon's Elymia (*Hellenika*, 6, 5, 13) is unacceptable, because Elymia was probably not a town but a territory. The identification of the chapel of the Virgin above the village to the east as the site of Artemis's temple is also dubious because unsupported and unconfirmed. For the cult, cf. Bk VIII, Note 39. At least one Orchomenos inscription has been found at Lebidion (*I.G.*, V (2), 344).

96. The Greeks thought queen bees were males; the word is *essen*. Various kinds of priestesses were called bumble-bees. Frazer was very interested in this question and has compiled a list of bee-priesthoods at this point in his commentary.

97. Orchomenos was a fortified town on a low isolated hill close to TRACHYS, Rough Mountain; the site is a little west of due north of TRIPOLIS, and a little east of due north of LEBIDION; the village of KALPAKI among the scattered ruins of the lower town has been renamed Orchomenos. Of all the remote and idyllic antiquities which characterize Arkadia so strongly, the ruins of Orchomenos were at one time among the most striking; there was a church 'entirely

their water from, and there are stone TEMPLES and statues of Poseidon and Aphrodite. Near the city is a wooden idol of Artemis, standing in a giant cedar; they call the goddess Cedar Artemis after the tree. [3] Below the city there are some separate CAIRNS of stones heaped together for the war dead. There are no inscriptions on the graves to say what Peloponnesian people the war was fought against, or whether it was against other Arkadians, and the Orchomenians have no records about it.

[4] Opposite the city is Rough Mountain.[98] The water from heaven runs in the bed of a gully between the city and Rough Mountain, and down to the plain of Orchomenos which is huge but mostly under water. Not quite half a mile from Orchomenos, the straight road to the city of KAPHYA takes you right past the gully, and then on the left past the lake water. The other road crosses the gully stream and passes below Rough Mountain.[99] [5] On this second road you come first of all to the monument of Aristokrates, who once raped the virgin priestess of Singing Artemis, and beyond his grave are the Teneian springs and then a mile or so from the springs is a place called AMILOS, which they say was once a city. At this place the road forks, with one road leading to Stymphelos and the other to Pheneos.[100] [6] On the Pheneos road you find

---

composed of the remains of a Doric temple', and the cottage that Dodwell lived in 'stood upon the remains of a Doric temple of white marble, some large masses of which are scattered about in the vicinity'; he excavated the capitals of some of its columns, but soon moved on because he hated the cottage 'where the snow and rain drifted through the fissures of the roof' (*Tour through Greece*, 1819, vol. 2, pp. 424–8). There was a German survey of the site in the 1900s and a French excavation in 1913 (*B.C.H.*, 38. 1914, pp. 71f. and 447f.).

98. Trachys means 'Rough Mountain'.

99. The water runs north into a plain where there are still marshes. Kaphya lay north-west of Orchomenos, and the first road went that way. The other road skirted Rough Mountain to the north-east. The best map of all this is in *Arkadische Forschungen* (1911) by Hiller von Gärtringen and Lattermann. There was no road going directly north because of the marshes.

100. For Aristokrates, cf. Bk VIII, 5 (11f.). There is a spring with some traces of antiquities a mile or two north-east of Orchomenos. The two roads

yourself on a mountain, and on this mountain the frontiers of Orchomenos, Pheneos and Kaphya meet. There is a high crag rearing above the boundaries which they call the Kaphyan rock. Beyond the boundaries of these cities lies a ravine with the Pheneos road running through it. Roughly midway along this ravine is a spring of water, and at the end of the ravine comes KARYAI.[101]

[1] The Phenean plain lies below Karyai, and they say it once flooded and the ancient Pheneos was drowned, so that even today there are signs left on the mountains where they say the water rose to. Mount Oryxis and Mount Skiathis are about half a mile from Karyai, and below each of these mountains is a pothole that takes the water from the plain.[102] [2] The Pheneans say these potholes are artificial, that Herakles made them when he lived at Pheneos with Amphitryon's mother Laonome: they say Amphitryon was the son of Alkaios by Laonome, who was Gouneos's daughter and a Phenean woman, not his son by Lysidike daughter of Pelops. If Herakles really came to live with the Pheneans, one may reasonably

are routes 61 and 94 of the old Admiralty *Handbook* (cf. Bk VIII, Note 42). Stymphelos (now Stymphalia) lies north-east, and Pheneos (now a dryish marsh) to the north. The roads cannot have forked much nearer to Orchomenos than the monastery of KANDELA, since the Pheneos road would have kept to the edges of the Orchomenos plain. To reach Pheneos from Orchomenos you started by travelling north-east instead of north, going out of your way along the Stymphelos road to avoid the marshes. Amilos has not been securely identified.

101. The mountain is probably KREKOZI, east of the mountain track northwards to GUIOZA, which has now been renamed MATION. The spring is just above this village, and north of this point the Pheneos plain opens out. In the nineteenth century it became for some years a spectacular greenish-blue lake; its underground outlets seem to have become blocked during the 1820s, but by the 1890s the water-level was falling and it is now almost dry in summer. Karyai has not been found.

102. The potholes are one near MATION (GUIOZA) which takes the water from the south and probably discharges into the Stymphalian lake, and a much more important one in the south-west corner of the plain taking the rivers from the north and north-west, which reappears to the south-west as the source of the Ladon which runs into the Alpheios. Perhaps one of the two mountains is SAITAS on the west, the other MAVROVOUNI on the east.

believe that when Eurystheus expelled him from Tiryns he went to Pheneos first instead of straight to Thebes. [3] In the middle of the Phenean plain Herakles dug a CHANNEL for the river Olbios to run in; some of the Arkadians call it Aroanios and not Olbios. The length of this excavation is about six miles, and the depth where it has not fallen in is thirty feet. But the river has gone back to its old bed and no longer runs in it: it has deserted Herakles' channel.[103]

[4] The city is six miles or so from the potholes in the mountains that I mentioned, and the Pheneans say its founder was an aboriginal native called Phenos. Their AKROPOLIS is precipitous on all its sides, and mostly left natural, but a few parts have been strengthened for safety's sake. In the akropolis there is a shrine of Tritonian Athene, though nothing is left of it but ruins.[104] [5] A bronze Poseidon with the title of Horse Poseidon stands up there which they say Odysseus dedicated, because he lost his horses and wandered around Greece to find them and founded a sanctuary of Artemis naming her Horse-finder at the place in the Phenean territory where he found his mares, and dedicated a statue of Horse Poseidon as well. [6] And they say when Odysseus found his mares he decided to keep a herd of mares on the Phenean territory in the same way as he raised heifers on the mainland opposite Ithaka; and the Pheneans showed me an inscription on the statue-base, which was apparently Odysseus's orders to the herdsmen of his mares.[105] [7] With this exception we shall

103. The Aroanios seems to be the PHONIATIKO (now renamed OLBIOS) to the north of the swampy area (cf. Bk VIII, 15 (6)). Herakles' channel used to be identified with a dyke which could be clearly traced in the early nineteenth century. There is an excellent drawing of it by Sir William Gell in his *Journey in the Morea* (1823, p. 380); it was at that time used as a causeway. The remains of it are now the line of a road; it shows up well on photographs taken from the air.

104. The site of Pheneos is a hill near PHONIA (now renamed PHENEOS). The hill is called PYRGOS because of a ruined medieval tower on top of it. There are traces of the walls and a temple of Asklepios has been excavated.

105. This was not the only sanctuary Odysseus founded in Arkadia (cf. Bk VIII, 44 (4)). The heifers he kept on the mainland are Homeric; Eumaios the swineherd gives an inventory of them (*Odyssey*, 14, 100–8). There were no herds

have probability on our side in accepting the Phenean story, but I cannot be persuaded that Odysseus dedicated a bronze statue: in those days they did not know how to make statues in complete bronze like seamless cloth. I have already explained their technique of bronze workmanship on the subject of the statue of Supreme Zeus in my Spartan treatise.[106] [8] The first smelters of bronze and casters of statues were the two Samians Roikos son of Philaios and Theodoros son of Telekles. The engraved emerald seal that Polykrates the dictator of Samos wore so much and took such extreme pleasure in was by Theodoros.[107]

[9] On the way down from the Phenean citadel you come to a STADIUM, and to the monument of Iphikles, who was Herakles' brother and Iolaos's father, which is on a hill. The Greeks say Iolaos shared most of Herakles' toils: but when Herakles was fighting his first battle against Augeas and the Eleans, Iolaos's father Iphikles was wounded by the sons of Aktor, who were named after their mother Moline.[108] His close friends brought him in a fainting state to Pheneos, where a Phenean called Bouphagos and his wife Promne showed him true hospitality and buried him when he died of his wound. [10] To this day they sacrifice to Iphikles as a divine hero, but the god the Pheneans worship most is Hermes: they hold Hermaian games, and have a stone statue and TEMPLE

in Homeric Ithaka itself except of goats and pigs. The herds and herdsmen probably did range very widely. There are still semi-nomadic herdsmen in several parts of Greece, but their movements are more and more restricted (cf. John Campbell, *Honour, Family and Patronage*, 1964). The connexion of Odysseus with horses, lost horses and herds of horses probably has to do with Poseidon.

106. Cf. Bk III, 17 (6).

107. Theodoros was a legendary artist even in the time of Herodotos (3, 41 and 60) from whom Pausanias takes the story of Polykrates' ring and the name of its maker; Polykrates threw his beloved ring into the sea to propitiate divine envy, but a fish brought it back and he ended unhappily. In Pliny's time you were shown Polykrates' ring in the temple of Concord at Rome; it was a green stone set in gold. For the artists cf. Bk X, 38 (6).

108. Cf. Bk V, 2 (1).

OF HERMES; the statue is by an Athenian called Eucheir son of Euboulides.[109] Behind this temple is Myrtilos's grave. The Greek legend is that Myrtilos was Hermes' son, and Oinomaos's driver, and whenever anyone arrived to woo Oinomaos's daughter, Myrtilos drove Oinomaos's mares skilfully, and as they raced Oinomaos speared the wooer when he came close. [11] Myrtilos was in love with Hippodameia himself; however, he was poor-spirited and agreed to the games and drove for Oinomaos. In the end they say it was Myrtilos who betrayed Oinomaos, because Pelops swore to let him lie with Hippodameia for one night, but when Myrtilos reminded Pelops of his oath, Pelops threw him out of the ship, and the Pheneans say they recovered his dead body cast up by the waves and buried him: and every year at night they consume his sacrifice with fire. [12] It is clear that Pelops did not go far by sea but just from the Alpheios estuary to the port of Elis, so the Myrtoan sea, which begins from Euboia and stretches to the Aegean past the desert island of Helene, would appear not to be named after Myrtilos son of Hermes; writers on the ancient history of Euboia seem to me to offer a not unlikely solution when they say the Myrtoan sea got its name from a woman called Myrto.[110]

15   [1] The Pheneans have a SANCTUARY OF ELEUSINIAN DEMETER, and hold a mystery of the goddess, claiming the Eleusinian rites are also established here: Naos grandson of Eumolpos came among them by command of the Delphic oracle.[111] By the sanctuary of the Eleusinian goddess is a con-

109. There was a Hellenistic Athenian family of sculptors who used these two names in alternate generations.

110. The race between Pelops and Oinomaos, in which Oinomaos was killed, was commemorated on the east pediment of the temple of Zeus at Olympia (cf. Bk V, 10 (6), and Bk VI, 20 (17)). The desert island of Helene (Helen's Island) is MAKRONISI; the concentration camp of the Karamanlis regime in Greece was on this island, and the screaming of prisoners could be heard on still nights at Sounion.

111. The persons are legendary. The place has not been found. There is no reason to believe that the legendary priority of the Eleusinian mysteries represents a real priority: many details of the cults of Demeter in Arkadia were independent of Eleusis until the end.

struction called the Rock consisting of two enormous stones
fitted together. [2] Once a year when they hold what they call
the greater mystery they open these stones, and take certain
writing from them which has to do with the mystery, read it
out to the initiated and then put it away the same night. I do
know that most Pheneans swear by the Rock about the most
important things. [3] It has a circular top with the mask of
Kidarian Demeter inside it which the priest puts on at the
greater mystery, and for some reason he beats the underworld
gods with rods.[112] There is a Phenean story that before Naos
Demeter came there in her wanderings, and the Pheneans who
took her into their houses and gave her gifts of hospitality
received lentils and so on from the goddess, but she gave none
of them the bean. [4] There is a sacred legend about the bean
and why they believe it to be impure. Those who entertained
the goddess in the Phenean story were Trisaules and Dami-
thales, who built a temple of Demeter of Right below Mount
Kyllene and established a mystery there which is still celebrated today. The temple of Demeter of Right is roughly two
miles away from the city.[113]

[5] On the way from Pheneos to Pellene and Aigeira in
Achaia after about two miles you reach a TEMPLE OF PYTHIAN
APOLLO: nothing is left of it but ruins and a big white stone
altar, where they still sacrifice now to Phenean Apollo and to

---

112. Kidaris means a special head-dress or, more appropriately here, a
special dance. We know from Theokritos (7, 107–8) that statues of Pan were
sometimes beaten in Arkadia, but with squills not rods. The beating was for
making fertile, like the ritual beatings at Sparta, and like the touching or
beating with boughs of particular trees on a given day which is still in the
children's folklore of a few English villages. Beating walnut-trees and shooting
shotguns into cider-apple-trees is a different matter, but some early agricultural
process is probably at the root of the superstition.

113. Kyllene is the big mountain on the east of the plain; this temple must
have been on the eastern side; I know no one who has searched for it. Sextus
Empiricus says beans were forbidden because the more you eat the more you
toot and this interferes with the spiritual functions; on the other hand the
Romans thought that if you ate beans and bacon on the first of June at the
feast of Carna nothing could ever hurt your stomach again (Ovid, *Fasti*, 6,
169–82).

Artemis.[114] They say Herakles built the sanctuary after he captured Elis, and there are monuments of the divine heroes who took part in Herakles' expedition against the Eleans and failed to come home safely from the battle. [6] Telamon is buried close beside the river Aroanios, a little distance away from Apollo's sanctuary, and Chalkodon not far from Oinoe's fountain.[115] Yet one cannot possibly accept that the fathers of Elephenor the Euboian commander at Troy and of Ajax and of Teukros fell in this battle; how on earth could Chalkodon have helped Herakles in this battle, when we have trustworthy evidence that Amphitryon had already killed him at Thebes, and [7] how could Teukros have founded the city of Salamis in Cyprus if no one threw him out of his own country when he came home from Troy? And who did drive him out if it was not Telamon? Obviously it was not the Chalkodon from Euboia and not Telamon of Aigina who marched with Herakles against the Eleians; there are still obscure men today who share illustrious names, and there always will be for ever and ever.[116]

[8] The Phenean borders and the neighbouring part of Achaia do not meet at one spot but meet at Porinas towards Pellene and at Artemis ... towards Aigeira. But inside

114. Pausanias is heading north-east towards Achaia and the coast, up the valley of the PHONIATIKO (now the OLBIOS). For Pellene, cf. Bk VII, 27 (1–12); for Aigeira Bk VII, 26 (1–9); they were both Achaian cities. The temple has not been found; it must have been in the valley above STENON.

115. For the Aroanios (now OLBIOS), cf. Bk VIII, 14 (3). Oinoe's fountain may be where she nursed the infant Pan (Bk VIII, 30 (3)) since it seems to have been on Kyllene that Hermes was working as a shepherd when he seduced Pan's mother.

116. Elephenor is Homeric (Iliad, 4, 463). Chalkodon was Elephenor's father; Telamon was Teukros's and Ajax's father. The city of Salamis was north of FAMAGUSTA on the east coast of Cyprus. Large-scale excavation is still going on under the Cyprus Department of Antiquities; at least two volumes of the results of this excavation have already been published (Karageorghis and Vermeule, 1964 and 1966) and there is now an illustrated general study by Karageorghis, Salamis (1969). Casual robbery of this site went on for many years; it was first excavated by a German photographer employed by the British as a forester, who was planting a forest of mimosas to stabilize the sand-dunes where the ruins lay. He came across the lost city when he sank a well.

Phenean territory if you go on a little way past the sanctuary
of Pythian Apollo you are on the road to Mount Krathis.[117]
[9] The springs of the river Krathis are on this mountain: it
flows to the sea past AIGAI, which in my time is a deserted
place, but in the old days it was an Achaian city.[118] There is a
river in Italy named after this river Krathis, in the territory of
the Brettians. On Mount Krathis stands a SANCTUARY OF
PYRONIAN ARTEMIS, and in even older times the Argives used
to fetch fire from this goddess for the Lernaian festival.[119]

[1] If you head east from Pheneos there is a mountain crest 16
called Geronteion in front of you with a road on it. Geronteion is the Phenean frontier with Stymphalian territory. On
the left of Geronteion as you travel through Phenean land
rises the Phenean mountain called Three Springs, and there
are three water springs on it where the nymphs of the mountain are supposed to have washed Hermes when he was born,
and so people believe these springs are sacred to Hermes.[120]
[2] Not far from Three Springs is another mountain called
Mount Viper, where they say Aipytos son of Elatos died of
the snake-bite and they made his grave here, because it was
impossible to carry the corpse with them. The Arkadians say

117. The frontier with Aigeira can be guessed but cannot be fixed. I believe
there is a slip in the manuscripts at or after the word Artemis; can it have been
something to do with Phelloe (Bk VII, 26 (10))? Mount Krathis is certainly the
mountain north-west of PHENEOS: the river AKRATA, which is the ancient
Krathis and has now been renamed KRATHIS, rises there. The mountain is
called LIBADAKI. The valley of the Krathis (or Akrata) lies west of this
mountain and runs northwards to the sea.

118. For the site of Aigai, which must have overlooked the river and seems
to have been near the sea, cf. Bk VII, 25 (12).

119. The Italian Krathis was modern CRATI, a powerful river that runs
north from Cosenza and into the gulf of Taranto just south of the site of
Thourioi. For the Lernaian mysteries, cf. Bk II, 36 (7), and 37 (2).

120. Pausanias is moving east from the plain of Pheneos, which is south-east
from the ancient settlement. The mountain called Three Springs must be the
little one north of the main mass of Geronteion and just south-east of GOURA
in the plain. These mountains are separated by a valley from the formidable
bulk of Kyllene to their north-east; Pausanias's route passes between Three
Springs and Geronteion into this valley, the modern track from Goura does the
same.

those snakes still exist on the mountain in our own times, though not in great numbers; in fact they are extremely rare, because for most of the year the mountain is under snow, and any snake the snow catches outside its hole will perish, and if they do get into their holes for refuge, the snow still kills some of them because the freezing cold creeps right down into the holes.[121] [3] I observed the GRAVE OF AIPYTOS with the greatest interest because in his verses about Arkadia Homer has told the story of Aipytos's monument. It is a tumulus of earth of no great size surrounded by a circular stone platform. Homer would never have seen a more notable monument than this and he seems to have been staggered by it, just as he wrote that the dancing engraved by Hephaistos on the shield of Achilles was like dancing carved by Daidalos, because he had never seen anything better.[122] [4] I know a lot of wonderful tombs, but I shall mention two of them: the one at HALIKARNASSOS and the one in the Jewish country. The one at Halikarnassos was made for King Mausolos of the Halikarnassians; it is of such a huge size and so marvellous in its whole construction that even the Romans have been utterly astounded by it and use the word MAUSOLEUM for their own grandest tombs.[123] [5] The Jews have the grave of a local woman called Helen in the city of Jerusalem, a city which the Roman king destroyed to its foundations. They have contrived to make the door of the tomb, which is stone like all the rest of it, so that it opens only on a certain day of the year

121. Mount Viper (the Greek word is *Sepia*) seems to be a shoulder of Kyllene (or *Ziria*), which is a magnificently snowy mountain. For Aipytos and the snakes, cf. Bk VIII, 4 (7), and Note 25.

122. Homer mentions this tomb 'under steep Kyllene' in the *Iliad* (2, 603–4). The reference to the shield of Achilles (*Iliad*, 18, 590f.) is to lines where Homer says Hephaistos engraved a dancing-floor on the shield like the one that Daidalos constructed for Ariadne. Pausanias believed that Daidalos's dancing-floor still existed (Bk IX, 40 (3)).

123. Mausolos was satrap of Karia; he died in the middle of the fourth century. The famous tomb was excavated by Sir Charles Newton in 1857, and most of it is in the British Museum, but some pieces which have turned up later are still in Turkey. The dismembered monument has not been accurately reconstructed, but scholars are working on it now.

at a particular season: at that moment the machinery opens the door on its own, holds it open for a little while, and then closes it up again. At the time you can get in like that, but if you tried to open it at any other time it would never open – you would have to break it down first.[124]

[1] Beyond the grave of Aipytos stands Kyllene, the 17 highest mountain in Arkadia. There is a ruined SHRINE OF KYLLENIAN HERMES on the crest of the mountain, which obviously got its name as the god got his title, from Kyllen son of Elatos. [2] In ancient times the materials used for human images here, so far as I have been able to discover them, were ebony, cypress, cedar, oak, yew, and Libyan lotos, but the statue of Kyllenian Hermes himself was a different timber: it was made of juniper, and by my reckoning it stands about eight feet high.[125] [3] And there is another wonderful thing about Kyllene: the blackbirds there are white.[126] (The birds the Boiotians call blackbirds are really some other species without any song.) At Sipylos around Tantalos's lake I have

124. This Helen seems to have lived in the first century A.D. and been the mother of King Izates of Adiabene; her bones and his were brought to Jerusalem by another son, Monobazos, and buried in three pyramids half a mile from the city. Pausanias sounds as if he has seen this tomb, in which case it must have survived the destruction; it would have been pulled down in the Byzantine period and its stone re-used. The door probably opened and shut on the anniversary of her death. The site of her monument is perhaps the supposed royal tomb north of the city.

125. Kyllene or ZIRIA is the easternmost of the three magnificent mountains of the northern Peloponnese; the central mountain is CHELMOS (or AROANIA), and the westernmost is PANACHAÏKON. The shrine has not been traced; can it really have stood on a peak so windy and so snowy? As for the kinds of wood, Theophrastos adds box-wood and olive-roots, and Pausanias elsewhere mentions fig-wood and wild pear. The Greek word I translate as juniper is *thuon*; Greeks usually called junipers cedar-trees, and still do so; *juniperus oxycedrus*, the common juniper and *juniperus phoenicea* are all native in Greece.

126. Aristotle talks about these blackbirds. I have seen albino blackbirds in England but not in Greece. Lindermayer has reported that they do exist in some strength on Kyllene, but this report must be regarded only with prudent curiosity, since it has never been confirmed, although a number of scholars looking for white blackbirds have visited the right mountain. Can Aristotle possibly have meant a snowfinch?

seen some eagles they call swan eagles, which are as white as swans, and particular individuals have sometimes owned white wild boar and white Thracian bears, [4] and the Libyan breed of hares is white and I have seen snow-white deer at Rome, and was astounded by them, though it did not occur to me to ask what coast or what island they came from. I am saying all this because of the blackbirds of Kyllene, to remove any doubts you might entertain about their colouring.[127] [5] Kyllene gives on to another mountain called Chelydorea where Hermes is supposed to have discovered the tortoise and stripped its shell and made the lyre out of it. This is the frontier of Pheneos and Pellene, and most of Mount Chelydorea belongs to the Achaians.[128]

[6] As you travel west from Pheneos into the setting sun the left-hand road leads to the city of KLEITOR, and the right-hand road takes you to NONAKRIS and the STREAMS OF THE STYX. In the old days Nonakris was an Arkadian town named after Lykaon's wife, but in our own times it lies in ruins, and there is not a lot you can make even of the ruins. Not far from these ruins is a high crag: I have never seen a rock face so high; the water falls sheer down it, and this is the stream that the Greeks call Styx.[129]

127. Swan-eagles are presumably the fine white Egyptian vultures that still visit Delphi. For Tantalos's lake, cf. Bk V, 13 (7). Albinism does occur in deer. The bear sounds like a yellowish kind of brown bear, which certainly exists. There is a large number of species of hares of all kinds of colours; Pausanias means the Egyptian hare. I have not been able to find anyone who has seen white hares in Egypt. The reliable historian Sau-ma-chien (tr. Watson, 1961), speaks of white deer and white wolves in central Asia.

128. This could be the northernmost peak of Kyllene, or more likely MAVRONOROS, to the north-west.

129. Pausanias is saying that if you head west from Pheneos you must then turn north for Nonakris or south for Kleitor. The falls of the Styx are now called MAVRONERI; the river falls six hundred feet down a sheer face of CHELMOS. The writers of the Admiralty Guide to Greece (?1916) appear to have the cliffs to the top of the falls. The ridge of CHELMOS itself is a nearly perpendicular cliff over 3,000 feet high. It hangs above the west side of the KRATHIS valley. Nonakris has not been found; it was probably somewhere between the Kranthis, of which the Styx is a tributary, and the falls of the Styx.

[1] Hesiod speaks of the existence of the Styx in his 'Birth 18
of the Gods' (there are some people who believe that poem is
by Hesiod), and in the poem makes Styx the daughter of
Ocean and the wife of Pallas.[130] Linos is supposed to have
written something similar, but I read it and it seems to me
utterly phoney. [2] Epimenides the Cretan has also made
Styx a daughter of Ocean, but instead of mating her with
Pallas he makes her the mother of Echidna by Peiras, whoever
Peiras was.[131] But it was particularly Homer who introduced
the name of Styx to poetry; in Hera's oath he writes

> Witness this earth, witness this heaven,
> and the down-dropping water of the Styx.

He seems to have written this in allusion to the Stygian water-
fall, and in the list of Gouneus's regiment he has the river
Titaresios drawing its water from the Styx.[132] [3] He also
makes it run in Hades: Athene says Zeus has forgotten it was
through her that he rescued Herakles from his labours for
Eurystheus:

> If I had known this with my mind's cunning
> when he was sent to Hades the gate keeper
> to fetch horrible Hades' watchdog
> from Erebos, he never should have escaped
> the steep streams of the Stygian river.[133]

[4] The stream that falls from the crag by Nonakris drops
first of all on to a high rock and down through the rock into
the river Krathis, and its water is death to men and to all
animals. They say once upon a time it brought death to the
goats which first tasted its water, and as time went by its
other extraordinary qualities became known. [5] The water
of the Styx dissolves glass and crystal and agate and all the
stone objects known to man, even pottery vessels. The water

130. Hesiod, *Theogony*, 383. Pallas seems to have been the moon's cousin
or father. The children of Styx and Pallas were Victory and Strength. It is not
certain whether this Pallas is the Arkadian hero or not; probably he is.

131. The poems attributed to these two legendary poets have not survived.

132. *Iliad*, 15, 36 and 2, 748f.          133. *Iliad* 8, 366–9.

corrupts horn and bone, iron and bronze, and even lead and tin and silver and the alloy of silver and gold. It treats gold just as it does all other metals, although the Lesbian poetess is a witness and the substance of gold demonstrates that gold is not subject to rust.[134] [6] The god has given the most rejected things power over those that are supposed to be strongest; it is the quality of pearls to dissolve in vinegar, and the blood of a billy-goat wears away a diamond, the most durable of all stones, and the only thing able to resist the river Styx is a horse's hoof, which will hold the water you pour in and not be destroyed by it. I have no actual knowledge that this water was the poison that killed Alexander son of Philip, but I have certainly heard it said.[135]

[7] Above Nonakris stand the Aroanian mountains, in which is a cave where they say Proitos's daughters took refuge during their madness, but then Melampous used mysterious sacrifices and purifications to bring them down to a place called LOUSOI, which is already inside the boundaries of Kleitor, although most of the Aroanian range belongs to Pheneos.[136] [8] They say Lousoi was once a city, and an Agesilas of Lousoi won a horse-race for a ridden horse at the eleventh Pythian games held by the League: but in our day there were not even any ruins of it that have survived. Melampous brought Proitos's daughters down to Lousoi and cured them of madness in a SANCTUARY OF ARTEMIS, and the

134. The reason for the modern name of the falls, which means 'black water', is the black water-stain on the face of the rock. Ancient superstitions about its deadliness were widespread in the Roman period and can be traced back to Theophrastos. They may have something to do with the formula for taking an oath by the river (Herodotos, 6, 74). The Lesbian poetess is Sappho. Aristotle (De Mirabilibus, 125) says the mice at Lousoi could swim.

135. According to the only other authority for this amazing belief about diamonds, a medical writer, the billy-goat had to be fed on bay-leaves and it had to take place in August. (The three hottest things are August, Apollo's bays and a billy-goat's blood?) The story about the horse's hoof is widespread in the ancient literary sources. Aristotle was supposed to have put Antipater up to sending Alexander some Styx water in a horse's hoof.

136. The mountain is CHELMOS. Melampous was the holy man who cured them. Lousoi sounds like a word meaning 'washing'.

Kleitor people have called her Artemis the Tamer ever afterwards.[137]

[1] There are some people of Arkadian blood called the 19 KYNAITHAIANS, the ones who dedicated the statue of Zeus at Olympia with the thunderbolt in each hand. They live about five miles from Lousoi, and in their market-place they have divine altars and a portrait of the emperor Hadrian.[138] [2] The most memorable thing there is a SANCTUARY OF DIONYSOS where they hold a winter festival in which men oil their bodies and take a bull out of the herd, whichever bull the god puts into their heads, and bring it to the sanctuary. The traditional sacrifice is this: there is a cold water-spring just about a quarter of a mile from the city, with a plane-tree growing over it. [3] Anyone wounded or hurt in any way by a dog with rabies can be cured by drinking this water: so that it seems the Arkadian stream by Pheneos called the Styx was invented for the destruction of human beings, and the

137. Lousoi even had games of its own in the Hellenistic period. Agesilas must have won at Delphi in 546. Polybios (4, 18, 9) says the sanctuary of Artemis was between Kleitor and Kynaitha (KALAVRYTA). Pausanias reckons it was five miles or so from Kynaitha (19 (1) below). For the site of Kleitor, cf. 21 (1) below. The site of Lousoi is at the north foot of HAGIOS ILIAS west of the AROANIOS and due south of Kalavryta. Several buildings including a temple of Artemis were excavated by Austrian archaeologists in 1901 (cf. *Jahrshefte des Osterreichischen Archäologischen Instituts* 4, pp. 1f. with excellent plans and maps). Vitruvius (8, 3, 21) says that in the land belonging to Kleitor there is a cave with a spring, where if you drink you become teetotal, and records and inscription inviting you to drink and forbidding you to wash. He quotes the poem in Greek; it appears to be late Hellenistic. Leake identified the spring (*Morea*, vol. 2, p. 109) as the middle of the three headsprings of the Aroanios: wrongly, I suspect.

138. For the statue at Olympia, cf. Bk V, 22 (1). Kynaitha was where Kalavryta is; it hardly existed in Strabo's time (8, 8, 2), but there was a statue of Hadrian and under Caracalla in the third century A.D. coins were still struck showing the city centre: a colonnade, a temple, a statue, and a tree (*Zeitschrift für Numismatik*, 2, 4, p. 66). The only inscriptions are in Latin. The place had been destroyed in 220 B.C. and was perhaps refounded as a Roman colony. The castle of TREMOLA, the picturesque ruins of which are a kind of backdrop to Kalavryta, looks purely medieval; it was named after Humbert de Tremouille, the feudal lord of these valleys. Mr Mastrokostas has excavated there and found classical antiquities; I do not know where this was published.

Kynaithaian spring is a counterweight of goodness to balance it.[139]

[4] One of the roads west out of Pheneos I have still to deal with, the one on the left, which leads to Kleitor, past Herakles' labour, the channel he made for the river Aroanios. Beyond that point, the road goes down to a place called Lykouria, which is the territorial boundary of Pheneos and Kleitor.[140]

20      [1] Six miles or so from Lykouria you arrive at the SPRINGS OF THE LADON. I had heard that the water of the Phenean lake which drops into the pot-holes in the mountains comes up again here to form the springs of the Ladon.[141] I am unable to say for certain whether that is the truth, but the Ladon has the finest water of any river in Greece, and besides this is famous in the world because of Daphne and her celebrated story.[142] [2] I will not dwell on the story of Daphne as the Syrians on the river Orontes tell it, but there is another story told in Arkadia and Elis.[143] Oinomaos the lord of Pisa had a son called

139. This spring may be one near Kalavryta that Leake saw and the old Baedekers used to mention. It is on the way from Kalavryta to HAGIA LAVRA where the Latin inscription (C.I.L., III, 528) was found.

140. Facing west from Pheneos Pausanias turns left, that is south-west, skirting the Pheneos plain and the causeway (cf. Note 103 above) and the OLBIOS (PHONIATIKO). Lykouria must have been somewhere below the mountain called DOURDOUBANA at the edge of the plain, probably south-east of the mountain. For the modern Lykouria, cf. the next note.

141. These springs are close to the modern village called LYKOURIA. Pausanias took roughly the track from LOUZION.

142. Frazer refers to 'a brawling impetuous stream of dark blue water', and to 'a deep greenish-blue tinge . . . flat and tepid to the taste'. Mr Roger Howell says the water is now 'a muddy green . . . it had dirty old goats in it; there was a cheese factory on the edge'. The water comes from what used to be the Pheneos lake. Lower down, the Ladon is certainly a fine river.

143. Pausanias is referring to the sanctuary of Apollo at Daphne (the word for a bay-tree) near Antioch, which was founded by Seleukos the Champion (Niketor), the Macedonian general who took Syria in the carve-up after Alexander's death. Its mythology was contemptibly derivative. The sacred forest of cypresses and bay-trees became impressive with time, and the architecture was magnificent. The roof of the Christian church at Antioch in the fourth century A.D. was made of cypress beams cut from the forest of Daphne.

Leukippos who fell in love with Daphne, and knew he could never have her by straight wooing because she ran away from all men whatsoever, so he thought of a trick. [3] Leukippos grew his hair long for the river Alpheios,[144] so he plaited his long hair like a young virgin and put on women's clothes and went to Daphne and said he was Oinomaos's daughter and wanted to go hunting with her. She believed he was a virgin girl of a much grander family and a much more brilliant huntress than the other girls, and besides he was extremely attentive to her, so that he and Daphne became close friends. [4] Those who celebrate Apollo as her lover add to all this that Apollo was jealous of Leukippos's success in love. So Daphne and the other young virgins suddenly wanted to swim in the Ladon, and stripped Leukippos against his will. When they saw he was not a young girl, they stabbed him to death with their hunting-knives and spears.

[1] That is how they tell the story. The city of KLEITOR is 21 seven or eight miles from the springs of the Ladon; the road is a narrow cliff path beside the river Aroanios and near the city you cross a river called the Kleitor which is a tributary of the Aroanios joining it under a mile from the city itself.[145] [2] Among the various sorts of fish you can find in the Aroanios there are what they call spotted-fish: these spotted-fish are supposed to sing like thrushes. I have seen them caught, but I

144. Cf. Bk VIII, 41 (3).
145. The Ladon rises at Lykouria, the Aroanios (KATSANA) runs into the Ladon five miles to the south-west, below SPELIA; Pausanias is following I believe the western bank of the Aroanios upstream, that is north-west, in the general direction of Kalavryta. He leaves the Aroanios at MAZEIKA (now called KATO KLEITORIA) and turns west up the KARNESI, which is a tributary; he probably thought it was the main stream. Two or three miles to the west the Kleitor runs into the Karnesi, and the ruins of Kleitor are in the fork between the two rivers. The Karnesi runs down from what used to be the village of Karnesi and is now ANO KLEITORIA. There is also a modern village of KLEITOR on the Kleitor river farther west. Kleitor is due south of AIGION on the gulf of Corinth and due east of CHLEMOUTSI on the west coast of Greece. The site is locally called ZAGORITSA or PALAIOPOLIS. There is a lot of it left; there was more in Frazer's time and even more in Leake's. For a plan, cf. Praktika, 1920, p. 113.

never heard them singing although I stayed beside the river until sunset, which is supposed to be their favourite time for songs.[146]

[3] The city of Kleitor was named after Azan's son. It stands on level ground surrounded by smallish mountains. Its most distinguished SANCTUARIES are of DEMETER and ASKLEPIOS, and a third of EILEITHUIA ... and fails to say how many, but at an early period Olen the Lykian composed some hymns for Delos, including one to Eileithuia, where he calls her the good spinner, obviously identifying her with Fate, and says she is older than Kronos.[147] [4] About half a mile from the city of Kleitor they have a SANCTUARY with bronze statues of the Dioskouroi whom they call the GREAT GODS. On the summit of the mountain four miles or so from the city they have built a SHRINE with a statue of KORIAN ATHENE.[148]

22    [1] My description brings me back to STYMPHELOS and the frontier of Stymphelos and Pheneos which is called Geronteion.[149] The Stymphelians are no longer classed as Arkadian; they chose to alter their nationality and now belong to the Argolid, though Homer is my argument that they were Arkadians by blood; in fact their founder Stymphalos was a grandson of Arkas son of Kallisto. The original settlement is

146. They are supposed to have whistled loudly like thrushes. Frazer was told at Kato Kleitoria in 1895 that the trout in the river quite often chirped like little birds, particularly when they were netted, and a local magnate told him whenever a lot of the fish came together they made 'un petit bruit harmonieux'. Dodwell noticed only that they were 'of a fine bright colour and beautifully variegated'. There are singing fish in a certain bay in Ceylon, which make a sharp, thin, chirping noise. (I owe a confirmation of their real existence to Father Paul Casperz, a Ceylon Jesuit.)

147. For Olen and his works, cf. Bk V, 7 (8). Eileithuia's temple at Delos has been found (Bk I, 18 (5)). Olen said in the same hymn that she was Love's mother (Bk IX, 27 (2)).

148. It is not absolutely certain which is the right mountain, and the sanctuary has not been found. Korian Athene probably means 'Athene of the Summit', but Athene is also Kore, Zeus's virgin daughter.

149. Pausanias is covering the whole of northern Arkadia in a series of long excursions from Pheneos. For Geronteion and the point to which he is now returning, cf. 16 (1) above. It stands above MOSIA on the east of the Pheneos plain, south-west of Kyllene.

said to have been elsewhere in the territory and not at the site of the modern city.[150] [2] They say the ancient Stymphelos is where Temenos son of Pelasgos lived, and that Temenos brought up Hera, and founded three sanctuaries of that goddess and gave her three titles: he called her the Child when she was still a young virgin, and Perfect when she married Zeus, and while she was quarrelling with Zeus and came back to Stymphelos, Temenos called her the Widow. [3] These are Stymphelian legends about the goddess that have come to my knowledge, but the modern city possessed none of these sanctuaries: here is what they did possess. There is a Stymphelian spring from which the emperor Hadrian has brought water to the city of Corinth. In the winter this spring at Stymphelos creates a small LAKE with the river Stymphelos running out of it, but in summer the river runs straight from the spring without any flooding at all. This river disappears into a chasm in the earth, and reappears again in the Argolid with a new name: they call it Erasinos instead of Stymphelos.[151] [4] There is a story about the water in the lake of Stymphelos that man-eating birds used to breed on it; Her-

150. *Iliad*, 2, 603f. The old city in a different place has never been found; Mr Howell has found traces of geometric and early classical occupation in the direction of LAVKA to the south-west of the lake. The proper name of the city is Stymphalos; Pausanias consistently spells it wrongly. The site is north of the lake and partly unexcavated. For a description and photographs, cf. *A.M.*, 40 (1915, pp. 71f.). For the excavations and a plan, cf. Orlandos in *Praktika*, 1925, pp. 51f. There is a small akropolis garnished with ruined walls from which the town plan shows clearly under the surface of the fields. The ruins of the Cistercian monastery beside the lake contain many ancient stones.

151. The spring is the KEPHALOBRYSI at KIONIA on the north-east of the big modern lake. Its classical name was Metopa. Like Pheneos (Bk VIII, 14 (1)) the lake has had different levels at different times. A public company undertook to drain it in 1881, and in Frazer's time (1896) its level was irregular. At present it is far bigger than the water Pausanias saw, and the level is rising. It has recently drowned an archaeological site excavated by Mr Orlandos. There are traces of a Roman conduit to the east of the lake, and Sir William Gell in the early nineteenth century observed the arches of an aqueduct north-east of the ancient city. For the Erasinos, cf. Bk II, 24 (6); its modern name is the KEPHALARI. It breaks out of a cliff in the mountains behind Argos, a long way south of this lake, but the ancient opinion is not impossible.

akles is supposed to have shot them down. Peisander of Kamiros denies that Herakles killed the birds: he says he chased them off with the noise of castanets.[152] Among the wild creatures of the Arabian desert there are some birds called Stymphalidai which are just as ferocious against human beings as the lion and the leopard; [5] if you come to hunt them they fly at you and tear and kill you with their beaks. They pierce through any kind of armour of bronze or iron, but if you wear clothing woven out of thick bark the bark holds their beaks just as the wings of little birds are held in bird-lime. These birds are the size of a crane, but they look like the ibis, only they have stronger beaks, and not curved like the ibis. [6] Whether the Arabian birds in my time have the same name as the birds once upon a time in Arkadia, but are not the same to look at, I have no idea: but if Stymphalidai have existed throughout history like hawks and eagles, they appear to me to be an Arabian breed: a flock of them could have flown to Arkadia and reached Stymphelos. The Arabs would originally have called them by some other name than Stymphalidai, but the fame of Herakles and the prestige of Greece over barbarians drove it out, so that today the birds in the Arabian desert are called Stymphalidai.[153] [7] At Stymphelos there is also an ancient SANCTUARY OF STYMPHELIAN ARTEMIS; the statue is a wooden image, mostly gilded. The roof of the temple has the Stymphelian birds on it: it was hard to make out with

152. Peisander is a lost epic poet probably of the sixth century B.C. who wrote about the foundation of Herakleia and the deeds of Herakles. Theokritos wrote a verse inscription (*Epigrams*, 22) for a bronze imaginary portrait in the market-square of Kamiros. Even Herakles was not strong enough to shoot such an enormous flock of wild birds, so he took a bronze castanet, and played it so loudly the entire flock flew away. We have this story from Apollonios of Rhodes, who almost certainly read Peisander. The point of the story is Herakles' strength as much as the cleverness of using a metal crow-scarer.

153. Three of these birds were carved on the metopes of the temple of Zeus at Olympia as well as at Stymphelos (cf. the next section). The Olympia birds are now in Paris. They occur on fifth- and fourth-century coins as tough-looking crested birds with thick, short, serviceable beaks (British Museum Catalogue, *Peloponnese*, p. 199). D'Arcy Thompson calls them 'Fabulous and mystical birds'. Can Pausanias possibly be thinking about egrets?

any certainty whether they were in wood or in plaster, but to my eyes they seemed to be wooden. There are also young virgins here in white stone with the legs of birds, standing behind the temple.[154] [8] There is a wonderful thing said to have happened in our own times. They were celebrating the feast of Stymphelian Artemis at Stymphelos rather unenthusiastically, neglecting most of what tradition dictated: and so a mass of wood caught in the mouth of the pothole where the river goes underground, and stopped the water going down; they

*13. The Stymphalian Bird*

say their whole plain flooded for fifty miles. [9] Then they say there was a huntsman following a running deer that leapt into the flood-water and the huntsman swam after the deer, raging behind it: and deer and man were swallowed down by the pothole, and the river water rushed down after them so that the whole flooded Stymphelian plain drained off in a day: and from that time on they have celebrated the feast of Artemis more magnificently.

154. Bird-legged girls or girl-faced birds are a conventional Greek weirdity; they can represent the spirits of the dead, or the creatures that take away dying souls. The sirens who sang to Odysseus were represented as bird-girls by early classical painters. The original bird-like water-nymph is the Assyrian Antaura, the evil wind-demon (cf. A. A. Barb, 'The Mermaid and the Devil's Grandmother', *Warburg Journal* 29, 1966, pp. 1f.).

23 **[1]** Beyond Stymphelos comes ALEA, which also belongs to the Argive league, though they recognize Aleos son of Apheidas as their founder.[155] There are divine sanctuaries of Ephesian Artemis and Alean Athene, and a shrine of Dionysos with a statue, where they hold the feast of the Rotunda every second year; women are beaten at the feast of Dionysos by the command of the Delphic oracle, just as they beat young lads at Sparta at the sanctuary of Standing Artemis.[156]

**[2]** I explained in dealing with Orchomenos how at first the straight road runs by the gully, and then on the left of the lake water. There is a mound of earth in the Kaphyan plain that prevents the water on Orchomenian ground from doing any harm to Kaphyan ground under cultivation. There is another stream of water that passes inside this mound, with volume enough to make a river: it goes underground into a chasm and rises again at Nasoi as they call it. The place where it rises is called Reunos; when it rises there its water produces the perpetual streams of the river Tragos.[157] **[3]** The city is

155. If he went farther west Pausanias would be on Corinthian territory; he either turns south past the outlet of the lake, keeps to the east of LAVKA, and crosses the pass east of Mount SKIPIZA, always heading south, or he goes round farther east and then south-west up the road to SKOTEINI. The ruins are farther south at BOUGIATI, now renamed ALEA. I wonder whether Pausanias did in fact approach Alea from Stymphalos; it would be as easy to reach by either of two passes north of Rough Mountain, from the Orchomenos plain (cf. Bk VIII, Note 99), or even by taking a road north-west from Argos. The phrase 'beyond Stymphelos' is not convincing. For a description and photographs of Alea, cf. Professor Ernst Meyer's *Peloponnesische Wanderungen* (1938). The ruins of this remote fortified mountain town have not altered since the war. They guarded the northernmost approaches to Arkadia from the Argolid. Gell and Dodwell saw the ruins of a less civilized fortress somewhere above Skoteini; no one has yet been able to find it in this century.

156. There were other mysteries of Dionysos not far south at Melangeia (Black Pots, cf. Bk VIII, 6 (5), and Notes there). Nilsson adopts the suggestion that the rites at Alea may have been connected with an oracle (*Griechische Feste*, p. 299). The Greek name of the festival is *Skiereia*.

157. For the road from Orchomenos, cf. Bk VIII, 13 (4). Pausanias is talking about the part of the plain north-west of Orchomenos between Mount Mainalos and Mount Kyllene, due west of Alea. The spring called Reunos was on the way to Psophis (23 (8) below). It seems to be north-east of CHOTOUSSA

obviously named after Kepheus son of Aleos, only the
Arkadian version of its name KAPHYAI drove the other version
out of currency. The Kaphyans say they came originally from
Attica, but Aigeus expelled them from Athens and they fled
into Arkadia and begged for kindness from Kepheus and
settled here. The town is built on the edge of the plain at the
foot of some not particularly high mountains. The Kaphyans
have SANCTUARIES of the gods POSEIDON and KNAKALES-
IAN ARTEMIS. [4] They also have a Mount Knakalos, where
they hold an annual mystery to Artemis. A little above the
city there is a water-spring presided over by a beautiful and
enormous plane-tree that they call Menelais, because they say
Menelaos came here and planted the plane-tree beside the
spring when he was gathering his army against Troy; nowadays the spring and the tree are both called Menelais.[158]  [5]
But if I were to number all the trees in Greek legends that are
still alive and flourishing, the most venerable of all is the
Samian *agnus castus* growing in the sanctuary of Hera, then
the oak at Dodona and the olive on the akropolis and the one
at Delos, though the Syrians would award the third prize for
antiquity to the Syrian bay-tree: but of all the rest this plane-
tree is the oldest.[159]

above ELATOS; if so Pausanias is wrong about its origin; the Tragos runs into
the Ladon. The ruins of the city of Kaphyai are evident at Chotoussa, which
lies south-east of LIMNI and north-west of Orchomenos. There is a geographical explanation of the site in Philippson's *Griechischen Landschaften* (vol.
3 pt 1, 1959, pp. 250–1). It used to be disputed but there is no real doubt.

158. Menelaos as Helen's husband had married into a tree-cult (cf. Note 160
below). Theophrastos says Agamemnon planted this tree, and so does Pliny.
Artemis and Poseidon figure on Kaphyan coins. What does *Knakalos* mean?
*Knax* means a white goat, and *knekis* means a white horse, a grey; another
derivative of the same word is the name of a herb. The word occurs fairly
widely in place-names, probably because of the herb, which was used for
colouring. Does it mean Whiteweed Artemis?

159. I have seen at different places in the Peloponnese a vine and a plane-
tree currently pointed out as having been there since Pausanias's time, and
people used to be told that the olives in the Garden of Olives were the ones that
Christ saw. There used to be and still are a large number of King Alfred's oaks
in England. But Pausanias's venerable trees are all religious. The Syrian bay-
tree is the one at Antioch that Daphne turned into (cf. Note 143 above).

[6] About two hundred yards from Kaphyai is a place called
KONDYLEA; there is a grove of Artemis with a TEMPLE here
which in ancient times was called the temple of Kondylean
Artemis, but for the following reason the goddess's name was
altered. Some children, it is not recorded how many, were
playing round the sanctuary and found a rope: they tied this
rope round the neck of the statue and said Artemis was
hanged. [7] The Kaphyans discovered what the children had
done and stoned them to death: as soon as they had carried
out the execution their women contracted a disease, and their
unborn children dropped dead out of the womb, until the
reply of the Pythian priestess came that they must bury the
children and burn annual offerings to them, because they had
died unjustly. The Kaphyans still carry out the commands of
that oracle to this day, and they have called the goddess
Hanged Artemis ever since, as they say the same oracle
commanded.[160]

[8] After you climb up from Kaphyai you come down to
Nasoi in something under a mile, and the Ladon is six miles
farther on from there. Cross the river and pass through
Argeathai and Lykountes and Skotane, and you arrive at the
oak forest of Soron, where the road leads towards PSOPHIS.[161]
[9] Like all the Arkadian oak forests, this one has wild animals
in it, wild boar and bears and gigantic tortoises: you could

160. The place has not been found. We know from Clement of Alexandria
that the story was told in the *Aitia*, a collection of stories like this by Kallimachos (*Fr.* 187). There is another mysterious story he told connecting Artemis
with hanging (*Fr.* 461), and we know of hanging Helen as a tree-divinity at
Rhodes (Bk III, 9 (10)). Usener believed *Kondyleatis* meant that Artemis was a
moon-goddess hanging in the sky, and on Kaphyan coins she has a crescent
moon on her forehead; the two are not irreconcilable.

161. Psophis is west-north-west. Pausanias follows the Tragos until it meets
the Ladon and then crosses over to TRIPOTAMO, south of the modern PSOPHIS,
where the head-streams of the Erymanthos come together, east of Mount
LAMPEIA and south-east of Mount ERYMANTHOS (OLONOS), almost due east
of GASTOUNI on the west coast, and almost due south of Cape DREPANON
which is north-east of PATRAI. None of the places has been found, but there
are still some oak-trees.

make a lyre out of one of these that would equal one made of an Indian turtle. On the edges of Soron are the ruins of the village of PAOS, and not far away is what they call Seirai, the frontier of the territory of Kleitor with Psophis.[162]

[1] Some say PSOPHIS was founded by Psophis son of Arron, 24 son of Erymanthos son of Aristas son of Porthaon son of Periphetes son of Nyktimos; others say Psophis was the daughter of Xanthos son of Erymanthos son of Arkas. This is the account given in the Arkadian records of kings, [2] but the truest version is that Psophis was a daughter of Eryx the Sicilian ruler: Herakles slept with her, but he decided not to take her home and left her pregnant with his friend Lykortas, who was then living in the city of Phegia, which before the reign of Phegeus was called the city of Erymanthos. So Echephron and Promachos, sons of Herakles and the Sicilian woman, were brought up there, and changed its name Phegia to their mother's name Psophis.[163] [3] The Zakynthian akropolis is also called Psophis, because it was a Psophidian who first crossed over to that island in his fleet and became its founder, Zakynthos son of Dardanos.[164] Psophis is four miles from Seirai; the river Aroanios flows past it and the Erymanthos is a little distance from the city.[165] [4] The Erymanthos

162. Herodotos called Paos a city, there was a cult of the Dioskouroi (6, 127), and the ruins have been identified and a village renamed after it about half-way between the LADON and TRIPOTAMIA. Wild boar and bears have died out in the Peloponnese, though they existed until recently. I have never seen a giant tortoise there. Kleitor (cf. 19 (4) above) was only a few miles east-north-east of Psophis, and the two are in fact linked by a modern road. There is even a mountain village called SEIRAI between them, but the real position of the frontier is unknown.

163. Erymanthos (the river's name) was once the city's name; then it became Phegia because of Phegeus, and finally Psophis. For Eryx, cf. Bk III, 16 (4).

164. Only Pausanias (and Stephanos of Byzantium who follows him) gives this name for the akropolis of the island of Zakynthos (ZANTE). Rather few classical antiquities have been found on the island, perhaps because its visible relics were stripped by the Venetians. There was a temple at MELINADO.

165. There is more than one Aroanios. The site of Psophis is in the fork of two rivers, above the place where the LOPESI joins them.

has its springs on Mount Lampeia, which is said to be sacred to Pan: Lampeia would really be part of Mount Erymanthos.[166] Homer has written that on Taygetos and Erymanthos . . . huntsman . . . [167] Erymanthos, and passes through Arkadia with Mount Pholoe on the right and Thelpousa on the left again, and joins the Alpheios.[168] [5] They say Herakles hunted a boar of unique size and strength beside the Erymanthos, at Eurystheus's orders. The people of Opician Cumae have a boar's tusks dedicated in their SANCTUARY OF APOLLO, which they claim are the tusks of the Erymanthian boar, but there is not the remotest probability attaching to this tale.[169] [6] In the city of Psophis there is a SANCTUARY OF ERYKINIAN APHRODITE, of which only the ruins survive today. The story is that Psophis's sons founded it, and in fact this is a probable story, because Erykinian Aphrodite has a sanctuary in Sicily in Eryx's country which has been most sacred from very ancient times and is as wealthy as the sanctuary at Paphos.[170]

166. The Erymanthos has springs in every direction. Lampeia is probably KALLIPHONI, the mountain to the north with Mount Erymanthos south-west of it; the two are joined by a range called the High Peaks (PSILAI KORYPHAI). The mountain west of Psophis now called Lampeia has perhaps been wrongly renamed. For Pan at Psophis, cf. perhaps Kallimach, fr. 412.

167. *Odyssey*, 6, 103: 'as arrow-playing Artemis goes over the mountains, long Taygetos or Erymanthos, enjoying the wild boar and the swift deer, and with her go the Nymphs . . . and Leto is very pleased . . .'

168. The course of the Erymanthos which turns south from Psophis. Pholoe was the mountain which has been wrongly renamed LAMPEIA, or else SKIADOBOUNI west of the Peneios, or both.

169. Cumae is in Italy: Opician was a word used for Italians. Apollo's temple was on a summit, probably the smaller eastern hill of Cumae; this is the temple described at the beginning of the sixth book of Vergil's *Aeneid*. Cumae is on the Campanian coast some miles north of Cape Miseno.

170. On the eastern tip of the great crag of MONTE SAN GIULIANO above Trapani in the far west of Sicily: *Vicina astris Erycino in vertice*. It was in the end utterly destroyed; the tattered remains of a big Norman castle now occupy the site. In Pausanias's time the temple was Roman; it had been restored by Tiberius. It has been excavated and planned, but not much has been recovered (*Journal of Hellenic Studies*, 56, pp. 218f., and *Notizie degli Scavi di Antichità*, 1935). Aphrodite of Eryx was the mother of the Caesars: the *Aineadum genetrix*. Horace calls her simply *Erycina* (*Odes*, 1, 2, 33). For Paphos, cf. Bk VIII, 5 (2) and the note there. For the sanctuary at Psophis cf. Ergon, 1968, pp. 12–16.

[7] The SHRINES of the divine heroes Promachos and Echephron sons of Psophis were no longer very impressive in my
time. Amphiaros's son Alkmaion is also buried at Psophis; his
tomb is a building of no great size or ornamental splendour.
There are cypresses around it growing so high that their shade
falls on the mountain above Psophis. They refuse to cut these
since they believe they are sacred to Alkmaion, and the local
people call them virgins. [8] When Alkmaion had killed his
mother and ran away from Argos he came to Psophis (which
was still called Phegia after Phegeus) and married Phegeus's
daughter Alphesiboia, and among the gifts you might
imagine he gave her the necklace.[171] But his disease was not
in the least relieved by life in Arkadia, so he took refuge with
the Delphic oracle, where the Pythian priestess instructed him
that Eriphyle's avenger would follow him everywhere except
to the youngest of countries, the one that had risen from the
sea since his mother's blood had stained him. [9] So he
discovered the alluvial deposits of the Acheloos and settled
there, and married Acheloos's daughter Kalliroe (as the
Akarnanians say), and had two sons Akarnan and Ampho-
teros. They say the people of that part of the mainland were
previously called Kouretes, and took their present name from
Akarnan.[172] A lot of men run their lives on to the rocks of
irrational desires, and women even more so. [10] Kalliroe
desired Eriphyle's necklace and sent Alkmaion to Phegia for it
against his will. He met his death there: he was treacherously
murdered by Temenos and Axion the sons of Phegeus, who
are supposed to have dedicated the necklace to Apollo at
Delphi.[173] They say it was during their reign at Phegia, as it
was still called, that the Greeks fought against Troy. The
Psophidians say they did not take part in that expedition

171. It was a venegeance killing, because his mother Eriphyle was bribed
with a necklace to cause his father's death; the necklace brought trouble to all
its owners; cf. Bk IX, 41 (2-5).

172. Akarnania, in the south-west corner of the main mass of Greece, north
of the gulf of Corinth.

173. There was another such necklace in Athene's temple; it was supposed
to be Helen's.

because their kings hated the Argive chiefs, who were most of them related to Alkmaion and had fought in his campaign against Thebes.

[11] The reason the ECHINADES islands have not been joined to the mainland by the action of the Acheloos is that the Aitolian people have been rooted out and their whole land devastated. Since Aitolia has been left uncultivated, the Acheloos has not deposited mud on the Echinades in the same way. I can confirm this from the fact that the Maiander flowing between the regular ploughland of Phrygia and Karia has turned the sea between Priene and Miletos into dry land in a comparatively short time.[174] [12] Beside the Erymanthos the Psophidians have a SHRINE and a statue of ERYMANTHOS. Except for the Egyptian Nile the rivers all have white stone statues, but people believe you should make statues of the Nile in dark stone, because he flows down to the sea through Aithiopia.[175]

[13] I did not really believe the story I heard at Psophis about Aglaos, a Psophidian contemporary of Kroisos of Lydia, that he was truly happy throughout his entire life. One may have smaller troubles to put up with than one's contemporaries, just as one ship may suffer less than another from

174. Certain farming methods cause erosion, particularly the grazing of goats. Herodotos said that half the Echinades had been joined to the mainland by his time (2, 10), and Thukydides said the rest soon would be (2, 102). The water round the outer Echinades is deep, and even in the bay just south of the Acheloos estuary the destroyer *Leander* anchored in 1904 in fifteen fathoms. But the mud the river carries down still discolours the sea as far as two miles out, and there are plenty of fresh mud and sand banks around its mouth, and only two feet of water on the bar. Slightly farther south, east of Cape Oxia at SKROPHA BANK, the shore is still silting up from year to year. Miletos is now miles inland.

175. There do exist basalt statues of the Nile; there are two in the Louvre. Obviously Egyptian statues are more likely than Greek ones to be made of basalt, since basalt is not a Greek stone. The association of whiteness with religious architecture and sculpture in Greece depends on the fact that the use of ivory and of white stucco is older than the architectural use of marble, and probably of unpainted, unplastered sculpture in Greece. Mud walls were already whitewashed in the seventh millennium.

bad weather, [14] but it is absolutely impossible to find a man permanently untouched by tragedy or a ship that always has a prosperous wind. And Homer has written about the jar of good that Zeus has and the other jar of evil: he learnt about this from the god at Delphi, who once called Homer himself both a cursed and a happy man, because he was born to be both.[176]

[1] On the way from Psophis to THELPOUSA the first place 25 you come to is TROPAIA on the left of the Ladon, immediately after that comes the oak forest of Aphrodision, and thirdly a stone tablet with archaic lettering, the boundary stone of Psophis with Thelpousan territory. The river Arsen runs on Thelpousan land; cross it and in three miles you will reach the ruins of the village of KAOUS and a sanctuary of Kaousian Asklepios which is on the road.[177] [2] The city is about five miles from this sanctuary; they say it was named after a nymph Thelpousa who was Ladon's daughter. The source of the Ladon is among the water-springs in the territory of Kleitor. As I have already showed in this discussion, first of all it flows past a place called Leukasion and Mesoboa and through Nasoi to Oryx, or Halous as it is sometimes called, and from Halous it flows down to Thaliades and a SANCTUARY OF ELEUSINIAN DEMETER, [3] which is inside the frontier

176. Aglaos lived on a little farm and never strayed off it; when the king asked the Delphic oracle who was the happiest man alive (meaning himself) the god said Aglaos of Psophis. The jars of good and evil come into the *Iliad*. For what the oracle said to Homer, cf. Bk X, 24 (2).

177. The identification of this site, which Leake had already found about 1806, was confirmed in 1878 by an inscription discovered by R. Weil (*I.G.*, V (2), 411, and cf. 412). It lies due south of Psophis, on the Ladon at what used to be called VANAINA, a mile above the old Ladon bridge at TOUMBITSI, which is just north of the modern bridge that carries the main road from Olympia to Tripolis. The castle on the hill was besieged by the Palaiologoi in 1417. For the classical site, cf. the report in *B.C.H.*, 63, 1939, p. 300. There is a large modern TROPAIA, but it has nothing to do with Pausanias's place. The mountain between Psophis and the Ladon had been renamed APHRODISION; it used to be called HAGIOS PETROS. Kaos was above the river at BOUTSIS below Mount Aphrodision, north-west of SPATHARIS, but there is not much left of it. (Meyer, *Peloponnesische Wanderungen*, p. 85, and *Arch. Ang.*, 1940, p. 223.)

of Thelpousa.[178] There are statues there at least seven feet high of Demeter and her daughter and Dionysos, all in stone. After passing the sanctuary of the Eleusinian goddess, the Ladon flows past the city of Thelpousa on its left; the site of the city is a big hill, but in our time most of it is deserted, so that they say the MARKET-PLACE on its fringes was originally constructed right in the middle of the city. There is a SHRINE OF ASKLEPIOS at Thelpousa, and a SANCTUARY OF THE TWELVE GODS, most of which is already reduced to ground level. [4] After Thelpousa the Ladon flows down to the SANCTUARY OF DEMETER at Onkion. The Thelpousans call the goddess a Fury, and Antimachos confirms this name in his poem on the Argive expedition against Thebes; the verse is:

*at the throne of Demeter the Fury.*[179]

According to the legend Onkios is Apollo's son, who ruled around the place called Onkion in the Thelpousan country, and the goddess got her title of Fury because [5] when Demeter was wandering in search of her child, they say Poseidon followed her lusting to have sex with her, so she changed herself into a mare and grazed among the mares

178. Cf. Bk VIII, 21 (1). The only one of these names we can place is Thaliades at DIVRITSA now renamed DEMETRA, which was identified by the finding of a bronze pot dedicated to the Maid (*I.G.*, V (2), 414). In the fifth century B.C. it had been a place important enough to strike its own silver coinage. If this is Thaliades then the ruins (*Palaiokastro*) at SYRIAMAKOS or SYRIAMOU must surely be Halous, as Meyer has suggested. But there have also been finds of antiquities at BACHLIA north of the river, and at two sites to which commentaries refer but which I am unable to pinpoint.

179. For Antimachos, cf. Note 180 below. The Furies are underworld women who avenge. Professor Meyer thought Onkeion was at KALIAMI which someone has now renamed DOXA (glory). This is surely too far east of the Ladon for the sanctuary though not for the town. Sir James Frazer had an enjoyable walk down the Ladon without finding it but thinking of Milton's line, 'by sandy Ladon's lilied banks'; he saw some sand but no lilies. Milton of course never came to Greece, though from Italy he intended to do so and was starting out when the outbreak of the English Civil War turned him back. Had he come he would unquestionably have been the discoverer of many antiquities and the revealer of a new age. But as things happened, his ideas of Greek geography are based on learned reading and an English imagination.

belonging to Onkios; but Poseidon saw how she tricked him and coupled with Demeter in the form of a stallion. [6] At that moment Demeter was very angry about what had happened though later on she got over her wrath and they say she fancied a wash in the Ladon: and this is how the goddess got her titles, the Fury because of her wrath, as the Arkadian expression for giving way to anger is to be furious, and Washing Demeter because she washed in the Ladon. The

*14. The Divine Horse*

statues in the temple are made of wood, but the faces and hands and feet are Parian stone. [7] The statue of the Fury has the basket in her left hand, and a torch in her right which I reckoned was nine feet long. Washing Demeter appeared to be about six feet high. People who think this is a statue of Themis and not of Washing Demeter had better realize they are mistaken. They say Demeter bore Poseidon a daughter whose name may not by holy law be repeated to the uninitiated, and also a stallion called Areion, which is why they were the first Arkadians to use the title of Horse Poseidon. [8] They bring as evidence for their story the verses of the *Iliad* and the *Thebais*; the *Iliad* refers to Areion himself,

> *Not if he drove back godlike Areion*
> *Adrastos's fast horse, blood of the gods,*

and so does the *Thebais*, when Adrastos was running away
from Thebes,

> *in foul clothing with blue-maned Areion.*[180]

They claim that those verses are an allusion to Poseidon
being Areion's father, [9] but Antimachos says he was a son
of Earth:

> *Adrastos son of Talaos, Kretheus's son,*
> *first of the Greeks whipped up his praised horses,*
> *swift Time and Thelpousaian Areion,*
> *whom Earth produced, holy and glorious,*
> *by Oñkaian Apollo's sacred wood.*

[10] Even if the horse grew out of the earth he could still be
the blood of the god with hair as blue as lapis lazuli. There is a
further story that when Herakles was fighting his war with
the Eleans he asked Onkos for this horse, and captured Elis
by riding into battle on Areion; later on Herakles gave the
horse to Adrastos. This is why Antimachos writes about the
horse as he does,

> *tame to his third master Adrastos.*

[11] The Ladon leaves the sanctuary of the Fury behind on
the left and flows past the SHRINE OF ONKAIAN APOLLO on
the left and the SANCTUARY OF CHILD ASKLEPIOS on the
right, where the tomb of Trygon is who they say was Asklepios's nurse: because they say Autolaos the bastard son of Arkas
came across the child Asklepios thrown out at Thelpousa and
picked him up, which is why they call him Child Asklepios
... I consider more probable as I explained in my treatment
of Epidauros.[181] [12] There is a river called the Touthoa that

---

180. *Iliad*, 23, 346–7. The *Thebais* is a lost epic of the Seven against Thebes,
attributed to Antimachos of Kolophon. The coinage of Thelpousa has Demeter's
head on one side and this amazing divine horse on the other.

181. Cf. Bk II, 26 (4). Attempts have been made to relate stray antiquities
to this Asklepieion, but they are not convincing.

joins the Ladon at the frontier of Thelpousa with the Heraians, which the Arkadians call the Plain. The point where the Ladon itself joins the Alpheios is called Crow Island. Some people think Enispe and Stratie and Ripe which are listed by Homer were once inhabited islands in the Ladon: anyone who believes this ought to realize it is nonsense: [13] the Ladon could never make islands even the size of a ferry-boat. For beauty there is no foreign river and no Greek river like it, but for size it is not big enough to produce islands like the Danube and the Po.[182]

[1] The HERAIANS were founded by Heraieus son of Ly-   26 kaon; the city stands on the right bank of the Alpheios, most of it on a gentle slope and spreading down to the Alpheios itself.[183] There are tracks beside the river lined with myrtle and various other cultivated trees, the BATHS are here, and there are SHRINES OF DIONYSOS, one of Citizen Dionysos and the other of Dionysos of Increase; [2] the building where they hold Dionysos's mysteries is also here. There is also a TEMPLE OF PAN at Heraia, Pan being a local Arkadian god, and the pillars still survive among the ruins of the TEMPLE OF HERA. The most famous of all Arkadian athletes was Damaretos of Heraia, the first winner of the race in armour at Olympia.[184]

[3] Roughly two miles down towards Eleia from Heraia you cross the Ladon, and from this point you can reach the Erymanthos in about two and a half miles. According to the Arkadians, the Heraian frontier with Elean territory is the

182. The Touthoa has to be the LANGADIA river; Crow Island still exists, in fact there are several islands here. The three places Homer mentions are in the list of Arkadians who went to Troy (*Iliad*, 2, 606). Strabo calls them difficult to find and unrewarding. The Ladon does make little islands, and it really is a most handsome river. But the construction of dams and barrages for the use of water power is altering Peloponnesian rivers as fast as big roads and depopulation are altering villages.

183. The site of Heraia is on the Alpheios a mile or two upstream of the point where the Ladon enters it. Pausanias is moving anti-clockwise round Arkadia. There was once a Greek excavation here; there are no visible monuments but there is no doubt about the site.

184. Cf. Bk V, 8 (10), and Bk VI, 10 (4). He won in 520 B.C.

Erymanthos, but the Eleans claim the limit of Elean territory is the GRAVE OF KOROIBOS.[185] [4] When Iphitos restored the Olympic games after they had died out for a long time, and they held the Olympic festival all over again, the only contest then was a race, and it was Koroibos who won it. An inscription on the tomb declares that Koroibos was the first man who ever won in the Olympic games, and that his grave was built on the edges of Eleia.

[5] There is a smallish town called ALIPHERA, which lost most of its population at the combined settlement of Great City. So to get to this town from Heraia you cross the Alpheios, pass over a plain for something like a mile and a quarter, and reach a mountain; you can climb the mountain to reach the town in another four miles or so.[186] [6] The city of Aliphera was named after Alipheros son of Lykaon; it has SANCTUARIES OF ASKLEPIOS AND ATHENE.[187] She is the god they worship most: they say she was born and reared among them. They have built an altar of Zeus in Bed, where Zeus gave birth to Athene, and a water-fountain they call TRITONIS, where they make the story of the river Triton their own.[188] [7]

185. The Elean–Heraian treaty inscribed on bronze in the sixth century B.C. and brought home from Olympia by Sir William Gell in 1813 is one of the earlier pieces of inscribed continuous Greek prose that now exist, though it is not so old as was once thought; cf. Jeffery Local Scripts of Archaic Greece, pp. 206f. and 216f. There is an instructive commentary on the status of Elis and of Heraia about 500 B.C. in Meiggs and Lewis, Greek Historical Inscriptions, pp. 31f. Pausanias moves west across Ladon along the north bank of Alpheios to the disputed frontier. The grave of Koroibos (cf. Bk V, 8 (6)) is lost; but there is a huge tumulus on the Elean side of the Erymanthos which was opened in 1845. It is common for a real or imaginary champion to be buried at a frontier.

186. Pausanias is still moving south down the western borders of Arkadia. The ruins of Aliphera are on a high, isolated hill above the modern ALIPHERA, the old name of which is RANGOZIO, and north-west of ANDRITSAINA. It was excavated by Mr Orlandos in the 1930s (Arch. Anz., 1933–6). Cf. now A.K. Orlandos, Alipheira (Athens, 1968).

187. Both of these temples were found by Mr Orlandos, with a number of coins, inscriptions and other miscellaneous antiquities.

188. Athene sprang from the head of Zeus. For the story of the river Triton, cf. Bk IX, 33 (7).

The statue of Athene is in bronze, by Hypatodoros, and worth seeing for its size and fineness.[189] They hold a night festival to some god, I think it must be to Athene, in which they sacrifice first to the Fly-hunter, and when they have performed this ceremony the flies are no further annoyance to them.[190] [8] On the way from Heraia to Great City is MELAINEAI, founded by Melaineus son of Lykaon, but deserted in our time and ruined by water. Five miles from Melaineai is Oxeating where the river Oxeater has its springs and flows down to join the Alpheios. The boundaries of Heraia with Great City are at the springs of the Oxeater.[191]

[1] GREAT CITY (*Megalopolis*) is the youngest city not only 27 in Arkadia but in Greece, except for those overtaken by calamity and resettled by colonists from the Roman empire. The Arkadians gathered here to mass their strength, because they knew that long ago the Argives had been in almost literally daily danger of being defeated and overrun by Lakonia, but then Argos had increased its numbers by breaking up Tiryns and Hysiai, Orneai, Mycenae and Mideia, and every other insignificant town in the Argolid, and at once Lakonian pressure decreased and the Argives were able to deal more strongly with

189. It stood on the hilltop; Polybios thought it a fine and beautiful object and was impressed by its enormous size (4, 78). Hypatodoros was a late-fifth-century bronze-caster.

190. As at Olympia (Bk V, 14 (1)).

191. The Greek name of this river is Bouphagos. Pausanias is headed off from the south by Mount LYKAION, so he goes back to Heraia and starts upstream along the Alpheios, moving south-east towards MEGALOPOLIS (Great City) (cf. the excellent survey in *B.C.H.*, 80, 1956, pp. 522f.). The Oxeater seems to be the stream just west of PALAIOKASTRO on the northern bank of the Alpheios, and Oxeating (BOUPHAGION) is the ruined fortification. Frazer believed Melaineai was destroyed by a spring called KAKOREOS, and he visited an unidentified akropolis at PAPPADAS (variously spelt) several miles north of the river. What bounded the territory of Great City was the gorges of the Alpheios, guarded in antiquity by Bouphagion and in the Middle Ages by the wild-looking castle of KARITAINA. An inscription with a place-name in it was copied by the Abbé Fourmount at Karitaina, but the interpretation is most dubious (*I.G.*, V (2), 495).

the provincials.[192] [2] Arkadia made a combined settlement
with the same idea, and Epaminondas of Thebes could justly
be called the founder of the city. It was he who incited the
Arkadians to come together, and he sent a thousand elite
Thebans under Pammenes to defend Arkadia in case the
Lakonians should try to prevent the settlement.[193] The
Arkadians chose as founders Lykomedes and Hopoleas from
Mantineia and Timon and Proxenos from Tegea, Kreolaos
and Akriphios of Kleitor, Eukampidas and Hieronymos of
Mainalos, and Possikrates and Theoxenos of Parrasia. [3]
There were as many cities as the Arkadians could persuade
whether out of positive enthusiasm or out of hostility to
Lakonia to abandon their native places: Alea, Pallantion,
Eutaia, Soumateion, Asea, the Peraitheans, Helisson, Orestha-
sion, Dipaia, and Lykaia, all from Mainalos; the Eutresians of
Trikolonoi, Zoition, Charisia, Ptolederma, Knauson and
Paroreia; [4] the Aigytians of Aigys, Skirtonion, Malea,
Kromoi, Blenina and Leuktron; the Parrasians of Lykosoura,
the Thokneans, Trapezous, the Proseans, Akakesion, Akon-
tion, Makaria, Dasea; from the Arkadian Kynouraians Gortys
and Theison by Lykaion, the Lykaians and Aliphera; from
those who belonged to Orchomenos Theisoa, Methydrion
and Teuthis; there were also the Three Cities, Kallia, Dipoina
and Nonakris.[194] [5] The rest of Arkadia had no reservations

192. This happened after the Persian Wars; for Tiryns, cf. Bk II, 25 (8);
Hysiai, II, 24 (8); Orreai, II, 25 (5); Mycenae, II, 15 (4); Mideia, II, 25 (9).
The word I translate as 'provincials' is *perioikoi*: it means the loosely organized
subject peoples on the borders of Lakonia; in particular the west coast of the
Peloponnese south of Argos was hotly disputed.

193. Epaminondas constructed a line of powerful and threatening cities
across the Peloponnese to keep the Lakonians quiet; Mantineia, Megalopolis
(Great City), and Messene. At Mantineia he started from ruins and at the other
two sites from nothing. The foundation of Great City was in 370, a few months
after the Spartans were broken in battle at Leuktra; it took three years to build.

194. Pausanias divides Arkadia into Mainalos, the Eutresians, the Aigytians,
Parrasians, Arkadian Kynouraia, Orchomenos and the Three Cities; these
divisions were something between a tribal or feudal community and a canton.
The places he mentions are not a comprehensive list of the cities in each canton;
they are the places each canton agreed to abandon. The list is obviously authen-

about the common decision, and joined the Great City with enthusiasm, only the Lykaians and the Trikolonians and Lykosourans and Trapezountians changed their minds, alone in all Arkadia; they withdrew their consent to abandon their ancient cities, and some of them were forced into the Great City against their will, [6] and the Trapezountians emigrated from the Peloponnese altogether, that is those survivors who were not angrily slaughtered by the other Arkadians. Some were rescued, and took ship and reached Pontos, where they were taken in by the people of Trapezous on the Euxine, because they came from the mother city of that same name.[195] In spite of their disobedience the Arkadians were ashamed to touch the Lykosourans because of Demeter and the Mistress in whose sanctuary they took refuge.[196] [7] Of all the other cities I have listed some are completely deserted in our time and the others are villages held by Great City: Gortys, Dipoinai, Orchomenian Theisoa, Methydrion, Teuthis, Kalliai, Helisson. Only Pallantion of all of them was still to experience a sweeter providence. Aliphera retains to this day its original status of city. [8] The Great City was founded in the year of the Lakonian defeat at Leuktra but a few months later, when Phrasikleides was governor of Athens, in the year after the

---

tic; there are forty places mentioned, which is the number Diodoros gives (15, 72). The source of Pausanias's information directly or indirectly is probably an inscription; though no such inscription has been found. Ptolederma and Krauson are never mentioned again and we know nothing else about them. The Three Cities are another problem. Malaia and Leuktron were in the mountains on the Lakonian border. Eutaia was probably near BARBITSA west of the north tip of Parnon. Xenophon speaks of the Eutresians as if of a city (*Hellenika*, 7, 1, 29).

195. The settlement was negotiated by cantons or through commissioners, but certain cities refused to be fed into the new metropolis. Trapezous in Pontos was a Sinopian not an Arkadian colony; it was probably named after its shape. It was a solid and important place, and is better known as the Byzantine city of TREBIZOND (from Trapezounta, like Negroponte from Ston Evripounta for Euripos). The site is on the south coast of the Black Sea, in the north-east corner of Turkey.

196. Cf. Bk VIII, 38 (1).

hundred and second Olympics when Damon the Thourian won the running.[197]

[9] As the Great City people had been enrolled as Theban allies they had nothing to fear from Lakonia, but when Thebes went to war in the Sacred war as it was called, and the Phokians who live on the Boiotian border and were not by any means poverty-stricken as they had captured the Delphic sanctuary, attacked the Thebans, [10] then the Lakonians were in a mood when they would have devastated Great City and all Arkadia to the foundations, but they met a spirited Arkadian defence, and the provincial peoples rose spontaneously to combine with it. At that time there were no important successes on either side, but Arkadian hostility to Lakonia contributed largely to the extension of the Macedonian empire under Philip, and Arkadia did not join in on the Greek side at Chaironeia or later on in Thessaly. [11] Not long afterwards Great City produced the dictator Aristodemos: he was of Phigalian descent and his father was called Artylas, but he was the adopted son of Tritaios, an influential figure in Great City. Even though he was dictator Aristodemos came to be called the Good. During his dictatorship a Lakonian army invaded under Akrotatos, the eldest son of King Kleomenes; I have already explained his ancestry and that of all the Spartan kings.[198] There was a fierce battle with many dead on both sides, but the Great City people won it. Akrotatos was among the Spartan dead, and he never inherited his ancestral crown. [12] Two generations after Aristodemos's death, Lydiades became dictator. He came from a quite distinguished family, he was naturally ambitious of honour and a patriot, which he proved later. He came to power young, but when he began to think he abdicated his dictator-

197. In 370. For the sweetness of providence to Pallantion, cf. Bk VIII, 43 (1f.). It was lavishly restored by an emperor because of its bogus link with the foundation of Rome.

198. Cf. Bk III, 6 (2). We are now in 265. Akrotatos was the son of King Areus; the other Akrotatos who was the son of Kleomenes was his grandfather.

ship although by that time his authority was absolutely secure. The Great City had then joined the Achaian League, and Lydiades' reputation rose so high among his own people and all over Achaia that it rivalled the glorious fame of Aratos.[199] [13] The whole Lakonian people under Agis son of Eudamidas the king of the other family[200] mounted a campaign against Great City more massive and more significant than the expedition under Akrotatos: the city people marched out against them, but the Lakonians won and brought a powerful engine against the fortifications and disjointed the tower they battered with it, hoping to use their engine to break it to pieces next day. [14] But the North-east wind who came to the assistance of the whole of Greece when he shattered most of the Persian fleet on the Sepiades was going to save Great City from its fall; he blew a continuous violent gale that broke up Agis's engine, and scattered its pieces in utter ruin. The Agis whom the North-east wind prevented from capturing Great City is the same man who lost Pellene in Achaia to Aratos and the Sikyonians and met his death later at Mantineia.[201] [15] Not long afterwards Kleomenes son of Leonidas captured Great City during a truce. Some of the people fell

199. Aratos of Achaia. Pausanias tells the story of the Achaian league in Book VII. These events were on the verge of the Roman conquest of Greece. The pedestal of a statue of Lydiades put up by the people of Kleitor has been found at Lykosoura. Pausanias has the dates muddled; it was not by any ordinary standard two generations after Akrotatos that Lydiades came to power. He resigned as he brought Arkadia into the Achaian league in 234. Pausanias's mistake has to do with the genealogies of Spartan kings, a slippery subject.

200. There were two royal families and two kings. Akrotatos had died before his father. King Agis is Agis the fourth.

201. Herodotos tells the story of the storm that destroyed the Persians (7, 188f.). The rocks are on the south-east tip of Thessaly, just above Euboia and opposite the island of Skiathos. There is a lighthouse on the point. Agis is supposed to have been killed at Mantineia in 242; Plutarch says he was killed at Sparta in 241. Pausanias is following a triumphalist Arkadian version. What is worse, unless I am mistaken, he has these events in the wrong order: Agis was killed in 241 before Lydiades had moved from dictator of Megalopolis to officer of the Achaian league: this happened when Arkadia joined the league after the battle of Kleonai, which was fought late in 235.

fighting for their native city during that night, and it was then that Lydiades after putting up an outstanding struggle met his destiny in the fighting.[202] Philopoimen son of Kraugis escaped into Messenia with others, about two thirds of the fighting men and some children. [16] But Kleomenes massacred everyone he caught and demolished and burnt the city. How the people recovered their country and what they did after their return home I shall explain when I come to treat Philopoimen.[203] The Lakonian people had no responsibility for the tragedy of Great City, since Kleomenes had altered their system of government from monarchy to dictatorship.

[17] As I have already said, the boundary of the Great City territory with the Heraians is at the springs of the Oxeater river.[204] They say the river was named after the divine hero Oxeater, a son of Iapetos and Thornax; she has the same name Thornax in Lakonia. They say Oxeater was shot by Artemis on Mount Pholoe, for an impudent and wicked assault on the goddess.

28    [1] On the way from the springs of the river, you find yourself first of all at a place called Maratha, and after that at GORTYS, a village in my time which in the old days was a city.[205] There is a TEMPLE OF ASKLEPIOS here in Pentelic

202. The city fell in 223, but Lydiades had been killed in battle at Ladokeia in 227 (Polybios, 2, 51, 3, and 55, 3).

203. In Chapters 49–51.

204. Cf. Note 191 above.

205. Pausanias has not yet reached Great City (Megalopolis); the historical introduction occurs immediately he reaches the border of its territory; the places in the next few chapters are on Megalopolitan territory though they were once independent; they are on the way from Bouphagion (Oxeating). The whole of Chapter 27 was a digression to explain the frontier. *Maratha* means fennel. The site is perhaps the ruins at HAGIOS NIKOLAOS, north-east of VLACHORAFTI (*B.C.H.*, 80, p. 538), which are at least on the right road from PALAIOKASTRO, but identifications like this are risky: we sometimes seem to have too many names to go round the ruins, but if one looks hard enough one always ends with too many ruins for the available names. Gortys is a formidable akropolis on a precipitous flat-topped hill west of the Gortys stream; it was evidently refortified as a frontier castle at the time Megalopolis was founded. There are no inscriptions, but R. Martin has been able to draw some important conclusions from a detailed study of the site (*B.C.H.*, 71–2, 1947–8, p. 81).

stone, with Asklepios as a beardless youth and a figure of Health, both by Skopas. The local people also say that Philip's son Alexander dedicated his breast-plate and spear to Asklepios, and in my time the breast-plate and the tip of the spear were still preserved.[206]

[2] There is a river flowing through Gortys that the people who live around its springs call the Wash,[207] because it was used for washing at the birth of Zeus, but people who live farther from the springs call it the Gortys river after the name of the village. The Gortys has the coldest water of any river in the world. In my view the Danube and the Rhine and the Hypanis and Borysthenes[208] and all the other rivers that freeze over in the winter really ought to be called winter rivers: they run through country that is under snow for most of the time, and the air around them is full of frost, [3] but what I call rivers of cold water are the ones that flow through temperate country and still cool you if you drink or wash in them in summer, without being affected by the winter. The Kydnos that flows through the territory of Tarsos and the Black river at Side in Pamphylia have cold water; and the coldness of the Ales at Kolophon has been celebrated by elegiac poets.[209] But the Gortys river is colder than any

206. The Asklepieion was south-east of the akropolis and south of the other, smaller fortified area. (The ancient city trailed down the south-west slopes.) Skopas is a fourth-century Parian sculptor; he was an architect, and built the temple of Athene at Tegea as well as making the Asklepios and the Health that stood there. There are pieces of his work from Tegea in the National Museum at Athens.

207. Lousios is the Greek word. This washing is mentioned by Kallimachos in his hymn to Zeus (16f.). The river used to be called DIMITSANA, but there has been an attempt to rename it Lousios.

208. Hypanis and Borysthenes are the Bug and the Dnieper which enter the Black Sea from the north near Greek Olbia west of the Eon estuary.

209. The Kydnos was a famous cold river, good for the nerves and good for gout. It was once navigable up to Tarsos. Side was on the gulf of ANTALYA north-west of Cyprus. The site used to be much visited and has been often described. Cf. now Bean, *Turkey's Southern Shore* (1968), pp. 78f. For Kolophon, cf. Bk VII, 3 (1–4), and for the Ales, Bk VII, 5 (10).

of them and particularly in the summer. Its springs are at Theisoa which shares a border with Methydrion, and the spot where it discharges into the Alpheios is called Raiteai.[210]

[4] Just across the border from Theisoa there is a village called TEUTHIS, which was once a town.[211] In the Trojan War it had a leader of its own, who was called Teuthis or some say Ornytos. When the Greeks were unable to get a carrying wind from Aulis, and a gale had pinned them there for some time, Teuthis came to hate Agamemnon and was going to take his Arkadian detachment home again, but [5] they say Athene disguised as Melas son of Ops turned him back from the road home; Teuthis was swelling with anger and hit the goddess in the thigh with his spear, and then brought his army home from Aulis. But when he got home they say the goddess herself appeared to him with her thigh wounded, and from that moment a wasting disease took hold of Teuthis and the earth refused its fruits only in this place in all Arkadia. [6] Later the oracle at Dodona told them ceremonies to perform to placate the goddess and they made a statue of Athene with a wound in her thigh. I have seen this statue myself, with its thigh bound in a crimson bandage. The other things at Teuthis include a sanctuary of Aphrodite and Artemis. [7] That is what there is. On the road from Gortys to Great

210. For Theisoa and Methydrion, cf. Bk VIII, 36 (1), and 38 (3). The remotest springs are a long way north above KALONERION, north of the mountain village of DIMITSANA, but Pausanias means a fortified site at KARKALOU north-east of Dimitsana. Many of the antiquities at Dimitsana were not found there but collected from considerable distances by a local schoolmaster in the last century, but the site of Theisoa does seem to be guaranteed (I.G., V (2), 510). It was excavated by G. Oikonomos. The modern Theisoa south of the Alpheios is many miles from the right place.

211. Teuthis is supposed to be at DIMITSANA, and there was certainly a fortified town there in ancient times. None of the inscriptions there name Teuthis, which ought to be near Methydrion, not far east of Karkalou. Teuthis must at least be east of the river to be in Methydrion territory; I am not convinced that either the Dimitsana site or Leake's suggestion (Morea, 2, pp. 60–5) is in the right place.

City is the monument of those who died in battle against Kleomenes. The city people call this monument the PARAI-BASION, because Kleomenes broke the truce.[212] It overlooks a plain of seven or eight miles. On the right of the road there are the ruins of the city of BRENTHE, where the Brenthe stream rises to join the Alpheios about half a mile away.[213]

[1] Across Alpheios is the territory of TRAPEZOUS and the ruins of the city. On your left as you come down again to the Alpheios from Trapezous not far from the river is the Depth, where they celebrate a mystery of the Great goddesses once every two years. There is a spring at this place called Olympias,[214] which ceases to flow in the other year, and near this spring they light a fire. The Arkadians say the legendary battle of gods and giants took place here and not in Thracian Pallene, and they sacrifice here to the lightning and the storms and the thunder. [2] Homer never mentions the giants in the *Iliad*, but in the *Odyssey* he writes of the Laistrygonians attacking Odysseus's ships like giants and not like men, and he makes the king of the Phaiakes say the Phaiakes were close to the gods, like the Kyklopes and the race of giants. That passage shows the giants were mortal

29

212. *Paraibasion* comes from a word that can also mean 'to pass by', a likelier derivation. I am unable to reproduce the ambiguity in English. I wonder if Paraibasion is not the odd little archaic fort at HELLENIKON north-east of Karitaina (*B.C.H.*, 80, p. 542). The place and its name may well be older than the tomb.

213. At the Paraibasion you were out of the gorge; Brenthe must have been on a stream near Karitaina.

214. These sites were identified easily and to some degree excavated by Mr A. G. Bather and Mr V. W. Yorke (*Journal of Hellenic Studies*, 13, pp. 227f.) in 1893, and by Mr K. Stephanos of the Archaeological Society of Athens in 1907. He found some little bronze and terracotta pigs, and apparently a miniature bronze statue of the Great goddess (*Praktika*, pp. 122–4). The sites are at what is still called BATHYREVMA below the chapel of St George, and at KYPARISSIA, north-west of Megalopolis and south-south-east of Karitaina. The spring was said in the last century to stop running one year in every nine. The pigs were found at both sites. There is a widespread popular story in Arkadia of an ancient golden treasure, a great gold sow and twelve gold piglets, said to lie buried at whatever is the local archaeological site.

and not a divine race, and this one shows it even more clearly:

> who was king of the high-spirited giants,
> destroyed his reckless people and perished.[215]

The word 'people' in Homeric poetry means the human crowd.

[3] Many other places in my discussions and particularly the present instance shows that the story of giants having serpents instead of feet is ridiculous.[216] The Roman king wanted to make the Syrian river Orontes navigable from the sea to the city of Antioch, though its natural course is not all over level ground – in fact it falls down a cliff – so with labour and expense he excavated a navigable canal and turned the river to run in it. [4] When the old course of the water had drained out they found a coffin in it more than sixteen feet long, and the corpse was the size of the coffin, and a human body in every detail. When the Syrians went to consult the oracle the gods at Klaros said the dead man was Orontes who was an Indian.[217] If the sun created the first men by heating the earth which was originally wet and still full of moisture, what other country is likely to have produced earlier or bigger men than India which even today breeds wild beasts of extraordinary size and peculiar appearance?

[5] BASILIS is something over a mile from the place they call the Depth; it was founded by Kypselos who gave his daughter to Kresphontes son of Aristomachos. In my day Basilis and

215. All these references are to the *Odyssey*: 10, 118; 7, 205; 2, 59.

216. Chthonic beings have serpentine lower limbs. There is a splendid archaic triple snake-bodied god from a pre-Persian temple on the akropolis at Athens; the convention persisted as late as the Roman period, and serpent-bodied giants held up the Odeon in the agora at Athens.

217. Tiberius had some interest in this river and he may be the emperor concerned. Philostratos (*Heroikos*, 2, 4) says the giant was called Aryades. Strabo says the river used to be called Typhon, after a dragon who was struck by lightning and cut the river-bed with his tail. I can discover no trace of the canal to Antioch, but the story may mean simply a dredging and levelling operation.

its SANCTUARY OF ELEUSINIAN DEMETER were in ruins.[218]
Proceed from here to the Alpheios and cross it again and you
reach THOKNIA, named after Thoknos son of Lykaon, which
in my time was completely deserted. Thoknos was said to have
built his city on the hill, and the river Aminios flows beside it
to meet the Helisson which not far away joins the Alpheios.[219]

[1] The Helisson begins from a village with the same name 30
of Helisson, and passes through the Dipaian and then the
Lykaian country and finally through Great City itself, to join
the Alpheios two or three miles from the city. Quite close to
the city is a temple of Overseeing Poseidon in which the head
of the statue has survived.[220]

[2] The river Helisson divides GREAT CITY (*Megalopolis*)
just as the narrows of the sea divide Knidos from Mitylene.
The MARKET-PLACE is in the northern part which is on the
right bank of the river.[221] In the market-pace there is a stone
enclosure and a SANCTUARY OF LYKAIAN ZEUS, but without

218. The akropolis is just above Kyparissia; cf. Note 214 above.

219. Thoknia was north of the Alpheios quite close to Megalopolis, but
downstream from the place where the Helisson and the Alpheios come together. It must have been near VROMOSELLA (Dirty Saddle), which has
now been renamed THOKNIA. Stray antiquities have been seen there. Mr
Stephanos dug a great number of trenches there in 1907 and since he observed
nothing but fragments of pottery believed there was no settlement, and casti-
gated Pausanias for mythological tomfoolery (*Praktika*, 1907, p. 122).

220. The springs of the Helisson are a long way to the north-east, on the
slopes of MAINALOS (MOURTZIA) north-west of Tripolis. For Lykaia cf. Bk
VIII, 36 (7). DIPAIA, which Pausanias never visits, was near PIANA due west of
the southernmost part of Mainalos. Overseeing Poseidon has been lost.

221. The site of GREAT CITY, just north of modern MEGALOPOLIS (which
has grown out of the village of SINANOU), is more or less south-west of
TRIPOLIS, which is its modern equivalent and was the Turkish capital of the
Peloponnese. Several generations before Pausanias Strabo says it was abandoned
in his time except for a few shepherds. Part of its remains were excavated in the
1890s and admirable plans made of the rest, since when rather a lot has disappeared. The excavators were British. There is not much left north of the
river but some interesting stone lying here and there in the fields. The market-
place was west of the modern Helisson bridge; it seems partly to have been
destroyed by the river. The publication of the digs of 1890–1 was issued by the
Society of Hellenic Studies in 1892. The map in Frazer's commentary is less full
but clearer.

any entrance. You can see everything inside: there are altars of the god and two tables and two eagles, and a stone statue of Pan. [3] He has the title of Sinoean Pan, which they say comes from the nymph Sinoe, because she and other nymphs (particularly Sinoe) were Pan's nurses. In front of this precinct is a bronze statue of Apollo worth seeing, which is twelve feet high, and was brought from the Phigalean territory to help to ornament the Great City. [4] The place where this statue was originally erected by the Phigaleans is called BASSAI.[222] The god still has his Phigalean title, and my discussion of Phigalia will explain how he came to be called the Helper. On the right of Apollo is a smallish statue of the Mother of gods with nothing left of the temple except the columns.

[5] In front of the TEMPLE OF THE MOTHER there are no human figures at all, but the pedestals where figures once stood are plain to see. A couplet inscribed on one of these pedestals says it was a portrait of Diophanes son of Diaios, the first man to include the entire Peloponnese in the Achaian League.[223] [6] The colonnade in the market-place called the PHILIPPEION was not built by Philip son of Amyntas: the city was paying him the compliment of naming the building after him.[224] The TEMPLE OF AKAKESIAN HERMES next to it had been demolished, and there was nothing left of it but a stone tortoise. There is another smaller COLONNADE next to the Philippeion, where are the six official buildings of Great City. In one of them is a statue of Ephesian Artemis and in another a bronze Pan eighteen inches high called Skoleitas [7] who was brought from the hill Skoleitas, which as a matter of fact is inside the fortifications; there is a stream of water that rises from a spring there and runs down into the Helisson.[225] Behind the

222. Cf. Bk VIII, 41 (7f.).    223. For this Diophanes, cf. Bk VIII, 51 (1).

224. It probably contained his statue. It was on the north side of the square, and has been excavated. It had been reconstructed in the third century B.C. (Livy, 38, 34).

225. Some remains of the offices were recovered in 1891. An inscription was found nearby that mentioned a records office, keepers of the records and legal secretaries. The hill Skoleitas is an unsolved puzzle; the excavators seem to have neglected the question.

offices is a SHRINE OF FORTUNE with a stone statue at least five feet high. The colonnade called the SCENT MARKET in the market-place was built from spoils of war at the defeat of Kleomenes' son Akrotatos and his Lakonian expedition, in their battle with Aristodemos who was then dictator of Great City.[226] [8] In the Great City market-place behind the enclosure dedicated to Lykaian Zeus, there is a stone tablet with a relief carving of a man: Polybios son of Lykortas. There is an inscription about him in couplets saying he wandered all over the earth and the sea, he was an ally of Rome, and he ended the Roman anger with Greece.[227] This Polybios wrote a Roman history including an account of how Rome went to war with Carthage, [9] with the cause of the war and how after a long time and after being in great danger the Romans ... Scipio, whom they call the Carthaginian, who put an end to the war and destroyed Carthage to its foundations. So far as the Romans followed Polybios's advice, things went well for them, but when they disregarded instructions, they say there were disasters. The Greek cities that belonged to the Achaian league managed to obtain Polybios from the Romans to establish their constitutions and make laws for them. The COUNCIL-HOUSE is on the left of Polybios's portrait.

[10] That is what is here. They say the market-place colonnade called the ARISTANDREION was built by a citizen called Aristandros. Very close to this colonnade to the east of it is a SANCTUARY OF ZEUS Saviour, ornamented with pillars all round it. Zeus is seated on a throne with the Great City standing beside him and a statue of Artemis Saviour on his left. These are all made of Pentelic stone, and the artists are Kephisodotos and Xenophon of Athens.[228]

226. Probably the colonnade on the east side of the market. For the battle, cf. Bk VIII, 27 (11), and Note 198.

227. The great Polybios; cf. Bk VIII, 9 (2). This inscription was more elaborate than the ones at Olympia and Kleitor (*I.G.*, V (2), 370).

228. Part of this sanctuary was eaten off by the river; what was left was excavated, but there is very little left of it now. The two sculptors appear to have worked in the early fourth century, so it looks as if the statues were

31 [1] The other end of the colonnade towards the west has a sacred ENCLOSURE OF THE GREAT GODDESSES. The Great goddesses are Demeter and the Maid as I have explained already in my description of Messenia, though the Arkadians call the Maid the Saviour. There are relief carvings of Artemis worked on one side of the entrance and Asklepios and Health on the other. [2] As for the Great goddesses, Demeter is completely

15. *Zeus Saviour*

in stone, but the Saviour has her drapery in wood; each of them is about fifteen feet high. ... He has also carved smallish statues of young girls in front of them, in ankle-length tunics, one of them carrying a basket full of flowers on her head; they are said to be Damophon's daughters, though some who favour a more god-haunted explanation believe them to be Athene and Artemis picking flowers with Persephone.[229] [3] There is also a Herakles beside Demeter about eighteen inches

commissioned with the temple, though there was also a younger Kephisodotos. For Xenophon, cf. Bk IX, 16 (2). This Zeus seems to be the one on coins of Great City.

229. Damophon of Messene made a big group at Lykosoura parts of which have been found, and worked at Messene when it was rebuilt (Bk IV, 31 (6f.). He probably worked at Great City around 180 B.C.

450

high. Onomakritos in his hexameters says this Herakles is one of the Idaian Daktyloi.[230] There is a table in front of him, with two Seasons worked on it and Pan with a reed-pipe and Apollo playing the lute. There is an inscription saying these are among the first of the gods. [4] The table also has a representation of Nymphs, Neda carrying the infant Zeus and another Arkadian nymph Anthrakia holding a torch, and Hagno with a water-jar in one hand and a drinking cup in the other; Anchiroe and Myrtoessa are carrying water-jars and in fact water is pouring down from them. Inside the enclosure is a SHRINE OF ZEUS of Friendship, with the statue by Polykleitos of Argis, rather like a Dionysos as he is wearing buskins and has a cup in one hand and a pine-wand in the other, only with an eagle perching on it, which is not consonant with the legends about Dionysos.[231] [5] Behind this shrine is a grove of trees of no great size surrounded by a stone barrier. No human being is allowed inside here, but there are statues of Demeter and the Maid in front of it about three feet high. Also inside the enclosure of the Great goddesses is a SANCTUARY OF APHRODITE. In front of the entrance there are ancient wooden idols of Hera and Apollo and the Muses, which they say were brought from TRAPEZOUS, and [6] the statues in the temple are by Damophon: a Hermes in wood and a wooden image of Aphrodite, with stone hands and face and feet. I thought their title for the goddess, the Contriver, was absolutely right; Aphrodite and her activities are the source of many, many devices and every kind of fresh resource of human language. [7] There are also portrait statues standing in this building, of

230. It was almost certainly the Herm of Herakles that occurs on Megalopolitan coins. Mr Dickins has pointed out that in this case as in others Damophon imitated an existing rather stylized type (cf. *B.S.A.*, 13, pp. 402–4). For Herakles and the Daktyloi, cf. Bk V, 7 (6f.). The best general discussion of what kind of god the Daktyloi were is by Dr Bengt Hemberg in his *Die Kabiren* (Uppsala, 1950). Onomakritos was an Athenian religious and ritual poet; he lived at the end of the sixth century and got into trouble for forging an oracle (Herodotos 7, 6).

231. This sounds very odd for the great fifth-century Polykleitos, but no doubt the statue is by his later namesake. This Zeus seems to have been a Zeus of alliance or confederation.

Kallignotos, Mentas, Sosigenes and Polos, who are supposed to have first established the mystery of the Great goddesses in the city, and the imitations of the Eleusinian ceremonies. There are also these square-shaped statues of other gods inside the enclosure: Hermes the Leader, Apollo, Athene, Poseidon, the Saviour Sun, and Herakles. There is a huge building where they celebrate the mystery of the goddesses.[232]

[8] On the right of the temple of the Great goddesses, there is another SANCTUARY OF THE MAID; the statue is in stone and about eight feet high, and the whole of its pedestal is festooned in ribbons. Women are always allowed into this sanctuary, but men go in only once in the year. There is a training-ground built adjoining the market-place on the west. [9] There are two hills of no particular height behind the colonnade named after Philip of Macedon, on one of which is the ruined SANCTUARY OF ATHENE of the City and on the other a TEMPLE OF PERFECT HERA which is also in ruins. Below this hill is a water-spring called Bathyllos which goes to swell the river Helisson.[233]

32 [1] Those were the important things. The part of the city over the river, that is the southern part, offers for the record the biggest THEATRE in Greece, which has a perpetual water-spring in it.[234] Not far from the theatre lie the foundations that have survived from the COUNCIL-HOUSE built for the ten thousand Arkadians; it was called the Thersilion after the man who dedicated it.[235] Near by is the house which belonged

232. The Herm of Poseidon was dedicated by Damophon; part of it has survived, with an ornamental trident in low relief on the block and the dedication to Poseidon of Safety inscribed on the crossbar of the trident (*B.S.A.*, 12, pp. 134–6). The mystery building was probably west of the market-place; at least there is one crumb of evidence that suggests this (*Excavations at Megalopolis*, 1892, p. 116).

233. The excavators reckoned this spring had disappeared; it is open to anyone who wishes to do so to make a conjectural identification.

234. The theatre used to have a crown of trees above it that nodded, but it has recently been stripped down like an old engine. The water was still there in the summer of 1963, west of the theatre, and there are still trees.

235. The theatre faces this big political building, which occupies the south bank of the river opposite the temple of Zeus.

in my time to a private individual but was originally built for Philip's son Alexander.[236] There is a statue of Ammon by the house in the form of one of those square figures of Hermes, with ram's horns on its head. [2] The SANCTUARY OF THE MUSES with Apollo and Hermes, erected for all of them together, does not offer much in the way of foundations for the record, but one of the Muses was still there and a statue of Apollo in the style of a square Hermes. APHRODITE'S SANCTUARY was in ruins as well, with the exception of the porch and three statues; Heavenly Aphrodite, Popular Aphrodite, and a third without a title.[237] [3] There is an altar of Ares not far away, but it was said that the god originally had a sanctuary as well. They have built a STADIUM above Aphrodite's temple which in one direction reaches to the theatre, where they have a fountain they believe is sacred to Dionysos, and at the other end of which a TEMPLE OF DIONYSOS was said to have been struck by lightning two generations before my own; in my day there was not much left of the ruins. The temple shared by Herakles and Hermes beside the stadium was no longer in existence; nothing was left but the altar. [4] In this half of the city there is a hill towards the east with a TEMPLE OF HUNTRESS ARTEMIS dedicated among other offerings by Aristodemos.[238] On the right of the Huntress is a holy precinct with a SANCTUARY OF ASKLEPIOS and statues of Asklepios and Health, and as you go down a little way some gods in the square style called the Workers: Working Athene and Apollo of the Road, and Hermes and Herakles and Eileithuia who have a reputation for work from Homeric poetry, Hermes for being the servant of Zeus and guiding the souls of the dead down to Hades, Herakles for completing many difficult labours, and Eileithuia in the *Iliad* looks after the birth-pangs of

236. It must have been between the spring and the river and opposite the temple of Zeus.

237. There is an inscription in verse recording the building of a wall round this temple and a banqueting room in the mid second century B.C. It was found in use as a sanctuary step in a church at the nearest village.

238. For Aristodemos, cf. Bk VIII, 27 (11). The site is problematic.

women.[239] [5] Under this hill there is another SANCTUARY OF CHILD ASKLEPIOS. His statue is standing and just eighteen inches high, but Apollo's is enthroned and all of six feet.[240] There are some bones dedicated here that seem too vast for a human being, and actually there was a story about them that they belonged to one of the giants that Hopladamos collected to fight for Rea, but I shall come to all that later.[241] Near this sanctuary is a water-spring that travels down into the streams of the Helisson.

33 • [1] I am not astounded that Great City which the Arkadians founded in all eagerness, and for which Greece had the highest hopes, should have lost all its beauty and ancient prosperity, or that most of it should be ruins nowadays, because I know that the daemonic powers love to turn things continually upside down, and I know that fortune alters everything, strong and weak, things at their beginning and things at their ending, and drives everything with a strong necessity according to her whim. [2] Mycenae which led the Greeks in the Trojan War, and Nineveh, seat of the Assyrian kingdom, are deserted and demolished, and Boiotian Thebes, once the chosen champion of Greece, has left its name to nothing but the fortified rock and a tiny population. Centres of overwhelming wealth in antiquity, like Egyptian Thebes and Minyan Orchomenos, are not so prosperous now in the power of riches as a single moderately wealthy individual, and Delos, the common marketing place of Greece, if you took away the sanctuary guards who come from Athens, so far as

239. This sentence is so awkwardly constructed in Greek as to be almost incoherent, and I am not certain there are not a few words missing. The references to Homer are *Odyssey*, 24, 1, and *Iliad*, 8, 362, and 16, 187, and 19, 103.

240. Loring thought this was north-east of the theatre; his arguments appear flimsy but he knew the alternative sites and their problems and possibilities extremely well.

241. Bk VIII, 36 (2). A number of fossil bones have been found at Megalopolis in this century. They are in the old petrological museum close to the University of Athens, a ruinous building that can be visited only by personal negotiation.

Delians are concerned would be utterly deserted. [3] The sanctuary of Bel survives at Babylon, but of that Babylon which was the greatest city the sun saw in its time, nothing was left except a fortress wall, like the one at Tiryns in the Argolid. The daemonic power annihilated all these, and Alexander's city in Egypt and Seleukos's city on the Orontes were built yesterday and the day before, and have risen to such greatness and such prosperity because Fortune is favouring them. [4] There is a way in which Fortune shows a still greater and even more astounding power than in the tragedies and the happiness of cities. The island of Chryse where they say Philoktetes suffered his tragedy from the water-snake was not a long voyage away from Lemnos: it was completely submerged by the waves of the sea, Chryse sank and vanished into the depths. Another island called Holy Island . . . during this time.[242]

[1] That is how temporary and completely insecure human 34 things are. On the way from Great City to Messene just under a mile along the road there is a divine SANCTUARY on the left of the highway. The goddesses themselves are called the Crazes and the country round the sanctuary has the same name.[243] I think this is a title of the Furies, and they say Orestes went crazy here over the murder of his mother. [2] Not far from

242. All these examples are mentioned again elsewhere by Pausanias, though never in such a torrent. Alexander's city is Alexandria and Seleukos's is Antioch. DELOS was not completely abandoned for some years, although at about the time Pausanias was writing the Athenians were so tired of it they tried to sell it (Philostratos, *Lives of the Sophists*, 1, 23). The island of Chryse seems to have been tiny; it existed as late as the first century B.C. and must have disappeared in some volcanic disturbances. Holy Island was a small island off SANTORINI that appeared out of the sea during a volcanic eruption; another one appeared near it between 1707 and 1709 (cf. Bk III, 1 (8); also Fouqué, *Santorin et ses éruptions*, 1879). The palace and city of THERA were overwhelmed in the Minoan palace period by an enormous upheaval of the same island. Most of Thera is still under a massive depth of lava, but erosion has now made some excavation possible. The site was abandoned before the final catastrophe but dead animals have been found on the upper floors of houses.

243. Pausanias is moving south-west; the place has not been found unless at some mounds observed by Curtius (*Pelop.*, 1f., 291).

the sanctuary is quite a small tumulus with a finger of stone standing on it, and this mound is called the Finger tomb. They say Orestes in his madness bit off a finger of his left hand here. There is another place adjoining this called Cure, because Orestes was cured of his illness there; the Furies have a SANCTUARY there. [3] When the goddesses were going to drive Orestes mad they are said to have appeared to him all black, and when he bit off his finger they suddenly seemed to turn white, and the sight of them sobered him and he consumed offerings in fire to turn away their wrath, and performed divine sacrifice to the white goddesses. They believe he sacrificed to the Graces at the same time. By the place called Cure is another SANCTUARY called the Barber because Orestes cut his hair there when he came to his senses. [4] The ancient historians of the Peloponnese say Orestes' adventures in Arkadia with the Furies of Klytaimnestra happened before the decision at the Hill of Ares, his accuser there not being Tyndareos, who was dead by then, but Perilaos, who knew law and sued him for his mother's murder as Klytaimnestra's cousin: Perilaos was a son of Ikarios, who later on had daughters as well.[244]

[5] The road from Crazes to the Alpheios is just about two miles. This is where the Gathean river into which the Karnion has already flowed falls into the Alpheios. The springs of the Karnion are in the Aigytian country below the SANCTUARY OF HORNED APOLLO, the springs of the Gathean river at GATHEAI in the Kromian territory, which [6] lies about five miles above the Alpheios: the ruins of the city of KROMOI in that area are not completely obliterated.[245] It is about two and

244. This piece of misplaced ingenuity is an attempt to explain how Orestes, whose home was in the Argolid and whose guilt was well known to have been purged at Athens, could also have had strong local connexions with these remote mountains. But a name like Orestes or Herakles is applied to such a local religious cult at a comparatively late stage; the making-up of stories like this is an even later rationalization. I do not believe that the finger was originally a finger.

245. The Gathean river and the Karnion combined are the XERILOPOTAMO or XERILAS. It joins the Alpheios near TRIPOTAMON. The main Xerilas rises

a half miles from Kromoi to Nymphas, which has been broken
up by water and is overgrown with trees. Two and a half miles
more from here is the Hermaion, where Great City has its
boundary with Messenia. Here as well there is a stone relief of
Hermes.[246]

[1] This road goes to Messene, another one leads from 35
Great City to the Messenian Karnasion; if you take it you will
find yourself first of all at the Alpheios where the already
combined streams of the Malous and the Skyros flow into it.
From this point you keep the Malous on your right and after
about four miles cross over it and climb up by a very steep
road to a place called Phaidrias.[247] [2] About two miles from
Phaidrias is what they call the HERMAION AT THE MISTRESS.
Here again is a frontier of Great City with Messenia, and there
are smallish statues of the Mistress and Demeter and also of
Hermes and Herakles. In my opinion the wooden idol of
Herakles that Daidalos made stands here on the actual frontier
between Arkadia and Messenia.[248]

---

on the north-west slopes of TAYGETOS, and a tributary rises east of Mount
BOUZOURI below the pass of the modern main road to KALAMATA and the
ancient road to Messene. Gatheai and Kromoi seem both to have been fortified
mountain towns. In this wild area no traveller seems able to find the same
ruins as another; several fortresses have been reported and none confirmed. The
best guide is still Leake (*Morea*, 2, pp. 295f., and *Peloponnesiaca*, p. 235).

246. Nymphas sounds like a powerful mountain torrent, but 'destroyed by
water' might mean a landslide. No one who has not seen a landslide in the
Greek mountains could perhaps imagine how completely it obliterates human
constructions.

247. This pass seems to be farther north. If so the fact is surprising, as Pausanias usually takes routes more in order. For Karnasion, cf. Bk IV, 2 (2).
Phaidrias has to be near Lykosoura (Bk VIII, 38 (1f.)). Pausanias is taking a
high pass, probably the one by ISARIS and BASTAS where a track still crosses
the mountains into Messenia, and where there seem to be suitable rivers, but
perhaps the track south from Bastas through the modern KARNASION (cf.
Valmin, *Messénie ancienne*, pp. 95–6).

248. Pausanias is very interested in the stiff and archaic works he attributes to
the legendary Daidalos (cf. Bk I, 27 (1) etc.). Among the smooth forests of
solemn classical and sweeter Hellenistic art with which he was familiar, these
sharp and powerful prehistoric works must indeed have seemed godlike.

[3] The road from Great City to Lakonia comes to the Alpheios in four miles and from that point it travels beside the river Theious, which is one of the tributaries of the Alpheios, and then leaving the Theious on your left you reach Phalaisiai five miles from the Alpheios. From Phalaisiai to the Hermaion at Belemina is two and a half miles.[249] [4] The Arkadians say Belemina belonged originally to them and the Lakonians annexed it, but this appeared unlikely to me, for one thing because I hardly think the Thebans would have overlooked a piece of Arkadia being chopped off in this way, if they could decently have redressed matters.

[5] There are other roads from Great City to places in the interior of Arkadia; it is twenty-one miles to Methydrion, and in just over a mile and a half you come to a place called SKIAS and the ruined SANCTUARY OF ARTEMIS of Skias, said to have been built by the dictator Aristodemos. A mile and a quarter from here there are a few relics of the city of Charisiai, and another mile and a quarter farther on is the site of TRIKOL-ONOI.[250] [6] It was a city once, and even today there is still a SANCTUARY OF POSEIDON left on a hill with a square statue, and a sacred wood growing round the sanctuary. Lykaon's sons founded these cities. ZOITIA lies about two miles from Trikolonoi, not on the direct road, but on the left.[251] They say it was founded by Zoiteus son of Trikolonos, while Trikol-onos's younger son Paroreus founded PARORIA, which is a mile and a quarter from Zoitia. [7] Both sites were uninhabited

249. South-south-east from Great City. Belemina was on Mount CHELMOS. The village of BOURA some miles north-west of LONGANIKOS has now been renamed PHALAISIA, probably wrongly since the site is likely to have been farther east, and the BOURA site is dubious. The Theious is the KOUTOU-PHARINA.

250. Methydrion is more or less north of Megalopolis and north-west of Tripolis. The sanctuary of Artemis Skias is lost. For Aristodemos, cf. Bk IV, 9 (6f.). Charisiai and Trikolonoi seem to be near TRILOPHON and near KARATOULA, but there are some inviting ruins at ZONE (ZOUNATION) and nothing at Trilophon so far as I can discover.

251. Zoitia might be ZONE.

in my time, though there is still a SHRINE OF DEMETER
left at Zoitia, and of Artemis. There are other ruined cities,
THYRAION about two miles from Paroria, and HYPSOUS
on a mountain overlooking the plain and called Mount
Hypsous.[252] The whole country between Thyraion and
Hypsous is mountainous and infested with wild beasts. I have
already explained that Thyraios and Hypsous were sons of
Lykaon.

[8] To the right from Trikolonoi there is a road precipitous
at first to a spring called the Wells. In something under four
miles down from the Wells you reach KALLISTO'S GRAVE, a
high mound with a lot of trees on it, barren and cultivated
trees alike. On the top of the mound is a SANCTUARY OF
ARTEMIS Kalliste. [9] Three miles from here and twelve or so
from Trikolonoi, on the banks of the Helisson and on the
direct road to Methydrion, that is on the one road from Trikolonoi I still have to discuss, there is a place called Anemosa and
Mount Phalanthos where the ruins of the city of PHALAN-
THOS lie.[253] They say Phalanthos was the son of Agelaos son of
Stymphelos. [10] Above this is the plain of Polos, and beyond
that SCHOINOUS, named after a Boiotian called Schoineus. If
this Schoineus emigrated to Arkadia, Atalante's tracks must
have been close to Schoinous, as they were named after this

252. Mount Hypsous must be KLINITSA, the mountain directly north of
Megalopolis. The sites have not been found.
253. The Helisson swings too far east to be a straight route from the city to
Methydrion. Pausanias has halted at Trikolonoi. He first turns west to Zone and
wanders into the mountains, and then east or north-east to the Wells (a
mountain-spring) and to Kallisto's grave; he then moves down to the Helisson
somewhere near PIANA north-west of Tripolis. He could have reached the
same point on the Helisson without visiting Kallisto's grave, though this
'direct' route would probably have followed the river and might have been
longer. As it is he visited the grave from Trikolonoi and found himself so close
to the Methydrion road he went straight to it without returning home to
Trikolonoi. Leake thought Anemosa was near ARKOUDOREVMA, west of
Piana and north-west of Tripolis (*Pelopponesiaca*, pp. 238f.). Frazer complains
about Leake's spelling of the name ZIBOVISI for LIBOVISI, but the word is
spelt in the same way on the *Carte de la Morée*. Phalanthos is west of ALONI-
STAINA and just south-west of the northern peaks of Mainalos.

man's daughter. Next . . . I think it took its name, and they say everyone calls this region Arkadia.[254]

36      [1] There is nothing else left to record from here except METHYDRION itself. The road to Methydrion from Trikolonoi is a journey of sixteen and a half miles. It was named Methydrion because of a big knoll in between the river Maloitas and the river Mylaon where Orchomenos built the city.[255] Before joining the Great City Methydrion on its own had men who won at Olympia. [2] There is a SHRINE OF HORSE POSEIDON at Methydrion on the Mylaon. Mount Marvellous rises above the river Maloitas, and the Methydrians claim that when Rea was pregnant with Zeus she came to this mountain and got help in case Kronos attacked her, from Hopladamos and his giants. [3] They admit that she gave birth in some part of Lykaion, but they say it was here she tricked Kronos by the legendary substitution of the stone. Near the crest of the mountain there is a CAVE OF REA, into which no person may ever enter except women consecrated to the goddess.[256]

[4] The spring Nymphasia is something like four miles from Methydrion, and the place where the boundaries of Great City and Orchomenos and the Kaphyans meet is as far again.[257]

254. Pausanias means that the man must be Atalante's father, Schoineus son of Athamas. The word *Schoinous* means 'the rushes'. He is talking about the district where Methydrion is, but Schoinous is another lost place.

255. Methydrion is in the angle of two mountain rivers, called NEMNITSA and BOURBOULISTRA west of Mount TZELATI, the north-west peak of Mount MAINALON. The two rivers run north to feed the TRAGOS and in the end the LADON. The site is quite near the main road from Tripolis to the west coast. Such ruins as survive are rather overgrown. *Methydrion* means 'between waters'.

256. The temple of Horse Poseidon is on the banks of a western tributary that joins the other two rivers just below Methydrion. This river is called KORPHOXYLIA. The temple was to have been excavated in 1859 by a Mr Tangopoulos, but no results were ever published so far as I know. The cave has not been found.

257. Great City owned all the central mountains including Methydrion. Nymphasia may be the powerful water-spring at BYTINA farther north. A village has been named NYMPHASIA as far north again near what must have been the border. For Orchomenos, cf. Bk VIII, 13 (2); for Kaphya, 23 (2).

[5] What they call the Marsh gates of Great City lead to Mainalos along the river Helisson; on the left of the road is a SHRINE OF THE GOOD GOD. If the gods are rivers of good to mankind and Zeus is the supreme god, one could logically conclude that this title belongs to Zeus. Not much farther on is a tumulus where Aristodemos is buried, whom even his dictatorship could not prevent from being called the Good, and a SANCTUARY OF ATHENE with the title of the Contriver, because this goddess invented all kinds of ideas and devices.[258]
[6] On the right of the road is a sacred precinct of the Northeast wind; the city people offer him sacrifices every year and they honour him as much as any of the gods, because he saved them from Agis and the Lakonians.[259] Next to this comes Amphiaraos's father Oikles' tomb, if in fact he met his fate in Arkadia and not on Herakles' campaign against Laomedon. Beyond this is the TEMPLE and the sacred grove of DEMETER in the Marsh, as they call her. You are half a mile or so from the city; only women are allowed in.[260] [7] Four miles on is the region called Paliskios; from here you leave the Elaphos, which dries up sometimes, on your left, and proceed two and a half miles, and among the ruins of the Peraitheans you will find a SANCTUARY OF PAN. Cross the dry gully which is a winter torrent, go straight on, and two miles from the river you come to a plain; cross it and you come to the mountain which shares its name, Mainalos. Below the skirts of the mountain there are traces of a city called LYKOA, with a sanctuary and a bronze statue of Artemis of Lykoa.[261] [8] To the south of

258. English archaeologists in 1890 dug a series of holes in a tumulus on the wrong side of the river called the Turk's tump (*Arapou magoula*) and seem to have found Hellenistic burials (*Excavations in Megalopolis*, p. 9 and p. 118).

259. Cf. Bk VIII, 27 (14).

260. None of these landmarks has been found.

261. The Elaphos is the stream that rises near ARACHAMITAI. The remains of a big Doric temple on top of HAGIOS ILIAS just south of ARACHAMITAI are probably Pan's temple. The plain is the valley of the upper Helisson northwest of Tripolis, under the shadow of Mainalos. The site of Lykoa is in the south-east corner of the valley. There seems to have been another Lykoa or Lykaia somewhere on the Alpheios north of Mount Lykaion, but Pausanias knows nothing about it (cf. Polybios, 16, 17).

the mountain stood SOUMETIA.[262] The Three Roads as they call them are on this mountain; it was from here the Mantineans fetched the bones of Arkas son of Kallisto by command of the Delphic oracle. There are still some ruins left of MAINALOS itself, traces of a TEMPLE OF ATHENE, and a stadium for athletic contests with another for horse-racing.[263] They believe Mount Mainalos is particularly sacred to Pan, so much so that people around it say they hear Pan piping.[264] [9] To the Mistress's sanctuary from the Great City fortifications is five miles; the banks of the Alpheios are half-way. Cross over the Alpheios, and MAKAREAI lies in ruins a quarter of a mile from the river; nearly a mile from Makareai there are the ruins of DASEAI, and as far again from Daseai brings you to the hill called AKAKESION.[265] [10] Below this hill there was a city with an Akakesian Hermes carved in stone which is still on the hillside today. The Arkadian legend is that the child Hermes was brought up here by Akakos son of Lykaon. But the Thebans

262. The small akropolis at SILIMNA west of Tripolis.

263. Opposite DABIA above the west bank of the Helisson.

264. This may be an inherited literary embellishment and not a piece of popular religious practice. But in an earlier age Pindar had heard Pan piping, and it is possible that such beliefs hung on in out of the way places. Pan's piping and its wildness is a theme of certain Hellenistic epigrams, Lucretius says you think you hear Pan when you get lost in lonely echoing mountains which terrify you, Vergil talks about the wind being never silent in the pinetrees of Pan's mountain.

265. Pausanias is moving west from Megalopolis. Makareai or Makaria (Bk VIII, 27 (4)) ought to be easy to pinpoint, but not a trace of it can be found. It could have been the name of some fields (cf. Strabo, 8, 4, 6), and the settlement site might have been engulfed in Great City. But compare also the problem of Thoknia (Note 219 above). More likely it was a small village and is lost now. Daseai is probably the vanishing ruins near APIDITSA, which I think is the old DELI-HASSAN on the north bank of a small stream (cf. 39 (1) below). Akakesion is the hill half a mile before the temple of Lykosoura, which is above the old chapel of St George. The village of STALA has been renamed LYKOSOURA. There are several ancient sites in the area, including a spring feeding a cistern with fine polygonal walling. Dodwell saw the pieces of a temple newly built into the *pyrgo* of the local Turkish ruler at Deli-Hassan.

have a different story and the Tanagrans disagree even with the Thebans.[266]

[1] The SANCTUARY OF THE MISTRESS is half a mile from 37 Akakesion.[267] First of all there is a SHRINE OF GUIDING ARTEMIS and a bronze statue holding torches (I reckoned them to be six feet long), and then the entrance to the consecrated enclosure of the Mistress. As you approach the temple, there is a COLONNADE on the right with white stone reliefs on its wall: first the Fates with Zeus Master of Fates, then Herakles taking Apollo's tripod. I will tell you what I heard about their history if we ever get to the treatise on Phokis and the discussion of Delphi.[268] [2] In the Mistress's colonnade in between these reliefs there is a little inscribed tablet to tell you about the mystery.[269] Then in the third position there are Nymphs and Pans, and in the fourth Polybios son of Lykortas. There is an inscription on him saying Greece would never have collapsed if they had taken all Polybios's advice, and after it did fail the only help that came to it was through Polybios.[270] In front of the TEMPLE is an ALTAR to Demeter and another to the Mis-

266. Stray finds have been reported but the settlement has not been excavated.

267. This is the Hellenistic sanctuary that Edward Dodwell discovered and drew and Kavvadias excavated (Dodwell, *Tour through Greece*, 1819, vol. 2, p. 394). A new French and Greek excavation had been planned here for 1967 and the preliminary work had been done. Parts of the circuit wall of the sacred area of Lykosoura survive, and there are foundations of a Doric colonnade with altars to Demeter, the Mistress and the Great Mother. The excavated temple was a fourth-century construction. It is a small site on a hillside terrace in very wild country, with the remnants of an oak forest stretching for miles eastward. The Artemis temple became a Christian church at the east end of the colonnade (its entrance), and the ruins of the temple can be made out in the ruins of the church, which is unexcavated.

268. Phokis is the subject of the last book Pausanias wrote (Bk X, 13 (7f.)).

269. An inscription of laws and conditions for people using the sanctuary has been found (*I.G.*, V (2), 514), but this is probably not the mystery inscription but a more general set of regulations. For a mystery inscription, cf. Bk IV, 1 (5).

270. The great historian was taken to Rome as a hostage and returned as one of the commissioners for Greek constitutions. These reliefs were probably all the same but with different verse inscriptions; cf. Bk VIII, 9 (2), and 30 (8); also 44 (5), and 48 (8).

tress, and beyond that again the Great Mother has one.[271] [3] The actual statues of the goddesses, the Mistress and Demeter and the throne they sit on, and the stool under their feet are all carved out of one block of stone. None of the drapery, and nothing worked on the throne is joined on with clamps or cement, it is all one block. This block was not brought here; they say it was discovered by excavation inside the precinct through a vision in a dream. Each of the statues is the size of the statue of the Mother at Athens, [4] and these also are by Damophon. Demeter carries a torch in her right hand and has her left hand on the Mistress. The Mistress has a staff and holds the basket on her knees with her right hand. Beside the throne Artemis is standing by Demeter wearing a deer-skin and carrying a quiver on her shoulder, holding a light in one hand and two serpents in the other. There is a hunting-dog next to Artemis. [5] By the statue of the Mistress stands Anytos as an armed man.[272] The people round the sanctuary say the Mistress was brought up by Anytos, who was one of the Titans as they are called. Titans were first introduced into poetry by Homer, who says they are gods in Tartaros: the

271. These have been found in a line in front of the colonnade, and between the colonnade and the temple.

272. Big fragments of this impressive group are in the National Museum at Athens and the rest in the local museum on top of the spur of hill above the temple terrace. The drapery of the colossal statue of the Mistress is elaborately carved in low relief with ornamental motifs, bay-leaves, Victories, eagles and thunderbolts, girls riding on sea-monsters, and a long string of most interesting animal-headed dancers. A large number of terracottas of similar beast-headed dancers were found by Mr Kourouniotis near an altar on the slope above the temple; two crates of them were discovered recently in the cellars of the National Museum at Athens (B.C.H., 23, 1899, p. 635). They had not been unpacked. There is a single terracotta of a ram-headed man in the Lykosoura museum. It also includes dedications to Hermes. There is a detailed discussion of the big statue by Guy Dickins in B.S.A., 13, 347f. There are still some mysterious animal-headed observances on certain days in remote parts of northern Greece, and the evidence of vases connects a similar tradition with the origins of Aristophanic comedy, but these rather diverse practices are not necessarily a historical continuity, although they do arise from a single level of popular superstition and expression; primitive feeling strongly characterizes even so Victorian an artist as Damophon of Messene.

verses are in Hera's oath. Onomakritos took the name of Titans from Homer for the revels of Dionysos he composed; he made the Titans responsible for Dionysos's sufferings.[273] [6] That is the story the Arkadians tell about Anytos, but it was Aischylos son of Euphorion who first told Greece the Egyptian legend that Artemis was Demeter's and not Leto's daughter.[274] I know but choose to pass over the story of the Kouretes, who are represented below the statues, and that of the Korybantes, who are carved on the base and are a quite different family from the Kouretes.[275] [7] The Arkadians bring the fruit of every kind of cultivated tree into this sanctuary except pomegranates.

On your right as you come out of the temple there is a mirror fitted to the wall; when you look into this mirror you see yourself very dimly or not at all, but you have a clear view of the statues of the goddesses and their throne. [8] Beside the Mistress's temple a little way up on the right is the HALL (as they call it) where the Arkadians perform the mystery and where they sacrifice generous and abundant offerings to the Mistress.[276] Everyone sacrifices whatever he has, only not by cutting the throats of the victims like at other sacrifices, but by each person chopping off whatever limb it may be. [9] The Mistress is the god the Arkadians worship most: they say she is the daughter of Poseidon and Demeter. Her public cult title is Mistress, just as Zeus's daughter is the Maid, whose private name is Persephone, as Homer and Pamphos before him have written, but I am frightened of writing down the Mistress's name for the uninitiated. [10] Above the Hall grows the Mistress's sacred wood, surrounded with a stone barrier;

273. *Iliad*, 14, 278f. For Onomakritos, cf. Bk VIII, 31 (3), and Note 230.

274. The information about Aischylos is not first hand; it comes from Herodotos (2, 156). The play is lost and its name unknown.

275. The Kouretes and Korybantes protected the birth and infancy of Zeus; cf. also Bk III, 18 (14), and Bk V, 11 (7). Probably Pausanias knows a piece of mythology which he has religious scruples about telling. It has something to do with chthonic religion perhaps; hence the train of thought about pomegranates. The pomegranate law is probably one of the lost provisions of *I.G.*, V (2), 514.

276. This has been identified and excavated.

among the trees inside it there are true olive and wild olive growing from the same root, and this is not due to clever cultivation. Above this grove there are altars of Horse Poseidon, being the Mistress's father, and of some other gods; the last one has an inscription saying it belongs to all the gods in common.

[11] From here you can climb up steps to a SANCTUARY OF PAN, which has a colonnade as well and a smallish statue, though Pan can answer prayers and give wickedness what it deserves as effectively as the most powerful of the gods. There is a never extinguished fire burning in front of Pan, and they say that in older days this god used to give oracles through the lips of the Nymph Erato, the same Erato who married Arkas son of Kallisto. [12] Erato's verses are recorded; in fact I have read them. There is an altar of Ares here, and there are statues of Aphrodite in the temple, one of white stone and the more ancient one wooden. In the same way there are wooden idols of Apollo and Athene, and ATHENE has a SANCTUARY as well.277

38 [1] A little higher up is the CIRCUIT WALL of LYKOSOURA, which has a few inhabitants. Lykosoura is the oldest of all the cities the earth and its islands have produced: it was the first city the sun ever saw. It was from here that the rest of mankind learnt to build cities.278

[2] To the left of the sanctuary of the Mistress is Mount Lykaion which some of the Arkadians call Olympos, and the Holy Peak.279 They say Zeus was reared on this mountain, and there is a region of Lykaion called Kretea, left of the grove of Parrasian Apollo; the Arkadians argue that the Crete

277. All this is unexcavated. Pan cannot be unrelated to the animal-headed dancers. He worked through Erato as Apollo did through the Sybil.

278. This is not the little rock above the temple, but the hill to the west. Part of the circuit wall is standing, but the city itself has hardly been excavated. Massive walls survive on the hillside, and lower down, close behind the museum there are baths and other buildings built on to a pre-existing heavy wall.

279. To the left as you turn down to the plain and to Megalopolis, which you can see; that is to the north.

where the Cretan legend says Zeus was brought up was this region and not the island of Crete.[280] [3] They name the Nymphs who they say reared Zeus, Theisoa and Neda and Hagno; a city named after Theisoa was founded in Parrasia, and in my time Theisoa is a village in the territory of Great City, and the river Neda took Neda's name, and Hagno's water-spring on Mount Lykaion has the same quality as the Danube of always producing the same volume of water in summer and winter alike.[281] [4] If a drought lasts a long time and the trees and the seeds in the ground are withering, then the priest of Lykaian Zeus prays to this water and sacrifices according to the holy law, dipping an oak-branch on to the surface but not into the depths of the spring; when he stirs the water, a vapour rises like a mist, and a little way off the mist becomes a cloud, collects other clouds, and makes the rain drop on Arkadian land. [5] There is a SANCTUARY OF PAN on Lykaion with a grove of trees around it and a STADIUM for horse-racing in front of it. In ancient times they held the Lykaian festival here. There are pedestals for portrait statues there, though the figures have gone. A couplet on one pedestal says it was a portrait of Astyanax, and that Astyanax was descended from Arkas.[282]

280. For Parrasian Apollo, cf. Section 8 of this chapter. His sanctuary was probably or certainly the one found by Kourouniotis at HAGIOS IANNIS STA MARMARA above ISOMA KARYON west-north-west of Megalopolis. The area called Kretea may be the site where there are fragments of pottery farther west (*Eph. Arch.*, 1910, pp. 29f.).

281. Theisoa was in the northern part of the Lykaion range (cf. Section 9). It has nothing to do with the other Theisoa of Bk VIII, 27 (4) and 28 (3). It could be the *palaiokastro* of LAVDA, also called St Helen's Castle, above the Alpheios north-east of ANDRITSAINA. The village below this fortified town has been renamed THEISOA. But Ross hesitantly suggested and Curtius accepted that Theisoa had been at Andritsaina, and that the Alpheios site was Polybios's Lykoa (16, 17 and cf. Note 261 above). There is no way of knowing without a coin or an inscription. The Neda rises on the southern slopes of Lykaion and swings away west. For Hagno, cf. Bk VIII, Note 10. The site has not been found.

282. There was a sacred cave of Pan and the moon on Lykaion (Porph. *Antr.*, 20). Pan called the moon down into the deep forests by offering her glittering white sheep's wool, and she was pleased to be taken in (Vergil, *Georgics*, 3, 392–

# BOOK VIII

[6] There are some amazing things on Mount Lykaion but the most astounding of all was this. There is a PRECINCT OF LYKAIAN ZEUS on the mountain, which no person is allowed to enter.[283] If you disregard this law and go in it is absolutely certain you will die within the year. And there was a further story they told, that things inside the precinct, man and beast alike, cast no shadow; so when a hunted beast takes refuge there the hunter refuses to jump in with it but stops outside watching the beast, and sees no shadow from it. As long as the sun is in the Crab in heaven, no tree and no living creature casts a shadow at Syene below Aithiopia, but the precinct on Mount Lykaion is always the same for shadows at any season.[284]

[7] On the highest peak of the mountain is a mound of earth which is an altar of Lykaian Zeus, from which you can see most of the Peloponnese. In front of the altar there are two pillars towards the rising sun; the gilded eagles on them are even older than the pillars. At this altar they offer a secret sacrifice to Lykaian Zeus. I could see no pleasure in pursuing

---

3; cf. Macrobius, *Saturnalia*, 5, 22). The race-track was found by Kourouniotis (*Praktika*, 1903, p. 51). It is in a small valley a little below the peak, called KATO KAMPOS. An inscribed list of winners of the Lykaian games in the late fourth century B.C. was found in 1905. The games were very elaborate, and the winners included an Athenian, Argives, Spartans and Akarnanians. Pan's temple (if that is what it was) has been dug for but not found.

283. Kourouniotis examined the altar, which contained a lot of bones, two iron knives, and some bronze tripods (*Praktika*, 1903, p. 50), and later excavated the sanctuary which yielded some fine small bronzes, including a splendid two-headed bronze snake (*Eph. Arch.*, 1904, pp. 152–214). One would wish to know what archaeological evidence there is for the earliest occupation of this site, but the question is easier to ask than to answer.

284. For Syene, cf. Bk V, 7 (4), and Bk VI, 26 (2), and the Notes there. The sun at Syene in midsummer was almost exactly overhead, and there was a sacred well there in which the full face of the sun blazed exactly at noon at the summer solstice. Theophrastos tells the same story about shadows; if you went in you were called a 'deer', and either stoned to death or if you entered involuntarily sent to Eleutherai (Plutarch, *Quaestiones Graecae*, 39). The pillars and eagles may well have had something to do with the solstice. The secret sacrifice was human (cf. the pseudo-Platonic *Minos*, 315c).

inquiries about this sacrifice; let it be as it is and as it was from the beginning.

[8] On the eastern part of the mountain there is a SANCTU-ARY OF PARRASIAN APOLLO, also called Pythian.[285] At the annual festival celebrated for this god they sacrifice a boar to Apollo the Helper in the market-place, and then once they have slaughtered it they take it straight to the sanctuary of Parrasian Apollo in procession with piping, cut out and burn the thighs and consume the victim there and then. This is their traditional observance. [9] On the northern part of Lykaion there is the Theisoan country, where the nymph Theisoa is particularly honoured.[286] The Mylaon, the Nous, the Acheloos, the Kelados and the Naliphos all flow through the Theisoan country to join the Alpheios. There are two other more famous rivers with the same name as the Arkadian Acheloos, [10] one that flows down to the Echinades through Akarnania and Aitolia, which Homer in the *Iliad* calls the lord of all rivers, and the other flowing down from Mount Sipylos which he mentions, both the mountain and the river, when he is writing about Niobe. And there is this third river called Acheloos by Mount Lykaion.[287]

[11] To the right of Lykosoura are the Nomian Mountains as they call them. There is a SANCTUARY OF NOMIAN Pan there; they call the place Melpeia, saying it was here that Pan first found the melody in his pipes. It is a very obvious con-jecture that the Nomian Mountains are so called because of Pan's tunes, but the Arkadians themselves say Nomia is a nymph's name.[288]

285. Cf. Note 280 above. Not a lot was found here, probably because the temple was too accessible. In some respects it resembled the temple of Apollo at Bassai.

286. Cf. Section 3 above and Note 281.

287. *Iliad*, 21, 194, and 24, 616. The Acheloos that divides Akarnania from Aitolia (the ASPROPOTAMOS) impressed Pausanias, and he often mentioned it. For the Acheloos at Sipylos, cf. Bk V, 13 (7), and the Note there.

288. Melpeia means music. Nomian could mean a tune, but it almost certainly means pastures; Nomia was a nymph who wandered through the pastures. The place must be south of Lykosoura; it has not been found.

39 [1] The river Plataniston runs west past Lykosoura; to get to PHIGALIA you are obliged to cross the Plataniston, and from there you have a climb of about four miles or not much more.[289] [2] I have already treated the story of Phigalos son of Lykaon, the original founder of the city, and how in the course of time the city changed its name to be called after Boukolion's son Phialos, and later recovered its ancient name again.[290] There is a further story which is not credible, that Phigalos was not Lykaon's son but an aboriginal child of the earth. Some say that Phigalia was a nymph who was one of the Dryads. [3] When the Lakonians attacked Arkadia and invaded Phigalia, they fought and beat the local people and settled down to besiege the city. As the defence walls were in danger of falling the Phigalians broke away, or perhaps the Lakonians let them go under a truce. The fall of Phigalia and the flight of the Phigalians took place when Miltiades was governor of Athens, the year after the thirtieth Olympics when Chionis of Lakonia won for the third time.[291] [4] The Phigalian refugees decided to go to Delphi and ask the god about their return home; the Pythian priestess said she could foresee no homecoming if they tried to return to Phigalia on their own, but if they took a hundred picked men from ORESTHASION those men would die fighting and through them the Phigalians would come home. When the Oresthasians heard of the oracle given to the Phigalians they struggled with each other for a place among the hundred men, to take part in the march on Phigalia. [5] When they met the Lakonian garrison they perfectly fulfilled the prophecy: they died fighting gloriously; and they drove out the Spartans and made it possible for the Phigalians to recover their native city.[292]

The site of Phigalia is mostly precipitous and high in the air, and the DEFENCE WALLS are built on cliffs, but if you climb up the top of the hill is quite level and unbroken. There is a SANC-

289. Pausanias retreats towards the south of Lykaion and crosses by the obvious pass north of PROPHETES ILIAS. Plataniston means the plane-grove. Phigalia is above the modern village of the same name, once called PAVLITSA, above the Neda.        290. Cf. Bk VIII, 3 (2).

291. In 659 B.C.        292. For Oresthasion, cf. Bk VIII, 44 (2).

TUARY OF SAVIOUR ARTEMIS here with a standing stone statue; tradition dictates that processions should start from this sanctuary. [6] The statue of Hermes in the TRAINING-GROUND seems to be wrapped in a cloak, but it ends in a square block instead of feet. There is a TEMPLE OF DIONYSOS with the local title of Neat Wine Dionysos, but the lower part of the statue is impenetrably obscured by bay and ivy. As much of it as you could see had been rubbed ... vermilion; this is said to be found with gold in Spain.[293]

[1] In the Phigalian MARKET-PLACE they have a portrait statue of Arrachion the all-in fighter, which is as antique in its stance as in other respects: the feet are not far apart, and the hands hang down the sides to the buttocks. The portrait is carved in stone and they say there was an inscription on it; the inscription has vanished through the processes of time, but Arrachion had won twice at Olympia in the games before the fifty-fourth, and he won again in the fifty-fourth by the just decision of the umpires and by his own fortitude.[294] [2] He was fighting his last opponent for the wild olive when the oppon-

293. Vermilion (cinnabar) was mined in Spain (in Andalusia) and processed in Rome under government contract. The antiquities of Phigalia have never been exhaustively surveyed; the site is in and above the village of PHIGALIA (the old PAVLITSA) east of KATO PHIGALEIA on the Neda. The village water-spring rises in classical marbles, hens live in a Byzantine frescoed chapel, the parish priest reads Pausanias, there is an unpublished archaic inscription built upside down into a barn wall, the akropolis used to be called 'the Princess's monuments'. It has yielded a variety of antiquities and buildings (RE, XIX (2), 2069). The road is not practicable except on foot; the mountain track is easier but requires a guide. There is an excellent short article on the late-fourth-century marbles of the water-spring by Orlandos in Peloponnesiaki Protochronia, (1962, pp. 8-11) with references to some other classical springs in Arkadia.

294. He won in 564 B.C., and his statue was one of the first recorded championship monuments. An archaic statue of a naked standing youth has been found at Phigalia; it is surely Arrachion even if the style is perhaps twenty years too primitive. It can be dated 590-570 B.C. (Richter, Kouroi, p. 77, and figs. 144-6). Miss Richter calls the inscription on the breast below the neck a clear and not a dim inscription; I am unable to solve the problems of this inscription, which is unintelligible and possibly phoney, but whatever must be said about it, the inscription will at least not invalidate the identification of this admirable, gawky statue as Arrachion. Frazer saw it in the fields when it had just been found, in May 1890. (Cf. also Hyde, Olympic Victor Monuments.)

ent, whoever he was, caught Arrachion and held him with a scissors grip and at the same time throttled him with his hands, so Arrachion broke one of this man's toes: and Arrachion died by strangling, and at the same time the strangler gave in from the pain in his toe. The Eleans crowned the dead body of Arrachion with the wreath and proclaimed it as the winner. [3] I know of a similar action of the Argives in the case of Kreugas, an Epidamnian boxer: the Argives gave the Nemean wreath to Kreugas dead, because Damoxenos of Syracuse who was fighting him broke the conditions of the match. Night was just falling on them as they boxed and they agreed in public hearing each to take one blow from the other in turn. In those days boxers were not yet wearing the toughened leather on both wrists, they were still boxing in soft gloves with the knot in the palm of the hand and the fingers left bare. Soft gloves consisted of thin strips of untanned ox-hide twisted together by an old-fashioned method. [4] Kreugas struck Damoxenos on the head, and Damoxenos told Kreugas to lift his hand, and then he hit him under the ribs with his fingers straight. With the sharpness of his nails and the force of the blow he drove his hand right into the man and gripped his guts and tore them right out. [5] Kreugas died at once, but the Argives disqualified Damoxenos for disregarding the agreement and hitting his opponent many times instead of once. They gave Kreugas his victory dead and erected a portrait of him at Argos, which was kept in my time in the SANCTUARY OF WOLF APOLLO.[295]

41    [1] At the Phigalian market-place there is also a common tomb of the Oresthasian elite, to whom the offerings due to divine heroes are consumed by fire every year. [2] The river Lymax flows past Phigalia and discharges into the Neda; they say it got its name from Rea's purification. When she had given birth to Zeus and the Nymphs cleaned her up, they flung the water they used into this river; the ancient word for it was *lymata*, as Homer proves, when he speaks of the Greeks

295. Cf. Bk II, 20 (1). We know about this revolting story from no other source.

being purified to put an end to the plague, and says they threw the *lymata* into the sea.[296] [3] The springs of the Neda are on Mount Kerausion, which is a subdivision of Lykaion. At the point where the Neda comes closest to the city of Phigalia, the boys cut their hair to the river. Near the sea the Neda is navigable by small ships. Of all the rivers I know the Maiander is the one that flows crookedest, and winds and turns back on itself oftenest, but the Neda takes the second prize for twisting about.

[4] A mile and a half above Phigalia there are HOT BATHS, not far from which the Lymax joins the Neda. Where the rivers join is the SANCTUARY OF EURYNOME, holy from ancient times and inaccessibly situated in broken country. A continuous, dense wood of cypresses grows round it.[297] [5] The religious belief of the Phigalian people has been that Eurynome is a title of Artemis, but students of ancient records say Eurynome is a daughter of Ocean, in fact Homer has written in the *Iliad* that she was with Thetis at the entertainment of Hephaistos.[298] On the same day in every year they open Eurynome's sanctuary, but for the rest of the time tradition dictates it should not be opened. [6] On that day though they offer sacrifices privately and publicly. I did not manage to be there at the moment of the festival and have not seen Eurynome's statue, though the Phigalians told me it is a wooden idol tied up with gold chains, like a woman down to the buttocks, and below that like a fish. There may be something about a fish that suggests a daughter of Ocean who lives with Thetis in the depths of the sea, but by no stretch of reasonable probability has it anything to do with Artemis.[299]

[7] Phigalia is surrounded by mountains: it has Kotilion on

296. *Iliad*, 18, 398f. Not the stream that runs down through the village of PAVLITSA (Phigalia), but the river east of the ancient site, or possibly the DRAGOI river.

297. There is every kind of extraordinary water effect in the gorges of the Neda but there are now no hot springs so far as I could discover. Eurynome's sanctuary is lost unless it is the ruins about a mile east of Phigalia, which is unlikely (*RE*, XIX (2), 2072–3).

298. *Iliad*, 18, 398.     299. She was a vigorously rustic water-nymph.

the left, and another mountain projecting on the right, Mount Elaion. Kotilion is just five miles from the city; there is a place there called BASSAI with the TEMPLE OF APOLLO the Helper, even the roof of which is made of stone. [8] Of all the temples in the Peloponnese this one could be considered second only to the temple at Tegea for its proportions and the beauty of its stone.[300] Apollo was named the Helper because of a plague, just as he was named Turner-away-of-evil at Athens for turning away a pestilence there. [9] His action at Phigalia as at Athens was during the Peloponnesian War. This is proved by Apollo's two titles having the same meaning, and the fact that Iktinos the architect of the temple at Phigalia was a contemporary of Perikles and built the Parthenon at Athens. I have already said that the statue of Apollo is in the market-place at Great City.[301]

[10] There is a spring of water on Mount Kotilion, and the

300. Bassai means 'the glens'; the temple site (STYLI or STYLOUS, which means the pillars) is on a high ridge east of Phigalia. It is best approached by the ancient track through DRAGOI and across the mountains, which I remember as considerably more than four miles. The temple of Bassai is really as fine as Pausanias says it is, but most of its wonderful frieze was stolen by the architect Cockerell and his partner Haller von Hallerstein, and ended up in the British Museum, where until recently it was kept in a locked room for twenty or thirty years. There is a curious plaster reconstruction in the library of the Travellers' Club, and another on the main stairs of the Ashmolean Museum at Oxford (by Cockerell, who also imitated a Bassai column in Oxford). I do not know whether it is the stone, the specially pleasing architecture, or its setting among high mountains that makes the temple one of the freshest and sharpest monuments in Greece. It was discovered accidentally by a French architect called Bochor in 1765, who was later killed for his brass buttons, which were believed to be gold, when he revisited the area.

301. Cf. Bk VIII, 30 (3). Iktinos also rebuilt the sacred building for the initiations at Eleusis, and Apollo's temple at Bassai. On technical evidence the Bassai temple cannot be much earlier than 420 B.C. and may be later; its ground-plan is strangely old-fashioned, perhaps because it imitated the old Apollo temple at Delphi. It is in several ways very unlike the Parthenon, which is also a structurally eccentric building, but if excellence is the criterion it is a fine enough piece of work to be by Iktinos. It is interesting that neither Apollo's temple at Bassai nor the Parthenon conforms to the rigid canons of Doric architecture, and that they were both decorated with continuous relief carvings that swirl like drapery. At Bassai the frieze was inside the temple, and the

man who recorded that this spring is the source of the river Lymax had neither seen what he was writing about nor heard about it from anyone who had seen it; personally I have done both. We saw the course of the river, and also the water of the spring on Kotilion; it does not travel far and soon disappears altogether. I have not studied where in Arkadia the head-spring of the Lymax is to be found. Above the sanctuary of Apollo the Helper there is a place called Kotilon, and an APHRODITE IN KOTILON; she had a temple which had lost its roof and a statue.[302]

[1] Elaion the other mountain is about four miles from 42 Phigalia; there is a CAVE OF DEMETER there with the title Black Demeter.[303] The Phigalians believe the same as they say

temple was oriented north–south; the statue stood against the west wall and faced the sunrise through a side door in the east wall. This arrangement probably has nothing to do with the impressive sunrise over Lykaion or with the lie of the land; there are other north–south temples in western Arkadia.

302. The spring is below the temple to the west. It still has some of its classical marbles, and was still running in 1963, although not strongly in summer. The bald crest above the temple is probably Kotilion. The sacred area was investigated and excavations carried out in the 1900s by the Greek archaeological service (*Eph. Arch.*, 1910, p. 271).

303. It is not clear which mountain Pausanias means. The cave of Demeter is surely one of the many caves in the Neda gorge; I believe a sacred cave was found by Orlandos upstream of STOMIO, but I can find no published reference to it; we cannot be certain of its not belonging to Eurynome or to Pan. There are several caves at Stomio itself, including a fine rocky pothole or cavern into which the Neda vanishes underground. The cult-cave might have been one of the caves on a rocky terrace on the north side of the gorge above the Neda cavern, where there is a chapel of the Virgin; the furthest, smallest cave, beyond the ruins of the old chapel, is the entrance to a cave-system which I have not thoroughly explored. There are other cave sanctuaries where a narrow or very narrow passage leads away into the rock (Trophonios's cave at Lebadeia for example), and there are some local superstitious practices and popular stories that suggest there has been a cult here from remote times. It may be the site of the Phigalian oracle of the dead (Bk III, 17 (9)) which did not exist in Pausanias's time; I cannot believe he would have scrambled down into the gorge and seen the Neda cavern without discussing it. The village of STOMION is not the same as the place I am talking about, which is best reached not from Phigalia but from PLATANIA south of the river, and SIDEROKASTRO farther south. One cannot get anywhere near it in a car.

at Thelpousa about the coupling of Poseidon and Demeter, though the Phigalians say Demeter gave birth not to a horse but the goddess Arkadians call the Mistress.[304] [2] They say she was furious with Poseidon and grieved at the rape of Persephone, put on black, and went into this cave and stayed there for a long time. All the earth produces was perishing and the human race was even worse devastated by famine, but none of the gods knew where Demeter was hiding. [3] At that time Pan came into Arkadia to hunt, now over one mountain and now over another, and at Mount Elaion he sighted Demeter, saw how she looked and how she was dressed. So Zeus found out from Pan and sent the Fates to Demeter; she obeyed them and put away her anger, and forgot her grief. The Phigalians say because of all this they considered the cave as sacred to Demeter, and dedicated a wooden statue there. [4] The statue was like this: she was sitting on a rock, and looked like a woman except for the head; she had a horse's head and mane, with serpents and other beasts sprouting out of her head; she wore a tunic down to her feet, she had a dolphin on one hand and a dove on the other. To anyone of intelligence with a good memory it is obvious why they made the wooden image in this shape.[305] They say she was named Black Demeter because the goddess also was dressed in black. [5] It is not recorded who made the statue or how it came to be burnt; when the old one was gone the Phigalians did not give the goddess another statue, and neglected most of the observances of festival and sacrifice, until the earth was struck barren, and the Pythian priestess answered their petition with this prophecy:

[6]  *Arkadian, Azanian acorn-eaters,*
 *people of Phigalia, O, people*
 *of stallion-mated Deo's hidden cave,*

304. Cf. Bk VIII, 25 (4f.).

305. The horse belongs to Poseidon or Demeter (who sits on a horse-skin in the Parthenon frieze), the serpents are chthonic, the dolphin belongs to Poseidon, and the dove to Persephone.

476

*you came for a cure of painful famine,*
*in exile twice, living wild twice,*
*no one but you: and Deo took you home,*
*made you sheaf-carriers and oatcake-eaters,*
*makes you live wild now, because you stopped*
*your fathers' worship, her ancient honours.*
*You shall consume yourselves, be child-eaters*
*if your whole people will not soothe her spleen,*
*and dress the deep cave in divine honours.*[306]

[7] When the Phigalians heard the oracle that was brought to them, they honoured Demeter more than they ever had before, and they persuaded Onatas son of Mikon of Aigina, whatever they had to pay him, to make them a statue of Demeter. The bronze Pergamene Apollo, one of the most astounding of all works of art for its size and fineness, is by the same Onatas.[307] So now he found a copy or a painting of the ancient wooden idol, and found out most, so they say, by a vision of it in his sleep, and made the Phigalians a statue in bronze, just two generations after the Persian expedition against Greece. [8] I can confirm this, because when Xerxes crossed over to Europe Gelon son of Deinomenes was dictator of Syracuse and Sicily, and when he died his brother Hieron succeeded him, and then Hieron died before consecrating the dedications he had vowed to Olympian Zeus for his winning horses, so Hieron's son Deinomenes offered them in his father's place.[308] [9] These were by Onatas, and there are inscriptions on them at Olympia, the first like this:

306. Wilamowitz (*Glaube*, 1, 402f.) disbelieves this story; the oracle would have been given in the mid fifth century. It seems to me acceptable. This exile has no connexion with the story of the Oresthasians (Bk VIII, 39 (3–4)); it is a question of economic hardship and a second exile.

307. Onatas's work and influence travelled all over Greece. The great bronze Poseidon now at Athens from the sea off Cape Artemision could conceivably come from his workshop (cf. Dorig in the Thames and Hudson *Art and Architecture of Ancient Greece*, 1967, pp. 277–8; cf. also Bk V, 25 (13), and the Note there). The pedestal of the Pergamene Apollo has been found (*Inschriften von Pergamon*, 48) and a poem about it exists in the *Palatine Anthology* (9, 238).

308. Hiero died in 467, but cf. Bk VI, 12 (1).

> *Olympian Zeus: Hieron who once*
> *won at your holy games gives you this thanks*
> *for one team-race, two ridden horse-races:*
> *which things Deinomenes of Syracuse*
> *dedicates for his father's monument.*

[10] The other inscription is this:

> *Onatas son of Mikon has made me,*
> *whose house is in Aigina the island.*[309]

Onatas's lifetime coincides with Hegias of Athens and Ageladas of Argos.[310]

[11] This Demeter was my principal reason for coming to Phigalia. According to the traditional local observance I slaughtered nothing to the goddess; the sacred law for her sacrifice dictates that private individuals and once a year the whole Phigalian community should take the fruit of cultivated trees, particularly the grape, and the honeycomb, and greasy unspun wool, and lay them on the altar constructed in front of the cave, with oil poured over them. [12] The ceremony is performed by a priestess with the youngest of the sacrificial ministers as they call them, who are three of the citizens. There is a sacred grove of oaks around the cave, where cold water springs out of the ground.[311] But in my time the statue Onatas made was no longer in existence, and most of the Phigalians had no idea there had ever been one, [13] though the oldest man we met told us there had been a fall of rocks from the roof that hit the statue three generations before his time. He said the statue was smashed and had completely

309. Cf. Bk V, 25 (13), more or less the same couplet on another pedestal.

310. Sculptors. This whole discussion represents the kind of argument on which Pausanias's ideas about the history of sculpture rested. It was a matter of establishing generations; only then would stylistic analysis proceed. He was right to want a chronology independent of the 'evolution' of style, but questions about generations are befogged by the recurrence of names.

311. There is such a spring near STOMIO; but there are too many springs and caves in the gorge for this to be significant. There are also a number of fine, tall plane-trees and at least one oak-tree.

disappeared. And in fact you could still see in the roof of the cave how the rocks had broken off.

[1] From here the discussion takes us to PALLANTION, sup- 43 posing there is anything there to be recorded, and to the reason why the late emperor Antoninus the First made a city out of a village at Pallantion and granted it freedom and immunity from taxes.[312] [2] They say the most intelligent Arkadian and the best soldier was Euander, the son of Hermes and a nymph, a daughter of Ladon. He was sent to found a colony with an Arkadian expeditionary force from Pallantion, and founded a city on the river Tiber: and part of the city of Rome today, which was founded by Euander and his Arkadian followers, was called Pallantion in memory of the city in Arkadia. At a later period the name was altered by dropping an l and an n. It is because of all this that the king made his grants to the Pallantians.[313] [3] Antoninus who was responsible for these kindnesses to Pallantion never willingly involved Rome in a war. The Moors began a war; they are the biggest subdivision of the independent Libyans, they are nomads and tougher fighters than the Scythians in so far as Scythians ride in waggons, but the Moors and their wives roam around on horseback: Antoninus swept them right out of their territory and compelled them to look for refuge in the farthest recesses of Libya, at Mount Atlas among the people of that mountain. [4] He annexed the greater part of the territory of the Brigantes in Britain, because the Brigantes started an invasion of Genounia, which is subject to Rome.[314] The cities of Lykia

312. Pausanias obviously regards the Roman connexion with Pallantion with a doubtful eye. The site is east-north-east of Megalopolis.

313. Mons Palatinus. There was a further connexion with Arkadia in that a statue of Pan was installed in the cave of Faunus under the Mons Palatinus called the Lupercal. (I have discussed the Roman interest in Arkadia and the relevant texts at more length in *Proceedings of the Virgil Society*, 1967–8.)

314. Where was Genounia? The Brigantes lived more or less in Yorkshire. This was a rising and a tribal war, not an invasion I suppose. A. L. F. Rivet (in *Civitas Capitals of Roman Britain*, ed. Wacher, 1966, p. 111, n. 11) has argued that until this time the Brigantes were a *civitas foederata* with some reserve of freedom.

and Karia and Kos and Rhodes were stricken by a violent earthquake: Antoninus saved them by colossal expenditure and enthusiasm for their restoration. Others have written in accurate detail about his gifts of money to the Greeks and to the barbarians who asked for it, his Greek, his Ionian, his Carthaginian, his Syrian constructions, but [5] the emperor has left another thing to remember him by. Those subjects who were Roman citizens, and whose sons were classified as Greek, were faced because of some legal provision with the alternatives of leaving their money outside their families or increasing the king's riches: Antoninus permitted their children to inherit, preferring to show his humanity rather than preserve a financially profitable law. The Romans named him the Religious because he showed such honour for the divine power, and [6] in my opinion he deserved to bear the title of Cyrus the elder, who was called the father of humanity. He left a son of the same name to succeed him, Antoninus the second, who marched out to take vengeance on the Germans, the most numerous and warlike barbarians in Europe, and on the Sauromatian nation for starting a war and for injuries committed.[315]

44    [1] What is left of my account of Arkadia is the road from Great City to Pallantion and Tegea, the road which leads to the Mound.   The area in front of the city along this road is named Ladokeia after Ladokos son of Echemos; beyond this in ancient times was the city of HAIMONIAI, the site of which has kept its name to this day.[316] [2] Among the remnants to be recorded of the city of ORESTHASION, on the right of the road

315. The father is Antoninus Pius (138–61) who succeeded Hadrian; the son is Marcus Aurelius Antoninus (161–80). The Sauromatians lived in south Russia.

316. East-north-east from Megalopolis by a rather circuitous south-tending route dictated to the Megalopolitans by the pre-existing route from Kalamata and Messenia to Tegea and the north-east. Pausanias more or less followed the upper Alpheios (PIGAI ALPHEIOU). The modern high road does the same essentially. Haimoniai was a mile south-east of modern Megalopolis, where some traces of it still exist on a low hill near PERIBOLIA, the old ROUSVANAGA (cf. I.G., V (2), 494).

after Haimoniai, some columns of the SANCTUARY OF ARTEMIS are still standing; the title of Artemis is the Priestess. Along the straight road from Haimoniai is APHRODISION and then another place called ATHENAION, on the left of which is a temple of Athene with a stone statue in it.[317] [3] Just two and a half miles or so from Athenaion lie the ruins of ASEA, and the hill which was once its fortress still shows traces of the defence wall.[318] Half a mile from Asea the head-spring of the Alpheios lies a little way from the road, and the source of the Eurotas is right at the roadside. At the Alpheios spring there is a roofless TEMPLE OF THE MOTHER of gods with two stone lions. [4] The stream of Eurotas mingles with the Alpheios and they run together for about two and a half miles, then they drop into a chasm, and Eurotas springs up again in the country of Lakonia and Alpheios at the Springs in the Great City territory.[319] There is a way up from Asea to the mountain called Boreion; on the peak of the mountain there are traces

317. Oresthasion (or Oresteion, Bk VIII, 3 (2)) was on an important road from Sparta to Tegea (Thukydides, 5, 64). It was possibly the site found by Loring between PAPARIS and MARMARIA south of the railway line and due south-west of Tripolis (Leake, *Peloponnesiaca*, 247; cf. *Journal of Hellenic Studies*, 15, pp. 27–31). It can hardly have been at RAPSOMMATIS east of PERIBOLIA, as has been suggested, since the road from Sparta would not cross the Alpheios here. A village farther north-east has been named ATHENAION; some ruins were noted here in the early nineteenth century, but have not been seen since.

318. This is a fine akropolis on an isolated rock. It seems to have suffered dilapidations during the late nineteenth century, probably in connexion with the building of the railway, which it overlooks. It is close to the village named after it. It was excavated by Scandinavian archaeologists before the Second World War.

319. The so-called source of the Eurotas seems to be FRANKOVRYSI; it unites with several other springs and runs south-west towards the Marmaria pass and Megalopolis. It disappears into a series of holes east of the gorge which it must once have formed and through which the railway passes. There are new springs that feed it at Rapsommatis, where it seems as if the old river is breaking out again. Sometimes when the potholes are blocked or the river swollen, it still runs in its old course down the gorge. I saw this from the air in the rainy spring of 1968. The Eurotas was supposed to reappear at BELEMINA on CHELMOS. The sanctuary at the Alpheios spring has not been found. Frazer (*Pausanias*, Vol. 4, p. 446) speaks of a statue of an enthroned woman, perhaps Demeter, being found at Frankovrysi.

of a SANCTUARY, which Odysseus was supposed to have built for Saviour Athene and Poseidon when he got home from Troy.[320]

[5] The Mound is the frontier of the Great City land with Tegea and Pallantion, and if you turn off left from the Mound you come to the Pallantian plain.[321] At PALLANTION[322] is a TEMPLE with stone statues of Pallas and Euander, a SANCTUARY OF DEMETER and the Maid, and not far away from that a portrait of Polybios.[323] In ancient time they used the hill above the city as a FORTRESS, and one SANCTUARY of gods still survives on the crest of the hill down to our own day, [6] with the title of the Pure gods; there is a tradition of swearing by them on very great issues. They either do not know or know and are not willing to reveal the proper names of these gods, but one might argue that they were named the Pure gods because Pallas sacrificed to them differently from the way his father sacrificed to Lykaian Zeus.[324]

[7] To the right of the Mound is the Manthourikon: this plain is already inside the boundaries of Tegean land, say about six miles from Tegea. On the right of the road is a smallish mountain called Kresion, on which the SANCTUARY

320. A Doric temple was recorded by Leake in 1806 at the top of the pass over Mount KRAVARI east of Asea. Most of it still existed in 1834, but by 1840 it had almost completely vanished. There are still some vestiges of it.

321. This seems to have been a causeway near EUANDRON on the edge of Lake Taka. This lake is marked on maps as a lake and a marsh; it was as dry as a bone in 1967 but in 1968 it was a wide expanse of green water. Loring (*Journal of Hellenic Studies*, 15, pp. 34f. with a useful map) would prefer the Mound to be a hillock, but the analogy with Herakles' dyke-like mound or causeway at Pheneos seems irresistible (cf. Bk VIII, 14 (1)).

322. Pallantion was identified by the Expédition scientifique de la Morée a century and a half ago; the akropolis was on a little green hill, and was excavated by the Italian School of Archaeology at Athens (*Annuario*, ns. 1–2, 1939–40, pp. 225f.). It is a few miles south of modern Tripolis.

323. Bk VIII, Note 227.

324. For Pallas and Lykaon's sacrifice, cf. Bk VIII, 3 (1) following on Chapter 2. The excavators investigated a *megaron* with an associated votive deposit near the chapel of St John on the hilltop, and found the remains of a fifth-century temple on the southern slope.

of the Abundant god is.[325] Ares slept with Aerope, daughter of Kepheus son of Aleos, so the Tegeans say; she died in childbirth and [8] the son clung to his dead mother and sucked generous and abundant milk from her breasts. Ares was pleased with this scene, and so they called the god Abundant; they say the child was called Aeropos. The Leukonian spring is also on the road to Tegea; they say Leukone was Apheidas's daughter, and her tomb is not far from the city of TEGEA.[326]

[1] The Tegeans say that in the time of Tegeates son of 45 Lykaon only the territory took its name from him, and the human population still lived divided into peoples: Gareatai, Phylakeans, Karyatai, Korytheans, Potachidai, Oiatai, Manthoureans, and Echeuetheans. In the reign of Apheidas, the ninth people – the Apheidantes – were added, but the founder of the modern city was Aleos. [2] Apart from the events in common to all Arkadia, like the Trojan War and the Persian War and the battle of Dipaia against Lakonia,[327] even apart from all these the Tegeans have the following glories. Ankaios son of Lykourgos stood up to the Kalydonian boar although he was wounded, and Atalante shot it and hit it first, and so Atalante was awarded the boar's head and hide as trophies. [3] When the children of Herakles returned to the Peloponnese, Aeropos's son Echemos of Tegea fought a personal duel with Hyllos and beat him.[328] The Tegeans were the first Arkadians to win a battle against the invading Lakonians, and took most of them prisoner.[329]

[4] The ancient Tegean SANCTUARY OF ALEAN ATHENE was made by Aleos. Later on the Tegeans built the goddess a great and impressive temple. It was wiped out by a fire that suddenly caught it when Diophantes was governor of Athens,

325. The hill is about two miles west of Tegea and traces of the sanctuary survive there.
326. The spring is at KERASITSA south-south-east of Tripolis. The site of Tegea is at AKRA south-east of Tripolis; the akropolis is called Akra.
327. In about 470 B.C.
328. For Hyllos, cf. Bk I, 41 (2).
329. Cf. Bk VIII, 48 (4).

the year after the ninety-sixth Olympics when Eupolemos of Elis won the running.[330] [5] The modern TEMPLE is by a long way first of all the temples in the Peloponnese for its size and its whole construction. The style of its columns is first Doric, then Corinthian, and there are Ionic columns standing inside the temple. I found the architect was Skopas of Paros, who made statues in many parts of ancient Greece and in Ionia and in Karia. [6] The figures in the front pediment represent the hunting of the Kalydonian boar, with the boar in the middle and on one side Atalante and Meleager and Theseus, Telamon, Peleus, Polydeukes, Iolaos who shared most of Herakles' labours, Thestios's sons and Althaia's brothers Prothous and Kometes. [7] On the other side of the boar Ankaios already wounded and dropping his axe and held up by Epochos, Kastor beside him, Amphiaraos son of Oikles, Hippothous son of Kerkyon son of Agamedes son of Stymphelos, and last of all Peirithous. The figures on the rear pediment are the battle of Telephos and Achilles in the Kaikos plain.[331]

46 [1] The ancient statue of Alean Athene and the tusks of the Kalydonian boar were taken by the Roman emperor Augustus after the victory over Antony and Antony's allies, who included the Arkadians except for Mantineia. [2] Augustus does not appear to have started the looting of dedications and statues of gods from the defeated, but to have employed an ancient and established tradition. At the fall of Troy when the Greeks divided the spoils, Sthenelos son of Kapaneus was given the wooden idol of Household Zeus, and many years

330. In 392 B.C. The sanctuary site was first sounded by Milchhöfer in 1879; Dodwell had already recognized this site, which was the point of arrival in Tegea from Pallantion. It was finally fully excavated by the French in the 1900s, and the results were published in 1924. Its foundations and the remnants of its columns are an impressive sight. There are still antiquities built into houses in the village, which is PALAIA EPISKOPI.

331. Many fragments of Skopas's heroic figures were recovered by the excavators and are now some of them in Athens and some in the local museum, which is an important Arkadian collection. Some pieces seem not to be on show. For references to the eight different reconstructions that have been suggested, cf. *Skopas* by P. E. Arias (Rome, 1952, pp. 115f.).

later when the Dorians settled in Sicily, Antiphemos the founder of Gela sacked a Sicilian city called Omphake and brought home to Gela a statue made by Daidalos.[332] [3] And we know that Xerxes king of Persia the son of Darius, even apart from all the things he carried away from the city of Athens, took the statue of Brauronian Artemis from Brauron,[333] and he blamed the Milesians for deliberate cowardice in the face of the Athenians in the Greek sea battle, and took the bronze Apollo of Branchidai; later in time Seleukos was to send that back to Miletos,[334] but in my day the Argives still kept a wooden idol with Hera and another dedicated with Wolf Apollo, that both came from Tiryns, [4] and the people of Kyzikos, who compelled the Prokonnesians to unite with them by force of war, took from Prokonnesos a statue of Mother Dindymene which is made of gold with a face not of ivory but carved out of hippopotamus teeth.[335] What the emperor Augustus did was an established ancient tradition observed both by Greeks and by barbarians. The statue of Alean Athene is in the ROMAN FORUM built by Augustus, as you come into it. [5] It is complete ivory, by Endoios, and that is where it is kept.[336] The keepers of the wonders say one

332. The image Zeus gave Sthenelos was a statue at Argos (Bk II, 24 (3)); for the statue at Gela, cf. Bk IX, 40 (4). Gela was a great city on the south coast of Sicily, east of LICATA (cf. Herodotos, 7, 153).

333. Bk III, 16 (8).

334. Cf. I, 16 (3). After the battle of Mykale in 479 Xerxes burnt the temple and took the Apollo. It came into Macedonian hands under Alexander. There is a bronze copy of the Apollo of Branchidai in the British Museum, and he appears on coins of Miletos. Cf. also Bk IX, 10 (2). Frazer in his commentary on Pausanias gives a list of other very similar figures of Apollo.

335. For the Tiryns statues, cf. Bk II, 17 (5). Strabo says the sanctuary at Kyzikos was founded by the Argonauts. The city lay on the neck of the big peninsula on the south coast of the sea of Marmara; Prokonnesos was MARMARA ADASI, the island just to the north-west.

336. Endoios was a late-sixth-century Ionian Greek who worked also in Athens (Bk I, 26 (4)). The Forum Augustum was vowed at Philippi in 42 B.C. and consecrated forty years later. It was built on land bought from the spoils of war, and included the temple of Avenging Mars. Pliny thought it one of the two or three most beautiful pieces of architecture in the world (*Natural History*, 36, 102), and it was full of loot, including an ivory Apollo, a series

of the boar's tusks is broken, but the surviving one is kept in the EMPEROR'S GARDENS in a SANCTUARY OF DIONYSOS, and it measures just three feet long.[337]

47   [1] The statue at Tegea at present was brought from the country town of the Manthoureans, where it had the title of Horse Athene because according to them she charged Enkelados with a chariot and team in the battle of the gods and giants. But she too has come to be called Alean by all Greece and even by the Peloponnese. On one side of Athene's statue stands Asklepios, on the other Health; they are Pentelic stone and both by Skopas of Paros.[338] [2] The most important dedications in the temple are the hide of the Kalydonian boar, which time has shrivelled and left without a single bristle, and the hanging chains, except those that have rusted away, that the Lakonian prisoners wore while they dug the Tegean plain.[339] There is a sacred couch of Athene and a painted picture of Auge, and the dedicated arms of Merpessa of Tegea who was called Sow, and whom we shall mention again.[340] [3] She was a child priestess of Athene, I do not know how long for, but her priesthood was before her maturity and not after it. They say the goddess's altar was made by Melampous son of Amythaon. Rea and the nymph Oinoe with the baby

of reliefs, and two statues which had held up the tent of Alexander the Great. There were also inscribed bronze statues of every Roman general who had triumphed since Aineias. Part of it is still standing, including several columns of the temple, and there are caryatids from the upper storey of its portico in the Sala della Loggetta of the Knights of Rhodes, whose Loggia is built on to the ruins of an extension of this forum by Domitian.

337. The tusk of a prehistoric animal; the temple was probably in Caesar's gardens beyond the Tiber, which he willed to the Roman people. Tiberius had built the temple of Fors Fortuna in these gardens. Shakespeare in *Julius Caesar* calls the gardens 'on this side Tiber', but he is following a mistranslation of Plutarch.

338. Enkelados was a giant; for the Manthoureans, cf. Bk VIII, 44 (7). The kindly head of what is almost certainly Skopas's Health is in the National Museum at Athens.

339. They had been already there in Herodotos's time (1, 66).

340. Bk VIII, 48 (5).

Zeus are represented on the altar, with four other figures on each side, Glauke, Neda, Theisoa, and Anthrakia on one side, and Ide, Hagno, Alkinoe, and Phrixa on the other. There are also statues of Muses and of Memory.

[4] Not far from the temple is a STADIUM of piled earth where they hold games, which they call the Alean games after Athene and the Capture games because of the battle when they took most of the Lakonians alive.[341] Somewhere north of the temple is a water-fountain where they say Auge was violated by Herakles, a different story from Hekataios's account of her. About six hundred yards from the water-fountain is a SHRINE OF HERMES Aipytos.[342]

[5] The Tegeans have another SANCTUARY TO ATHENE of the City, which is entered by a priest once in the year. They call it the Holy Wall, and tell you Athene granted to Kepheus son of Aleos that Tegea should never fall, and they say the goddess cut off some of the hairs of Medusa to preserve this city.[343] [6] This is the story they tell about Artemis the Guide. Aristomelidas was dictator of Arkadian Orchomenos, and he fell in love with a young Tegean girl and by one means or another he got hold of her, and put Chronios to guard her. Before they brought her in to the dictator she killed herself from fear and shame, and Artemis appeared to Chronios and made him rise against Aristomelidas; he murdered him and fled to Tegea and built a SANCTUARY FOR ARTEMIS.[344]

[1] The MARKET-PLACE is the shape of a brick;[345] there is a 48

341. Cf. Bk VIII, 48 (4).

342. Hekataios thought it was not rape but seduction; cf. Bk VIII, 4 (9). I am not clear about the identification of the spring.

343. Athene handing over the hair figures on Tegean coins; but the temple has not come to light. Medusa's hair was a bronze snake, and 'Gorgon's hair' was a proverbial phrase.

344. The story sounds like fiction and the characters are unknown to history, but St Jerome tells the same story (*Against Jovian*, P.L. 23, 284) calling the dictator Aristokleides of Orchomenos, and the girl a Stymphalian. Those who take the story seriously date it in the mid third century B.C.

345. West of the church of PALAIO EPISKOPI, cathedral of the medieval bishops of NIKLI when it was one of the greatest cities in the Peloponnese.

TEMPLE OF APHRODITE there called Aphrodite's brick temple, and it has a stone statue. There is a stone tablet with relief sculptures of Antiphanes, Krisos, Tyronidas and Pyrrias, who laid down the laws of Tegea and whom the Tegeans still honour to this day. On the other tablet Iasios is represented, holding a horse with one hand, and a palm-branch in the other. They say that Iasios won a horse-race at Olympia, when Theban Herakles held the Olympic games. [2] I have already given the reason why the winner at Olympia is given a wreath of wild olive in my Elean treatise, and later I shall explain why the winner at Delphi gets a laurel wreath.[346] At the Isthmus the traditional observance is pine, and at Nemea wild celery for the tragic fate of Palaimon and Archemoros.[347] But at most games they use a wreath of palm, and everywhere the winner has a palm-branch put in his right hand. [3] The reason for the tradition is this: they say when Theseus came home from Crete he held games at Delos for Apollo, and crowned the winners with palm. They say it started from there, and even Homer mentioned the palm-tree at Delos in Odysseus's prayer to Alkinoos's daughter.[348]

[4] There is a figure of Ares in the market-place of Tegea, in relief on a stone tablet; they call him the Woman-feaster. At the time of the Lakonian War and the first expedition of King Charillos of Lakonia, the women laid an armed ambush below the hill now called Wardress hill; the main forces had engaged with acts of daring and memorable male courage on both sides [5] when the women appeared and broke the Lakonian line; the most daring of them all was Marpessa whom they called the Sow, and Charillos himself was one of the Spartan captives. They let him go without a ransom, under oath to the Tegeans that the Lakonians would never

346. Cf. Bk V, 7 (7), and Bk X, 7 (8).

347. Cf. Bk II, 1 (3). Archemoros is the same as Opheltes (Bk II, 15 (2–3)).

348. *Odyssey* 6, 162f. Cicero says he supposes the palm at Delos they showed to tourists was not really the one Odysseus saw (*On Laws*, 1, 1.2). The Romans took over palms from the Greeks at the beginning of the third century B.C. (Livy, 10, 47, 3).

campaign against Tegea again: an oath that he broke. The women on their own with no man present slaughtered a victory sacrifice to Ares and gave the men no share of the sacrificial meat. This was how Ares got his title.[349] [6] There is an altar of Perfect Zeus with a square statue; the Arkadians appear to me to take some extraordinary delight in this shape. The monuments of Lykaon of Tegea and Maira the wife of Tegeates are here; they say Maira was Atlas's daughter whom Homer mentioned in Odysseus's speech to Alkinoos about the journey to Hades and the souls he saw there.[350] [7] The Tegeans call Eileithuia, whose temple and statue they also have in the market-place, Auge-on-her-knees; the story is that Aleos handed over his daughter to Nauplios with orders to take her out to sea and drown her, but when he took her she fell on her knees and gave birth to a son, just where Eileithuia's sanctuary now is. This story is not the same as another one which is just as much told at Tegea, that Auge bore a child (Telephos) without her father's knowledge, whom he ordered to be exposed on Mount Parthenion; and the abandoned child was given milk by a deer.[351] [8] Beside Eileithuia's sanctuary there is an altar of Earth; next to the altar stands a tablet of white stone with Polybios son of Lykortas on it,[352] and Elatos one of the sons of Arkas on another tablet.

[1] There is a THEATRE not far from the market-place with the pedestals for bronze portraits beside it, though the figures are not there now. A couplet on one of the bases says this was a 49

349. The *prima facie* oddity and the strong religious overtones of this story, with its women's cult of Ares who had other functions besides those of war-god, and the even stranger oracle story that goes with all this (Bk VIII, 1 (6), and Bk III, 7 (3)), do not necessarily mean there was never such a war, although Charillos is a suspiciously early king. But compare also Bk VIII, 53 (10).

350. *Odyssey*, 11, 326. Eustathios calls her a daughter of Proitos (and cf. Bk X, 30 (5)).

351. There was a famous ancient painting preserved in a fine copy from Herculaneum of a personified Arkadia with Herakles on one side and the little Telephos suckled by the deer in the foreground.

352. The historian; cf. Bk VIII, 30 (8), etc.

statue of Philopoimen.[353] Philopoimen is not the least, in fact he is the most remembered man in Greece, both for the wisdom he showed and for the courageous achievements he undertook. [2] So far as illustrious blood is concerned, his father Kraugis was second to no other Arkadian in Great City. Kraugis died when Philopoimen was still a baby, and his guardian was Kleander of Mantineia, an exile living in Great City because of his misfortune at home, and a friend of Kraugis's family by mutual hospitality for generations. Among the masters Philopoimen went to they say two were Megalophanes and Ekdelos, both of whom were pupils of Arkesilaos of Pitane.[354] [3] He was as big and as tough as any man in the Peloponnese, but his face was no picture; he disdained training for public games, but he worked the land he had, and took the trouble to put down the wild beasts on it. They say he read books by famous philosophers, and war history and everything that teaches military leadership. He wanted to make his whole life an imitation of Epaminondas and of Epaminondas's achievements, but he was not able completely to equal his original: one of Epaminondas's spiritual qualities was a quiet restraint of anger, but this Arkadian had a temper. [4] When Kleomenes captured Great City, Philopoimen did not panic at the unexpectedness of the catastrophe, and escaped with two thirds of the men of fighting age and with women and children to Messene, the Messenians being their allies and friends at the time.[355] Kleomenes announced to some of the refugees that he regretted what he had done, and wanted the Great City people to come home and make a truce with him, but Philopoimen persuaded the citizen community to obtain their homecoming by force of arms and refuse any truce or agreement. [5] Philopoimen

353. Philopoimen lived from about 253 to 182 B.C. There is a life of him by Plutarch, and a lost life in three books by Polybios. The theatre has been found; the cathedral at PALAIO EPISKOPI was built on to a buttress of it.

354. Arkesilaos was the founder of the new Academy; he was preoccupied by problems about the grounds of knowledge and by polemics against stoicism. Pitane is in Asia Minor, at CHANDARLI east of the southern tip of Lesbos.

355. Bk IV, 29 (7f.), and Bk VIII, 27 (15).

fought in the cavalry at the battle of Sellasia, where all the Achaian and Arkadian cities along with Antigonos with his Macedonian army combined to fight Kleomenes and the Lakonians.[356] When Philopoimen saw that the decision would depend mostly on the infantry, he volunteered as an infantry-man, and was taking extraordinary risks when one of the enemy spitted him through both thighs. [6] Pinned as he was he bent his knees and forced himself forward until the move-ment of his legs snapped the spear. After Kleomenes and the Lakonians were beaten and Philopoimen came back to camp the doctors took the stub-end out of one of his thighs and the point out of the other. When Antigonos saw and heard his courage, he did his best to get Philopoimen to Macedonia. [7] But Philopoimen was not the man to care much for Antigonos; he crossed over by ship to Crete, where there was a civil war, and served as a mercenary commander. As soon as he returned to Great City he was chosen to command the Achaian cavalry, and he proved them the best horsemen in Greece. When the Achaians and their allies fought the Eleans and their Aitolian relations and allies at the river Larisos, first of all he personally killed Demophantos the enemy cavalry commander, and then broke the Aitolian and Elean cavalry.[357]

[1] As the Achaians were already looking to him and he 50 was in fact already doing everything for them, he was now in a position to change the equipment of their infantry. They were carrying short little spears and long shields like Celtic targes and Persian *gerra*; Philopoimen persuaded them to put on body-armour and wear leg-guards, and to use long spears and Argive shields. [2] When the dictator Machanidas came on the scene in Lakonia, and war broke out again between the Achaians and the Lakonians, Philopoimen was Achaian commander. There was a battle at Mantineia; the Lakonian light infantry beat the Achaian light-armed troops, and as they ran Machanidas pressed them hard; but Philopoimen's column broke the Lakonian regulars, and he met and killed

356. Cf. Bk III, 10 (7). It was in 221.
357. The battle at the Larisos was fought at the frontier of Achaia and Eleia.

Machanidas returning from the pursuit. So the Lakonians lost the battle and won a greater success than the defeat they suffered: freedom from the dictator.[358] [3] Not long afterwards when the Argives celebrated the Nemean games, Philopoimen happened to be present at the instrumental singing contest, when Pylades, a Great City man by origin, the most famous instrumental singer of his generation and winner of a Pythian wreath, was singing an oratorio by Timotheos of Miletos called *The Persians*. When Pylades began to sing,

> *Creator of freedom, the glorious ornament of Greece,*

the entire Greek assembly turned to look at Philopoimen and applauded, to show they took it to refer to him.[359] I heard of something like that happening to Themistokles at Olympia, where the whole theatre stood in his honour.[360] [4] Philip son of Demetrios king of Macedon, the one who poisoned Aratos of Sikyon, sent some men to Great City with orders to murder Philopoimen. The attempt failed, and he was hated all over Greece.

The Thebans had fought and beaten the Megarians in a battle, and were already assaulting the walls of Megara, when the Megarians tricked them into thinking Philopoimen had entered the city: and they were so nervous that they marched away home without finishing the campaign. [5] Another dictator appeared in Lakonia called Nabis, and the first people in the Peloponnese he attacked were the Messenians. He attacked at night quite unexpectedly and took the city except for the citadel, but when Philopoimen arrived the next day with an army he retreated from Messene under a truce.

[6] When Philopoimen's time as general was up and other Achaians were chosen for commands, he crossed over to

358. In 207.

359. Plutarch says he marched in at the right moment with soldiers wearing red cloaks. It has to be said that Timotheos was a dreadful poet. The prologue of *The Persians* is said to have been by Euripides.

360. After the Persian defeat at Salamis, the subject of Timotheos's oratorio.

Crete again and helped the war-distressed Gortynians.[361] The Arkadians were furious with him for going abroad, so he came home from Crete and found the Romans had declared war on Nabis. [7] The Romans had fitted out a fleet against Nabis, and Philopoimen was most eager for a share of the fighting. But having no naval experience whatever he made the mistake of going on board a warship that leaked, which reminded the Romans and their allies of the verses of Homer in his list of ships about Arkadians ignorant of the sea.[362] [8] A few days after the sea battle Philopoimen and his company chose a moonless night and burnt down the Lakonian camp at Gythion.[363] At this moment Nabis caught Philopoimen and his Arkadians in some difficult country; they were good soldiers, but not numerous. [9] But Philopoimen altered the dispositions of his men for the retreat and contrived to use the strongest natural positions to his own advantage and the disadvantage of his enemies; he beat Nabis in a battle and massacred a lot of Lakonians in a night attack, so that his reputation in Greece rose even higher. [10] After this Nabis obtained a truce with Rome to last a stated time, and then died before the renewal of the war. He was killed by a Kalydonian who came under the pretence of an alliance, though he was really an enemy and was actually sent to do the murder by the Aitolians.

[1] At this juncture Philopoimen dropped on Sparta and 51 compelled the Lakonians to join the Achaian League. Not long afterwards Titus the commander of the Romans in Greece and Diophanes son of Diaios of Great City, who was the elected Achaian commander at the time, marched on Lakonia, on the excuse that the Lakonians were plotting against Rome.

361. Gortys had an alliance with Arkadia in the previous century (*Insc. Creticae*, 4, 171). Philopoimen's second visit was from 200 to 193. The Gortynians were probably as usual at war with Knossos. In 192 or so there was a Cretan mercenary force, probably from Gortys, fighting against Nabis (*I.G.*, IV (2), 244).

362. *Iliad*, 2, 614.

363. Gythion is at the head of the Lakonian gulf. For the ancient site, cf. Bk III, 21 (6f.).

Philopoimen, even though he was just a private citizen then, shut the gates against them. [2] For this and for his acts of fortitude against both the dictators, the Lakonians gave him Nabis's house, worth more than a hundred talents; but he disdained the money, and told the Lakonians not to flatter him with their presents but to keep them for the public persuaders in the Achaian League, by which he is said to have meant Timolaos.[364] He was accepted as Achaian general. [3] The Lakonians had now reached the point of civil war, and he expelled three hundred ringleaders of the revolution from the Peloponnese, sold off as many as three thousand serfs, dismantled the walls of Sparta, and forbade the young lads to follow the laws of Lykourgos: he made them train in just the same way as young lads in Achaia. The Romans were to restore the educational traditions of the Lakonians in a later generation. [4] When Manius with the Romans at Thermopylai had beaten Antiochos the descendant of Seleukos the Champion at Thermopylai, and Aristainos of Great City was advising the Achaians to approve whatever the Romans liked and never to stand up to them over anything, Philopoimen looked furiously at Aristainos and said he was accelerating the doom of Greece. Manius wanted Lakonia to take back the exiles, and Philopoimen opposed him on principle; when Manius went away, Philopoimen let the exiles come home to Sparta.

[5] But Philopoimen's turn was coming when the punishment for pride would catch him. When he was re-elected as Achaian commander for the eighth time, he insulted some not undistinguished figure because the enemy had captured the man alive. The Achaians had a complaint against Messenia at that time, and Philopoimen sent off Lykortas with the army to devastate the Messenian countryside; just two days afterwards in a high fever and at the age of over seventy, he rushed to take a share in Lykortas's operations. He took sixty

364. This is a jumbled story. It was Timolaos who was deputed to come to Great City and make him the offer; when he dared to do so Philopoimen went to Sparta and made the speech Pausanias is talking about.

cavalry and slingers. [6] By then Lykortas and his army had already turned home without doing much damage to the Messenians and without sustaining much themselves, but Philopoimen was hit on the head in the fighting and fell off his horse, and they took him alive to Messene. The Messenians called an assembly immediately, but all their opinions turned out to be in utter disagreement. [7] Deinokrates and the Messenian rich demanded Philopoimen's death, but the people were most eager to treat him well: they said he was higher than the father of all Greece. Deinokrates meant to do away with Philopoimen whether the Messenians liked it or not, and sent him poison. [8] Meanwhile Lykortas quickly collected a force from Arkadia and the Achaian League, and marched on Messene; the Messenian people immediately came over to the Arkadian side. Those responsible for Philopoimen's death were taken and suffered the penalty, except for Deinokrates who died by suicide, and the Arkadians brought home Philopoimen's bones to Great City.365

[1] From that time onwards Greece ceased to produce 52 courageous men. Kimon's son Miltiades who beat the barbarians that landed at Marathon and stopped the Persian expedition in its tracks was the first communal benefactor of Greece, and Philopoimen son of Kraugis was the last. Those whose achievements were illustrious before Miltiades, Kodros son of Melanthos, Polydoros the Spartan, and Aristomenes the Messenian and anyone else there may have been, can be seen to have done good to their native places, but not to the whole of Greece.366 [2] After Miltiades, Leonidas son of Anaxandridas and Themistokles son of Neokles drove Xerxes out of Greece, one at the battle of Thermopylai and the other in two naval battles, Pausanias son of Kleombrotos and Aristeides son of Lysimachos commanded at Plataia, but Pausanias's subse-

365. They were carried by Lykortas's son, the young Polybios. When a tomb had been built for Philopoimen, the Messenian prisoners were stoned to death at it.

366. Kodros was a fable (Bk IV, 5 (4)); Polydoros (Bk III, 3 (1–3)) and Aristomenes (Bk IV, 6 (3)) were legendary but real.

quent crimes and the taxes Aristeides imposed on the Greeks
of the islands took away their right to be called benefactors of
Greece. Before Aristeides no Greek people paid a tax. [3]
Xanthippos son of Ariphron with Leotychides king of
Sparta destroyed the Persian fleet at Mykale, and Kimon's
achievements for Greece are numerous and enviable, but one
might well say that the generation of the Peloponnesian War,
and particularly its most famous members, were the murderers
of Greece and came close to throwing her overboard altogether. [4] Konon son of Timotheos and Epaminondas son of
Polymnis restored injured Greece: Konon threw out the
Lakonian colonists and put an end to governing boards of ten
in the islands and coastal territories, and Epaminondas did the
same in cities remote from the sea; Epaminondas added
materially to the greatness of Greece by founding Messene
and Great City in Arkadia. [5] I also regard Leosthenes and
Aratos as benefactors of all the Greeks: Leosthenes rescued by
ship, in spite of Alexander, the fifty thousand or so Greek
mercenaries in Persia who had reached the sea; I have already explained the history of Aratos in my treatment of
Sikyon.[367]

[6] The inscription on Philopoimen is this:

GREECE KNOWS HIS COURAGE AND GLORY:
HIS MANY DEEDS OF STRENGTH AND OF WISDOM:
PHILOPOIMEN, ARKADIAN SPEARMAN:
HONOUR WENT WITH HIS WAR-COMMANDING SPEAR:
THE DOUBLE TROPHY FOR FALLEN DICTATORS
SPEAKS TO SPARTA: HE DESTROYED
INCREASING SLAVERY: THEREFORE TEGEA
ERECTED KRAUGIS'S GREAT-TEMPERED SON:
SOVEREIGN OF UNSPOTTED LIBERTY.

53    [1] The Tegeans say they put up statues of Apollo of the
Road for the following reason. The story is that Apollo and
Artemis were taking revenge on all the people of all the
countries who had despised Leto when she was pregnant and

367. Bk II, 8f.

visited them in her wanderings. [2] When the gods came to the Tegean country, Tegeates' son Skephros went to meet Apollo and spoke with him secretly: Leimon, who was another son of Tegeates, suspected he was inculpated by what Skephros said, and so he assaulted and killed his brother. [3] Leimon was punished for the murder immediately because Artemis shot him; Tegeates and Maira at once sacrificed to Apollo and Artemis, and then when a terrible barrenness of the earth followed, an oracle came from Delphi commanding them to lament for Skephros. And among the ceremonies they perform at the festival of Apollo of the Road in honour of Skephros, the priestess of Artemis chases someone as if she were Artemis chasing Leimon. [4] And they say Kydon and Archedios and Gortys, Tegeates' surviving sons, migrated willingly to Crete, and the cities of Kydonia and Gortys and Katreus were named after them. The Cretans contradict the Tegean legend; their version is that Kydon was the son of Minos's daughter Akakallis and of Hermes, Katreus was Minos's son, and Gortys was the son of Radamanthys.[368] [5] Homer says of Radamanthys in Proteus's speech to Menelaos that Menelaos would come to the Elysian fields, and that Radamanthys had arrived there before him; Kinaithon writes in his epic that Radamanthys was the son of Hephaistos, who was the son of Talos, who was the son of Kres.[369] Greek legends mostly disagree, and as much about lineage as about anything. [6] There are four of these Tegean statues of Apollo of the Road, one erected by each tribe, the tribes are called Klareotis, Hippothoitis, Apolloniatis, Athaneatis. The names are derived from Arkas making his sons cast lots for the territory, and from Hippothoos son of Kerkyon.

[7] There is also at Tegea a SHRINE OF DEMETER and the Maid, whom they call the Fruit-bringers, close to one of

368. KYDONIA is CHANIA in north-west Crete; GORTYS is near Phaistos in the south of central Crete. Katreus not only has no obvious connexion with the name Archedios, but appears not to exist. (Stephanos of Byzantium copies Pausanias here as elsewhere.) I am unable to suggest a solution.

369. *Odyssey*, 4, 561f. Kinaithon is an epic genealogist; cf. Bk II, 3 (9).

Paphian Aphrodite which was founded by Laodike.[370] I explained before that she was the daughter of Agapenor who commanded the Arkadians against Troy, and she lived in Paphos. Not far from here there are two SANCTUARIES OF DIONYSOS, an altar of the Maid, and a TEMPLE OF APOLLO with a gilded statue [8] by Cheirisophos of Crete, whose period and whose teacher are unknown to us, though the time Daidalos spent at Knossos living with Minos made Crete famous for a very long period for the carving of wooden idols. Beside the Apollo stands a stone Cheirisophos.

[9] There is a place the Tegeans call the common HEARTH of the Arkadians, where there is a statue of Herakles with the wound carved on his thigh from his first battle with Hippokoon's sons. The high ground where most of the Tegean altars are is called Klarian Zeus; the title obviously comes from Arkas's sons casting lots. [10] The Tegeans hold an annual festival here. They say the Lakonians once marched on them at the moment of this festival, and as it was snowing, the Lakonians were shivering and fatigued in their armour, but the Tegeans secretly lit their fire, and (so they say) untroubled by frost put on armour and went out to meet their enemies and had the best of the action.[371] Here are the other things I observed at Tegea: ALEOS'S HOUSE and ECHEMOS'S MONUMENT, and the battle of Echemos with Hyllos carved on a stone tablet.

[11] As you go from Tegea towards the Lakonian border there is an altar of Pan on the left of the road, and one of Lykaian Zeus, and you can still see the FOUNDATIONS OF

370. The sanctuary of Demeter on the north-east slope of the akropolis (?) was among the first sites at Tegea to be investigated. (Cf. also Romaios in *Praktika*, 1910, pp. 274f.) This small akropolis is some distance from the city in the plain, but there is no doubt that the little hill is an ancient site. The site of the excavation is lost in the fields, but the many fragments of broken small terracottas rejected by the excavators can still be traced and marks the place. The better pieces are in the museum at Tegea.

371. At Bk VIII, 48 (5), there is another of these cult stories which verges in the same way on what sounds like a real event. The coincidence is in itself suspicious.

SANCTUARIES. The altars are a quarter of a mile from the ramparts; about a mile farther on you come to a SANCTUARY OF LAKE ARTEMIS with an ebony statue in the style of workmanship the Greeks call Aiginetan.[372] A mile and a quarter from here there are the ruins of a SHRINE OF ARTEMIS Knakeatis.[373]

[1] The frontier of Lakonian and Tegean land is the river 54 Alpheios. It rises at Phylake, and not far from the source another stream joins it from springs of no great size though there are more of them; because of this the place is called the Meeting.[374] [2] The Alpheios appears to have a special quality different from other rivers: it has a way of disappearing underground a lot of times and reappearing again. Proceeding from Phylake and the Meeting it disappears into the Tegean plain; then it rises at Asea and mingles its streams with the Eurotas and then goes underground for the second time;[375] [3] it comes up at a place the Arkadians call the Springs and flows out past the Pisaian territory and past Olympia, and discharges into the sea above Kyllene the port of Elis. Not even the Adriatic could hold it back: it swims right across this extensive and violent sea, and in Quail Island off Syracuse it proves itself the true Alpheios by uniting its streams with Arethousa.[376]

[4] The straight road from Tegea to Thyrea and the villages of the Thyrean territory presents for description the monument of Orestes son of Agamemnon; the Tegeans say it was from here a Spartan took his bones: today the tomb is no longer enclosed.[377] The river Garates flows by the road; if

372. It means just stiff and pre-classical.

373. A study of the 1907 excavation of this shrine was published by K. Romaios late in his life (*Eph. Arch.*, 1952, pp. 1f.). It was an archaic Doric temple with a running goddess in relief over the front.

374. This is the SARANTOPOTAMOS.

375. Cf. Bk VIII, 44 (3f.), and the Notes there. The meeting is probably KRYAVRYSI ten miles south, where there are ancient marbles and two streams do unite.

376. Cf. Bk V, 7 (2f.).

377. For the Thyrean territory, cf. Bk II, 38 (4). Pausanias is heading east. For the story of Orestes' bones, cf. Bk III, 3 (5f.).

you cross it and travel a mile and a quarter you find a SANCTU-
ARY OF PAN with an oak-tree growing beside it which is also
sacred to Pan.378

[5] The road to Argos from Tegea is excellent for traffic,
mostly a real highway. First of all on this road there is a SHRINE
and statue of ASKLEPIOS.379 Later if you turn off left for two
hundred yards there is a collapsed SANCTUARY OF PYTHIAN
APOLLO, utter ruins. Along the main road there are a lot of
oak-trees; there is a SHRINE OF DEMETER in the sacred oak-
wood called Demeter of the Korytheans, and nearby another
SANCTUARY OF MYSTIC DIONYSOS.380 [6] It is from this
point that Mount Parthenion begins. They show you a precinct of Telephos on the mountain, where they say he was
found abandoned as a child and reared by a deer. A little way
on is a SANCTUARY OF PAN where Pan appeared to Philip-
pides; the Tegeans tell exactly the same story as the Athenians
do about it.381 [7] Parthenion has tortoises which are excellent
for making lyres, but the mountain people are always terrified
to take them, nor do they let strangers catch them either; they
believe the tortoises are sacred to Pan. When you have passed
the crest of the mountain and got into cultivated land, you

378. If we are west of the Sarantopotamos this must be the stream
from PSILI BRYSI or ANO DOLIANA. The sanctuary of Pan has never been
found.

379. North-east to ACHLADOKAMPO on the line of the modern main road.
The Asklepieion has not been traced and the exact line of the road is not
certain at this point.

380. The site of the Demeter temple and the Dionysos temple was dis-
covered by M. Bérard in 1889 (B.C.H., 14, pp. 382-4). The broken statue of
Demeter enthroned was found on the spot, east of HAGIORGITIKA and of
TRIPOLIS, on level ground below the mountains.

381. The precinct of Telephos was identified by L. Ross, who found some
marble blocks at the south of the hill below the PALAIOMOUCHLI castle, in
the bed of the river. The site of the sanctuary of Pan was apparently fixed
through an inscription on bronze near the first arch of the old railway viaduct
below the same castle and hill; but I cannot at present trace this inscription.
The old viaduct was bombed in the Second World War and is now in ruins.
The story is the one told by Herodotos; Pheidippides ran between Athens and
Sparta before the battle of Marathon and met Pan on the way.

come to the boundary-stone of Tegea with the Argives of Hysiai in the Argolid.[382]

Those are the divisions of the Peloponnese, and the cities in each division, and the most memorable and interesting things in every city.

382. For Hysiai, cf. Bk II, 24 (7). I have seen the shells of small tortoises on this mountain.

# Select Bibliography

There are some general books it will be useful to list in one place. The classical English translation and commentary by Sir James Frazer in six volumes is still invaluable. It was first issued in 1897, and slightly revised just before the First World War; a volume of maps and plans was added under the title *Graecia Antiqua* by Frazer and Van Buren (1930).

The best edition of the Greek text, a Greek edition with an important commentary in German, was produced by Hitzig and Blümner (Leipzig, 1896). Their topographical information is less valuable than Frazer's, but they can never be ignored on points of scholarship.

The standard Greek text is the current Teubner text, edited by Spiro in 1903, and reissued in 1959. It has its drawbacks, but this for reasons of convenience was the text I used. The Loeb Pausanias provides the useful service of confronting a Greek text with an English version; the most useful volume is the fifth, a volume of maps, plans, and index put together by Professor R. E. Wycherley. This volume was revised in 1955, and it is essential to use the revised rather than the 1935 edition. There is an abridged one-volume translation of Pausanias into German with particularly useful notes by E. Meyer (1954), and a very serviceable translation and commentary in modern Greek in several volumes by N. D. Papahadzis (1963, 1965) is still appearing. But the only writer so far as I know ever to have covered the whole of the ground that Pausanias covered in Greece was the greatest of all Greek travel writers and topographic scholars, Colonel William Leake, who was seconded to the Turkish government to inspect the defences of Greece between 1804 and 1809. His *Athens*, his *Northern Greece*, and his *Morea* are required reading for students of Pausanias. There is also a useful mass of information in Smith's *Classical Dictionary of Geography* (1857), in the standard encyclopedias of mythology and *realia*, and in Imhoof-Blumer and Gardner's *Numismatic Commentary on Pausanias*, recently reissued in a slightly enlarged edition but with inferior plates (1964).

For specific questions and particular parts of Pausanias I have tried to give references in the footnotes to the most useful books. The journals of the foreign schools of archaeology in Athens as one might expect contain important articles; in particular one should mention almost all the recent numbers of *Hesperia*. The publications of the Archaeological Society of Athens and of the Greek Archaeological Service are indispensable. For the last ten years the French School at Athens has issued an important and comprehensive *Chronique des Fouilles en Grèce*. It has now ceased to appear, but the less full *Archaeological Reports* annually issued by the Hellenic Society continue, and there is now an important new periodical with short notices of the most important Greek finds, *Athenian Annals of Archaeology*, issued by the Greek archaeological service. In 1890 Harrison and Verrall commented on Pausanias's Athens in their *Mythology and Monuments of Ancient Athens*, and in 1958 G. Roux did the same for Corinth and its neighbours in his *Pausanias en Corinthie* (Paris, 1958). Individual digs and sites have been covered by formal publications, the greatest of them in long series of volumes which will continue to appear as long as work goes on: notably the American *Agora* volumes and the French *Fouilles de Delphes*. There is an excellent short official guide to the Agora excavations, of which it is important to have the 1962 edition. J. Travlos's important recent study of the topography of the city of Athens was issued only in Greek and is already out of print; a translation is being prepared by Professor Wycherley. But the fundamental work on Athenian topography is still Judeich's very detailed *Topographie von Athen*, which has never been translated into English. I should perhaps mention here an important bibliography of articles on Athenian archaeology printed since Judeich, down to June 1960, made by Mr S. L. Glass of the American School of Archaeology at Athens; there is a copy of it in the British School library. For Pausanias's cities in Asia Minor the only modern guide with any authority is G. E. Bean's *Aegean Turkey* (1966), but it is still essential to refer to the works of Sir William Ramsay.

The best general handbooks on Greece are the British Admiralty official three-volumed *Handbook* to Greece (1944), and for footpaths and tracks the rarer and earlier edition of the same work issued in one volume about 1916 (a projected second volume seems never to have appeared). The best tourist guide is the *Guide Bleu*, which has a series of site plans that suit most ordinary purposes, though it does of course have lapses. It is essential to have the most recent edition. The old *Murray's Guide* is not to be despised. Almost all maps except old hoarded military-staff maps get you into more trouble than they get you out of.

# BIBLIOGRAPHY

Some useful reference books have appeared recently: John Travlos, *Pictorial Dictionary of Ancient Athens*, F. E. Winter, Greek Fortifications, A. Mallwitz, *Olympia* (in German only), a new Teubner text of Pausanias (ancient Greek) and a fine commentary by Papahadzis (modern Greek).

# INDEX

# INDEX

# INDEX

# INDEX

Phlious and the Phliesians, 264-6
Phlyos, 104, 106
Phoenicians, the 274, 276, 339
Phoibe, 54, 178
Phoinikous, harbour of, 187 and n.
PHOIZON (Arkadia), 397-8
Phokis and the, Phokians, 166, 175, 179n., 186, 274, 281, 301, 377: quarrel with Lokrians, 32-3; occupation of Delphic sanctuary, 34, 115; war with Thessaly, 270 and n.
Pholos, 65
Phorbas, governor of Athens, 200, 342
Phorbas,-son of Lapithos, 200
Phormion of Halikarnassos, 259
Phormion of Sparta, 54
Phormis of Mainalos, 279-80
Photios, 70n.
Phradmon of Argos, sculptor, 307
Phraortes, king of Ekbatana, 158 and n.
Phrasikleides, governor of Athens, 298, 439
PHRIXA (Eleia), 350-52, 487: grave of Hippodameia's wooers, 351-2; sanctuary of Artemis Kordax, 352; temple of Kydonian Athene, 350
Phrygia and the Phrygians, 57n., 262 and n., 274
Phylake and the Phylakeans, 483, 499
Phyleus, Messenian general, 134
Phyleus, son of Augeas, 200, 202 and n.
Physkoa, 246
Piera, fountain of, 247
Pig Valley, 103, 112n., 171
Pindar, 93 and n., 108 and n., 173 and n., 222, 238 and n., 266 and n., 288
Pisaia and the Pisaians, 199 and n., 201-2, 205, 211, 223 and n., 246, 265, 295, 352-3, 499
Pison of Poros, sculptor, 291-2
Pisos, 250, 352
Pitanatai, the, 47
Plastene, see Kybele
Plataia, battle of, 20, 27, 31, 39, 47, 61, 266, 292 and n., 326, 382, 495: column at Delphi, 267n.; Plataian Zeus at Olympia, 266-8
Plataians, the, 166 and n., 266
Plataniston, river, 470
Plato, 13n., 71n., 179, 202n., 205n., 308n., 314n., 384n.
Pleistaines, Aitolian commander, 329
Pleistarchos, 20
Pleistoanax, 20
Pleuro, 46
Pliny, 67n., 189n., 193n., 230n., 256n., 285n., 296n., 300n., 301n., 308n., 318n., 332n., 360n., 364n., 373n., 399n., 407n., 425n., 485n.
Plutarch, 2, 13n., 17n., 32n., 45n., 48n., 56n., 61n., 97n., 115n., 136n., 147n., 173n., 206n., 240n., 316n., 332n., 396n., 441n., 468n., 486n., 490n., 492n.
Pluto (Plouton), 67: statue, Olympia, 257
Po, river, 238 and n.
Podaleirios, 100 and n., 178
Podares, 393 and n., 395

Polemarchos, 15
Polemo, 63n.
Polichne, 182
Polites, companion of Odysseus, 303 and n.
Polites of Keramos, Olympic winner, 320
Polos, 452
Polos, plain of, 459
Polyainos, 138n., 142n., 147n., 188n.
Polybios, son of Lykortas, historian, 69n., 82n., 154n., 167n., 171n., 174n., 325n., 327n., 390 and n., 417n., 437n., 442n., 461n., 482, 490n., 495n.: inscription, Akakesion, 463; tablets: Megalopolis, 449; Tegea, 489
Polyboia, 67
Polychares of Messenia, 114-16: Olympic winner, 114; murders Lakonians, 115; Messenians refuse to hand him over, 115
Polydektes, 15
Polydeukes (Pollux), see Dioskowroi
Polydora, 108
Polydoros the Spartan, 15, 40 and n., 137, 495: his house in Sparta, 40n., 41; in Messenian war, 121, 124
Polykaon, 9, 103-4, 106, 110
Polykleitos of Argos, sculptor (I) 64 and n., 248, 285n., 289, 290n., 297 and n., 307., 308n., 321 and n.
Polykleitos of Argos, sculptor (II), 301 and n.
Polykles, 287
Polykles of Athens, sculptor, 296
Polykrates, dictator of Samos, 407 and n.
Polykrates, orator, 334
Polyktor of Elis, 263, 357
Polymedes of Argos, sculptor, 313n.
Polymestor, 381
Polyneikes of Elis, Olympic winner, 218
Polyneikes, son of Oedipus, 109, 123, 254-5
Polypeithes of Lakonia, 331
Polysperchon of Aitolia, 210
Polyxenes, 203
Polyxo, 70
Pompos, king of Arkadia, 381
Porinas, 410
Poroselene, island of, 95 and n.
Porphyry (lapis lacedaemonius), 77n.
Porthaon, 187
Poseidon, 52, 59, 65, 67, 104n., 107, 158, 199, 224n., 229, 249n., 250, 266, 269, 314n., 351n., 362, 385 and n., 387, 396, 432-4, 465, 466, 476, 482: and Demeter, 431-3: Horse Poseidon, 47, 242, 347, 394, 406, 433; altar, Olympia, 242; sanctuaries and shrines: Kaphyai, 425 and n.; Mantineia, 380, 394; Messene, 175; Methydrion, 460 and n.; Sparta, 40, 42, 47, 49, 53; Therapne, 72n.; Trikolonoi, 458; statues: Cape Tainaron, 94 and n.; Gythion, 79-80; Megalopolis, 452; Nymphaion, 85; Olympia, 277; Pheneos, 406; temples: Megalopolis, 447; Orchomenos, 403; Samia, 210n.

# READ MORE IN PENGUIN

In every corner of the world, on every subject under the sun, Penguin represents quality and variety – the very best in publishing today.

For complete information about books available from Penguin – including Puffins, Penguin Classics and Arkana – and how to order them, write to us at the appropriate address below. Please note that for copyright reasons the selection of books varies from country to country.

**In the United Kingdom**: Please write to *Dept. JC, Penguin Books Ltd, FREEPOST, West Drayton, Middlesex UB7 0BR*

If you have any difficulty in obtaining a title, please send your order with the correct money, plus ten per cent for postage and packaging, to *PO Box No. 11, West Drayton, Middlesex UB7 0BR*

**In the United States**: Please write to *Penguin USA Inc., 375 Hudson Street, New York, NY 10014*

**In Canada**: Please write to *Penguin Books Canada Ltd, 10 Alcorn Avenue, Suite 300, Toronto, Ontario M4V 3B2*

**In Australia**: Please write to *Penguin Books Australia Ltd, 487 Maroondah Highway, Ringwood, Victoria 3134*

**In New Zealand**: Please write to *Penguin Books (NZ) Ltd,182–190 Wairau Road, Private Bag, Takapuna, Auckland 9*

**In India**: Please write to *Penguin Books India Pvt Ltd, 706 Eros Apartments, 56 Nehru Place, New Delhi 110 019*

**In the Netherlands**: Please write to *Penguin Books Netherlands B.V., Keizersgracht 231 NL–1016 DV Amsterdam*

**In Germany**: Please write to *Penguin Books Deutschland GmbH, Friedrichstrasse 10–12, W–6000 Frankfurt/Main 1*

**In Spain**: Please write to *Penguin Books S. A., C. San Bernardo 117–6° E–28015 Madrid*

**In Italy**: Please write to *Penguin Italia s.r.l., Via Felice Casati 20, I–20124 Milano*

**In France**: Please write to *Penguin France S. A., 17 rue Lejeune, F–31000 Toulouse*

**In Japan**: Please write to *Penguin Books Japan, Ishikiribashi Building, 2–5–4, Suido, Tokyo 112*

**In Greece**: Please write to *Penguin Hellas Ltd, Dimocritou 3, GR–106 71 Athens*

**In South Africa**: Please write to *Longman Penguin Southern Africa (Pty) Ltd, Private Bag X08, Bertsham 2013*

# READ MORE IN PENGUIN

## A CHOICE OF CLASSICS

| | |
|---|---|
| St Anselm | **The Prayers and Meditations** |
| St Augustine | **The Confessions** |
| Bede | **Ecclesiastical History of the English People** |
| Geoffrey Chaucer | **The Canterbury Tales** |
| | **Love Visions** |
| | **Troilus and Criseyde** |
| Marie de France | **The Lais of Marie de France** |
| Jean Froissart | **The Chronicles** |
| Geoffrey of Monmouth | **The History of the Kings of Britain** |
| Gerald of Wales | **History and Topography of Ireland** |
| | **The Journey through Wales and The Description of Wales** |
| Gregory of Tours | **The History of the Franks** |
| Robert Henryson | **The Testament of Cresseid and Other Poems** |
| Walter Hilton | **The Ladder of Perfection** |
| Julian of Norwich | **Revelations of Divine Love** |
| Thomas à Kempis | **The Imitation of Christ** |
| William Langland | **Piers the Ploughman** |
| Sir John Mandeville | **The Travels of Sir John Mandeville** |
| Marguerite de Navarre | **The Heptameron** |
| Christine de Pisan | **The Treasure of the City of Ladies** |
| Chrétien de Troyes | **Arthurian Romances** |
| Marco Polo | **The Travels** |
| Richard Rolle | **The Fire of Love** |
| François Villon | **Selected Poems** |

# READ MORE IN PENGUIN

## A CHOICE OF CLASSICS

ANTHOLOGIES AND ANONYMOUS WORKS

**The Age of Bede**
**Alfred the Great**
**Beowulf**
**A Celtic Miscellany**
**The Cloud of Unknowing and Other Works**
**The Death of King Arthur**
**The Earliest English Poems**
**Early Irish Myths and Sagas**
**Egil's Saga**
**The Letters of Abelard and Heloise**
**Medieval English Verse**
**Njal's Saga**
**Roman Poets of the Early Empire**
**Seven Viking Romances**
**Sir Gawain and the Green Knight**

# READ MORE IN PENGUIN

## A CHOICE OF CLASSICS

| | |
|---|---|
| Aeschylus | **The Oresteian Trilogy** |
| | **Prometheus Bound/The Suppliants/Seven Against Thebes/The Persians** |
| Aesop | **Fables** |
| Ammianus Marcellinus | **The Later Roman Empire (AD 354–378)** |
| Apollonius of Rhodes | **The Voyage of Argo** |
| Apuleius | **The Golden Ass** |
| Aristophanes | **The Knights/Peace/The Birds/The Assemblywomen/Wealth** |
| | **Lysistrata/The Acharnians/The Clouds** |
| | **The Wasps/The Poet and the Women/The Frogs** |
| Aristotle | **The Art of Rhetoric** |
| | **The Athenian Constitution** |
| | **Ethics** |
| | **The Politics** |
| | **De Anima** |
| Arrian | **The Campaigns of Alexander** |
| St Augustine | **City of God** |
| | **Confessions** |
| Boethius | **The Consolation of Philosophy** |
| Caesar | **The Civil War** |
| | **The Conquest of Gaul** |
| Catullus | **Poems** |
| Cicero | **The Murder Trials** |
| | **The Nature of the Gods** |
| | **On the Good Life** |
| | **Selected Letters** |
| | **Selected Political Speeches** |
| | **Selected Works** |
| Euripides | **Alcestis/Iphigenia in Tauris/Hippolytus** |
| | **The Bacchae/Ion/The Women of Troy/Helen** |
| | **Medea/Hecabe/Electra/Heracles** |
| | **Orestes/The Children of Heracles/Andromache/The Suppliant Women/The PhoenicianWomen/Iphigenia in Aulis** |

# READ MORE IN PENGUIN

## A CHOICE OF CLASSICS

# READ MORE IN PENGUIN

## A CHOICE OF CLASSICS

| | |
|---|---|
| Plautus | **The Pot of Gold/The Prisoners/The Brothers Menaechmus/The Swaggering Soldier/Pseudolus** |
| | **The Rope/Amphitryo/The Ghost/A Three-Dollar Day** |
| Pliny | **The Letters of the Younger Pliny** |
| Pliny the Elder | **Natural History** |
| Plotinus | **The Enneads** |
| Plutarch | **The Age of Alexander** (Nine Greek Lives) |
| | **The Fall of the Roman Republic** (Six Lives) |
| | **The Makers of Rome** (Nine Lives) |
| | **The Rise and Fall of Athens** (Nine Greek Lives) |
| | **Plutarch on Sparta** |
| Polybius | **The Rise of the Roman Empire** |
| Procopius | **The Secret History** |
| Propertius | **The Poems** |
| Quintus Curtius Rufus | **The History of Alexander** |
| Sallust | **The Jugurthine War** and **The Conspiracy of Cataline** |
| Seneca | **Four Tragedies** and **Octavia** |
| | **Letters from a Stoic** |
| Sophocles | **Electra/Women of Trachis/Philoctetes/Ajax** |
| | **The Theban Plays** |
| Suetonius | **The Twelve Caesars** |
| Tacitus | **The Agricola** and **The Germania** |
| | **The Annals of Imperial Rome** |
| | **The Histories** |
| Terence | **The Comedies (The Girl from Andros/The Self-Tormentor/TheEunuch/Phormio/The Mother-in-Law/The Brothers)** |
| Thucydides | **The History of the Peloponnesian War** |
| Virgil | **The Aeneid** |
| | **The Eclogues** |
| | **The Georgics** |
| Xenophon | **Conversations of Socrates** |
| | **A History of My Times** |
| | **The Persian Expedition** |